Landscapes of War and Memory

# Landscapes of War and Memory

## The Two World Wars in Canadian Literature and the Arts, 1977–2007

SHERRILL GRACE

The University of Alberta Press

Published by

The University of Alberta Press
Ring House 2
Edmonton, Alberta, Canada T6G 2E1
www.uap.ualberta.ca



LIBRARY AND ARCHIVES CANADA CATALOGUING IN PUBLICATION

Grace, Sherrill E., 1944–, author
Landscapes of war and memory : the two world wars in Canadian literature and the arts, 1977–2007 / Sherrill Grace.

Includes bibliographical references and index.
ISBN 978-1-77212-000-4 (pbk.)

1. Canadian literature—20th century—History and criticism. 2. Canadian literature—21st century—History and criticism. 3. Arts, Canadian—20th century. 4. Arts, Canadian—21st century. 5. War in literature. 6. War in art. 7. World War, 1914-1918—Influence. 8. World War, 1939-1945—Influence. I. Title.

PS8101.W37G73 2014 C810.9'358282 C2014-906091-2

First edition, first printing, 2014.
Printed and bound in Canada by Houghton Boston Printers, Saskatoon, Saskatchewan.
Copyediting by Jean Wilson.
Proofreading by Joanne Muzak.
Indexing by Judy Dunlop.



The University of Alberta Press is committed to protecting our natural environment. As part of our efforts, this book is printed on Enviro Paper: it contains 100% post-consumer recycled fibres and is acid- and chlorine-free.

The University of Alberta Press gratefully acknowledges the support received for its publishing program from The Canada Council for the Arts. The University of Alberta Press also gratefully acknowledges the financial support of the Government of Canada through the Canada Book Fund (CBF) and the Government of Alberta through the Alberta Media Fund (AMF) for its publishing activities.

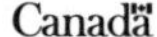

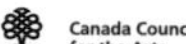

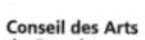

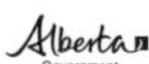

To the thirsty ghosts,
and to all those who remember
what we never knew.

People are the landscape of memory.
Without the benefit of time and place,
they are forced to play
the scenery themselves.

**Timothy Findley**
*Inside Memory*, 11

History is amoral; events occurred.
But memory is moral;
what we consciously remember
is what our conscience remembers.

**Anne Michaels**
*Fugitive Pieces*, 139

Lest we forget. Remember me.
To you from failing hands we throw.
Cries of the thirsty ghosts.
Nothing is more difficult than to
understand the dead, I've found;
but nothing is more dangerous
than to ignore them.

**Margaret Atwood**
*The Blind Assassin*, 638

# Contents

PART IV

## Testing the Nation in the Second World War



PART V

## A Peaceable Kingdom in the Twenty-First Century

# List of Illustrations

# Preface and Acknowledgements



OVER THE SEVERAL YEARS spent on research for this book, I have learned an immense amount about Canada, the twentieth century, and the two world wars. The most memorable of my research trips was the one I took in the spring of 2009 to the battlefields and cemeteries of France, Belgium, and the Netherlands, but other journeys have also been moving—to memorials in Germany, France, England, Belgium, and Hong Kong—and these foreign journeys have made me see the memorials in Canadian towns and cities in a different light. However, my interest in the subject of Canada's representations of the wars began in an art gallery, the Vancouver Art Gallery to be precise. Before the Canadian War Museum officially opened in 2005, the exhibition "Canvas of War" toured the country to its major public galleries, and it was at the VAG that I saw this stunning show. I had students with me on my first visit, and watching them discover this art and their heritage, about which they knew next to nothing, started me on my search. That visit to that art together with a few of the finest novels written in this country about the wars—Timothy Findley's *The Wars* and Joy Kogawa's *Obasan*—stimulated my desire to know more. The rest, as people like to say, is history. Except that our history is not well known among Canadians and I quickly realized I had much to learn.

I began with the history and Canada's military historians and from there worked with increasing fascination through the literature in English, films, plays, and visual art relevant to my interest. Several years of reading and research confirm that Canadians have created a great, and too little appreciated, cultural history about the wars. My cut-off dates of 1977 to 2007 are discussed in the book, but I quickly gravitated to what my generation—and younger ones—had to say about those twentieth-century cataclysms. Studies already existed of work published, performed, or produced during and immediately after each war, and by 1977 and Findley's *The Wars*, anglophone Canadians were reassessing what war meant for Canada and for its place in a wider world. This was the work I wanted to explore.

There are many groups and organizations I wish to thank for their support and help with the preparation of this study. I am, however, especially grateful to my students in several graduate seminars because I was able to share in their urgent discovery of what, for them, was unknown territory. Next, of course, are the artists themselves, those who are still alive and granted permission for me to quote from or reproduce their work, and those no longer alive who have given so much. They are named and acknowledged formally in the text. Among the organizations whose help has been invaluable are the Canadian War Museum, which I visited several times; Trent University, where I was Ashley Fellow in 2010 and where I was able to air some of my research findings in public lectures to sophisticated and knowledgeable audiences; and UBC for a sabbatical that gave me badly needed time to write. I am also grateful to Playwrights Canada Press for their keen interest in publishing the two volumes of plays about war contained in *Canada and the Theatre of War*. These volumes forced me to think critically about such plays and to teach them as a body of work about war. My thanks, as well, to my co-editors of *Bearing Witness: Perspectives on War and Peace from the Arts and Humanities* (2012) Patrick Imbert and Tiffany Johnstone, and to McGill-Queen's University Press for permission to reprint my discussion of Michael Crummey's

*The Wreckage* and Marie Clements's *Burning Vision*. Preparing that volume added to my understanding of some of the issues involved in discussing war. By far the most important institution to recognize, and with deep appreciation, is the Social Sciences and Humanities Research Council of Canada. Without the research funds to support me, my graduate student assistants, and a study of this scope—over several years—the work could not have been begun or completed. I hope the finished product is worthy.

Then there are individuals to whom I owe much gratitude for their interest, their permission to quote from their works, their help with photography, films, paintings, and discussion, as well as their patient attention to my obsessive stories, and their practical help with my travel and with the manuscript: Laura Brandon, Peter Blow, Glenn Deer, Susanna Egan, Elizabeth Grace, John Grace, who accompanied me to European cemeteries and to more war films and plays than he would have liked, Trevor Greene, Fraser Jackson, Tiffany Johnstone, Elena Lamberti, Jan Lermitte, Mary-Ellen Perley, Jim and Betsy Struthers, Peter van Wyck, Susan Vella, and William Whitehead. It is a special pleasure to thank Alicia Fahey for her patient and expert assistance in tracking down illustrations and permissions, and to Jean Wilson, who read and commented so helpfully on the entire manuscript and whose keen editorial eye and equally keen interest have been very encouraging. It has been such a pleasure to be able to work with you, Jean. To the fine folks at the University of Alberta Press—Peter Midgley, Alan Brownoff, and Linda Cameron—three cheers for helping see this project through to publication so well. Your support has been invaluable.

I have dedicated this book to the ghosts and the artists who tell their—and our—stories. There are many more stories to tell, I am sure, and hopefully other students of Canada and its arts will tell them.

S.G.

*Vancouver*

PART I

# Landscapes of War/ Landscapes of Memory

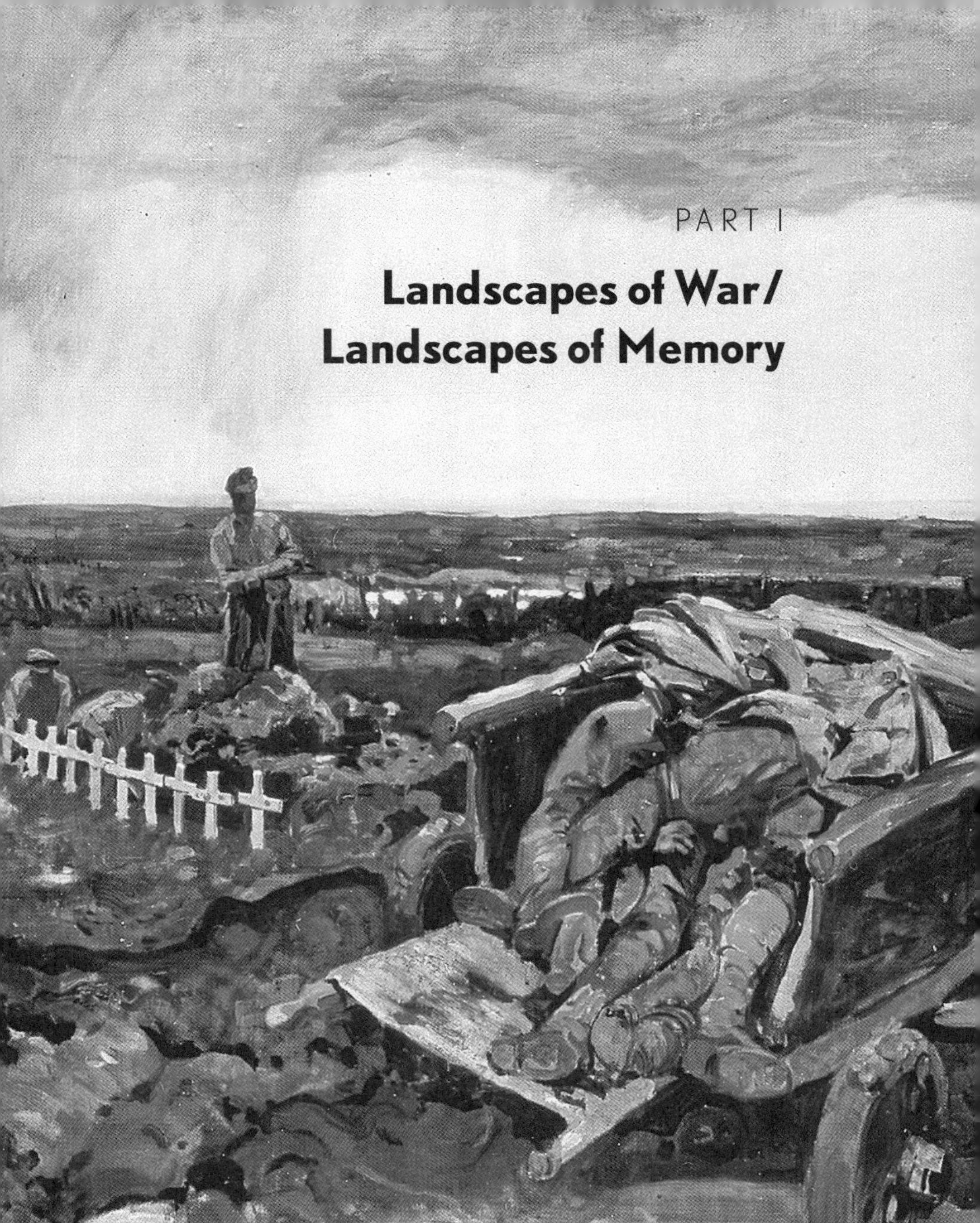

We live in a period in which memory of all kinds, including the sort of larger memory we call history, is being called into question. For history as for the individual, forgetting can be just as convenient as remembering, and remembering what was once forgotten can be distinctly uncomfortable. As a rule, we tend to remember the awful things done to us, and to forget the awful things we did.



**Margaret Atwood**

*In Search of* Alias Grace, 8

Memory—along with its lapses
and tricks—poses questions
to history in that it points to
problems that are still alive or
invested with emotion and value.



**Dominick LaCapra**

*History and Memory after Auschwitz*, 8

Landscapes of memory are given shape by the personal and social significance of specific memories but also draw from meta-memory—implicit models which influence what can be recalled and cited as veridical.

**Laurence J. Kirmayer**

"Landscapes of Memory," 175

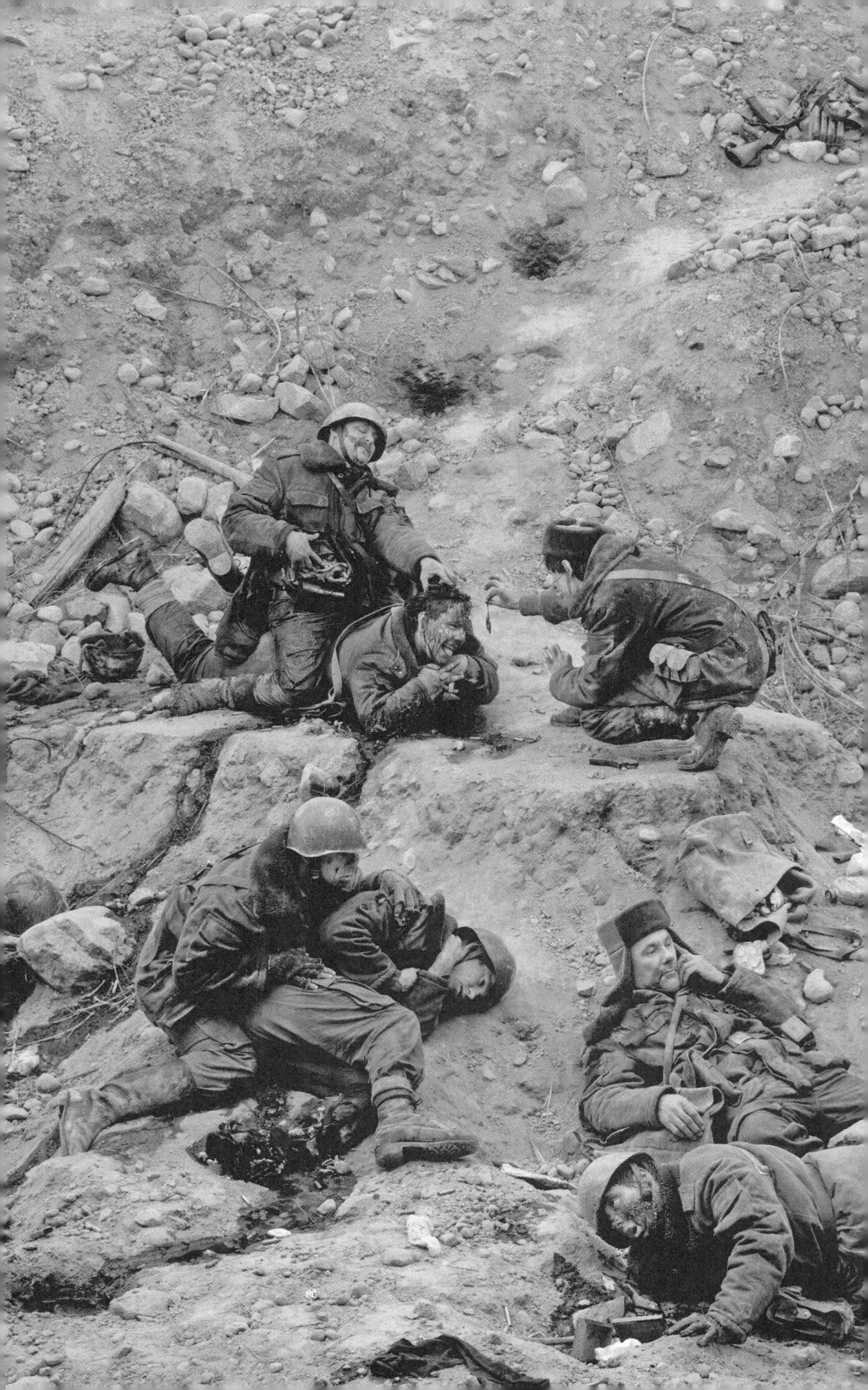

1

# Landscapes of War



"AS A RULE, WE TEND TO REMEMBER the awful things done to us, and to forget the awful things we did." When Margaret Atwood said this in her 1996 Bronfman Lecture on Canadian historical fiction, she was not thinking primarily of war.[1] She did, however, go on to point out that, as Canadians, we remember the German blitz of London during the Second World War but prefer to forget the Allied fire-bombing of Dresden. Moreover, when reminded about "things that society has decided are better forgotten," we tend to respond with "cries of anguish and outrage" (Atwood, *In Search*, 8), as the McKenna brothers discovered when their documentary film about that war, *The Valour and the Horror*, was shown on CBC Television in 1992.[2] Since 1977 Canadian writers have insisted on remembering the two world wars, both to honour and to challenge and reassess "things that society" decided to forget. Emerging from this work is the realization that what Canadian society, in the shape of official history and popular culture, decided to forget about the wars has not gone away.

Forgetting is a trap, and it is as much my subject in the chapters that follow as remembering. While inconvenient stories about the wars were pushed aside—or in the case of war art hidden from public view in storage for decades—they have always *haunted* the dominant Canadian narrative, waiting to surface, waiting for us to pay attention, waiting, even, for resurrection. "We are the dead," the soldiers in our most famous war poem tell us every 11 November; "we shall not sleep," they warn. What the soldier-poet John McCrae did not tell us is what *they* would do to us if we broke faith, or how the meaning of breaking faith would change with the years. Like ghosts with warm hands, as First World War veteran Will Bird called them, and as so many of the writers I discuss demonstrate, these ghosts clamour for recognition. They are, to recall Atwood in *The Blind Assassin*, "thirsty ghosts" (638) who want their stories told, who want us—we who are alive now and are their largely unknowing inheritors—to listen.

In order to *hear* these ghostly voices and stories, however, it is never enough merely to read about them because such a passive and passing acquaintance leaves no room for engagement with the past, for seeing our connection with these ghosts and realizing that they haunt us, for understanding the meaning of history—its trauma and difficult subjects—and for what Dominick LaCapra calls "empathic unsettlement" in *Writing History, Writing Trauma* (41). Truly to hear and see, to accept and understand, and then to move on by incorporating this new knowledge into who we are in the future (as individuals, communities, or a nation), demands that we create what I call a "landscape of memory," and later in this chapter I explain this term, why I find it so important, and where I locate this landscape. But there are three other questions to introduce first because each affects the terrain of a "landscape of memory." Why worry about this now, or more precisely, why and how did Canadians start worrying about this in 1977? *Who* (which groups of Canadians) was doing that worrying and continues to explore the subject? And to what end, or to use Frederick Varley's haunting and still relevant question: for what?

Although fixing dates is always arbitrary, I begin with 1977 because it signals a turning point or breakthrough in a general English-speaking Canadian awareness—or fresh reassessment—of the two world wars. Timothy Findley published two major works in 1977: *The Wars* and *Can You See Me Yet?* The novel has become a Canadian classic, very widely read, translated, and studied in schools and universities at home and abroad. As I demonstrate in Chapters 2 and 3, *The Wars* set the stage for a re-examination of the impact and significance of the Great War and established a number of tropes and narrative strategies for remembering and representing that war. Findley's play, set in the late summer of 1938, as Europe armed for another war, premiered at the National Arts Centre in March 1976 and was published in 1977. I attended that premiere, with the incomparable Frances Hyland in the role of Cassandra Wakelin, and I shall never forget the experience. I can still hear "These Foolish Things" playing softly from the wings or the voice of Hitler screaming from an offstage radio, followed by a crescendo of "Sieg! Heil!" *Can You See Me Yet?* takes place in the long shadow of the Second World War, but it is also haunted by the First World War and by the atrocities taking place in China (the Rape of Nanking began in December 1937).





One other book that appeared in 1977 heralded, along with these two works by Findley, the advent of a new understanding of the past; Heather Robertson published her well-illustrated study *A Terrible Beauty: The Art of Canada at War* that year, twenty-eight years before the Canadian War Museum opened its doors and before the art she discussed became familiar to Canadians. I vaguely recall hearing about Canadian war art (Was it Varley who painted something? What about Colville?), but I had never seen this war art because it was stored in vaults, unavailable for viewing, and I could not imagine it to be of artistic value or cultural importance. The Canada I grew up in was a "peaceable kingdom";[3] no Canadians I knew personally had been in a war, and my parents rarely spoke about the Second World War. The shock I received as a teenager, when my mother, without prior warning or preparation, took me to see the film *Judgment at Nuremberg* in 1961 has never left me.[4] But even then, what happened was in the past and over there; I did not *see* the connection with my Canada. Opening *A Terrible Beauty* in about 1979, I was stunned. In her groundbreaking study, Robertson placed reproductions of paintings side by side with excerpts from memoirs, letters, and media dispatches, and with quotations from fiction and poetry—English-Canadian *war* poetry. Prior to 1977 there were a few scattered novels, plays, and memoirs in print, especially from the Second World War, and the first of Barry Broadfoot's populist oral accounts of Canadians in the war, *Six War Years, 1939–1945*, had appeared in 1974, but the only Canadian war poem my generation learned was McCrae's "In Flanders Fields."[5] Since 1977, however, many excellent works of literature and history have appeared on stages and in bookstores, and the serious study of Canadian war artists has blossomed. Findley and Robertson pointed the way back to a forgotten past and forward to present and future remembering. Their year was 1977. My goal is to chart developments in Canadian cultural memory since then.

I have selected 2007 as my end date, at least for those works I analyze closely. In the final chapter I come forward to 2010 to demonstrate the continuing productivity of the subject, but 2007 is especially significant for one reason. On 9 April 2007 the restored Canadian National Vimy Memorial on the Douai Plain near Arras, France, was rededicated in a massive and moving ceremony that was broadcast live to millions of viewers back home by CBC Television. This day marked the ninetieth anniversary of the beginning of the Battle of Vimy Ridge in the Great War, the battle in which—so we have been endlessly told—Canada came of age as a nation. Vimy marked our coming of age because our troops fought together *as Canadians*, albeit under the command of the British Lieutenant-General Sir J.H.G. Byng (a Canadian, General Arthur Currie, was appointed commander of the Canadian Corps in June 1917), and because we won. *We won*, or so the official story goes, although who exactly *we* were and precisely what was *won* were not widely scrutinized, at least not publicly, until 1977 and after. Those gathered around the monument in 2007 certainly expanded the concept of who we are today; veterans attended, of course, as did current troops representing today's armed forces and those soldiers killed in Afghanistan just days before the ceremony, but children were also present, choirs sang, ethnic diversity (notably Inuit and First Nations) was well represented, and the dignitaries (the Queen, the Canadian and French prime ministers of the day, Stephen Harper and Dominique de Villepin) seemed less important than the youthful faces surrounding them. The carefully staged spectacle—for that is what it was—was performed in English and French, with some Cree and Inuktitut, and it took place under a warm sun in a clear blue sky with the cheerful sounds of bird song clearly audible. The scene could scarcely have been more different from the battle in April 1917 or the day in 1936 when the monument was unveiled.[6]





But this ceremony and its coverage were only one, albeit a highly visible, aspect of Canadian remembrance of war in 2007. Brian McKenna's 2007 film *The Great War* was released on CBC Television to coincide with the April rededication of the monument, and this film is a *tour de force*. More than two years in the making, *The Great War* presents the re-enactment of First World War battles culminating in the battle of Vimy Ridge, the interweaving of archival images with actors' recreations of actual events and people (Justin Trudeau's portrayal of Talbot Papineau is one example), and interviews with descendants of Great War veterans, a number of whom were chosen to perform in the Easter Sunday re-enactment of the taking of Vimy Ridge. One of these descendant re-enactors, Joel Ralph, described his reaction to the performance in troubling terms. For him, the return to Vimy in *The Great War* focused attention on—that is, it *remembered*—the violence Canadians suffered but ignored "the violence that was dispensed" (41). In words that echo Margaret Atwood's comments about selective forgetting quoted at the start of this chapter, Ralph acknowledges that the "effects of the violence administered by Canadians are still as profound as the effects of the violence they suffered" (41). As far as I know, Ralph's is one of the few voices raised publicly to alert Canadians to the complex, selective, and problematic recreation of history in the film; I have not found, to date, any critical assessments of the rededication ceremony. But Ralph's insights and my own ambivalence about the politics and narrative construction of memory, forgetting, and history in both productions lead me to my next two questions: who does this remembering and why, for what, or to what end or purpose do we engage in this remembering?



These questions, as much as my respect for the quality of the art and literature about the world wars, motivate my inquiry and inform this book. Both wars produced political tension and resentments within Canada. Chief among them was the sharply different position held on both wars in Quebec compared with most of the rest of the country. Military historians, political scientists, and political biographers (of King and Trudeau, for example) always address the reasons for these differing views, which include Quebec's reluctance to fight *for* England in a foreign war that was not our business and the widely felt opposition to conscription; when conscription was introduced, despite federal promises to the contrary, the official response in Quebec was to feel betrayed.[7] Given this complex background, it is not surprising that Quebec literature, film, and art produced between 1977 and 2007 have largely ignored the representation of the two wars. Quebec did not come of age on Vimy Ridge; Quebec identity was not consolidated at Dieppe or in Normandy, despite the valour of the famous Royal 22nd Regiment—the Van Doos. Those artists who are remembering the wars live *hors de Québec* and work in English. Although they come from many different ethnic and immigrant backgrounds and address the two wars from varying positions, they rarely include Quebec or French Canada. Consequently, those who do so much of the cultural work of remembering, and produce the texts I discuss, construct personal, community, and national landscapes of memory that make room for First Nations experiences of war and its aftermath, alongside the voices of Italian, Japanese, Dutch, German, Eastern European, and Greek

Canadians, and, of course, Jewish Canadians. Which is not to say that French-Canadian perspectives and voices are entirely absent from this narrative landscape; there are fine examples of *representations* of these voices in a play like *Vimy* or a film like *The Valour and the Horror*, but there are very few works produced from within the Quebec domain. In this book, therefore, I focus on the wealth of material created by non-francophones and comment in passing on a few examples of French-Canadian self-representation. Nevertheless, I do not lose sight of this characteristically Canadian challenge to an imagining of one, unified, pan-Canadian, all-inclusive national landscape of memory. Aspects of this challenge surface in my discussion from time to time; for example, with Louis Caron's 1977 novel *L'Emmitouflé* (*The Draft Dodger*), with Sandra Gwyn's hero Talbot Papineau in *Tapestry of War*, with Vern Thiessen's play *Vimy*, and with the memories of the eloquent Second World War veteran General Jacques Dextrasse in *The Valour and the Horror*.





Finally, what is the purpose of this remembering and why is it happening now? What distinguishes the period from 1977 to 2007 to make it so productive for the Canadian reimagining of the wars? Just as Varley asked "for what?" of the Great War itself, so I ask a parallel question of this cultural activity in my time. Canada is by no means unique in this concentration on the twentieth-century military past. A large number of important novels, plays, historical and cultural studies, films, memoirs, and biographies have appeared over the past thirty years in several languages in many different countries. Much of this cultural production has taken place in the West (especially regarding the Holocaust), but Asia, most importantly China, has begun to explore its tragic experiences leading up to and during the Second World War.[8] One quick answer to the question "why now?" is that enough time has passed for the immediate pain of war to have dissipated and for those who fought, especially in the Great War, to have died, and this passage of time allows for objectivity and greater freedom for critical analysis. Judging from the hostile reaction to *The Valour and the*

*Horror*, Canadians still need greater distance from the veterans and the events of the Second World War before they are ready to re-examine what happened. That said, the opposite may be equally true: we may be rushing to remember while there is still time, before those with first-hand experience of the two wars have all gone. Or, and this is an intriguing possibility, *we* are the ones who are in a position to appreciate the aftermath of both wars through what Marianne Hirsch calls "post-memory."[9]

Such claims, however, immediately raise a host of questions that I explore in the following chapters. For example, does distance in time assure objectivity? Can new information (sometimes previously classified or deliberately hushed up) radically alter the historical record and public, or private, memory? And why do we attribute—or do we?—special credence to eyewitnessing and first-hand experience? Most importantly, I do not want to imply that the narrative constructions of the past emerging between 1977 and 2007 are all singing from the same songbook. The represented memories on page, canvas, screen, and stage compete with each other and with received interpretations of the past; the stories are multiple, contradictory, and often ambivalent; the strategies used to recreate these stories are complex and bring with them a range of crucial aesthetic and ethical challenges like the one Adorno put to the arts many years ago: how can one write poetry after Auschwitz?[10] If I can offer one generalization here, before turning to the works themselves, it would be this: most of the post-1977 Canadian works I discuss insist that we critically re-examine, through memory, our understanding of our role in the two world wars, and most invite us to reflect upon what it means today to be Canadians with this military history and, by extension, what it means to be human. Few of the works I consider can be simply classified as anti-war, let alone pro-war; few provide cut and dried answers to serious questions about war and peace. All urge us to remember and think, to pay attention and listen.

Why? Just as Varley felt compelled to depict the battlefields of the Great War, with their corpses and devastated landscapes in paintings like *For What?* (1918), *Some Day the People Will Return* (1918), and *The Sunken Road* (1919) and to ask why, so I am troubled by this question almost a century later. Why do so many contemporary Canadians (and people around the world) seem obsessed with the two world wars, and what can we hope to gain by continuing to study, remember, and reimagine them? Although Varley had no answer to his question because the war seemed so utterly wasteful and devastating, he knew why he decided to paint these shocking scenes.[11] In a letter to his wife, he insisted that "You in Canada...cannot realize at all what war is like. You must see it and live it" (qtd. in *F.H. Varley* 38), but in a letter to fellow artist Arthur Lismer he was more explicit: "I tell you Arthur, your wildest nightmares pale before reality. How the devil one can paint anything to express such is beyond me. The story of war is told in the thousand and one things that mingle with the earth—equipment, bits of clothing almost unrecognizable, an old boot stuck up from a mound of filth, a remnant of a sock inside, and inside that—well, I slightly released the boot, it came away in my hand and the bones sifted out of the sodden rag like fine sand" (qtd. in Oliver and Brandon 69). Understandably, this eyewitnessing of truth, or "reality," is one way of expressing "such" things, but I think there are many others, some of which are particular to a given text or writer/artist, while others are more general and reflect late twentieth-century and early twenty-first-century concerns. Moreover, some of these answers are especially significant for Canada, even though they involve international issues, as indeed they must, given the scope of both wars.

My choice of framing dates throws a critical and theoretical light on second- and third-generation remembering and on the extensive research required by postwar generation artists who choose to look back at the events that shaped the lives of their parents and grandparents, but had only an indirect impact on their own lives. All my major novelists, poets, filmmakers, and playwrights were born after the Second World War (or in a few cases just before or during it); therefore, each of them made a deliberate decision to revisit the past and each was obliged to do research, sometimes extensive research. As quickly becomes clear, an artist cannot examine an actual war (or any other historical event) by fabricating dates and events. Insofar as it is known, the historical record must be respected and readers will not tolerate errors; the London Blitz cannot be moved to Paris, and the Battle of the Marne cannot be relocated to the Somme. Moreover, this demand for historical accuracy by both reader/audience member and artist has consequences for the style of representation and the mode of art to be created, and I will return often to these aesthetic issues.





Given such limits on the free flow of creative imagination, why then write about a war you did not experience first-hand? Because the first-hand, eyewitness account by combatants or non-combatants is not the whole story and because such accounts, whatever they may claim in authenticity or legitimacy (and these claims are open to debate) usually lack context, critical distance, and the reflection necessary to weigh the impact of events; because new information may surface along with new perspectives on information, and these can prove immensely productive, if the artist wishes to find meaning in cataclysmic past events; and because the traumatic, life-changing impact of each war only began with those who lived through it. As we have come to realize, especially regarding the Second World War and the Holocaust, these wars continue to haunt us, whether we know it or not. While much of this afterlife, or after-effect, has been analyzed and much debate has erupted (and continues to do so) over who has a right to speak about atrocity and war, writers and artists, readers and scholars choose to explore the ever-receding, yet ominously present, past. They do so because, as Adorno said later in his 1962 essay "Commitment," as if in response to his famous 1951 pronouncement that to write poetry after Auschwitz was barbaric: "It is now virtually in art alone that suffering can still find its own voice, consolation, without immediately being betrayed by it" (*Essential Frankfurt School Reader* 312).

Certainly, I believe that artists are uniquely positioned to bear witness to the wars and their repercussions, and to Varley's question I would add the claim by the great German painter Otto Dix (1891–1969), a First World War veteran who understood Varley's revulsion, that "the painter is the eyes of the world."[12] I also believe that readers and audiences can learn important lessons from their works. I would not have undertaken this study without this conviction. My emphasis here is on learning and understanding (which is more than gaining knowledge), and the demands *placed by the subject matter* on both those who create and the rest of us who receive and respond are ultimately ethical. By reading, studying, watching, and talking about works like Findley's *The Wars*, Varley's *For What?*, R.H. Thomson's *The Lost Boys*, Anne Michaels's *Fugitive Pieces*, Marie Clements's *Burning Vision*, or Miller Brittain's *Night Target, Germany*, we too are asked, in some senses, to bear witness, to respond, to remember. Ultimately, *we* are asked to reflect upon, if not answer, the artists' cry—for what?





Because *we* are asked to *bear witness*, to respond, by the works we read or look at, I want to reflect briefly on this process; detailed discussion of concepts follows in Chapter 2, with specific examples of the witnessing process highlighted throughout the book. To begin with, the little pronoun *we*, in its sweeping assumption of inclusivity (and exclusivity) calls for attention. By "we" I mean all Canadians living now (including French Canadians and Quebecers), but especially those Canadians who have a professional responsibility to teach younger generations—parents, families, communities, artists, governments, media, and other institutions also fulfill (or should) these responsibilities—because teachers are entrusted with the transmission and interpretation of knowledge. In my experience as a humanist, teaching senior English undergraduates and graduate students Canadian literature about the two world wars has involved me in a double responsibility (a double witnessing) in that I have had to explore the primary materials with their historical contexts *and* guide

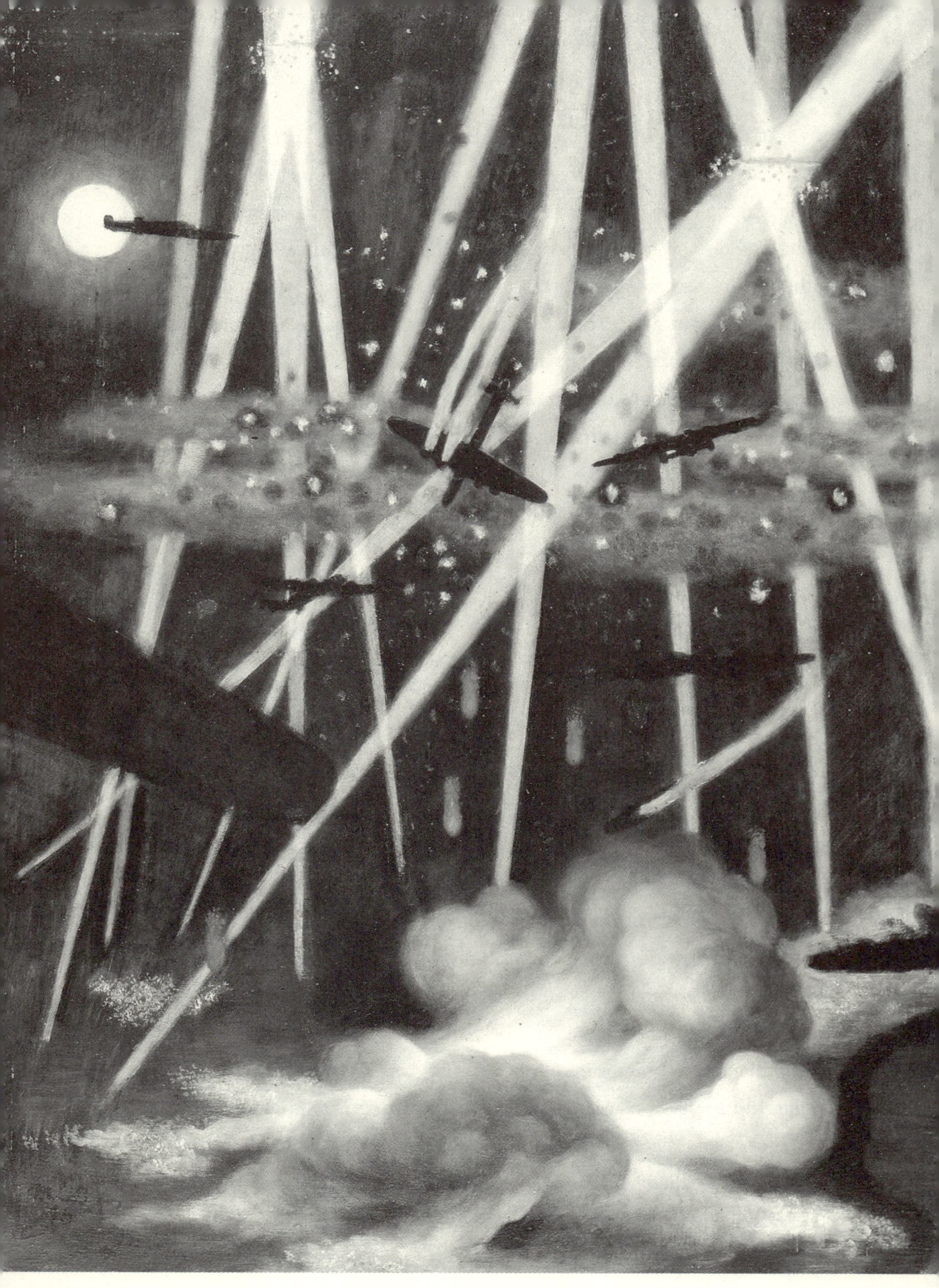

*Miller Brittain,* Night Target, Germany *(1946). o/c 76.5 x 61 cm.* CWM *#19710261-1436. Beaverbrook Collection of War Art. © Canadian War Museum. Brittain was a bomb-aimer with the* RCAF *during the Second World War, and the devastation of Dresden after bombing missions haunted him all his life. He became an official war artist in 1945.*

my students' exploration of challenging materials on extremely difficult subjects, while managing my own reactions and facilitating theirs. Asking young people, so few of whom have much prior knowledge of twentieth-century history or any direct living family connection with either war, can seem to them like an affront. They may well—indeed, they have—responded with shock, disbelief, compassion, silence and a refusal to engage, anger, bursts of speech, and even tears. Some left my classes when they encountered Findley's descriptions of the trenches or the gas attacks in the Great War or Michael Crummey's scenes in a Japanese POW camp from *The Wreckage*. They did not wish, or choose, to be confronted with the kind of horrors Varley witnessed and described in his letters and paintings. Secondary readings in theory and abstract theorizing in class failed to address—to be commensurate with—the material being studied.



Those who stayed, however, often completed their seminars by writing deeply thoughtful essays and, I believe, having not only learned by listening—to the texts, to each other, to themselves—but also having worked through their initial unease with the works we studied. Above all, they encountered and acknowledged facts and events from their own history as Canadians (or about Canada for those who were visiting from the United States, Hong Kong, Switzerland, Germany, Belgium, or France), about which they had never heard. Without question, the most significant aspect of this new-for-them information was Canada's racist treatment of European Jews before, during, and after the Second World War. They already had some awareness of the Japanese internments (*Obasan* has been widely taught in high schools for several years now), but works like Irving Abella and Harold Troper's *None Is Too Many* or Jason Sherman's play based on that book, and also called *None Is Too Many*, were a major shock. Part of their angry response was aimed at their own ignorance: why had they not been taught this history?

My experiences with classes on war, memory, and trauma over the past ten years are not unique. Shoshana Felman has described one exceptionally powerful example of teaching a comparative literature seminar at Yale called "Literature and Testimony" in which she used a variety of texts, mostly literary, to test the claim that "testimony is the literary—or discursive—mode par excellence of our times" (Felman, 17). Seminar work proceeded smoothly, academically, until the class encountered reality in the shape of "life testimonies" by Holocaust survivors from Yale's Fortunoff Video Archive.[13] At this point, she describes the class as being "in crisis" while students wrestled with how to manage their own witnessing. Although I did not bring my students to such a state of crisis, the parallels are clear. Where Felman used two filmed interviews as examples of testimony, I drew on documentary films like *Canvas of War, The Valour and the Horror, Return to Ortona,* and *Village of Widows* to contextualize and historicize the literature.





All four films, each made post-1977, rely on survivor testimony and personal witnessing and focus tightly on the faces and gestures of elderly men and women as they struggle to articulate memories of pain suffered and of pain inflicted. The case of war artist Aba Bayefsky was especially moving because he recalled how he felt as a young Jewish-Canadian soldier-artist entering the liberated concentration camp of Bergen-Belsen, and he quietly asserted that what he saw *made* him become an artist, so that he could bear witness to what must never be forgotten or denied: "It was the determining factor in everything I have done since."[14] Even more than the plays, memoirs, and novels dealing, in my seminar, with the Second World War, these films elicited such powerful reactions from students that group discussion could only resume the following week. A two-hour meeting ended in silence as each person left with his or her private thoughts. I suspect that many of my colleagues who have taught examples of Canadian (or other) war literature have had similar experiences. Surely the same must be true in Canadian history seminars, not to mention those devoted to the Holocaust, but I also suspect that such experiences are relatively recent in Canadian literary studies.[15]

This silence in Canada about the country and its war arts, especially in university settings where one might expect the subject to be part of a standard literature, history, and cultural studies curriculum, highlights some provocative issues. A quick survey of English-Canadian literature anthologies reveals scant attention paid to any form of writing about either war. Even if one had wanted to teach the material, the primary texts were lacking (out of print and not reprinted or even excerpted). It is only after 1977, and with the attention Findley brought to the First World War with *The Wars*, that the slow process of filling in the literary history and critical blanks could begin. Paradoxically, the post-1977 works, which differ in so many important ways from earlier ex-soldier or eyewitness narratives, shed new light on the wider field of war literature in Canada. Four major scholarly studies demonstrate this sea change: Peter Buitenhuis's *The Great War of Words: Propaganda and Fiction, 1914–1933* (1987), the first study of its kind to feature Canada (unlike Fussell's *The Great War and Modern Memory*), Evelyn Cobley's *Representing War: Form and Ideology in the First World War* (1993), with its discussion of *The Wars*, Modris Eksteins's *Rites of Spring: The Great War and the Birth of the Modern Age* (1989), a cultural, interdisciplinary *tour de force* by a Canadian scholar who is usually overlooked in favour of Fussell, and finally Dagmar Novak's study of combatants' writing up to 1977 in *Dubious Glory: The Two World Wars and the Canadian Novel* (2000).[16]



The appearance of *Obasan* in 1981 did for the Second World War what *The Wars* did for the First—it shocked Canadian readers into rethinking their wartime past and reassessing works that had been published only to be forgotten, works like *Barometer Rising* (1941), *Turvey* (1949), *Execution* (1958), *The Deserter* (1964), *The Betrayal* (1964), and *Fifteen Miles of Broken Glass* (1975).[17] The situation for history was similar. Barry Broadfoot's first-hand oral accounts of that war based on eyewitness interviews in books like *Six War Years* (1974) and the later *The Veterans' Years: Coming Home from the War* (1985) served unapologetically and uncritically to celebrate Canadians' efforts in the war. The first generation of important academic military historians such as Desmond Morton, Jack

Granatstein, and David Bercuson did not begin publishing until the 1970s (Morton's comprehensive *A Military History of Canada* appeared still later in 1985) and popular historians like Pierre Berton, who are much more widely read than the academics, did not publish his magisterial *Vimy* until 1986 and *Marching as to War* until 2001. The journal *Canadian Military History*, which has contributed so much to our awareness of Canadian war artists (as a glance at Laura Brandon's publications indicates), began publishing in 1992, and Canadian war poetry is still neglected in our anthologies, although Raymond Souster was publishing his stunning poems about the Second World War in the early 1970s and Robert Service's poetry, including his First World War poems, has never gone out of print.[18] The situation for Canadian plays has been even more belated: despite the enormous popularity of John Gray and Eric Peterson's classic *Billy Bishop Goes to War*, which premiered in 1978, Canada's plays about war have been ignored. The first volume of these plays, *Canada and the Theatre of War*, appeared in 2008, with volume two published in 2010 (see Coates and Grace). As for stories about Canadian children and war, the first study of this subject did not appear until 2011: Susan Fisher's *Boys and Girls in No Man's Land: English-Canadian Children and the First World War*.



As so much recent discussion about memory, commemoration, witnessing, and testimony demonstrates, the entire subject of who can (or *may*) bear witness, and of how, when, and in what form remembering, bearing witness, or giving testimony about trauma in general, but more especially in war, takes place is extremely sensitive and complex. My claim that readers and viewers of post-1977 Canadian war narratives are, in fact, bearing witness to history—or, at least, that we are positioned by writers and artists so we can do so, if we choose to engage—is influenced by my reading of historians, cultural and literary theorists, and psychologists like Dominick LaCapra, Cathy Caruth, Marianne Hirsch, Laurence Kirmayer, Jan and Aleida Assmann, and Ansgar Nünning.[19] In the next chapter I examine my critical framework in detail. At this point, I wish only to stress that the texts I analyze and deem important were created by non-eyewitness, non-combatants, and that many of them (*The Stone Carvers*, *Soldier's Heart*, and *Mary's Wedding*, for example, or *Obasan*, *The War Between Us*, and *Burning Vision*) take place, for the most part, on home fronts, not battle fronts. Moreover, it is these home fronts that matter. No doubt, some readers, including scholars, would refuse to call these works *war* plays, novels, and films because they lack *real* eyewitnesses, *real* survivors' voices, or first-hand accounts of battles and because they are fictional, imaginative recreations of experiences, memories, and research. However, I describe them as works about war, and I insist on this point. I also insist on the personal voice and perspective, both as writer and reader and as a scholar with a theoretical/analytical position. As I realized with my students and continue to learn from the artists, it is only through the personal that I (that anyone) can listen, respond, and participate in the process of remembering and bearing witness. When the biographer in *The Wars* says "you" or the character/actor in *Burning Vision* looks at the audience (at me) and says "you," then I must either shut the book or look away, or acknowledge this address. To turn aside with the passive voice or plural pronouns is to retreat from the challenge. Therefore, on several occasions, I analyze texts by performing my interlocutory/interpretive role as honestly and directly as possible.



If war has taught us anything it is that battles and battle fronts never stay put *over there* or *back then*. The ghosts cannot simply be pushed aside; as Atwood warns us, they are "thirsty." Soldiers return home bringing their memories and trauma with them, people are displaced and immigrate to countries like Canada bringing their memories with them, and nations create myths of a glorious past, as Jonathan Vance shows in his study of Canada's First World War *official* history in *Death So Noble*. Such an official history, constructed from selected memories, stories, and events, becomes a foundational narrative of nation that works in the present and underpins a future understanding of identity, moral purpose, ideology, and social values—for *culture* in the broadest sense of that term. In Canada, the dominant cultural discourse of the First World War claims that we came of age, gained our identity (while glossing over grievances within the province of Quebec), helped save the world for peace, and sacrificed nobly and willingly. According to this discourse, we were tried and proven in the blood of battle and we emerged united as a people. As Vance argues, we created a "positive, light-hearted" account of ourselves in the war (74) because we needed a "mythic version" from which "to fashion a usable past" (9)—usable, that is, for the socio-political present of those postwar years. But Vance, in *Death So Noble,* is not the only historian to challenge Canada's official First World War story. *Vimy Ridge: A Canadian Reassessment*, edited by Geoffrey Hayes, Andrew Iarocci, and Mike Bechthold, tackles the central tale of heroism, and Suzanne Evans exposes the propaganda and coercion that produces the rhetoric of willing mothers in *Mothers of Heroes, Mothers of Grief.* However, I believe that it is the artist who most unequivocally and movingly exposes the hypocrisy, lies, and expediency of such myths. What all these post-1977 texts have in common is a bearing-of-witness to the past, a gathering of memory, imagination, and research that asks us to reconsider, to look again at what we took for granted, and to listen anew for the silences, the *forgotten* history, the absent (but not lost) people and their stories.

The dominant discourse of Canada in the Second World War is similar to that about the Great War in that it also demands forgetting and also produces a glorious record to support present needs. Thus far, however, no historian has done for this war what Vance has done for the First World War; the McKennas began the process of critical investigation and demythologizing in their film, *The Valour and the Horror*, but subsequent films have largely aimed at damage control.[20] One of the most telling, and to my mind chilling, summaries of the idea that Canada emerged from the Second World War stronger and better and without blemish is captured by the unnamed veteran in Broadfoot's *Six War Years* who insists that "it was a good war":

> *I am not talking about a good war from the standpoint of any high moral purpose. If going out and killing millions of Krauts to get Hitler off his goddamn pedestal is a high moral purpose, then I am all for it.*
>
> *But it was a good war for Canada too, because it made us a great nation. I mean, hell, it showed us what we could do. We weren't just a bunch of wheat farmers and Nova Scotia fishermen and lumbermen in B.C. We were a nation. A big and tough and strong nation.*
>
> *And another thing. Listen to this. If you take the terror and the horror and the death and destruction out of it, it was a good war. It was a party. I enjoyed myself. I'll never have so much fun again in my life. I mean it. Ask anybody. It was a good war.* (Six War Years 11)





And Broadfoot seems to agree. Nowhere in this book or in the 1985 one, *Veterans' Years*, does he weigh what is missing from his selected interviews, provide a wider social context, or review the history surrounding the war, Quebec's views on Canada's role or on conscription, or the reasons for Canada's entry into the war. Instead, he dismisses these absences in his narrative setting of the interviews by saying that "Canadians did not seem to care about the major events [presumably the Holocaust]" (*Six War Years* viii) and takes pride in the view that "Canada's war effort was massive [it was], heroic [really?] and done of her own free will [whatever this means]" (ix).

In his epilogue to *The Veterans' Years*, Broadfoot concludes that "the Canada we know today [he is writing in 1985] is largely the creation of the veterans of World War Two" (249). If this is true, as I think it partially is, albeit often in ways that Broadfoot does not consider, then all the more reason why it is important to ask what our writers and artists have to say about who we are now—and have been post-1977—and where we might be headed in the twenty-first century. Although a history of who those veterans were who went on to shape the politics, institutions (most importantly educational ones), businesses, and culture of Canada has yet to be written, it seems clear that such a story could not be told without the experiences of a composer like Harry Somers who returned from his war to seek solace in Algonquin Park and write *North Country* (1948), or a writer like Farley Mowat, who was so traumatized by his experiences as a soldier in Italy that, shortly after his return, he fled an uncomprehending, celebrating southern Canada for the Northwest Territories and eventually wrote several books about his experiences there, or painters like Aba Bayefsky, Alex Colville, Charles Comfort, or Miller Brittain, who died in his prime at fifty-four in 1968 (after battles with alcoholism). Then there is Raymond Souster, whose poem "The Dresden Special" might stand for Canada's response to the Second World War, much as McCrae's "In Flanders Fields" stands for our response to the Great War:





*The R.A.F called it*
*The Dresden Special*
*...*
*One hundred thirty thousand*
*Charred bodies jammed together*
*Between two bread slices.*
*("The Dresden Special" 108)*[21]

The vast distance between Broadfoot's veteran and Souster, also a veteran, serves to remind us of the parameters of what and who has made Canada and that it is essential to listen to the dead, to acknowledge the ghosts, to recover the stories we prefer to forget and to reinstate them within our landscape of memory so as to understand who we are now by bearing witness to as complete a history as possible. Just as Canadians after the First World War needed a positive, uplifting tale about the war in order to mourn and move on with hope, and just as Canadians needed a similarly reassuring story about their contributions during the Second World War, both at home and abroad, so do we now need a story that serves current expectations and demands. Since 1977 writers and artists have been imagining that story. But to do this they have first had to create a landscape of memory.

The term "landscape of memory" is one I initially came across in my reading of Findley (see my first epigraph) and later in an essay by Laurence Kirmayer to which I have often returned when thinking through how an artist connects with his or her readers or viewers. I discuss the theory behind Kirmayer's use of the metaphor in the next chapter, but the metaphor itself is too important to pass over here. To speak of memory as (like) a landscape is to realize that one moves safely, comfortably through a landscape that is familiar, where the markings and signposts are remembered, understood and, therefore, meaningful. Such a landscape is a domain or territory for which the traveller has a legible memory map because the markings on that map are traced in and by memories, which are, in turn, connected to produce a meaningful narrative pattern and shape. The *narrative*—the forming of stories and history, of myths, and discursive formations—is *the* crucial step in creating landscapes of memory. We *read* such maps; we *read* our way through such landscapes. But what happens if there are blank expanses in the landscape or areas of the map without familiar signposts? What if the story is interrupted, erased, forgotten, or buried? What if another story—one that is widely accepted, sanctioned, dominant, and official—already occupies the available space so that one's memories and stories can find no room, location, grounding, or accepted place in the landscape? How then can the traveller find his or her way? How can others see, hear, or read these absent stories? The person I am calling the traveller, this person with the memories and stories that need to be understood and validated, will be lost; his or her stories will be laughed at, denied, rejected, especially if they involve experiences the official story has decided to forget. The stories, memories, and the person who bears them will, quite simply, be silenced.

Which does not mean that the stories, memories, and rememberers go away. Throughout this book I demonstrate that hitherto silenced stories, with their burden of memory and forgetting, persist like ghosts just below the surface of our personal landscapes of memory or in the backstory and subtexts of our official history. Moreover, these landscapes exist in landscape paintings from the wars, are produced by the settings and tropes of novels and memoirs, through the diegesis and set designs of plays and films, and in the rhythms, repetitions, and tonalities of music. The artists create new landscapes or recreate familiar ones so that the buried, forgotten, or repressed and denied memories can surface. When the story to be told is about war, many of the landmarks are firmly identified and cannot be altered. Nevertheless, the landscape of war memory is, uncannily like an actual battlefield, still a mnemonic minefield.





As Jack Hodgins tells us through the remembering of his main character, the returned soldier Matthew Pearson, in *Broken Ground*, "the only crop those fields produced was a harvest of arms and blown-off feet and lost buttons and helmets and the surfacing rotted corpses of the dead" (104). Or as R.H. Thomson comes to appreciate in his play *The Lost Boys*, the "Iron Harvest" will never end; he picks up an "H.E. detonator head from the war," holds it out to the audience, and explains, "The frost pushed this remnant to the surface of the fields several springs ago. It's called the Iron Harvest. But when I walked in the fields [they] looked peaceful to my immediate eye. Peace and order were what I saw but they were just a small part of the story. The larger part of the story was that everything beneath my feet was moving. Through seasons of rain and heaving frosts, bits of rifle, detonators, barbed wire, helmets, artillery shells are slowly being pushed to the surface....The larger story is that the earth is not at peace. The earth is reworking its memory of the war" (46).

At this point in the actor's remembrance and re-enactment, the actor/Thomson begins to dance accompanied by the skeletons of the long-dead soldiers (images projected on scrims). As he dances he speaks of the thousands of unclaimed skeletons hidden in the landscape, some of which "break company" with the dead and "come to the surface" to contribute to "the larger story" (47). In other words, Thomson, like Hodgins's Matt Pearson, or like Varley decades before him, is keeping faith with McCrae's dead by unearthing their stories from landscapes of memory created on canvas, page, or stage.

The landscapes of memory traversed in the chapters to come are not safely located elsewhere in a dim past. They are *here* and *now*. The narrative and narrators of Hodgins's novel are located in 1990s Canada, in a small returned soldiers' community on Vancouver Island; Thomson performs his dance of remembering, his vigil, before—and for—us; the main character in Jane Urquhart's *The Stone Carvers* is a woman who lives in a quiet farming community in Ontario, and like the young, prairie women in the plays *Mary's Wedding* and *Unity (1918)*, she inhabits a landscape of memory troubled by a war fought far away. This recuperation of times past and distant places operates in the Second World War works as well. In Marie Clements's play *Burning Vision*, for example, a contemporary Dene widow evokes Dene memories of uranium mining before and during the war, and through her visions she connects the Dene (and us) with a vision of the past and the future. In novels like Crummey's *The Wreckage* or Kogawa's *Obasan*, the stories surface in and through landscapes and memories that erupt in the present with both terrifying and comforting results. The landscape of memory metaphor, therefore, is an image of the broken ground of our history as we recall and rework it. This metaphor effectively captures the sense in which history is like a field hiding stones/stories that continue to surface and, as they surface, they *change* the story, alter the landscape, make room for new, for more, stories, and allow us to see/hear the repressed, forgotten memories excised from the official story of Canada and the wars.

The Canadian landscape of memory in the works I consider holds the present potential of a larger, more inclusive history that complicates, provokes, and challenges what Jonathan Vance calls the "myth" of the Great War and what I call the discursive formation of Canadians-in-war.[22] In describing my landscape of memory metaphor, I mentioned signposts, markings on the landscape that enable it to be read, and this notion of signs is also a metaphor for the many tropes I find at work in the texts I examine. Some of these tropes have already put in an appearance: the dead as ghosts; the *things* or mnemonic remnants of the past that surface over time and which stand, metonymically, for what Thomson calls a larger story; the pervasive sense of haunting; the complex connection, often figured as disconnect, between home front and battle front. But there are other tropes, some very specific ones such as barbed wire, trains, suitcases, and wounds, and more general ones like borders and webs, which recur obsessively, until they come to seem essential tools in an artist's kit bag. The best way to consider how this set of signs functions is to study it at work in the landscape of an actual text, but two preliminary examples may be useful at this point.

I have chosen two works through which to introduce my landscape of memory metaphor, one from before 1977 and one from after 2007. The first, Varley's 1918 painting *For What?* (page 36), strikes me as standing for, as *addressing*, all the later works; it casts a long shadow forward into the present. The second, a 2008 sound installation piece by Janet Cardiff and George Bures Miller, *The Murder of Crows* (pages 33–34), looks backward to the Second World War while remaining dramatically located in the twenty-first-century present; it speaks (literally) to us about current, small international "new wars" (Mary Kaldor's term), genocide, terror, and atrocity. When I look closely at Varley's *For What?* what do I see and can I speak of this painting's effect on me in terms other than the visual? Although I cannot remember when or where I first saw the actual painting or even reproductions of it (perhaps in Heather Robertson's *A Terrible Beauty*), I know it disturbed me. If it was ever hung as part of a Group of Seven or Varley exhibition in the National Gallery or in the Frederick Varley Art Gallery of Chatham, as is entirely possible, I do not recall seeing it there.[23] In other words, I remember strong emotion conveyed by the painting and elicited from me decades after it was painted, or originally exhibited after the First World War, and then stored, *because* it was textually reproduced in a

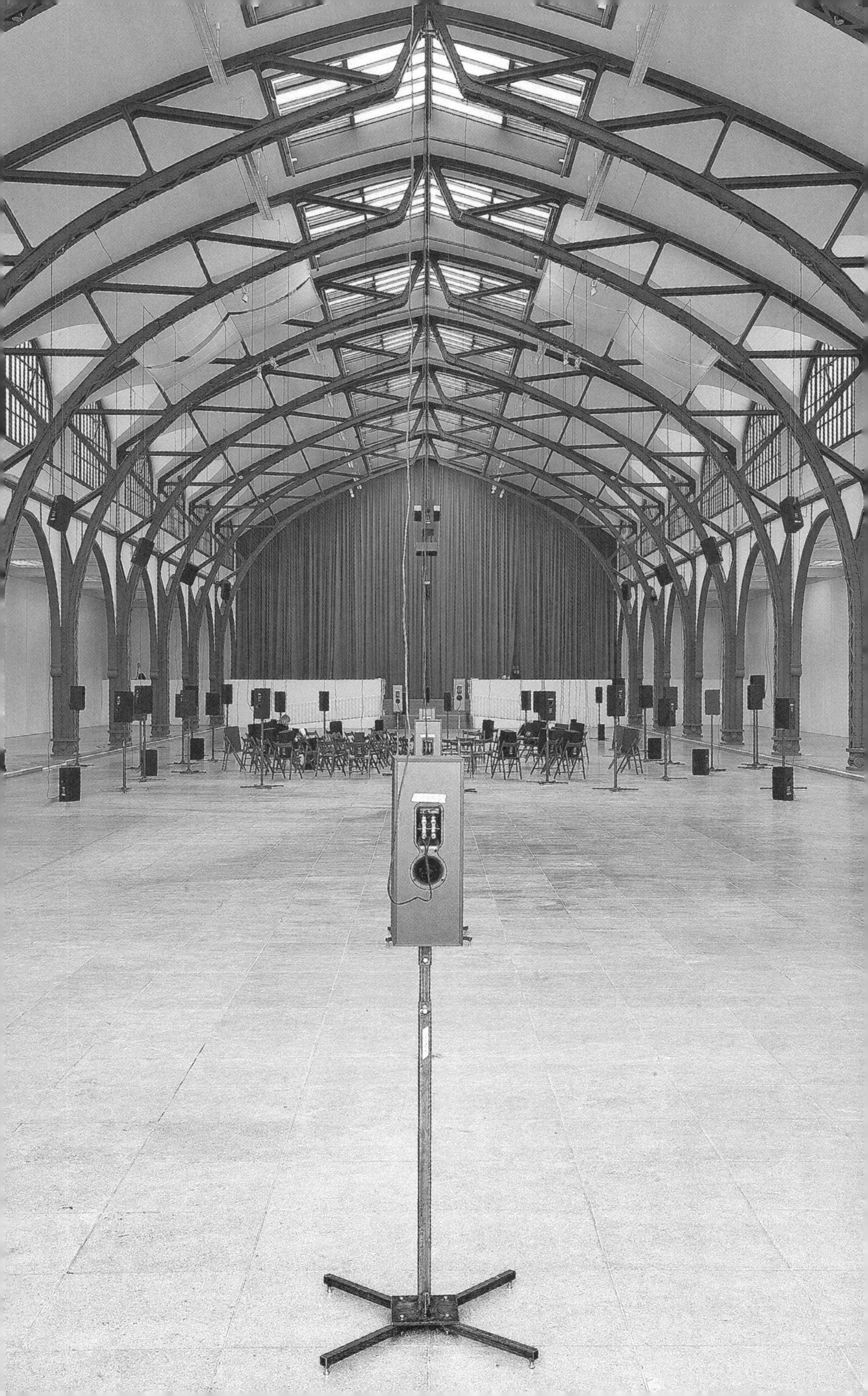

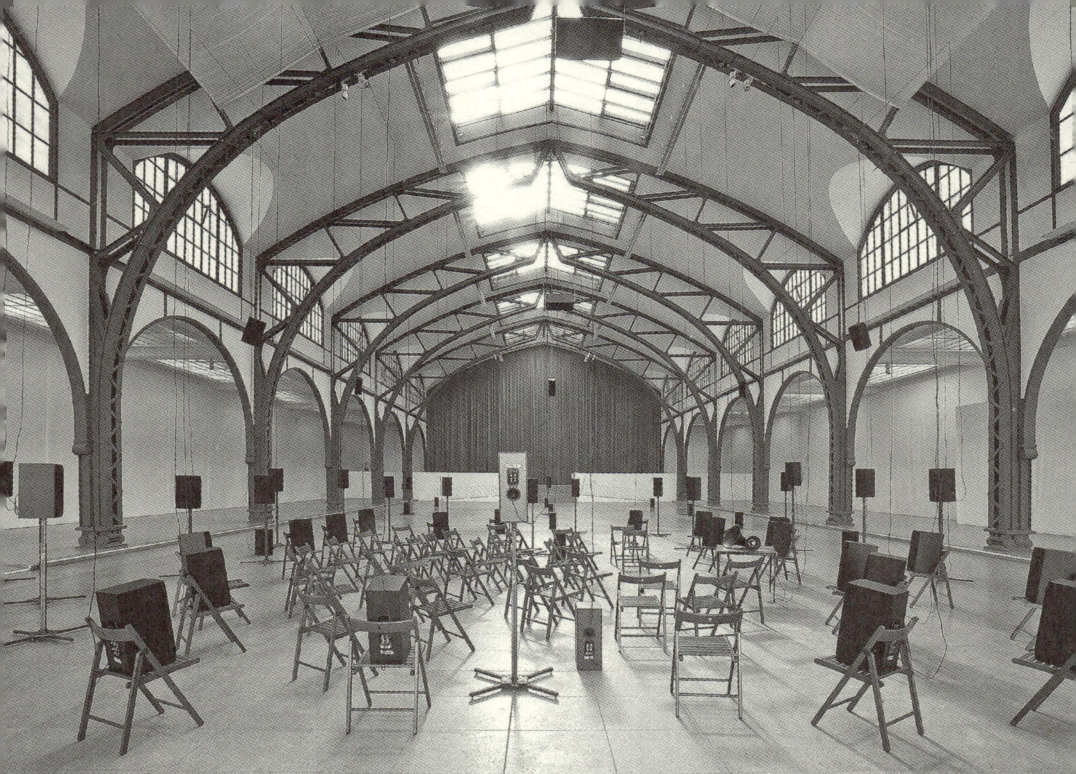

*Pages 33–34: Janet Cardiff and George Bures Miller,* The Murder of Crows *(2008). Mixed media installation with 98 audio speakers, 20 amplifiers, 1 computer, electronics, 1 desk, 1 horn speaker, chairs. Duration 30 mins; dimensions variable. Reproduced courtesy of the artists, Luhring Augustine, New York, and Galerie Barbara Weiss, Berlin.*

book and because its reproduction occurred in the context of Canadian war art, where narrative and poetry framed its presence.

It is impossible now to determine what Canadian gallery visitors might have thought they saw or felt when the picture was shown in touring exhibitions immediately after the war. Reviewing one exhibition in 1920, Augustus Bridle called another of Varley's works, *The Sunken Road—August 1918*, "his cadaver picture" (Osborne, "Warscapes" 321), and Bridle's reaction to A.Y. Jackson's somber *A Copse, Evening, 1918* was equally blunt. In his autobiography, *A Painter's Country*, Jackson praised Varley for producing some of the finest Canadian First World War canvases, and by "finest" Jackson meant that they were both powerful and true to the felt experience of war, unlike the large, celebratory, heroic studio pictures by Richard Jack (such as *The Taking of*

*Vimy Ridge, Easter Monday 1917* [1919]) or Derwent Wood's controversial bronze called *Canada's Golgotha* (1918).[24]

What I first saw and still see in Varley's painting echoes Jackson's verdict. There most certainly are corpses in *For What?*—they occupy the centre, focal point of the composition—but they are emphatically part of a landscape painting, or what is barely (yet *still*) recognizable as a landscape. Two-thirds of the picture is filled with a seemingly endless flat expanse of mud, slime, and eerily familiar but not quite discernible objects (perhaps just rocks or lumps of pockmarked earth?). The only upright things in this landscape are the two rows of tiny, fragile white crosses and the figure of a weary soldier, who leans on his shovel; kneeling to his right is another soldier. Together they form the burial crew, the gravediggers charged with preparing a resting place for their fellow soldiers. Although the standing soldier's facial expression is invisible—the sickly light in the sky is behind him, his cap casts a shadow, and he is too far away, too small for his features to be seen—he appears to be gazing towards that ugly wheelbarrow in the foreground with its grisly contents. I, however, am positioned in front of this scene, where I must witness (unless I turn away) the forlorn graves, the sodden terrain, the strangely illumined sky, the tired soldier and his comrade and, above all, the shocking contents of that barrow. Several aspects of Varley's depiction of the barrow with its corpses produce its shock value for me. While the bodies are unquestionably recognizable as human beings, as dead First World War soldiers from their boots and puttees, I cannot see them wholly because their upper torsos and heads are covered; they are piled in such a manner that I cannot even determine exactly how many there are, and they are—in terms of colour—indistinguishable from the ground in which they will soon be laid. Who are they, how old are they, how did each man die and where did he come from? How, in fact, did he end up here like this? Where are all those myriad small things that identify and distinguish these men as individuals? What is hidden by the tarp or filthy blanket that partly covers them? Varley refuses to show me the full picture,

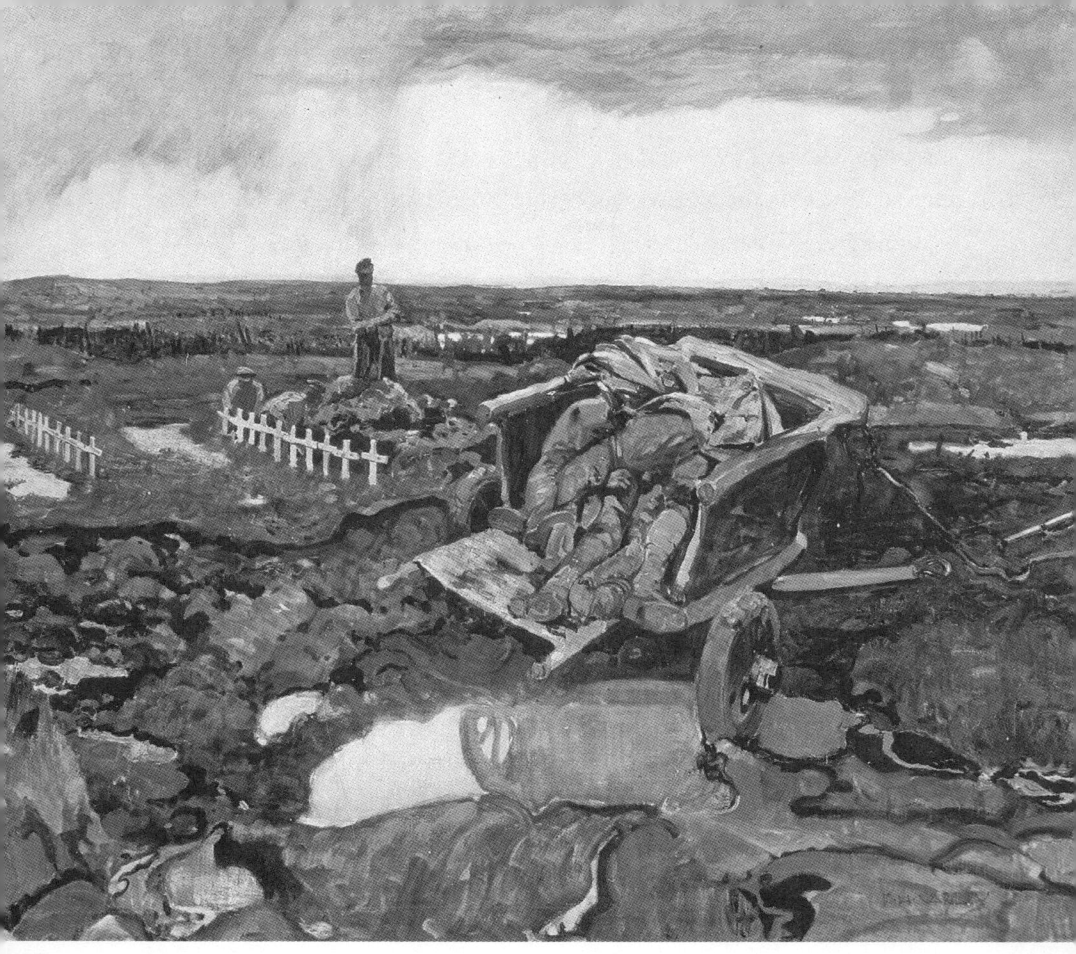

*Frederick Varley,* For What? *(1918). o/c 147 x 183.8 cm. CWM #19710261-0770. Beaverbrook Collection of War Art. © Canadian War Museum. Varley painted several memorable pictures of the First World War battlefields, but this burial scene is especially powerful. The haunting question of its title is as pertinent in this century as it was one hundred years ago. To varying degrees all the works discussed in this book grapple with this question.*

which is surely his point and part of the source of this painting's power to disturb and haunt.

But if I *can see* the contents (or most of it) of the wheelbarrow, it is because I am forced to do so. The two soldiers in the background do not need to see inside it, not just yet; in any case, they already know what lies there awaiting their attention. It is the rest of us, back in Canada, who must be enabled to see, *to see* and remember. This painting *speaks* to anyone who stands before it (or opens *A Terrible Beauty* or *Canvas of*

*War*) of human frailty and vulnerability, of what we share with the men and bodies in the picture—our ephemeral humanity—and it asks us to bear witness to its silent eloquence. If human beings can be reduced to this jumble of legs and boots (and we know they can, and worse, because by now we have seen images from Bergen-Belsen, Dachau, Shanghai, Vietnam, Rwanda), where does that leave us? I do not feel I can walk away from this picture saying that it does not implicate me or address me. I must respond to that weary soldier, to those dead men, to the image of that barrow mirrored in the crater-hole of repulsive water. I am quite simply seized by this painting, as Coleridge's Wedding Guest was seized by the Ancient Mariner; I am asked to provide answers, above all to the painting's title: for what reason have these men died and once dead why should they be buried there in such a place? This painting haunts me. It haunts me because it is a landscape (and I am sure I know the landscape genre) but not one I recognize and, therefore, I feel ill at ease. It haunts me because it reflects back to me an image of my own mortality. It haunts me because it urges me to remember what I could never have seen with my own eyes (it happened before my time and far away), and it haunts me because of what I see in it and in other, more recent, images. It haunts me because it evokes memories of reciting "In Flanders Fields" ("We are the dead"...), of visits to galleries, ceremonies, monuments, of many snatches of conversation or suppressed discussion (not suitable for young ears), and of very recent witnessing that I finally undertook by visiting Vimy Ridge, Beaumont-Hamel, Ypres, and a few of the 956 cemeteries and monuments from the two world wars that exist in Belgium, the Netherlands, and northern France. *There* I stood in another landscape of memory made real to me by this painting and wondered—for what?

Today that landscape is green, fertile, almost pastoral, as it must have been before the war, but its hundreds of cemeteries, thousands of crosses, and many monuments belie this seeming calm.[25] As R.H. Thomson put it, "the earth is not at peace." Back *here*, where time, distance, and "imposed amnesia" (K. Oliver 322) gloss over the real horror and waste of the war, I must return to works of art like *For What?* to help me remember. This painting succeeds where official history and politically approved rhetoric (what Vance calls the myth of the Great War) fail because it is a landscape of memory, one so powerfully synaesthetic that I can almost smell and hear the scene. It is one in which the dead are not yet decorously hidden from view in a groomed and verdant landscape, and where they and the earth continue to address me, to tell me parts of their story. That this story will always be incomplete, a fragment only, produces the need to know more and provokes my attention; it elicits from me that quality of "empathic unsettlement" that LaCapra finds essential to bearing witness. I cannot answer Varley's question because this ugly waste of human beings and nature seems utterly pointless to me. Worse still, his haunting question never seems irrelevant, never becomes fixed in a past war, and cannot be consigned to the vaults of forgetting. And this topicality or persistent relevance also contributes to the haunting power of the scene. This landscape of memory is one I (we) continue to inhabit, if only we take time to appreciate the fact, to read and listen to its ghosts and stories.

My next example of a landscape of memory is contemporary—the stunning sound installation piece by Janet Cardiff and George Bures Miller called *The Murder of Crows* (2008). The title of this work reminds listener-viewers that flocks of crows (the murders) are known to gather around a dead crow and caw, as if in lament at a funeral, for up to twenty-four hours, but it is people who gather around and within the space of the installation to listen to what the artists have to say. The installation comprises ninety-eight audio speakers, twenty amplifiers, a computer and electronics, plus a desk, a megaphone, and about two dozen empty folding chairs for visitors to sit on. The sound program lasts for thirty minutes and includes a variety of pre-recorded sounds, voices, and music emanating in a programmed sequence from the speakers distributed around the exhibition space. Listeners hear the sounds of crows cawing, of wind, waves, dripping water, footsteps, and machines separated by taut moments of silence as they wait and strain to hear the next sound and determine where it is coming from. There are also songs, most notably one in Russian by a male choir that is, unmistakably, a war song sung by marching soldiers, and three narratives delivered by Cardiff as she tells us fragments of her dreams and nightmares. Her voice emanates from the megaphone placed on a table near the centre of the installation. *The Murder of Crows* is, in effect, a theatrical performance with an aura of ritual in which an audience sits among, and is surrounded by, the speakers' eerily disembodied sounds, stories, and songs that transform a huge exhibition hall into an intimate acoustic landscape or soundscape that envelops a listener.





Although a detailed analysis of this extraordinary work is beyond my expertise, I can describe the impact it made on me when I stumbled upon it at Berlin's Nationalgalerie im Hamburger Bahnhof museum for contemporary art in the spring of 2009. I felt, at first, acutely disoriented as I approached the huge exhibition hall defined spatially, but very loosely, by the chairs and speakers: the usual border between art and the museum visitor, that dividing line that helps one play one's familiar, rule-governed role, seemed so uncertain and permeable. Once I sat down and joined, as it were, the performance, I felt by turns included by some of the surrounding sounds (birds, waves, wind, and dripping water) but pushed back, even excluded from the scene, by other sounds, especially the marching men singing a battle song; I did not need to understand Russian to get that point. When Cardiff's voice emerged from the megaphone near the centre of the gathered chairs, I was both attracted—she was speaking directly to me—and yet repulsed: her voice was dreamlike in quality, almost soothing, while her remembered dreams and words were terrifying, none more so that her description of finding a severed leg sticking out from under a blanket on a bed. "I try to scream and I want to wake up," she says in the present tense, "but I can't scream and I can't move" (qtd. in *The Murder of Crows*).

This dream story is followed by an opera singer who sings about her leg which has been blown off by a bomb. In another sequence, involving a jarring juxtaposition, Cardiff describes her dream in which a boy with an injured foot is dragged before an army commander who orders the amputation of his leg; the child screams and screams as the story fades into the Russian army singing their patriotic marching song. By this point, I realize that I have entered a land-sound-scape that I shall never leave behind insofar as the memory of the experience will stay with me long after precise details from the piece are forgotten. Afterwards (the thirty minutes felt like two hours), I bought a pamphlet about the work in which art historian Carolyn Christov-Bakargiev tells me that "the piece is a requiem to a world of positivity and utopia that—although heralded at the end of the Cold War after 1989—seems to have disappeared in our time of pathological 'war on terror' and 'ethnocidal' violence that mark the darker side of globalization" (21). Christov-Bakgarviev also identifies the Russian marching song as Aleksandr Aleksandrov's *Svyaschennaya* (*The Sacred War*), a famous, patriotic song composed in 1941 to boost morale for the Soviet army as it prepared to meet Hitler's invading forces: "Rise up, huge country / Rise up for a mortal fight / with the dark fascist force," the deep voices sing, "A people's war is going on / A sacred war" (20). And she explains that *The Murder of Crows* was inspired in part by Goya's etching *The Sleep of Reason Produces Monsters* (ca. 1799).

In 2010 *The Murder of Crows* finally came home to Canada, where it was first exhibited in the Art Gallery of Alberta from January until May, but Cardiff's work, as well as important pieces like this one created with her husband, is not well known here. In one sense, the piece escapes classification as Canadian because it addresses an international audience about a global crisis of nightmare, war, atrocity, terror, and the failure to achieve peace since the Second World War. But in another sense, *The Murder of Crows* is profoundly Canadian, deeply personal, and even local—local, that is, to British Columbia, where Cardiff and Miller live for part of each year. This acoustic landscape of memory, with its cawing crows, seagulls, waves, wind, and dripping water, is as much a part of the BC coast as are the ominous, physical traces that are still visible, but forgotten, from the Second World War (the coastal gun emplacements, bunkers, and memorials) and of present terrors (aerial surveillance and sea- and airport security screening).

When Cardiff was asked by Francesca von Habsburg if the work was "autobiographical," despite being so "abstract" in style and presentation, Cardiff replied that it was "quite personal": "I'd been recording dreams for about a year, keeping a recorder beside the bed. At one point I had a series of dreams about strange situations in foreign countries... I was also having violent, apocalyptic dreams. Strangely enough two of the dreams I recorded dealt with a severed foot and on the way to Australia to install the piece George opened the paper and it was about a fifth foot being found, washed up on the west coast [of a British Columbia] beach" (from "Collecting: The last temptation," an interview with von Habsburg). In other words, the landscape of memory informing an exhibition space holding *The Murder of Crows* is home ground (geographical, psychological, emotional), even as it reaches out across borders of time, space, medium, and language to haunt anyone who falls under its spell.[26]

*The Murder of Crows* brings the subject of war, history, and memory into the immediate present. It achieves this *presence* (and presentness) in two ways: by incorporating familiar, natural sounds and Cardiff's personal address and by involving each witness (a gallery visitor, an audience member, even a passerby) as an active listening participant in the story process. At the same time, it recuperates and recontextualizes history—the past of Goya's art, the history of the Second World War, and the more recent past of contemporary wars, including the war on (and of) terror. Although it cannot answer Varley's question, it does demonstrate how deeply implicated in and haunted by past wars we all are. Moreover, like *For What?*, *The Murder of Crows* addresses us and asks us to respond. Both works use their landscapes of memory

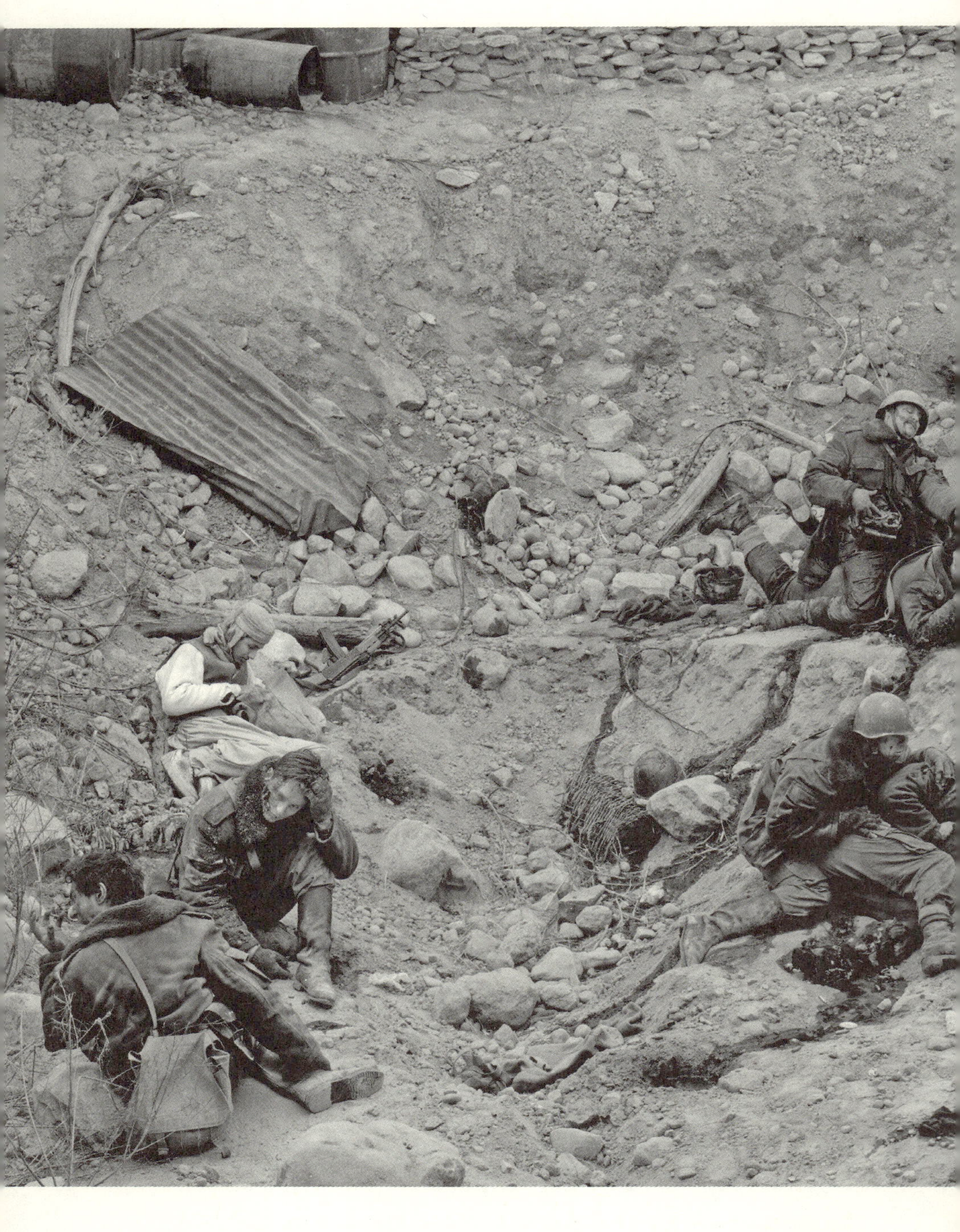

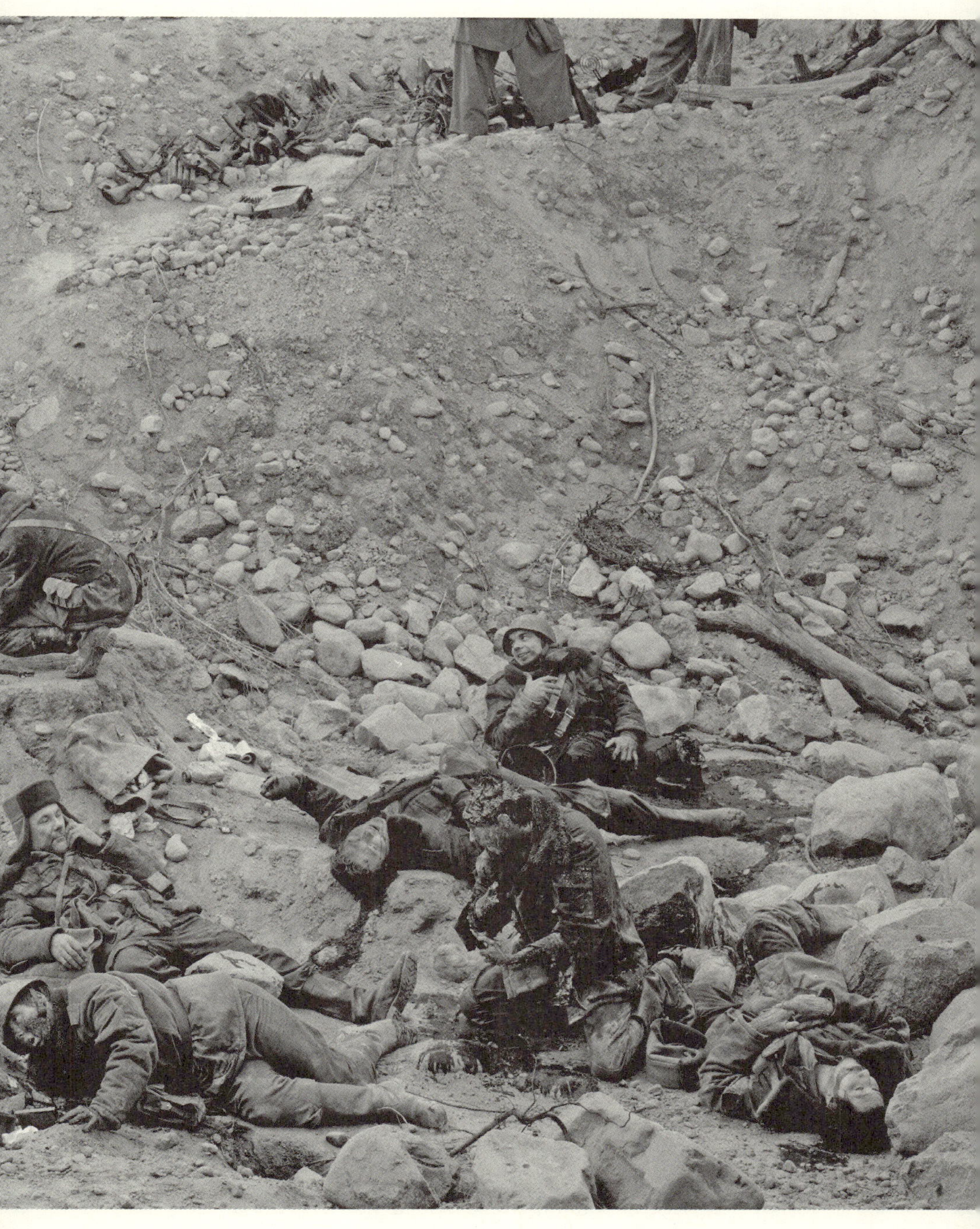

*Jeff Wall*, Dead Troops Talk (A Vision After an Ambush of a Red Army Patrol, Near Moqor, Afghanistan, Winter 1986) *(1992). Transparency in light box. 229 x 417 cm. Wall created this tableau over several weeks in a studio in Burnaby, BC. He calls this type of work a "cinematic graphic" because the photograph uses enactment and captures a performance of the scene depicted. The image is reproduced with permission, courtesy of the artist.* 

to create the conditions under which their interlocutors (a term I prefer to ones like viewer, spectator, or audience member, each of which implies passive non-response) can experience the empathic unsettlement that promotes thoughtful reflection and recognition, a degree of understanding and accountability, and a hope for change in the way individuals, communities, and nations approach others. It is perhaps too soon to say what twenty-first-century Canadian war art will contribute to an evolving landscape of memory and whether today's visual artists can achieve (or would want to) what war artists like Varley did. But if Jeff Wall's *Dead Troops Talk* is any indication, then I would say that they have much to tell us. I would say this as well of Gertrude Kearns's paintings of Shidane Arone and of casualties in Afghanistan. About Althea Thauberger's photographs, especially her recent ones of women soldiers in Afghanistan, I am less certain.[27]

Walls's 1992 iconic tableau photograph called *Dead Troops Talk (A Vision After an Ambush of a Red Army Patrol, Near Moqor, Afghanistan, Winter 1986)* shows a group of what appear to be dead, dying, and wounded soldiers lying in contorted positions or crouching or struggling in a blasted landscape of dirt, rocks, and fragments of *matériel* (see pages 42–43). However, the scene was staged; it represents the combined forces of photography and performance that took Wall several weeks to shoot. He calls this kind of work a "cinematic graphic," and from his recent comments about the piece it is clear that his theatre of war tableau is meant to be seen as a landscape of memory: he explains that, when he began working on the image, the Soviet-Afghan war had been forgotten; it was in "a faraway place" and had "dropped from the public eye" (qtd. in Lederman). This distance in time and space freed Wall to construct his "hallucinatory image" that would haunt viewers by reminding them, not only, I would argue, about the failure of the Red Army in Afghanistan, but also, and very pointedly, about Canadian war art going right back to Varley and to John McCrae's "In Flanders Fields." The title of the tableau after all is *Dead Troops Talk*, and we are enjoined to listen (to listen in). Looking at and reflecting upon this piece intensifies the urgency with which we must pay attention and the hope that we might learn before it is, once more, too late.

Gertrude Kearns's war art has been much more controversial than Wall's *Dead Troops Talk.* In 2006 Kearns spent five weeks in Afghanistan with the Canadian Forces, and after returning to her Toronto studio she painted six huge, somber canvases of what she had witnessed there. These powerful images would have left Augustus Bridle speechless because they are much more disturbing than Varley's pictures. In *What They Gave* (2006, see pages 46–47), for example, she depicts the deadly result of a suicide bomber attack through the medical treatment given three severely wounded Canadian soldiers. Works like this, based on Kearns's own witnessing and photographs, pose Varley's question all over again, and make it virtually impossible for me to think the sacrifice worthwhile. Her earlier painting of Master Corporal Clayton Matchee torturing the Somali teenager Shidane Arone (*Somalia 2, Without Conscience,* 1996, see page 475) led the National Council of Veteran Associations to threaten a boycott of the Canadian War Museum when they exhibited the painting.[28] Such attempts to repress versions of the events recall the post–First World War era when Canadian war paintings were stored away from the public eye and government, media, and a growing veterans' movement were consolidating an official story of Canada and the Great War, or the more recent furor over the McKennas' film *The Valour and the Horror.* Raised against the kind of witnessing provided by Kearns are the voices and sensibilities of those in Canada who reject images and stories that create landscapes of memory in which ugly facts and horrifying events exist beside more heroic and celebratory ones.

Althea Thauberger brought this confrontation with war images and stories into the public space of a university library, with predictable results. For several weeks in 2008, her life-sized, staged photomural called *The Art of Seeing Without Being Seen* (2007–08, see pages 48–49) filled a wall in the Koerner Library at the University of British Columbia. In some ways this dramatic piece recalls the strategy of Wall's *Dead*

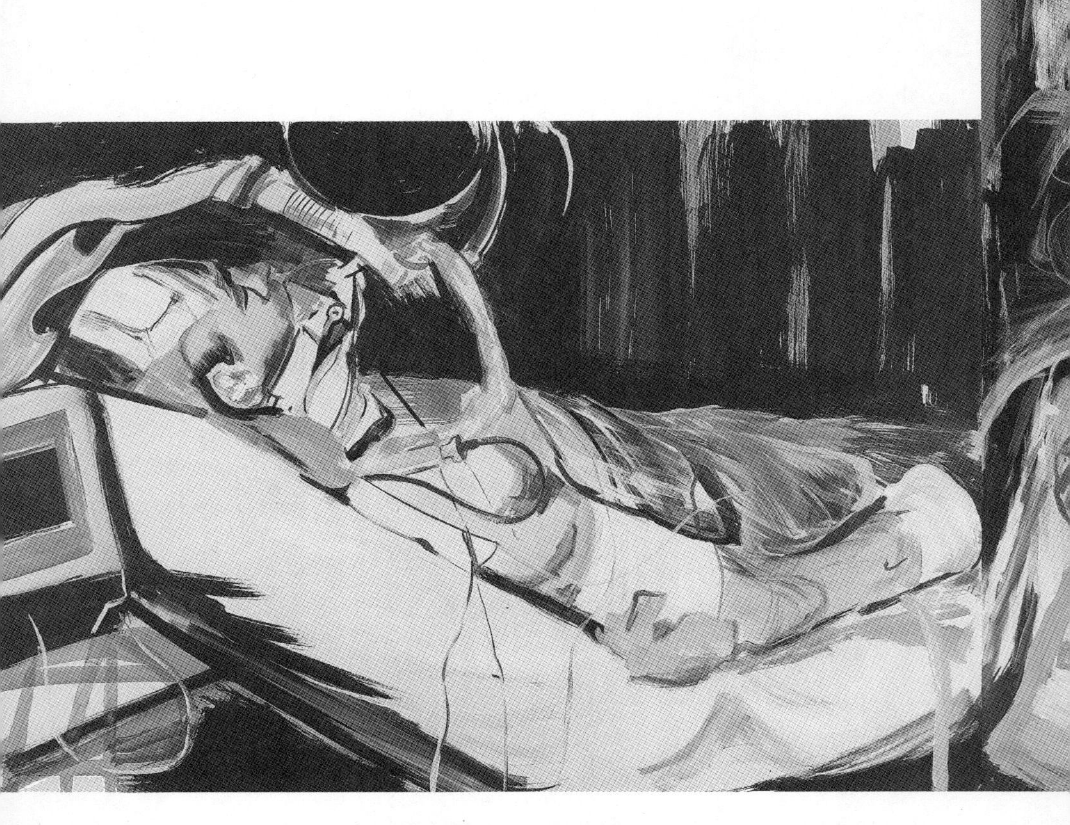

*Gertrude Kearns,* What They Gave *(2006). Ink, acrylic, and crayon on 4-ply board. Three panels, each 152 x 102 cm. #20120019-001. Beaverbrook Collection of War Art. © Canadian War Museum. Kearns was a war artist in Kandahar in January 2006 when a suicide bomber attacked a Canadian vehicle. Three soldiers were seriously injured and Kearns was allowed to photograph one of them—Master Corporal Paul Franklin. These paintings were inspired by this event and her photographs of Franklin.*

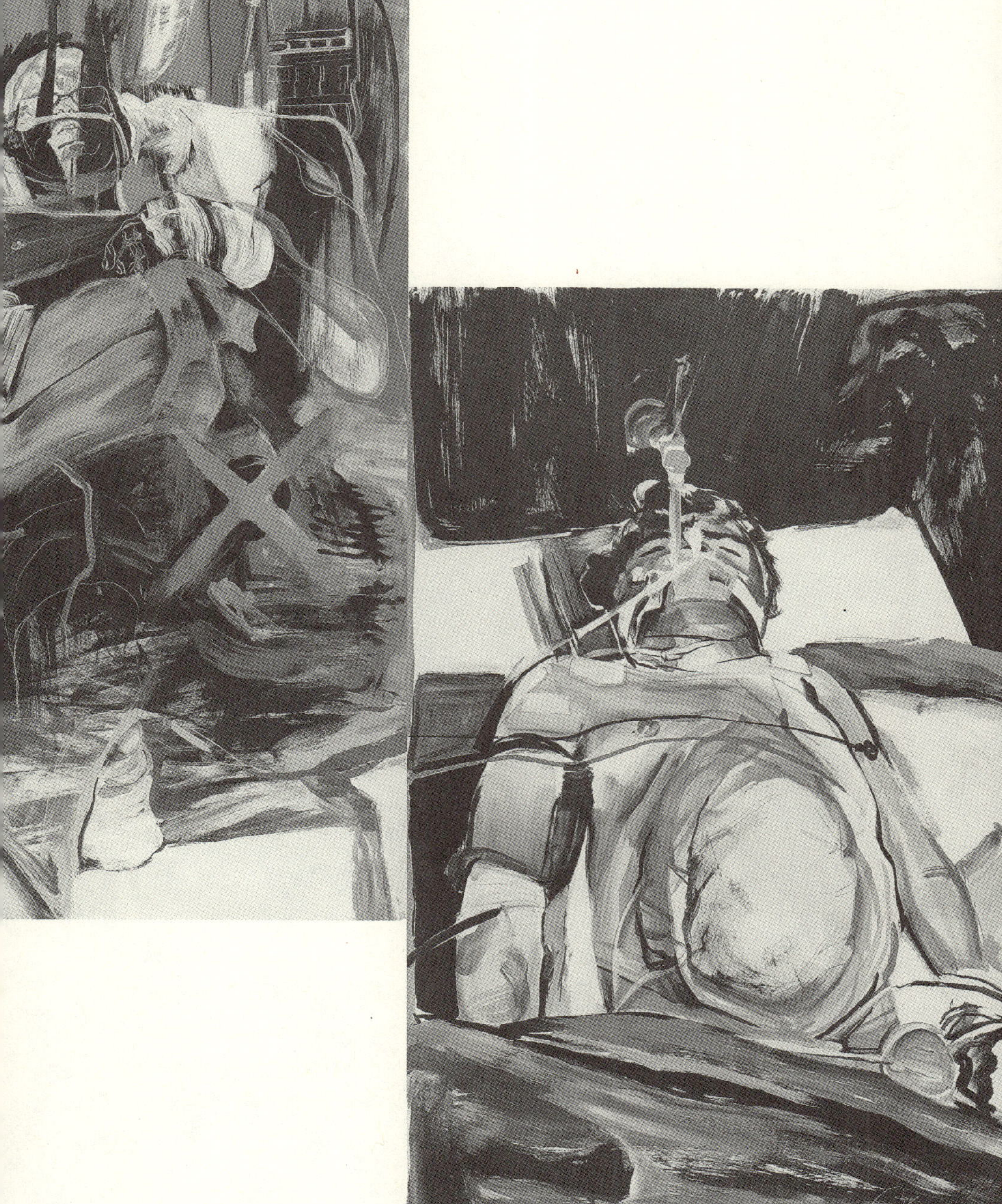

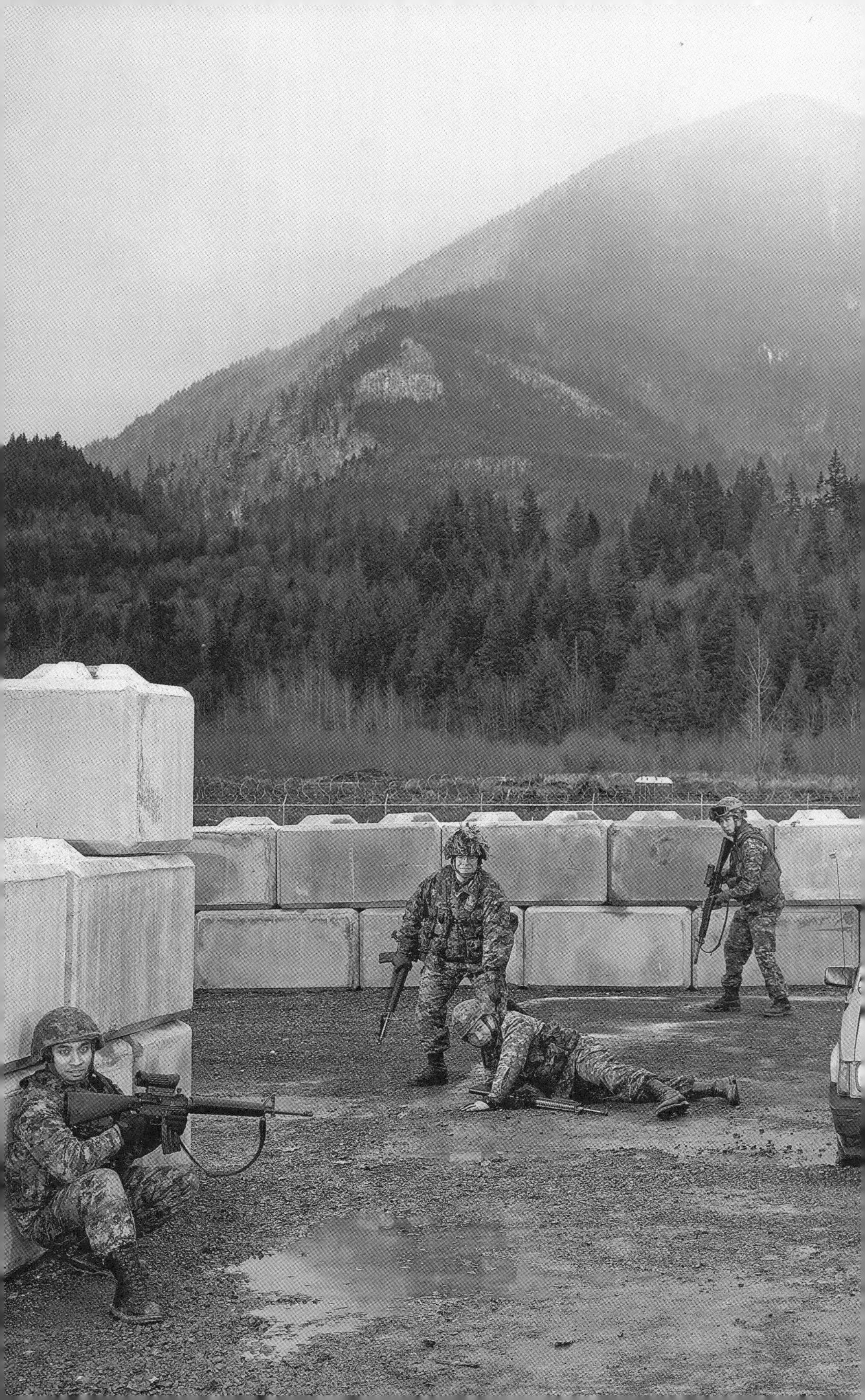

*Althea Thauberger,* The Art of Seeing Without Being Seen *(2007–08). Photographic mural, 216 x 173 cm. Courtesy of the artist. © Althea Thauberger.*

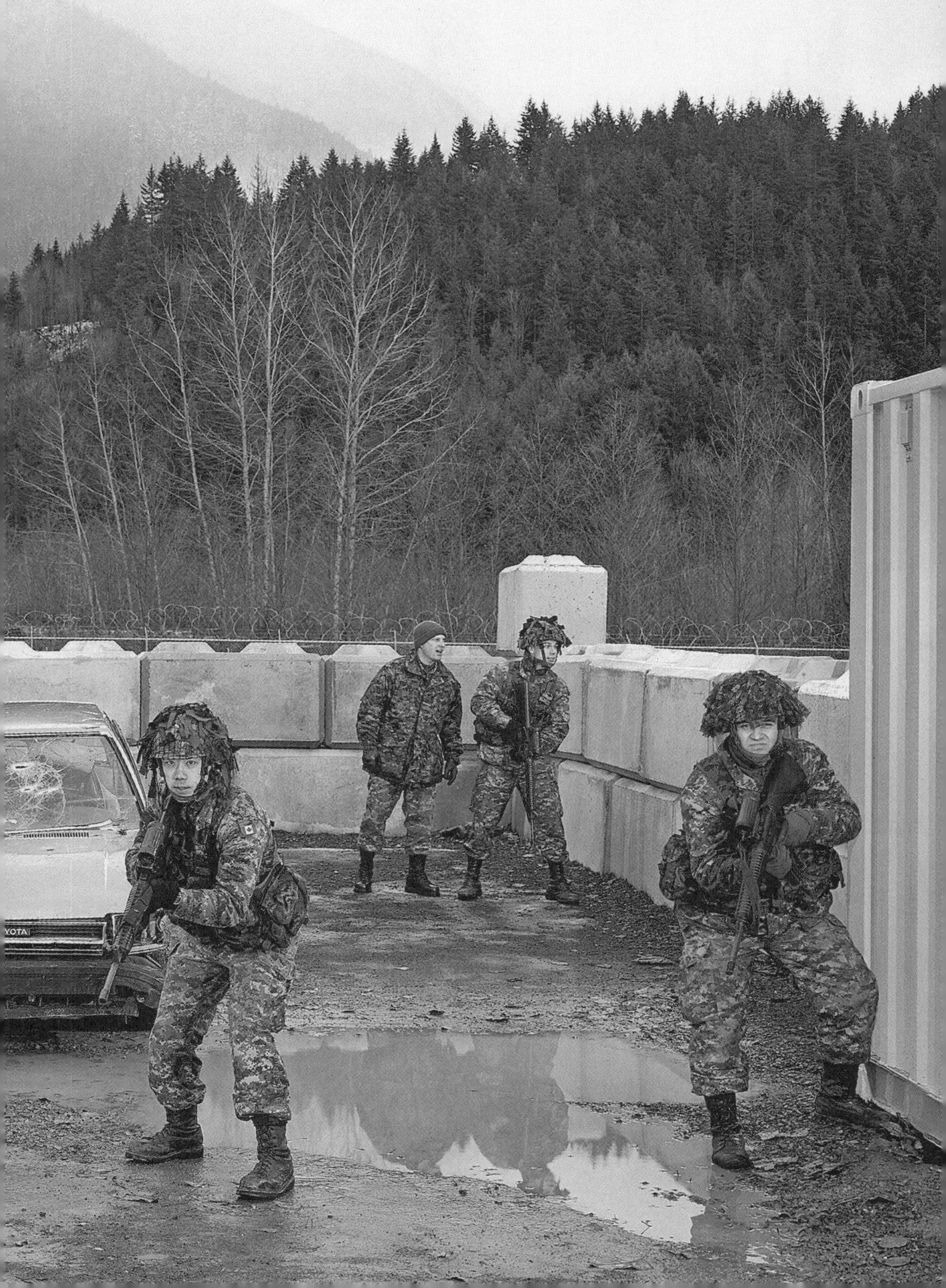

*Troops Talk*, but the resemblance ends there. Thauberger's troops are not dead (yet); they are very young, still in their teens; they appear to be playing a game, complete with battledress, in a parking lot or street; and the background is a familiar Canadian (possibly even Britsh Columbian) landscape. They are Canadians. The maple leaf is clearly visible on the left shoulder of the centre figure and, what's worse, this kid and the other one to his left seem about to point their guns at us. Scott Watson, the director of the university's Belkin Art Gallery, set up a comment book for people to express their reactions and opinions, and these responses arrived in the hundreds. Some viewers were disgusted that such a violent, military image would be hung in a library sanctuary for quiet study: "Violence and libraries don't mix!"[29] Some comments reveal that people saw the piece as mocking the armed forces; others show that people interpreted the piece as praising "these cute boys" before they go off to "kill Afghanis for imperialism" (qtd. in Deborah Campbell 64). My reaction to this highly provocative work of art is that there was no better place to exhibit such an image than on a university campus and in a library, where young people go to do their research, to think, and to question received dogma on all subjects.

*The Art of Seeing Without Being Seen* (which is precisely what we practise when we stand in front of the photomural) challenges us to see more clearly, to take our own position into account, and to look again at things we thought we understood or simply took for granted. It is another landscape of memory, but one so recent, so fresh, so very close and intimate that it destabilizes memory and history to remind us, not about forgotten war stories, but about the desire to forget that war involves us, that war can never be kept over there, that "cute boys" playing war games could kill us or other human beings, and that they may well end up dead themselves, forgotten in their turn. And they will be forgotten unless or until they remind us that they are thirsty ghosts who *will* speak. There may not be any answers to Varley's question here, but there are other questions. If the two world wars made Canada, then what kind of Canada is it, and what kind of country are we making now?

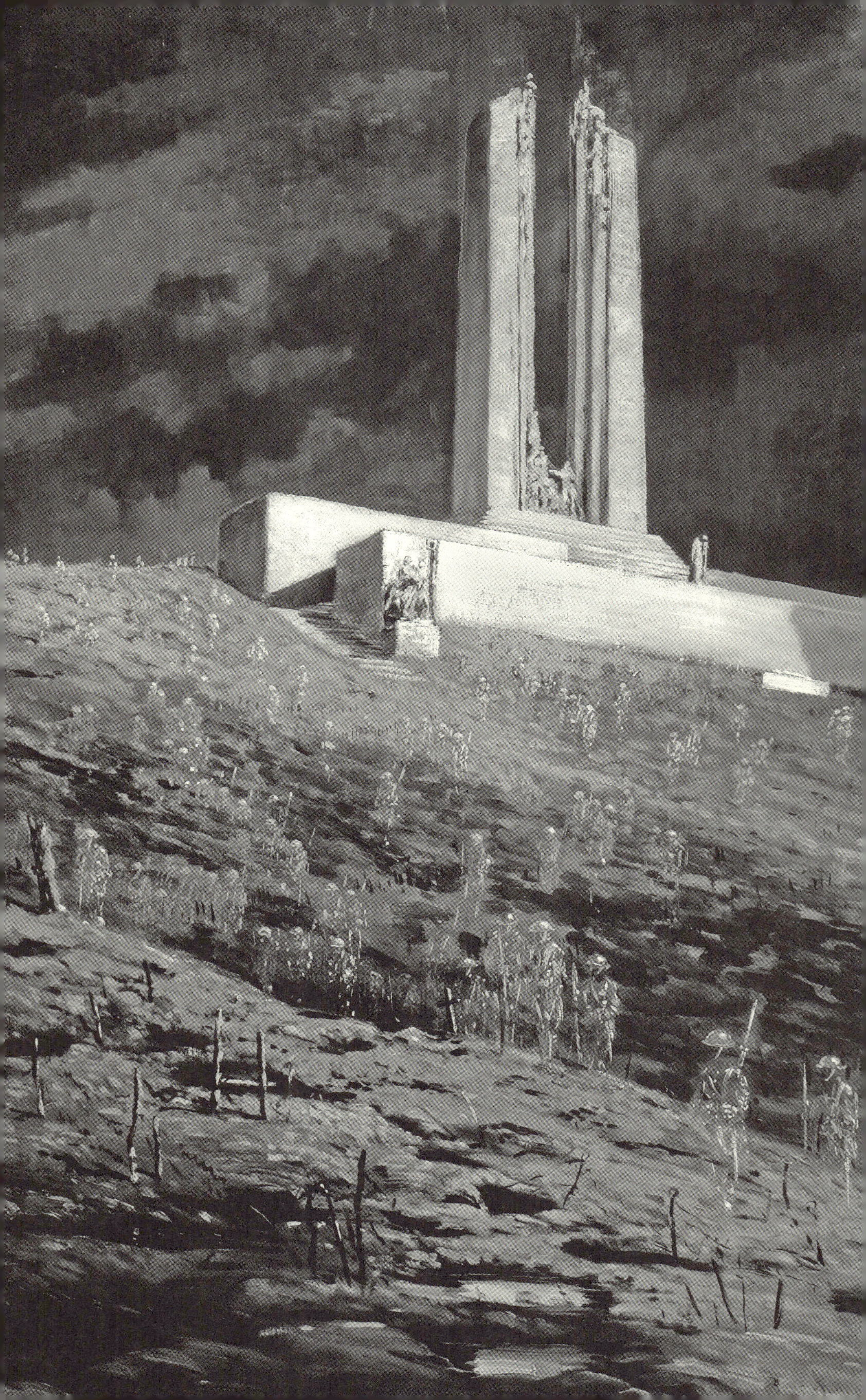

# 2
# Landscapes of Memory



IN THE FINAL SEQUENCE of Abel Gance's classic film *J'accuse* (1938), the dead soldiers from the Great War rise from their graves with all their bleeding wounds, lost limbs, disfigurements, and horror-stricken, traumatized and vacant stares—and march.[1] Europe is about to plunge itself and the world into another war and the dead soldiers have risen from their graves, where they had been so quickly forgotten after the last war, because they are needed once more—this time to stop war. What is so remarkable about the final ten minutes of the film is less the cinematic techniques used to create this effect than the reason for the soldiers' return from the dead and the clearly visible fact that the dead of *all* the warring nations have risen together *en masse* in this march for peace. The hero of the film, Jean Diaz, a First World War veteran whose closest comrades were wiped out in a futile patrol of a ravine at Verdun just hours before the Armistice, vowed that he would never forget them and that there would never be another war. As the sole survivor of this ill-fated patrol, he has devoted his life to inventing tools for peace and to protesting the rise of militarism and the escalation of weapons manufacture in France.

Traumatized by his war experiences and increasingly alarmed by the signs of another war, he often returns to the graves of his friends to remember and commune with them. At times he seems to go mad with rage and despair because no one wants to listen to his warnings, so intent are those around him on resuming a normal life, making money, and obliterating the past. When he finally realizes how futile his efforts are and learns that his peaceful inventions have been commandeered for war, he hurls a series of accusations against the men of today for "not listening to the dead" of the First World War, and he returns to the cemeteries of Verdun to call out the dead. A violent storm erupts as Jean stands bare-headed before the graves and screams for help to stop the approaching war: "Dead of Verdun arise," he shouts in French, German, and English, and they do. The entire landscape seems to shift and heave, the crosses melt away, layers of earth disappear before our eyes, memorial statues of warriors come to life, and the dead reappear. This filmic landscape remembers its dead.

Of course, the coming war will not be stopped. Not even these ghastly spectres can bring the living to their senses. Instead, a civilian mob captures Jean and hangs him, and the film ends with the armies of the dead marching, marching, marching towards the camera and the viewer. We are the dead, they might be saying, but they are definitely not asking anyone to take up their quarrel with the foe. Nor are they asking for revenge as does the ghost of Hamlet's father when he rises from the grave fully armed to insist that the younger generation never forget him. German, French, Italian, Russian, English, they march side by side; officers march with foot soldiers, and no man points an accusing dead hand at the generals, politicians, or capitalists who caused the war. On the contrary, these dead armies march to remind the world of their staggering numbers and appalling deaths so that such a cataclysm will not happen again. They march because they have been forgotten; rising from the earth, they disrupt the tidy, decorous landscape of neat crosses, flowers, and sanctimonious memorials; they perform this communal remembrance ceremony for future generations. By doing this (or so Gance wants us to understand), they warn us about the consequences of forgetting and they remind us of the importance of memory.

Many post-Second World War films, especially documentaries and anti-war films, employ this image of the dead rising or returning (from the grave or the past) to remind the living of what they want to forget. Artistically, this return of the dead is a powerful device because of its roots in ritual and myth, its shared cross-cultural familiarity (what human community does not fear, honour, propitiate, and commemorate their dead?), and its long, distinguished use in literature and art. In the representations of the two world wars this trope of ghostly return is inextricably combined with landscapes depicting shattered scenes of destruction (it is with reason that we describe natural disasters as resembling war zones) or serene, peaceful scenes, usually pastoral, where few traces remain of past violence and upheaval. The juxtaposition of past and present landscapes from which the dead appear and to which we return is nowhere more emphatically and strategically employed than in Claude Lanzmann's excoriating *Shoah* (1985). The film opens and closes with Holocaust survivor Simon Srebnik, who still carries within him the bullet meant to kill him, returning to the Polish village of Chelmno. His survival is a miracle. The Nazis intended to destroy him, along with all the other Jews who might testify to the horror of their extermination at Chelmno, but Lanzmann found him alive in Israel and persuaded him to return to the site of extermination and mass graves—to return and to sing. I had no clear idea what to expect when I began to watch *Shoah*; therefore, I was charmed and seduced, as I was meant to be, by the long opening sequence of a lovely pastoral scene with a misty river from which drifts the haunting sound of singing.

*Shoah* takes place entirely in the present time of filming—no archival footage is used—and as the narrative slowly unfolds, some now elderly villagers hear this voice too and it reminds them of a thirteen-year-old Jewish boy they knew in the 1940s who had a sweet voice and to whose songs they and the German soldiers enjoyed listening. Simon Srebnik's return to this village and this now calm, lovely landscape is iconic. This real man, who survived by sheer accident, embodies and performs, thanks to his enormous generosity and Lanzmann's persuasion, a ghostly return, within a landscape that has erased him and others like him, in order to make room, to locate and make possible the telling of a story we would rather not hear and for which so few signposts remain to show us where, when, and how things happened *back then*. In Lanzmann's hands, this voice, the quiet river, and the green fields, become an exemplary instance, a recreation, of what I call a landscape of memory.



*J'accuse* and *Shoah*, as works of art, illustrate almost all the narrative techniques, tropes, and themes found in Canadian novels, plays, films, and memoirs created after 1977. From the ghosts and deceptively pastoral landscapes to the larger sense of the First World War haunting the future and our present to the stress on trauma, especially cross-generational trauma, and the need to bear witness to history and to remember the past, these films, like the Canadian texts, operate on the assumption that the reader/viewer/audience member will accept their appeal to an ethics of memory and take up the challenge to *listen*, to pay attention, and respond to the stories being told. All these works mobilize a coherent set of tropes to produce their narratives and capture our attention; some of these are as obvious or concrete as the ubiquitous images of trains, barbed wire, wounds, and deafening noise, or the shorthand of resonant, and historically specific, dates, place names, songs, quotations, facts and events: Ypres, Beaumont-Hamel, Vimy, D-Day, Dachau, Hiroshima, Stalingrad, 11 November, 9 April, "Keep the Home Fires Burning," "Daddy, what did YOU do in the Great War?" Others are more complex or elusive: for example, the evocation of borders, which can fix or blur distinctions between life and death, past and present, here and there (home front/battle front), the powerful and strategic fragmentation of diegesis with a reliance on asyndeton to involve the reader/viewer in the process of recovery and discovery, or the creation of direct address in disturbing moments of prosopopoeia that break through the ominous silences of war experiences and the aporias of history to demand personal attention and response.

But the concept—the metaphor really—that holds all these aspects of narrative discourse together and marks them as relevant, even essential, to the representation of war is that of a landscape of memory. As I suggested in Chapter 1, even our best war artists, although working during the wars, reproduce this crucial trope, and their paintings, now so often seen for the first time by younger generations, function as landscapes of memory for today's viewers. The term "landscape of memory" does not belong exclusively to the creative artist (like Findley), and the concept, while central to the fiction, drama, and films I discuss, has a life outside of literature and art. I have borrowed the landscape of memory concept from Laurence Kirmayer, a psychiatrist and mental health expert, who provides a clear and useful discussion of the term in his essay "Landscapes of Memory: Trauma, Narrative, and Dissociation."[2]



As his title indicates, Kirmayer moves beyond the confines of his own discipline to embrace mine, and he finds in literary and cultural studies much of the terminology he requires to analyze the impact of trauma on the lives of his patients—survivors of the Holocaust and of child sexual abuse. Thus, his understanding of memory and its twin, amnesia, is based on what he calls narratives or life stories and on social contexts *for* remembering, or on what I am more comfortable calling narratology or genre and cultural memory. His choice of an example to illustrate "the links between narrative, memory, and the moral order." is not a clinical case study but a novel: Martin Amis's *Time's Arrow*, in which a former Nazi doctor and concentration camp murderer *must* live his life in reverse, thereby reliving his crimes, and Kirmayer concludes that in this novel Amis "drives home the impossibility of moral life under circumstances where history is denied"

(192–93). Questions of narrative conventions, memory, trauma, "moral order" (I prefer *ethics*) and history, along with the need to bear witness *and* to listen empathically (both also discussed by Kirmayer), are all elegantly accommodated by this landscape of memory concept, and all these questions are integral to my analyses of representations of the two world wars. Of equal importance is the fact that Kirmayer's handling of this metaphor facilitates a crucial move back and forth between the psychological and the social, or, to put this another way, between the narrow space of the individual haunted by his or her private memories of trauma (atrocity, violent death, or extreme deprivation, fear and suffering) and the wider domain of public collective remembering shared by a group, a community, or ultimately a nation.[3]





Throughout his essay, Kirmayer stresses the absolute need for a socially acceptable, publicly recognized context if an individual's story is to move from the silence of repression or dissociation or, indeed (to extrapolate from Kirmayer's work), from the deliberate suppression, the willed forgetting of uncomfortable or shameful past events, into the spoken, disruptive narratives of revelation and disclosure. It is by no means only the individual's memories that must find fertile ground for storytelling; a nation too must make room within its official narratives—its approved history and myth (as Vance calls it) of the Great War, its accepted version of actions taken and not taken (or openly admitted to) in the Second World War—if it chooses to face what Atwood calls those "things that society has decided are better forgotten" (*In Search* 8). And this fertile ground is precisely what a landscape of memory provides. Put very simply, if no one believes your story or wants to listen to you, then your story is forgotten, denied, repressed, or even suppressed. If the terms, narrative conventions, cultural frameworks, and tropes needed to construct and communicate your memories in a more coherent form than mere broken fragments are not accessible to you, then your memories, your story, might as well not exist. Society has chosen to forget and ignore, or even to deny and falsify, them. (A classic instance of such forgetting and falsification is the Polish story of Katyń and the lies and suppression that shrouded that massacre for decades until the public truth could be represented in Andrzej Wajda's 2007 film.)[4] Moreover, as many theorists, besides Kirmayer, insist, there must be a listener, an interlocutor, an *other* who acknowledges the teller, who responds with "empathic unsettlement" (LaCapra, *Writing History* 41) for memories to find a narrative shape and thereby become part of an individual's, or a society's, landscape of memory.[5] Or, as Kirmayer puts it, "memories are most fully and vividly accessed and developed when they fit cultural templates and have a receptive audience. Societies then must provide cultural forms and occasions for remembering [and] the moral function of memory depends on the constraints of social and cultural worlds to provide a limited range of narrative forms with which to construct the coherent stories of ourselves" (193). Despite the constraints and "limited range" that Kirmayer acknowledges, the landscape of memory is not a static or fixed paradigm; like a map, such a landscape may be altered, added to, changed and, thereby, made to accept new information and correct old errors.





This is the work of literature, theatre, and the arts: to develop, expand, open up, reach out, to cultivate the landscape (as it were), to make occasions for remembering those things we prefer to forget. There is a strong ethical motivation (what Kirmayer calls "moral function") to this memory-work and an unquestioned assumption that knowing is preferable, even therapeutically valuable, to refusing to know. And this ethics of memory, as I think of it, which drives post-1977 representations of the wars, participates in a wider, international ethical turn in late twentieth-century thought and calls for a vigilant, historical contextualization and specificity in all such representation.[6]

The memory-work performed by literature and the arts draws on and addresses several categories of memory and necessitates the recreation of witnessing (or of bearing witness) by means of specific strategies for narrating and performing the witness figure, be he or she a character in the story (Jakob in *Fugitive Pieces*, Esau in *Soldier's*

*Heart*), a narrator of the story (the Actor in *The Lost Boys*, Charlie in *Broken Ground*), a fictional autobiographer (Naomi in *Obasan*, Bethune in *The Communist's Daughter*), or a biographer-cum-researcher like the unnamed man conducting interviews and visiting archives to find Robert Ross in Findley's *The Wars*. Then, and this is crucial for most of the works I examine, this memory-work posits (often by creating and including in the narrative) someone to receive the story—the reader, the audience member/viewer, the interlocutor, who must also be a *listener*, and this fictional, hypothetical, yet also always real, listener is asked to listen with empathy and to bear witness. To accomplish a successful interchange or sharing of the remembering process, whether it is read silently, watched in live performance, or viewed on a screen or a gallery wall, the artist must respect history. This is not to say that the fictional characters and narrators will not forget or lie or withhold important information, or simply be ignorant of facts, contexts, and consequences: on the one hand, there cannot be an engaging story, a gripping scene or image, without such narrative strategies; and, on the other hand (and even more importantly), these post-1977 memory-works are *about*—they both perform and thematize—the processes of forgetting, remembering, willfully suppressing and self-protectively repressing traumatic experience, and the necessary coming to knowledge, working through mourning, and accepting a landscape of memory that contains others' new stories. In other words, we (as interlocutors and listeners) will work through the remembering *with* the fictional characters/narrators/autobiographers. As we do so, we will learn much because in these representations of war, the ethics of memory involves learning, but what we learn cannot be based on the careless (or deliberate) misrepresentation or misleading decontextualizing of documented history.

If, as LaCapra suggests, the memory-work of such texts poses questions to history (*Writing History* 204–07), and if, as Günter Grass insists, memory can prevent "the past from coming to an end" (qtd. in Egan and Helms 39, 49), then the facts of history and geography must be accurate. This expectation of historical accuracy (or what are felt to be the truths of history and of life stories) is a salient feature of all war representation. Even post-1977 works created (and received) by those with no direct involvement in either war will be judged by standards of realist conventions, or what Michael Rothberg calls "traumatic realism," that are not required of other modes of representation (such as fantasy, science fiction, surrealism, or abstraction).[7] To resist official history, to insert new voices and experiences and memories into the already acknowledged record, to challenge lies, myths, and stereotypes associated with war, entails staying as close as possible to the known facts, the documents, dates, and actual names of participants. As Robert Ross's biographer tells us, "You begin at the archives with photographs. ...As the past moves under your fingertips, part of it crumbles. Other parts, you know you'll never find. This is what you have" (Findley, *The Wars* 11).





Findley's *The Wars* captures perfectly the complexities and ironies of all post-1977 Canadian representations of the wars. We are directly addressed; we have data to work with; the past can be recovered, at least in part, and we have something—a sketchy landscape of memory—with which to begin. Although everything Findley creates here is fictional, a story, an artistic trap to catch our attention, neither he or his researcher/biographer, nor we, can stray too far from the events of the First World War. Historiography, memory-work, and the conventions of realism come together in these texts to varying degrees, of course, but always in gestures of truth-telling, fact-finding, listening-to-learn. To the degree that we have a right to expect (or feel we do) accurate reporting of actual events, especially events of such terrible import as, say, the first use of chlorine gas by the Germans in the First World War or the bombing of Hiroshima in the Second World War, the artist remembering such events and representing them is expected to adhere to claims of referentiality and accountability, and to deploy with care and discretion the parodies and self-conscious textual reflexivities we associate with postmodernism.[8] The stakes in the *real* world are simply too high. Too many lies, subterfuge, and denials (the Russians about Katyń, the Japanese about Nanking, the Canadians about uranium mining, not to mention the obscenity of Holocaust denial) exist to allow free experimentation with stories about the wars. To call official history to account one must know what that history claims and, thus, if and where it fails.





But history is only one side of this representational equation. The other side is memory, and the famous Historians' Debate that took place in Europe during the 1980s and 1990s was as much about memory as about history.[9] One of the more influential participants in this debate is Pierre Nora, whose term "sites of memory" provides an appealing formulation of a complex late-twentieth-century understanding of history as "a reconstruction, always problematic and incomplete...of the past" (*Les lieux de mémoire* 7–8) and, therefore, as distinct from memory as "life" located within "real environments of memory" (*milieux de mémoire*). For Nora, it is essential, even urgent, to mobilize history and/with memory, to harness the two forces in a combined experiential-narrative effort, if we hope to construct and maintain national identities (22–23); the more a country loses a cultural, collective, shared, and lived-in memory, the more it must rely on memorializing institutions (museums, archives, libraries, databases—or worse: *Wikipedia* and Google) and practices (re-enactments, remembrance rituals, monuments—or the virtual domain of games and blogs). For Nora, this loss of living memory and the concurrent dependence on substitutes, which are merely second-hand, artificial modes of remembering, is a negative sign of the time. However, I retain Nora's terms for sites of memory (*lieux* and *milieux*), while repositioning them solidly within the domain of artistic representation because the texts I examine in the following chapters hold the potential to revivify shared, lived memories, to recuperate lost stories, and to create landscapes of memory that are more complex, more complete (though never finished) than either official history or private recollection. I will go further and say that cumulatively they produce Canadian cultural memory, and they do this by complicating what is meant by History and Memory.

Since at least the mid-1990s, and with increasing frequency in this century, scholars in Europe and North America have debated and theorized a range of important issues gathered under the categories of History and Memory. Indeed, the so-called Historians' Debate dating back to German reunification was marked by the phenomenon Andreas Huyssen called a "memory boom" in his 1995 study *Twilight Memories: Marking Time in a Culture of Amnesia*. This was his catch phrase for a resurgence of attention to remembering that would shake up the prevailing culture of amnesia in a "struggle for memory [that] is also ultimately a struggle for history" (5). Three years after Huyssen published *Twilight Memories*, LaCapra published *History and Memory after Auschwitz* (1998) in which he explored the contemporary obsession with memory (notably in the United States) and its relationship to history that showed no signs of abating as the twentieth century drew to a close. By situating his analysis in an explicitly ethical context of trauma, atrocity, and "limit experiences" (12) as he calls them, like the Holocaust, LaCapra mounts an effective critique (and warning against) Nora's polarization of history and memory and his valorization of, or nostalgia for, a folkish, embodied, excessive memory, a sort of "chocolate-covered madeleine of the psyche on which one overdoses" (*History and Memory* 14). LaCapra rejects Nora's *opposing* of memory to history in favour of an approach to the past, especially to traumatic events like war, that recruits memory—the primary memory of those who lived through such experiences *and* the secondary memory of critical analysis (as in historiography)—to work through (in Freud's sense) post-traumatic mourning hand-in-hand with and always in the context of the historical record. To achieve some understanding of the "belatedness" of past traumas and their "aftereffects" and "aftershocks" (*History and Memory* 9), which haunt society at large, and not just individuals, and to separate (partially if never completely) the past from the present in the effort to move forward into a clearer, constructive future, requires the mediation of both forms of narrative recall: what is *reconstructed* as memory (for memory is never an unmediated conduit to the past) and what is *represented* as history. "Memory," LaCapra explains, "is a crucial source for history and has complicated relations to documentary sources," but "history serves to question and test memory in a critical fashion and to specify what in it is empirically accurate or has a different, but still possibly significant, status" (*History and Memory* 19–20).

This is not the place to review LaCapra's arguments in detail, but I wish to acknowledge the influence his *History and Memory after Auschwitz* and the later *Writing History, Writing Trauma* (2001) have had on my attempt to organize and clarify what I see taking place in the post-1977 Canadian works that are my subject. LaCapra is by no means the only one to address these large issues of history and memory, and I have also benefited from others' work. However, his formulations of concepts like "empathic unsettlement," his critique of "harmonizing narratives" that offer "redemptive" answers to past atrocities, and his belief in the possibility that articulating *affect* and representing the past "may to some viable extent counteract" the destructive repetition (Freud's "acting out") and re-enactment of the past (*Writing History* 14), encourage me to claim that literature and the arts are excellent sites for resisting willed forgetting, for exploring the most difficult and repressed events from the past, for distinguishing the past from the present, and thereby imagining a new, ethically responsible future. Perhaps the most useful of these three concepts, for me, is LaCapra's notion of "empathic unsettlement," which he describes as the reader's/writer's/listener's state of "being responsive to the traumatic experience of others, notably of victims" without "the appropriation of their experience" (*Writing History* 41).

While LaCapra would not share my faith in the arts (his two examples of redemptive, harmonizing narratives are *Schindler's List* and *The Reader*), he does allow that some literature (his examples are Flaubert, Woolf, Kafka, and Beckett) (*Writing History* 105), can produce effective narratives that bear responsible witness to history and memory. Where "redemptive narrative," according to LaCapra, "denies the trauma that brought it into existence...more experimental, nonredemptive narratives are trying to come to terms with trauma in a post-traumatic context" (*Writing History* 179–80). My task is to illustrate how such narratives function and to consider their role in refusing merely redemptive closure and in addressing, without appropriating, the trauma of both world wars.

By virtue of the fact that my chief examples (with the exception of war paintings that occupy a unique doubled position—produced *then* but widely received *now*) are created post-1977 by writers and artists without direct eyewitness/combatant experience, these works must engage with the historical record, work with and from post-memory, and provide representations that resist nostalgic over-identification with past suffering (an empathy that privileges its own trauma), on the one hand, or that objectify or over-generalize events (thereby erasing real, documented distinctions and particularities), on the other. Insofar as these writers and artists participate in and contribute to the "memory boom" and the renewed attention to the history of both wars, they also negotiate ethical positions in relation to both memory and history. In many cases, these texts resist a simple (and simplistic) repetition and endorsement of accepted, official narratives. Vern Thiessen's *Vimy* is a case in point. This play is a fascinating example of artistic juggling with history and memory because it takes as its subject one of the most revered and culturally entrenched (mythic, if you will) stories from Canadian First World War history and manages to respect the official memory of Vimy Ridge while opening up our remembering of it, our bearing witness to it in our time, to new historical insights. I analyze the play closely in the next chapter and consider it in the context of recent rememorializations of Vimy, which not only fail to resist redemptive versions of the battle but actually work to reinstall its unproblematic, nation-building story of sacrifice and heroism. And I suspect that the hostile response to *The Valour and the Horror* was a direct result of that work's refusal of redemptive narrative and its insistence on eliciting an empathic unsettlement that facilitated a viewer's ability to sympathize with and yet criticize the past.

To accomplish the work of resistance and unsettlement, texts construct modes of witnessing and bearing witness, establish positions for active listening, and develop many techniques for incorporating (narrating, dramatizing, visualizing) what Ross Chambers calls haunting or "hauntedness" (*Untimely Interventions* xxv). Since I need each of these terms (bearing witness, listening, and haunting/hauntedness) in order to explore the landscapes of memory created by the works I discuss, I want to establish my theoretical parameters and unpack some of the thinking involved in each of these key terms to demonstrate how they produce remembering. It is first important to distinguish between the terms *primary* and *secondary witness* as these are used by trauma theorists. In *real* life, so to speak, the primary witness is usually thought of as the survivor (although Primo Levi has called the true primary witness the one who has been exterminated; see *The Drowned and the Saved* 83–84), and the secondary witness is the one who sees from a distance or hears the story after the fact (a doctor, a parent or friend, a psychiatrist, a lawyer). In created life, that is in works of art, both the primary and secondary witnesses within the work are fictions. The secondary witnesses outside a text—you and I—are *real* and we too have an important role to play as readers and viewers. This rather obvious, but fundamental, distinction does not mean that actual witness positions are not constructed or mediated—indeed *created*—but that they are located in extra-textual, historical (real world) contexts and events; what they bear witness to and how they do so are open to interpretation and conditioned by many factors such as gender, language, class, ethnicity, level of education, and physical and psychological health (especially in stories about war). We too exist extra-textually and, as reader response theorists have argued since the early 1970s, we are prompted and guided by the text into producing interpretations that stimulate ethical awareness and empathic unsettlement and that encourage resistance to and expansion of received versions of events.[10]

My concern is with the artistic representation and creation of primary and secondary witnesses and the process of remembering and telling what has been witnessed. Here lies the central activity of remembering: one character (the primary witness) will speak/tell/depict and another character will listen, pay attention, *hear*. This activity of interlocution, of bearing secondary witness, acknowledges the other's voice and story and thereby legitimates that story and makes room for it in a shared landscape of memory. Cathy Caruth calls this activity "a creative act of listening" (*Trauma* 154); I call it a co-creative, collaborative one, and the fact that this co-creativity takes place in the realm of art, of fiction, does not make it any the less real. However, the goal of this *real* activity is not psychotherapeutic or legal. There are several goals for the artistic representations of the two world wars, and I will consider these in a moment. First, I need to note some of the ways in which remembering is produced because creating landscapes of memory is the chief purpose of these works. Although the ideal way to accomplish this task is to examine specific works—as I already have and will do in the following chapters—a few additional points provide a compass for travelling through the landscapes ahead.

As I noted in Chapter 1 and earlier in this chapter, accurate facts are critical. All the artists, regardless of medium or genre, honour historical fact. They also rely on a familiar set of images (several mentioned earlier), extended metaphors, and tropes of which the most important is landscape. Descriptions, depictions, and designs of physical landscapes—so often of remembered homes or sites of trauma and loss—play central roles in these works, whether they are invoked in familiar, descriptive or innovative (experimental, highly technical, imaginative) ways. Landscapes in these works (to be sure, not only in works about the wars) are never just backdrop; they are active participants in their story and they will change/be changed by the end of the tale. The novels, memoirs, films, and plays (and an installation work like *The Murder of Crows*), rely heavily on a category of devices or narrative strategies loosely referred to as intertexts: letters, visual documents (such as photographs or paintings), transcribed tapes, and direct address to a reader or viewer: YOU. Most important, however, is the creation of characters who bear witness because the remembering process must be located in a relationship of interlocution, of speaking to and being actively, creatively listened to. Therefore, there will always be a primary witness inside the text—often a first-person narrator—and there may well be several primary witnesses who take turns remembering. More often than not, there is a secondary witness inside the text, and when there is this character provides a role model, to a degree, for the reader and viewer (this doubled witnessing can also be nicely captured in visual art as well). The secondary witness either inside or outside the text or both is essential for the creation of a landscape of memory that is successful, by which I mean more complex, convincing, and more inclusive *for the reader* than it was before the process of remembering and bearing witness began.





While the overarching goal of such texts is to produce a landscape of memory—individual, community, national—there are other goals involved. None of these is the preserve of the post-1977 war texts I examine, but together they form a powerful centre from which to advance creative and cultural interests on the subject of memory and the two world wars. They include the pedagogical, ethical, political, imaginative, and, of course, artistic. These works inform readers and viewers about actual events, people, and relationships either not known about or forgotten—or erased from public, official memory. They also urge an ethical response from readers and viewers willing to accept the role of secondary witness. Insofar as these works reveal—discover, uncover—new factual information or problematize accepted versions of Truth and History, or even personal experiences, they prompt reflection, empathic unsettlement, a curiosity to know more and a resistance to the unquestioned acceptance of received facts. By constructing us as co-creative listeners, they foster an engaged and shared sense of responsibility to work through the trauma and haunting of the past. While claims to political influence must be tentative, I think it is possible to see a political dimension to many of these works. Certainly, some authors and artists—Findley, for example, or Clements, Kogawa, Thiessen, or Wheeler (to name just a few)—are overtly political in their work in that they expose political injustices, legal inequities, historical erasures, and social prejudices. Moreover, they invite us to change things as we find them, to make our world a more fair and inclusive place, and to celebrate a Canada that is open to new information and to others' experiences and stories. But it is the imaginative goal of these works that I find the most intriguing and personally challenging. By the term *imaginative* I mean that they stimulate the receptive imagination to see beyond the easy and the familiar; ultimately, as Findley, Michaels, Crummey, Varley, and all the others insist, society will falter—has already—when human beings fail to imagine a better world (a world without wars, torture and terrorism, ethnic cleansing, degradation of the environment, etc.). Failure of the imagination—or so I read/see/witness these works—is the most dangerous failure of all failings. Finally, these works aim for artistic integrity. Some are highly innovative; others less so. But being avant-garde is not the main goal here; making us see—as Joseph Conrad so aptly put it—is. And it takes creativity, artistry to accomplish that.





As Shoshana Felman insists, "art inscribes (artistically bears witness to) *what we do not yet know of our lived historical relation to events of our time*" (*Testimony* xx). What's more, the art I am concerned with inscribes that bearing of witness at multiple discursive levels: the work itself bears witness, but it may also perform the witnessing process through its characters, themes, tropes, and narrative structure (in live theatre its staging), thereby involving us in the process. In other words, we become constitutive actors in the witnessing, helping to produce the textual witnessing impact simultaneously with our experience of pleasure in the artistry. We are constructed (at least in some of the more complex, overtly self-conscious texts) as witnesses at a remove, at second hand (which is not the same as being second-hand, second-rate, or lesser witnesses); we are imagined as fully engaged, ethically responsive witnesses rather than as mere observers or consumers of events who are free to indulge in the emotion evoked (LaCapra's chocolate-covered madeleine) or to dismiss the story as unimportant or false, as just fiction and, therefore, frivolous entertainment.

In *Seeing Witness: Visuality and the Ethics of Testimony* (2009), Jane Blocker explores what we have come to understand by witnessing and how it relates to identity and memory. She draws heavily on the theories of Giorgio Agamben (notably in *Remnants of Auschwitz*), Judith Butler, and Cathy Caruth to explore the ways in which history, "an authorized form of witnessing" (3), and works of art (especially theatre, installation works, and photography) illuminate the dialogics of testimony.[11] As I understand her argument, bearing witness is a complex process that functions along a trajectory from seeing with one's own eyes (which in the case of the Holocaust means death)[12] to bearing witness to what cannot, or can no longer, be seen, to telling another what we recall having witnessed, and then being acknowledged, responded to by the listener, who in turn participates (by bearing witness) in a sharing of and dealing with the subject, so often traumatic, of memory and history. Or, as Kelly Oliver puts it in *Witnessing Beyond Recognition*, "It is impossible to bear witness without an audience" (91). As a philosopher, Oliver is keen to challenge the clichés about eyewitnessing as truth ("seeing is believing" or "what you see is what you get") (147) which are based on subject/object separation, but also, and more importantly, to search for an ethics of non-adversarial, non-hierarchical relational identity that incorporates address-ability and response-ability in what I call interlocution.[13]

Oliver is motivated by one extremely important and pertinent question: "From the assumption that human relations are essentially warlike, how can we imagine them as peaceful?" (4) One part of her answer is that we can learn to carry our bearing of witness beyond mere visual recognition into a more multisensory, contextualized witnessing founded on touch, smell, and especially hearing. We must learn to listen, she argues, "for the unfamiliar" (2), and her distinction between full and partial listening (between simply hearing and paying active listening attention) is drawn from the famous instance recounted by Dori Laub about the woman who survived Auschwitz and told her story of the camp uprising when the inmates set fire to "four" chimneys (Oliver 1–2; Laub, "Bearing Witness" 59–63). This woman claimed that she saw *four* chimneys burning, but historians knew there was only one and, therefore, tended to dismiss her account. However, Laub and Oliver insist that because they were focused on empirical facts, the historians could not hear what else this woman was telling them about survival and resistance. Taking this as her starting point for a new exploration of witnessing, Oliver concludes that the "tension between recognizing the familiar in order to confirm what we already know and listening for the unfamiliar that disrupts what we already know is at the heart of contemporary theories of recognition" (2). Which returns me to Shoshana Felman's remark that works of art inscribe, or bear witness to, "*what we do not yet know*." My task as a secondary witness is to interpret that message, and with Oliver I suggest that we can improve our interpretive skills by listening.

Clearly, the term *listener* is a metaphor, at least as regards those genres/media we read silently like novels, memoirs, and autobiographies, photography, and painting, but it is a metaphor I want to keep, even though I may *seem* to be mixing my metaphors when I speak (write) of listening for voices in a landscape of memory. For live theatre, film, and music (or installation work like *The Murder of Crows*), of course, metaphor gives way to contextualized, lived experience, even when the sound is pre-recorded (as with the singing that rises from the river at Chelmno), but even in novels the position of listener can be posited: think of that direct address to "You" in Findley's *The Wars* or the pleading, confessional speaker who opens *Obasan* ("I hate the stillness, I hate the stone...I ask..." [n.p.]). Listening takes place in what Eric Santner calls a "social space" (25), and such a space, like a landscape of memory, is by

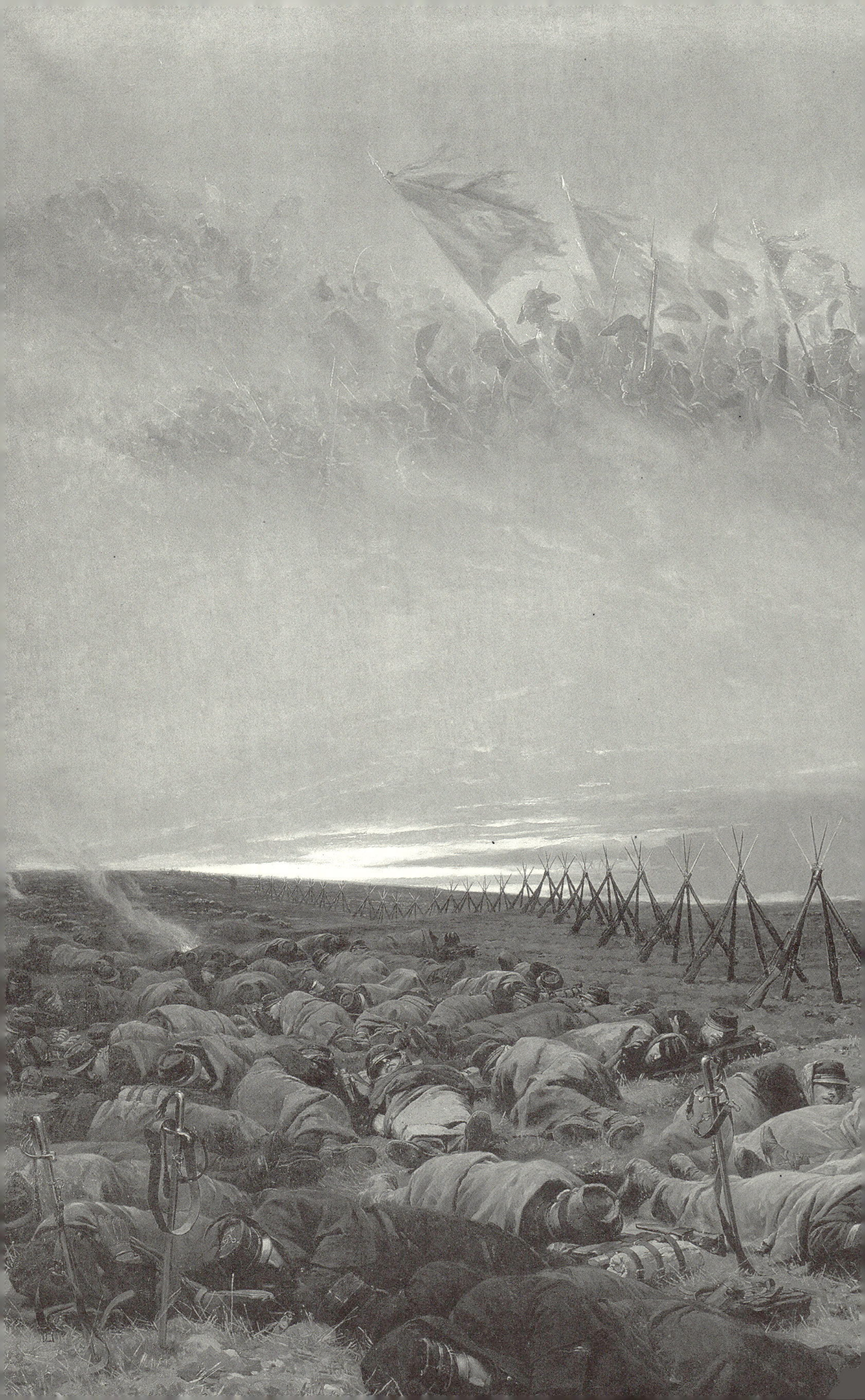

*Edouard Detaille*, Le Rêve *(1888). o/c 300 x 400 cm. Musée d'Orsay, Paris. D00025271/ ART175528. Photograph: H. Lewandowski. © RMN-Grand Palais/Art Resource, NY.*

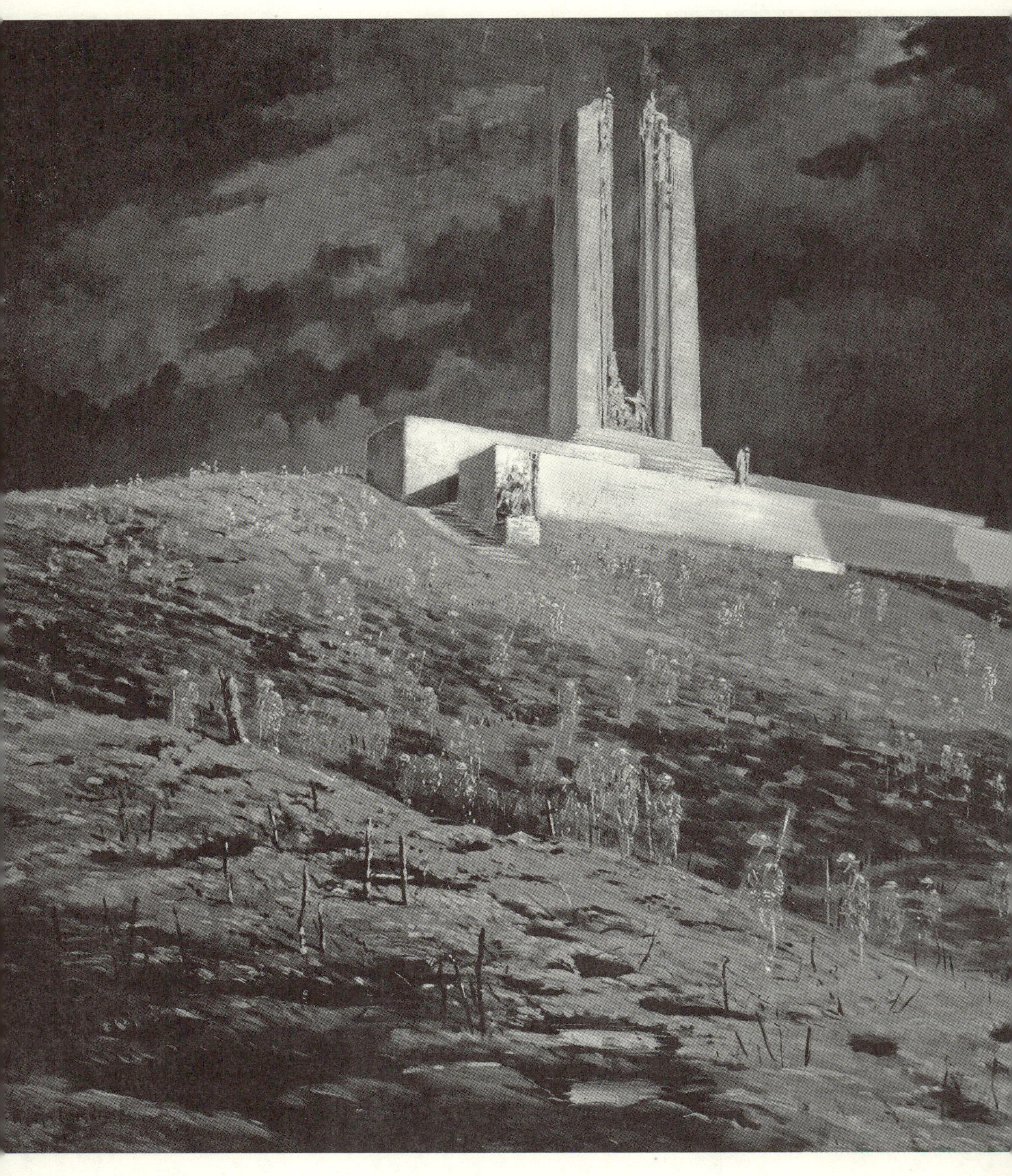

*William Longstaff,* The Ghosts of Vimy Ridge *(1931). o/c 138 x 270.2 cm. CWM #19890275-051. This painting was popular in its day, with prints sold across Canada and the British Empire. In his dream about the Vimy monument that he would design, Walter Allward claimed to see the ghosts of the dead soldiers marching towards the ridge.*

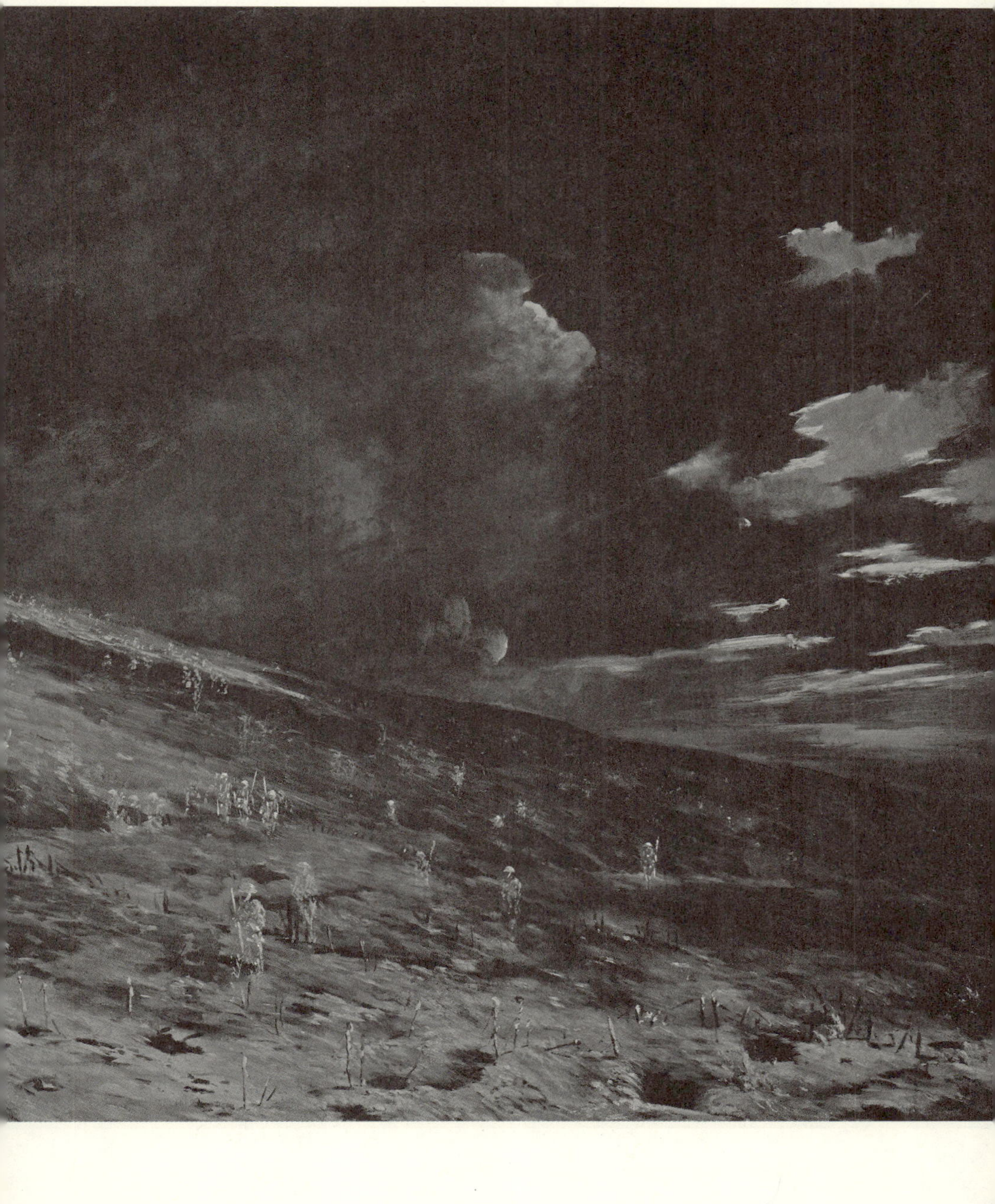

definition private *and* public, shared, and full of sound (and other sensory stimuli). Just as we must forget in order to remain sane, so we must block out unwanted noise, although some of the noise and the memories remain waiting for us to tune in, to perform our past as witnessing listeners. But I want to keep my metaphor of listening not only because it connects my genres and media, not only because it co-exists in productive ways within my umbrella term, landscape of memory, but also because it facilitates an end-run around the dominant trope of seeing as eyewitnessing with its all too often unreliable truth claims.





Ghosts and references to haunting or feeling haunted by the past and the dead are among the most common and familiar of all images found in writing about or depicting war. I have already noted the cinema's most dramatic example of the dead rising from their graves in *J'accuse*, and John McCrae's comparatively simple poem "In Flanders Fields" turns on the trope of the speaking dead, whom we cannot see but can certainly hear. War paintings also resort to this powerful iconography: Edouard Detaille's *Le Rêve* (a key intertext in *The Lost Boys*) and William Longstaff's *Ghosts of Vimy Ridge* are two especially striking examples of this form of haunted and haunting landscape.[14] Wars, and the extreme experiences associated with them, leave individuals, survivors, combatants, civilians, descendants and future generations, and entire communities haunted by these experiences. But it is survivors, in particular, who are haunted by the past, its inexplicability, their own survival, and often a sense of guilt for having survived, and then by a sense of moral duty to remember, to never forget, and if possible to bear witness. And they pass that complex haunting on in a myriad of forms. Writing, whether as non-fiction or fiction, and storytelling are effective ways to cope with haunting in daily life, so it is not surprising that artists employ intertextual examples of writing (such as diaries, journals, actual documents, and letters) and telling (in the form of oral reports, interviews, and confessions) to represent the state of being haunted. And it should not be surprising to find authors of post-1977 texts developing strategies to transfer their own personal haunting and their fascination with the wider cultural hauntedness of society to their readers.

In *Untimely Interventions*, Ross Chambers singles out Pat Barker's *Regeneration* as a paradigmatic contemporary novel for representing what he calls repercussive, chain-reaction "hauntedness": "As a *historical* novel, it fulfills the historian's supposedly secondary task by performing a kind of 'archeological' going back to the past. But as a historical *novel*, it functions as...a report of an event that it carries forward" into the present, to us. For Chambers, Barker's work constitutes a meta-witnessing that becomes its own form of witnessing (104). And this *relay* in bearing witness from one layer of narrative to another, from one fictional generation to the next, and from the world of the text to the world of the reader is a distinctive feature of all the materials I am examining, and a factor to which I shall often return. What further interests me in Chambers's study of haunting is the connection he carefully establishes between society and art (in this case the novel, although he also examines poetry and memoir). He begins from the assumption that haunting is real (not some figment of the imagination, but a phenomenon we actually experience) and that ways must be found to acknowledge testimonial writing about this condition and to move it from "a cultural periphery where it must make do, catachrestically, with genres [like the novel, the feature film, the autobiography, the play] that scarcely admit it" (33). He also assumes that as readers and scholars (he includes himself) we have an ethical responsibility to break through the cultural deafness around us so that we are able to acknowledge and discuss—to listen acutely, responsibly—to those works that ask us to listen. If we refuse (turn a deaf ear, if not a blind eye) to these works, then what he calls our "aftermath cultures" (xxix) will remain trapped in melancholic re-enactment and fail to take up the working-through process of mourning.

The task, according to Chambers, of those who know they are haunted (survivors and those close to them who come after and have been obliged to feel this condition) "is to transmit their own sense of aftermath (as a state of acknowledged hauntedness) to those survivors who seem not to know, or at least to fail to acknowledge, that they too, as survivors, are haunted" (xxv). While I want to be cautious about extending the term *survivor* too broadly (as I think Chambers finally does) and thereby levelling off or diminishing the trauma of immediate survivors (of the Nanking massacre, of the Nazi death camps, of the Rwandan genocide, and other extreme, or limit, events), I believe that Chambers has put his finger on an extremely important contemporary condition that recalls Shoshana Felman's comment and directly addresses the representation of war. *We*—those survivors several times removed from catastrophe who seem not to know, who refuse to see what Felman says art inscribes—must "become ghosts" in our turn and "haunt the living with [our] own hauntedness" (Chambers xxv).

Although Chambers protests the marginalization of testimonial writing to the cultural periphery of contemporary society and suggests that literary genres begrudgingly incorporate ("scarcely admit") such writing, or evidence, within their conventional narrative boundaries, it seems to me that a significant number of artistic works not only accept testimonials to witnessing and hauntedness as relevant and integral to their stories but actively create ways in which such evidence (be it historical or fictional) can be recruited to pose questions to history and challenge assumptions about truth claims. To be sure, many of the narrative techniques that destabilize such claims and undermine socio-cultural and epistemological certainties are familiar from postmodern fiction and art, as Linda Hutcheon demonstrates in the *Poetics of Postmodernism*; however, when the subject is war, these techniques usually expose serious gaps and suppressions in the historical record and in ideologically motivated or expedient obfuscations of events and experiences. Moreover, many post-1977 works participate in a system of cultural retrieval, reconstruction, and rewriting of official history, and they do so not only to revise history, to set the record straight (as if that were even possible), but also to rework ideas of nation, national identity, and national memory. Insofar as haunting touches all of us, as

Chambers insists, then works that represent war and related extreme events will either silence the ghosts who haunt us with redemptive visions of peace and reconciliation or—and this is much more the case with my texts—they will allow the ghosts to speak from within a landscape of memory, and they will make room at centre stage for the witnessing experience.

Chambers is only one among many recent cultural theorists to identify the connection between issues of war on the narrow individual level of trauma, bearing witness, and hauntedness, and on the wider level of community and nation, but he is especially succinct in his formulation of this connection: "National cultures," he writes, "seem increasingly aware of the sense in which they are haunted, both by past atrocities and by the continuing injustices those atrocities spawned" (*Untimely Interventions* 34). It is ideas of the nation as haunted, imagined, defined, narrated, and produced that I want to examine next, before I situate my analysis of memory, history, and the representation of war in its international, intellectual context.





Between the first phase of scholarly attention to the links between the two world wars, memory, history, and national identity that began with Paul Fussell's *The Great War and Modern Memory* in 1975 and Modris Eksteins's *Rites of Spring: The Great War and the Birth of the Modern Age* in 1989 and the present, an enormous amount of effort has gone into mapping these connections. By 1990, when George Mosse's *Fallen Soldiers: Reshaping the Memory of the Two World Wars* appeared, or 1991, when Benedict Anderson published his revised and extended 1983 study, *Imagined Communities: Reflections on the Origins and Spread of Nationalism*, Huyssen's "memory boom" about the wars was already in full swing. To go back now to Fussell, Mosse, and Anderson is to experience a sense of déjà vu, but this sense of already knowing what they have to say is an index of the impact these authors have had on the past twenty years of scholarship in the field. Whether one disagrees with Fussell, as Jonathan Vance does (*Death So Noble* 48, 90), or disputes his findings as extremely limited, which David Williams does (20–22), or argues with Anderson about his failure to grasp the postcolonial complexities of nationalism, we have all benefited from and built on these early studies.[15] It was Anderson, after all, who pointed out that "no more arresting emblems of the modern culture of nationalism exist than cenotaphs and tombs of the Unknown Soldier" and that such sites are "saturated with ghostly *national* imaginings" (9).

If I find Eksteins's *Rites of Spring* less dated than Fussell or Mosse and still invigorating, it is because of his immense interdisciplinary sweep. Few cultural historians can match his capacity to incorporate Stravinsky, Wagner, Max Planck, and Fritz Haber (the German chemist who invented chlorine gas and Vern Thiessen's protagonist in *Einstein's Gift*), German expressionist painting, Picasso, Handel's *Largo*, McCrae's "In Flanders Fields," Remarque's *All Quiet on the Western Front*, Sherriff's *Journey's End*, films like *What Price Glory?*, Robert Graves, Charles Lindbergh (who will make a cameo appearance in Findley's *Famous Last Words*), Mackenzie King, and Hitler (to mention just a few of his *dramatis personae*), in a three-act study of the Great War and its formative influence on the twentieth century. He is quick to remind his readers that, "from its start, the war was a stimulus to the imagination. Probably no other four years in history have produced as much testimony on public events. Artists, poets, writers, clergymen, historians, philosophers, among others, all participated fully in the human drama being enacted" (*Rites of Spring* 208). As I hope will become clear, *Rites of Spring* is something of a model for the type of interdisciplinary analysis of cultural history and the Canadian nation that I am undertaking here. In his 1999 book, *Walking Since Daybreak: A Story of Eastern Europe, World War II, and the Heart of Our Century*, Eksteins explicitly juxtaposes official historiography with personal testimony, autobiography, and biography and addresses, *avant la lettre*, Chambers's worries about generic marginalization.

Among other important contributors to the discussion of war, history, memory, and nation are British scholars like Paul Connerton and Sue Malvern, Americans like Jay Winter and Marita Sturken, and

Canadians like Laura Brandon, Daniel Francis, and David Williams. Connerton's *How Societies Remember* (1989) is of particular interest for its emphasis on performance and performativity and the central importance of these activities for creating a shared "social memory" (3), or what he also calls "communal memory" (17). Connerton's attention, however, is not on the arts as such and certainly not on theatre; his focus is on embodied, or incorporated, forms of commemoration and re-enactment.[16] What he identifies is the socially and culturally conservative production of collective identities "as represented by and told in a master narrative...a kind of collective autobiography" (70). Among his chief examples are the commemorative rituals and public performances of Nazism, but he also discusses a range of religious festivals that serve to remind participants where they came from and who they are. As a rule, and when taken together, cyclical repetitions of such rituals, performances, and festivals support and reinforce the more linear narratives of official history that define a nation. Given the immense power of this combination—of commemoration/re-enactment/communal memory/official history—in performance and discourse, it is necessary to ask *how* literature, or any of the arts, can intervene in this process of remembering and consolidating identity to challenge or disrupt the established boundaries (the inclusions and exclusions) of a national story.





By drawing attention to this dynamic, Connerton also makes it possible to see more clearly what plays like *Vimy* or *Burning Vision* and novels like *Three Day Road*, *Obasan*, or *Broken Ground* are up against and how they perform their resistance to the received wisdom of national mythology. Did Canada come of age as an independent, united nation on Vimy Ridge? Were Canadian soldiers heroes, honoured and well-treated, after either war? Were Canadians—military or civilian—only and always the good guys during the Second World War? Our post-1977 texts, far from obeying official marching orders, provide some complex and troubling answers to these questions.

Studies by Sue Malvern, notably her *Modern Art, Britain and the Great War: Witnessing, Testimony, and Remembrance* (2004), and Jay Winter, especially his *Sites of Memory, Sites of Mourning: The Great War in European Cultural History* (1995), and to a lesser extent his *Remembering War: The Great War Between Memory and History in the Twentieth Century* (2006), are useful in different ways. In her study of British war art, Malvern analyzes painting practices (so sharply challenged by the horrors of trench warfare) and the legitimizing rhetoric of the so-called *authentic* eyewitness accounts, which manufactured hierarchies of knowing and telling (I *was* there, therefore I know, and you don't). She identifies the regimes of socio-political power invested in representation (the control of who gets to represent what, and who doesn't) and mobilized after the war by means of reinventions and suppressions of events, as well as the heated, ideologically inflected debate about the distinctions between art and history. If artists did not "subscribe to the fiction of sacrifice and redemption" (110), which was the dominant narrative of the Great War in Britain and the Commonwealth, if they created jarring modernist or personal interpretations of the war, then their pictures might well be classified as failing to meet the benchmark of an accurate historical record. Malvern's work embraces far more than I can comment on here, and in *Art or Memorial?* Laura Brandon does for Canada what Malvern does for the UK, but Malvern's arguments that the continuing narrativization of the First World War brings its legacies and meanings into the present (177) and that such narratives produce national identities, are compelling. As Malvern puts it, "nationhood is informed by telling stories, manufacturing fictions, and inventing traditions in a ceaseless and selective process of inclusion and exclusion, remembering and forgetting" (5). And the arts are central to this process.

Like Eksteins in *Rites of Spring*, Jay Winter explores literature, sculpture, painting, film, and music in *Sites of Memory, Sites of Mourning*. He also criticizes nationalist approaches to the Great War as "distorting," and calls for approaches (like the one he uses) that "leave behind national boundaries," in contrast to the one taken by Pierre Nora, whose tight focus on France and French national identity he critiques (10–11). However, a national perspective should not be so quickly dismissed. Despite his comparative methodology, or perhaps because of it, I find his discussion of issues superficial at times. Moreover, he is often obliged to acknowledge the nationalist narratives that grew increasingly strident and powerful as a result of that war. Indeed, if Margaret MacMillan's monumental *Paris 1919* reminds us of anything, it is that ferocious new nationalisms emerged with the shifting boundaries resulting from the war, and that the older, established powers (Great Britain, France, Germany, Italy) were aggressively determined to defend their status (in Germany's case to re-establish theirs) in the precise terms of national identity.



Nevertheless, in *Sites of Memory, Sites of Mourning*, Winter mounts a convincing argument for what I call the long twentieth century by demonstrating the many ways in which traditional nineteenth-century beliefs in religious and romantic rhetoric continued through and well past the end of the war to structure private and public expressions of mourning, commemoration, and history. One of the most interesting examples Winter gives of this phenomenon of a persistent nineteenth-century belief system is the popularity of spiritualism after the war. He argues that spiritualist ideas fuelled the uncanny sense of the dead returning to haunt the living that still, to this day, characterizes so much war literature and art (see Winter, *Sites of Memory* 54–72). In other words, he maintains that a true rupture with past modes of thought and the representation of loss, trauma, atrocity, and mourning came with the Second World War, not with the First. Certainly, his description of British, German, and French poets as forming "a long line of twentieth-century romantics, who walk backwards into the future, struggling to understand the chaotic history of this century" (222), rings true. The evidence within Canadian culture illustrates the gradual development of modernism alongside more traditional, romantic attitudes until well after the second war, which suggests, quite apart from the historical realities MacMillan describes, that a national perspective that respects an international context is important and must be retained to trace the subtle (and sometimes not so subtle) cultural distinctions and priorities that surface within a landscape of memory.

In his 2006 book *Remembering War*, Winter returns to many of the issues he explored in *Sites of Memory, Sites of Mourning*, but he adds two new components—or vectors, as he calls them (20)—to his analysis of memory and war that are noteworthy.[17] One is his delineation of two distinct stages in the twentieth-century memory boom that produced a cult of mourning after the Great War, but then changed both its form and focus after the Second World War; the other is his view that the upsurge in local or small-scale memory is a result of identity politics, which presents serious challenges to the authority of collective memory as promulgated in officially sanctioned stories "formed by or about the state or about nations as a whole" (35).





According to Winter, the "Second World War and the Holocaust broke many of the narratives at the heart of the first 'memory boom'" (18). Where the first phase of attention to memory could trace its roots, concepts, and imagery back to thinkers shaped by the nineteenth century (to Freud, Henri Bergson, Maurice Halbwachs, and Aby Warburg, for example), the second phase emerged belatedly in the 1970s and 1980s well *after* enough time had elapsed to make discussion of a host of complicities and atrocities possible. Chief among the troubling aspects of the Second World War that Winter identifies are the collapse of "idealizing remembrance" of resistance movements (Ophuls's *Le chagrin et la pitié*, 1969, is a stunning index of this shift in the memory boom in France), and what he calls the arrival of "the age of the witness," signalled in part by the publication of works like Primo Levi's *The Drowned and the Saved* (the original, *Sommersi e i salvati*, appeared in 1986; the English translation came out in 1988). As Winter clearly acknowledges here, the "grand narrative of nation-building, out of which the first memory boom had emerged, bore little resemblance to the fault lines of the later twentieth century" (33), and the rhetoric of the second phase of remembering has been inexorably influenced by the moral pressures and the search (so often frustrated) for meaning prompted by the accounts of Holocaust survivor-witnesses. Or, as Winter puts it, "the Holocaust appeared to be an event without a meaning. It was a giant black hole in the midst of our universe of meaning" (32). On the subject of small-scale, or local, memory, Winter argues that "cultural history is now all around us" (48) in the plethora of individual and group witnessing of trauma, of family memories published or displayed (photographs, letters, and other memorabilia) in museums, in the multidisciplinary study of both trauma and memory, and in the general attention and respect accorded to memoirs, autobiographies, and oral histories. What these two phases of the memory boom have in common, says Winter, is their "focus on the authority of direct experience, on the words and images we have [from] those who went through...the Great War, or through the concentration and extermination camps of the Second World War" (50).





To a considerable degree, national perspectives on the Second World War have come to include, and *respect*, a host of local perspectives, family histories, and personal accounts of loss, dislocation, and suffering, and such stories cannot simply be subsumed within official history. National perspectives and the exploration and troubling of national boundaries and identities are central concerns in Marita Sturken's *Tangled Memories: The Vietnam War, the AIDS Epidemic, and the Politics of Remembering* (1997), Daniel Francis's *National Dreams: Myth, Memory, and Canadian History* (1997), Laura Brandon's *Art or Memorial?* (2006), and David Williams's *Media, Memory, and the First World War* (2009). For Sturken, cultural memory, as distinct from personal memories or official history, is "an inventive social practice" (259) that produces a *national* story from what she sees—in the American context (which is her subject)—as "a field of contested meanings" (2). Moreover, she sees cultural memory as essential to the creation of "national meaning" (12) because such meanings converge on who we agree to tell ourselves we are. She explores the role of re-enactments, feature films, and television docudramas as mediators and facilitators of "collective national witnessing" (25): "Participation in the nation," she notes, "often takes the form of watching or taking part in reenactments" (43). Given the high degree of cultural market saturation, in Canada, England, and even in France, Germany, Italy, or parts of Asia, by American war films, one inevitable conclusion is that an American version of the Second World War competes with Europeans' perspectives on their own twentieth-century war history. Thus, Pierre Nora's concern for the preservation of French identity in *milieux de mémoire* (instead of in history or even in *lieux de mémoire*) arises not only from the pressures of postwar de-territorialization in Europe, the collapse of previous state nationalisms, the unmasking of myths about resistance movements, and the proliferation of minority identity politics, but also from this dominance of what is, after all, a foreign national story in which the French or Germans (or Canadians) cannot recognize themselves. In other words, the social practice of cultural memory in the twenty-first century is open—perhaps even vulnerable—to national and nationalistic scripts because of their capacity to reach and influence young, mass audiences.

Daniel Francis is unapologetically nationalist in his perspective; he is also sharply critical of Canada's incapacity to generate its own cultural memory through history and biography (he has less to say about the arts). While agreeing with scholars like Edward Said that narratives consolidate the social space of the nation (*Culture and Imperialism* 77), which is also Marita Sturken's position, he describes Canada as being one of the few nation states in the contemporary world to teach its citizens that "national independence" was "irrelevant" (54) and national pride suspect. Although the two world wars are not his primary focus, Francis sees the Great War as the apogee of the British Empire, with little to offer Canadian identity, which did not emerge with any force until after the Second World War. During the postwar years, as he notes, Canada adopted its own flag (the Maple

Leaf), repatriated its constitution, and renamed the 1 July holiday of "Dominion Day" as "Canada Day."[18] Although I find Francis's argument that contemporary Canada is postmodern in its diversity, multiculturalism, and decentralization, an oversimplification of both history and cultural memory, the fact that he explores the challenges presented to national identity in Canada through myth, memory, and history, is significant. I see his *National Dreams* as part of a longstanding debate in Canada about who we are that intersects with more focused contributions by Jonathan Vance (in *Death So Noble*), Laura Brandon, and most recently David Williams and myself in *On the Art of Being Canadian.*[19]



As curator of war art at the Canadian War Museum, historian Laura Brandon is ideally placed to assess both the importance of this art and its meaning for today's citizens, what it tells Canadians about who they are now because of who they were and what they did then. In *Art or Memorial?* she provides a wealth of art historical information, which is her primary goal, but she also touches on complex, contemporary questions of patriotism, military history and who has the right to represent this history, cultural memory, and national identity. On the one hand, she recognizes the extreme sensitivity and controversy surrounding attempts to contextualize and exhibit war art or write about its creation; on the other, she is intrigued by the high degree of public interest shown for a touring exhibition like "Canvas of War" and in the permanent installations at the War Museum. As someone working closely with the representation of war, Brandon's perspective is important. She argues that 1995, the fiftieth anniversary of the Second World War, signalled a key turning point in Canadian national identity, at least insofar as it is constructed through the cultural memory of war. That year saw a host of public celebrations and commemorative events specific to the war, but it also marked a sharp increase in general attention to both world wars as crucial indices of contemporary Canadian identity: in 2000 Canada entombed its Unknown Soldier; in 2001 the Department of National Defence announced a new war art program; in

2005 the Canadian War Museum opened its doors; and in 2008 a restored Vimy Monument was rededicated in the massive, televised ceremony I described in Chapter 1. Brandon does not comment on whether she sees this upsurge in national feeling so closely tied to war (with Afghanistan a persistent and haunting backstory) as a positive or negative phenomenon. However, what she reports on—her *dispatches* from the front lines of war art and memorial—confirm that Sturken's tangled web of memory, war, and the nation (whether Canadian, American, French, or German—or Serbian, or Israeli, for that matter) continues to ensnare and constrain us.





In *Media, Memory, and the First World War,* David Williams says much the same thing through his focus on films, selected novels and plays (his main Canadian texts are Hugh MacLennan's *Barometer Rising,* Findley's *The Wars,* and Thomson's *The Lost Boys,* but he also discusses British and German texts by Pat Barker, Wilfred Owen, and Remarque). For my purposes, however, his most original contributions to a discussion of the memory boom are his analyses of episode three, about Vimy Ridge, from the film *For King and Empire* (2001), and of the digital archive known as "The Memory Project: Stories of Service and Sacrifice." As Williams explains, *For King and Empire,* especially in the Vimy episode, contributes to the construction of a myth of national identity through war. He calls this episode a "text of the 'birth of the nation'" (225) that makes "Vimy Pilgrims of us all" (233, but see also, 217–33). "The Memory Project" serves a similar purpose but on quite a different scale. Begun as a website formed in 1997, "The Memory Project" is a digital archive of Canadian voices, memories, and documents from the Great War; it is operated by Historica Canada (formerly the Historica-Dominion Institute) and was jointly sponsored by the provincial government of Ontario and the federal government's Canadian Heritage Program. This archive is a quintessential example of Canadian First World War cultural memory in our time. With a mere click of a mouse on their website you can call up and listen to a voice from the past telling you his story of the war. The experience is uncanny, to say the least, because this spectral, oral presence, conjured up from one's personal computer in the privacy of one's study, is entirely "a product of new information technologies that digitize a voice and send it around the world" (237).

I cannot delve deeply into the impact of this project—digital archives are beyond my expertise and, thankfully, Williams has done that work—but I do want to emphasize my sense that "The Memory Project" adds significantly to the Canadian narrative of the Great War and its place within the cultural memory of the nation. As Williams notes, the archive has a haunting power and, although he does not cite Chambers, I would argue that, based on my own response, it has the capacity to transfer *hauntedness* to the digital listener because we are recruited *as listeners*, not just as viewers or readers, to whom the dead seem to speak. In Williams's words,

> *What is most telling in this digital version of an institutional medium like the archives is its extension of the boundaries of the family, handing on our cultural heritage as an expression of a national, and, one hopes, human family, where ancient foes may be united in the never-ending sound waves spreading out from the event....We need to remember that, as listeners and viewers, we are voluntary witnesses to the event, a volunteer "army" of witnesses who choose, like the original volunteers of 1914–17, to make ourselves part of a mass movement [and to] keep faith with "spectral images" of the past...as John McCrae first called on us to do in "In Flanders Fields." (266–67)*

By speaking of ghosts, haunting, bearing witness, and listening, I have come full circle, back to where I began this chapter, but it is still necessary to situate my research in the increasingly important international field of cultural memory studies. The term *cultural memory* is explained in detail by Ansgar Nünning and Astrid Erll, who trace its evolution back to Maurice Halbwachs and Aby Warburg, and from there forward to the work of Renate Lachmann and Jan and Aleida Assmann, among others.[20] In the introduction to *Literature and Memory:*

*Theoretical Paradigms, Genres, Functions*, Nünning defines cultural memory "as a virtual space which is organized by rituals, semiotic objects and systems, and processes of oral, written and visual communication" (3). The work of Nünning and his colleagues at the Research Centre on Memory Cultures at Giessen focuses attention on the wide international and collaborative nature of cultural memory studies, but also demonstrates some of the important distinctions I find among scholars working in this field in different countries and within differing intellectual traditions. While many similar studies conducted in other European countries, the United Kingdom, or in North America also stress the importance of literature and the arts as constitutive media for the production and transmission of cultural memory, their differences in perspectives and emphases are important to keep in mind. For example, the contributors to *Literature and Memory*, along with Nünning and Erll, *tend* to stress the historical and socio-political parameters of cultural memory, and when they explore the subject of war they have relatively little to say about trauma or the Holocaust. By contrast, as is clear from the work of Caruth, Felman, LaCapra, Laub, and others (including studies like James Young's *At Memory's Edge: After- Images of the Holocaust in Contemporary Art and Architecture*, 2000), trauma studies and the connection between trauma and witnessing, especially in the context of the Holocaust, are defining topics in American studies of culture and memory. In other words, where American research *tends* (and I am identifying tendencies, not absolute categories here) to begin with individual psychology, as a basis for wider theorizations about war, Europeans *tend* to begin with societal concerns and philosophical (notably ethical) questions in their approach to cultural memory.

The same socio-philosophical tendency is apparent in three other recent texts that deal extensively with literature and the two world wars—Peter Middleton and Tim Woods's *Literatures of Memory: History, Time and Space in Postwar Writing* (2000); *La Grande Guerre: Un siècle de fictions romanesques* (2008), edited by Pierre Schoentjes, and an important collection of essays edited by Elena Lamberti and Vita Fortunati called *Memories and Representations of War: The Case of World War I and World War II* (2009). Middleton and Woods argue that after a long period of post-Second World War numbness among British writers, memory and history gradually emerged as major narrative concerns in British novels and plays that interrogate the national past to a degree that seemed impossible in the immediate postwar decades. Interestingly, although they do discuss Pat Barker's *Regeneration* and others' novels, they privilege live theatre as an especially effective way of presenting and debating twentieth-century British history (see Chapter 5 of *Literatures of Memory*). And in his introduction to *La Grande Guerre*, Pierre Schoentjes describes Belgian and French novelists born after 1945 and, thus, with no direct experience of war ("des écrivains nés après 1945 et qui n'ont donc connu aucune guerre," 7) as turning back to the Great War in their novels. *La Grande Guerre* is the product of an international conference held in Ypres in March 2008, and the issues discussed by the contributors to the volume include, among other matters, the cathexis between writing and witnessing, the question of realist modes of representing war, the apparent need for fidelity to historical fact, the delicate balance required between aesthetics and ethics when representing war, and the current popularity of the subject (whether in novels, films, illustrations, or photography).[21] In the conference and the book, the Second World War attracted less attention but, according to Schoentjes, there was a very moving account given by the Belgian filmmaker Raoul Servais of his childhood memories of that war (12). Perhaps the Second World War is still too close for artistic, public, and scholarly comfort, but both wars, as Servais insists, haunt us—"Oui, l'inquiétude, voire la hantise, persiste longtemps, très longtemps...!" (396).

The Lamberti and Fortunati volume, *Memories and Representations of War*, is also the result of a recent European conference that brought scholarship in several European countries together under the aegis of the European Commission's thematic network on cultural memory.[22] The editors organized an international conference in Bologna in 2003 to examine the "contested memories" of war and develop a "shared ethic of memory" (11) through critical examination of literary, cinematic, and other representations of the two wars. Many of the contributors to this volume *do* focus on novels and films and in her introduction Lamberti describes this analysis as "a conscious must" (4) in a post-1989 Europe. That said, she also views the two world wars *together* as a complex "crossroads leading to the definition of the new European (and world) reality" of the twenty-first century (5). As is clear from so many recent discussions of the artistic and literary representations of the wars—studies by Williams and Winter are examples—films are crucial mediators and producers of cultural memory. They are at least as important as novels because of their capacity to reach mass audiences quickly and without the same need for language translation. One contributor to *Memories and Representations of War*, Sara Pesce, provides a compelling and thought-provoking analysis of the Hollywood "combat" film and its "powerful influence [in Europe] on the collective imagination of the war [the Second World War]" (224). According to Pesce, it is ironic that the influence of films like *Saving Private Ryan* authorizes an American perspective on the war which, like the prevalent American discourse on the Shoah, "implies...[that these events have] special importance for American national identity" (233), and that such discourse although transmitted from a "distance...to those who are culturally close to the theatres of war, namely ourselves, European audiences...affects the imaginary that...inhabits the collective understanding of war" (234).

As I reflect upon this very recent European scholarship on literature, the arts, war, and memory, it seems to me that Cultural Studies is, as it were, catching up, or making up for time lost—necessarily, inevitably—in dealing with the past, especially the past of the Second World War. Lamberti and Fortunati give 1989 as the year when the dam broke (it was the year the Berlin Wall came down and Jürgen Habermas published *New Conservatism: Cultural Criticism and the Historians' Debate*), producing a flood of attention by European historians, writers, filmmakers, and other artists. Finally, humanists could step back, take a deep breath, and engage in the debates that characterized the twentieth century and continue into this one. I am not suggesting that literary scholars completely ignored what writers had said or were saying about the wars; studies by Franz Stanzel and Martin Löschnigg in Austria, by Peter Buitenhuis and Evelyn Cobley in Canada, and, of course, by Fussell in the United States, paved the way for the research that would follow.[23] However, the work being done in cultural memory studies by Nünning and his colleagues, and by the contributors to the volumes edited by Schoentjes and Lamberti and Fortunati, signals a forceful reclaiming by humanists of history and memory and of representation and cultural meaning when dealing with the wars. As a Canadian born at the end of the Second World War, I am, like most of the writers and artists I study, distant in time and space from those who, as Sara Pesce puts it, "are culturally close to the theatres of war." I have tried to respect that distance by drawing on the theories and publications of European scholars and combining their insights, as much as possible, with Canadian and American perspectives and methods. The questions raised by post-1977 representations of the two wars know no boundaries; they are transnational, international, and interdisciplinary, like the novels, films, memoirs, and works of art. Therefore, I situate my investigation of Canadian texts within the broad paradigm of cultural memory studies, with its sensitivity to national identities, and I strive to practise, *as a literary scholar and humanist*, that complex ethical "act of listening" called for by Lamberti and Fortunati (23) and evoked by the artists I discuss.

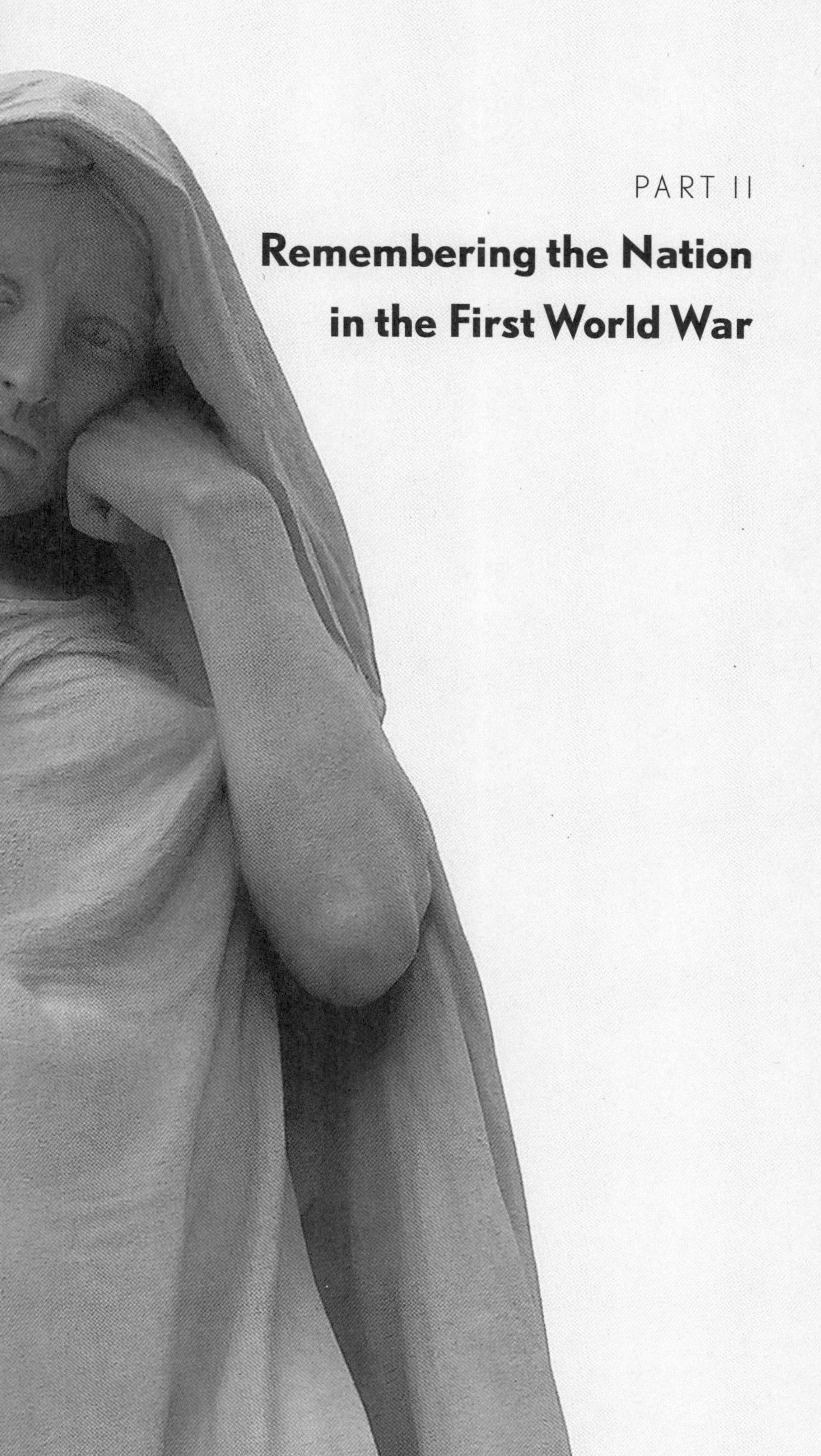

PART II

# Remembering the Nation in the First World War

Remembrance is more
than honouring the dead.
Remembrance is joining them—
being one with them in memory.
Memory is survival.



**Timothy Findley**

*Inside Memory*, 7

LAURIE: *April 9, 1917.*
*Somewhere in France.*
And when I come back,
I'm gonna have some story
to tell, Clare. We're gonna
get married on the cliffs at
Five Islands...and I'm gonna
tell you the story of Vimy
over and over and over.
'Til we're old and grey.



**Vern Thiessen**

*Vimy*, 77

"Why is he dead? And why, when he is dead, do I remain alive? Why?" asks one of the characters in this book after watching a friend die from a random shell burst. Almost all who survived asked themselves that same question and then set out consciously to try to answer it by developing the kind of Canadian institutions and Canadian spirit that would serve as memorials to those who had fallen in foreign fields.



**Sandra Gwyn**

*Tapestry of War*, xviii

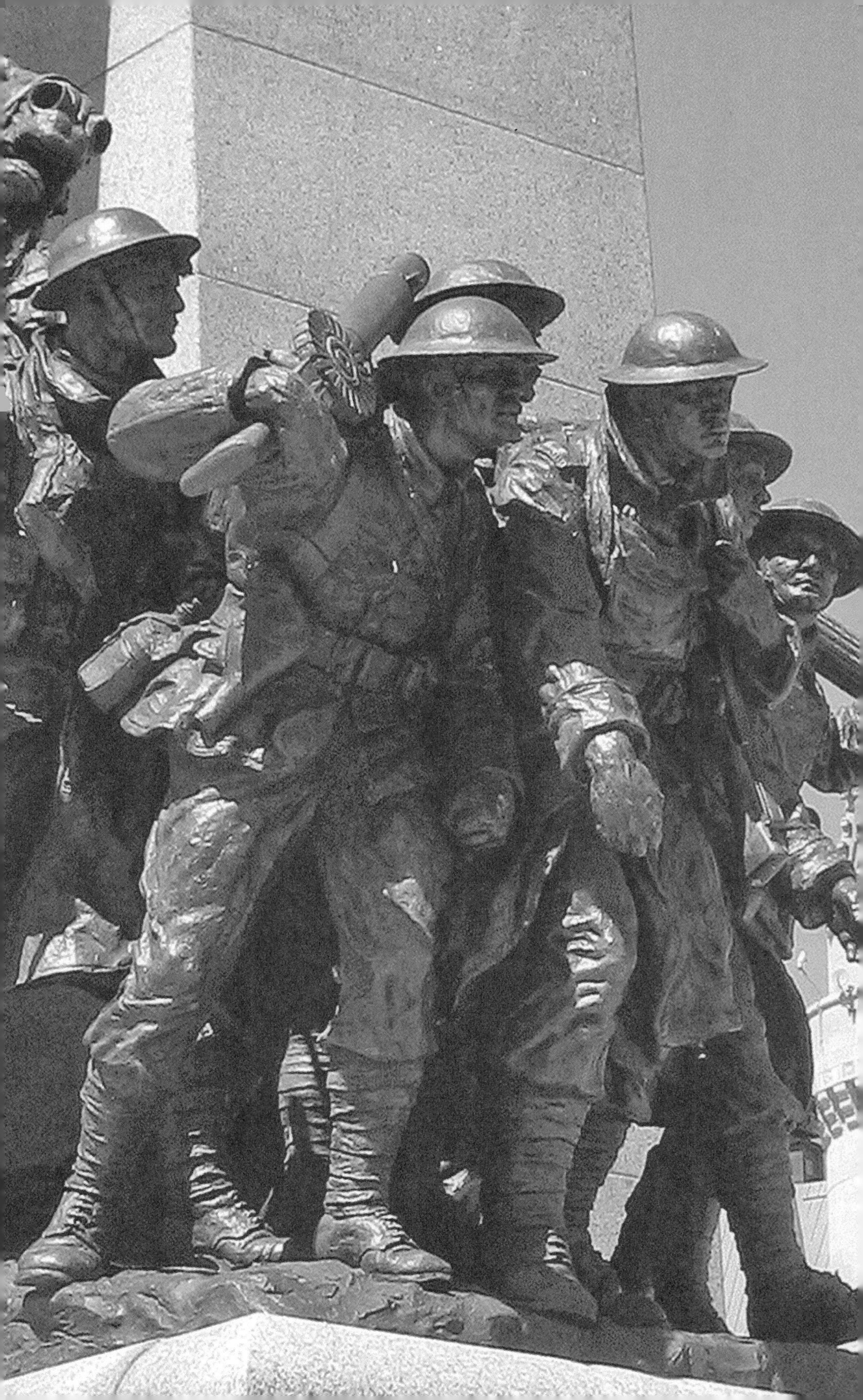

# 3 Novels

## From *The Wars* to *Three Day Road*

### MAPPING THE LANDSCAPE



In an important 1995 essay, Jan Assmann remarked that "through its cultural heritage a society becomes visible to itself and others" (133), and few literary examples of Canada's cultural heritage have made us more visible than *The Wars*. This novel represents that rare phenomenon, a work of art which, in Lorraine York's words, we "look back on as a singularly important moment in the writing life of a nation" (*Introducing Timothy Findley's* The Wars 14). How curious it is, then, for a country that has never initiated a war, invaded or tried to conquer another country, never had a civil war or a major, protracted conflict fought on its own soil since 1812—or 1885[1]—and that has, since the Second World War, defined itself as peaceable and peacekeeping, to find itself made visible in a work called *The Wars*. A closer look at this novel, however, nicely complicates easy assumptions about war and peace, and I will say more shortly about why I agree with York and how the novel functions as a national mirror and an influential narrative.

The phenomenon that begins with this novel has grown to include an impressive range of responses to the Great War, and these occur in fiction, non-fiction (memoirs, biographies, and history), drama, poetry, and film. Because I can only examine a few of these works in depth, I will focus on three novels (*The Wars, Broken Ground,* and *Three Day Road*), four plays (*Billy Bishop Goes to War, The Lost Boys, Mary's Wedding,* and *Vimy*), three films (*Going Home, The Great War,* and *Passchendaele*), and two works of non-fiction (Sandra Gwyn's *Tapestry of War* and David Macfarlane's *The Danger Tree*). My reasons for making this selection are many. Each of these works represents excellent to very fine work in its genre or medium, and all, to one degree or another, are post-memory works that evoke and create Canada as a landscape of memory. This last point is crucial because, despite the fact that all these works revisit the battlefields of France and Belgium as they recreate the war, they also focus on home ground, Canadian life, the history of the nation, and the meaning of that history as it is remembered now.

The fictional map on which to place *The Wars, Broken Ground,* and *Three Day Road* extends from coast to coast, north to Hudson Bay, and south of the border into Vermont. Other texts exist on this map and some of them deserve a mention. For example, Louis Caron's *L'Emmitouflé* was first published in 1977 and then translated as *The Draft Dodger* in 1980; it coincides with *The Wars.*[2] Set in the 1970s, in the shadow of the Vietnam War, a family of French Canadians living in Vermont remembers their Quebec roots and the story of Uncle Nazaire, who went into hiding in 1917 to avoid conscription. The character who establishes the remembering framework is the young American draft dodger Jean-François, "the grandson of a French Canadian who'd immigrated to the States" (11), who has been hiding in Montreal to escape the American army and Vietnam. Some of the most powerful scenes in the novel portray the physical landscape of fields, forests, farms, and riverbanks where the First World War draft dodger hid, and these scenes remind the young American, not only of his family's past, but also of the capacity of Canada, with its vast terrain, scattered population, and bilingual identity, to shelter those who choose not to fight. The irony of these memories, however, lies in the fact that for a man like Nazaire the war is never over because he remains haunted by his isolating experience and always feels guilty for refusing to fight. His trauma ends up resembling that of those returned soldiers who cannot talk about what happened.

For the reader, the irony goes deeper. Anyone reconsidering the view that Canada came of age as a nation because of the war will be reminded by this novel that the Khaki Election of 1917 and the introduction of conscription, which was deeply resented in Quebec, nearly split the country apart. Sandra Gwyn explores this crisis in *Tapestry of War* through the story of Talbot Papineau, who is her hero and will be the hero of McKenna's film *The Great War*, but the resistance to the war and to conscription by some French Canadians in Quebec is often overlooked in nation-building stories or else held against them in the mistaken belief that the rest of the country—to a man and a woman—fully supported Canada's war effort. Not until 2006, when Michael Poole published *Rain Before Morning*, is there a novel in which anglophone Canadians from British Columbia escape conscription by hiding in remote places along the northern British Columbia coast.



Although Poole has created a fiction with characters and places he imagines, *Rain Before Morning* is based on historical facts about the 1917 election, about a Canadian nurse working in Number One Canadian Hospital at Étaples, about the Military Police who pursue draft dodgers north to their hideaway, and about the Spanish flu that sweeps through even remote communities. In his Author's Note, Poole explains that he has given the name of "Silva Landing" to his fictional community, with its cemetery (and the grave of the young man killed in a shootout with the Military Police), because descendants of the people who were actually involved still live there and "so enduring is the stigma of desertion in World War One, their lips remain sealed to this day about the events of 1918" (319). Poole's "events" also include memorable scenes in France, where his heroine Leah Jamieson is a nurse. As we see with Thiessen's nurse, Clare, in *Vimy*, or Urquhart's Augusta in *The Underpainter*, Poole's Leah witnesses the horror of wounded and dying soldiers, but her situation is made impossible when she decides to help a sixteen-year-old deserter suffering from shell shock and starvation. When the boy is caught and her assistance is discovered, she is dismissed from the army's Medical Corps and sent home because not even the doctors will acknowledge the reality of shell shock, especially when mutiny is breaking out around Étaples. The young soldier will face execution for desertion, and Nurse Jamieson is told that she is "damned lucky not to go before a court martial" (140). Although *Rain Before Morning* is not narrated as a memory-work through the recollections of a narrating character (like Findley's biographer or Caron's Jean-François) and in this key way is a more conventional, realist novel than *The Wars* or *The Draft Dodger*, it is a valuable addition to the larger corpus of works remembering Canada in the First World War: it exposes events silenced and all but erased from our history of the war, both at home and abroad; it features the experience of nurses, whose stories are often ignored; and it represents a powerful indictment of the war itself.[3] While Poole's characters, especially Leah, bear witness to what they see and refuse to hide the truth, it is Michael Poole who remembers her story, resituates it in our landscape of memory, and reminds us that many men and women, for a variety of reasons, objected to the war.

Among other interesting novels that represent the Great War but present their stories without the complex narrative framing of *The Wars* and *Broken Ground* or the contrapuntal remembering structure of *Three Day Road* are Alan Cumyn's *The Sojourn* (2003) and *The Famished Lover* (2006), Frances Itani's *Deafening* (2003), Kevin Major's *No Man's Land* (1995), and Jane Urquhart's *The Stone Carvers* (2001). All these works are firmly situated in the narrative present of the war and its aftermath, and each uses a relatively straightforward, conventional third-person narration and a linear plot. Which is not to say that they are uninteresting novels or poorly written. *Deafening* and *The Stone*

*Carvers* are, in my view, fascinating texts with unusual perspectives on the war, and both are beautifully written. Cumyn's two connected novels follow the experiences of a Canadian soldier, Ramsay Crome, during the war and after his return home, and Major's *No Man's Land* retells the story of Newfoundland's "Blue Puttees" and their betrayal by the British command. Major provides a rather formulaic treatment of battle and male-bonding set against the tragic history of the decimation of the Newfoundland Regiment at Beaumont-Hamel on 1 July 1916. Cumyn, however, creates a larger, more complex narrative about the war and the fate of a soldier-artist (Crome), who falls in love with his English cousin during a leave. This love is doomed because the woman is already engaged, and shortly after his return to the front Crome is captured by the Germans. He spends the duration of the war as a POW, and we learn about these experiences and his longing for his cousin in *The Famished Lover*. After his escape, the war's end, and his return to Canada, Crome is unable to put his memories of the war behind him and settle into a normal, married life back home. The second novel follows his life story up to the Spanish Civil War and the approach of the Second World War.[4]

Without question, Major's and Cumyn's novels present realistic, powerful scenes of trench warfare and the filth and starvation of a POW camp, and Cumyn draws striking comparisons between home and battle fronts, as well as illustrating the problems faced by a returned soldier who is haunted by his memories. But this type of novel, while based on careful historical research, does not challenge a reader's assumptions about the status of official history or question the authority of those who guard it as unassailable and complete truth. Nor do these narratives complicate the characters' perspectives on their lives or ask the reader to bear witness or engage actively in a search for meaning in the men's war stories and in the dubious purposes of war. Certainly there is trauma, suffering, and death in these works and the men are haunted by their memories and resentful of those on the home front who will never understand their ordeal, but these crises and problems are described rather than presented as an occasion for critical reflection on history or as a chance to heal through mourning.[5]

*Deafening* and *The Stone Carvers* belong in a very different category. They are not war novels in the same narrow sense and, although they both feature soldiers and veterans, women are central characters and the landscapes explored in each text are complex amalgams of home front and remembered battle front. *Deafening* features a young deaf woman and her stretcher-bearer medic husband, who leaves for the war shortly after their marriage. The first third of the novel develops the life of Grania, describes her struggle to cope with her loss of hearing in childhood, the loving support of her family, and her courtship by Jim, a young man with normal hearing. Inevitably, the war reaches into small-town, rural Ontario in Prince Edward County, where the home front is set; it seeps into the peaceful lives of these people through the newspapers and the departures of the young men who enlist. The war is discussed and worried over in the community, and Grania, who by 1914 is an expert lip-reader, can speak clearly, and does not miss any of the information or gossip. Soon her brother-in-law has left for the war and Grania "knew, and Jim knew, that within months he would be leaving" (114). Once Jim has departed from the Belleville train station, Grania waits for his letters, and through the device of letters and quotations from *The Canadian* (the actual newspaper published by the Ontario School for the Deaf), we get regular updates on the progress and casualties of the war. Itani incorporates one further strategy into her otherwise linear, third-person narration when she shifts the focalization from this external position into the letters Jim writes "in his head" (257). These internalized passages are diary-like and confessional in their style and intimate tone, and from them we (but not Grania) are granted insight into Jim's private response to the horrors of the war.[6]

As time passes, we shift back and forth between home front and battle front as Itani establishes the myriad ways in which the war infiltrates every aspect of life at home without ever becoming fully real or understandable to those waiting for news. When her severely wounded and traumatized brother-in-law is returned to Canada, Grania sees that "everyone has lost something in this war" (282) and that neither she nor her sister will understand what this young man went through because he refuses to speak or leave his house. "Everything," Grania realizes, "was war, even the cookbooks" (284). By creating the character of the wounded veteran who will not speak, Itani intensifies what I see as the underlying and determining dualities of the *deafening* symbolism—silence and speech, hearing and not hearing, knowing and not knowing. In Itani's hands, this is more than a matter of imagery, or of choosing a deaf heroine, and much more than describing the often literally deafening cacophony of war. When Jim and Grania meet again, on another of those train-station platforms that seem integral to war stories, it is 1919. She has survived the Spanish flu and Jim has returned "from the land called *War*" (377). She knows he has lost friends in that land and she can see that he has changed; he cannot believe he is home, but he sees that she is "pale, thinner than he remembered" (378). It is the narrator who reminds *us* that "She would never know where he had been. Nor would he know where she had been" (377). The war has produced such a separation, such a gulf or, in this novel's terms, such a cultural deafening that even those closest to each other, if they were on different fronts, will never *hear* or fully comprehend what war meant for the other. Speech seems inadequate and listening intolerable.





Nevertheless, Itani tells us this story about war and peace, death and survival, battle front and home front. Clearly, she believes it is necessary. Through her narrator and her handling of narrative perspective, she invites us to listen to her story about ordinary young Canadians and how their lives were affected by history. Paradoxically, yet inevitably, the contemporary novelist believes that we can and must lip-read the past and that by doing so, with imagination, we will hear something important and better understand the burden of those years and how we today were shaped by them. She does not suggest that the losses and traumas of war can be overcome—no one can force the silent veteran to speak—but she does insist that the past is still with us despite the gulf of time and that, like her, we can bear secondary witness to it.

Jane Urquhart's *The Underpainter* and *The Stone Carvers* belong in a class of their own as far as my study of war fiction is concerned. They are both stunning novels, exquisitely constructed landscapes of memory that embrace Canadian history while creating unforgettable fictional characters. Neither is a war novel in the narrow sense of combat fiction, although both contain deeply moving scenes to remember and represent the war, and both explore many other themes and situations besides war. For these reasons I have not chosen either one for my central texts. Nevertheless, some attention must be paid to their perspectives on the war. *The Underpainter* is definitely a memory-work in which the narrator bears witness, against his will, to the past, and *The Stone Carvers* is a historical novel that traces the building of Canadian communities by German, Italian, and Irish immigrants who then find their children and grandchildren sucked back into European conflicts that their families chose to leave behind. Both novels are ghost stories—a genre Urquhart excels in—and some of the most restless, disturbing ghosts in these novels are directly connected with the war and with others' attempts to forget and ignore their sufferings. In *The Underpainter* these ghosts are two Canadians, the soldier and veteran George Kearns and the nurse Augusta Moffat; in *The Stone Carvers* the most heartbreaking ghost is Eamon O'Sullivan, who will go missing in action somewhere in France or Belgium and will haunt the main character, Klara Becker, until she carves his name on Walter Allward's Vimy Monument.

Although both works rely heavily on memory and on the metaphor of landscape as the ground, or map, of memory, they differ significantly in narrative structure. *The Underpainter* is a first-person autobiographical fiction presented by the elderly American painter Austin Fraser who, at the end of his life, tries to atone for his failures as an artist and a man by telling others' stories within his own: this is a fine example of fictional auto/biography, life writing that doubles as biography within autobiography.[7] Austin's story contains many powerful characters and memories besides those connected with George and Augusta, and these include the real American painter Rockwell Kent and the fictional Sara Pengelly, who is Austin's model and lover for fifteen summers from 1920 to 1935.[8] The Austin/Rockwell/Sara configuration carries the dominant theme of aesthetics and ethics (the responsibility of the artist to the people and world around him) and produces the main source of imagery in the text, notably the irresistible attraction of northern Canadian landscapes along the north shore of Lake Superior. Like Kent (in real life), Austin Fraser is drawn to this Canadian landscape, which he sketches behind and around Sara's figure during each summer visit; but when he returns to his New York studio, he reworks elements of her underpainted figure and the surface of his canvases until he has all but erased her presence. Both Sara and her northern landscape are mere subjects for Austin, never his love, never his home.

In a climactic confrontation, Rockwell Kent will call Austin's work "cold...as...hell" and, therefore, fatally "flawed" (261) because Austin has destroyed all signs of his personal, emotional connection with the northern landscape and the woman whom he refuses to love or respect. It is only in this text, his final confessional work called "The Underpainter," that the ruthless, self-absorbed artist will admit that his technique of pentimenti produces "ghosts of formerly rendered shapes" that threaten "to rise to the surfaces of my pictures like drowned corpses" (181). And pentimenti is a perfect metaphor for the entire novel; indeed, it is a metaphor, and a technique, that nicely complements my concept of landscape of memory.

Two other ghosts who will rise through Austin's attempt to forget them are George, his Canadian friend from before the war, and George's companion after the war, the shell-shocked nurse Augusta. As part of his atonement, Austin will pay homage to George and Augusta by retelling their traumatizing experiences during the war. However, he is not jolted into doing so until he bears witness to their deaths and accepts the fact that he is partly responsible. The scene of secondary witnessing comes in the winter of 1937 when Austin travels north with a woman George had loved and lost before the war. By 1937 George has re-established a quiet life in his hometown of Davenport (today part of northwest Toronto); he has recovered from his physical injuries and his own shell shock sufficiently to establish a relationship with Augusta that seems solid and loving. What he has not fully recovered from is the memory of this woman who, he believes, betrayed him, and when Augusta grasps the depth of his angry entanglement with his pre-war past, she gives herself a fatal injection of morphine. Before she does so, however, she tells her unwilling listener-witness, Austin, the story of her life, and to my mind the most compelling and unforgettable part of *The Underpainter* is Austin's testimony, his re-narration, of what she told him about the war during that winter night in Davenport, Ontario, in 1937 when she believes George has left her.

Augusta's story of destruction, loss, and anguish, rises from her witnessing of war at Étaples and from her confession that she killed her closest friend, another young nurse, who had been wounded and broken beyond recognition in a German bombing raid on the hospital. Augusta kills her friend Maggie, as she lies a bloodied unconscious wreck on a stretcher, by placing the ether mask over her crushed face and then "causing the amount of diethyl ether to rise well above the level of safety" (240). In 1937 this memory is still so overwhelming, so vividly present to Augusta that she can shock Austin out of his lack of understanding—as an American he did not fight, even when the United States finally entered the war—and self-protective insularity by telling it. Gradually, he will begin to appreciate the sufferings of others and, when he finally reports what Augusta said, he begins with—"Augusta said something I will never forget" and then quotes her testimony: "What were any of us to do with the rest of our lives anyway? After all that. We were only in our early twenties and our lives were finished. And yet here we are, George and me, right in the middle of the aftermath. What makes it just continue and continue? I had no answer for this" (298–99).

By imagining Augusta and her story, Urquhart has picked up where Findley left his nurse, Marian Turner, in *The Wars* and moved her life closer to centre stage, where we also find Thiessen's Clare. George's tragedy is also relayed to us by Austin after (and because) he witnesses the scene of double suicide and comes to understand his role in their deaths (see *The Underpainter* 309–12). This narrative construction of testimony by a primary witness for an increasingly empathic listener, who will assume his burden as a secondary witness, represents nicely what I outlined in Chapter 2 as the process of witnessing inside the text. Austin first listens to Augusta's story, then he relays her story to us; by telling us, he performs his role as secondary witness inside the text and constructs (Eco would say *models*) us as listening-readers with the potential to perform as secondary witnesses outside the text.



When George does return to Davenport in the early morning and finds Augusta dead, he smashes his prized china collection, injects the rest of the morphine into himself, and lies down beside her to die. This is how Austin finds the pair, dead, casualties of the war and its aftermath, surrounded by broken porcelain. His first response, after gathering up George's broken collection—something he had viewed as a mere craft instead of real art—is to "drive north" (313) to Lake Superior and Sara, and in another context I would discuss *The Underpainter* as a Canadian "northern" in which the landscape of memory is the North.[9] But Austin in 1937 is still incapable of facing the woman he abandoned two years earlier and he refuses to meet Sara when he spies her approaching him across the snow. He jumps into his car and flees south back to the States and his safe distances. Only in retrospect, years later, when Sara is dead and has bequeathed him her home, can he face the past. And it is only in this narrative, this testimony and memory-work of secondary witnessing, that he can make amends because this narrative is his self-portrait and his portrait of the others and of an era that he, like we his readers/listeners/viewers, must remember if we want to understand how we arrived here from there. The First World War is only one aspect of this haunted remembering, this ghost story, but it seems (at least I suggest this is the case) that Urquhart created an American artist as her narrator to maintain the kind of distanced and distancing lens she needed for this story about art, human relationships, the Canadian landscape, and a war that insists on its aftermath, on rising like ghosts, like drowned corpses, through our erasures.

*The Stone Carvers* is both a more exclusively Canadian story and a more conventional historical novel. The narrator is omniscient; the focalization shifts from character to character and from nineteenth-century Bavaria to 1930s Ontario; and the story of the First World War emerges from the history of immigration, settlement, family life, art and architecture, and, finally, from a woman's grief. The stories of the two main characters, Klara and her brother Tilman Becker (third-generation Canadians of German descent), diverge before the war when a young Tilman escapes his farming family and the village of Shoneval. He leaves Klara behind to fall in love and be left once more when her lover, Eamon O'Sullivan, enlists in 1914 with a dream of flying aeroplanes. First we are told Klara's story, her passion for Eamon, her anger when he leaves, and her paralyzing grief when he is reported missing. Then the narrator shifts to Tilman, his life as a child hobo, his loss of a leg at Vimy Ridge, and his miserable existence making wooden prostheses in a Toronto factory after the war. When the brother and sister are reunited in the early 1930s, neither will speak much about the war years. Instead, they recall their early training by their grandfather in woodcarving, their grandfather's hope that Tilman would be successful at this ancient, old-world art form, and his reluctant praise for Klara's obvious talent even though, in his eyes, she is a mere woman and cannot be a real artist. When Tilman tells Klara about the Canadian architect Walter Allward, who is building a monument to the memory of Canadian soldiers whose bodies were never found, the narrative lines converge around the aftermath of the war and Klara's need to remember the young man she tried to forget, but whose ghost haunts her still. Although the novel opens in June 1934 "in the shadow of the great unfinished monument" (1) and in the presence of the formidable Allward, we do not return to this crucial scene and to this *milieux de mémoire* until Part 3, called "The Monument," and more than two hundred and fifty pages later.

It will take a great deal of persuasion on Klara's part to convince her brother to travel to Vimy with her. He does not want to return or remember. But he is moved by her regret and love, her need to make amends for refusing to speak to Eamon before he left, and her frank obsession with memory and commemoration. Disguised as Tilman's brother, this forty-year-old spinster will get to France under his watchful eye, but once there the larger significance of their journey will slowly surface as both of them move through denial, anger, and melancholy withdrawal into mourning, and from there to new lives based on remembrance. Tilman will fall in love with French food and with the French chef, Recouvrir (a symbolic name indeed), whose body bears the scars of Verdun and whose flesh continually pushes bloody fragments of shrapnel through the surface of his skin. This image of embodied war memory surfacing unbidden, stark, and painful, echoes the physical landscape around the monument site and across northern France and Flanders, where even today fragments of bone, metal, and other *momenti mori* surface in farmers' fields.

Urquhart imagines two splendid scenes in which Klara works on Allward's monument—something the real man would never have permitted—and she also allows her Klara to fall in love with an Italian-Canadian sculptor whose main task is to inscribe the names of the missing on the marble walls of the monument. By conflating historical facts with imaginative fiction in this way, Urquhart insists on the power of human feeling (so lacking in Austin Fraser) and individual creativity to heal past trauma enough to allow a future to take shape. Art, she is saying, cannot redeem us, but it will provide us with enough hope to move on. Urquhart's Allward will catch Klara early one morning carving Eamon's beautiful features (as she remembers them) on his Torchbearer, but instead of firing this intruder on the spot, he talks with her—for he quickly realizes she is a woman—and allows her excellent carving, her private monument to an individual death, to remain. When her new lover, Giorgio, helps her inscribe Eamon O'Sullivan's name on the monument wall, Klara will be freed from his ghost and able to return home.

In many ways, the chief protagonist, the hero even, of *The Stone Carvers* is the monument itself. Although the novel does not mediate our reading through a witnessing narrator inside the text, it does make us see Klara, Tilman, Giorgio, and the fictional Allward at work on the monument, and what we see is the artistic passion, creative skill, dedication, and remembering that produce peace instead of war. Klara and Tilman Becker will return to Canada, each with his and her new love, at peace with themselves and the past. They will never forget, but they will no longer be trapped by melancholy and repression. Of course, Jane Urquhart cannot bring the same peace to Walter Allward, who went unheralded in his lifetime and was promptly forgotten, but she can, and has, created her monument to his memory by her own testimony. Through an act of empathic unsettlement, the novelist makes us see what happened during the war; she takes us underground into the labyrinth of tunnels beneath Vimy and gazes thoughtfully across the grass-clad mounds and cavities around the ridge; she caresses with words the marble figures as they emerge from the white stone under the skilled hands of Allward's carvers and brings us close enough to touch forms few Canadians have ever seen and cannot actually touch, even on site. Above all, Urquhart reminds us of what the Vimy Monument means, and for her, as for Tilman, this has nothing to do with military victory or a national coming-of-age myth. In the closing paragraph of the coda that ends the novel, Urquhart moves back in time and space to reflect on how the farmers of Shoneval created Canada, on how a Canadian architect, who we need to remember, dreamed "the stone that [would] be assembled and carved to expiate the sorrow of one country on the soil of another" (390), and how those in political power "hoard their coins for the machinery of war" (390). As if to *expiate* this greed and violence, she gives the final words to art and the Vimy Monument, which "disperse light and strength and consolation long after the noise of the battle has ended, and all the warriors have gone home" (390).

This business of bringing war memories home to Canada where they will infiltrate, if not poison, all aspects of home front life, both during and after the war, crops up in a surprising number of recent novels that appear to have no direct or special connection with the war. Where my three main texts focus on the war, and the other novels I have touched on—particularly *Deafening*, *The Underpainter*, and *The Stone Carvers*—treat the war as a violent backstory and as a source of traumatic memories and disturbing ghosts, these other works suggest that the First World War has become embedded in the life of the nation like a cancer, that later generations, families, and entire communities are affected by it even though they are unaware of its lasting impact. In Ann-Marie MacDonald's *Fall On Your Knees*, for example, the Great War seeps into the family's story of incest, blood, and death through the father and returned soldier, James, bringing tragedy in its wake.[10] In Allan Donaldson's *Maclean* the memory of the war is more pervasive. We spend one day with this man, Maclean, who lives in Wakefield, New Brunswick, is shunned by his family, and spends most of his waking hours drunk. He was gassed at Ypres and is so haunted by his memories that he has slipped into an existence of despair and uselessness. The fictional present of the narrative is set during the Second World War as bad news arrives home from the front, but Maclean's depressive state has rendered him ineffectual as either a warning against war or as an example of its long-range consequences.

June Hutton's *Underground* is a far more complex historical novel than Donaldson's. It follows the life story of its protagonist, Albert Fraser, from 1914 when he enlists at the age of seventeen until 1975, when he digs a small splinter of metal out of his neck: as he does this he thinks that "each time...he has dug out the last of them [until] another eventually appears" (239). But while Fraser's life is framed and determined by the Great War and "the memories heaved up by the shrapnel" (289), *Underground* covers much more territory than the war. Fraser will fight on the Somme and then return to Vancouver Island only to become an impoverished and discarded war veteran. He will end up living as a hobo during the Depression, join the On to Ottawa Trek, but then get caught up in Vancouver street riots and attack a policeman. This turn of events causes him to hide in the tunnels under Vancouver's Chinatown until he can escape to Whitehorse and a new identity. When he signs on to fight in the Spanish Civil War, the threads of his family past begin to reconnect in his present life and pull him back, finally, to Vancouver, where he will live with his Spanish wife in comparative peace observing Hitler's rise to power and events in Franco's Spain from a distance. But as the closing image of this now elderly man, recently widowed and once more grieving his losses, and with shrapnel surfacing from his flesh, reminds us, the war is always *there*, always a ghostly presence that shapes our lives. Moreover, the fragment of shrapnel reminds us—the readers—not only of the war, but also of the prefacing quotation Hutton chooses for her story. This is a quotation from Frederick Varley's 1919 letter to Arthur Lismer (see Chapter 1, page 17): "The story of war is told in the thousand and one things that mingle with the earth." In *Underground* one man's story illustrates the history of Canada and of working-class Canadian life from the first twentieth-century war to the uneasy peacetime of the 1970s, and his story raises an important question: if the First World War could have such a lasting impact on this man, what did it do to his generation?

To my mind, however, the novel that best captures the long-term, devastating impact of the Great War on twentieth-century Canada and on the lives of Canadians is Margaret Atwood's *The Blind Assassin*. This fictional memoir by an elderly woman called Iris Chase from small-town Ontario is so complex in narrative structure and so rich in themes and characters that it comes as a surprise to realize that war, especially the First World War, plays a decisive, pernicious role in her personal history and (as Atwood tells it) the history of the country. I am not for a moment suggesting that *The Blind Assassin* is *about* the war, or even about war in general, although the Second World War and late twentieth-century new wars trouble Iris's memories.[11] There are many ways of reading and analyzing this text. But it is important to pause and reflect on the omnipresence of war when Iris, sitting alone before her television, watches the news and tells us that "there's another war somewhere, what they call a minor one, though of course it isn't minor for anyone who happens to get caught up in it" (599).





On a first reading, I was hooked on the novel's whodunit qualities: who really wrote "The Blind Assassin" intertext? Who really fathered Iris's child? How did sister Laura really die, and why? But I came away from this reading haunted by something else, by a profound sense of grief and loss, not for the past—this novel is *not* nostalgic—but for the presence of ghosts, of events and lives forgotten, not accounted for or listened to. After several rereadings, I believe that the quality of hauntedness (as Ross Chambers would call it) that transferred itself, that spread as it were, from the pages of the book to my extra-literary life, has myriad subterranean links with the two world wars. For example, the opening sentence of this 655-page story begins, "Ten days after the war ended, my sister Laura drove a car off a bridge" (3). A few pages later, we come upon a 1947 obituary from the *Globe and Mail* notifying us that a Toronto businessman has died after having a "distinguished career...supplying Allied troops with uniform parts and weapons" (17). Then, a mere fifty pages into this auto/biography, this elderly woman's memory-work and confession, it seems quite *natural*—one scarcely even notices the image—for Iris to describe "orange tulips" as being "crumpled and raggedy like the stragglers from some returning army" (53).

Such images come easily to Iris because they are part of her mental baggage, her vocabulary, her outlook on the world. But surely this is a disturbed (and disturbing) perspective to hold. How did this elderly woman acquire her relentlessly honest gaze, her sibylline insight, and her Cassandra-like voice? The answer Atwood slowly reveals goes back to Iris's birth in 1916, to her family life in Port Ticonderoga, to her severely war-wounded father—injured three times during the Great War, at the Somme, Vimy Ridge, and Bourlon Wood (95)—and to her growing up in a home where her father, raging and drunk, would stump around in the tower above her bedroom like a helpless Wotan. As Iris remembers her father, his dead brothers (lost in the war), the sight of her parents meeting again on the train station platform, where it is obvious, even to a child, that *everything* is amiss, she is confessing that she cannot "cause the war to end" simply by writing down "*1918. November 11. Armistice Day*" (94–95). What's more, she cannot erase her memories of the "Weary Soldier" war memorial commissioned by her father for his hometown in 1928. The locals want something noble and uplifting; they want an inscription that reads: "For Those Who Willingly Made the Supreme Sacrifice." But Captain Norval Chase refuses. He gets, because he has paid the bill for it, a "dejected-looking" soldier and the inscription "Lest We Forget" because, as he points out, the memorial is for the dead, and "too many people had been a damn sight too forgetful" (185–86). In a narrative that is all about remembering a history that is neither "winsome" nor "clean," but that carries the stench of reality (66), and about memorializing and witnessing (118), Atwood wants us to think backwards in order to see where we are now and where we are (inevitably?) headed. To achieve this end, she has created Iris's landscape of memory in which war lurks everywhere—from bedraggled tulips to the fantasies set in the imaginary land of Sakiel-Norn in the intertext.





When Iris moves beyond her father's part in her story and on to the story of the man she will love, we learn that he was orphaned somewhere in Europe during the Great War (238–39) and that she will lose him somewhere in Holland in 1945 (612). As she watches the television news in the present, visits the cemetery, the war memorial, what remains of the family home, and writes the auto/biography of her life, her family's life, her lover's life, and her county's and country's life, she keeps her father's First World War medals and asks herself, and us: "How did the war crop up? How did it gather itself together? What was it made from? What secrets, lies, betrayals?" (581). She is thinking here of the Second World War, but the main answer to these questions is the same for all wars: by forgetting—forgetting the stench of reality, the lies about honour and sacrifice, the greed for military might and wealth, the fathers' betrayals of their sons. Iris's message, if that is what this is, her memorial and commemoration, is to tell this story as she lived it, witnessed it, before she dies. Her final advice to us is: "Nothing is more difficult than to understand the dead, I've found; but nothing is more dangerous than to ignore them" (638).





### *THE WARS*, *BROKEN GROUND*, AND *THREE DAY ROAD*

Few Canadian novels have received the amount of attention devoted to *The Wars*. There are extensive analyses by critics who locate it in the context of pre-1977 war fiction or discuss its place within Findley's oeuvre or identify some of its chief themes and narrative strategies.[12] Three decades after its publication, the novel has come to occupy what Lorraine York calls "a singularly important moment" in Canada's literary history (*Introducing* 14). As I suggested in Chapter 1, the year 1977 is important for several literary and cultural reasons, and *The Wars* captures that moment of cultural and historical awareness by re-presenting Canada's early twentieth-century past from a late twentieth-century perspective. When Jane Urquhart looked back at the war years, she saw an innocent, unselfconscious, even naïve, nation (Ferri, "A Conversation with Jane Urquhart" 29); when Sandra Gwyn looked back, she too saw this innocence, which would be trampled in the mud of Flanders and France, but she also saw a generation of survivors who felt duty-bound to build a nation that would represent "the Canadian spirit" and be a fitting memorial "to those who had fallen in foreign fields" (*Tapestry of War* xviii).

The notion that everything after the war was different from everything that came before, that the Great War caused a profound rupture in Western civilization, and that all who survived lost an innocence they had once possessed, is hardly new. Most writers, artists, and scholars—until quite recently, that is—repeated that mantra.[13] In Canada, this version of the war's destructive force carried the additional narrative burden of a coming-of-age story, of a nation growing up into a proud, tough, independent country. Findley was fully aware of that narrative; he grew up in a family haunted by the Great War (Aitken interview, "Long Live the Dead" 82). Near the beginning of his novel he has Robert Ross's biographer point to the research materials in the archive and observe that "a whole age lies in fragments underneath the lamps" (11). But like Gwyn and her characters, Findley assumes responsibility for these fragments and takes it upon himself—or rather he gives the biographer this task—to reassemble the fragments, to put the crumbling past together as best he can, and to produce meaning from the fragments. Why? Because these fragments are Canada's "cultural heritage," because, as Jan Assmann argues, they make a "society visible to itself and others" (133). They make us pay attention and, by paying attention, learn the value of remembering the past.

The cultural heritage, the society, reflected back to us from the pages of this text, was one that Findley believed Canadians had betrayed in the Second World War, the Korean War, and Vietnam (the immediate war context for the writing of *The Wars*). For Findley, this heritage was one that had been *comparatively* peaceful and non-violent, one in which a man like Robert Ross might have lived and flourished; it constituted a heritage worth remembering, treasuring (despite failures and faults), and understanding, even if it could never be recuperated. Therefore, in *The Wars*, Findley is at pains to create battle scenes, terrifying gas attacks, bombing, and trench life, scenes of destruction and violation, not for their own sake but so that his readers will be forced (as long as we keep reading) to bear witness to this history and its devastating impact on one young man, his family, his fellow soldiers, two women who loved him, and the man who is constructing the biography of a young man shaped by this historical context of time and place.

That the narrator in the text is a man is certain. However, this fact is not revealed until the end when Marian Turner, the Canadian nurse who cared for Robert until he died, responds to her sister Bessie's prompting that she confess her wish to help Robert die: "*Why don't you tell him Mernie? Why don't you say it and get it off your chest?*" (188). This voice and comment are captured by the tape recorder used by the narrator, the man I am calling Robert's biographer.[14] This man, this narrator-witness within the text, will only be identified once as male and he is never named. Critics usually call him a historian or a researcher, and he is, of course, both. I call him Robert Ross's biographer because he is piecing together the facts of Robert's life and death, his family and national background, within the context of the Great War, while insisting that Robert's life amounts to more than a war story. At many points, he departs from his tapes, interviews, historical facts, documents (like letters and photographs), to tell a story, to imagine an inner life for his biographee, to visualize the impact of the war and Robert's fate on his family, especially his mother. And this is where a compelling biography separates itself from social history, particularly from that subgenre known as military history. A good biography *must* tell a story. A good biographer will create a fiction—a story that draws on and is faithful to the known facts—but that interprets the facts by breathing life into them, by telling what Findley calls elsewhere *lies*.[15] He could have chosen a more conventional narrative voice, the kind used by Itani in *Deafening* or Cumyn in *The Sojourn*, but he created a biographer as his intradiegetic narrator and a fictional secondary witness, and the consequences of this choice are central to the meaning and purpose of *The Wars*.[16]

*The Wars* tells the story of a well-to-do upper middle-class young Canadian from Toronto who enlists, trains, and then ends up in France and Flanders for the Somme push in the summer of 1916. Robert Ross is only nineteen when he is sent overseas; he will be twenty-five (almost twenty-six) when he dies in 1922. Although he is the elder son in a family of four—two sons, two daughters—he is neither the most aggressive nor the most conformist member of the family. Indeed, judging from what we are told about his youth, he was a delicate child, a gentle person, and devoted to an older sister, Rowena, who is hydrocephalic and confined to a wheelchair. It is her accidental death in a fall from the wheelchair, not peer pressure or the sight of his sister Margaret's boyfriend in uniform, which precipitates Robert's decision to leave his family and enlist. He is a solitary man who likes long-distance running and whose idol is the famous Indian runner Tom Longboat.[17] Robert is increasingly traumatized by his boot-camp training on the Prairies, the claustrophobic conditions on the troop ship SS *Massanabie*—which carries the 39th Battery of the Canadian Expeditionary Force plus a cargo hold full of horses across the Atlantic in December 1915—and then by the horrors of trench warfare and the seemingly mindless hierarchy of the military. Robert's love of animals is firmly established through his relationship with Rowena and her rabbits and through his compassion for the horses crammed into the ship's hold during the crossing. His affection for his fellow soldiers—not unusual in war stories—is complicated by his recognition of their sensitivities and vulnerability; many of them, like young Harris, Rodwell, or Clifford Purchas, are non-adversarial human beings like himself. In short, Robert Ross is a most unlikely warrior. Although he is able to lead his men through danger, advise them during a gas attack (for which they had no gas masks),[18] and bear up under the pressures that are incapacitating many, he is finally driven to the breaking point by the violence and madness around him. He shoots a commanding officer and a private in his desperate attempt to save horses from a German barrage along the road to Bailleul near Magdalene Wood. Robert is severely burned in the holocaust that ensues, court-martialled, and then left to suffer and die of his injuries.

This is the main fabric of story that his biographer will stitch together from documents, primary witnesses, court records, and interviews many years later. Summarized in this fashion, Robert's story seems straightforward, even familiar: an inexperienced young Canuck is thrown into the cauldron of the First World War, survives for a while, but finally *loses it,* disobeys orders in a futile effort to save some horses, mutinies and kills his superior officer, and suffers a painful and ignominious end. However, such a summary is almost a mockery of *The Wars* because the manner in which Robert's story is told, the impact of his life on others, and some of the things that are imagined for him by his biographer far exceed a simple plot summary. This novel is as much about the biographer's, and reader's, search for meaning in the fragments and from the ghosts of the past as it is a story about the Great War and one young man. It is also the story of Robert's family, particularly of his mother, and of a community and a country swept up in events they do not understand.



My question then is: why should Robert's story matter? Why does a biographer need to tell it and why must so much effort go into reconstructing his story? One answer—and for me the most important one—is that Robert matters as an individual, as a young man full of promise who joins Canada's citizen army, as a much-loved son (I see Mrs. Ross as a crucial figure in the novel), and as a human being who, despite his own capacity for anger and violence, is a gentle, loving, and thoughtful soul. Robert matters because he represents much of what is *potentially* best in human beings and in being Canadian, so that if a man like this can be thrown to the dogs of war, reduced to futile gestures of violence and failure (for neither he nor the horses will be saved from conflagration), with what are we left? What hope can be wrung from this devastatingly honest look at the Great War and its consequences? Moreover, in my present context, I cannot forget that Robert's story is far from the one I was told about the war. He is not the epitome of noble sacrifice for our superior way of life; he may be a "glorious laddie," but he is *not* given gladly by his mother; he does not go to war pumped up with patriotic zeal; he does not, finally, agree with or wish to mindlessly contribute to the slaughter around him (his mistake in shooting the young German at the crater's edge [130–31] haunts him); and he does not come of age because of the war. Findley's—or the biographer's—Robert Ross shatters the myth of "death so noble."

Which turns the question why back on us and on the biographer because it matters that we remember Robert and all he meant and what we lost; "memory is survival" as Findley insists (*Inside Memory* 7). To appreciate the power and significance of *The Wars*, we must consider the purposes and strategies of this biographer. As several scholars have noted, his is not the only narrating presence in the text. There is also a fairly traditional voice that opens and closes the narrative from a distant perspective and with impersonal, chronicling omniscience. This narrator sets the stage—"She was standing....Twenty feet away, Robert sat.... Behind him, the railroad track stretched....He stood up" (9)—and brings the tragedy to a close: "Mister Ross was the only member of his family who came to see him buried" (190). This narrator also takes over from, fills in for, the more limited biographer at crucial points in Robert's story to describe events and private feelings no biographer has access to, except through a leap of imagination derived from empathic unsettlement. The most intimate of these imagined events is the rape scene, which takes place when Robert is returning to the front for the major Allied push in June 1916, just days before he will disobey orders. On a symbolic level, this scene is not difficult to interpret: after visiting the baths at Désolé, Robert is attacked in the dark by his fellow soldiers—"Maybe even his brother officers. He'd never know. He never saw their faces" (169); therefore, his violation enacts a betrayal of an especially heinous kind (brother turning on brother) and represents the larger betrayal of an entire generation of young men by their countries, their governments, their churches, and their fathers.[19] It also functions psychologically as an explanation for Robert's revolt against the army with its rigid chain of command. When he makes it back to the safety of his hotel room, he erupts in frantic gestures of violence, represented in the expressionistic prose style of the narrative, but imagined and invented for him so that we can witness his distress. The scene closes as Robert burns Rowena's photograph in "an act of charity" (172) because this world of men at war is unworthy of her image. By destroying this photograph, Robert cuts a crucial link between himself and the home front.

Other events occur in rapid succession to push Robert towards his revolt: he spends several days under heavy bombardment conveying supply wagons and animals from Bailleul to the front near Wytsbrouk; the roads and ditches around him are "piled with corpses and carcasses" (174); he stumbles upon a body on the road—the body of a friend and fellow officer, Clifford Purchas, who has been with him since training camp in Canada and now lies in the mud "shot in the back and...sprawled face down" (176); he has had no proper food and only eight hours of sleep in three days. Then the Germans begin shelling the barnyard and stables where Battalion Signals is stationed. Robert decides he must break ranks to save the horses and that Captain Leather "is insane" (177). This is the climax of Robert's life and life story: he will shoot the captain between the eyes, kill the burned and wounded animals, and escape the fire and chaos with the horses that have survived. At this point in our reading and witnessing of events, as presented by the observing narrator, things seem clear enough. Robert has acted wisely and bravely in a crisis. Leather is a maniac. Before we are allowed narrative time to reflect on what he has done in the context of army rules, let alone that he has executed his captain, we are abruptly returned to the home front and to Mrs. Ross, who collapses at the news that Robert is "missing in action" (178). No explanation is provided for this sudden shift or for how we get to the Ross home on South Drive in Toronto, but by this late stage in the novel we do not need help. We are accustomed to these narrative breaks, interruptions, and sharp juxtapositions—a narrative strategy I attribute to the fictional biographer who, on the one hand, addresses us, and on the other, slips behind this wider, chronicling perspective, and who is ultimately responsible for assembling all the fragments with which the reader must work.

These fragments include most of what is needed for a biography, among which historical facts are crucial.[20] I have already noted the reliance of war fiction on accurate facts about battles, casualties, and weapons, but with *The Wars* Findley established one of the hallmarks of his creative work—his ability to set historical facts beside fictional *facts* and give them equal weight and legitimacy. For example, to return to that scene of Mrs. Ross's collapse, we are told, as a matter of fact, that Robert's photograph in the drawing room has started to fade and that "This was the sixteenth of June" (180). The year is 1916. Or, in another example, one for which the biographer openly takes responsibility, we are told precisely how many people have died thus far in the story. Lady Juliet d'Orsey has just finished her last interview with him; in her final words she quotes her brother who said he hoped future generations would "*remember we were human beings*" (158), even though he reckons that his generation will never be forgiven for the war. Then there is a blank space on the page, a pause in our reading, a moment to take a breath and reflect before we are (as has happened before) *spoken to* and expected to listen: "So far, you have read of the deaths of 557,017 people—one of whom was killed by a streetcar, one of whom died of bronchitis and one of whom died in a barn with her rabbits" (158).

Since these three deaths occur on home fronts, if not exactly in peacetime (young Harris's death from bronchitis occurs in a London hospital after he has made it overseas), and are fictional, that leaves 557,014 as the casualty count from war. By running this staggering figure together in one breath with the deaths we know belonged to much-loved individuals (albeit fictional ones), Findley and the biographer invite us to transfer the humanity granted fictional characters to the faceless, nameless statistics of real, extra-literary people. This emotional transfer is a result of the secondary witnessing (from primary to secondary within the novel to secondary outside it) that

Findley handles so expertly. Because "you"—that is, me, you, and we—saw Mrs. Ross's brother through her loving eyes and Rowena and Harris through Robert's devotion, their deaths matter. We do not grieve them as Mrs. Ross and Robert do, but we remember them as valued human beings. We have seen human faces on people loved and lost and are, as a result, better able to understand the enormity of a nameless statistic.

But I want to examine this interview with Lady Juliet more closely because it comprises one of the most extensive and complex examples of the biographer's appearances in the text. It also provides evidence of how a biographer works to present material from an interview, actual or imagined, and it captures in one concise scene the modalities of witnessing, bearing witness, listening to/listening in, and legitimation, or truth claims, that accompany eyewitness accounts. That we can also locate moments of trauma and the remembering of trauma within Lady Juliet's story and that we can recognize the ghosts that inhabit her landscape of memory, only makes this scene especially productive for analysis. At almost twenty pages (139–58) it is far too long to quote, but rereading it is instructive. The biographer begins by addressing us to explain when and where the interview took place and to apologize for background noises picked up by his tape recorder. Then he expresses keen regret over "an aspect of this interview which, alas, cannot survive transition onto paper—and that is the sound of Lady Juliet's voice" (139). To compensate for this absence, he describes her voice and how it changes, almost as if she is singing, when she reads from "the diaries she wrote when she was twelve years old" (139). He dutifully informs us that he will present her readings from the diary—her self-quotations and authentification—in regular font and her spoken interjections or comments to him in italics. In this way we cannot be confused by the degrees of presentness, the difference between recalling and reflecting, by what was witnessed *in situ* and what she thinks now during the interview. Here we have the old lady reading what she wrote about how she felt and what she saw at twelve:

"Robert Ross, another Canadian, came up from town today" (144); here, she speaks directly to the biographer: "*I never took part, you see. Not ever, I was a born observer. Boswell in bows*" (143).

This establishing of narrative levels and intertexts—interview transcript within biography/diary excerpts within taped interview within transcript within biography/biography within-*as* novel—provides a replica, a sort of set design, for the structure of the novel and it positions us very cleverly, inobtrusively, as secret sharers. We are granted the privilege of *listening* to this tape, as well as reading the transcript; we are constructed as secondary witnesses to the biographer's bearing of witness to Lady Juliet's remembered experiences of what she saw and cared about so deeply. This elaborate performance of witnessing, however, is much more than clever on Findley's part. It is deliberate and meaningful; it encourages us to pay attention, to look closely again and again; it allows us in to listen. By paying attention and listening to this voice from the past with its deeply moving memories, we become part of the story with an invested interest of emotion and curiosity in the human beings and events. A connection between us and them has been established, one of, what I call (after LaCapra), empathic unsettlement.



A great deal of useful information is also conveyed in this interview section—not a word is gratuitous. We learn that diaries are going to be consulted (for any biographer such documents produce an exquisite *frisson* of anticipation); history is carefully set forth for us (Stourbridge-St. Aubyn is this far from Cambridge, the nearby towns are such and such, St. Aubyn has been in the d'Orsey family since 1070); by March 1916, Juliet's mother has converted the place into a convalescent home for "these poor young men" wounded in the war or seeking peace, which explains why Robert arrives there on leave after the Battle of Saint-Eloi (140–42). From Lady Juliet's account, we learn about Captain Taffler's injuries, about Robert's affair with Barbara d'Orsey—a primal scene the blundering twelve-year-old confesses to having witnessed—and about Robert's departure from St. Aubyn. Indeed, we watch her watch him disappear down the drive (158). Before she reads her diary entry on what she saw in the bedroom, however, Lady Juliet makes another confession, as her elderly, present self, to the biographer. She intuits his curiosity about the relationship between Robert and her sister, and she excuses herself for what she is about to impart because "*it seems to me to have some bearing*" on Robert's state of mind when he returned to France (154). If she still feels so uncomfortable about this episode decades later, why has she not destroyed the evidence? Her answer is ready: "*Many times, I have wanted to destroy this portion of my diaries but I always remind myself it is a part of someone's life: someone I loved and respected*" (154). That someone, of course, is Robert, but in reading "*this portion*" of her diary she is telling her own life story and something of Barbara's as well. She is also asserting the importance of someone's life and at the same time staking her claim to accurate information (represented in words written and read) that illuminates that life. But before the biographer releases her information, he too pauses. In a parenthetical aside visually represented by block capitals, he describes how she paused: "A GREAT LONG WHILE BEFORE SHE READ" (154). Then the regular typeface for Lady Juliet's first-person reading resumes.

Findley achieves a number of things in a sequence of passages like this. Quite apart from the technical distinctions in typography, the biographer separates three different time frames from each other—the distant past of 1916, the recent past of this interview with Lady Juliet, and the present when he speaks to us, or when we read his aside—while simultaneously connecting them on the page for our reading experience. In this way the present (of reading, writing, interviewing, and biography) is animated by the past and the past lives in the process of remembering and reconstruction. But this past is not part of official history; Lady Juliet may have been a "*Boswell in bows,*" but she is not a professional historian, let alone an expert on the Great War. Hers is an oral history (or so the textual presentation makes us think), a private, deeply personal perspective on the past. She has kept this portion of the diary and she shares it now because it sheds light, provides insight and meaning, for her and for us, on what happened to human beings back then. The biographer—and Timothy Findley—clearly agree with her about the importance of her testimony in part because what she provides is ignored in the official history.

That said, and while I agree entirely with those who characterize *The Wars* as a postmodern text that challenges, even undermines, the dominant view of history as truth—the story of what really happened—the *art* of a sequence like this lies in its realism. We must want to know, says Lady Juliet, and she can tell us what actually took place because she "*knew at first hand*" and she will tell us how she came by this first-hand knowledge. The fact that this is a fiction is beside the point. In this biography, this novel, the old lady's presence is as palpable as Robert's, and her fiction helps make him real.[21] To confirm and consolidate the status of the bedroom scene, as well as the context for it, we are told it is recorded in a diary, which is now read aloud while the biographer, and we with him, watch and listen. Therefore, we too can say we know what happened because we are witnessing its retelling. To reject the truth in this telling is to behave like those historians who rejected the Holocaust survivor's story about the chimneys at Auschwitz (see Laub, "Bearing Witness" 59; see also page 71, this volume). However, to accept this story of Robert Ross as *true* in all its elements, not in just this one instance of spying on him with Barbara, is to accept our responsibility as secondary witnesses, which in turn entails validating a landscape of memory—Lady Juliet's. And that landscape of memory, while concisely conveyed in this scene as hers, extends far beyond her to include Canada, France, the trenches of Flanders, Mrs. Ross sitting blind and appalled on the stairs in her Rosedale home, and the memories of Marian Turner.

I see Mrs. Ross as an extremely important character in *The Wars*. She is not portrayed as an easy woman to love, although her husband adores her. She is strong-willed, intelligent, independent, opinionated, and within the straitjacket of her time and place, a non-conformist.

By the time we meet her she is also an alcoholic disgusted with her world—a world that inflicts hydrocephalus on an innocent child, that strikes down a beloved brother in the street, that expects her to bear children willy-nilly, and a world that goes to war. She sees right through the sexism, greed, and hypocrisy around her, not least when it is preached at her from Christian pulpits. Robert is a lot like his mother. She is, moreover, the central representative of the Canadian home front, through whose eyes Findley wishes us to see it. With Mrs. Ross we rage against Robert's enlisting when, as few mothers dare to do, she admits that she can neither stop nor protect him, that she can give him his birth but nothing more (28). We experience her revulsion at church on 19 December 1915 to be exact—the second Christmas of the war—as she surveys her fellow worshippers congratulating themselves "that all their sons" have gone to the wars (33), and she is obliged to kneel and pray and sing. She breaks ranks, however, when the bishop begins to speak "about flags and holy wars and Empire" (53), and she marches from the church in protest. "What she needed was an empty cathedral in which to rail at God" (54), but instead she sits on the church steps, smokes and drinks from her silver flask in public, and weeps: "I do not understand. I don't. I won't. I can't. Why is this happening to us Davenport? What does it mean—*to kill your children*? Kill them and then...go in there and sing about it! What does that mean?" (54).

As 1915 marches into 1916 and the war to end all wars that was supposed to be over in a few months worsens, and Robert is dragged deeper into the horrors of the war, Mrs. Ross begins, or so we are told, "to seek out storms" (135). She calls Davenport, her constant companion, wraps herself in furs and scarves, and braves blizzards (as if to suffer an equivalent of what her son is suffering?), and walks the streets and ravines of Toronto. She reads and rereads her son's letters, and she writes to him every day—"long, meandering epistles angled down the pages of her blue notepaper—often (more often than not) completely indecipherable" (136). When the Parliament buildings in

Ottawa burn to the ground, as indeed they did in February 1916, Mrs. Ross believes "her country [is] being destroyed by fire" (136); she studies the news reports, then clips them to store and annotate.[22] She finds more than mere coincidence in the fact that the bells in the central tower collapsed just as they were striking twelve (they had tolled eleven times), but exactly how she interprets this omen is unclear. Perhaps she hopes that because midnight did not toll, some ultimate catastrophe had been averted, or perhaps she hopes she would not have to face another new day with what it might bring, or perhaps she finds solace in the thought that she will not have to sleep, only to be haunted by nightmares of death and loss. Mrs. Ross is Findley's figure of maternal grief trapped in a suffering so overwhelming that she will never recover, never be able to work through her depression and anger into mourning and reconciliation with the world of men and their wars. She is like Cassandra (who will appear by name in Findley's 1977 play *Can You See Me Yet?*) prophesying Canada's *destruction* by fire, rather than her country's *ordeal* by fire that would transform its young men into seasoned soldiers and its status into an independent nation.

One wonders what she would say about the Peace Tower (named in 1933) that now adorns the Parliament buildings, or the massive National War Memorial, with its tomb of the unknown soldier, that dominates the political and business core of Ottawa's Confederation Square, or the statue of the Spirit of Canada, better known as "Mother Canada," grieving her sons on the Vimy Monument. By creating Mrs. Ross with her clear-sighted resistance and honesty, and by making her see the razing of the Parliament buildings as an omen of the country's fate, Findley exposes one of the most oppressive home front myths of war as a violently coercive lie. In her unequivocal rejection of the propaganda calling upon loyal mothers to sacrifice their sons who, in turn, will be martyrs for Mother Britain (or for all home front mothers), she throws the lie back in a patriarchal society's teeth. As Suzanne Evans so ably demonstrates in *Mothers of Heroes, Mothers of Martyrs: World War I and the Politics of Grief*, "recruiters and propagandists in

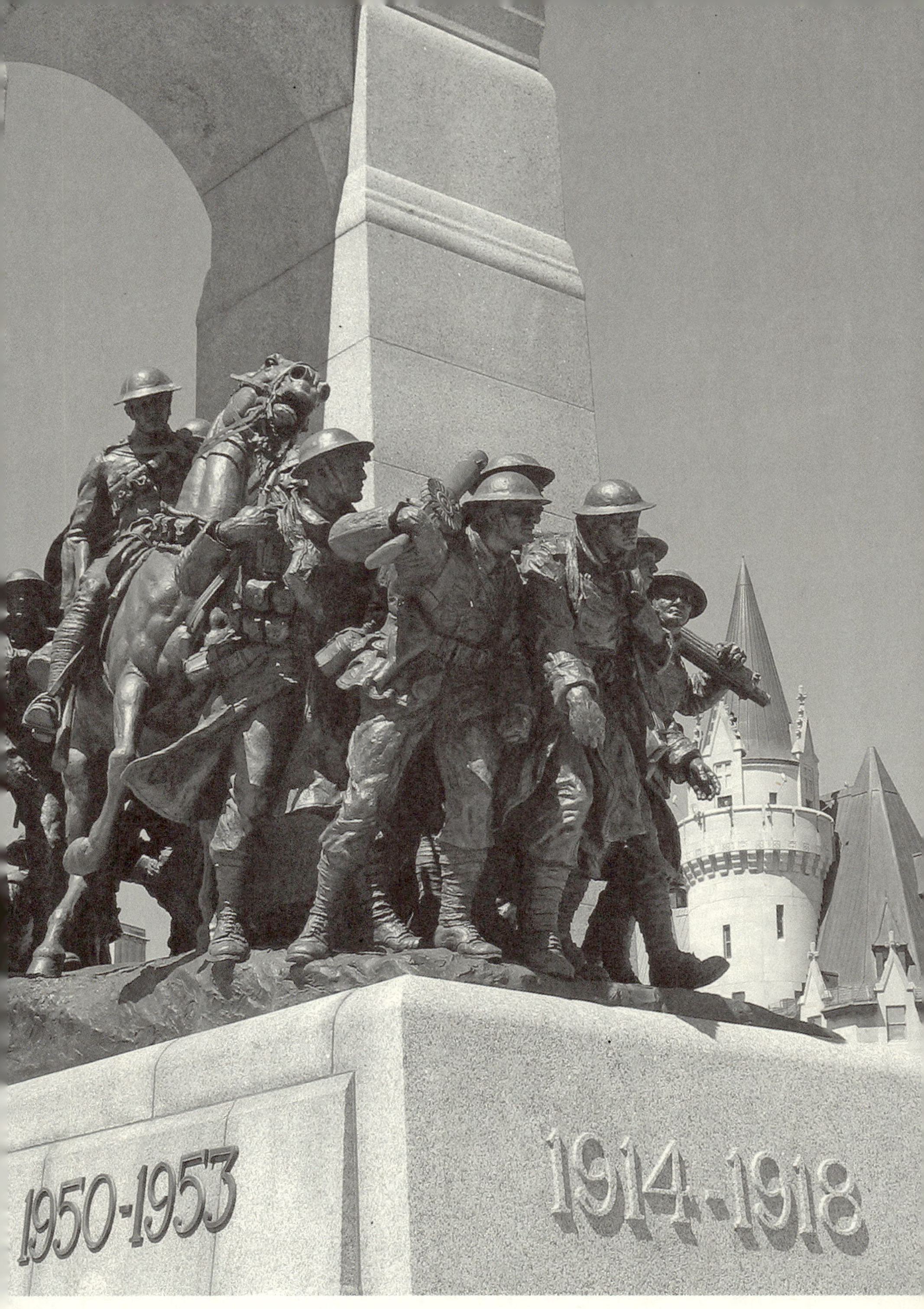


*Canadian National War Memorial, Ottawa. This massive monument, designed by British sculptor Vernon March to commemorate Canada's contribution to the Great War, was unveiled in 1939 at the convergence of Sparks, Wellington, and Rideau Streets in Ottawa. Today it also commemorates the Second World War and the Korean War. Photograph: M.-E. Perley.*

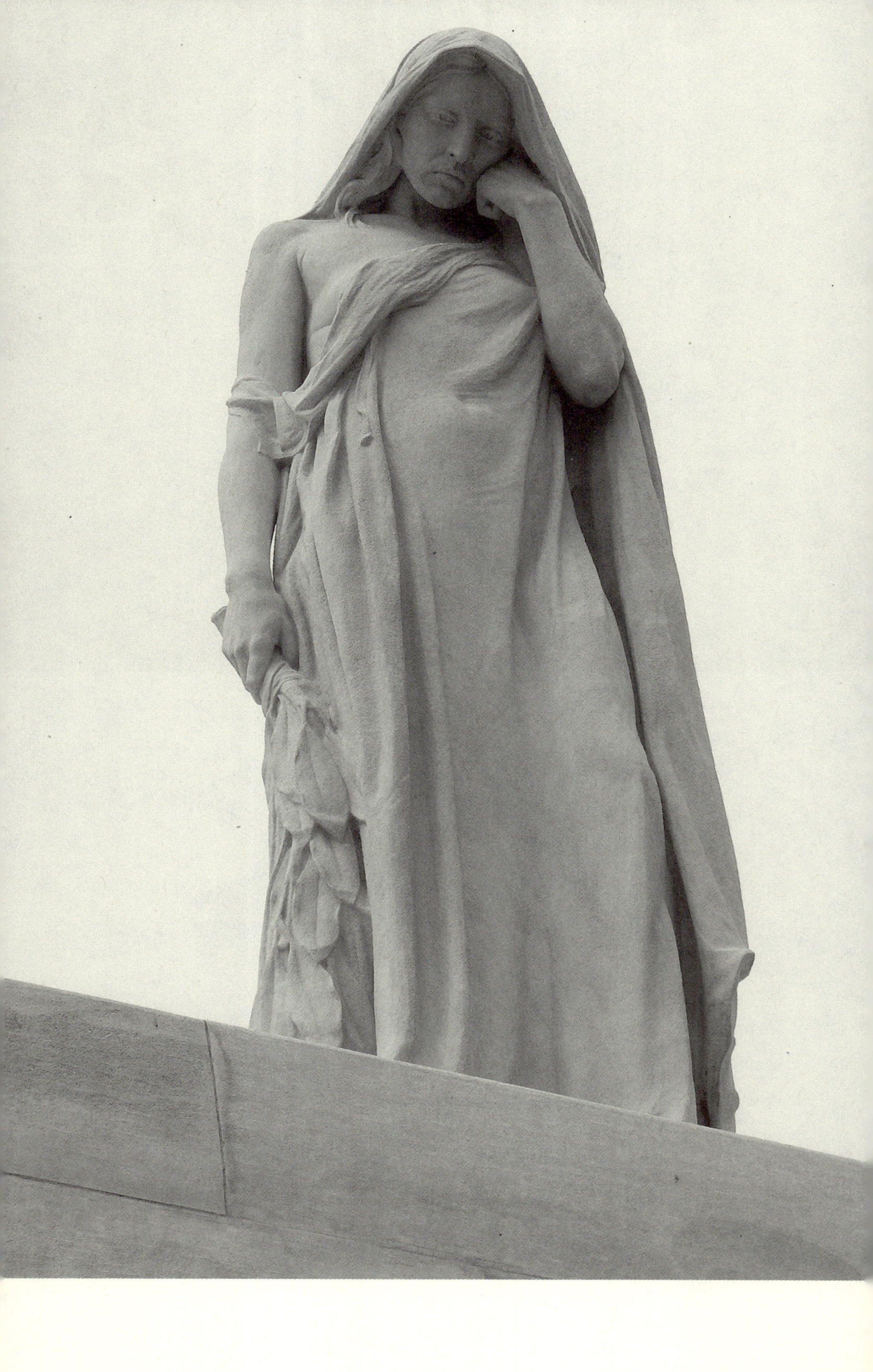

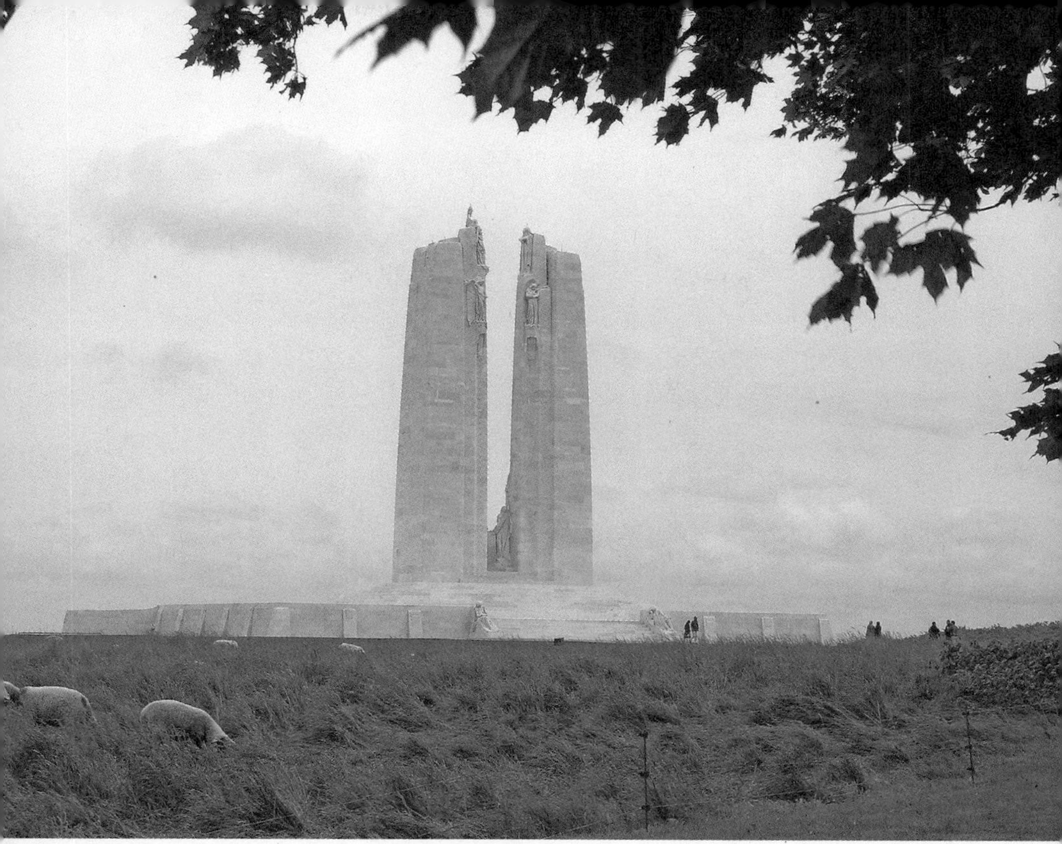

*Pages 136 and 137: The "Spirit of Canada" (sometimes called "Mother Canada") grieves for her war dead on the Vimy Monument in France. Photographs: J. Grace.*

this new industrial war realized the power of the *role of the mother* [as defined for her] both to sanctify what might be a paralyzing loss and to encourage even greater effort in the battle against the foe" (42, emphasis added).[23] To the best of my knowledge, Findley's Mrs. Ross is the first fictional example of a home front maternal revolt that must have (*really*) existed, but that has been erased from our official war history. As such she is a tragic but formidable ghost in a national landscape of memory, and we refuse to listen to her, we spurn her anguish, or we dismiss her as unloving at our peril. Mrs. Ross is a Canadian equivalent of France's war memorial called *Picardie Maudissant la Guerre*, and she evokes, for me, Käthe Kollwitz's powerful life-sized sculpture *Die Eltern*, depicting a father kneeling beside a mother (representing Kollwitz and her husband) in penitence and sorrow. In Findley's *The*

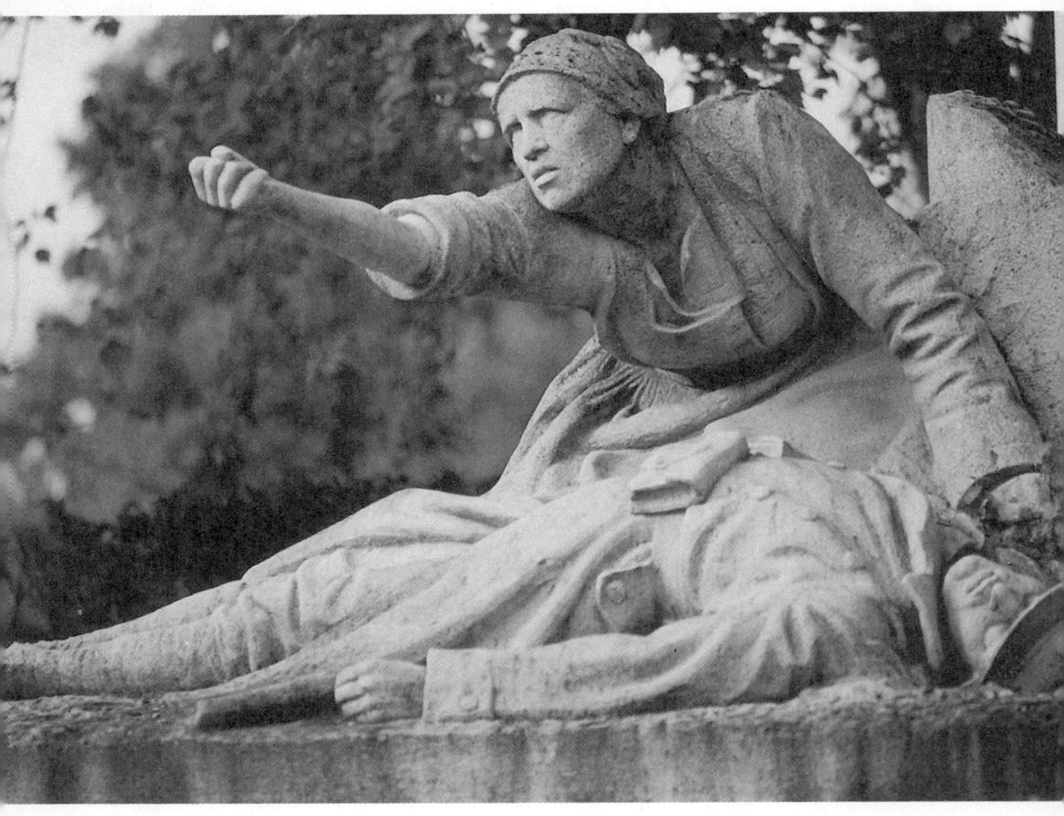

*This war memorial in Picardy, France, is called* Picardie Maudissant la Guerre (Picardy Damns War)*; it bears the inscription "À nos morts." Photograph: Alan Cumyn. Reproduced from Suzanne Evans's* Mothers of Heroes, Mothers of Hope *and with thanks to Evans and Cumyn. © Alan Cumyn.*

*Wars*, Robert's biographer insists that we pay attention to other war stories than those blessed by church, state, and official history.

In *Broken Ground* Jack Hodgins revisits the First World War in many ways, not the least of which is on the broken home ground of a Returned Soldiers' Settlement on Vancouver Island.[24] However, because the war stories and traumatic memories of its first settlers have all but been erased from the settlement's landscape of memory, Hodgins creates an octogenarian witness and storyteller, Charlie MacIntosh, who preserves their histories by placing one particular returned soldier, Captain

Matthew Pearson, at the fulcrum of his remembering. He also imagines another soldier, Donald McCormack, who hovers in the margins, where he will haunt the landscape, literally and figuratively, and ignite the spark of recollection that becomes Charlie's *Broken Ground*. Since this other soldier, Donald, is so crucial to the story, I had best explain his presence right away, even though Hodgins—or rather Charlie—does not fully reveal him until very near the end. Donald MacCormack is a severely wounded veteran and the brother-in-law of the main protagonist, Matthew Pearson. We catch distant glimpses of Donald or hear references to him from the beginning of Charlie's tale because Matthew and his wife, Maude, have brought him with them from their pre-war home in Owen Sound to Vancouver Island. Maude is the only one who tends to him, but her children and the neighbours regularly see him sitting on the front porch in his wheelchair, his head bobbing and most of his face covered by a leather mask. He cannot speak, and no one is certain how much he grasps of life around him. Understandably, such an apparition arouses curiosity, as well as fear and revulsion: the returned soldiers can imagine only too well what horrors lie behind the mask, but the children and women can only speculate. However, everyone is busy getting on with life and Donald is easy to ignore and ultimately forget. Forget, that is, until he demands recognition.

Years after the returned soldiers of Portuguese Creek and their wives have died, a young man descended from one of the community's few first families not directly caught up in the war, makes a film about the pioneering past. The year in the fictional present is 1996 and he is screening his film for the contemporary townsfolk, some of whom can recall hearing about the early 1920s and important events of 1922–23. Folks "went out to watch the filming" (259) whenever they could, and they have now gathered in 1996 to see the result but, as Charlie tells us, the young filmmaker has captured only one version of this complicated history, one that features *his* family, the Mackens, his Aunt Nora, and the great fire of 1922 that had such an impact on her life story. Charlie's version of this history, the one we read, is different. It does not end in 1922 before Matthew Pearson returns to France and then comes home for the second time. Charlie's version is prompted by Donald MacCormack's reaction to the film. Now in his nineties, Donald is looked after by his nephew's family, and they have brought him along to the screening, even though he is not expected to understand what is going on. However, as the movie gathers towards its close with Nora Macken's ill-fated love story as its main subject, a "subdued disturbance" is heard "several times" from the middle of the auditorium. A voice rises making growling noises; other voices try to hush it. But the voice will not be hushed. Donald is making this appalling sound as he tries to talk: "He *was* talking—I was close enough to know that [writes Charlie]—though it was the kind of talk that made no language sense" (332).





Finally, Donald stands up; he refuses to be silenced or taken away. The film is stopped and the house lights come up, and there he is waving one arm around and "making sounds in the language that some race had learned to talk without benefit of teeth or lips or maybe even tongues" (333). Then the unimaginable happens. Still screaming, still standing, Donald rips off his leather mask:

> *Will's son leapt over seats to retrieve it. Donald's mask. I suppose [the Pearsons] may have been the only ones in the room who had seen behind it. The rest of us had only imagined, if we had thought of it at all, and we'd got so used to the mask that it might as well have been his real face. I don't know if it was Donald or the rest of us the Pearsons thought they protected by making sure he was never observed without it.*
>
> *He was observed without it now. It could not be avoided, though many turned away. Some were later ashamed of being ill, without enough warning to get to a washroom in time. Courtesy demanded that we look away, but one quick glimpse was enough to imprint the image forever, I think. You don't forget a collapsed hole in the middle of a face where a nose ought to be, or a mouth that falls inward shapelessly like the crumbling entrance to an abandoned coal-mine shaft. It was hard to believe*

> *this calamity had been amongst us all these years without our seeing it.* (333–34)

The "calamity amongst us" is Donald, of course, but it is also what he represents and what those around him have preferred to forget: the war, what it did to an entire generation, and its impact on the future. Donald's protest, for that is how Charlie explains Donald's outburst, is against our collective, willed forgetting of wartime tragedy. By focusing on the Macken version of the community's history, the film totally ignores Donald MacCormack, the Great War, and the reason for a community to exist at Portuguese Creek. As Charlie puts it, the film is coming to an end without providing a glimpse of him sitting on the Pearson's porch in his wheelchair: "If the man was able to make any sense of what was happening on the screen he must have thought that someone had erased him from his own life" (333). Certainly, Charlie interprets the outcry in this way and, therefore, sets himself the task of telling his version of the returned soldiers and their settlement at Portuguese Creek. In Charlie's version, the First World War surfaces surreptitiously from the very beginning, and then with increasing frequency and urgency until it overtakes everything else to produce a landscape of memory that is profoundly shaped by the war and, as a consequence, maps the future not just for one small community on the far western edge of the country but for the entire nation. Charlie's purpose in telling his version (like Hodgins's) is not merely to set the record straight or fill in gaps in the movie's version of the past but also, and more importantly, to pay tribute to the soldiers and their families and demonstrate the extent to which the war and the battle front shaped peacetime Canada and home front life.

To make these points, Charlie goes back to 1922 when he was twelve and the day when a stranger called Wyatt Taylor rode into town and his father Mac was killed trying to blow up a stump to clear his land. These two events take place against the backdrop of a massive bush fire raging in the mountains above the community. Within the first thirty pages, Charlie has set *his* stage for a story about violent death, trauma, calamity, and a war no one wants to talk about, but no one can forget. His father's death causes Charlie to see in Matthew Pearson a surrogate father, and it causes everyone in the community, especially the men, to wonder how they can pay their respects to a fallen comrade like Mac when they have lost their faith in religious rhetoric and ritual, the function of clergy and churches, and the intentions of their government which sent them to this remote, dangerous locale in the first place. As Matthew reflects, shortly after Mac's death, the Canadian government deceived the returned soldiers with their Land Settlement Act by sending them from one disaster to another—the near impossible task of clearing such land to make a living—and, "if this was supposed to be our country's thank you, a man can only wonder if he's been made a fool of" (34). One way or another almost everyone in Portuguese Creek has been damaged by the war: Matthew carries the worst scars (apart from Donald), but another man has ruined lungs, another loses his British war bride, another's general health is poor, and so it goes. The women are also victims: the teacher's husband is missing in action, another woman was injured while nursing in France, and Maude Pearson will have to live with and carry on around and in spite of her husband's war memories and ghosts. Names like Passchendaele, Vimy Ridge, the Somme, the Canal du Nord, along with the comically ironic names the soldiers gave to the trenches (see pages 106–07), surface repeatedly in the men's conversations, usually without explanation or detail because such information is simply part of who these people are. However, they are crucial *aides-mémoires* for Charlie, part of the landscape of memory he is charting, and essential to the lives he chooses to tell us about.



*Broken Ground* provides a stellar example of the complex narrative witnessing that I find in many of the best post-1977 Canadian novels about the war. In some ways, Charlie MacIntosh recalls Robert Ross's biographer: he has taken upon himself the responsibility for reconstructing Matthew Pearson's biography as part of the community's history and, to a degree, as part of his autobiography. He describes himself from the outset as both observer of and actor in the drama about to unfold: "I was in the attic window again...keeping an eye on things" (9). And as if to prove true the maxim that the onlooker sees most of the game, Charlie watches, spies on, and then remembers what he sees and overhears from his various vantage points. At one point, Matthew jokingly asks Charlie, "You planning to be a sniper?" (10). And if one takes the term sniper metaphorically, one could say that he is because he will intervene unilaterally, directly, at a critical juncture, in his hero's story when he writes the letter that brings Matthew back from France.



Much further along in his narrative, Charlie informs us that he has become a reporter for a local newspaper (241) and that Maude Pearson has allowed him to read some of her husband's letters from the war and a notebook he kept when he returned to France in 1923. He has a remarkable memory for conversations he overheard as a boy, and he conducts further research into the oral history of the community and into the ordeals of the war. From these materials, Charlie pieces together the story of the Returned Soldiers Settlement of Portuguese Creek, the war memories of its inhabitants and, above all, the tragic story of Matthew Pearson. In the long first part of *Broken Ground*, Charlie presents his "Voices from Portuguese Creek, 1922" (9–197), and in most of these snatches of oral history and recollection, each speaker provides his or her perspective on the lives around them and the events of 1922. Matthew's is only one of these voices, but it is clear from the start that Charlie idolizes the man and grants him pride of place in the story. In the short second section, "The Fields of France, 1918–1919" (201–24), we read one of Matthew's letters to Maude and some excerpts from the notebook he kept in 1923. These first-hand testimonials (fictional and yet entirely convincing, given what we learn about the man in part one) lie at the heart of Charlie's version of this history. The third section, "A Helmet for the Bees, 1996" (227–357), brings us back to Vancouver Island and the Macken boy's movie to fill in many gaps in the history of the settlement. Two of the most significant events, in Charlie's eyes, are the funeral for Matthew Pearson's little daughter Elizabeth, who died in the fire of 1922, and the aftermath of the war.

Matthew Pearson is the main character and an iconic figure in *Broken Ground*. We learn enough about him from Charlie's primary and secondary witnessing and the evidence provided by Matthew's recollections, those of his wife, Maude, and his personal documents (letters and notebook excerpts), to see him in several dimensions—as soldier, school teacher, farmer, husband, and father—and over several years so that he can serve as the emotional and ethical lodestone of the story. In Charlie's eyes he is admirable, brave, and wise; in his own eyes, he is a guilty failure haunted by the war. He feels guilty for having survived when so many others were killed, but he feels especially guilty for having failed to save one young man, Hugh Corbett, from a military execution and for being unable to protect his young brother-in-law from crippling injuries. As a schoolteacher in Owen Sound before the war, Matthew encouraged his students to read imperialistic, warmongering poets like Rudyard Kipling, and when some of his former students enlisted he felt responsible for them and almost personally to blame for planting dangerous ideas in their minds.[25] But his sense of failure and guilt does not end there. During a brief liaison with a young French woman who has returned, destitute and almost deranged, to her ruined village where his battalion is stationed, he fathers the child whom he will ask Maude to accept into their postwar, reunited family. This is the child Elizabeth, who comes to Canada with Matthew in 1919. When she dies in the great fire of 1922, Matthew is devastated because in his eyes she was the one good thing he had salvaged from the destruction of war (203). Her loss, and his share of responsibility for not saving her, drives him back to France, to the battlefields now returning to farmers' fields, where the French *poilus* are slowly resuming a normal life and where the aged grandparents of the girl live in poverty. Matthew's return to help the old couple represents his effort at atonement for failing to save yet another child from destruction. In short,

Matthew Pearson is a sort of Canadian Everyman—good at heart, educated, and by disposition peaceful, but also physically strong and capable, sensitive, and responsible.[26] Neither a war hero nor a war victim in any obvious way, he is your fairly average, decent human being who is caught up in events beyond his control.

The worst event beyond his control, in my view, is not the fathering of Elizabeth and almost accidental betrayal of Maude; indeed, he could have stopped himself from meeting the young Frenchwoman and he was not forced to acknowledge the child or bring her back to Canada. Once he had responded to the grandparents who asked about him after the war, however, he began a process that would place extreme pressure on Maude and their children in a conscious decision to make amends for his actions and inactions as a soldier. By bringing Elizabeth to Canada and passing her off as his and Maude's child, he brought into the bosom of his family and into their postwar future a constant reminder of the past and the war. That he is haunted by his war memories is abundantly clear from his sleepless nights, his notebook, and his conversations, but the event that stalks him waking and sleeping is the execution of young Hugh Corbett. This appalling event is the key to Matthew's guilt and postwar behaviour, his refusal to return to teaching, and his unrealistic sense of responsibility for everyone around him. Hugh Corbett was Donald MacCormack's closest friend. Indeed, the relationship between the two was probably a homosexual love. Every time Matthew sees Donald sitting in his wheelchair, he is forcibly reminded, not only of Donald's injuries, but also of Hugh's death and of how Hugh had cried out for Donald before he died. Although Charlie does not put it this way (such speculation is left to the reader), I see Elizabeth's adoption as Matthew's attempt to make up for Hugh's abandonment.

Hugh Corbett's story is given to us in three versions. The official, public one is that he deserted, was court-martialled, and executed by firing squad; this is what the army records state and what the young man's parents are told (311). However, Matthew knows more about what really happened because he was there and witnessed events. The version he gives to Maude and then recounts for Wyatt Taylor—the first version Charlie then repeats for us in his account—*is carefully edited to protect his deepest feelings* and the truly horrifying aspects of what he saw. I emphasize this point because there is no need to protect the feelings of Taylor who, as a soldier himself and an explosives expert during the war, saw much that was appalling. All the same, this version of the story is shocking. In one of his "Voices from Portuguese Creek" recollections (passed on to us by Charlie), Matthew describes how he and Taylor sat in the Pearson kitchen shortly after his arrival in the community.[27] They fell to reminiscing about the war, but when Taylor remarked that these returned soldiers had created "a little Eden here, well away from the world" (91), Matthew replied that what he saw from his window was a scarred and blasted landscape that reminded him of France. Taylor next asked if the men still discussed the war among themselves, to which Matthew answered that "most of us are trying to forget it. And, anyway, the others wouldn't know what we were talking about" and that people do not talk about something they suspect has made fools of them (91).





Finally, Taylor asked what happened to Donald, and Matthew explained that on "his first day at the front, a mortar shell blew half his face away and embedded shreds of metal in his brain" (93). Then, at Maude's urging, he continued with the story of Hugh Corbett's fate (93–101). Hugh and Donald had enlisted together in their late teens; they were little more than boys. After Donald was severely wounded, Corbett was moved to Matthew's platoon, where he carried on until the night that two Jack Johnsons hit their trenches and Hugh was spattered with the blood, flesh, and brains of the soldier beside him. By the next day, when a Canadian counterattack was underway, Hugh had gone missing. He had wandered off to the nearest field hospital complaining of headache and pain. However, as Matthew explained to Taylor, this excuse was rejected and he was court-martialled; the sentence was execution by a firing squad composed of his fellow soldiers—a practice the Canadian army, like the British, followed in both world wars. What Matthew described for Maude and Taylor in this version of events is grim: the guards got the boy drunk so when Matthew was allowed to visit him he was incoherent, but he did call out for Donald and he wept (99). In the morning, as Matthew watched, he was dragged out and tied to a post, where he vomited behind the gas mask that had been pulled over his face, and then was shot. Except that the firing squad bungled the job and a colonel from HQ had to shoot Hugh in the head.



All these years afterwards, Matthew still believes "that [he] was meant to be [Hugh's] witness" (100), but his personal shame over the episode leads him to conclude *this* telling of what happened by exclaiming that he and his teaching caused boys like Donald and Hugh "to sign up willingly for the slaughter" (100), and that now "we should all...be like poor Donald...hiding behind a mask" (101). And no wonder he feels this way because what he did witness at the time but can only bear witness to later still, when the elderly Charlie is collecting his data, is much worse. In the context of his return to France in 1923—as he will eventually tell Charlie—Matthew testifies that Hugh Corbett was not so drunk after all that night and morning, that he was fully aware of what was happening to him, that he insisted he had done nothing wrong and begged Matthew to save him, that he had confessed his love for Donald, that he had cursed and wept, that he had asked the older man to shoot him privately in his cell, and that, finally, when he realized nothing could or would be done, he had asked Matthew to pray with him (309-10). Matthew could do nothing to intervene—unless he had led a mutiny—and can no longer remember what prayer he recited. But he is haunted by the memory of his failure and by his rage over "the murder of a confused and frightened boy who had volunteered to fight for his country" (310).

When Matthew returns to France after Elizabeth's death, he understands that he has joined "this year's crop of ghosts, haunting the scenes of war" (302), but what Charlie's *Broken Ground* makes clear is that these ghosts also haunt the Canadian landscape. What else is Hugh Corbett if not such a terrifying ghost? Charlie leaves open the possibility that just before Matthew returns to his Vancouver Island home, his marriage, and his future, he will have grasped this profound truth. In an excerpt from the 1923 notebook—a passage quoted for us by Charlie—Matthew did connect the two landscapes (French and Canadian) through the ghostly presence of Hugh Corbett. This insight came to him late one day as he paused to gaze across the fields of France at "the outline of a roofless barn" in the distance that could have been "poor Hughies's abattoir," and he was struck by the resemblance of this ruined building to the abandoned sawmill at home in which he often took refuge on sleepless nights: "I wondered with a cold shock if it had been Hugh Corbett's building that the abandoned sawmill at home reminded me of, and not the village church as I'd supposed" (314). All Charlie reveals at this juncture is that Matthew must now return home to find himself; the fields of France with their surfacing bones and *matériel*, their ghosts and memories, have nothing further to tell him. The ghosts from home, however, wait for him, and one of the most challenging of these is his own eldest son Tanner, whose sense of abandonment rises directly from Matthew's neglect and his obsession with Elizabeth, Hugh, the war, and his deep-seated guilt. In other words, the father's war trauma has been inflicted on the next generation, and neither Charlie McIntosh nor Jack Hodgins pretends things could be any other way.

*Broken Ground* is the story of how twentieth-century Canada was shaped by the Great War through the memories of its returned soldiers, through their ghost stories and traumas, and their postwar work, and through the impact of their witnessing on future generations. What's more, the narrative carefully retraces a landscape of memory with all its scars, events, and voices, and shows how the battles fought over there are replicated in the battles waged here. From the blasting of stumps, violent deaths, raging fires, muddy roads and drenching rains in the Returned Soldiers Settlement on Vancouver Island, to the sodden, rat-infested trenches, blasted fields and horrifying deaths in Flanders and France, is a short step after all—a shockingly short step. From Charlie's perspective (and no doubt Hodgins's too), this short step must not be forgotten because to forget is to deny what produced you, the home ground created for you by those who came before. It is, then, not so much the horrors of actual warfare that concern Charlie as it is the burden of bearing witness to the consequences of these horrors and the acceptance of responsibility—his and ours—to listen closely, to pay attention, to acknowledge the Donald MacCormacks, Matthew Pearsons, Elizabeths, and Hugh Corbetts as part of who we are here and now. Charlie's message, if I can put it this way, is that Canada came of age, not on Vimy Ridge but in the *aftermath* of the First World War on home ground and only through a long, painful process of transforming broken ground into a rich landscape of memory.



For Hodgins (as for Charlie and the folks from Portuguese Creek) that landscape is both real and imagined. Hodgins's imagination creates a Charlie for us and Charlie creates Matthew Pearson. But for Hodgins the landscape is real, physically *there* on the east coast of Vancouver Island in the Comox Valley just north of Courtenay. It is called Merville and was named by the returned soldiers for the tiny French village of Merville-au-Bois near Amiens in Picardy, France. I will let Jack Hodgins explain this because in the early 1990s he was taken to visit the French village he believes inspired the soldiers' name for their Canadian settlement:

> *The village was the scene of a good deal of fighting during what the French call the Grande Guerre. The inhabitants were evacuated to the west. The nearest trench of the Western Front was just a few yards from the buildings. Because the village sits on one of the highest rises in this area of low rolling hills, the Germans shelled it until most of the buildings were ruins....In a nearby Australian cemetery we find rows of Canadian gravestones. Many of these young men died on August 8, 1918, the day of the "big push" when Canadians and others drove the enemy back eight*

*miles—the beginning of the end of the war....So, standing in the midst of this village, I can only guess at reasons [for the choice of name by our soldiers]. Perhaps some of them had spent time in the nearby trenches and found the abandoned buildings to be places of relative safety and warmth when they weren't fighting. Maybe some of them found comfort in the ruined church. Or drank milk from a left-behind cow. Or struck up a friendship with a local farmer who may have crept back at night to check on his home....I have no trouble seeing the red brick buildings of Merville-au-bois as places of temporary privacy and shelter for soldiers weary of the crowded life below ground. Perhaps when they named their new settlement they were evoking memories of brief rough shelter in that home away from home.*[28]



While watching Macken's film, Charlie wonders "what effect this movie would have upon future accounts of the War's survivors and the Fire of '22. Was this the 'true' story?" (329), and he worries about what is inevitably lost in any mode of telling, any remembering, any version of the past because, in his view, "behind the colourful parade of this century's gains and losses was a huge absence of something that was neither identified nor regained nor replaced" (325). As Charlie knows, there are as many true stories as there are storytellers, and even a collective remembering like the narrative of *Broken Ground* will miss things. Nevertheless, this novel has recuperated a great deal we did not know or forgot or ignored as unpleasant by acknowledging Donald MacCormack, admitting the existence of Elizabeth, and bearing witness to the "murder" (as Matt Pearson calls it) of Hugh Corbett. Through Charlie's honest and empathic remembering of Pearson, we are able to see what Charlie saw as he listened to, spied upon, and talked with this man. Perhaps that "huge absence" Charlie worries about at eighty-four years of age is less an absence (something never there) than a lingering presence, a haunting that only seems like absence until we learn how to listen to an eyewitness like Matthew or a secondary witness like Charlie who can report on the past. Inevitably, the truth claims implied by such witnessing, as well as by the facts of the war, the letters, notebook, and the actual existence of a Returned Soldiers Settlement called Merville beside Portuguese Creek, lend authority to Charlie's version of things, even as he admits that no story is a complete or accurate representation of reality.

This haunting, which permeates *Broken Ground*, passes from Donald and Matthew to Charlie and then to the attentive, *listening* reader because of the skillful combination of imagined recreation of the past with historical facts conveyed through realist narrative strategies like witnessing, autobiography, and intertextual documentation. It operates like a wake-up call urging readers to seek out more information about their immediate surroundings and their histories and to open themselves to supplementary histories that expand upon, alter, or sometimes contradict and undermine official versions of such cataclysms as the Great War. How many contemporary Canadians know that the Canadian Army executed young men like Hugh Corbett? After reading *Broken Ground* they do.



By the end of the novel, Charlie can tell us that once Johanna Seyerstad left the community with Wyatt Taylor to begin their new life, a schoolteacher was badly needed and that Matthew Pearson finally returned to his former profession (327–28). He could not teach the old poets—Tennyson and Kipling—in the same way as before, and he did try to teach new ones like T.S. Eliot, but his chief contribution was to teach the stories of the Great War: "Eventually [says Charlie] he would use the War to issue warnings to younger generations" (329). It is not hard to imagine what these warnings would be, although Charlie only provides a brief summary of them, because the whole of *Broken Ground* testifies to these warnings. Never forget, Charlie's narrative insists; always listen for alternative stories; never accept one version as the truth; always remember (as Juliet d'Orsey's brother Clive wanted future generations to do in *The Wars*) that those who fought, died, or returned were human, and do not be too quick to judge them. Above all bear secondary witness to others' testimony and primary witnessing so

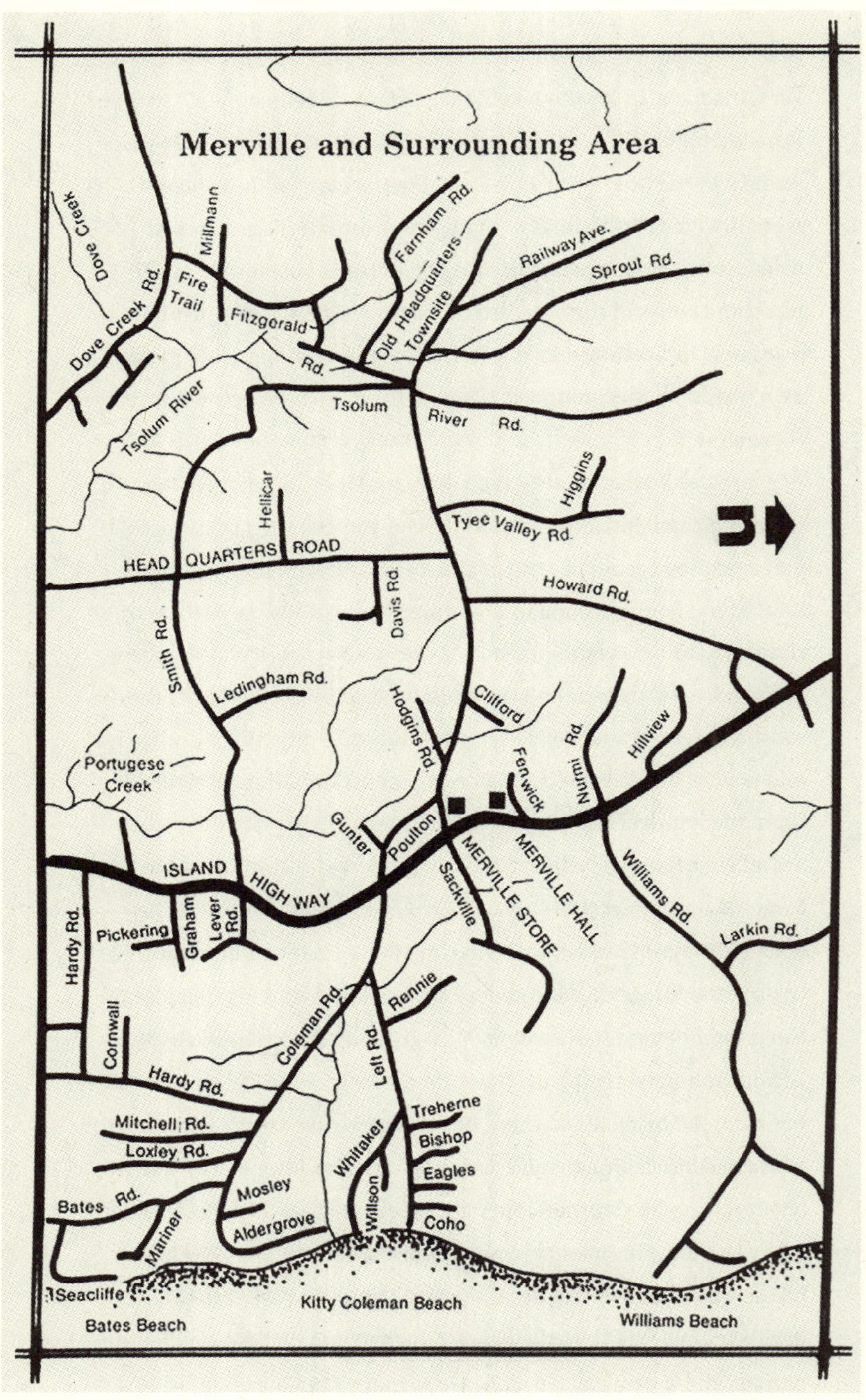


*This map of the town of Merville, Vancouver Island, BC, and the surrounding area, is reproduced from the back cover of* Merville and Its Early Settlers, 1919–1985, *edited by Reta Blakely Hodgins (1985). My special thanks to Jack Hodgins and the Merville Community Association.*

that a shared landscape of memory can tell you who and where you are. For Canadians, in *Broken Ground*, that landscape is incomplete without Donald, Hugh, Elizabeth, the Pearsons, Charlie, and Merville/Merville-au-Bois. What was literally true in France is born out in Vancouver Island's Comox Valley, and in many other communities across the country: the ground is fertilized, made rich and sustaining, by the blood and bones of the past, and the nation is defined not just in or by war but by peacetime efforts (often deadly and traumatizing in their own way) on home ground. It is also defined by the artists who create these stories.





*Three Day Road* is another such story, and it brings more hitherto forgotten participants onstage to present some of the most exacting and appalling scenes of combat and traumatic remembering yet created in English-Canadian literature. One way of summarizing the novel is to call it a combined horror-ghost story in which the source of the horror is the war and the ghost, unleashed by the war, is the most terrifying Canadian variety: a Windigo.[29] Who this Windigo is and how he became one, are among the most important ethical and dramatic issues of the story. Joseph Boyden's three main characters are all First Nations people: Niska is an elderly Cree woman from the James Bay region and the aunt of Xavier, her sister's son, who she rescues from the residential school in Moose Factory and raises in the traditional way as far removed as possible from white people and those home-guard Indians who have given up life in the bush to stay in and around white towns. The third character is Elijah, another Cree boy from the residential school, who comes to live with Xavier and Niska and also learns to hunt and trap in the traditional way. The two boys grow up like brothers; they are excellent shots (although Xavier is the best) and inseparable companions. When the First World War breaks out and news reaches them that Canadians are enlisting, they decide to travel south to the nearest town to join up because they are curious and seeking adventure. Like so many Canadian boys in 1914, they have no idea why a war has broken out, what they will be fighting for, how they will be treated, or what will happen to them. Like other Canadians, they believe the war will be over soon.

Despite having so much in common and spending their teenage years together, these two young men are fundamentally different from each other, and this difference is the pivot on which the novel's plot turns. Xavier is quiet, reserved, thoughtful, an introvert; he is devoted to Niska and loves his northern bush home and life. Elijah is a trickster and an extrovert; his second name is Weesageechak or, as his fellow soldiers call him, Whiskeyjack, and he is well named. He talks constantly and rapidly, seeks attention and praise, is quickly bored and always looking for excitement and danger. Xavier speaks little English and during his service will exaggerate and hide behind this lack of fluency to insulate himself from the white man's violence and madness; Elijah not only speaks fluent English, he is also a clever mimic who can imitate British accents to amuse his friends. To call Elijah a clown, however, would be to seriously misread the man's character and personality. He wants credit for his skill as a top sniper with the Southern Ontario Rifles, even though he knows Xavier is a better shot, and he boasts of returning to Canada as a war hero who will become an important chief. The two Cree soldiers stay together through their years of training and combat, and they work together—Xavier as a spotter of enemy targets and Elijah as the sniper who gets most of the kills.

As the war drags on from one appalling battle to the next, Xavier loses his hearing due to the constant din around him and becomes increasingly revolted by the brutality of war. Elijah, by contrast, is in his element. He is inordinately proud of his marksmanship, his medals, and the attention he gets from officers and fellow soldiers. But as Xavier will recognize with disgust and fear, Elijah becomes more than proud of himself: he enjoys the hunt for Fritz; he likes making his kills; in fact, he becomes obsessed with stalking and dispatching his human prey. To make matters worse, Private Elijah Whiskeyjack is addicted to morphine, and all Xavier's efforts to warn him away from the white man's terrible medicine fail. The two soldiers have not been in the field for long before Xavier realizes that he is "not enjoying this war like Elijah is" (187), but he continues to work with Elijah, to rely on his friend's ability to understand English and to hear, and he accepts the responsibility of watching out for Elijah and serving as "his listener" (197). By late 1916, however, Xavier's sense of alarm has grown acute. He begins to think of the war as a monster devouring men and of the battle-hardened soldiers around him as "*windigoes*" (207). He admits to being "sick with worry" that Elijah is going mad (229), and he is right. Elijah is becoming a Windigo, infected by the white man's insatiable hunger for violence and slaughter, and Xavier watches the transformation of his friend from a man into a fiend with horror and profound sorrow because he knows that, sooner or later, he will have to stop Elijah.



The crisis strikes not long before the end of the war after the Allies have broken through the Marcoing Line and Canadians take part in pushing the Germans out of Cambrai. By this late stage in the conflict, Xavier knows that not even a sweat lodge can purify Elijah because he "crossed the line [between being human and going Windigo] long ago" (347). But Xavier hesitates: "Is it up to me to stop him? I wish that I had you here to ask, Niska" (347). Ironically, and because of a mistake in punctuation, Niska has already told her nephew what he must do if necessary; her one letter to Xavier, written by another elderly Cree in broken English, seems to have told him that "God understands if [he] must kill Elijah."[30] Xavier has known for months now that Elijah has been scalping the Germans he kills to prove his score and storing the evidence in his pack, but when he stumbles upon Elijah apparently cannibalizing a dying—but still living—German soldier—he realizes he cannot wait any longer, that he and Elijah have seen "things that men should not be witness to" (346). Beyond experiencing the horrors of war, to witness a Windigo eating human flesh is both terrifying and extremely dangerous. The Windigo knows he has been identified; the witness understands the extent of his own risk of being eaten or of being infected by the Windigo spirit. These two close friends, this sniper team of near brothers, now face an ultimatum: one must kill the other.

As the fight to take Cambrai continues, the two men find themselves trapped in a crater in No Man's Land with all hell breaking loose around them. Xavier calls on Niska for help and crawls towards Elijah to kill him. In the struggle that ensues, Elijah admits that he has "gone too far" (369) and he reaches for Xavier: "Elijah's hands reach for my throat. He squeezes it hard, and the words from that letter come back to me, Niska. *Do what you have to.* I can't breathe. He is killing me. My good arm grasps at the ground beside me. My fingers grab a rifle. I swing the butt of it awkwardly at Elijah. The hard wood of it cracks the side of his head. He falls over" (369). But this fight to the death is not yet finished. Elijah struggles fiercely. Xavier presses down with all his weight on the rifle stock across Elijah's neck. Xavier weeps as he does this and whispers to his friend that he has gone mad and that there is "no coming back" from where he has gone: "I have become what you are, Niska" (370); Xavier is now a Windigo-killer.





If *Three Day Road* ended there in 1918 in that crater near Cambrai, we would have a horror story. The extra *frisson* of cannibalism has simply ratcheted up the monstrosity of war to new heights. Look what war can drive good men to do, we might conclude as we turn away in disgust from witnessing such an unimaginable sight. But *Three Day Road* does not end there, and to understand fully what we have just seen we must go back to the beginning because this is not a straightforward combat narrative, for all its detailed, accurate, shocking evocations of battle. Everything we read (or see or listen to) is, in fact, remembered after the fact. Everything Xavier and Elijah experienced during the war is now, in the fictional present of remembering, as Xavier's story rises from the depths of his landscape of memory. We are not actually at Saint-Eloi or the Somme, or at Vimy Ridge or Passchendaele; it is 1919 and we are in Niska's canoe as she paddles her nephew north to his Mushkegowuk home. We have been travelling through this landscape with Xavier as he fights, with Niska's help, for his life, but he will not survive his three-day road unless he works through his trauma and finally faces the ghost that haunts him more than all the others from the war. Even when he was recuperating in a London hospital, mistaken by the nurses and officers who visit him, for the famous Cree sniper Elijah Whiskeyjack, he remembers calling out for Elijah and hearing a rhythmic, pounding noise: "Elijah pounding to be let in? I want my friend beside me. I need to say I'm sorry" (371). Now, on the third night of his journey downriver with Niska, he must come to terms with this ghost. He must regain the identity he threw away in anger on the battlefield when he ripped off his dog tag, left his precious Mauser rifle on Elijah's body, and removed Elijah's dog tag and medals (370).[31]



The story of *Three Day Road* begins in the summer of 1919 as Niska waits in Moose Factory for the train that will deliver her nephew's friend, Elijah, home from the war. Official word reached her some months earlier that Xavier had died of his wounds near Cambrai on 3 November 1918, but that Elijah Whiskeyjack would return a decorated war hero with only one leg. When the right train pulls up and a one-legged veteran gets off, she nearly faints because Xavier stands with crutches before her. He believed she was dead because of that one letter, with its faulty punctuation, telling him he was the last surviving member of his family and he could kill Elijah if he had to. Now, as these two face each other, Niska understands that mistakes have occurred but she will wait to learn more because it is clear that Xavier is seriously ill with something she cannot understand: "My body hums with Nephew's pain and with the realization that he has come home only to die" (9). However, Xavier will not die. He will survive the ordeal of his three-day road and emerge on the morning of the fourth day weak but purified so he can begin a new life. His survival hinges on his and Niska's memories and the sharing of these memories in the healing process of storytelling. Xavier's memories surface in spite of his terror and resistance—"the dead friends I don't want to see come to visit" (10). Although he quickly uses up the last few vials of morphine to ease his pain and escape the past, the river and northern Canadian landscape around him constantly blend with and disappear into that other landscape. "This is where my life has led me," he thinks. "It's as clear as if I've been walking a well-marked trail that leads from the rivers of my north home...ending right here in this strange place where all the world's trouble explodes" (22). Niska, who sees that the needles he sticks in his bruised arm are part of what is killing him, also intuits that "something far worse is consuming Xavier from the inside" (34). She has two traditional Cree methods for saving her nephew, one of which is the sweetgrass and heat of the sweat lodge, and the other, most crucial method, the strategy that will keep him alive long enough to finish the morphine, to eat a little food, and to begin to have faith in life once more, is storytelling.



As Xavier lies in her canoe shaken by his memories of the war, terrified by the ghosts that haunt him, slipping in and out of his drug-induced state, Niska begins by telling him (and us) stories from her own childhood, when her father's "stories were all that we had to keep us alive" (35). Her first story is about a winter drama she cannot forget, when her family's group of Cree was starving and a young man killed a bear for food. Because this kill broke a prohibition against killing a creature considered to be a brother—an animal that even looks human when it is skinned (38)—the carcass is brought to Niska's parents for what amounts to a blessing and purification ritual. These starving people must ask for forgiveness before eating the bear. However, something evil has entered the space of this group and before the winter is over one of them will become a Windigo; she will eat her husband to save herself and her baby. There is only one recourse for the group: the Windigo must be killed before she kills or infects others with her madness. Niska's father is the *hookimaw*, a holy man and a Windigo-killer, and he allows Niska to watch him kill the woman and baby because after his death he knows she "might have to do the same" (45). By remembering this powerful scene from her past and making it a story for Xavier, Niska is both alerting him to the need to share even the most difficult memories and to the fact that a person blessed with the power of the *hookimaw* also bears the responsibility that comes with it. Niska knows that Xavier has inherited this power (48).

Once the narrative counterpoint has been established, Niska's and Xavier's stories unfold in tandem, side by side. He will remember scenes from the war and his life as a soldier; Niska will remember her youth, her life in the bush, and her adoption and training of her nephew. His memories, although presented in a present-tense, first-person voice, come from his inner consciousness, whether he is physically awake, sleeping, or lulled into semi-consciousness by the morphine. In this way, Boyden creates Xavier's landscape of memory as he relives it because, in the present of his canoe trip north with Niska, he speaks aloud rarely and she asks him few questions. The result is an excruciatingly vivid, detailed eyewitness account of several famous battles from Saint-Eloi, the Somme, and Vimy Ridge, to Passchendaele, Amiens, and Cambrai from the perspective of the individual soldier. But Xavier will also recall, as memories within the larger landscape of war memory, some of his pre-enlistment experiences with Elijah such as their first hunting excursions when he had to teach his friend how to shoot and skin an animal, or the canoe trip south they took to enlist, when they were trapped and almost died in a raging forest fire. Xavier's memory of this fire is triggered by "the acrid scent of charred wood" in the forest as Niska paddles north.[32] Her stories are *framed* as deliberate present-tense, first-person attempts to communicate with Xavier, to show him that she is remembering for his sake. At one point, she *says*, "I know that Xavier wants to talk to me" (88), but she cannot make sense of what he says in his dreams when he cries out in English. Because he must but cannot yet talk to her, she talks to him: "In this way maybe his tongue will loosen some. Maybe some of the poison that courses through him might be released in this way. Words are all I have left now" (89). And words are her chief power, her way of feeding him when he cannot swallow other food. "I feed him with my story instead. He's listening," she says (130).

In teaching *Three Day Road*, I have often had students wonder why the novel contains so much of Niska's voice. They want the active through line, the bloody history, reported by Xavier, and his memory-work is without doubt galvanizing. But Niska's stories are integral to the larger purpose of the novel; we cannot have Xavier without her, just as we cannot have Joseph Boyden's story about First Nations soldiers in the First World War without the story of home front peace, family traditions, and community responsibility. While Xavier bears witness to the war, its horror and agony as well as its comradeship and victories, Niska bears witness to the Cree past, as it was lived before the colonizing interference by white missionaries, fur traders, and settlements. Her stories remind Xavier of his Cree identity and his responsibility to that identity. Although Boyden has not depicted Canadian soldiers in a negative light—indeed, Xavier acknowledges their courage and suffering, and he is proud of Canadian victories such as the taking of Vimy Ridge—he is not writing a novel in praise of war. On the contrary, this war is portrayed as a madness akin to the Windigo turned loose upon everything and everyone it touches, and Elijah in his lust for killing embodies that madness. This is why Xavier must destroy him. To balance and make sense of this vision of the war, we need Niska's vision of a northern Canadian home in which life may be difficult but where those who know how to live there can survive in peace, with wisdom and dignity. From a reader's perspective, the two narratives support each other. For Xavier, Niska's stories keep him alive by reawakening memories of the home front and lessons learned by living a traditional Cree life. For Niska, his war stories, insofar as she can grasp them, help her to assume her role as guide and saviour; they harden her resolve to defeat the Windigo threat that hovers over him in the morphine, in his traumatic memories of battles and of people he killed as Elijah's accomplice or shot by accident (like the mother and child near Passchendaele), and in Elijah's ghost.[33]

As the hours and days of paddling north pass, Xavier's war memories approach closer to the end and to the crisis near Cambrai.

Running in parallel, from distant to more recent memories and from her own life story to Xavier's, Niska finally arrives at the critical juncture in her remembering—and his—when she tries the last thing she can think of to save him: "Maybe he won't last through the night. I cannot let him go without telling him his story. I lie down with him and gently place my arm over his thin frame....I put my mouth close to his ear so that he can hear me whisper....Listen to me, Nephew, when you were no more than five winters I came and took you away from their school, from them....And this story that I tell you is the story of you" (354–55). In this story, little Xavier becomes separated from Niska while they are out hunting. He is frightened but struggles through the snow following a moose and hoping to kill it. As night falls he begins to imagine a story he will tell his Auntie about stumbling upon the tracks of a Windigo and hearing it stamp and whistle. He prepares to shoot the Windigo and creeps up on it only to discover he is watching a rare grouse mating dance; the dancing birds move in a circle and reverse the circle when the lead bird calls. These circles and dancing remind the child of the circles in Cree culture. As Niska retells this story, and the story within it that the child told her many years ago, Xavier becomes calmer. She resumes her telling and reminds him, "do you remember...do you remember?—how they feasted, praised the boy, and gave him his name: Little Bird Dancer" (362–63).

Niska has become "desperate now"; "Now is when he will decide. I can feel him struggle" (362). Then the narrative shifts to Xavier, who admits, "I can no longer escape him....I remember our last day together" (364). What Xavier now remembers, whether he speaks these memories aloud or dreams them with Niska, is his slaying of the Windigo Elijah has become, his removing of Elijah's identity tag and medals; his leaving the Mauser, with which he killed Elijah and which his friend had long coveted, across his body. He remembers scrambling from the crater, being struck by something, and then waking in a hospital to find that he is mistaken for Elijah and that his leg has been amputated. He allows himself to believe he is indeed Elijah because "in this way he is still alive" (375).

Except that he is not Elijah. He is not a Windigo but a Windigo-killer. To live he must admit that Elijah is dead. He must, as it were, confess and seek forgiveness. In the sweat lodge, Niska prays and bends over the steaming rocks until a presence joins them in the *matatosowin*. It is Elijah's ghost come to hear Xavier ask for forgiveness and to forgive him. However, this ghostly presence cannot "forgive everything" Xavier did there, so although Xavier has now atoned for killing Elijah, he will have to carry on with his memories of other killings. Boyden makes it clear that Xavier will live because Niska has one final vision before they complete their cleansing ceremony and in this vision she sees the future and Xavier's children. By drawing on Cree belief and tradition, Boyden has imagined a war story full of haunting and enacted on a landscape of memory that imprints battle front horror on a home front of northern sanctuary and peace. He does not imply that Cree ways are so powerful that they can remove all remnants of trauma and free his Indian sniper from the guilt of the survivor or the terrible memories of what he witnessed and did. Xavier will have to carry on with one leg, living a bush life that is challenging, even for the young and healthy, with white culture intruding further and further into Cree life. But with the help of Niska he has rediscovered his own story, his true identity; he has faced his most dangerous ghost and accepted the responsibility that comes with being a Windigo-killer. *Three Day Road* does not have a happy ending because the past cannot be changed, but it concludes on a stronger note of hope, I think, than either *The Wars* or *Broken Ground*. Boyden gives the closing words to Niska who says, or tells us, or possibly just communicates her thought to Xavier: "By tomorrow we'll be home" (382).

In this remarkable novel, Boyden imagines the First World War in new ways for Canada. Yes, the battles, the facts and dates, the terrible losses in combat and the exhilarating victories are there, and Boyden's snipers fight on all these occasions. Indeed, the imagined, on-the-ground witnessing of Vimy is spectacular: Boyden's Xavier is pleased that by now the Germans "know their opponent is worthy" (229); he finds comfort in the falling snow as he crouches in his sniper's nest waiting for his target to appear (236); he is enraged when his comrades die around him. But there is something more here, something not encountered in other Vimy stories. In the midst of this terrible battle, with men screaming and the earth exploding in mud and fire, a memory of home and "the muddy shore of the Great Salt Bay" floods him until he feels Niska's presence protecting him—"I begin to mouth your name over and over, like a protection against the bullets. *Niska,* I whisper as I run up the hill and approach a stretch of barbed wire. *Niska. Niska. Niska. Niska. Niska*" (237). This is a remembering of Vimy Ridge as we have never had it before, in part because the soldier-witness-rememberer is an Indian, and in part because two landscapes merge; Xavier's personal home front of northern Canada, falling snow, and muddy shoreline sustains him on this French battlefield in April 1917. That he is remembering Vimy, where he remembered Niska and home, while lying in Niska's canoe on a Canadian river flowing north to take him home completes the fusion of these landscapes and returns Xavier to Canada with the war firmly embedded in his mind and, like his missing leg, always with him. In this scene at Vimy Ridge, as in many others in the novel, and in the parallel rememberings of Xavier and Niska, Boyden insists that the returning soldier brings the war home even as home sustained him over there, and this stresses his point through the creation of overlapping, complementary landscapes of memory.



In *Three Day Road* the bearing of witness by both Xavier and Niska is extreme. By telling their stories, which grow from memories and the pervasive haunting of the present by the past, they make listeners of each other and of us. These two complex, fully imagined human beings—really I should say *three* because Elijah comes to life with irresistible energy—command our attention; they ask us to perform our role of secondary witness with empathic unsettlement. That said, it is, finally, Elijah who is the most seductive, dangerous presence in this novel because he represents what war can do, how it can appeal to the worst in human nature—human pride, vanity, obsession with winning, and violence. By making this charismatic, deadly figure a Cree sniper, Boyden can emphasize the negative influence of white culture on native Canadian culture and draw on the awe-inspiring and ethically empowering myth of the Windigo to condemn war without denigrating the Canadians who fought in the war. Choosing native characters, then, is new but is in no way a mere add-on. If younger generations of Canadians know little about the Great War or how it influenced the country, they know less still about the role played by First Nations soldiers or how they were treated when they returned home, regardless of their medals. Lying behind the fictional Cree snipers is a real Indian sniper, the famous Corporal Francis Pegahmagabow, who will crop up in rumours and estaminet gossip about a man called "Peggy," but whose achievements and actual existence after the war were ignored.[34] *Three Day Road* reminds Canadians of much we have chosen to forget, repress, or even reject. It restores the story of courageous Cree people to their rightful place within Canadian memories of the war and brings their experiences to the surface of a landscape in which they were buried. Certainly, Elijah is a powerful ghost who haunts the narrative and the landscape until he gets his due, but Niska and Xavier also haunt this story of the First World War, and if we listen to their stories and learn from them, we will not only expand our understanding of the past but also better understand how to mourn and heal, how to live now and in the future.

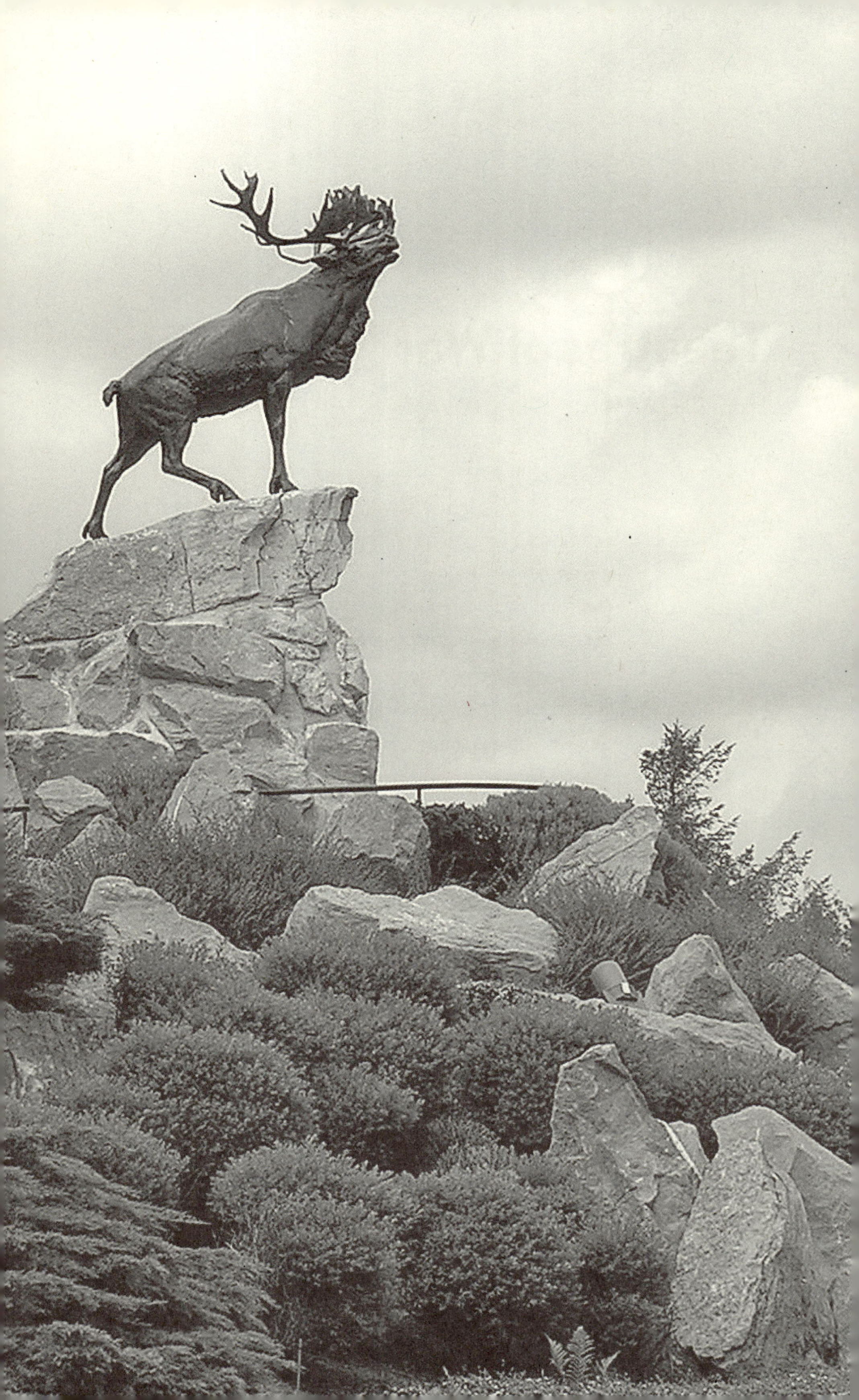

# 4 Theatres of War

## From *Billy Bishop* to *Vimy*

### SETTING THE STAGE



#### *Ways of Performing the War*

Canadian plays about the Great War burst upon the scene with the 1976 premiere of John Gray and Eric Peterson's tour de force *Billy Bishop Goes to War*. Since then the play has become a much-loved classic continuously remounted, and in a 2011 production it was reimagined by the two men who created it almost forty years earlier. The play is a two-hander with one actor playing an old upright piano and singing, while the other, "Billy," tells us his story. In this narrative sense, the play resembles the novels because it is a performance of storytelling.[1] Moreover, like the novels and like the plays to be written later, it draws heavily on historical facts, documents, and other personal information from the war. Indeed, staging a play about the war places unique demands on designers because they cannot afford to make mistakes with the sound effects or songs, or make a muddle of uniforms, flags, and other props needed onstage. Even when the play uses dream sequences or extended memory scenes (as most of these plays do), what we see onstage, whether a rifle, helmet, uniform, or civilian dress, must be historically accurate and convincing for contemporary audiences. Theatre is even more constrained by present reality and by credibility than fiction, despite its being a collaborative effort in illusion. But live theatre has advantages over the novel and narrative forms that we read silently and privately. In the theatre, the audience can be *constructed* as a live secondary witness or an accomplice, experiencing the telling, remembering, and suffering *with* live actors, and unable to escape or turn away from what they see. An audience *shares* in a public experience of watching and, on occasion, of being watched back and directly addressed; it is a phlegmatic audience member who is not viscerally, emotionally engaged in a well-written, well-performed and staged play. When that play asks us to remember painful experiences from the First World War, experiences we did not have (any more than those who embody them onstage), we can find ourselves facing degrees of horror and awareness, of sorrow, haunting, and revelation, never dreamt of in our histories.[2] It is one thing for a Robert Ross or a Matthew Pearson to be described as haunted by the past, or an Xavier to tell us that Elijah's ghost is beside him, and quite another to share in an expertly staged experience of haunting.

*Billy Bishop Goes to War* set the bar for Canadian war plays very high. The role of Billy, created by Peterson, is truly a star turn, a role so demanding that only a top actor can handle it. It is also, unlike every other Canadian play about the war, extremely funny. Although the inspiration for the play comes from the story of real First World War flying ace William A. Bishop and draws on his autobiography *Winged Warfare*, Peterson's Billy rarely takes himself seriously and has a splendid time imitating every stuffy Brit he comes across during his war: the actor playing Billy entertains us by performing everyone, from himself to the upper-class Lady St. Helier, who decides to mould this thick-skulled colonial into a well-mannered gentleman fit to be introduced to the king, and an efficient killing machine for the empire.

He also plays her exceedingly snooty butler, Cedric, several officers, and the "Lovely Hélène," a French chanteuse. In its comic turns and lusty songs, *Billy Bishop* resembles Joan Littlewood's *Oh! What a Lovely War*, but Billy is a Canuck through and through.[3]

The real Bishop was from Owen Sound, so the play's Billy must sound like such a fellow. As the opening stage instructions explain: "*His speech pattern is that of a small town Canadian boy who could well be squealing his tires down the main street of some town at this very moment*" (19). He is quick to tell us that the army must have been desperate to take him because he was the worst student RMC ever had (20); he is also accident-prone, so when the First Contingent of the Canadian Expeditionary Force leaves for England, Billy is in a Halifax hospital, writing to his sweetheart. Once he gets over to England he is disgusted by the rain and mud in Shorncliffe Military Camp, when suddenly, in the skies above him, a little single-seat fighter plane appears with a clean, elegantly attired pilot, who has no superior officer breathing down his neck. Billy is enthralled (shades of poor Eamon O'Sullivan from *The Stone Carvers*). But becoming a pilot is another matter. As he reminds us (speaking directly to the audience), "I'm Canadian. I'm cannon fodder. You practically have to own your own plane to get into the R.F.C." (34). In the interview scene that follows, Billy plays his part and the part of Sir Hugh Cecil at the War Office, who must examine Billy's qualifications for flying. The questions asked are ludicrous, Sir Hugh is a twit, and the canny Canuck lies through his teeth. Billy is made an observer (he goes up with a pilot) with the Twenty-First Squadron, better known as the "suicide squadron" (41).

But Billy is still accident-prone, and before he gets his first taste of bombing runs he finds himself in a London hospital and, with the piano player, sings about home:

*Nobody shoots no one in Canada,*
*At least nobody they don't know*
...

*Nobody drops no bombs on Canada*
*Wouldn't want to send no one to hell.*
*Nobody starts no wars in Canada,*
*Where folks tend to wish each other well.* (44)

Gray and Peterson do not use this song to moralize: *Billy Bishop Goes to War* is not an anti-war play. Instead, Billy segues directly to Lady St. Helier, a personnage whom Peterson captures in delightful caricature. *She* reminds Billy, who reports her speech to us in one of the play's most satiric scenes, that he is a "rude young man," which is "perfectly acceptable" for a Canadian, but she will improve his "rustic mind" and make him famous. No more "colonial mentality" will be allowed because "Beneath this rude Canadian exterior, there is a power that you [Cedric] will never know. Properly harnessed, that power will win wars for you" (52–53).





During the rest of his story, Billy describes his rise to fame, his pleasure flying, and his pride in shooting the Hun out of the sky. The young Billy who seemed so silly and inept at the beginning transforms before our eyes—and his own—into a single-minded, aggressive killer who can watch an enemy plane crash and burn and scream—"I win, I WIN, I WIN!" (63). And because Billy performs this dogfight scene for us, complete with his own energetic sound effects, we relive the entire bombing raid with him (62–63). Having seen this play performed three times, I can attest that I forgot my scruples and was swept up in the sheer excitement of the drama (only to come down later with a thud). Those around me seemed to be similarly seduced. By the second act, Billy has begun to reflect on what he is doing in this war and on who he has become: "I don't want to sound bloodthirsty," he tells us, but "if you want the machine to go down every time, you aim for one thing: the man. I always go for the man" (69). In a novel, this might well be a moment of truth, the point at which a listening narrator steps away from the eyewitness character to provide an ethical perspective on the action. But in a play, the action and dialogue—or, in this case, the monologue—must move forward. Our Billy confesses to his sweetheart, in the letters he reads out to us, that he hates the Hun for killing his friends and enjoys killing him. His "score" is getting higher; he's being promoted and winning medals; he outlives Albert Ball, and he mourns the British hero in a duet that conveys the shift in mood without any need for narrative explanation: "*I remember the faces; / I remember the time. / Those were the names of friends of mine*" (80).

*Billy Bishop Goes to War* is, in fact, a memory play in which an older Billy remembers his life in the war and retells and reimagines it for us. When he remembers making kill number forty-six he briefly describes the horror he felt as he watched two Germans fall, still alive, while their plane disintegrated around them. He believes they were looking back at him, and his full reaction to this vivid memory can only be conveyed through facial expression, tone of voice, and gesture—through excellent acting. The mood of the play, like the atmosphere in the theatre, plummets with those men. The play draws to its close with an older Billy singing the opening song—"We're off to fight the Hun"—again, only this time "*The song has a bitter edge...for it is World War II we are talking about*" (99), and in the final moments Billy Bishop is speaking to young Second World War recruits. He will then look at and speak directly to us, as if no longer performing his life for our entertainment, and say: "It comes as a bit of a surprise to me that there is another war on. We didn't think there was going to be another one back in 1918. Makes you wonder what it was all for?" (101).

No other Canadian play about the First World War is quite like *Billy Bishop Goes to War*; no other is so hilarious, even as it waxes darkly satiric. However, this play employs many of the staging strategies and overall theatrical aesthetics that are found in the later plays. It also addresses some of the crucial themes that would be explored in the plays by David French, Stephen Massicotte, and Vern Thiessen. After all, Billy is remembering his war story for us; he relies on letters, facts and dates, music, and re-enactments to *re*-present his life, and he does have moments of shocked recollection and even regret that the war changed him from a happy-go-lucky Canuck into such a focused killer. Perhaps most importantly, Billy wants us to listen to him, to hear him out, to be secondary witnesses to his bearing of witness. If that position means we laugh at his mimicry, his fake British accents, his childlike performances with toy planes, it also means we laugh with Billy and are all the more chastened and impressed by the changes in the man.[4] In light of the stress placed on being an uncouth colonial in Britain's war—mere cannon fodder for the glory of the mother country—the play insists, through memories and humour, that we think carefully about what it meant to be Canadian then and what might have changed over the years. Billy is like Mary in Massicotte's *Mary's Wedding* (a play I discuss below) in this one sense: he symbolizes Canada and Canadian identity, a remembering of but also a carrying on after the war. Clearly, speaking to us from his older present during the Second World War, Billy Bishop remains haunted by those two Germans pilots falling, still alive, to their deaths and looking up at him, but this haunting contributes to who he has become and to what the country must always acknowledge as part of its history.

Apart from the year it premiered (1976) and then was published (1977), and its long-term success, *Billy Bishop Goes to War* has little in common with *The Wars*: the play's Billy Bishop is no Robert Ross. And the plays that follow this one are all fairly grim, even tragic. Their mood and perspective on the war owes more to the novel than the play. Beginning with Anne Chislett's *Quiet in the Land*, these plays explore the causes and consequences of the war and tend to focus on the traumas and negative impact of the war on the home front. Most of them belong in the special category of memory play, which is appropriate, given that they are all created by playwrights born during or after the Second World War and that none of them has fought in a war. But even when they are not, strictly speaking, structured as memory plays, they stage moments of remembering and remembrance at key points in the plot, and they urge audiences and readers to reflect on what these war memories tell us about being Canadian. Ghosts haunt these plays—one or two are comforting, but most are terrifying—and audiences are made to confront hard truths about the war. However, just as there are too many fine novels that address or reimagine the Great War for me to discuss each in detail, there are too many excellent plays to examine: a selection must be made. When compiling the plays to include in volume one of *Canada and the Theatre of War*, I was surprised to find such a wealth of material and sorry to have to leave out several works. Therefore, before I turn to the three I examine closely—*Mary's Wedding*, *The Lost Boys*, and *Vimy*—I want to linger a bit with *Quiet in the Land*, *Dancock's Dance*, *Unity (1918)*, and *Soldier's Heart*.





Chislett's play premiered at the Blyth Festival in 1981 and went on to win several awards. Inspired by the title of Glenn Gould's third composition in *The Solitude Trilogy* (*Quiet in the Land*), it presents the story of an Amish family near Kitchener, Ontario, that will be torn apart by the war. The sons in this pacifist, traditional community are sorely tempted to enlist because of surrounding social pressures, and the Military Service Act (introducing conscription) weighs heavily on their minds.[5] When one young farmer, Jacob Bauman, insists on becoming a soldier to fight for his country, he alienates himself from his parents, the young woman he loves, and the entire community. The question that hovers over the play boils down to this: how can one remain true to pacifist beliefs when faced with what seems to be an urgent, national call to arms? Jacob (or Yock, as he is called) will distinguish himself as a soldier and return home a decorated *Canadian* hero, but his community sees him as a bloodstained traitor, and they reject him. The play closes with Yock leaving his home as an outcast, but in the final scene with his father he confesses that the old man was right about war; he recalls standing by the body of a German soldier he has killed and finally understanding that pacifism is the better way. As theatre, this is a straightforward, realist piece that turns on accessible issues of family tensions and intergenerational conflicts in a farming community, but the questions Chislett poses about the role of the state in coercing young men to fight, the propaganda used to inflame or shame ordinary farm boys, and the violence of combat (described instead of staged), emphasize the ethical dilemma faced by many Canadian families and expose the resistance to the war that many on the home front felt but that has been largely erased from the official story. When the play ends with Jacob forced to leave his community, the lonely future he faces in postwar Canadian society hangs over the final curtain like a pall.





Guy Vanderhaeghe's *Dancock's Dance* did not get its premiere until 1995 with Persephone Theatre in Saskatoon, and general forces at play in Canadian society between 1981 and 1995 may well have contributed to the savage content of this play. By 1995 Canadian peacekeepers had been involved in the disgrace of Somalia and the horror of Rwanda; atrocities, genocide, and war-related trauma were on the front pages of newspapers and on the television news. By revisiting the Great War, Vanderhaeghe was determined to throw light on the aftermath of war and on Canadian society's inability to deal with the effects of post-traumatic stress disorder (PTSD) and the role of the authorities in twisting or hiding truths. The main character in this play is a decorated veteran of the war who has been wounded and sent home to Saskatchewan, where he is incarcerated in the Saskatchewan Hospital for the Insane; the year is 1918, the war is ending, and the flu is breaking out. But is Lieutenant Dancock insane? In some respects, the answer is yes because he is so severely haunted by the war that he compulsively scratches his hands until they bleed and he believes a Canadian soldier he executed on the battlefield visits him, threatens and accuses him, and wants to drive him to suicide. In most other respects, however, Dancock is entirely lucid. He suffers immensely from survivor guilt and for killing the young private whose sin was to be too terrified to obey the order to advance, and it is hard to call a man mad for feeling guilt over such an event. Moreover, Dancock has become vociferously critical of all authorities, from lying politicians and army generals to the hospital superintendent, and he blames those in power for sending young men off to die for nothing but lies.

To make matters worse, he is not anti-German. On the contrary. As he says in the angry opening confrontation with the superintendent, "The German soldier did his duty. I did mine. He was an honest enemy. I save my hatred for the dishonest enemies" (13). The man Dancock befriends in the hospital is a German Canadian who is mad, but harmless, and who is taunted and abused by the hospital staff. Dancock's committal to the hospital and his treatment while there, especially when he is put in the cage to control his behaviour, soon begin to appear as society's punishment for his daring to speak out, to tell the truth as he sees it, for bearing witness, and for condemning those in authority who caused the war. Dancock is incarcerated to shut him up and to correct his behaviour so he will conform and obey.





At the core of the theatrical presentation of this drama is the "Soldier" who haunts Dancock, who appears behind him and is visible only to Dancock (and the audience) and who reminds Dancock of what he did. When he speaks to this figure, others believe he is crazy, but Dancock knows full well he is struggling with a terrible ghost who has come to get revenge and to remind him of how he behaved in the war and the injustice and cruelty of what he did. This ghost insists that Dancock admit what he did, take responsibility for his actions, and be honest with himself and others. He also serves as a spur to Dancock's despair and wish to die. The crisis of remembering, bearing witness, and confession comes in an excoriating scene in Act 2 when Dancock, exhausted by helping inmates ill with the flu, relives the confrontation with the soldier on the battlefield, how he orders the young private to stand to, fix bayonets, and advance, and how the young man refuses, cries for mercy and begs not to be forced to go, and even prays to his commanding officer. Dancock, aware of the mutinies in the French army and that his orders are to shoot any soldier who refuses an order in battle, puts his revolver to the man's head and executes him on the spot. In this appalling scene, he tries to insist that the gun's going off was an accident, but the ghost is relentless. He calls Dancock a "Liar" (66) and a "murderer": "I couldn't say no to you and live. You can't say no to me and live. There's no denying me, Dancock, or what you did" (67).

If Dancock is to survive this accusation, if he is to live, he must be able to tell his story to someone who will listen, and Vanderhaeghe gives his protagonist a listener and witness inside the play in the character of Dorothea, a young woman who suffers from delusions, but who in her tenderness and gentleness is capable of hearing what Dancock says. She senses the presence of the past that haunts Dancock and she provides the legitimating secondary witnessing that will help him to save himself. Dorothea does not recoil from him, when she witnesses his reliving of the past, or argue or deny his torment and guilt; she simply says, "It's all right. He's [the ghost] gone....Darkness and fire! That's what we've seen and what matters!" (67–68). She performs, within the play, the empathic unsettlement that at least some audience members will also feel. After this crisis, the Soldier never appears again. He does not have to because Dancock has told his story and been believed. He and his guilt and atonement—worked out by risking his life to help those who are sick—are out in the open, firmly situated in a shared landscape of memory. What's more, the play has situated some very ugly truths about the war, about military policies, about blind acceptance of authority that hides behind the excuse of following orders, and about a man's capacity to lie to himself about his past, right out onstage for all to see. Although Dancock stands condemned in his own eyes (and to some extent forgiven by the end), the politics of war and the manipulations of ambitious men in power and of governments must still be called before the court of conscience. It is the agonies suffered and crimes perpetrated in the name of authority (in the name of Canadian citizens) that *Dancock's Dance* with death asks us to think about and face.

Kevin Kerr's *Unity (1918)* is also set on the home front, in a small Saskatchewan town, at the end of the war and as the flu epidemic spreads across Canada. It premiered in 2001 at the Vancouver East Cultural Centre and was an instant hit with audiences.[6] The large cast features six women from Unity—two sisters, a friend, two telephone operators, and a woman who takes over the mortician's work when the local undertaker dies—and three men, one of whom is a blind soldier home from the war and another, a young farmhand, who will be an early casualty of the flu. We move through the final months of the war with the women who wait at home, and the action is guided by the dated entries in Beatrice's diary. One by one the characters die, but not before Hart, the returned soldier, corrects Beatrice's views about what really happened over there. Beatrice will also die from the flu and her younger sister, a doomsday prophet, will be left alone onstage to read out her final diary entry. Unlike *Dancock's Dance*, this play is much gentler, even romantic, but Kerr is making some of the same points as Vanderhaeghe. Among them are the concentration on the home front and the focus on how the war affects small communities and the women who wait there. As the play unfolds and time passes, the emphasis shifts from the war, or even reports of the war, to the impact of the flu which, as history tells us, killed many millions more than all the war dead together. In other words, Kerr seems to be saying that the flu was the war fought by civilians, that this contagion and its devastating costs outweigh the war itself and are as much responsible for the Canada that emerged after 1919 as what happened between 1914 and 1918. Hart, the blind soldier who arrives in Unity, brings another kind of message, however, because in an important scene with Beatrice he refuses to hear any of the war stories from the newspapers that she offers to read to him. "They have this section where they write stories of Canadian bravery," she explains, but he becomes agitated and tells her "They're not true" (96–97). Then he tells her that such stories are stupid and never about the ordinary soldier stuck in a trench "with his head between his knees and his pants full of his own shit because he's been there for three days in the same position between the corpses of a couple of guys who looked up when he said 'Heads Down'" (97).

Of course, the true war story in Unity is the story of the young men who do not come back, the women who wait, and the arrival of the flu. As Beatrice, in her role of town historian, notes at one point, "The enemy was in our midst and it was everyone's favourite son" (77). The enemy in David French's *Soldier's Heart* is also at home, in the midst of his family and community, but the difference between these two plays is striking. *Unity (1918)* is a women's play and battles are rarely described and never relived. *Soldier's Heart* is a men's play in which one veteran and survivor from the Royal Newfoundland Regiment will remember and relive the most excruciating events of his war experience. This is also a deceptively simple, realist play that can be enormously powerful in performance when the actors are up to the task. The cast is minimal: the three men onstage are sixteen-year-old Jacob Mercer, his father Esau Mercer, and a fellow veteran, now in charge of the local train station, Bert Taylor. The action is equally economical; indeed, with the exception of the terrible memories that will surface, *Soldier's Heart* obeys all the Aristotelian unities.

The entire play takes place in one act on the station platform at Bay Roberts, a tiny Newfoundland community, and covers only that amount of time required for the performance. The three men are waiting for the local train, the *Caribou*, to arrive and it is, as usual, late; ominous word comes down the line that a crippled veteran has tried to commit suicide on the track. The date is Monday, 30 June 1924, and in case this date does not immediately resonate with audiences, it soon will. Jacob has decided to leave his home for good because Esau tried to kill him earlier that day and his mother is terrified of her husband, who came back from the war suffering from such terrible nightmares and shell shock that he has been unable to speak about what happened, has violent nightmares (he broke her arm in one), and will turn with violence on anyone who approaches him suddenly from behind—even his own son. Bert, who was with Esau during the war but has managed to come to terms with the past and carry on a normal life, talks to young Jacob, tells him bits about the war, and tries to intercede between father and son. Jacob is headed for St. John's, where tomorrow, on 1 July 1924, the Newfoundland Memorial to the war will be unveiled. The delayed train allows Esau enough time to make the confession he must make and tell the story his son needs to hear. Only Esau can tell his story, as Bert warns Jacob: "It's just that each man's experience was his own. Take me, now. I never lost a brother at the Somme. Nor was I badly wounded there like Esau...The Newfoundland Regiment was wiped out at Beaumont-Hamel, but I got off without a scratch" (18).

And so the scene is set. Only a revelation about what happened to the Mercer brothers on 1 July 1916 will satisfy Jacob and the audience. We already know from history that what happened at Beaumont-Hamel was catastrophic because the regiment was all but destroyed when they were sent in to confront a crack German regiment that had not been softened up by advance shelling. General Haig (the British officer in charge at the Somme) will be showing up in St. John's for the unveiling on 1 July, but as far as Esau and Bert are concerned the man should be shot instead of feted. But this play is not about Beaumont-Hamel as such and certainly not about the stupidity of British officers. It is about Esau and Jacob and how they can carry on living as a family after the war; it is about how Newfoundland can carry on outside of—or within—Canadian Confederation.[7] While the men wait for the train and Bert's wife plays old First World War songs on her gramophone—"Keep the Home Fires Burning" is the ironic theme song of this play—the truth about the Mercer boys and Beaumont-Hamel slowly surfaces. Through a masterful handling of dramatic tension and release, French builds the suspense and suspicion to fever pitch: the train is late, Esau is drunk and refusing to talk, the train approaches, and Jacob will leave unless....And finally Esau becomes so caught up in remembering the past that the story of what happened in No Man's Land on the day following the massacre of the Royal Newfoundlanders pushes to the surface of his memory.

This story is horrifying on the realistic level and immensely important on a symbolic and ethical level. When Esau finally loses himself in his memories of the war, the story he tells is one of confusion and mistaken identity because out in No Man's Land, with men crying out for death, German snipers watching for the slightest movement, and big, fat rats looking for a meal, he will mistake his own brother Will, who has come out when night falls to search for his brother's body, for a German soldier. In the dark he will kill this soldier by stabbing him through the heart with his bayonet. To quote this scene of remembering in full and out of context is unfair; the play must be seen to do Esau's memories justice. But one anguished speech captures something of the intensity. As Esau holds the body of the man he stabbed, a flare lights up the sky just enough for him to see the man's face: "A red foam bubbled from his mouth...He was looking at me, puzzled. He couldn't speak, but I could see the question in his eyes: *Why? Why had I done this? Why had I killed my own brother?*" (90). Once Esau has told this story, he is, *to a degree*, freed from his melancholic withdrawal and obsessive repetition of the past in dreams (or when startled by noises behind him), into a possible present and future with his son at his side.

In performance, the play positions the audience as the secondary witness to Esau Mercer's trauma, but it is Jacob, the listening, secondary witness within the play, who has the chief power of empathic unsettlement and forgiveness. Jacob now understands, at least to some degree, what has shaped this man he calls his father, and the play ends with the three men singing "Keep the Home Fires Burning." This singing of the famous, familiar song is bittersweet and profoundly ironic, however, because the future of Newfoundland, never mind the Mercer family, which represents the province, was determined at Beaumont-Hamel. The monument that presides over that place in France is eloquent in its silence; it is a bull caribou calling out against the sky while around it, to this day, one sees the grass-covered craters and trenches from the war and one remembers the story of the Newfoundland Regiment. They were, to recall the words of Billy in *Billy Bishop Goes to War*, cannon fodder, lambs to the slaughter, and their thanks from a grateful nation (Great Britain or Canada) was small.

To reflect on this play and recall that it is one in French's sequence of five Mercer family plays, prompts me to look beyond *Soldier's Heart*

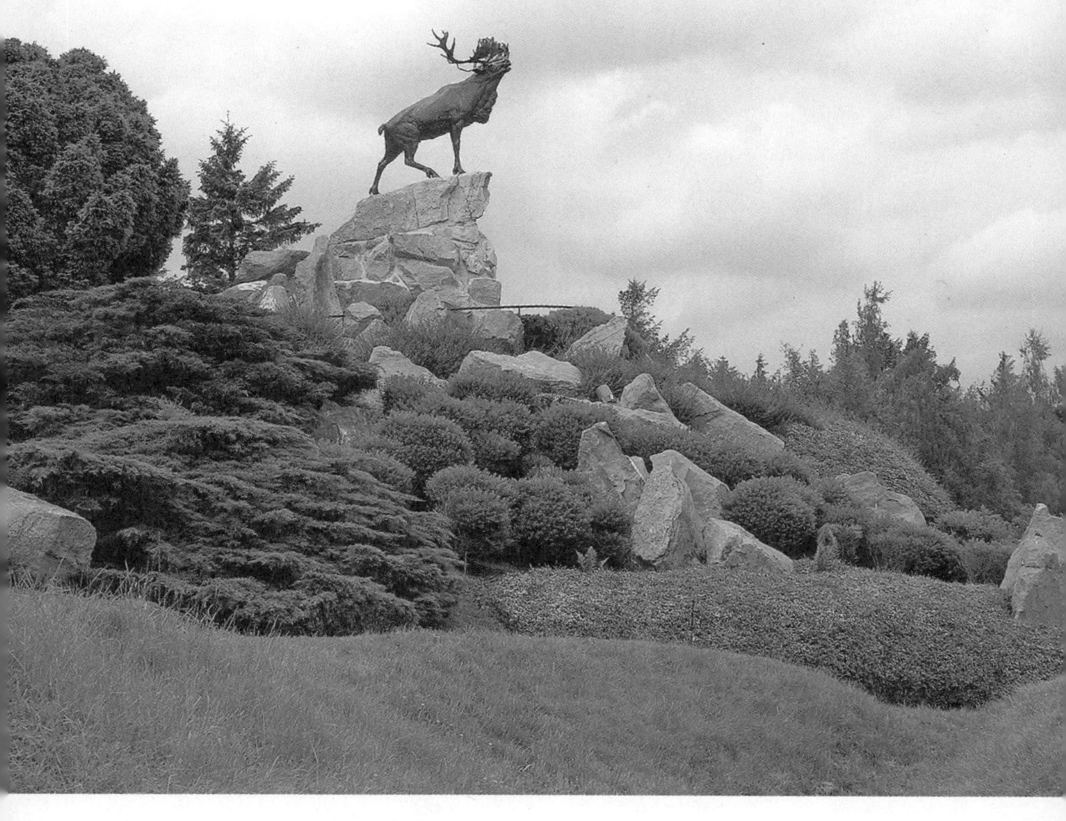

*This monument to the Newfoundland Regiment, which was decimated on 1 July 1916, overlooks the former battlefield at Beaumont-Hamel, France. The bull caribou and the rocks, shrubs, and trees (all native to Newfoundland and Labrador) represent the province. The grass-covered mounds and craters remind a visitor of the blasted earth and trenches from the First World War. Photograph: J. Grace.*

to *Leaving Home* and *1949*, where French revisits Newfoundland's entry into Canadian Confederation. Many Newfoundlanders believe to this day that their loss of a generation of sons, husbands, and fathers at Beaumont-Hamel so weakened the British colony that it had to join Canada to survive.[8] Certainly, in his other Mercer plays, most notably in *Leaving Home*, David French examines the resentment, frustration, and sense of exile experienced by Newfoundlanders who had to leave the island for places like Toronto. But I think French is describing something even more important in *Soldier's Heart* than the fate of one family or one province damaged by the war. That war and the killing of that one soldier—a brother—produces a haunting that exceeds the personal or national because that brother could also have been someone's German brother. To be sure, Esau is tormented by the memory of Will, but his landscape of memory includes a battle front massacre that persists in a peaceful-seeming home front, outport town long after the war is over, and our secondary witnessing includes the wider reality of man's slaughter of his fellow man.





## STAGING A NATIONAL LANDSCAPE OF (WAR) MEMORY

*Mary's Wedding*, *The Lost Boys*, and *Vimy* are all very much about being Canadian *because of* and *after* the Great War. None is a war play in the sense of *Journey's End*, and none of them is as much *about* war as about questions of forgetting and remembering, and the exploration of truths and lies surrounding the First World War. And yet, each plays involves staging battle scenes, and recounting deaths in battle and from injuries: shell shock features prominently in these plays as does mourning and the working through of grief to healing. Inevitably, these plays share much with the others, such as the reliance on facts, references to historical places and events, carefully invoked aspects of the period, and the use of key dramatic strategies like letters, songs, and familiar quotations and slogans. But as creative fictions about the war they are more reminiscent of the novels and memoirs. They have a certain scope, a breadth of narrative reach, of symbolic resonance, and a rich complexity of vision that puts them in a special category as theatre and as case studies in my discussion. They are big plays, technically difficult to stage, demanding to perform, and exhausting to watch. We cannot sit back and smile or be entertained; we are expected to leave the theatre questioning what we thought we knew and how we feel, not because these plays are Brechtian (they are not epic satire like *Mother Courage*) but because the issues they raise are ethically important and the ways in which they involve an audience are subtle, even surprising.

The plot of each play can be quickly summarized: In *Mary's Wedding* a girl dreams about the young soldier she loved and lost in the war on the night before she marries another; in *The Lost Boys* a descendant of five men from his family who went to the war reads their letters and reconstructs their experiences so he can enact a vigil; and in *Vimy*, four injured Canadians being nursed in a field hospital remember home and realize how much they have in common *as Canadians*. So simple. And yet what fascinates me is how each play establishes exactly what Ross Chambers identifies as haunting and how each produces this hauntedness in and for us through the imagining of a landscape of memory that includes the audience (or the reader).





*Mary's Wedding* opens with a ghost. His name is Charles Edwards and he died in March 1918 after the infamous cavalry charge at Moreuil Wood. Ironically, he survived the charge only to be killed the following morning when the Germans shelled a field in which he was standing with his horse, but we do not know this at the beginning. When Charlie speaks directly to us, it is a July night in 1920; he tells us that it is the night before Mary's wedding and that she is about to dream a story about him and the war that she has relived many times since learning of his death. Charlie invites the audience (and the reader) to share this dream *with* her, and then "*a barefoot girl in a nightgown enters*" (3). In her first speech, she describes her memory of how the dream always begins—at the end of the story with Charlie's death. She *sees* him standing in a field with his horse; she screams to him to run, but as we all know in such dreams our cries are not heard. The image of Charlie in a field with his horse triggers her memories of first meeting this Alberta farm boy as they sheltered from a thunderstorm in a barn. This vivid memory of a young man, a horse, a barn, and a violent storm with thunder and lightning marks the beginning of her description of a landscape of memory in which she will fall in love and then lose the man she hoped to marry after the war. This boy-meets-girl plot, with love thwarted by historic events beyond their control, is as old as the Alberta foothills, but it is not the plot that gives the play its power. *How*

Mary dreams and *what* she remembers within her dream transform an otherwise sentimental love story into an experience of haunting and remembrance with a much larger meaning.





Mary and Charlie are very much products of their time and place, and each has been raised on the kind of British poetry Matthew Pearson taught his boys in Owen Sound. Charlie's favourite poem is Tennyson's "Charge of the Light Brigade," which the two recite together as they wait for the storm to pass. But like so many other innocent-seeming allusions or intertexts in this play, the poem will come back—it will haunt the play, along with "The Lady of Shalott"—at completely inappropriate moments to highlight the shocking contrasts between illusion and reality, romantic poetry and the facts of a twentieth-century war. From time to time, Mary will speak to herself (and to us) about events that she remembers from before the war—meeting Charlie in the barn, or at a social gathering, or in her home when he comes to tell her that he has enlisted—and she will assume the role of another character in the story, Canadian Lieutenant Gordon Muriel Flowerdew, VC, of Lord Strathcona's Horse, the officer in command of "C" Squadron, Charlie's unit, a kind man who keeps an eye on young Charlie and about whom Charlie writes home to Mary.[9] In fact, within her dream Mary performs herself remembering and reliving the past and the ghost of the gentle lieutenant because Flowerdew died from the wounds he suffered in leading that bloody charge on 30 March 1918. His fate functions as part of the larger back-story in *Mary's Wedding*; it hovers there surfacing from time to time in Mary's dreaming imagination as an *aide mémoire* of the tragic stupidity and senseless slaughter of the Great War. Like Charlie, who writes constantly to Mary, and Talbot Papineau in *The Great War* (film), or like the uncles in *The Lost Boys*, Flowerdew wrote home and his last letter to his mother, dated 30 March 1918, will reach her after his death.

Stephen Massicotte does not include much explanation of what he intended in his play. It is up to a director, a designer, the actors, and the audience to work with the scenes they are given.[10] However, in the published text he does reproduce a photograph of Flowerdew beside his last brief letter to his British mother, and he tells us when and how the man died and where he is buried. He concludes his "Historical Note" as follows: "The first day of rehearsal for the first production of this play [February 2000 by Alberta Theatre Projects] took place on January 2nd, 2002. This was the 117th anniversary of his birthday" (n.p.). Without doubt, the story of Flowerdew resonates in profound ways for Massicotte, as does the betrayal represented—in March 1918 when the generals knew better—by calling for a nineteenth-century cavalry charge against the kaiser's modern weaponry.





This complex mixture of romance, nostalgia, and courage in the context of insane waste (of men and horses) and tragedy, symbolized by Flowerdew and the charge at Moreuil Wood, are captured with a poignancy laced, in retrospect, with anger and incomprehension, in Alfred Munnings's canvas *The Charge of Flowerdew's Squadron.*[11] How exhilarating, how noble the image is. One can almost see Charlie charging behind his commanding officer, just as Mary can:

CHARLIE: *We round the back of Moreuil Wood, out in the open. Fields of blue and green, waves like the ocean. And men in waves. Flowers stands up tall in the saddle to see. Enemy troops set in two lines, fixed bayonets, a cannon. Machine guns on the flanks. An ambush.*

MARY: *Oh, god, they're waiting for you.*

CHARLIE: *They open fire. There are hits among us. My mare's ears flick. The cannon fires and dirt spits up, a horse screams, things fly through the air. We can't turn back. Flowers rings out his sabre.*

MARY: *It's a charge, Charlie, it's charge.*

CHARLIE: *We flash all our sabres bare and our horses race to catch up with him. The long blades of grass blend together and blur with speed. I crouch low with my head beside hers. She breathes.*

MARY: *Shh ha, shh ha, shh ha.*

BOTH: *CHARGE! CHARGE! CHARGE!* (55–56)

186

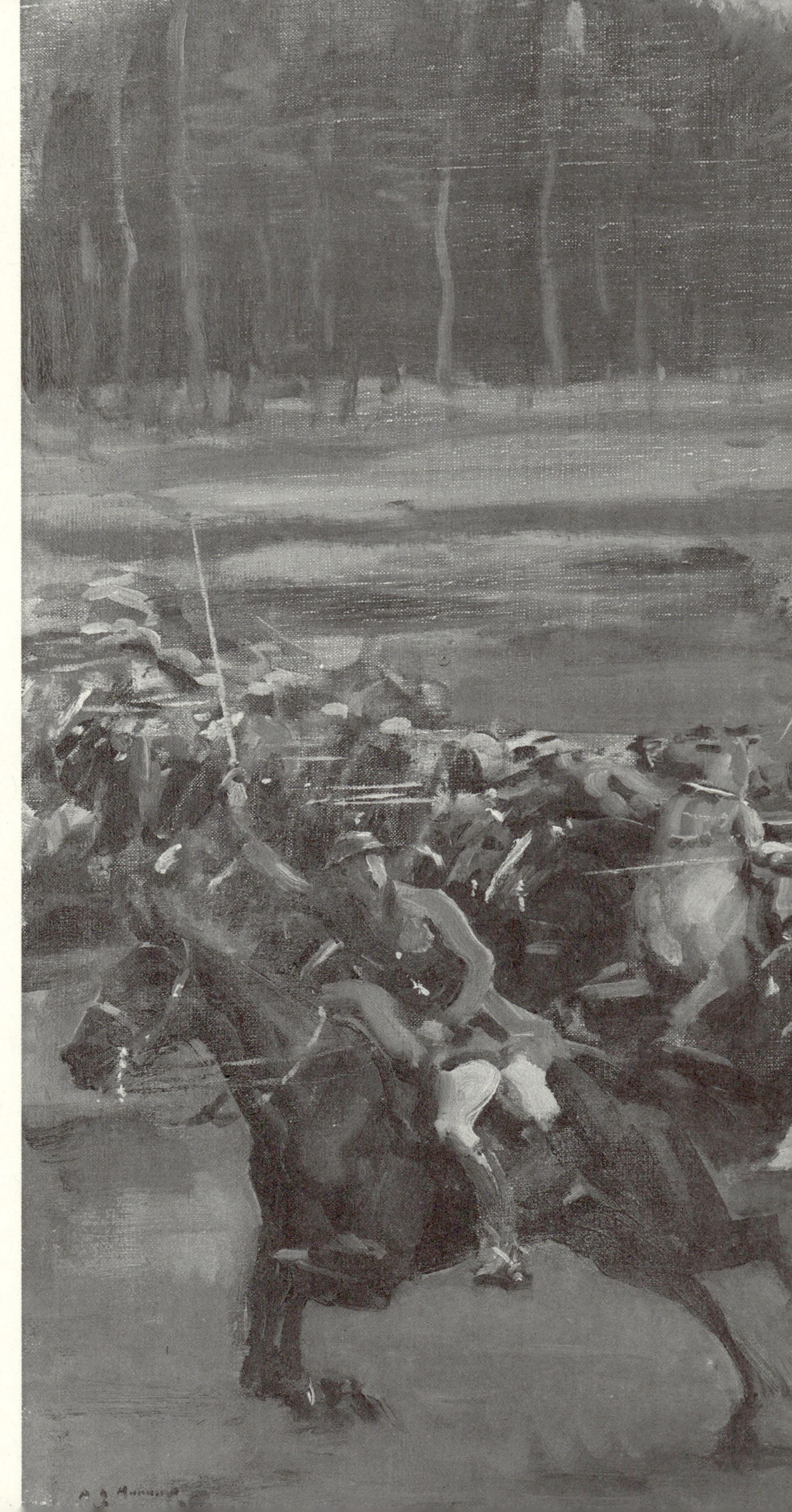

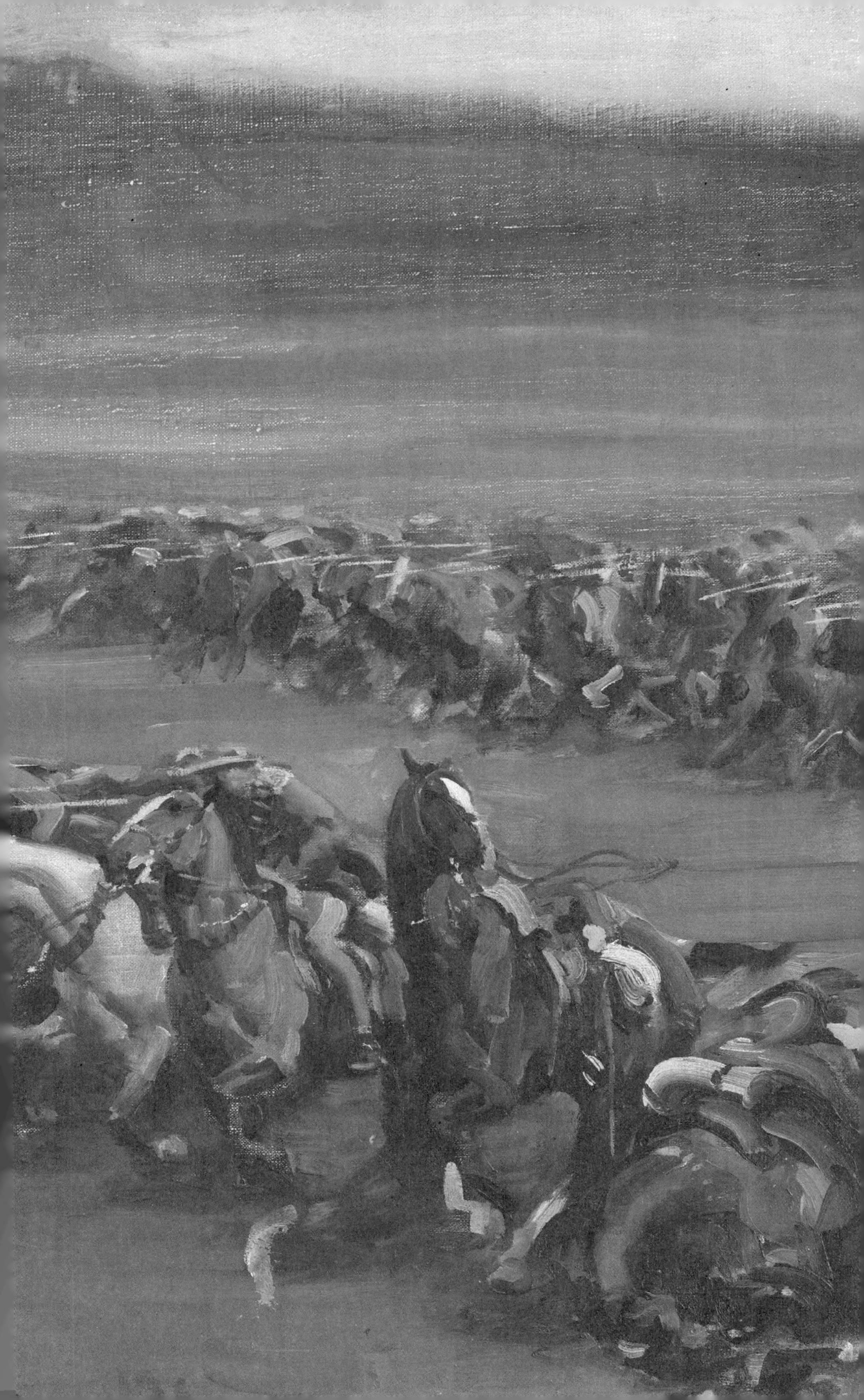

*<< Pages 186 and 187: Alfred Munnings,* Charge of Flowerdew's Squadron *(1918). o/c 51 x 61 cm. CWM #19710261-0443. Beaverbrook Collection of War Art. © Canadian War Museum.*

Except the charge is not poetry or genre painting, as Charlie will admit in Mary's dream; Flowerdew dies along with most of his men, and Charlie Edwards wants desperately to come home (59). What Mary remembers by reimagining this battle is the stunning difference between rhetoric and reality, as well as the power of words to inspire—and deceive.





In the course of her dream, Mary, Charlie, and Flowerdew will remember and relive the war from Ypres to Moreuil Wood, but what she failed to do before the war continues to haunt her and she will carry these memories forever. Mary's deepest regrets are not having stopped Charlie from going and not having met him in the barn on the night before he left. Perhaps, had she met him, they could have made love; perhaps they would simply have sworn to love and marry after he came home. Perhaps she could have stopped him. Years later, she recalls these two things as the worst things she ever did (63) and she cannot forgive herself or forget Charlie. As the dreaming draws to its end, however, Charlie's ghost comforts her. She confesses that after months immobilized by grief at his death, she did not die of heartache like the Lady of Shalott. In reality one lives and must carry on—or one dies in a cavalry charge that is anything but glorious—but in the play carrying on does not mean forgetting. When Mary tells Charlie she is unable to forget, he advises her not to forget but to "Just let go," to be as happy as she can with the man she is about to marry (63). He tells her to wake up and that she "will never have this dream again" (64). In effect, Charlie's comforting ghost tells her to live *with* his memory, which survives in the landscape around her, in the wind and the flowers. As her dream ends, "he rides off into the fields" (65).

By calling the play *Mary's Wedding*, Massicotte gestures towards the future of one young woman and to how she will live her life after the war, but she cannot wake up and marry—and the play does not close with a wedding—until she imagines a landscape of memory to live in, until she tells Charlie's (and Flowerdew's) story, until she experiences as best she can the horror and anguish of his battle front life. By rereading his letters so intensely that she can enter into them, she listens to him, pays homage, and comes to understand what happened to everyone involved. She bears witness faithfully, with empathy, and this enables her to move forward. However, I would not rest the play's significance there on a personal, individual level. In his opening speech, Charlie invites us to dream with Mary, to remember with her. The imaginative, emotional outcome of that sharing is to make us listeners to her storytelling, to position us as secondary witnesses. After all, we *are* the future beyond the end of the play. Canada, like Mary, lived on, built its future, and let go of the war past. If we have forgotten where we are, then the play reminds us. Insofar as Mary represents Canada and Charlie represents the war, the play stages a landscape of memory in which we can see, respect, and cherish the past, grant the soldiers of the Great War their due, but also face reality. War is not poetry; grief does not kill us. Truth is, finally, a firmer foundation for life than lies.





As if in response to the promise of truth and hope held out at the end of *Mary's Wedding*, *The Lost Boys* reminds us of this possibility by quoting another British poet: "If any question why we died, / Tell them because our fathers lied." These bitter, famous lines are by Rudyard Kipling, written after the death of his only son in the war, and they serve as one of two prefacing quotations chosen by Thomson for the published text; the other is from Thucydides: "There were a great number of young men who had never been in a war and were consequently far from unwilling to join in this one" (*The Lost Boys* n.p.). And there it is in a nutshell, so to speak. Our fathers present war as glorious, ennobling, a patriotic duty, even when they should—or, in fact, do—know better, and young men with no first-hand experience of combat are susceptible to persuasion, pressure, propaganda, and appeals to patriotism. By the time the truth is out, and the reality of war faced, it is too late—too late for the likes of Hugh Corbett, Robert Ross, Donald MacCormack, Will and Esau Mercer, Charlie Edwards, Talbot Papineau, and thousands more. I am not suggesting, nor are the novelists, playwrights, filmmakers, and memoirists, that propaganda and love of country were the only or major reasons that men enlisted; there were many other more pedestrian ones such as boredom, poverty, a thirst for dangerous adventure, or merely doing what others were doing so as not to miss out and feel left behind. Jonathan Vance has explored this complex question of motivation thoroughly, but Bert Taylor in *Soldier's Heart* sums up the situation especially well when he reminds young Jacob that a "soldier doesn't die for King and Country, Jacob. He doesn't want to let his friends down. That's why he dies" (72). In *The Lost Boys*, R.H. Thomson revisits the Great War through the letters of five great uncles in an effort to understand why they went, how two of them really died, how the other three carried on after the war, and what their experiences mean for him in the twenty-first century. He is obsessed by the murky past revealed so fleetingly and partially in the letters, and he is profoundly haunted by these "boys" who have been lost in the war, lost in the passage of time, and lost to a general forgetting we call cultural amnesia. But he is especially haunted by one of these uncles, Lieutenant George Stratford, who, he believes, looks very much like him.





R.H. Thomson is best known as an actor on stage, television, and in film. He has also performed as the narrator in documentaries like *Canvas of War* and *Canada Remembers*, and in November 2008 he co-created with Martin Conboy the "Vigil Project, 1914–1918," the projection of the names of Canadians killed in the war on the National War Memorial in Ottawa and on the façade of Canada House in Trafalgar Square. For Thomson this was a way of bringing the soldiers home on Remembrance Day and of reminding Canadians of who they were. All these activities, together with his family's story and the seven hundred letters preserved by his great-grandmother and great-aunt, make Thomson an ideal voyager into this past, which is at once deeply personal and broadly national. When we add to these credentials his background in science and his decidedly philosophical turn of mind, we get a play that is a *tour de force* of passion and intellect performed by one of the country's finest actors. Thomson, who not only wrote the play but created the central role of the Man who searches for the past at the 2001 premiere, is a lot like the biographer in *The Wars*, with one crucial distinction: the story of those lost uncles is also Thomson's autobiographical story of self-discovery through a landscape of memory he constructs onstage before our eyes so that we can witness events with him, grasp the meaning of remembrance, and share in the vigil he performs. He explains this theatrical gesture of staging memory very clearly in his "Playwright's Foreword," when he writes that despite the play's "minutia of war": "I never intended it to be about the war. The journeys which we undertake define us. I did not recognize the country which I was traversing until my feet were on the path. The landscape of our experience changes forever with our aging. What was possible in our youth is no longer possible now. Yet there are possibilities that exist in age which were never apparent in youth. I used to think my great uncles, being dead, would have no meaning in my life. I now know that there is nothing without meaning" (n.p.).



To design and stage *The Lost Boys* is a challenge. The play opens in partial darkness as a man wanders across a dark stage with a First World War cavalry sword that he uses to "*unearth a half-remembered vigil from his youth*" (3). The "*war landscape*" will appear on "*scrimmed screens*," along with certain faces, to create what Thomson calls a "*dreamscape*" (3). The story unfolds through the reading and performance of excerpts from each uncle's letters to his mother both onstage and in offstage voice-overs. For example, no woman appears onstage, but we hear Mrs. Stratford's recorded voice (she is Thomson's great-grandmother and the boys' mother), while a projection of her photograph appears on a screen. Throughout the play, providing the aural context for the action onstage and the performance of the letters, are frequent sounds of battle, from distant artillery to deafening mortar explosions, gas alarms, and the surrounding cries of wounded men and horses. Music is essential here, as in the other plays, and Thomson builds a memory scene on the Christmas 1914 singing of "Stille Nacht" by German and Allied soldiers (14–15).[12] The visual qualities of the play are equally complex and powerful. Sometimes we are left in near darkness; at other moments there are bright flashes or slow fades to emphasize the onstage lighting and extinguishing of candles. Moving across this multimedia landscape is the Man, whose dream we share and whose search we witness.





The motivation behind the Man's journey is a vague memory—"I've buried this memory. It was a vigil. I was 16...and I was in Belgium" (3)—from a tour he took as a teenager, when the reality of war and the significance of participating in a vigil in an actual battle chapel were simply beyond him. "I didn't get it," he tells us, although among his group he was the only one whose family had such a massive connection with the war and two of his uncles were buried in Europe (4). He finds it easier to remember home front moments such as playing with his toy soldiers when he was six, listening to stories told by his "mysterious and favourite uncle," Arthur Stratford, or staring in wonder at a big picture that hung in his grandmother's hall: "The picture fascinated me....It was called 'Le Rêve'" (6).

The picture was a reproduction of Edouard Detaille's *Le Rêve* (1888), a famous depiction of an imagined scene of French troops before the Franco-Prussian War of 1870–71 (see pages 72–73). A projection of the painting appears on a screen, and a black-and-white illustration is included in the published text, along with many other images used in the production.[13] As a teenager, Thomson imagined that the real soldiers sleeping on the ground were dreaming about marching to battle and achieving glory, but now, as an adult, he sees that those soldiers marching in the clouds are dead (8). The ones sleeping are dreaming their imminent death. Detaille's painting serves (like Flowerdew's story in *Mary's Wedding*) as an *aide mémoire* that enables the Man to draw distinctions between art and reality, truth and lies, dressed-up fictions about war and the brutal facts of trench warfare in the war. That the Man (and Thomson) is building his own *art*ifact, his elaborate theatre illusion, to represent the war and to attempt, at least, a partial unearthing of truths, cannot escape an audience or readers, any more than it does R.H. Thomson. But theatre and the tools of performance and live production are what he must—by profession—work with. Like most Canadians of his generation, he has never fought in a war. But unlike most of us, he is determined to remember and understand how the Great War shaped him, his family, and the country.

To do this, he will stage a new vigil, one in which he makes amends for *not getting it* when he was sixteen. Preparation for this vigil, and then its re-enactment, form the backbone, or through line, of the play. As the Man moves through his landscape, he enters the trenches, unearths five helmets, locates the marks of detonators (even picking one up from the battlefield [48]), searches the family trunk for his uncles' letters and the "night letter" announcing George Stratford's death (50). He finds photographs and other mementoes, and finally lights the candles sitting in each of the five, unearthed helmets (68). He is ready to *re*-perform his vigil, but some final steps are still necessary. Having found a letter written by Rick, the sixth and youngest uncle, to his mother in 1923, he realizes that this young man, who did not go to the war, visited the French countryside to search for the graves of his brothers George and Joe. George's body was never found, so he has no specific grave; Joe was originally buried at Dommartin in France, and the Man makes his pilgrimage to the site (as Thomson did): "I walked in through the cemetery gate as Rick did. I followed his footsteps to where Joe's grave had been" (66). Onstage he can now arrange "*the grave for a vigil*" and he keeps watch. The play ends as the Man rises from his vigil to join in the larger story of the universe, of history, of the cycles of life and death, by dancing: "as the men dance beneath this earth so too do the stars above my head....So I can only dance, as I might have danced through the vigil of my youth" (70).

A great deal surfaces in this play, from shell casings, helmets, and belts with the inscription *Gott mit uns*, to the uncles' letters and the half-truths they convey. As the Man asks himself, and us, "How much do you want your mother to know?" (44). But the Man has done his research on attestation papers, casualty forms, hospital admissions, and historical statistics, so he can read between the lines and fill in certain blanks. Time out in hospital could mean venereal disease; after all Canadians were known for "the highest rates" (45). Killed instantly was often a euphemism for a death too horrible to inflict on a grieving mother or family. The letters, with their trivial details and offhand tone, are deceptive; they leave "a world unspoken," and the Man grieves at the basic humanity he fears his uncles had to bury in order to carry on (46). The stories *not* in the letters kept so lovingly at home, lie hidden, but *there*, like the Iron Harvest in Flanders fields, and in an especially poignant, resonant passage, the Man reflects on this persistence of the past in both the present physical and remembered landscapes. He describes walking in Belgian fields where everything seemed verdant and peaceful, but acknowledging that even the fields are in a sense a lie: "Peace and order were what I saw but they were just a small part of the story. The larger part of the story was that everything beneath my feet was moving. Through seasons of rain and heaving frosts, bits of rifle, detonators, barbed wire, helmets, artillery shells are slowly being pushed to the surface. There are a quarter of a million tons of unexploded shells still buried in the fields of Belgium. They will continue to surface for centuries. The larger story is that the earth is not at peace. The earth is reworking its memory of the war" (46).





Perhaps the most startling truth to surface in the play, however, is R.H. Thomson's discovery that he resembles his Uncle George, the uncle who had VD, the uncle killed at Passchendaele, whose body was never found, but who was officially reported "killed in action" on 17 November 1917 (52). George is the ghost who walks beside the Man on this journey. As he reads George's attestation, he comments, "Height? 6'1" [My height.] Complexion? Fair [My skin.] Eyes? Grey Blue [My eyes.] Hair? Fair [My hair.]" (26). In other words, the Stratford genes surface in the body of this fortunate descendant who has never had to attest to his willingness to fight a war, but who owes it to the past and to those who did fight, to remember, to bear witness, to keep vigil. If this is survivor guilt, it is symbolic, and of a kind we all share.

In his "Playwright's Foreword," Thomson claimed that he did not intend the play to be about the war, but inevitably it is, at least insofar as he makes of the war and his uncles' service a monument to remembrance on personal and family, psychological, cultural, and national levels. By imagining, and literally staging, a landscape of memory, he demonstrates the value of keeping faith through the process of remembering, of finding meaning in the things that wait in that landscape to be found, and in always reaching for the great story, the larger vision. Part of that vision is Albert and his wisdom, and by Albert Thomson means Albert Einstein, who in 1915, in Berlin, was a colleague of Fritz Haber, the chemist who developed the chlorine gas that was first used at Ypres and on Canadians (23–24). In 1915 Einstein was not much older than George Stratford, but unlike Haber Einstein saw the great story of humanity, the insanity of war, and the need for peace. Thomson invokes Einstein to contradict and balance Haber, poison gas, and the brutal regression of war, and to remind himself, and us, that there *is* a larger story about humanity and peace. He ends the play and the vigil with a dance that mirrors time, the motion of the stars, and those dead soldiers who dance to the surface and often dance down again, biding their time. This dance is eerie, but gentle; it is a dance of life and peace, not a dance of death, and it fades away into an empty stage: "*Blackout*."

At first glance, *Vimy* seems to be a much more specific play than *Mary's Wedding*, *The Lost Boys*, or *Soldier's Heart*. The title is iconic; it names a time and place of mythic importance for Canadians, or at least for Canadians who know the history of the First World War and agree with historians like Pierre Berton and Jack Granatstein, or filmmakers like Brian McKenna, that Canada came of age on Vimy Ridge. However, Vern Thiessen has said that in writing this play he wanted "to crawl inside one small corner of a large offensive...to discover how small actions can define us as individuals and as a nation" (v). He was not trying to write a war play or defend or criticize war or even to pose large ethical questions about the value of sacrifice in war. Instead, he was curious about "the no-man's-land," as he puts it, "between reality and memory, truth and dream, history and mythology" (v). And so, *Vimy* is about Vimy Ridge, the battle fought there between 9 and 12 April 1917, when four divisions of Canadian troops fought together for the first time. It is also, and much more so, about five people and a sixth, who is a ghost, and how they remember their lives before and during the war up to, and just after, the battle to take the Ridge. To be sure, these people will come together as Canadians to fight, but they will also come together to remember, and the totality of their memories is what makes them Canadians, as individuals and as representatives of their country—and in *Vimy* that country includes French Canadians.

As with every text discussed thus far, this one observes the facts. Not only has Thiessen done his research, he has also provided "Historical Notes" for the published play: 97,000 Canadians assembled for the battle; 15,000 men, most of them Canadians, went over the top in the first wave early Easter Monday, 9 April; of 10,602 casualties, 3,598 men died; four Canadians were awarded the Victoria Cross; at least four of the twenty-three Canadian soldiers executed during the war by their fellows were shot for failing to take part at Vimy Ridge (vi). And yet, Thiessen reports that in a 2002 poll conducted by the *Globe and Mail* "only 36 percent of Canadians could name Vimy Ridge as the most significant Canadian victory of the Great War" (vi). Thiessen's purpose in this play is not to dwell on facts but to tell the story of Vimy as a story about Canada by opening it up beyond cold fact to reveal the lives of his characters and, through their memories of home, of battles, of guilt and suffering and love, create a composite, or collective, story about what it meant (and might still mean) to be Canadian. Vimy is just one place, a short time in history, a name in a foreign country. The *story* of Vimy is something else.

To introduce this ambitious project, Thiessen chose three prefacing quotations for the published text, and house programs should always, in my view, reproduce them. The first is a quotation, a warning really, from American historian and anti-war activist Howard Zinn that nations are never homogeneous communities, and that official histories conceal internal conflicts. The second is a poem written by Sergeant Sid Unwin from the 6th Brigade, Canadian Field Artillery, Second Division; it was written on 27 May 1917 and Unwin died a month later. In his poem, the solider writes of being wounded at Vimy Ridge and then finding himself being cared for by angels—the Canadian Bluebirds who nursed the injured men. The third quotation recalls Ted Chamberlin's 2003 study *If This Is Your Land, Where Are Your Stories? Finding Common Ground*, and I believe it is the most important of the three, so I want to repeat it here:

> *"If this is your country [sic], where are your stories?*
> *Tell me your stories..."*
> —attributed to a Blood elder, speaking to a newly arrived white man, claiming Canada as "his country."[14]

I see this quotation as the most important index to the meaning of the play because, like Chamberlin, Thiessen is telling us that we can only know ourselves as Canadian (indeed, as human beings) if we know our stories—not the facts, the dates, the numbers, the names of leaders, but our felt, embodied stories.

The nurse, Clare, puts this precisely when she insists that she "wants to hear the *story* of this place, not how tall it is....What's in its heart. What does it remember" (30). She is not speaking here about Vimy but about Mont Royal in Montreal, where she trained to become a nurse, but she is remembering this comment in the field hospital near Vimy and reliving the time of a conversation, before the war, with a man who has died at Vimy. I have another reason, however, for singling out this quotation above the others, but I must first introduce the *people* in this play. I call them people because, although they begin as characters, *dramatis personae*, they transform before our eyes into people thanks to the quality of Thiessen's writing and the impact of live performance.[15] I stress this point, recognizing that, of course, this entire phenomenon is illusion, because so much depends on this vitality—this embodied reality that is even capable of making a ghost seem as alive as the men who are still living—for the successful bearing of witness and the empathic listening to voices from the past in the play.





There are five live people in the play, one of whom will die at the end, and one ghost, who will come back from the dead because he is so deeply loved and mourned by the woman remembering him. Clare is the woman, a nurse with the Canadian Army Nurses' Corps and is named for Clare Gass, whose war diary Thiessen read.[16] She is from Shubenacadie, Nova Scotia, and at several points she longs to be home, sitting on the cliffs at Five Islands overlooking the Bay of Fundy with her lover, Laurence (Laurie) McLean, from Upper Stewiacke, Nova Scotia. Laurie is a mining engineer, a graduate of McGill, who enlisted with the Nova Scotia Highlanders, 85th Battalion, 11th Brigade, 4th Division. As an engineer he was not expected to fight, but at Vimy he was called forward, and he went; the Highlanders took the Ridge that April 1917, but Laurie was shot and killed. The four severely wounded soldiers are Mike Goodstriker, a Blood Indian from Standoff, Alberta, who is suffering from a poison gas attack; Jean-Paul (J.-P.) Metivier, a butcher's son from Montreal and an infantryman with the newly formed "Van Doos," who is suffering from shell shock; Will Saunders, a canoemaker from Renfrew, Ontario, who has shrapnel wounds to an arm and his upper body; and Sid Polson, who was a construction worker in Winnipeg, but is now blinded and suffering from head injuries and tuberculosis. I think it fair to say that not one of these ordinary guys is aggressive or bloodthirsty, not one enjoys killing "Fritz," not even Mike, who has dreamt of becoming a warrior, like his ancestors, and will receive a Distinguished Conduct Medal for risking his life to help another soldier with his gas mask (76)—the assistance that has led to his own injuries. Those who survive to come home, like J.-P., who receives his discharge in the final scene, will never be the same. To understand why they are so profoundly changed and what they must live with—and without—I need to go back to the beginning and listen to the stories they tell.

*Vimy* is a two-act play that is unified by careful repetition of key lines, songs, and images, and by memory scenes that move inexorably from pre-war to early war to post-Vimy experiences. The setting is a space in a primitive field hospital. Four beds are arranged "*as if a cross*" (3), and they will later be turned on their sides to suggest trenches and wire. Five men appear "*as if spirits*" (3). Clare speaks to Laurie recalling the beauty of sunrise at home, but the war with its casualties overtakes her memories, and in the dramatic present four of the men sink into the beds with "*their injuries taking hold*" (3). Clare then identifies each man by his injuries: "Broken bones and blindness. Gas and gangrene. Shrapnel and shredded flesh. Shell shock and shaken" (3). As the men waken, they struggle to speak and remember what happened to them, but they cannot. They begin, instead, to introduce themselves by telling each other where they are from; they eat their "*first real meal in days*" (7); they sleep, have nightmares, and are haunted by those not present. Clare thinks she *sees* Laurie (the actor playing Laurie is visible), who repeats one of the key lines in the play: "It's all stuck in here" (8). It is all stuck in here for each of these people, and "it" means the war, "stuck" means remembered forever, and "here" means in their minds, hearts, and bodies. Memories are now as much a part of them as the shrapnel lodged in their flesh—an image that recalls Albert in *Underground* or Recouvrir in *The Stone Carvers*, Donald in *Broken Ground*, or the bones and metal surfacing in Flanders' fields described by the Man in *The Lost Boys*.

As they gradually learn more about each other and regain enough strength to talk, they release fragments of their stories (the process mimics the surfacing of shards of metal through the flesh and skin or the earth). For J.-P. this means remembering his friend Claude and how he talked Claude into joining the "Van Doos"; it also involves recalling English and French antipathies at home. Clare will remember meeting Laurie in Montreal, when she was training and he was at McGill, and how they fell in love. Sid, who recognizes the voice of Will as the man he met before the war and thought might accept him and love him, remembers and relives that meeting and Will's invitation to join him on a canoe trip. However, Will is refusing to remember this past scene or to acknowledge Sid; he is in pain from his injuries, but all he can say to Clare is this: "Listen...I got this...mess. Stuck inside me. And I feel like it ain't ever gonna leave" (24). Mike's memories stretch back well before the war to when he was camping at Chief Mountain with his older brother Bert and hoping for a vision to guide his future. When the vision came, Bert said it was telling them both to "fight under a sky of fire" (29), and both men do. Bert will be invalided out of the war after being gassed three times at Ypres, and the train will bring him home dead; Mike promised to follow Bert, and does so, only to dream of his brother as he suffers from gas poisoning himself.





In the course of these memories, each person explains why he or she is in this war: J.-P. wanted something better than a life in his father's butcher shop, with his hands always smelling of blood and meat; Will's father fought in the Boer War and thinks it is now his son's turn; Mike kept his promise to Bert; Clare wanted to use her training to help the men; Laurie wanted to be close to her and to serve as an engineer, not a soldier. Sid?—well, his reasons are not given but we can guess that his rejection by Will had much to do with his decision to enlist; perhaps he wanted adventure, or perhaps he felt he was an outcast as a gay man and didn't care about his fate. With plays it is crucial for the playwright to provide enough information about the *backstory* to help actors interpret their roles and even decide how or when to move onstage. What Thiessen does, piece by piece, is bring the backstory forward to centre stage to make it visibly part of the action—indeed, to make this storying the action. This is quite a feat, but it is, more importantly, essential to the meaning of the play.

Throughout the play, and all around the hospital beds, we hear and see distant signs of war. Thiessen is careful to insist that most of the time these signs must be distant, muffled, as if penetrating the minds and memories of these people. *Vimy* is not a play about war after all, but a story about remembering. In his production notes, Thiessen stipulates that this is "not a naturalistic play," and he calls for "non-realism" in all aspects of staging and design (x). Nevertheless, realistic moments occur in the dialogue—in the men's speech, grammar, and references to home—and in the arguments that erupt amongst them. One of the more amusing arguments involves the loss of a Canadian hockey team to an American one (33–35); they are all disgusted at losing *their* Stanley Cup to Seattle, but quickly fall to bickering over who invented the game. Clare says it began in Nova Scotia; Will insists it was started in Kingston; J.-P. is sure it began in Quebec, but Mike says "It was INDIANS first played it" (34), and this sparks a more serious dispute between Mike and J.-P., with racial slurs slung back and forth until Clare shouts at them to stop. This too is part of the Canadian home story, and part of who these people are. But by the end of Act 1, they will have put their differences aside to remember a more immediate experience, one they shared: the months of preparation for fighting at Vimy Ridge.

In this extended sequence (40–55), the men remember the past in the form of a re-enactment. They perform the preparations within their shared memory-work, and we are positioned as witnesses to this process of remembering. The dialogue is rapid; Clare calls off the passing of time, the count down to Zero Day; they practise the famous Vimy Glide (43–44);[17] and they work together:

WILL: *[...] We need to work fast.*
*We need to work smart.*
*We need to work together.*
*Understand?*

*J.-P.: […] Nous devons travailler vite.*

*Nous devons travailler intelligemment.*

*Nous devons travailler ensemble.*

*Comprenez?*

*ALL: Oui. Monsieur! (44–45)*

Then it is the day before the battle and they wait and softly sing: "Here we are, here we are, here we are again" (54). Act 1 ends with "*the flash of a flare*" followed by "*Darkness*" and with everyone (and that means an audience and readers) "*Holding their memories tight*" (55).





Act 2 is shorter than the first and very tightly structured. After the high point at the end of the first act and the pause between the two acts, memories and remembered action almost stampede to the finish. We are caught up in the tide of war and swept along with these men. At the same time, the memories that push up into the present give us more of the information—more of that essential backstory—we need in order to understand what it means to say "we are here." For two of the men, and for Clare, this remembering entails speaking with a ghost (the roles of Claude and Bert may be doubled with Mike and J.-P.), reliving painful moments of human connection. For J.-P., this means bearing witness to Claude's fate. Unlike J.-P., who has accepted the reality of speaking only English with superior officers, Claude refuses to do this. As a result, he is picked on and he rebels; worse still, in this memory scene, Claude asks J.-P. why he is here when he "never wanted to join in the first place," and then he challenges J.-P.: "which language you gonna speak to the Hun…[and] when he dies in front of your eyes…? You gonna pray in English, my friend?" (58). J.-P. is haunted and tormented by these memories and by another, almost intolerable, memory because Claude refused to fight at Vimy Ridge. We are not told what happened until others' memories are relived—this dramatic process is akin to those shrapnel fragments surfacing over time, piece by piece—but when we do reach this telling, the truth is appalling.

Claude is court-martialled "for cowardice and missing battle" (69) and he is sentenced to death. One of his fellow soldiers chosen to serve on the firing squad is J.-P.:

> J.-P.: *They blindfold him, tie him to a tree. Captain pins*
> *a white circle to his heart.*
> *And I look at him. And I...*
> Hammers being cocked.
> *And I...*
> Aim being taken.
> *They always give one guy a blank, eh.*
> *So you walk away.*
> *Hoping you're not the one. Not the one who—*
> Shots—more memory than sound.
> His hands shake—his illness once again present.
> *My hands, they smell like blood, they smell like...*
> He weeps.
> *Ah, Claude...pardonne-moi.* (69)

To describe this moment in the theatre as heartbreaking is inadequate. J.-P. has now confessed, in a sense; he has inscribed this event in his landscape of memory and, like Clare, who comforts him, we listen.

By listening we acknowledge his grief and help him mourn, although we can change nothing. But we do so with that crucial quality of empathic unsettlement that does not usurp his pain or turn away from it claiming that such knowledge is too painful for us. Our listening grants J.-P. the right to tell his story and be heard. He is discharged, honourably, in the final scene, so he and we know he will be going home. However, nothing suggests that he will forget Claude or that his shell shock will be cured. Claude's death has found its place in his story, and in all likelihood J.-P. will carry the burden with him for the rest of his life. Claude, and Vimy, and the firing squad are now part of who Jean-Paul Metivier is as a veteran with the "Van Doos," as a Québécois, and as a Canadian. It is left to the audience (or the reader) to reflect on the significance of Claude's fate and J.-P.'s responsibility by accepting the role of secondary witness.

When Clare relives the last time she spoke with Laurie before the battle, and before she learns of his death, her memories, while less traumatic than J.-P.'s are nonetheless striking. The two escape their duties briefly to drink rum and swim in the ocean. They are peaceful and happy, remembering the pine trees of home. When she asks him to marry her, she sees that he is distracted, and wants to know, "How is it. Where you are" (64). He begins to answer by making light of her question; he has a shower, he says, then a brunch of steak and eggs, and then it is "time to murder some Bosch!" (64). But his tone quickly shifts to one of bitterness and horror: "ya drag a friend out of a crater. Oh, but the poor bugger's drowned in the muck see, so you best leave him there to rot" (65), and the details he describes get worse. She asks him to stop the story of where he is—either because she cannot bear to listen or cannot bear to see his bitterness and how he has been changed (this nuance can only be captured in performance)—but he replies that this is who he is now and, therefore, who she would marry: "You're not just getting me. You're getting all the...mess what's inside me now. And it ain't never going to leave, Clare. Never. It's stuck. In here. (*his heart*) For good" (65). Sid and Will share the reliving of what happened before the war on that canoe trip: Sid remembers touching Will's cheek; Will remembers refusing to respond and aborting their trip (59–61). Mike remembers Bert's return to the reserve, with the entire community waiting to welcome home their "first Indian veteran" (62), but Bert comes home in a coffin. It was right then and there, with his brother's body, that Mike vowed to join up and make his brother proud. Once these distant memories are out in the open, the play shifts into the more recent past and the men remember what they could *not* dredge up at the beginning of Act 1: the fighting at Vimy Ridge and what happened to each of them. These memories come in the form of short

*In this scene from Vern Thiessen's* Vimy*, we see Daniela Vlaskalic in the role of Clare. The play had its world premiere in October 2007 on the Maclab Stage at Edmonton's Citadel Theatre. It was directed by James MacDonald and co-designed by Bretta Gerecke and Narda McCarroll. Photograph: David Cooper.*

monologues as Mike, J.-P., Will, and Sid testify to what they saw, felt, and did. Clare listens to each man's story, but when it is Sid's turn, Laurie appears for the second-to-last time in the play and Sid *sees* this fellow Canadian—this Nova Scotia Highlander—who tries to help him, who holds him, tells him he will be all right, and then suddenly "goes cold" (73). Sid is remembering and bearing witness (with his body instead of his eyes) to Lieutenant Laurie McNeil's kindness and death.





It is finally over, all this memory-work and the *story* of Vimy, so now all these injured men can do on their beds in the field hospital is sing together "*slowly, softly*": "Here we are, here we are, here we are again" (74). When the song ends, they realize that Sid has just died. The stage instructions call for time to pass, Sid to slowly vanish (there is a gradual fade to a darkened stage), and a new day begins with the arrival of mail. Mike receives news of his medal, J.-P. learns of his discharge, but Will's mail is the postcard Sid asked J.-P. to write for him at the beginning of the play: Will is "*speechless*" (77). The final speeches are Laurie's and Clare's. His is, in fact, the oral delivery of the brief note he wrote dated "April 9, 1917. Somewhere in France," and in it he promises to tell her the story of Vimy over and over and over. "Til we're old and grey" (77). And she speaks *to him* before his ghost fades: "Us. There. Together.... Let's go home" (77). *Vimy* ends there, with Clare alone onstage holding her letter. All the men have vanished as the "*thundering of guns*" (78) grows closer and louder. On the night I attended the premiere, the audience sat absolutely still and quiet for what seemed ages but was, no doubt, only a few minutes. Even when the house lights came up, no one moved. Everyone needed to hold their memories of this play (and other memories it may have called up) close and tight. This is, in my experience, an exceedingly rare occurrence in the theatre. It seemed wrong, improper, disrespectful, to break that silence so full of emotion and reflection.

I have dealt with this play in such detail because on that night I shared in the empathic unsettlement that LaCapra asks us to search inside ourselves for when we listen to others bear witness to horror and trauma: the artistic strategies of witnessing *worked*. We all knew we had been watching a play and that the stories we listened to were fictions created by the playwright and performed by actors. We knew the actors were not dead. When they did come back onstage for their bows, the audience stood for them out of respect. But why were we so moved? What is it about a First World War story like *Vimy* that is so important in this century? This was not the Vimy of glorious laddies dying for king and country; this was neither a coming-of-age story nor a celebration of a bloody victory over the enemy. I would wager that most audiences, and especially any audience member under fifty, would have no idea that young Canadian men died in such ways, that the Canadian military executed its soldiers for failing to go over the top, that Indians fought bravely in the war and were decorated for their courage, or that some soldiers, like Claude, rebelled against killing their fellow human beings at the command of a British (or Canadian) officer. All these men were volunteers in a citizen army; they all wanted to come home. But those who made it back alive would bring their stories of Vimy with them because it was stuck inside them forever. And this, finally, is what *Vimy* achieves: the work of art restores the stories of Vimy to our national landscape of memory and makes them integral to a vision of Canadians today.

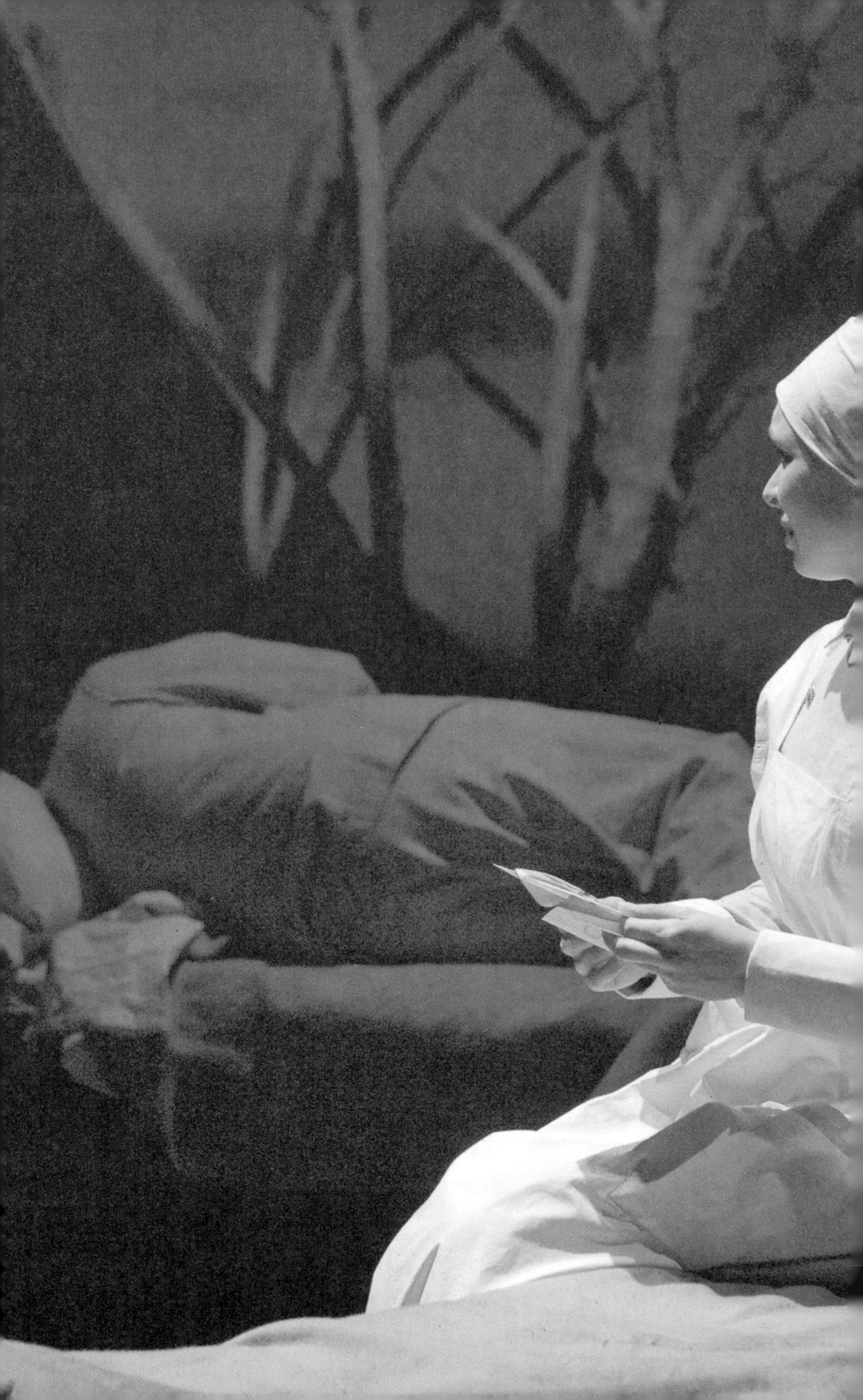

# 5
# "Away to the War and Back Again"

## Remembering Canada in Film and Auto/Biography

### DOCUMENTING CANADA AT WAR ON FILM



The plays and novels I have considered thus far all remember Canada through fictional stories, even when they draw on *real* ones as do *Broken Ground*, *Billy Bishop Goes to War*, and *The Lost Boys*. The works I turn to now are much more centrally documentary and auto/biographical.[1] They have, however, much in common with the plays and novels in that all these works reflect on the nature and meaning of the Great War for Canadians and dramatize the *connections* within the separation between home and battle fronts. None of them glorifies war or represents the soldier as a conquering hero, and most prompt us to think carefully about the root causes of war, about how peace-loving citizens get caught up in war, how survivors manage to carry on after war, and why it is important to remember. These works take the long view by emphasizing the responsibility to remember and by leaving us with more questions than answers. While they all explore the importance of the First World War for Canadian cultural history and identity, they also include the broader picture of family conflicts, guilt, and mourning, intolerance, the decimation of communities by the flu or by the loss of men, the values of forgiveness and peace, and the making of the nation. Moreover, these works are as full of ghosts as the novels and plays, and they work with the phenomenon of haunting just as powerfully as the fictional texts.





In fact, this business of ghosts haunting real and imagined landscapes of memory is paramount in the films and memoirs, despite our intensely scientific, rationalistic age, and the utilitarian, no-nonsense nature of public discourse in today's Canada. I was surprised to hear Prime Minister Stephen Harper speak of ghosts around him at Vimy during the CBC's live broadcast of the 9 April 2007 rededication of Walter Allward's monument. And Harper is not alone in evoking the past by calling up Canadian ghosts. Walter Allward saw dead soldiers at Vimy rise from their graves (or from the earth in which they lay) to help the living in a dream he had about creating his monument; and William Longstaff depicted these ghosts in his painting *The Ghosts of Vimy Ridge* (see pages 74–75). Ghosts haunt the film footage and the pages of Canadian representations of the war. "We are the dead," say the soldiers in McCrae's poem, and like the dead in Gance's *J'Accuse*, they keep returning, even as we try to shut them out.

Among the many recent documentary films about the First World War, I will discuss just two: *The Great War* and *Vimy Ridge 90*, both shown on CBC Television and released on DVD in 2007.[2] Of the three truly fine feature films I might examine—*The Wars*, *Going Home*, and *Passchendaele*—I have decided to examine only the last one.[3] A more extensive analysis of the full range of documentaries and feature films deserves a separate study by a film historian because even to a non-specialist's eye it seems clear that much has changed in the filmic representation of the war, from an earlier emphasis on boosterism and a narrow focus on fighting men to a wider perspective inclusive of the racial mix of our actual soldiers and the roles of women to a full-scale reconstruction of some of Canada's major and most costly battles—such as Passchendaele. Auto/biographies (and memoirs) have become enormously popular over the past twenty years; new examples of such works that deal with the two world wars are published every year and are widely read. To my mind, however, two stand out as especially noteworthy—Sandra Gwyn's *Tapestry of War* and David Macfarlane's *The Danger Tree*, which gives me the title for this section ("away to the war and back again," 3)—a phrase that encapsulates the movement and motivation of the films, as well as of the auto/biographical works, the novels, and the plays. In them we leave home for the war and return with a better understanding of home.





*The Great War* mini-series, written and directed by Brian McKenna, is one of those documentaries that combines archival images, historical facts, and voice-over narration with re-enactments and dramatizations of events or scenes using actors who perform scripted material often based on actual letters. But it does something more and something new within the field of Canadian war documentary. McKenna selected a group of 150 descendants of First World War veterans to participate in the film through the re-enactments of the kind of basic training, fighting, and nursing their ancestors would have experienced and by touring the cemeteries, monuments, and battlefields with fourteen of these young people. To find these descendants, train, interview, and film them was a lengthy, complex process but, as McKenna explains, "the army of [veterans'] grandchildren have come to awaken Canada's sacred places," and he believes they are "transformed" by reliving this history (liner notes, n.p.). No doubt he hopes his viewers will be transformed by watching his army and listening to contemporary Canadians bear witness to their personal and national journeys because, as much as the film captures the stories and reactions of certain individuals, it is clearly meant, in McKenna's words, as "the saga of a Northern people, who came...to fight a war not of their own making, but in doing so, created a country" (liner notes, n.p.).

Among the fourteen featured Canadians are descendants of John McCrae, Talbot Papineau, and Canon Frederick George Scott, all famous names in the history of the war. Others are chosen to represent a Mohawk soldier, an Afro-Canadian soldier, and several soldiers whose names have been forgotten by history. Talbot Papineau, a captain with the Princess Patricia's Canadian Light Infantry, is without question the hero of this film, as he is in Gwyn's *Tapestry of War*, and to play his role McKenna chose Justin Trudeau, whose youthful good looks, French- and English-Canadian ancestry, and political cachet, made him seem perfect for the part. Trudeau does a good job as Papineau, who was thought of as a future prime minister of Canada and as a man whose vision of a united and proud country inspired many. When Papineau was killed at Passchendaele (under gruesome circumstances), his mother was devastated but so were his friends at home and at the front because it seemed that Canada's hope for a bright, unified future had been dealt a serious blow. The scenes dramatizing Talbot Papineau's story, his close relationship with his mother and with a young woman to whom he also wrote regularly, and his political debate with his cousin, the Quebec nationalist Henri Bourassa, come alive through memories and his letters. These exchanges and the double love story (with mother and sweetheart) provide the thematic through line for the film: Papineau (Trudeau) is constructed as a symbol of Canadian qualities of courage, love of country, self-sacrifice, belief in freedom and democracy, and national commitment to peace.

There are, however, many other galvanizing scenes in this film as it follows Canadian troops from Ypres and Saint-Julien to the Somme and Beaumont-Hamel, Vimy, Passchendaele, and Courcelette. Possibly the most moving of these for the descendants and the viewer is the visit to Beaumont-Hamel. As the group of fourteen witnesses (each of them both primary—experiencing the present landscape—and secondary—remembering and retelling the earlier stories of the place) stands on the site, which is still scarred from the battle fought there almost 100 years ago; now grass-covered but unmistakable are the trenches, craters, and mounds of earth thrown up by shelling. Then a young woman, who was born in Newfoundland, tells the story of 1 July 1916 and sings the "Ode to Newfoundland" through her tears. None of her companions is dry-eyed as they listen, and I imagine many viewers, whether Newfoundlanders or not, are equally moved. This is a key moment in the film, not only because it retells a tragic story but also because the storyteller has an audience of listeners within the film who register the experience of being there with her and bearing witness as she speaks and sings. Beyond the obvious appeal to sentiment, this scene demonstrates the power of bearing witness, even when that witnessing can only take place at a remove of ninety years by people too young to have known any of the men who died. As film viewers, we are swept up in this remembering and we share in what is not presented as a performance but as a live impromptu act of mourning.



*The Great War* is unquestionably aimed at encouraging today's Canadians to remember the First World War and to trace their roots back to the veterans, nurses, and families at home who lost so much in the war. It is also emphatically about national pride and it rehearses and re-presents the idea that the Canadian nation was born as a result of the war—on Vimy Ridge most dramatically, but in other battles as well. With its combination of archival documents, narration, actors performing roles, re-enactments, and intimate camera work with the fourteen descendants who tell their own stories, this film creates a story of origins for Canada, a mythic narrative of birth and baptism in and through war. Although it touches on a few controversial or shocking details—that Canadian soldiers were insubordinate, that 325 were executed for what was called desertion, and that they used gas (after experiencing it themselves at Ypres) as much as, or more than, other armies, and that thousands died horrible deaths (like Papineau or Canon Scott's son Harry), and although it notes in passing that some sensitive First World War records were destroyed and others are still secret (what records? why secret?), the overall tone of the film is patriotic and uplifting. For all its gruesome realities, I would describe it as trying to be a *feel-good movie*. Sir Robert Borden is portrayed as a bold, proud statesman when he accuses the British of attacking Canadians at Passchendaele (they did, in the sort of tragic blunder we now call "friendly fire") and threatening the British prime minister, Lloyd George, that he would recall *his Canadian troops*. Where were our current leaders, we are nudged to ask, when Americans mistakenly killed Canadian troops in Afghanistan? The closing scene is not given to Talbot Papineau's grieving mother who, we are told, never recovered from his death, but to a young, handsome Talbot in spotless uniform returned from the dead to embrace his sweetheart in the green fields of home. This is a ghost with a difference! Justin Trudeau is very much alive and this romantic scene can only mean that, in him, Canada's hope for the future is reborn.



If an extended analysis of the film has been made to date, I am not aware of it. Therefore, in assessing the film I must rely on my personal reactions to it, on my discussions with students, and on a short, thoughtful article by Joel Ralph, a great-nephew of a soldier who fought at Vimy Ridge and one of the young men chosen to join McKenna's army. As Ralph so wisely points out, these descendants were not fighting a real battle, were not risking death in their re-enactment, and were not killing real German soldiers. Ralph was keenly aware of the fact that Canadian soldiers had become efficient killers by the time of Vimy and that they delivered as much violence as they received; however, the film does not explore that reality (41). Like Ralph, the film left me with very mixed feelings. Yes, the war was a major event for Canada and, yes, Canadians were successful at Vimy, where the British and French had failed. Nevertheless, in becoming secondary witnesses to the descendants' stories, even ones as terrible as Beaumont-Hamel or as horrifying as the discovery of Papineau's torn and shattered corpse identified by his puttees, I am invited to legitimate the making of a myth that, as these kinds of narratives always do, leaves huge blanks in the landscape of memory.

While I applaud the ambitious scope of *The Great War* and respect the enabling of fourteen young Canadians to bear witness to a distant past and reconnect with it as part of their own story, I remain unconvinced that one battle can or should be given such status and become the time and place that our nation came of age or, indeed, that Canada's myth of origins lies in the blood and loss—even the courage—of soldiers in a war. A more convincing claim to such a myth can be made by Russia, France, Poland, Great Britain, and the United States, countries whose populations and physical landscapes have been ravaged by civil wars, catastrophic foreign invasions, and massacres. In the last analysis, it is films like this that produce the myths by repeating, reproducing, and performing a story—if this is your *country*, where are your stories?—and it is the peacetime creations of artists working on the home front that transform the stories into a national narrative. Happily, this film with its strengths and weaknesses, innovations and clichés, integrity and sentimentality, is just one of many texts that show Canadians who they are today by remembering the past because the making of a nation like Canada, which has never had a world war fought on its soil, occurs over time on a comparatively peaceful home front by the people who *work* to build and imagine it.





*Vimy Ridge 90* returns us to France on the occasion of the ninetieth anniversary of the battle. It is the commemorative DVD prepared by the CBC from the April 2007 rededication of Walter Allward's monument. Peter Mansbridge is the host because he covered the live broadcast of the actual ceremony, but other well-known CBC reporters like Dan Bjornson, David Common, Ioanna Roumeliotis, and Adrienne Arsenault are featured narrator-interviewers for specific parts of the final film. According to Mansbridge, the DVD format is intended as "a lasting keepsake" for Canadians because what happened on Easter weekend in April 1917 and is being remembered in April 2007 is "a story every Canadian should know."[4] All the familiar touchstones are revisited in interviews with historians like Ted Barris and schoolteachers like Dave Robinson, who led a group of high school students in their research on the battle: we are told once more that the Great War was a young man's fight in a young country, that Canada came of age at Vimy, that the four Canadian divisions fought together for the first time here using new techniques developed by Canadians, that 3,598 Canadian soldiers died in the fighting, and that 11,000 names for men whose bodies were never found across the battlefields of France, are inscribed on the monument. A constant presence in the film, and the reason for its making, is the Vimy Monument, which was painstakingly restored at a cost of $20 million over three years of work by architects, engineers, and carvers. According to Julian Smith and Jacqueline Hucker, the monument is Walter Allward's masterpiece, a structure of elegance and majesty, and a "cathedral to Canadian valour" (quoted from the film; see also Hucker, "Vimy" 43). It represents a sacred place of sadness and remembrance for Hucker, who speaks of the "vibrations" from the dead she felt while there. And while the cameras pan the landscape and the whole structure or zoom in for close-ups of the pylons and the sculptures—especially of "Mother Canada"—Mansbridge reiterates the story of Allward having a dream in which the dead soldiers rose from the shattered landscape to help the living soldiers in their fight. The stage is set, then, for the main purpose of the film, the rededication ceremony, by calling up the dead.





The actual ceremony was exceptionally grand for Canada and, on the whole, tasteful and moving. The usual players appeared: the Canadian prime minister, the French prime minister, and Queen Elizabeth, in that order because the monument stands on land ceded in perpetuity to Canada by France; it is a piece of Canada on foreign soil. For the great majority of Canadians who will never visit this distant part of their country, twenty-first-century technology brings television viewers (and now DVD owners) right into the ceremony. The officer presiding over the official ceremony begins by reminding assembled veterans and guests that the ghosts of 3,600 Canadians are present on this day, and Harper calls upon these ghosts, our ancestors, to make all Canadians feel at home in this foreign place. Inevitably, he too repeats Allward's dream; he recalls the "enormity" of what Canadians achieved here ninety years ago; and he goes further than simply calling Vimy the site where a nation was born by describing the battle as "our creation story." He closes his remarks, visibly near tears, by pronouncing that the dead speak to us today of love of family, freedom, and country. The prayers that follow are in French, English, and three First Nations languages, and a young Métis fiddler plays the "Warrior's Lament" as she stands silhouetted beside the towering figure of a mourning "Mother Canada." This is, possibly, the simplest, most genuine, and therefore most sincerely moving scene in the drama. It is rivalled only by a girls' choir, led by Susan Aglukark, singing "Dreaming of Home," the song made famous by the First World War film *Joyeux Noël*. There are other rituals to perform—making pledges, laying wreaths, a royal inspection of the troops, a military band plays, and a flyby is executed by four French jets—but throughout the ceremony, as represented in this film, it is Allward's monument that dominates the scene. It is more than a backdrop or a stage set because it is lovingly captured by the cameramen from every angle. The film ends with Peter Mansbridge and military historian Jack Granatstein reflecting on the war and its significance for Canadian history and on the importance of making students aware of their country's past through events like this ceremony, school projects, and Historica Canada's "Memory Project" website.[5] In one of the few more somber moments in their conversation, Granatstein reminds viewers that in 1917 the day was bitterly cold with snow (unlike the warm blue skies of 2007) and that Canadian troops used gas a lot after Ypres "because it worked."

No doubt each person watching or rewatching this story could have criticized this or that aspect of things: why was $20 million spent to clean a structure in France few Canadians even know about? Why was the Red Ensign chosen to fly beside the Canadian and French flags? Why did French President Jacques Chirac not attend instead of, or with, their prime minister, Dominique de Villepin? What about the Germans, French, and others who died here ninety years ago? What did today's

Quebec sovereigntists think of this ceremony—if they watched it? And so on. No doubt skeptics dismissed the rhetoric about a creation story and the making of a nation or the presence of ghosts, and Canadians opposed to war and glorification of the military must have deplored the emphasis on military protocol, the bearing of arms, the salutes. Whatever our individual views, however, millions of Canadians bore witness to a grand, public ceremony in honour of the past and, most interestingly, to a work of art commemorating peace and freedom and hope at the site of a bloody battle. By watching and listening, we became secondary witnesses, and I imagine that many responded to the solemnity of the occasion with emotion, perhaps even empathic unsettlement.





In retrospect, I am more critical than I was during the broadcast because now I can reflect on what the event forgot rather than on what it remembered. I am especially uncomfortable with its pandering to a political agenda and a type of patriotic nationalism that is dubious, even dangerous. The scenes constructed by the CBC for the DVD (and to an extent in the live broadcast) tell a simple and powerful story with a populist appeal that a difficult novel like *Three Day Road* or a complex play like *Vimy* do not have. For this reason, *Vimy Ridge 90* needs to be discussed and placed in the broader, richer, more troubling landscape of memory that these other works provide.

After Vimy Ridge, Passchendaele is seen as one of the most important, albeit deadly, pyrrhic victories for the Canadian Corps. The week-long struggle to reclaim the shattered Ridge and the Belgian town took place between 26 October and 6 November 1917 in a sea of mud, rotting corpses, heavy rains, and cold; it was an indescribable nightmare causing 15,654 casualties with 5,000 men killed, one of whom was Talbot Papineau. It was also an indecisive and ambivalent victory because the town was scarcely worth fighting for and the Germans quickly retook it.[6] When Gross chose this battle for his film he did so with these aspects of the battle in mind, but his inspiration for the story came from his own grandfather's memories of the war and the fact that he felt haunted all his life by a German he had killed.

The auto/biographical motivation enhanced the subject for Gross and brought the war home in much the same way as it did for Thomson in *The Lost Boys* and for McKenna and his army of descendants in *The Great War*. *Passchendaele* premiered at the 2008 Toronto International Film Festival amid a flurry of media attention and high expectations; it was released for general viewing on Remembrance Day that year. But the film was disappointing in a number of ways, even though it won awards and its ratings gradually increased over the following year. It is not the first Canadian feature film to explore the First World War—*The Wars* appeared in 1982 and *Going Home* in 1986—but it is at least as good as these two and, like them, it embraces key ethical issues. And this is what distinguishes Canadian feature film treatments of war from the more familiar and popular American genre of combat movies: the enemy is not faceless or demonized, and the representation of staggering ethical contradictions and dilemmas faced on both home and battle fronts takes precedence over simple win-lose scenes of combat.





Paul Gross wrote and starred in the film as Sergeant Michael Dunne—his grandfather's actual name—and the film opens smack in the middle of a vicious, deafening battle, captured with close-up camera work, in the rubble-strewn streets of a town from which the Canadians are trying to drive the Germans. It *feels* almost as if Gross is quoting from *Saving Private Ryan*. We are given no indication of where we are, but move rapidly to a scene in which a nervous German soldier shoots a young Canadian who is trying to surrender and then to a companion scene in which a young German is trying to surrender to Sgt. Dunne. The action pauses as the camera cuts back and forth between their two faces; the German tentatively, hopefully reaches out saying "Kamerade," but Dunne drives his bayonet into the man's forehead. This appalling murder—it is hard to know what else to call this, even in a battle—this take-no-prisoners act of revenge, will haunt Dunne for the rest of the film, just as a similar act haunted Gross's grandfather all his life. The young German's death becomes the *memento mori* and underlying force behind everything that propels the plot from that point on. It is the act, the crime even, for which Dunne feels he must atone. The need to tell his story, coupled with his guilt, obliges him to make amends in every way he can and leads inexorably to the climax of the story and to Dunne's self-sacrifice and death. After the opening minutes of horror (shot mostly in black and white or with muted sepia colour, as are all the battle scenes), we cut abruptly to the sunny, cheerful streets of 1917 Calgary, where life goes on almost as usual albeit in the context of anti-German propaganda, a recruitment drive, and the anxious waiting for news from Europe.





Dunne has been sent home because of his physical injuries, but he is held there because he is suffering from neurasthenia—shell shock—a condition viewed as cowardice by many in the military and by some civilians. He will fall in love with Sarah Mann, the nurse who cares for him, and this love will eventually pull him back into the war and allow Gross to examine the critical issue of prejudice at home because Sarah and her younger brother David, who were born in Canada, are of German descent. To make matters worse, their father Martin Mann returned to Germany in 1915 to fight for the fatherland and he died at Vimy Ridge. As she will tell Michael, their father chose Germany over Canada, fighting for the kaiser over serving with Canadians. This choice, she feels, was one she forced on him, although how she did so is not clear. What is clear is that this is what haunts her, causes her private grief and prompts her to use morphine to dull her pain; she feels responsible for her father's death and is desperate to keep her asthmatic brother out of the war. As recruitment pressures build up and propaganda intensifies, David (an obnoxious teenager who has fallen for the daughter of the local doctor), pesters the authorities to accept him. But Sgt. Dunne blocks his efforts because he loves Sarah and because he knows that the war has nothing to do with courage or patriotism and everything to do with blind violence that obliterates ethical decision making and idealism. When the Mann house is attacked by locals and defaced with graffiti calling them Huns, the time has come for Sarah and David to leave the only home they have ever known. That they are Canadians, that their mother is buried in Canada, and that Sarah's nursing work with returned soldiers is her way of supporting the war effort, mean nothing to the inflamed citizens of Calgary. She is fired from her job and David gets a clean bill of health from the doctor, who wants the boy away from his daughter; he is accepted into the Canadian army, where he believes he can make up for his father's mistake.

This is the plot line that accounts for the strength of *Passchendaele*. The home front scenes provide the ethical lens through which we witness what happens during the battles. The revelations that German Canadians were ostracized and persecuted during the war (and in some cases interned), that public meetings were held at which young men were shamed into signing up, and that the truth about what was happening in Europe was hidden from the public in favour of laundered reports of valour and success, should come as no surprise. Military historians know these things, of course, but most Canadians do not, and the film stresses these revelations through highly charged scenes that oblige us to bear witness to unsavoury aspects of the past. Moreover, moviegoers expecting a combat flick—and the opening sequence suggests that is what we are in for—will be caught off guard, forced to listen to some truths they might prefer to ignore.

Where the film becomes problematic is in the closing scenes of the battle, and diffficulty has nothing to do with historical accuracy and much to do with ethical complexity and art—storyline, imagery, camera work, soundtrack, and acting. Gross has scripted a scene in which Michael Dunne stumbles across No Man's Land to rescue David Mann, whose body the Germans have strung up on what looks like a cross. The scene is long and melodramatic. As Dunne weaves through the knee-deep mud and between water-filled craters towards the German line, he is wounded, but he staggers to his feet and carries on to reach the man on the cross some hundred yards ahead. Amazed, but sympathetic, a German officer halts the shooting and allows Dunne to hoist David, still tied to his makeshift cross, onto his back and start his return to the Canadian trenches. The mud and detritus are indescribable, the weight of the burden he drags is palpable, Dunne is seriously wounded: he collapses and the camera moves in for a close-up on his haggard, blood- and dirt-streaked face. Above him fly birds of prey, kestrels, returning to the scene of carnage because of the lull in the fighting. He sees these birds of ill omen above him and staggers to his feet. He will make it to his line, where stretcher-bearers are waiting to carry him and David to the field hospital. Sarah is working there—a coincidence explained (if unconvincingly) by her firing in Calgary and her desire to be close to Michael and to watch over David—and Michael will die, almost, if not exactly, in her arms.





To be fair, the film does not end there. The closing sequence returns us home to the foothills and grasslands of Alberta. The war is over and the day fills with glorious sunshine as a small group of people gathers in front of a homemade wooden cross bearing Michael Dunne's name and dates. They are Sarah, David in a wheelchair, David's sweetheart, and two of Michael's buddies, one of whom is an Indian veteran who fought with him at Passchendaele. The moment seems surreal, serene in its peaceful beauty and sharp contrast with the preceding scenes of slaughter. It is also, importantly, symbolic of a home front landscape of memory because soldiers' bodies were not allowed to be returned to Canada; their actual graves are in Europe. Presumably, David will marry the doctor's daughter, so the doctor has failed in his attempt to kill off the upstart Canadian Hun; very likely Sarah will carry on alone cherishing her memories of Michael's valiant self-sacrifice. And Michael will no longer be haunted by the young German he killed; he has atoned in a Christian ritual akin to that of a pilgrim following the stations of the cross. While this may be true to the Christian sentiment that dominated Canadian thinking of the period, it seems exaggerated and overwrought when reduced to a scene in a film. Moreover, this business of making amends by dragging a man on a cross through No Man's Land has other, highly ambiguous, associations that are brought to our attention more than once.

During the war a rumour surfaced that Germans had nailed a Canadian soldier to a barn door and left him there to die.[7] At two points in the film, this rumour is raised, but Dunne dismisses it as propaganda; he witnessed no such atrocity, and those who were not fighting have no right to spread such gossip. What then are viewers to make of this scene in No Man's Land? There is Private David Mann strung up on bits of duckboard and trench ladder that resemble a cross. Why did the Germans do this and then display him to the Canadians? Why, finally, is Dunne allowed to rescue him and why does he not free David rather than haul the whole contraption back through the mud? Does this complex scene present what (viewers are asked to believe) really happened, as opposed to the brutal anti-German propaganda?





The simple answer is that I do not know. In the brief scene in which a crazed David charges into a German trench, he is immediately captured and challenged about who he is—"Sind Sie Deutsch?"—to which he stammers what sounds like "Yes, *nein*!" This is the young man's moment of truth. He is and is not German, so perhaps the Germans see him as a traitor and make an example of him. Are we to believe, then, that the appalling story of a crucified Canadian is true after all? Or is this the symbolic fate of all immigrants to Canada who are not accepted as loyal citizens, unless they are of British origins, or is David a symbol of that psychic split that must be overcome to make a person Canadian? Margaret Atwood once said of Susanna Moodie that "we are all immigrants to this country" and must choose to become Canadian (Atwood, "Afterword" 62), so perhaps this is also Paul Gross's point. But where does this speculation leave Michael Dunne? Despite the Christian trappings of martyrdom that hang over that rescue scene, I think it is safe to conclude that Dunne is not a conquering hero who can live comfortably with his guilt and violence. He is, instead, a much more human—dare I say, Canadian?—hero who has a conscience and suffers from the trauma of killing one helpless young man rather than from the general conditions of a filthy war. The roots of his shell shock resemble those of Esau Mercer's in *Soldier's Heart* and they recall Robert Ross's remorse over shooting the German who was holding binoculars instead of his rifle at the crater's edge. Had Dunne lived, this ghost would have remained beside him forever. Once he is dead, that haunting is transferred to us, along with the warning about blind ethnic-based prejudice and the hysteria of wartime propaganda.

That *Passchendaele* is a fable about the causes of war in violence, prejudice, and lies, and about the way to peace lying in acceptance of differences, sacrifice, and love, is one possible way of characterizing the film. But it could also be described more simply as a historical film about Canadians during the First World War that tries to uncover unpleasant truths and forgotten activities on both home and battle fronts. In its juxtaposition of landscapes on both fronts, the film creates that much larger landscape of memory that I am tracing in this book. Visually, what remains with me after watching the film is precisely this landscape imagery. The chiaroscuro effects, with the black, grey, and white landscapes of No Man's Land, shift and fade into the warm sun-filled colours of the Canadian prairies and foothills, the winding rivers and distant mountains of home. Through an aerial view of No Man's Land near the end of the film to the long distance, wide-angle panorama shots of home at the very end, we are positioned to see and remember just how intimately connected these landscapes were—and are. The closing frames move from a close-up of Dunne's wooden cross to a field of crosses and then to a shot in which the official white stellae of a First World War cemetery fill the screen to reinforce this connection. Michael Dunne is remembered at home, his loss marked by this simple cross, but he died at Passchendaele and he is buried in a war graves cemetery with other Canadian soldiers whose bodies could be identified and buried.



## PERSONAL REFLECTIONS

### The Danger Tree *and* Tapestry of War

Auto/biographical writing about the Great War comes in various forms, from full-scale biographies like Dianne Graves's *A Crown of Life:*

*The World of John McCrae* or Alexander John Watson's *Marginal Man: The Dark Vision of Harold Innis*, in which Innis's experiences in the war are seen to have shaped his life and his vision of Canada, to editions of letters, personalized histories of events, and auto/biographies. One of the more interesting collections of war letters published recently is *The Wartime Letters of Leslie and Cecil Frost, 1915–1919*, edited by R.B. Fleming. Both men survived the war, but Leslie Frost became the long-standing premier of Ontario, and we learn much about the period and how the war shaped a man who played a prominent role in public life, from these letters and from Fleming's introductory essay. Laura MacDonald's *Curse of the Narrows: The Halifax Explosion, 1917* is a popular history of this catastrophe based on eyewitness accounts gathered by a woman who is a former Haligonian with roots in Halifax history, and her intimate look into the explosion makes this home front event come to life as a formal history cannot; indeed, her approach makes a fine companion piece for Hugh McLennan's novel *Barometer Rising*.





Michael Ignatieff's *True Patriot Love: Four Generations in Search of Canada* can be read in this context of war auto/biography because of the emphasis he places on the impact of the Great War on his maternal grandfather, William Grant, who in turn influenced his family and others he met during his postwar life (especially as a Master at Upper Canada College). As Ignatieff puts it, "the memory of war influenced everything he did" (104). Then there are the personal journeys undertaken by Canadians keen to understand what caused or what happened during the war, to bear witness to what they find, and to explore how that distant war and their quest affects how they see themselves. Two recent examples of this kind of auto/biographical writing are Stephen O'Shea's *Back to the Front: An Accidental Historian Walks the Trenches of World War I* and Tony Fabijančić's *Bosnia: In the Footsteps of Gavrilo Princip*.

In both books a Canadian man sets out to retrace the past in an attempt to find meaning, if not quite to make sense, of what happened. For the former, the search unfolds along a line that stretched across

Europe for hundreds of miles; for the latter it is a search for the man who fired the opening shots of the war. O'Shea walked the Western Front from town to town, cemetery to cemetery, and monument to monument in what he finally decides was war's "macho romance" with "futility" (6), but he provides little insight into the war beyond that conclusion, and he believes that the best way to remember the war is to walk through the landscape once shattered by fighting and to search for signs of this past in that landscape. Fabijančić also walks (and drives with his father), through a landscape of memory, but his journey is always linked to his own ethnic identity (Croatian) and his search for the solution to cycles of hatred and violence. His perspective, as a Canadian, is what provides the balance and sense of hope in the story. Like the other types of auto/biography, this personal journey into the root causes of the war underscores the extent to which, whether due to Canadian soldiers who fought and returned or through waves of postwar immigration from Europe, the home front would be shaped by a war fought far away. This is a phenomenon that recurs with the Second World War and with more recent wars, as I demonstrate in following chapters. However, I will not linger over these examples of First World War auto/biography because there are two texts that I have chosen for closer study. *The Danger Tree* and *Tapestry of War* are exceptionally well written and, within the genre of life writing, innovative. In both works, their authors provide a wealth of information and insight into how the war influenced Canada and how it marked a watershed in our history. In both we find a mixture of biography and autobiography, a fabric of others' stories interwoven with the author's story, and this composite strategy contributes much to the story of the nation.





David Macfarlane sums up the impact of the war succinctly when he writes that "the greatest change the war brought was one that no one could measure. It was an absence" (189). *The Danger Tree: Memory, War, and the Search for a Family's Past* is his attempt to address that absence by imagining a landscape of memory in which his

Newfoundland ancestors, the Goodyears, come back to life and he can find himself, his *place*, beside them in that landscape. Macfarlane is haunted by this "constant and disastrous absence" and by the *presence* of the old black-and-white photographs of the dead soldiers that hang on the family's walls: "They are the missing pieces" (191). But *The Danger Tree* does not move in a straight line to identify those ghosts or to explain (for readers who do not know) the significance of the title. Instead, he creates narrative loops that circle these absences. He includes reproductions of the old photographs but delays discussion of them so that a reader frequently turns back to contemplate the image and ponder its meaning. He moves in close to a name, a date, an event that links his family to the war, then backs away and turns his attention to something else—a childhood memory, a detail from Newfoundland's long history, a family dinner in Hamilton, where he grew up. Then he is pulled back by desire and memory to Newfoundland, to the generations of Goodyears and to their home in Grand Falls. He longs to know who they were, especially who those dead men were, and what their stories have to tell him about himself, about his family, about Newfoundland, and about Canada.





David Macfarlane is not a Newfoundlander; he is a Canadian born after the Second World War and after Newfoundland joined Canada in 1949. He was raised in southern Ontario and only saw his mother's home on summer holidays and his maternal grandparents on their rare visits to Hamilton. The Newfoundland part of his identity is something of a mystery to him, something of a ghost story, and he feels compelled to uncover the story of his (and Canada's) roots before the stories, traces, and memories vanish with time. His narrative begins and ends with a return to Grand Falls (one of many he has made) on 1 July—Memorial Day in Newfoundland, Canada Day for the rest of the country—and to Gander to visit his elderly grandmother who now lives in an old-age hospital and has lost her memory. She is the last remaining member of her generation of Goodyears, and he sees her as lost in a barren landscape, where she has "passed the last gnarled landmark on her horizon and found herself in No Man's Land" (295). By this point, near the end of the remembering, we recognize that gnarled landmark as the Danger Tree at Beaumont-Hamel, and we grasp the full significance of No Man's Land for the Goodyears and for Newfoundland.

At the centre of *The Danger Tree*, hovering over the family history and functioning rather like a vortex or black hole pulling everything toward it, is the war: Newfoundland was a British colony, proud of its unique identity and its relationship with the mother country. It coined its own money, had its own stamps; raised its own regiment, the Royal Newfoundland Regiment, at its own considerable cost; no Newfoundlander allowed anyone to call him or her a Canadian or a Brit, for that matter. Five of Macfarlane's six great uncles went to war, three died, and by the end of the war eight hundred Newfoundlanders were gone. The island country was left with crippling debt, its social and economic fabric in tatters, and a population decimated by the war. Macfarlane's self-appointed task is to push back against the silence of forgetting, the erasure of memory, by reconstructing their lives in Newfoundland as best he can, using the photographs, letters, and other documents he can find, so he can bear secondary witness to their absence and to the meaning of their loss. The achievement of his auto/biography is the restoration of the dead soldiers, their family, and their sister (Macfarlane's much-loved great-aunt) Kate to a personal and national story. Before he reaches the Canadian era, however, he journeys into the past and comes forward as far as 1 July 1916. The youngest Goodyear son, Raymond, died at Beaumont-Hamel, and this disaster sits like an ugly open wound in the cultural memory of Newfoundland. As a small battle in the massive Somme offensive, Beaumont-Hamel is easy to forget, but Macfarlane insists that it must never be ignored. His description of this battle is among the simplest, most direct, and eloquent I have read: "At Beaumont-Hamel, the Newfoundlanders had hoisted themselves over the lip of a trench called St. John's Road and had walked into a cross-fire of machine guns....Casualties were horrendous. Advances and losses were measured in yards," and at home "the newspapers spoke of valour and determination and gallantry in the face of difficult odds" (146). The St. John's trench was named for that city at home from which the "Blue Puttees" (143) sailed to the war. Private Ray Goodyear was only seventeen.

Macfarlane's assertion that twentieth-century Canada took shape around a "constant and disastrous absence," haunted by the ghosts of the dead, is further borne out by the loss of two more Goodyear men. On the night of 9 October 1917, near Langemarck, Lieutenant Stan Goodyear, the most handsome (his picture appears on page 182, forty pages before we learn his fate) and seemingly lucky of the brothers, is killed by German shelling as he rides with his party along a mud-clogged road in torrential rain towards the Newfoundlanders' line. Because he has no facts beyond these general ones of time and place, Macfarlane must imagine the scene and create a story for this man. To do this, he describes the soldiers, the road, their slow progress, the distant thud of shells, and "Stan riding at the front of the column" (235): "He heard the rising screech. Christ, he thought. He turned to his left, behind a low rise of mud and just beyond the dead stub of a tree. His shoulders were square and his expression seemed untroubled. He was thinking Christ, the bugger's coming in close. He was thinking about leave and shepherd's pie and a music hall near Piccadilly" (235). Stan Goodyear "was thinking Jesus Christ..." and Macfarlane ends there, with an ellipsis that speaks of an absence transformed by memory and imagination (and fine prose) into a flash of presence.

But one more ghost remains: Captain Hedley Goodyear, a graduate student at the University of Toronto who enlisted with the *Canadian* army and who, by the summer of 1918, was with the Canadian 102nd Battalion near Amiens. Hadley Goodyear is to *The Danger Tree* what Talbot Papineau is to *Tapestry of War* (and to McKenna's *The Great War*); he is the hero of the story, the man whose vision of the future was based on Newfoundland joining Confederation to help build a greater, unified country. He will be killed by a German sniper, but not until

Macfarlane gives us an almost forensic description of the mechanism of a German Mauser 98, known as "the Sniper," and the consequences of a bullet fired from this rifle when that bullet strikes a soldier's head (268–69): in short, a human skull is blown to pieces. But wait. Macfarlane is still not ready to tell us Hedley's story. Next we learn about the significance of the number three and the army's superstition that if three soldiers light a cigarette from one match, the third becomes a perfect target for a sniper: "Military threes were prophetic, and every soldier knew it. They packed up their troubles in their old kit bags and smiled, smiled, smiled" (271).





Macfarlane wonders if Hedley thought about the power of the number three and whether he noted the "ominous numerology" of the serial number on his .455-calibre Webley Mark VI revolver: 332137 (273). He cannot know, of course, but he can attest that for his great-grandparents the number three summed up who they were because their "three dead sons paraded past" them "on through the century" (272). Their deaths, says Macfarlane, cast everything he knew about his mother's family and Newfoundland "into high relief" (272). Hedley Goodyear wrote a letter to his mother on 7 August 1918 before the battle at Amiens. In it he spoke of his hope for the future and his belief that he was fighting for freedom and a better world. He expected to come home and work towards building a Canada that included Newfoundland. In his master's thesis, "Newfoundland and Its Political and Commercial Relation to Canada," he wrote that "a patriot's first duty to his country is to know the truth about it" (284). When 110 men of the 102nd Battalion were killed in the battle on 8 August 1918, Goodyear was listed among them, and the family believed what the army reported, but Macfarlane discovers that Hedley survived that battle. He finds a long-forgotten letter, buried at the bottom of a cardboard box, from Hedley to his mother dated 17 August 1918 in which he tells his parents he is "Hun-proof" (290). But then Macfarlane says that two Australians who were with Hedley on the early morning of the next day confirmed that he was shot just before dawn by a German sniper, probably using a Mauser 98, from his nest three hundred yards away: "it looked as if a bomb had exploded inside his head" (290). Why has this truth been forgotten or hidden, even in the family? Macfarlane doesn't speculate, and he doesn't tell us how he gleaned the gruesome information from two Australians. Perhaps the letter really was just lost; perhaps, however, this inglorious, frightful death, even though mercifully instantaneous, was less palatable, less bearable even, than a death with comrades in battle.

There are other personal stories in *The Danger Tree*. Aunt Kate's is almost as important as her brothers' because she nursed returned soldiers in Ottawa and on one memorable occasion she defied the hospital authorities to make a young private, left in a cold corridor, more comfortable (see pages 255–59). She did this in the name of her own brothers and in the hope that someone would show them compassion. For the rest of her life Aunt Kate could not speak about her dead brothers without weeping, and her story reminds me of the Stratford boys' sister, Mayden, saving their letters home, of Clare in *Vimy*, Sarah Mann in *Passchendaele*, and, inevitably of Nurse Marian Turner in *The Wars*. The largest story, however, the one that reverberates behind all the others and shadows every page in the book, is the story of the Newfoundland Regiment at Beaumont-Hamel and of "an old gnarled tree [standing] among the shellholes like a skeleton" (133). When Newfoundlanders saw such trees, like the charred skeletons at Ypres and along the Western Front, they thought of the landscapes of home, but this tree, the Danger Tree, was special because it stood where so many died in a hopeless, futile, botched campaign at the Somme. Macfarlane believes, along with many, that Newfoundland's contributions to the war led, via bankruptcy and abandonment by England, to confederation with Canada (193). He does not say whether he believes, as his great-uncle Hedley did, that this was for the best. What he does instead is bring the dead to life so we can listen to them. He tells their stories and in doing so he writes them into *Canadian* history. In the final sequence of the film version of *The Danger Tree*, Macfarlane stands beside the monument at Beaumont-Hamel and tells his viewers that going back to recall things he did not experience himself was "about learning who you are."[8] The "you" in this statement is us, all Canadians, and his bearing of witness makes twentieth-century Canadian history more complete.

*Tapestry of War* is neither a history nor a biography; it is a national auto/biography of Canada. Subtitled *A Private View of Canadians in the Great War*, it tells the story of ten Canadians who lived during the war, one of whom would not survive it. The book is packed with information on what Canadian society was like in the summer of 1914, how the war was fought and at what cost, and how Canada would emerge on the world stage after the war. But this kind of information can be found in many other places, and it is not what I find fascinating about Gwyn's work. Often speaking in her own voice about her views on Canadian society, her favourite characters, and her hopes for the country, Gwyn draws extensively on the diaries and letters of her ten individuals to present the story of Canada and the First World War as a first-hand, eyewitness account. Her role is that of secondary witness; she listens carefully, often with a personal response of empathic unsettlement, and she offers her composite story containing their voices to us. Her main characters are Ethel Chadwick, Agar Adamson, Mabel Adamson, Max Aitken (soon to be Lord Beaverbrook), Talbot Papineau, Beckles Willson, Harold Innis, Grace MacPherson, John Gallishaw, and Brooke Claxton. But many other figures—minor players in her story but major ones for a military or political history of the war—crowd the margins of her narrative and the borders of her main characters' lives. These include such men as Arthur Curry, a former British Columbia real estate agent with a shady past who would become, in the war, one of our greatest generals; Sam Hughes, now infamous for championing the unreliable Ross Rifle and for maligning Curry; the Canadian prime minister Robert Borden; General Douglas Haig, Sir Julian Byng, Sir George Perley, the war artists gathered by Beaverbrook (some of whose paintings are reproduced in the book), and Caroline Papineau. The end result of such a production—for I prefer the theatre metaphor of active staging to the static one of tapestry—is an astonishingly broad, yet intimate and revealing, look at a past landscape most Canadians had forgotten by 1992 when the book first appeared.

*Tapestry of War* has had, I suspect, a direct influence on post-1992 remembering of the Great War, most obviously on McKenna's film *The Great War* and the portrayal of Talbot Papineau, but quite possibly on the novels and plays published since 1992. Jane Urquhart, for example, dedicates *The Stone Carvers* to "the memory of Sandra Gwyn." Since *Tapestry of War*, artistic use of personal memoirs, diaries, letters, and old family photographs has become common in Canadian war memory-work in all media. It is for these reasons that I conclude my exploration of Canadian representations of the Great War with Gwyn. To map Canada's landscape of memory, she focuses on individuals forgotten by history, people who served at home and abroad but whose lives had not been placed, until now, in such a prominent light. Moreover, Gwyn turns to their eyewitness accounts to capture and re-present their voices in an effort to bring them alive once more as examples of who we were then and what we would become. Of course, her drama—or her picture—is not complete. It is hard to imagine how any one composition could meet that standard. She passes lightly over some of the darker issues of the war, such as racism and resistance at home, or mutiny and execution on the front, and she pays scant attention to Canadian writers who preceded her with works like *Barometer Rising*, *Billy Bishop Goes to War*, and, most significantly, Findley's *The Wars*. Nevertheless, hers is an important and innovative approach to remembering the war, and its strength lies in the stories within her story, in the empathetic way she testifies to them, and in her desire to pass them on to us.

Two individuals surface in this landscape with special prominence. Talbot Papineau is, she tells us, her hero (389), but the somewhat unlikely figure of Brooke Claxton emerges towards the end to take up a crucial role—rather like Fortinbras to Papineau's Hamlet—because he survives and returns home haunted by the war and determined to make Canada a country worthy of those who died in the war. Among the others, the two Adamsons, Agar and Mabel, grow to fill sympathetic roles as members of an older generation—older that is than so many of the soldiers—and as guardian angels. He was forty-eight when he enlisted with the Princess Patricia's Canadian Light Infantry (PPCLI), and he spent three years in the trenches; she came from a wealthy Toronto family, but refused to stay safely at home and worked in England and Belgium to establish the Belgian Canal Boat Fund that brought relief to a starving population. After the war, their marriage failed due to his shell shock and her impatience with his autocratic ways, so their personal story is finally a sad one, but the war years are brilliantly captured through their almost daily correspondence. Max Aitken would be a colourful character in any story about the war, and his performance in *Tapestry of War* is at once entertaining and commanding. Aitken, always *there* for his own interests, saw himself as an official eyewitness to the war (260), and through his creation of the Canadian War Memorials Fund he was without doubt responsible for the existence of one of our most precious records of the war. It is thanks to this ambitious, energetic, self-important little man that we have Varley's *For What?*, Jackson's *A Copse, Evening*, and so many other pictorial treasures. As Gwyn puts it, "no other Canadian carved his name so large upon his times" (238).

While future scholars and writers like Harold Innis and Beckles Willson become important presences in Gwyn's landscape, she is equally, if not more, drawn to her three women. Mabel Adamson is a complex, mature example of Canadian womanhood rising to the challenge of her times; Grace MacPherson, a girl from Vancouver who would train as an ambulance driver and serve with the Canadian Field Hospital at Étaples, shines as an inspiring example of the future that lay ahead for her generation, and her postwar story is a happy one (see pages 459–60). Ethel Chadwick, however, is at first glance an odd choice. A very proper, conservative young Ottawa lady who enjoyed parties, especially winter skating parties, she was also an astute observer of the times and kept a detailed diary for most of her long life. It is through Chadwick's eyes and words that Gwyn represents the home front scene as Canada plunges into the war (a scene that recalls the life of the Ross family in *The Wars*) and basks in its newfound pride and independence afterwards.

However, it is in Papineau and Claxton that Gwyn finds the most important examples of a future *Canadian* identity. Both men were Canadian nationalists and both honed their sense of national pride and hope for a Canadian future in the war. In Papineau, a captain with the PPCLI (not with the newly formed "Van Doos"), she sees the future we might have had if he had survived Passchendaele, and she dwells, at length, on his letters home and on his vision for the country. Chapter 18, called "The Soul of Canada," presents the public debate between Talbot and his cousin Henri Bourassa, the founder and editor of *Le Devoir*. Bourassa opposed the war and argued in his editorials that the deaths of French Canadians fighting with the "Van Doos" would make no difference to "the Bosches of Ontario" who made war against the French language (318). Talbot replied by writing an open letter to Bourassa in which he made his claims with great passion from the battlefield: "Canada," he said, "was suffering the birthpangs of her national life. There, even more than in Canada herself, her citizens are being knit together into a new existence [and] united in bonds almost as strong as the closest of blood ties" (319). (How prophetic this is of Thiessen's *Vimy*.) He concluded this letter by insisting that the sacrifices of Canadians "fighting and dying side by side" (322) would be for nothing unless Canada emerged from the war united, independent, and committed to the ideals of humanity and peace. This was 1916. In a year Talbot Papineau was dead.

Gwyn describes Passchendaele as "unmitigated military madness" (390) and Papineau's death as Canada's loss of a leader—"the Pierre Elliott Trudeau who never was" (401). Papineau himself is reported to have said, before going over the top, "This is suicide" (399). Apparently his friends and men like Mackenzie King saw him as a future prime minister (400–01), but it is his mother's response to his death that is most profound and moving. After receiving the news and a letter of condolence from Agar Adamson, she replied, "The courage and readiness with which he faced what I am told was a desperate attack, fills my heart with pride, but also with great bitterness. I've nothing. Nothing can console me for the loss of my boy who had been the joy and comfort of my life" (403). If only, I am tempted to add, if only her words took precedence over the rhetoric of warmongering, the slogans, lies, and saccharine sermons, *perhaps* there would be fewer wars. Caroline Papineau, like Findley's Mrs. Ross, saw things clearly and spoke honestly. Gwyn gives us a chance to listen to her voice.





With Papineau gone, Gwyn needed another standard-bearer for the country, and while a somewhat plain, twenty-year-old Anglo-Canadian may not have seemed a likely replacement for Papineau, Claxton actually came from a similar privileged Montreal background and his war experiences transformed him into a serious, dedicated Canadian nationalist. After the war, he went on to become a senior cabinet minister with the Liberals and then, in 1957, the first chairman of the newly created Canada Council, the organization Gwyn praises as "the most creative institution that Canada has ever produced" (491). Claxton fought at the Battle of Amiens and survived, but what he saw in the war appalled and motivated him. In an article Gwyn found with his scrapbooks, he describes witnessing the random death of a close friend on a sunny summer day as he was bathing; a shell struck the place and shattered a young, happy life, leaving nothing but bloody fragments behind: "He is dead now. The world and I have lost a gallant soul....Why is he dead? And why, when he is dead, do I remain alive? Why?" (487). Immediately after the war, Claxton contracted the flu, but once more he survived an assault that would kill many millions more than had died in the war. Clearly, his life was blessed and he recovered, determined to dedicate that life to Canada, to "the Canadian Movement," and to federal politics.[9]

As she did with Papineau, Aitken, the Adamsons, Harold Innis, and her other protagonists, Gwyn found a defining metaphor in Claxton's life: "Claxton's subsequent career can serve as a metaphor for all those Canadians who had gone to war as blithely and innocently as he had done—Lester Pearson as the best-known fellow member of the breed, Harold Innis as another—and who returned wiser, broader, far more mature. It can serve also as a metaphor for the maturing nation that had emerged from the war on the brink of its coming of age and that then went on growing up on the foundation created by that hard-earned experience" (486).





And this is, finally, what I see as her most astute observation about the war. The men and women who lived through it were profoundly shaped by their experiences, and whether they returned to take up important positions in the arts, government, universities, or business, they consciously (as with Claxton) or unconsciously brought those experiences to bear in what they did. It is impossible to uncover the myriad ways in which this influence was transferred to the shaping of the country or how a vision for the future would emerge from a widely disparate cross-section of lives, personalities, and careers, but *Tapestry of War* is a map of that process of transference. Through the writing of an auto/biography of Canada, Gwyn exposes a backstory for a national drama that retains its internal conflicts, failures, and contradictions while celebrating successes, achievements, imagination, and the winning of home front battles. She is not saying that Canada came of age on Vimy Ridge but that what was learned on the battle front came home with those who returned—or indeed with those who had stayed home and were now left with absence and loss, with Atwood's "thirsty ghosts." That generation of Canadians, with its traumas and memories, worked at home to build the country.

As the works I have examined demonstrate, the real story of the Great War is not only about patriotism, noble sacrifice, glory, and goodness. These post-1977 works all expose the violence of war and many of the lies and prejudices hidden behind propaganda and the pressure to conform, to fall into line. At the same time, none of these works is simplistically anti-war or focused on criticizing what Canadian soldiers endured and achieved under unspeakable conditions. In most cases, they draw our attention to the average man, not the big shots, to those forgotten or ignored in earlier accounts (the women at home, the nurses, the First Nations soldiers), and to the connections (including the inconsistencies and outright contradictions) between life at home and life at the front. Above all, they imagine and celebrate a more complete landscape of memory in which things we have been told are modified and complemented by new stories and voices. By bearing witness to the past in all the different generic ways they do, they add up to an extremely powerful testament to the meaning of a renewed, more complete, national story influenced by the war. In the witnessing process they give us some remarkable figures to remember and ponder—Robert Ross, Billy Bishop, Hugh Corbett, Xavier Bird (and his indomitable aunt), Esau Mercer, Clare and her wounded men, Sarah Mann, Michael Dunne, and Talbot Papineau. When Charlie tells Mary to wake up at the end of *Mary's Wedding*, I hear our playwrights and novelists, our filmmakers and painters telling Canadians to wake up, to listen with empathic unsettlement, to remember, but also to build forward and to be proud.

Although these writers and artists do not—cannot possibly—keep faith with the dead in the way John McCrae intended in his poem, they have nonetheless remembered the dead by recreating them, by putting them back in the larger story of the First World War. But I do not wish to close my exploration of this landscape with McCrae because there is another poet who addresses the memory of the dead from a contemporary, retrospective position, and he speaks more directly to the later twentieth- and early twenty-first-century world in which we now live. This poet is Alden Nowlan and the poem is "Ypres: 1915."[10] In this long, highly personal narrative piece, Nowlan describes his visit to the crypt in St. Paul's Cathedral containing the tombs of Nelson and Wellington. As he moves forward in time to the Great War, he repeats the words "I know": he knows the picture of war as glorious is a "forgery" (100); he knows that the stories he's grown up with of noble Canadians marching to war belongs with "Kitchener's mustache" and old movies; he knows, when he watches an old First World War veteran on television being asked what it was like to fight at Vimy Ridge, that no one wants to hear the old fellow talk about rats and "water up to our middles." He knows all these things, and yet he also knows and testifies to this: that "they stood there at Ypres / the first time the Germans used gas," that they "did not break and run" (101). "Sometimes," Nowlan tells us "I'm not even sure I have a country" (101). But then he assures us he does know and he takes quiet pride in that knowledge because a certain Private Billy MacNally faced the Germans and said,





*You squareheaded sons of bitches,*
*you want to take this God damn trench*
*you're going to have to take it away*
*from Billy MacNally*
*of the South End of Saint John, New Brunswick.*

*And that's ridiculous, too, and nothing*
*on which to found a country.*

*Still*
*It makes me feel good, knowing*
*that in some obscure, conclusive way*
*they were connected with me*
*and me with them.* (102)

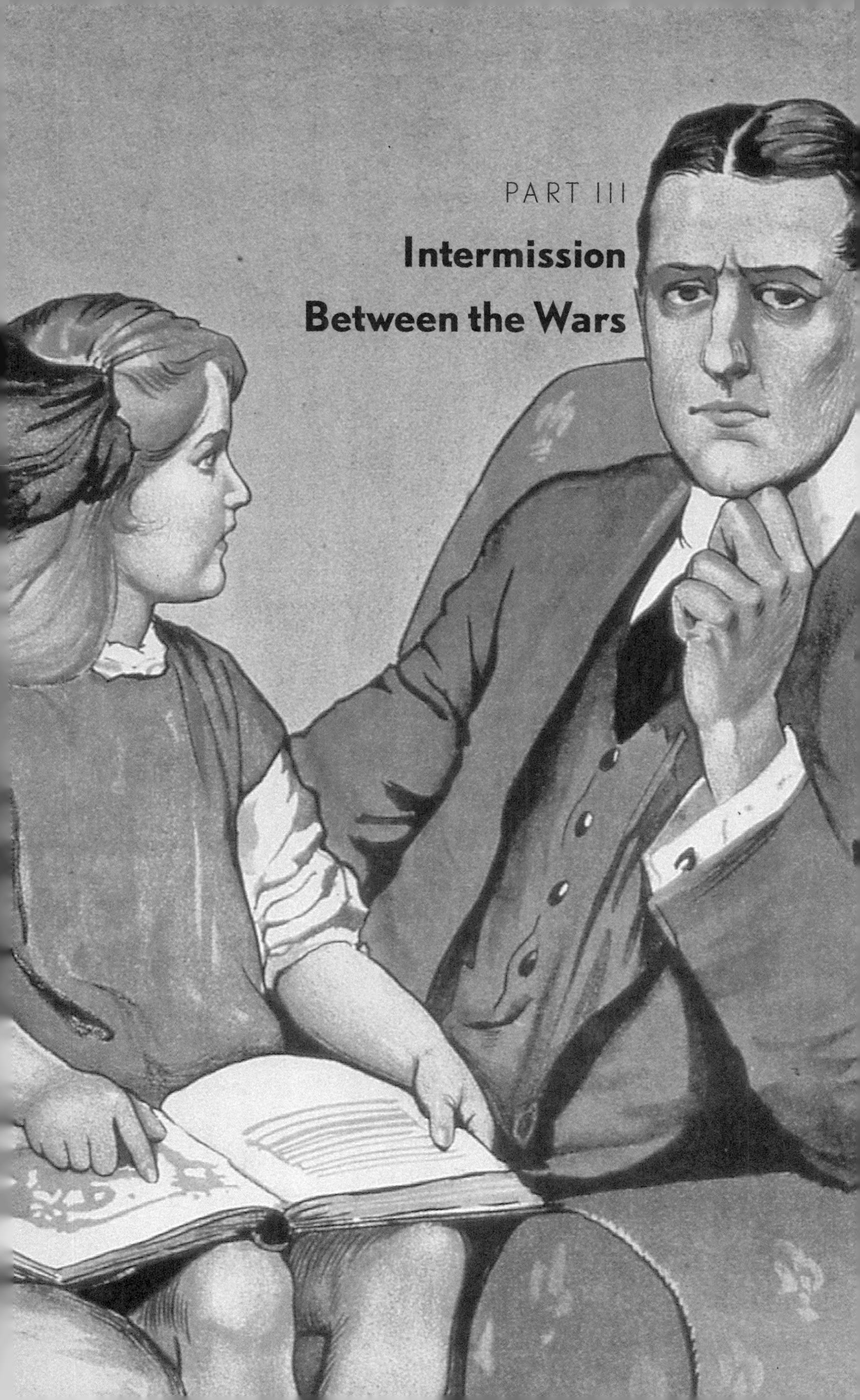

PART III

# Intermission Between the Wars

The peacemakers of 1919
believed they were working
against time. They had to draw
new lines on the map of Europe...
but they also had to think of Asia,
Africa and the Middle East....
If they could, they had to create
an international order that would
make another Great War
impossible.



**Margaret MacMillan**

*Paris 1919*, xxix

We will never know everything that happened in the many cities and small villages that found themselves prostrate beneath the boot of this conquering force. Ironically, we do know the story of Nanking because some foreigners witnessed the horror and sent word to the outside world at the time, and some Chinese survived as eyewitnesses.



**Iris Chang**

*The Rape of Nanking*, 4

They are everywhere,
these ghosts of empires past.
I live in a haunted world.
The question is: Have I joined
the ghosts or have
the ghosts joined me?



**Modris Eksteins**

*Walking Since Daybreak*, 4

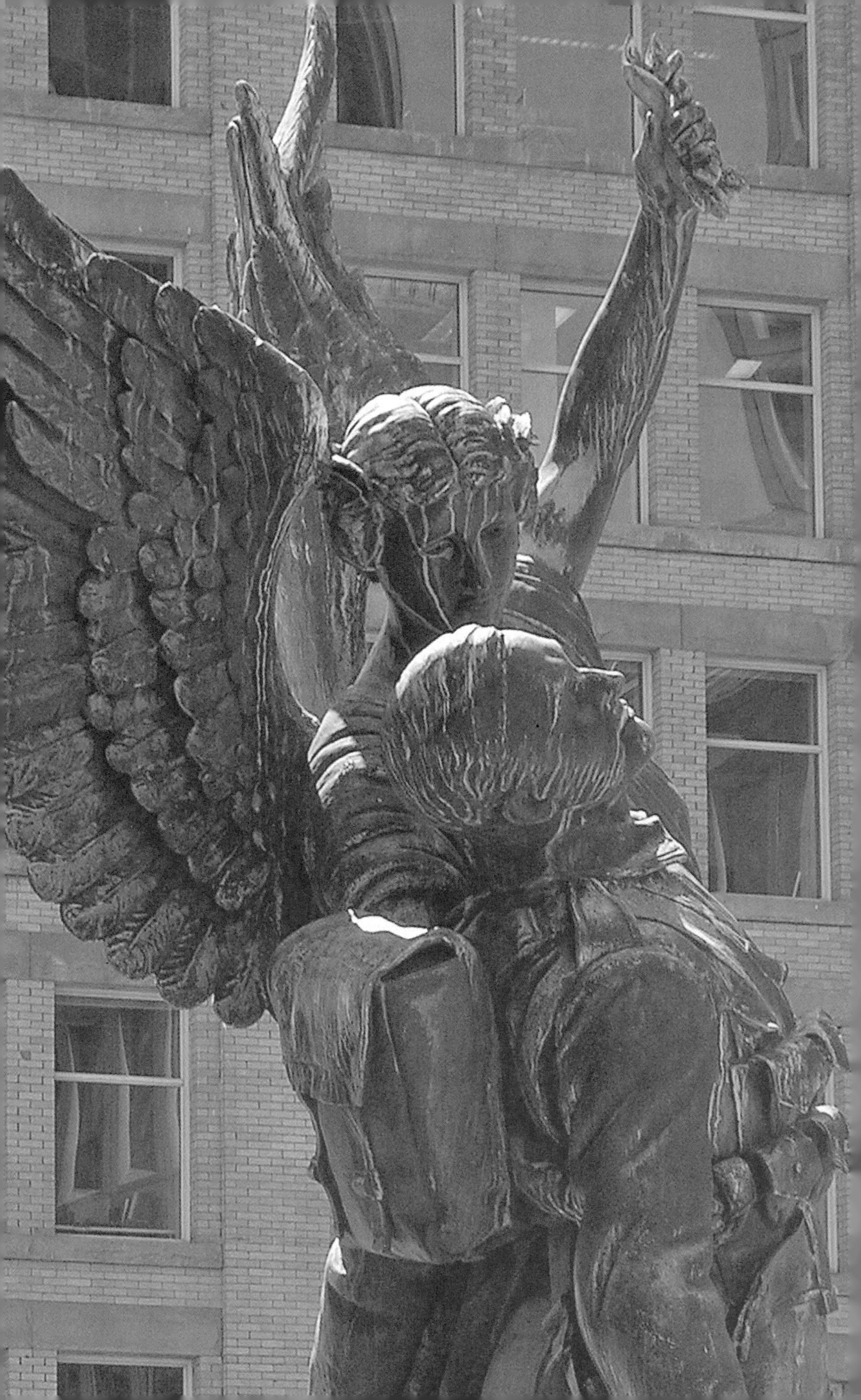

# 6
# Living in a Haunted World

AT THE END OF *Under the Volcano*, Malcolm Lowry leaves his readers with this apocalyptic vision of destruction: "yet no, it wasn't the volcano, the world itself was bursting, bursting into black spouts of villages catapulted into space [and] the inconceivable pandemonium of a million tanks [and ] the bursting of ten million burning bodies" (375). From one perspective, this *scene* exists only in the drunken imagination of the dying consul, Geoffrey Firmin. But from another, it represents Lowry's warning about the looming threat of the Second World War. *Under the Volcano*, published in 1947 and one of the masterpieces of twentieth-century literature in English, is not a Second World War novel. Neither is it a First World War novel, nor a novel about the Spanish Civil War, although all three conflicts crowd its pages. *Volcano* is about the tense, ominous, threatening years between the two wars.[1] It depicts some of the ways in which the Great War haunts those years and how too few Westerners paid attention to the warnings heralded by the rise of fascism in

Spain. Indeed, *Under the Volcano,* its very title symbolizing the condition of life in Europe during the post–First World War years, is one of the most portentous works of fiction in twentieth-century English literature. It is, quite simply, haunted, and it projects the condition of hauntedness on everyone who reads it. Everywhere the consul turns, he is confronted by the ghosts of his past, be they the Germans he ordered burned alive in the First World War or the accusatory memories of his many other failures and betrayals. He is haunted by voices from his past life and from his present conscience. He refuses to accept responsibility for events unfolding around him—in Mexico, in Spain, in Germany, and even in England. He refuses to bear witness, to listen with empathic unsettlement—until it is too late.

Lowry was writing *Under the Volcano* during the late 1930s and into the mid-1940s. He knew what had happened in the Great War and in Spain, and he was well aware of events in the Second World War, despite living in comparative seclusion on Burrard Inlet near Vancouver.[2] So, although Lowry does not belong to the generation of novelists I am most concerned with, and although he was not Canadian, even though he wrote *Volcano* in Canada and often called himself Canadian, he does herald the kind of Janus-facing fiction that later Canadian writers would produce after 1977. These are stories about the years between the wars, about the warning signals that were largely ignored, about Western society's determined will to forget the past, to live in the present and for an immediate future, to deny (for as long as possible) the rising tide of fascism and rearmament. These texts are disturbing reminders of how perversely blinded the between-the-wars generation insisted on being, and they dramatize those ghostly presences whose voices, warnings, and stories were silenced, repressed, and erased from a landscape of memory that, had it made room for them, *might* have halted the world's headlong rush into another world war. "We are the dead," McCrae's soldiers told us. "My secrets are of the grave," confessed Lowry's consul. "Dead of Verdun arise!" cried Jean Diaz, Abel Gance's hero, in *J'accuse*. But who was prepared to listen?

In this chapter, which serves rather like a bridge (if not a respite) between the horrors of the First World War and the catastrophe of the Second, I will consider a few recent Canadian texts that pick up the burden of warning and witnessing where Lowry left it in *Under the Volcano*. They are Findley's play *Can You See Me Yet?*, Dennis Bock's novel *The Communist's Daughter*, and Marjorie Chan's play *A Nanking Winter*. Inevitably, there are many other texts I can only mention in passing, such as the recent memoirs by Fred Bruemmer and Modris Eksteins.[3] In *Survival: A Refugee Life* (2005), Bruemmer takes his readers back to a world most Canadians never knew and to his childhood in Latvia as a Baltic German. As the Second World War drew closer and then exploded around him, he fled with his family into an ordeal of exile, military camps, forced labour, starvation, illness, escape, and ultimately survival and a new life in Canada.[4] By the age of twenty, he had lived (and nearly died) several lifetimes over. Eksteins, also from Latvia, but of Latvian ethnicity, would also emigrate to Canada, but his memoir *Walking Since Daybreak* (1999), traces his family history well back into his Baltic roots to create a landscape of memory where ethnic violence, atrocity, and persecution helped pave the way to the Second World War: the Holocaust, he reminds us, "was a state of mind [in the Baltic States] before it was a Nazi policy" (151).[5] In these powerful stories, both men demonstrate the degree to which life in Europe between the wars (indeed, well before the Great War) came with them to Canada, as former lives do with all immigrants, and that, once here, these memories must find their place within a Canadian landscape of memory. My answer to Eksteins's question in the passage I included with my prefacing quotations to this chapter is this: the ghosts have joined him in *this* country, and now they live here.

These memoirs, both written long after their authors had built secure, successful lives in Canada, are acts of remembrance. As such, they alert us to the degree of forgetting that shrouds the interwar years. During the 1920s and 1930s, Canada focused on its internal problems—a massive debt left from the First World War, the Great Depression, devastating droughts on the Prairies that we still recall as the "dirty thirties," severe unemployment across the country, internal political divisions caused by simmering resentments in Quebec toward the federal government, and major labour strikes. These years from 1919 to 1939 were turbulent enough at home, without worrying unduly about disputes in an ungovernable Europe, fascist muscle-flexing in Spain, Stalin's vicious brand of Communism in Russia, and the rise to power of a German veteran of the First World War called Adolf Hitler, who was democratically elected in 1933. The Second Sino-Japanese War, which began in July 1937, was covered by the newspapers but seems scarcely to have caught the general public's attention. Reconstruction on the home front was of paramount concern. The Spanish flu epidemic led to the creation of our first federal Department of Health, millions of dollars were dedicated to returned soldiers' settlements, and veterans' organizations quickly emerged to fight for their interests. Before the end of 1919, thirty thousand Winnipeggers went on strike, and this in turn led to *recommendations* for so many of the improvements for working people that would eventually take effect (a minimum wage, unemployment insurance, and so forth). By 1922, Canadian women were eligible to vote in every province except Quebec.





William Lyon Mackenzie King, the "great conciliator," as Granatstein and Morton call him (163), came to power in 1921 and would be there through the Second World War. King worked to rebuild Liberal Party fortunes in Quebec, to unify Canada, and to manage the economy. The burned Parliament buildings that Mrs. Ross lamented as a sign of doom in *The Wars* were rebuilt; Allward's magnificent monument was completed and unveiled in 1936; defence budgets were slashed until a professional Canadian armed forces barely existed (Granatstein and Morton 173). The 1931 Statute of Westminster made Canada an independent nation—at least, on paper—within the British Commonwealth. But few people in Canada wanted to talk about the last war, let alone contemplate another. "Peace in our time" was Neville Chamberlain's mistaken pronouncement after the four great powers met in Munich in September 1938. Canada was not present at that meeting, but King believed, with Chamberlain, that Hitler could be, and should be, appeased.

In *Going Home*, the film I mentioned in Chapter 3 about Canadian troops demobilized and held in camps in Wales to wait for transport home, the perceived threat facing the postwar Western world was Communism. There were plans to keep Canadian soldiers abroad and send them to fight the Bolsheviks; one of the young men slaughtered in the film's depiction of the mutiny, when the officers turned their guns on them, was seen as a "Commie" sympathizer. In fact, all he wanted was to go home to Canada. Today, it is hard to believe that trade unionist and secretary of Canada's Communist Party, Tim Buck, would be jailed (1932–34) for his views and be forced to go underground during the Second World War, but hatred of Stalin would prove well-founded, and fear of "Commie" infiltration became widespread during the 1920s and 1930s.[6] Harassment was common. Duplessis's infamous Padlock Laws came into effect in 1937 as one extreme example of the attempt to stamp out Communism. Another example of anti-Communist hysteria was the fate of the play *Eight Men Speak*. A piece of theatre may seem innocuous when compared with the Winnipeg Strike, the On to Ottawa Trek, or labour agitation and demonstrations, but *Eight Men Speak* was closed by the Toronto police on the night of 4 December 1933 after its first and only performance in the city. It was an openly left-wing play about the loss of civil rights by leaders of the Communist Party of Canada (CPC), and it was deemed by the authorities to represent a threat to civil order and good government. In fact, it told the truth. Despite harassment at home and the League of Nations (of which Canada was a member) ruling against intervention in Spain, the CPC helped organize the Canadian contingent (the Mackenzie-Papineau Battalion) that fought for the Republican cause during the Spanish

Civil War, and Dr. Norman Bethune, who had joined the CPC in 1935, would become our most illustrious Communist hero—*in China*.

Timothy Findley's play *Can You See Me Yet?* is set on home ground, and there are no heroes in it. The story unfolds in the Asylum for the Insane, in Britton, southern Ontario, during one late summer day in 1938, but despite this setting *in an asylum*, or perhaps, inevitably, because of it, the play provides no safe sanctuary from the world beyond its walls or the despair within. The main character, a would-be missionary to China, Cassandra Wakelin, is haunted by her memories of a destructive family past and of the First World War, and she is acutely aware both of events in the wider world—in Europe and China—and of the rapidly approaching catastrophe of the Second World War. In her final "sermon," when she calls on an absent God to see her—"See me! *See* us!"—she realizes that "the world is ending all around us, and we need each other now. And yet there is no sanctuary. Nowhere. None. In all the world" (162). The play premiered at the National Arts Centre on 1 March 1976, with the great Frances Hyland as Cassandra.[7] Findley dedicated the published text, in part, to Hyland, and it is Hyland I remember speaking these lines, struggling to be heard over Hitler screaming from an offstage radio, remembering her brother killed at Passchendaele, grieving for her dearest friend who died on her way to serve in China, and delivering her "War Sermon" in which she rages against a neighbour who made millions from the war but treated his own children like objects. Cassandra, as her name suggests, sees what the world is coming to, and she tries to warn us. But she is mad, after all, incarcerated for her seering visions and accusations. And she will die in the fire that destroys the Britton Asylum in September 1939, just as the Second World War became a declared fact. For all that this play constitutes a prophecy of the horror soon to engulf the world, it is constructed as a memory play in which the Great War haunts the present because it destroyed the lives and the sanity of the Wakelin family. The remembering takes place in Cassandra's mind as the Asylum's inmates become members of her former family. This doubling of roles—present inmates, past family—transforms the garden of the Asylum into Cassandra's landscape of memory, a landscape within which ghosts gradually rise to the surface to reveal some appalling truths.

Cassandra herself is a complex character, weak and ineffectual on one hand yet honest and brave on the other. How she ended up in an insane asylum, or who committed her, is never made explicit, although her father, Edward Wakelin, is the likely culprit. She remembers this father as loving only his eldest son Patrick, who died in the trenches at Passchendaele, and he is portrayed as a callous tyrant. In the penultimate scene of the play, Cassandra *remembers* (and stages) a confrontation between her father and her brother Franklin in which we see the extent of this father's destructive influence on his children. He gloats over his success in marrying off his younger daughter to the son of that neighbour who made millions from scavenging the battlefields of Europe, and he dismisses his surviving son as a weeping, drunken boy. He has no time for Cassandra because she refuses to be married off and resists his authority. But the key moment in this memory scene comes with Franklin's accusation, which evokes the full haunting power of the war. In a speech laced with bitter irony and pain, Franklin describes his trip to Europe to visit "the very best battlefields. The Somme, and Passchendaele. And Vimy Ridge" (156). He finds his brother's grave—"that graveyard you [his father] worship from afar—in the field, by the woods—where Patrick and my manhood are buried" (157), and he grieves, not only for his brother, but also for the rows and rows of dead boys sacrificed by their fathers. Then he asks the fundamental questions: "Why is he over there? Dead. And, why do you wish that we were there instead of him?" (157). The father has no answers. Instead, he refuses to listen or acknowledge his role in the past or in the present disaster destroying his family. He refuses to accept the fact that he helped to kill his son. Cassandra, however, takes up Franklin's cause. In response to her father's excuses—"I wasn't even there [in Europe, in the trenches]"—she replies, "You were as much there...with Patrick in that trench—as you were here, this morning" (158).

But if Cassandra blames her father, and all the fathers like him, she also blames herself for failing to save anything from the ruins of her family or the flames threatening her immediate world of 1938. Her crucial scene of self-accusation arrives earlier in the play (in scene 11), when she delivers what Findley calls "The War Sermon." This brief scene is a monologue in which Cassandra sits in the Asylum garden and addresses her fellow inmates, and us, while the offstage radio voice of Hitler speaking at the famous Nuremberg rally provides a chilling counterpoint. This radio broadcast is first audible as little more than a faint rhythm of German words, but it will gradually increase in volume until the "*sounds of someone shouting 'SIEG!' and of thousands responding 'HEIL!' rise like ocean waves: SIEG! HEIL! SIEG! HEIL! SIEG! HEIL!*'" (123). In her "sermon," this would-be, failed missionary to China describes the acquiescence she finds in herself and in all of us. "Why do we listen," she asks, to the voices of men like Hitler and Mussolini, or even to Aimée Semple McPherson, with her false promises of comfort? "Why do we obey?" (121). Her answer is that we all yearn to cringe and obey; we are victims of such people, yes, but also of "our willing weakness." And why are we so weak, so compliant? "Because we are afraid to be ourselves. To *listen* to ourselves" (121). With this revelation, or accusation, Findley's Cassandra names the root problem that so many of the texts that I am discussing confront and explore: too many people choose to forget the past, to ignore present warning signals; they acquiesce before apparent power and sleepwalk through dangerous times. And some, like the man who scavenged dead horses from the battlefields for glue, this neighbour who made his millions from the war and is now marrying his son to the youngest Wakelin daughter, profit from war.

*Can You See Me Yet?* is not a long play. It is hard to imagine either the actors sustaining or an audience enduring the intensity of its rage and grief for very long. It has just two acts and fifteen scenes, with a unity of setting made possible by the force of memory, which collapses the here and now in the Asylum into the then and there of the Wakelin family home. But its economy of structure reinforces its impact and makes its meaning all the more clear. As Cassandra knows, there is no such thing as asylum from the world. Violence, tyranny, war, greed, and betrayal cannot be held at a distance, safely removed from our lives, even though we cannot bear to face that reality for too long at one stretch. Just beyond the visible stage—the Asylum's garden and Cassandra's landscape of memory—we hear the *noises off* of barking dogs, gunshots, radio news, and fire engines, and we listen to the characters' tragic stories against that aural backdrop and within that larger context. Together, these two domains, on and off stage, connect the First World War with the Second and a haunting by the past with a fear for the present and future. Nothing in this play suggests that the years between the wars were safe or peaceful. To the contrary. In the final scene, Cassandra confesses that she has never been to China (162); her friend died on her way to serve there, but Cassandra was not with her. She knows she has failed to act, to intervene, to help, and she asks for forgiveness and help, although who could provide either remains a mystery. In the closing speech of the play, Alma, the head nurse in the Asylum, comes downstage to tell the audience that Cassandra Wakelin died in the fire that destroyed the Asylum at Britton. The only consolation we are offered is to learn that "she did not die alone. As she had lived" (166). But surely this is cold comfort because these lines, spoken in the past tense, reach us from a present time *after* the Second World War, and in retrospect the fire, the Asylum, and Cassandra's life symbolize the failures of our society to wake up, to listen, to act while there was still time.

It is also, emphatically, about Canada. The Asylum for the Insane that cannot provide sanctuary, healing, or even much compassion among its inhabitants, symbolizes Canada between the wars. It represents a prison for those inside and a fortress to keep unwanted realities and people out, even as it becomes clear that world events cannot be held at bay. To make matters worse, the shock treatments to which its inmates are subjected serve to pacify them and strip away memory, so it is something of a miracle that one patient can still remember the past and the world beyond the Asylum gates. Focused inward after the Great War, and turning blind eyes and deaf ears to the warnings from Europe and Asia, *most* Canadians refused to acknowledge the dangers, and our governments tried to pretend that all was well. For Findley, this kind of willed forgetting and acquiescence are almost a crime and certainly amount to a moral failing. In this disturbing play, he suggests that our world is a madhouse and that we are crazy, unless, of course, we step forward to answer Cassandra's question by saying: yes, we can see you and, in you, ourselves living in our contemporary post-1977 world. If a play like *Can You See Me Yet?* serves any practical purpose—if works of art can be said to function in society (as I believe they can, and do)—it is to warn us, to make us see and hear, to wake us up to the urgent need to come together, to remember and bear witness, and above all to act.





Action provides the motivation and meaning of the text I examine next—Dennis Bock's *The Communist's Daughter*. This fine novel takes the form of a fictional auto/biography prepared by Norman Bethune during his months in China providing medical help to Mao's Eighth Route Army during 1938–39. We read it long after Bethune's death, at forty-nine, from septicemia on 12 November 1939, and Bock presents it as a found manuscript contained in seven envelopes, which have been preserved by his loyal Chinese colleagues until the Chinese authorities decide to reveal their revered doctor's confessional story. The narrative is addressed to the daughter Bethune never knew but fathered with Kasja von Rothman, a woman he loved and lost during the Spanish Civil War.[8] In it he describes his family life in Canada, his experiences in the First World War, his failed and unhappy marriage to Frances Penny, his medical work in Spain, and then his fieldwork with the army in war-torn China. At every turn, Bock draws upon historical facts, names, dates, events, and actual documents, such as Bethune's letters, speeches, and poetry. Hence Robert Capa, the famous photographer, John Rabe, the good Nazi who saved thousands of Chinese from the Japanese during the Rape of Nanking, Mao Zedong himself, Bethune's assistants, Ho and Mr. Tung, Jean Ewen, the Canadian nurse who worked with him in China, and many others appear to play their parts, large and small, in his drama. Indeed, reading this novel is like plunging into an actual past that is scarcely remembered today and listening to the voices of the dead that complement Bethune's ghostly first-person telling. Through Bethune's memory and his lost and found auto/biography, an entire landscape of memory rises before and around us, and its inhabitants spring to life with amazing vitality. Reading *The Communist's Daughter* is a truly uncanny experience. The real Bethune crowded a staggering amount of travel, medical work, and other activities (not to mention action in three war zones) into his forty-nine years, so it is not surprising that Bock's fiction should be so full. However, the novel is also wonderfully unified by Bethune's voice, by the conceit of a found document, and by the forceful presence of three wars: the First World War, the Spanish Civil War, and the Second Sino-Japanese War, with the last two pressing forward into the Second World War. Unlike any of the other between-the-wars texts I am considering, with the possible exception of *Under the Volcano*, *The Communist's Daughter* recreates interwar conflicts in Europe and Asia while, like *Volcano*, using the Spanish Civil War as its narrative-historical pivot.



In a 1936 letter Norman Bethune declared, "It is in Spain that the real issues of our time are going to be fought out. It is there that democracy will either die or survive" (qtd. in Clarkson 115). He was right, of course, as Malcolm Lowry, among other artists, intellectuals, and activists, also realized, but for Dennis Bock events in China between 1937 and 1939 were equally significant. His choice of hero, therefore—a Canadian Communist doctor who served in both theatres and is still marginalized at home—is important. Bock's Bethune becomes the voice and eyewitness who connects both war zones (Spain and China) while also answering Findley's question to Canadians: now you can see and hear me; *now*, in this address to "you." And this *you* is strategic because at the very start of the narrative it seems to refer to me or to us, the readers of this newly revealed document, which is prefaced by a typed note (the typeface suggesting an old typewriter with a worn ribbon) from Major Lu Ting-yi, Director of Propaganda of the Central Committee of the Chinese Communist Party, Yan'an, Shensi Province.





Major Lu explains that the "enclosed manuscript" was "likely written" between May 1938 and November 1939 in a border region of northern China. Apparently it contains 448 pages, with medical illustrations, drawings, and other documents besides the "personal letter" we will read. Then the Major notes that a committee will be asked to recommend when the manuscript should be translated and distributed. We turn the page with the expectation that we are about to read a translated document, to find "ENVELOPE ONE" typed by the same machine in capital letters on an otherwise blank page. We turn the page again and are directly addressed (happily in a clear, contemporary font): "It is my fond hope that your understanding will win out against any mistrust or anger you may harbour against me when you finally read this" (3). Although this opening may represent one of the oldest ploys in the history of storytelling (a personal, original document found and revealed for the first time—think of novels from *Robinson Crusoe* or *Clarissa* to *The Handmaid's Tale*), I find the temptation wrapped up in this discursive gesture hard to resist: someone is speaking/writing to *me* and asks for my understanding about something he or she has done. Such power this request grants me, such importance, and how it piques my curiosity! The writer—almost a speaker—goes on to say that he or she has been trying to communicate with me for some time, that this document that I hold in my hands is a letter, but also a history. However, the author seems anxious: "Heaven forbid these pages return to you without me"—*return?* Who is this person whose return I am to expect and recognize? But we read on and see that this person promises that "I will recount my life as faithfully as I recall it, nothing added, nothing lost" (3). Even before I turn another page I am seduced. Seduced by this mysterious presence, this plea for my attention and sympathy, and above all by this promise of truth about a life story remembered "faithfully."

However, there is a tiny caveat that slips by almost unnoticed: the innocuous phrase, "as I recall it." We cannot, do not, recall our lives faithfully or completely; we recreate them through our stories, we invent ourselves, and never more so than when we need an empathic listener and fear that we may be harshly judged or worse—ignored and forgotten. Before long this ruse of address is cleared up. The author claims that "we Bethunes are fighters" and that the first-person voice belongs to a man, a father in fact. Apparently this is Norman Bethune's story and the daughter of the title—the Communist's daughter—is his, even if we had no idea that Bethune had a daughter (or a son for that matter). How she came to be his child and why he must write to her from China gradually become clear as the story develops, which it does in a fragmented, interrupted, metaleptic manner. Meanwhile, this powerful opening gambit makes me his empathic listener/reader and secondary witness, a position I never quite relinquish while reading.

*The Communist's Daughter* is a memory-work, a narrative predicated on recalling a life story, or personal history, and on the presumption of truth: I saw and experienced this and that; therefore, I can and will tell you the truth. All auto/biography, whether non-fiction or fictional, involves these two manoeuvres of remembering and truth claims. But auto/biography involves a further move insofar as it speaks from a present about a past that is to be listened to in a future moment; it is addressed forward in time in anticipation of being received. This address to the future is especially important for *The Communist's Daughter* and it establishes several dramatic connections between the narrator and his audience. Addressed forward to a child never seen who may never receive it but, if she does, will read it many years after the time of its creation (as we do), the story pulls us back into its world of forgotten and unknown events and then pushes us, repeatedly, into the present process of reading because we want to learn more about what happened back then and why it matters now. Because the telling is interrupted when the demands of Bethune's immediate work in China intrude on those quiet moments when he can sit at his old typewriter, we are constantly shifting back and forth across his life and, in particular, across the years between 1914 and 1939. Moreover, he withholds information that he finds painful to record, ostensibly because he is distracted by medical emergencies or because he shrinks from shocking his daughter with ugly facts, until late in the narrative. Nevertheless, he is haunted while he writes by certain events and will refer to them, shy away from explanations or descriptions, return to the topic to reveal some details, and then back away again. We are constantly left hanging, wondering what really happened and when we will be told. The result is that we too become haunted. Three of these painful events are an experience in the Great War, the fate of Kasja after he left Spain to raise relief funds in Canada and the United States, and the appalling trauma witnessed by Ho, his young Chinese assistant.





Norman Bethune interrupted his medical training at the University of Toronto to enlist in September 1914 with No. 2 Field Ambulance Army Medical Corps. He served as a stretcher-bearer, was badly wounded at Ypres in April 1915, sent to hospital in England, and then discharged. He returned to his medical studies determined to put what he had learned about surgery, blood loss, and trauma in battle, to use. In this he was not alone. Medical science as we know it today made advances by studying the trauma, infections, deaths, and diseases encountered in trench warfare. But Bock's Bethune brings much more away from the war than medical curiosity and a burning desire to develop blood transfusion techniques that would save lives on a battle front. In the fictional autobiography, Bethune is haunted by the ghosts of that war and shaped by his realization that he was deceived about it. Remembering one night's search for wounded soldiers on the battlefields of Ypres, as he listened for the weeping, the groans or screams that identified those still living who might be saved, he describes the "moving green worms" (78) of poison gas, the shelling, the nauseating smells and sights of exploded bodies. Remembering "the horror upon horror" (80) all around him, he admits that he was desperate "to find heroism in my blood. But by now I knew that it was all—the gallantry, the romance, the glory—a great deception" (80). But these difficult memories are only the prelude to the memory of a man he can never leave behind.

In a scene that recalls some of those in *The Wars* or the final battle sequence in the film *Passchendaele*, Bethune describes trying, but failing, to save young Robert Pearce, a badly wounded Canadian farmer who he had known in northern Ontario. Slowly, painfully, he remembers dragging and carrying Robert across No Man's Land, hiding in filthy craters during shelling, fighting to keep the man alive but also to keep him quiet so his moans would not reveal their presence to snipers. He whispers to Robert that he needn't worry, that they are "brothers" and will make it to safety because "my life is in your hands and yours is in mine," that this ordeal and rescue will make a story they can tell afterwards (88–89). But Robert is dying and when Bethune is shot he abandons his burden in the mud, wraps Robert's blood-stained tourniquet around his leg, and crawls towards the Canadian line. The hard lessons here are that he survives when another dies and that he and Robert were abandoned by their God. During his convalescence, he tells his nurse that he will do his best "to forget" about the war (95), but he will not forget. He has been changed forever and must make his being alive worth something to the world. In short, Bock imagines this scene from the First World War as the motivating force, as well as the medical challenge, that determines Bethune's postwar life. His death years later on another battle front, caused by blood poisoning contracted while operating on a Chinese soldier, seems to respond to, even answer for, those terrible lessons at Ypres.

The lessons of Spain are less traumatic for Bock's Bethune because this time he has fewer illusions about war and is better equipped to be of practical help. As with his memories of the First World War, he recalls many of his activities during his months in Spain and describes in detail his meeting with Kasja and their love affair, but he also circles around the central questions of his experience there until late in the telling when he confesses how and when he learned about his daughter's birth and her mother's fate. One particular event holds special significance for him—the dangerous road trip to a Republican front somewhere near Guadalajara that he makes to bring blood supplies to the wounded. He introduces this story as follows: "It's dark now [in China], and quiet, which makes remembering an easy thing" (221). Kasja had insisted on accompanying him, and along the way she photographed a tank column travelling in the same direction (221–30). During the night, however, they were obliged to hike into the mountains, where the Partisans were hiding, but Kasja collapsed on the rough trail and was taken down to an observation post and left in the care of an old Partisan man.





As we have come to expect by this stage in his auto/biography, Bethune stops his remembering of this journey abruptly, only to pick up the thread of his story five days later when he and Kasja met again in Madrid. Then he shifts once more, this time to another story about his efforts to establish a medical training school in China. We are left wondering what was wrong with Kasja? What took place during those five unaccounted-for (at this point in the narrative) days? What happened to her camera, and why were the men she travelled with, except for Bethune, so uneasy about her presence among them? The answers will emerge in due course and after considerable evasion on Bethune's part. In the meantime, he writes about his unhappy marriage, his fight with tuberculosis in 1926–27, his writing—medical essays, poetry, and "confessional letters" (250), which seem to be his preferred epistolary mode. When he returns to his memories of Spain (these pages are contained in ENVELOPE SIX), it is to tell us that he "left Madrid in springtime, gathered my few things and retreated" (217). He had convinced himself that he could raise money for the Republican cause in North America, and Kasja told him to go

(267). The historical-biographical record of Bethune's life has never explained, definitively, why he left Spain, and Bock refrains from inventing reasons beyond the suggestion that he was hounded out of Spain because he was arrogant and bad-tempered with his Spanish colleagues and some of them became suspicious of his loyalties. Bethune recreates (Bock imagines for him) a scene in which he was confronted in Madrid by three Spaniards who questioned him about Kasja and especially about her photographs, which they could not now have in their possession unless they had taken them from her. These Partisans are angry and suspicious of both the good Canadian doctor and his Swedish lover. What's more, they are dangerous.





But once again our storyteller drops the Spanish thread in his auto/biography to return to his immediate situation in China and his troubling memories of Robert Pearce and the First World War. The parallels between his ordeal in No Man's Land at Ypres, his nighttime trail in the mountains before Guadalajara, and his recent terrifying experience in the northern hills of China, when his medical unit was attacked by the Japanese, are inescapable. In each event, he was alone at night trying to bring medical aid to others and failing, but it is not so much the failure as the fact of being alive that troubles him: "I was wondering about the odds of my survival, alone and unarmed, with very little food and water, when again I thought of that nighttime journey through the mud-fields of Belgium a full lifetime ago. Was it my turn to die now? Why had I survived these extra twenty years when others had been in the ground all this time? Why, in my third war, was I still alive?" (276). Only now, after this nearly hallucinatory connection is made in his memory between Belgium and China, can our reluctant author remember his second war—Spain—and fill in those empty places in his landscape of memory.

The truth is (if this *is* the truth) that after he left Spain Kasja was arrested and interrogated. Because she was pregnant (the reason she had collapsed on the trail and nearly miscarried), her jailors allow her to live until the baby is born, after which she is executed and the baby placed in a Spanish orphanage (280, 302–04). At this stage in his confession, having faced a good part of what he betrayed, abandoned, or at least lost, he warns this unknown daughter and, of course, us: "I think you know Spain was my great disappointment, the death of my idealism and of part of me. But I can assure you there will be no second failure. I have learned my lesson. There are rumours that things again are teetering on the edge in Europe. Will there soon be a time when only the dead enjoy their peace, when one war will follow another, with another after that, with no end in sight? War might be for your generation as it was for mine, but I certainly hope that is not the case" (282–83). If Bethune sounds a bit incoherent in this passage, his thoughts a bit unclear or wandering (was Spain his first failure or was Ypres? Was Spain the end of idealism for him, or did that happen with the First World War?), we must remember his condition as he writes this confession letter-cum-life story: he is weak, exhausted, and malnourished.





The present scene of his remembering and telling is China, and descriptions of the country, the people, the young Chinese soldiers he labours to save with blood transfusions and antiseptic (albeit never sterile) surgeries, provide the narrative foreground for his earlier life. It is abundantly clear that he has grown to love China and its people because he feels needed there—"My life has never seemed so crucial" (200). And he believes in the Chinese fight against the Japanese aggressor and respects the courage of Mao's soldiers, so many of whom are boys like Robert Pearce. The beauty of China's Yan'an area landscapes reminds him of northern Canada, and he feels almost at home in this foreign land. The wisdom of Mao, Chairman of the Central Soviet Government, inspires him and strengthens his ambition. After an all-night interview with Mao (the only time Bethune is reported to have met Mao) in his cave headquarters at Yan'an, he confesses that "I felt more purposeful than I'd ever been.... I have been absolved of all frailty and self-interest. I would devote myself exclusively to the fight ahead.... The great man's passion had taken hold of me" (196). Although Chinese history is not explored in detail by Bock's Bethune, he knows enough about what is happening to understand that the Chinese military is divided between those fighting with Chiang Kai-shek and those supporting Mao.[9] For both groups, the chief enemy in the late 1930s was the Japanese Imperial Army. Civil war in China would follow, and Bethune would not live to observe its course. He has become a secondary witness inside the text of his own story, thereby modelling a reader's position and responsibility.

Fragments of information about Japanese atrocities reach Bethune in his isolated front-line field hospitals; he hears rumours about what happened in Nanking, when the city fell to the Japanese, and about the German—a Nazi—called John Rabe who worked tirelessly to protect Chinese women and children (310). But the full horror of the Second Sino-Japanese War comes home to him when his medical assistant, Mr. Tung, tells Ho's story. Bethune is planning to leave China for North America, where he hopes to get fresh medical supplies and funds to continue his field surgery, but he cannot take young Ho with him. This is when Mr. Tung intervenes and, in a story within the story, Bethune repeats what he is told so that we and his daughter will know too. When Ho's village was overrun, the Japanese captured his mother and two sisters and incarcerated them in a "House of Consolation." When the boy, who escaped during the massacre, returned to search for them, he found them in this place of shame and horror, where they were strapped to beds and repeatedly raped by the soldiers. He tried to free his mother but could not do so before the next group of men arrived, so he hid beneath her bed, where "he remained frozen...until nightfall" (288). Of all the appalling stories within Bethune's life story, this is possibly the most painful and brutal. Here the doctor realizes the extent of the war's violence; he bears secondary witness (from inside the text of his life story) and by doing so he models our role. As a result, his responsibility to protect Ho becomes undeniable. If he leaves China without Ho, the boy will be swept back into the fighting and perish.

Would Bethune have stayed in China had he lived? Would he have taken Ho with him when he left? These questions cannot be answered.

Instead, in the seventh, and final, envelope we read Bethune's increasingly disoriented reflections about his life. Norman Bethune is dying because he has been fatally infected by a knife cut received while operating on a soldier's broken leg (295–96). As he lies ill, feverish, trembling, cold, and weak, Ho finds a pencil stub to replace the typewriter, so that he can continue to record his rambling thoughts, which are really memories, a "thick blanket of memories": "It warms me, this simple act of memory and reconstruction. I am sustained. I have a voice in this silent land" (300). *Now* he imagines Kasja's "terror" as she gave birth, knowing that the baby's life would signal her death; *now* he remembers his anger at feeling he was forced out of Spain; *now* he recalls the "moral panic" he perceived in Canadians who listened to his speeches and donated to the Spanish cause; *now* he describes how he warned them that Spain was the "staging ground for the gathering war in Europe that [would] consume the lives of our sons and daughters" (306); and *now* he explains how he learned where he might find his child (307). In the final analysis, Bock's Dr. Norman Bethune puts his trust in memory and auto/biography, and he claims to be "content": "Now I sit here content, polishing these fragments of memory in an attempt to make something of a life pitted by failure, abandonment and war. This is the one perfection remaining for me after a lifetime of compromise and fallen ideals. No, these musings shall not diminish that which is lost. You cannot fail in memory as you can, so horribly, in the operating theatre" (308).

I am not prepared to judge which is the worst failure—the surgical or the mnemonic. Both can lead to suffering and death. But Bethune's point here is less that memory can fail than that forgetting is a failure. Remembering cannot restore what has been lost or left undone, but forgetting is unforgiveable, and *The Communist's Daughter* is a plea to remember, to resist forgetting those uncomfortable things it is so much easier to forget. You cannot fail in memory *if* you choose to remember and in remembering create a landscape of memory that invites empathic unsettlement because it bears witness (secondary as much as primary) to the unbearable. By addressing his autobiographical confession to me, by entrusting me—his listening reader—with his "fragments of memory," he makes me, and all his readers, secondary witnesses. And as such, I, we, become responsible for his and our shared landscape of memory. To my mind the most remarkable feature of this text is the remembering it provides for those years between the wars when so many warning signs in Europe and Asia were apparent, but ignored. This Canadian ghost whose experiences encompassed both hemispheres and three wars has come back from the dead to remind us of the importance of remembering while there is still time in today's world.





Dennis Bock's choice of Norman Bethune as the narrator-autobiographer of this novel strikes me as exceptionally astute. Even in this century, when it is manifestly clear how important China is on the world stage and how relevant the country and its reverence for Bethune are to contemporary Canada, with its large Chinese-Canadian population, Norman Bethune and what he achieved are neither widely known nor celebrated by Canadians. The reasons for the comparative neglect (compared, for example, with iconic figures like Tom Thomson, Louis Riel, or Glenn Gould) are many.[10] Communism has always been suspect in Canada, so making a hero out of a sympathizer is, at best, *awkward*; Bethune died far away in a country little understood and viewed with suspicion, and he died helping a Communist cause; in any case, he was arrogant and difficult, a rather unlikeable character who ruffled feathers and rubbed people the wrong way (notably his fellow doctors in Montreal and Spain). But in addition to these rationales for forgetting Bethune, I think there is another factor that contributes to his neglect: the Second Sino-Japanese War and its overshadowing (in the West) by the outbreak of the Second World War. North American attention to events in China from the mid-1930s to the mid-1940s has been scant. Although news about Japanese atrocities in China certainly reached Canada and the United States, our main concerns have been with Japan, the war in the Pacific, the cataclysmic ending of the war by atomic bomb, and then the long process of Cold War forgetting, evading, even prevaricating over the treatment of Japanese Americans and Japanese Canadians during and after the war. China's internal history during these years and the Cultural Revolution barely surfaced to catch popular or general public attention. To further obscure the past, Japan continues to deny its wartime atrocities, and China remains cautious about pressing for apologies.[11] The wall of silence in the West finally fell in 1997, when Chinese-American historian Iris Chang published *The Rape of Nanking: The Forgotten Holocaust of World War II*. Another decade would pass before Chinese-Canadian writer Marjorie Chan would tackle this difficult subject head-on.





In her play *A Nanking Winter*, Chan creates a theatrical exploration of both Iris Chang's life and of events in the winter of 1937 in Nanking (today the city is called Nanjing, but Chang and Chan use the name current in the 1930s). This important play premiered at Toronto's Factory Theatre Mainstage in February 2008 and deserves to be toured across Canada. However, I have not been able to see it in performance, so must limit my observations to the published text. But first, I must go back to Iris Chang because Chan dedicates her play to Chang—"for Iris"—and bases one of her main characters on Chang. *A Nanking Winter* stages a commemoration of Chang as a way to remember Nanking and, in the process, constructs us as witnesses to the recuperation of a terrifying *double* landscape of memory. Iris Chang (1968–2004) was born in the United States to parents who had emigrated from China. Her grandparents told her stories about their escape from the massacre in Nanking, and these stories continued to haunt her until she undertook the research for *The Rape of Nanking*.[12] Although this was not her only book, it was the one that brought her fame and notoriety. The reception of the book, the publicity, the harassment she suffered after its publication, and possibly the horrors she uncovered in her research contributed to her growing depression and mental health problems. Chang shot herself on 9 November 2004 on a country road in California. She was thirty-six years old, married, and with a two-year-old son. Chan's Irene Wu is loosely based on Iris Chang insofar as she is harassed by hate phone calls, bullied by her publishers, who are worried about how to market her book, married—albeit in the play to a man of Japanese-American descent—and commits suicide. The Irene character also suffers from depression and has been sent away for treatment, but in the play the cause of her depression is directly linked to her research into what happened in Nanking and to the fact that her publishers sanitize the book by changing its title behind her back. They refuse to allow the word "holocaust" to be used on the title page, opting instead for the innocuous-sounding "The Nanking Incident." This name change, however, is a device in the play; the real book is not camouflaged behind such a trivializing term as "incident."



In *The Rape of Nanking*, Chang describes in relentless detail the scale of Japanese atrocities over a period of a few weeks, the sheer ferocity of their attacks on helpless women, children, and civilian men, and the measures taken to suppress the facts. She also addresses the phenomenon she sees as a refusal to believe by both those in China and in the West (officially, Japan has always denied these war crimes), and she criticizes China's postwar politics of forgetting as an effort to advance economically by developing trade relations with Japan. Chang demonstrates, through quotations and photographs, that the Japanese officers and soldiers viewed the Chinese as subhuman and treated killing them as a form of ethnic cleansing that prefigured the Nazi policy towards the Jews of Europe. What's more, she uncovered another story within the story of Nanking with which the Western world has yet to come to terms—the story of John Rabe, the good Nazi who risked his life to save hundreds of Chinese women and girls. When Nanking fell to the Japanese Imperial Army on 13 December 1937, after six months of fighting against Chiang Kai-shek's army, it was the capitol of Nationalist China. Chang claims that approximately one-quarter million non-combatants were slaughtered by Japanese troops (*Rape of Nanking* 4), and she insists that Nanking represents one of the largest-scale rapes in history (89). To substantiate this claim, she not only relies on statistics, which are debated, but on interviews with

Chinese eyewitnesses and survivors, and on the documentary evidence provided by Western photographers and witnesses such as nurses, doctors, missionaries, and the German businessman working for Siemens AG, John Rabe. In addition to Rabe's diary testimony (which Chang tracked down and was granted access to by Rabe's descendants), she quotes from the diary kept by the American missionary and teacher Minnie Vautrin, the head of Ginling Women's Arts and Science College, which became the refuge for Chinese women who escaped the ravages of the Japanese soldiers. Others' diaries, letters, and reports also support Chang's claims, but Rabe and Vautrin are of particular interest for my discussion because Chan draws on their stories in her play and creates two characters based on their experiences during that terrible Nanking winter.





Vautrin (1886–1941) committed suicide not long after her return to the United States, and Rabe (1882–1950) was detained by the Gestapo shortly after his return to Germany in 1938 and then denounced as a Nazi and arrested by the Allies after the war. In *A Nanking Winter*, the characters called Anna Mallery and Niklas Hermann are based on these two historical figures.[13] As they did with Bethune, the Chinese honour Rabe and Vautrin in today's Nanjing, even though official policy is not to demand an apology from Japan. Rabe's former residence in Nanjing was renovated and opened as a memorial hall in 2006, and Vautrin is hailed as a heroine for sheltering thousands of girls and women within Ginling College. But this attention, like the films about the massacre and memorials to the victims and their supporters, is very recent. Behind this attention, informing and inspiring it, is Iris Chang's *The Rape of Nanking*.

If one were to ask why a Canadian playwright would decide to create a play about this subject or why Canadian audiences should be interested, an answer might be that such an important and terrible occurrence needs to be better known than it is. Another answer, especially in view of the way Chan constructs her play, is that racism, rape as a weapon of war, and the practice of ethnic cleansing are not bad things that only happened in the past or that were the exclusive prerogative of Nazis. For me, yet another reason for my interest is that *A Nanking Winter* is above all about memory, about bearing witness, and about listening to the ghosts of past wars *now* because the conditions that led to those wars are still with us and the ghosts from that past haunt the present. It is this memory-work that makes this play so pertinent for my investigation and such a critical segue to the Second World War texts examined in the next chapters. In many ways, this Canadian play, with its Chinese, American, German, and Chinese-American characters, recreates the winter of 1937, while the world teetered on the edge of an abyss, to remind and warn us about the dangers of forgetting just how haunted the 1930s were, how much we need to remember those years, and how interconnected we are as human beings. By virtue of its non-Canadianness, it signals Canada's growing awareness of the larger world and its position within that world. Even more than *Can You See Me Yet?* but more still like *The Communist's Daughter*, this play alerts the country (or, at least, those who see or read it) to Canada's position within that global context, a position with its distinct responsibilities that the Second World War novels, plays, films, and memoirs investigate. Where contemporary First World War texts continue to examine the parameters of an internal sense of national identity, Second World War texts often take place beyond national borders and highlight behaviour, political decisions, and failures at home. By creating this play, Marjorie Chan shoulders a share of Canadian responsibility for remembering that larger world history and for remembering the dark years between the wars.





*A Nanking Winter* has two acts, but instead of moving forward in time as we expect plays to do, the second act predates the first. Act 1 is written in English and takes place in the California apartment of Irene Wu and her husband Kurt Tagasaki. It is November 2004 and Irene's book about the Nanking massacre and mass rape is being released; author's copies are expected to arrive at any moment. The apartment is still full of boxes containing Irene's research, and during the opening sequences of the play she will bring more boxes into the living room: the past literally materializes in the present onstage for all to see. Irene's husband comes home with champagne for a private celebration; her sister, an artist, arrives full of chatter and excitement, and then Irene's publisher shows up accompanied by a lawyer for the publishing house. Act 2 takes place in Nanking in December 1937, and the playwright calls for variations in language and the assumption that Mandarin is being spoken extensively, even though English is necessary to communicate with a non-Chinese audience. How we arrive in Nanking in December 1937 from California in 2004 is central to the form and meaning of the play. Technically, this shift is straightforward enough: the actors double their roles so that the Audrey of Act 1 becomes the Big Mei of Act 2, a young woman, who is pregnant and will be killed, and Irene becomes Little Mei, a teenager who is raped but survives her ordeal to thank Niklas Hermann (the John Rabe character, who is played by the same actor who performs Irene's husband in Act 1) and to bear witness to what took place during those weeks of 1937. The brief Epilogue, set backstage in a lecture hall, takes place in 2005, approximately one year after Act 1. A more mature, responsible and serious Audrey enters and prepares to do a reading from "*The Nanking Incident* by Irene Wu" (84). The only other onstage character in this brief scene is Julia, Irene's publisher, and the two women agree that this public occasion for the story of Nanking is "what [Irene] would have wanted" (13). Irene Wu is not there to do this reading herself because she is dead. She killed herself near the end of Act 1.

In Act 1, Chan presents her version of what happened to her character Irene Wu and how December 1937 in Nanking returns in the performing present of the play. The act runs through without scenes or interruptions, and this seamlessness is strategic because the transition from present to past happens at the end of Act 1, when we are all carried forward by being taken back in time. There is very little action as such in Act 1. Irene and Kurt are clearly experiencing marital problems brought on, it seems, by her discoveries about Nanking and exacerbated by his parents' commitment to visiting the Yakunsi Shinto shrine in Tokyo, where Kurt's grandfather is enshrined. This shrine is highly controversial because it honours soldiers who fought for the Imperial Army in the Sino-Japanese War and in the Second World War. 1,068 men are honoured there who were convicted of war crimes by the international tribunal held in Tokyo after the war, and among these men are fourteen who were charged with the highest level of responsibility for atrocities. Kurt's grandfather is among the larger group; he was at Nanking in 1937. Now that Irene knows the extent of what happened there, she is appalled by her husband's refusal to recognize what this man was like when he was not being the kindly grandfather Kurt remembers from his childhood. Audrey arrives, vibrating with excitement; Irene protests that she does not want a party and retreats to her office; and the phone rings—repeatedly. Each time it rings, the sense of dread and alarm increases because Irene has been receiving vicious hate calls about her book. One caller has threatened to rape, mutilate, and kill her just as the Japanese did to Chinese women in Nanking. According to Kurt, who accompanied her, she was constantly harassed on research trips to China and Japan, and he is dubious—perhaps influenced by the hate calls—about Irene's claims: "Irene says that the rapes were systematic and deliberate but I just don't know. War is messy. Bad shit happens. The violation of women is tragic, yes. But calculated? I don't know. I've never been in a war" (10). In other words, Irene's husband blames her in part for making the claims that lead to her harassment, and he undermines her arguments, her research, and her confidence. "War is messy. Bad shit happens" might just be the most accurate and yet the most simplistic comments made in this play or made by any character in any of the works I have examined. At the same time, Kurt's speech illustrates the enormous challenge faced by anyone who tries to create a landscape of memory that others simply refuse to see or acknowledge. Kurt speaks for most of us who need to downplay, or even ignore, the evidence so we can carry on with our lives.

When the publisher, Julia, and the lawyer, Frank, arrive, things go from bad to worse, and then to a crisis. The tension escalates when Irene realizes that her husband, her sister, and her publisher conspired to change the book's title, delete the word "holocaust" in its title and replace it with "incident." Frank is the most obnoxious and threatening of the people confronting Irene because he represents the legal interests and marketing agenda of the publisher. He insists on producing a book that will sell, rather than turn people off, and together with Julia he wants Irene to tour the country to maximize publicity and sales. "We want you to be the go-to Chinese writer," Julia chirps (21). Frank is more blunt: her book is too controversial, she levels accusations at "the current Japanese government and the royal family!" and her hero is a Nazi: "I thought, a Nazi hero, what the fuck! [...] Never start talking about Nazis in polite company, it's bound to go badly" (22). In the next breath, he praises Irene for her research, for getting her hands on that Nazis's diary: "What a great story. It'd make a great movie....You could call it 'Nazi of Nanking'" (23). As if this crass idea of commodification is not enough, Frank and Julia go on to praise Irene's ability "to tell [the story] from a Western point of view" (24) because it transforms the white missionaries ("Americans and Germans, even Nazis") into the saviours of the Chinese people. To Irene, this is appalling. Her book will be marketed to represent Westerners as heroes, so it will be "more palatable for a Western audience....Bad Japs rape and kill dumb Chinks. Good white people save the day. Is that more the slant you were going for?" (25). What should have been a quiet celebration at home has deteriorated into a bitter power struggle. She demands that her original title stand—*Nanking: The Other Holocaust*—but Frank refuses: "Absolutely not." (26). In this present of 2004, the term *holocaust* can only be used to refer to the Nazi genocidal persecution of the Jews; the Second World War haunts and controls the twenty-first-century present. In any case, it is too late.

While Irene was in an institution being treated for depression, her publisher, with her husband's consent, changed the title. *The Nanking*

*Incident* is a *fait accompli*, and boxes of the books are about to arrive at the door. Irene's response is twofold. First she tells them, "You're helping...to erase history. You're aiding a denial of war crimes on a massive scale. Diminishing any culpability, any responsibility" (28). Then she accuses Frank, Julia, even her husband and sister, of denying that a holocaust took place in Nanking:

> IRENE: *[...] It's been forgotten for so long—I don't want people to forget! The numbers from Nanking are real. The Japanese army kept records, the Red Cross kept records, the journalists from all countries kept records. They established numbers—from a number of sources—during the initial six week invasion period, twenty thousand women and children raped. At least three hundred thousand dead! In six weeks! [...] and to dismiss Nanking—to dismiss the three hundred thousand dead, to dismiss three hundred thousand individuals—to treat them as trivial, to refer to their deaths as an "incident," well—it's as bad as denial of the Holocaust. (30–31)*



As this excruciating act draws to a close, Frank and Julia leave, Kurt leaves—the marriage as well as the apartment—the books arrive, and Irene looks at them with her sister, who tries to be positive about the cover. Then Irene goes to the bathroom and we hear water running while Audrey chatters about the gift she has made for her sister; it is a statue created from the clay of the riverbank at Nanking, a statue of Kwanyin who heals those with "suffering in their souls" (39). This speech is followed by silence. Then we hear "*a single gunshot from inside the bathroom*" (39). Audrey realizes what has happened beyond the locked bathroom door because Irene has tried to commit suicide before, and she screams for help. Her screams become hysterical and "*her language shifts to Mandarin, if possible*" (39). A man enters and approaches her; he is wearing a Nazi armband. He speaks Chinese and offers to help her, and we realize we are beginning to move back in time and place because this man is Niklas Hermann and Audrey is now Big Mei, a young woman who he is rescuing from her ruined house in Nanking and will take to the refuge at Ginling College: "*They exit through the door and into the past*" (42).

Concluding Act 1 with this transition and juxtaposing it with Irene's suicide accomplishes at least two things. Theatrically, it allows for an intermission, a release of tension, before portraying the horrors of the past, while at the same time establishing the *presence* of that past and its continuity with the present. An audience can leave the theatre, go to the washrooms or buy drinks, knowing the second act is already in place. Thematically, and symbolically, this transition, strategically juxtaposed with Irene's suicide, is already suggesting that the trauma of past events reaches into the present, that the struggle to remember and make others remember is a life-threatening one. The ghosts of Nanking, as Atwood might say, are thirsty, but regardless of the personal cost we must go back to the past, to Nanking, to the rape and massacre of December 1937. Living safely in Canada with Marjorie Chan in the twenty-first century does not protect or absolve us. What was in Act 1 a personal journey of reconstruction through memory and pain for Irene is now poised to become a collective journey of cultural remembering. When Act 2 opens, we are in Nanking in December 1937; the set is "*imagistic and simple*" but suggests dirt and chaos. The Japanese have invaded the city.

The first character to speak is Little Mei (played by the actor who was Irene). She has been raped, her throat cut, and left for dead on a heap of women's bodies, but she has survived and will be taken to Ginling College, where hundreds of girls and women are kept safe from marauding soldiers. The nineteen short scenes that comprise Act 2 provide us with a variety of eyewitness reports on what is happening in the city and how Niklas Hermann and the headmistress of the college, Anna Mallery, are working to safeguard the girls and provide basic necessities. Little Mei often slips outside the gates, at great personal risk, to see things for herself. A Japanese diplomat arrives at the gates demanding that Mallery and Hermann hand over women for a Japanese army "Comfort Station"; he will accept prostitutes, but tends to see all Chinese females as prostitutes (71-72). His rationale for such a grotesque request is that such places will reduce attacks on Chinese women and that he wants to "alleviate the number of 'incidents'" (71)—the exact term used by Irene's publishers to market her book. Niklas bargains with the man and writes to Hitler begging for Germany to reason with Japan. Anna prays, while hiding Chinese soldiers in the college attic and scrounging for food. One by one, Little Mei, Big Mei, Niklas, and Anna describe what they have seen. As Little Mei says, "I wanted to see them [the dead]. See them with my very own eyes. Look at every face" (53). Act 2 moves inexorably to its close as Big Mei and Little Mei are taken to the "Comfort Station." Big Mei, who is pregnant, is rejected by the soldiers and killed; Little Mei is raped and slashed as she relives the scene that opened Act 2. Many of the Ginling College refugees will survive but very few of the women outside its gates will. Little Mei is an exception, and in living she assumes the burden of telling and resisting those who prefer to forget. Through the doubling of actors' roles and the carefully positioned transition from present to past, Chan suggests that Little Mei's spirit—her ghost—inhabits or inspires Irene until Irene's job is done. She also makes it clear that the past lives on in both personal and cultural memory, that one woman's story is a much larger, even a sadly universal, story. By ending the second act with Little Mei, who speaks directly to the audience to tell us that she "walked from Shanghai to Nanking to escape the Japanese, [was] captured, raped and left for dead, December 1937 [and] survived" (82), Chan leaves us with an image of life instead of death (Irene's suicide) and with some modicum of hope that the ghosts will be heard, the past remembered.



Two of the Canadian texts I have discussed deal directly with the aftermath of the First World War; all three portray the years between the wars as deeply disturbing and characterized by warnings that largely fell on deaf ears. Just as the ghosts of one war stalk their pages, so too do the spectres of more wars, even another world war, cast their long and ominous shadows across the stories they tell. Of course, Findley, Bock, and Chan—even Lowry—were writing with the benefit of hindsight, but they use that hindsight strategically to focus on the task of remembering the past. *Can You See Me Yet?*, *The Communist's Daughter*, and *A Nanking Winter* are complex memory-works that engage their readers (and audiences) in the process of remembering history in order to insist that we assume some responsibility for the desire to forget and take part in the effort to rediscover the past. By recreating the years and the events between the two world wars, these works fill in some of the gaps in a Canadian landscape of memory that stretches far beyond national borders to acknowledge and embrace a wider world, and this step across the border parallels the direction taken by many Second World War texts. Each of these three works also anchors memory and warning within an individual—Cassandra, Bethune, Irene/Little Mei—while establishing a *more than personal* accountability to the past and for the future. Each insists that personal memory contributes to and is shaped (or distorted) by collective memory and that the landscape we call *cultural* memory—of a family, a community, a nation—must make room for personal stories previously denied or erased if we hope to learn from the past or to heal the traumas of war.



And it is with this connection, essential and indissoluble, of the personal and the collective that I close my brief exploration of the haunted world between the wars. Poetry achieves this kind of succinct yet provisional closure better than any other literary genre, and so I turn to poems for my closure. Frank Davey revisits his childhood memories in *Back to the War*, especially in poems like "The Battleship"

> *This war memorial was erected in 1921 outside the* CPR *station on Cordova Street in downtown Vancouver. The* Bronze Angel *was intended to commemorate* CPR *employees who enlisted and died in the Great War, but a plate carrying the dates for both wars was attached to the base after the Second World War. Today this traditional, religious memorial depicting a dead soldier borne heavenwards by an angel seems like an incongruous reminder of an earlier, simpler era now lost in a bustling, commercial urban setting. Photograph: J. Grace.*

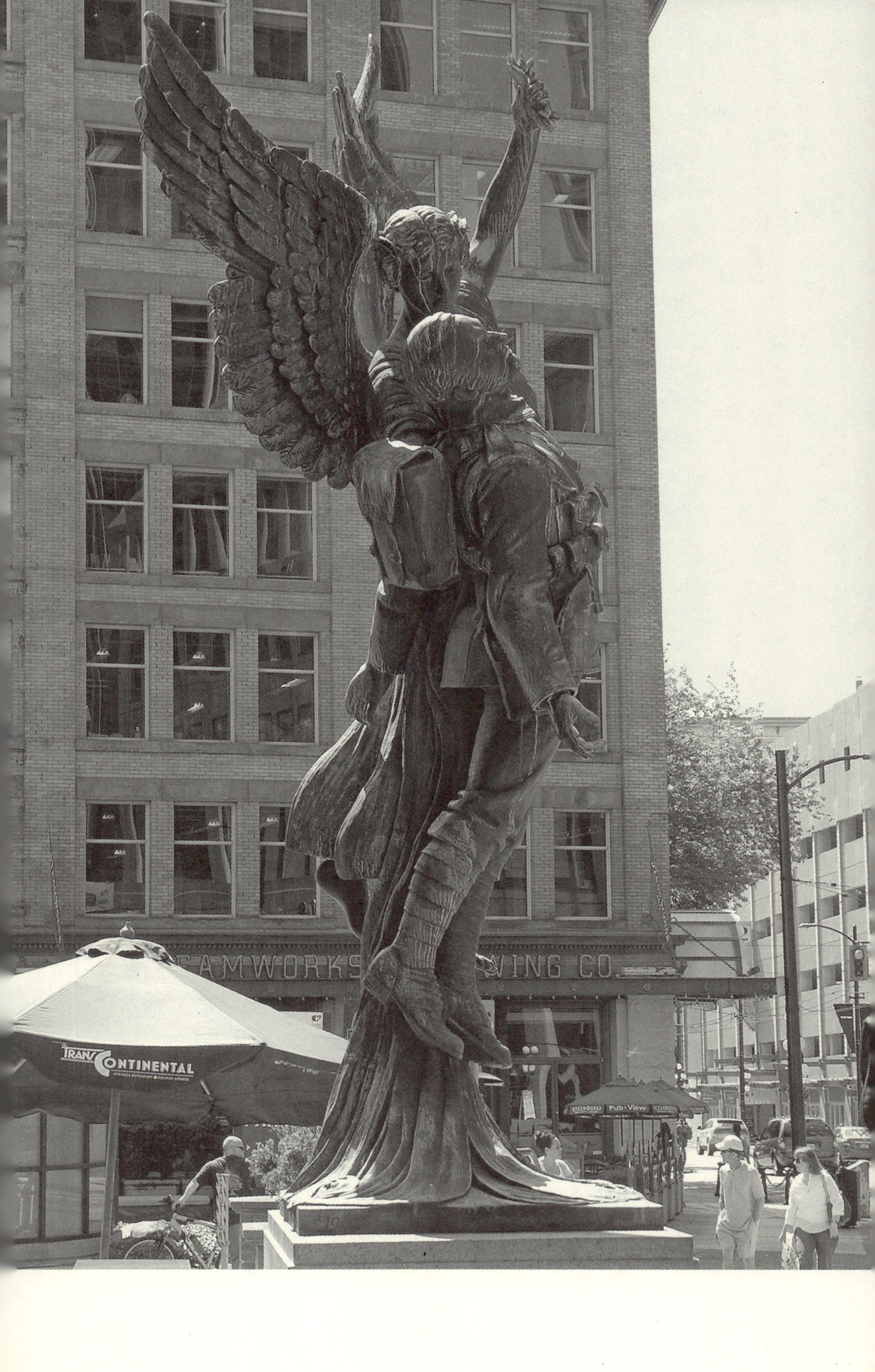
TRANSCONTINENTAL
Pub·View

(11), "The News" (14), and "The Gun" (73). The entire volume recalls the beginning of the Second World War, the duration, and the aftermath, through the eyes of the child Frank was, and so he remembers himself as a "small boy sitting in his crib" (11) colouring a battleship green, blue, yellow, and red. Or he remembers asking his parents: "Who are the Japs?" and "Why does Hitler hate us?" (14). The answers he remembers getting are cultural clichés, ill-informed accusations, or evasions: The "Japs" are "Small & sneaky"; Hitler hates us "Because he's German"; and "You don't want to find out" (14). But the poem that moves me most deeply, perhaps because it evokes a familiar landscape of memory, perhaps because it speaks to the child in me as well as the adult who has stood before war memorials puzzled and troubled, is Bill New's "My Vancouver Starts."





To appreciate this poem, try to imagine a war memorial, preferably the *Bronze Angel* erected in 1921 on Cordova Street outside the old CPR station in downtown Vancouver. Like so many Canadian memorials, it was originally created to commemorate the dead of the Great War, but two decades later new dates had to be incised on the pedestal: 1914–1918, and then 1939–1945. The poem, like the statue, speaks for itself and to us. The personal voice includes the collective experience in an elegiac remembering of time and place, war and death, events that have shaped us all:

*my Vancouver starts*

*my Vancouver starts somewhere behind blackout curtains,*
*starts in a fenced-garden*
*with the canopy cloth on a wooden toy truck,*
*camouflaged,*

*starts with a street-car ride*
*and the dead soldier on cordova street,*
*limp on an angel's arm,*

*dragged upward*
*beside the southeast corner*
*of the* CPR *station:*

*the soldier never moved:*

*every childhood trip to town, there he stayed, hanging:*
*heaven as close as maybe*
*the north shore mountains,*
*out of reach,*
*the coastline dissolving in war and death,*
*as clear as fear and rain.*

# PART IV

# Testing the Nation in the Second World War

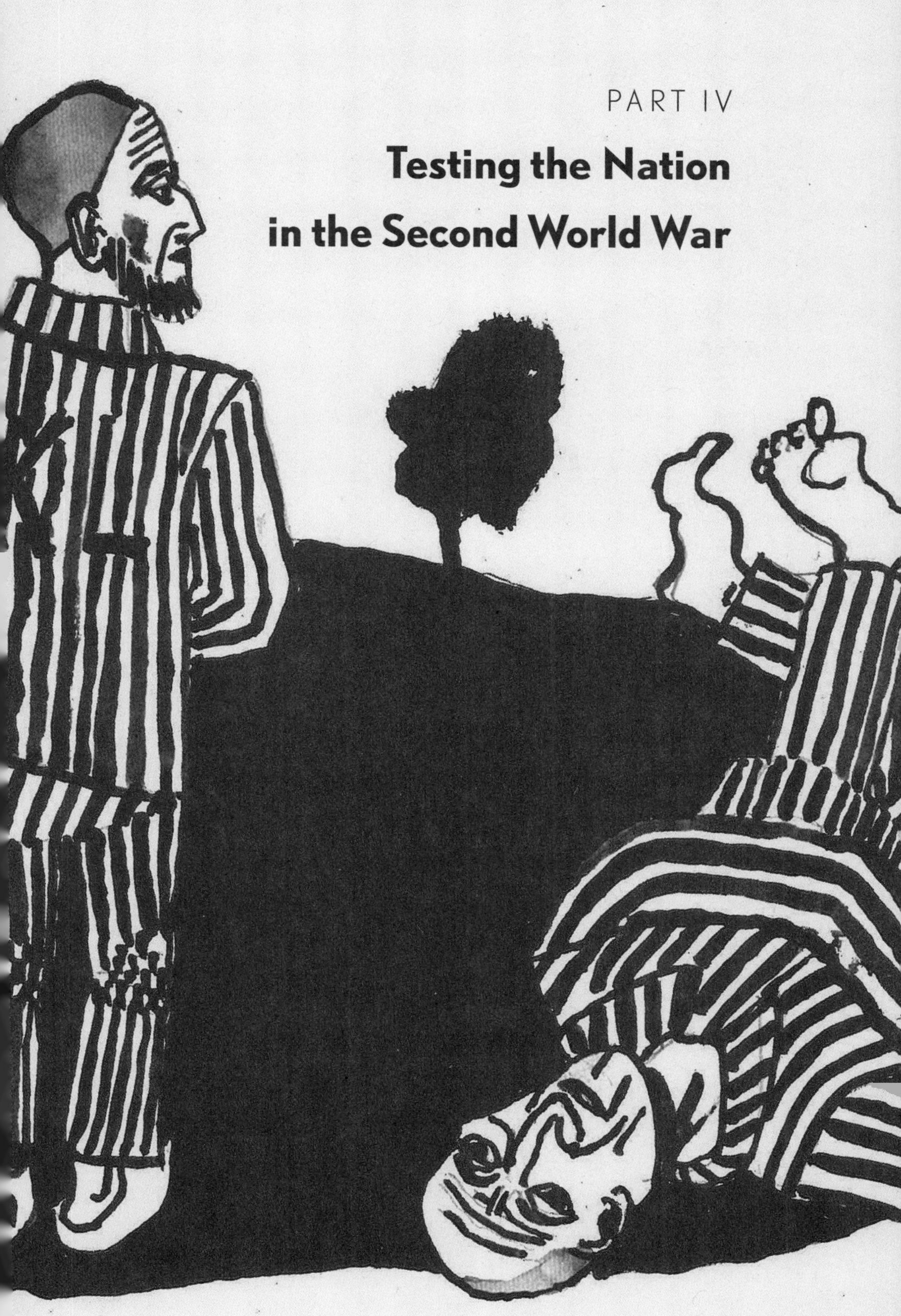

Where do any of us come from
in this cold country? Oh Canada,
whether it is admitted or not,
we come from you, we come
from you....We grow where
we are not seen, we flourish
where we are not heard,
the thick undergrowth of an
unlikely planting. Where do
we come from Obasan?...
We come from our
untold tales that wait for
their untold telling.



**Joy Kogawa**

*Obasan*, 226

But the end of summer 1939
is a line drawn down through
the memory of everyone who was
then alive. We were all about to
be pitched together into a
melting pot of violence
from which a few of us
would emerge intact and
the rest of us would perish.



**Timothy Findley**

"Stones," 198

Memory, like history,
is uncontrollable. It manifests
itself in unruly ways. It cascades
through the generations in a
series of misplaced fears,
mysterious wounds, odd habits.
The child inhabits the texture
of these fears and habits, without
knowing they are memory.



**Lisa Appignanesi**

*Losing the Dead*, 8

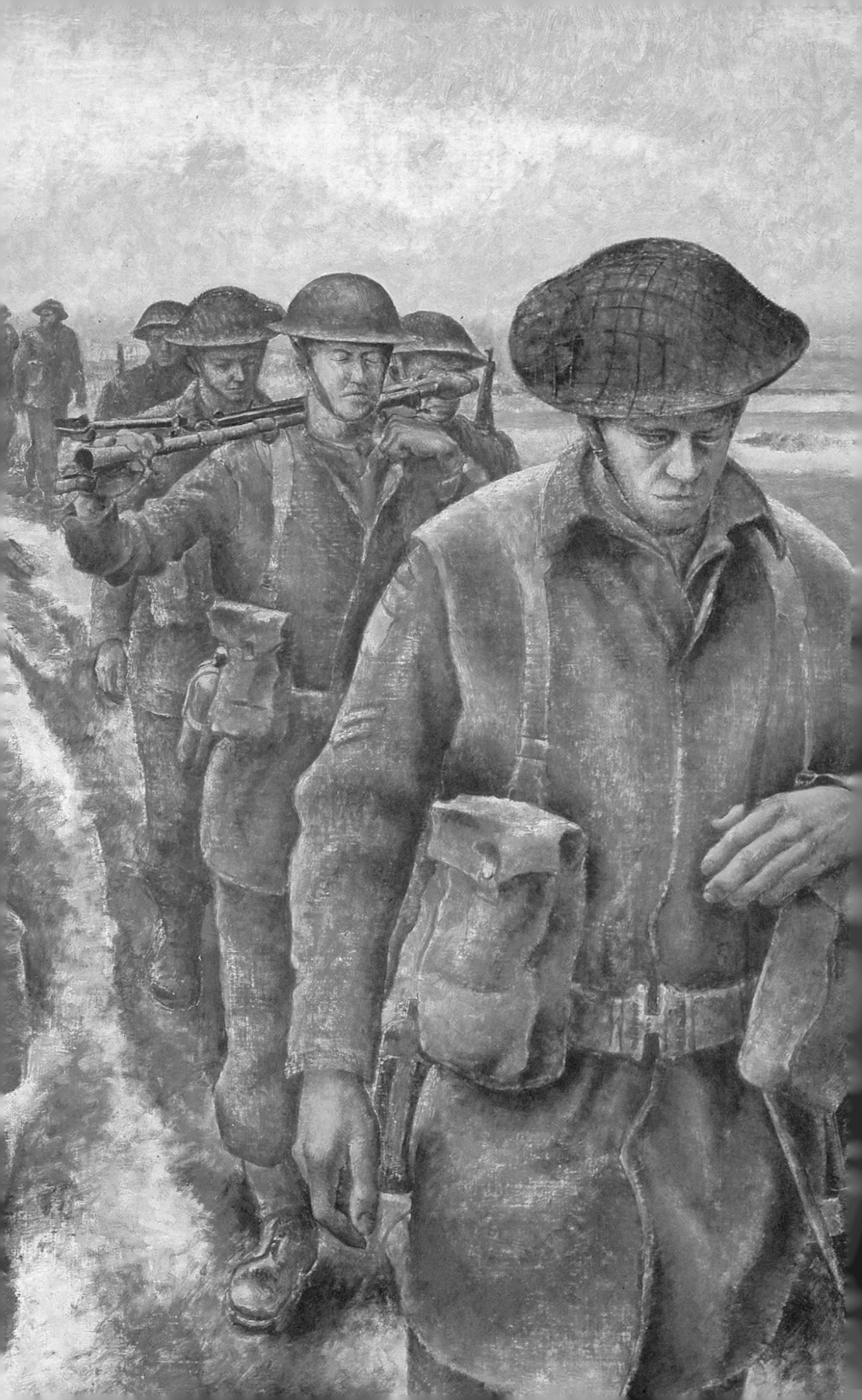

7

# "Made in Canada"

## The Second World War in the Pacific



MOVING FROM the literary and artistic representations of the First World War through the years between and into the subject of the Second World War in the next chapters necessitates a shift in focus from the concept of nationmaking *abroad*, or coming of age on the battle front in the first war, to that of being made-in-Canada in the second. This is not to suggest that the label "made in Canada" refers only to the Second World War or only to the experience of war; it simply indicates my shift in perspective from a discourse that stresses foreign events as shaping a young country's identity on the national and international stages to a discourse that puts Canada, Canadian policies and practices abroad and at home, and Canadian ideas about identity under a microscope—often, in fact, on trial. To a degree, the national identity question is taken for granted in the works I turn to now, but what that identity means and who can claim it are the troubling issues that surface with clarity in the context of remembering the Second World War. Where the story of Canada in the Great War can still, today, be told and read as celebratory, foundational, and even heroic, the same cannot be said about representations of the Second World War. Instead, the novels, plays, films, poetry, and even the memoirs and paintings tell a different story. When Margaret Atwood said that "we tend to remember the awful things done to us, and to forget the awful things we did" (see the epigraph to Chapter 1), she might have been thinking about the differences that characterize Canadian representations of the two wars: Ypres, Vimy, Amiens, Passchendaele still remind us of suffering, tragedy, loss, bravery, and ultimate victory; stories about Canada's response within her own borders to Jews fleeing the Holocaust, to Japan and all Canadians of Japanese ancestry after Pearl Harbor, or to German cities like Hamburg and Dresden are less amenable to redemptive retellings or glorious versions of fighting the good war. Works about this war make it impossible "to forget the awful things we did."



The Second World War was very different from the First. It was more complex, fought on a truly global scale, and it involved a direct, ruthless assault on civilians in every country the Nazis attacked or invaded, or against which the Allies retaliated, in cities like London, Coventry, Dresden, Hamburg, Stalingrad, Hiroshima, Nagasaki, and in those Chinese (and other Asian) cities invaded by the Japanese Imperial Army—Hong Kong, for example, or Nanking. The Second World War was a *good* war because this time the Allies really were fighting for freedom. Fascism and Nazism were serious threats to a democratic way of life, and they fomented the racial hatreds and other forms of bigotry that still surface and threaten human rights in the early twenty-first century. With ever more sophisticated technology at the service of war—improved air power, faster, better submarines, and finally the atomic bomb—war was no longer a matter of military combat or protracted trench warfare. With such weapons, a state could wipe out entire populations within its own borders as well as in the countries it invaded. The First World War ended in an armistice, not in German surrender, and the Treaty of Versailles left seething resentments in

Germany, which paved the way for Hitler's rise to power in a democratic election, and increased suspicions and dissatisfaction in the other major European powers. Where would Canada stand on any of the issues left unaddressed by the treaty? With no understanding, or living memory, of what it meant to live through a war fought on our soil, and with no open acknowledgement or discussion of our own prejudices, but with easily invoked patriotic memories of rising to the military occasion for the Great War, there could be no hesitation. Canada stood quickly and unequivocally with the Allies as soon as Britain, France, and the Soviets realized that Hitler could not be appeased. Canada declared war on Germany in her own name on 10 September 1939. However, warning signs that we also harboured extremist views and racist attitudes and could and would legislate fascist-like state controls over groups of Canadians were there for those who cared to pay attention to them. They were *there* in the general populace, among politicians and educators, and in the media. They were *there* in the repression of Canadian Communists who were harassed or imprisoned during the war and even in the police closure of the play *Eight Men Speak*.[1] They were *there* in novels like Gwethalyn Graham's *Earth and High Heaven* (1944) and would continue to surface in other novels like Henry Kreisel's *The Betrayal* (1964) and A.M. Klein's *The Second Scroll* (1951).





*Earth and High Heaven* may have achieved its popularity because of its love story, but that love story involved an upper middle-class Anglo-Saxon, Christian woman from Westmount and a middle-class, professional Jew, a lawyer, who grew up in northern Ontario. Neither family encouraged an inter-ethnic marriage, but Erica Drake's bigoted father refused to meet the Jew and came close to rejecting his daughter for her stubborn insistence on loving Mark Reiser. Drake was enraged at the very thought of a Jewish son-in-law. What's more, his attitudes and serious misunderstanding of people not from his class or exactly like him were not unique or isolated in 1940s Canada. No one knew this better than A.M. Klein. In *The Second Scroll*, he creates a Canadian-born-

and-raised Jewish writer whose parents praise Canada as a land of freedom even as they experience anti-Semitism in Montreal and carry their own sense of pain and guilt about being safe in Canada while family and friends in Poland are swept up in pogroms, massacres, and eventually the Holocaust. The narrator of the story, haunted by references to an Uncle Melech Davidson back in Poland, decides to find his uncle immediately after the war, and his biographical search enables him to tell his own life story and to explore what it means to be Jewish, whether in Canada or elsewhere, after the Second World War. Uncle Melech becomes the beckoning ghost who haunts the narrator and draws him into a journey in search of the family's European past and the 1949 present in the newly formed state of Israel. This is very much a novel about haunting, bearing witness, and remembering a past that has profoundly shaped the present.[2]



Compared with the large number of post-1977 works devoted to the Great War, literary and artistic attention to the Second World War has been belated. In part, this is because we are still closer in time to that war and because remembering and representing it are painful. But there are other factors that contribute to this belatedness, among them the scope and complexity of the war, American domination of the discourse in novels like *Slaughterhouse-Five* or *Gravity's Rainbow* and the pervasive influence of American combat films (including thoughtful ones like *Saving Private Ryan* [1998] or *The Thin Red Line* [1998]), and the sheer difficulty caused by military aspects of what happened during the war and the "awful things we [the Allies as well as just Canadians] did." Important Canadian historical discussion and debate on the war only began in the mid-1980s with military historians like Desmond Morton, and the journal *Canadian Military History* began publishing in 1992, thereby providing a venue for basic information about Canada's role and descriptions of events and participants. But it has not been until the early twenty-first century that critical attention and reassessment have focused intensely on the war with works like Pierre Berton's

*Marching as to War: Canada's Turbulent Years 1899–1953* appearing in 2002, Jack Granatstein's *The Last Good War: An Illustrated History of Canada in the Second World War, 1939–1945* published in 2005, and Randall Hansen's *Fire and Fury: The Allied Bombing of Germany, 1942–45,* precipitating its own form of fury in 2008 because Hansen criticized Allied area bombing practices between 1942 and the end of the war.[3] Canadian pilots were part of the bombing raids; they were under orders, and Germany's blitzkrieg horror over England called for a total war response. As Hansen points out in *Fire and Fury,* the British public was not informed about Bomber Command's attacks on civilians (neither were Canadians) in Hamburg, where many women and children were "sunk into the asphalt, burned to death, and cooked" (117), and he describes the American Air Force treatment of Dresden, in February 1945, as "terror bombing" (246).





Hansen's description of Allied bombing bears an eerie resemblance to the imagery and emotion of Canadian poet Raymond Souster (1921–2012), who served with the RCAF for four years during the war. In his poem "The Dresden Special," Souster creates the poetic equivalent *for World War Two* of McCrae's "In Flanders Fields." The profound differences between the two poems are obvious and acutely disturbing because there are no ghosts of the dead urging the living to keep faith in Souster's remembering, just "charred bodies":

*The Dresden Special*

*The R.A.F. called it*
*The Dresden Special...*

*One hundred thirty thousand*
*charred bodies jammed together*
*between two bread slices.*

*But even at that*
*jolly old Sir Winston*
*had no trouble lifting it*
*in his pudgy fingers.*

*After a bite or two*
*he smacked his lips, grunting,*
Just the way I like Nazis
Very well done...





Except that the few major strategic military targets (railways and munitions factories) were outside Dresden, and the babies, children, and mothers living in the city's historic centre were not Nazis.

No other work I know has the force of this little poem, but other Canadians who fought in the Second World War remembered and depicted it with similar feelings of guilt and despair. Earle Birney's "The Road to Nijmegen" is a moving example that captures the sense of weariness and bleak survival portrayed in Alex Colville's famous painting *Infantry, near Nijmegen, Holland* (1946):

*Numbed on the long road to mangled Nijmegen*
*I thought that only the living of others assures us*
*the gentle and true we remember as trees walking*
*Their arms reach down from the light of kindness*
*into this Lazarus tomb.*
...
*Over the clank of the jeep*
*your quick grave laughter*
*outrising at last the rockets*
*brought me what spells I repeat*
*as I travel this road*
*that arrives at no future*
*and what creed I can bring*

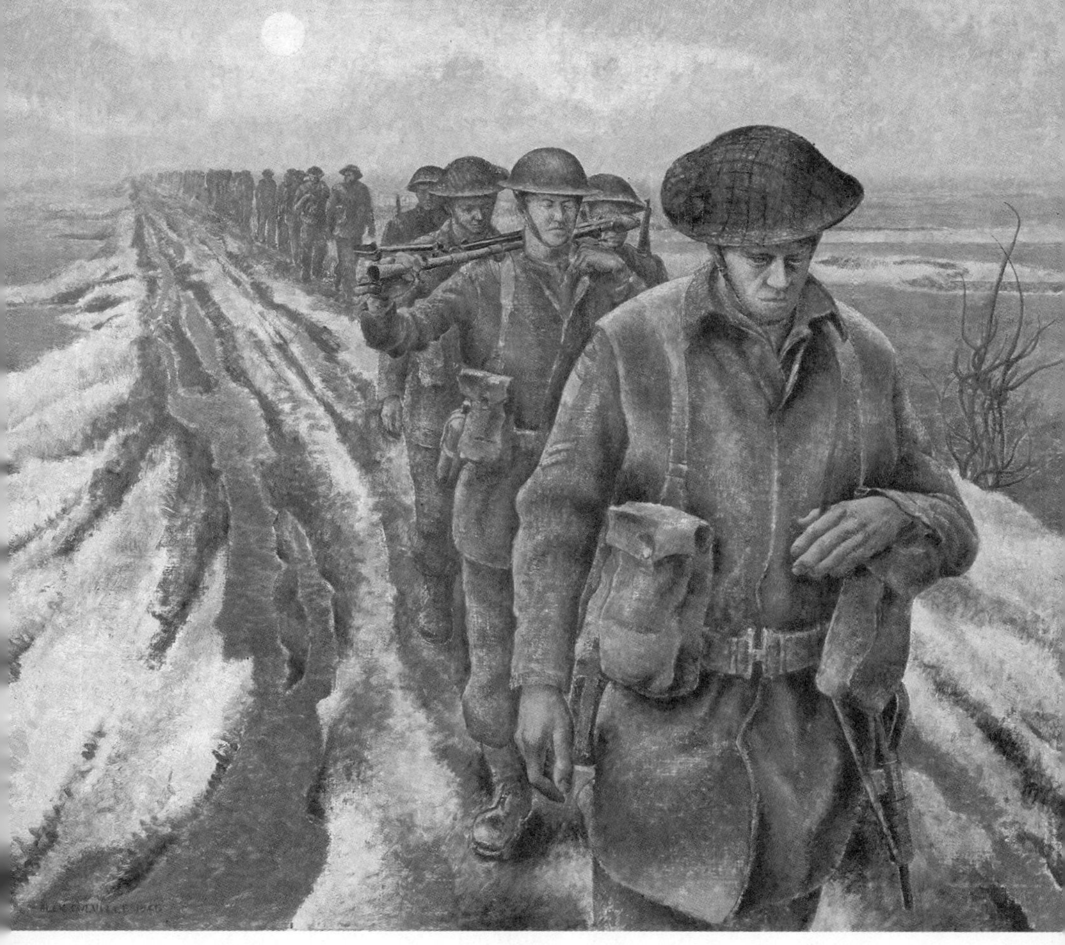

*Alex Colville,* Infantry, near Nijmegen, Holland *(1946). o/c 101.6 x 122.9 cm. CWM #19710261-2079. Beaverbrook Collection of War Art. © Canadian War Museum. Laura Brandon describes the genesis of this canvas from Colville's sketches in* Art or Memorial? *(71–73). The lead figure has Colville's own hand and his father's face.*

*to our daily crimes*
*to this guilt*
*in the griefs of the old*
*and the graves of the young*[4]

This poem and painting must be understood in the context of that disastrous Allied campaign of September 1944 (Operation Market Garden) depicted so honestly in the film *A Bridge Too Far*.

Colin McDougall's novel *Execution* exposes other horrifying aspects of the war, including his response to the Canadian military's execution of a young Canadian soldier,[5] and in his play, *Fifteen Miles of Broken Glass*, Tom Hendry, who was born in 1929 and therefore too young to fight, presents his condemnation of war and its brutal realities in contrast to the home front propaganda that encourages a young man to dream of becoming a pilot so he can get the Japs. Two of the finest eyewitness auto/biographies to come out of the war are by Charles Comfort and Farley Mowat. Both men were with the 1st Canadian Infantry Division in the Italian campaign, Comfort as a war artist and Mowat as a young infantry lieutenant. This bloody and appallingly destructive campaign has been neglected until fairly recently: Comfort's *Artist at War*, first published in 1956, was not reprinted—and then only in a small print run—until 1995; Mowat first published *And No Birds Sang* in 1979 and has returned to his war experiences in later volumes (especially in *Otherwise*, 2008) of his serial auto/biography. But it is Mark Zuehlke who has situated this campaign in Canada's landscape of memory with his important study *Ortona: Canada's Epic World War II Battle* (1999). He has done for Ortona what Berton did for Vimy Ridge. Because the two auto/biographies, together with Zuehlke's history, are making their impact in a post-1977 context, I examine the Italian campaign and the documentary film *Return to Ortona* (2001) as aspects of the contemporary process of remembering the war. But I begin, in this chapter, with novels, notably with *Obasan*, which stands in relation to the remembering and representation of the Second World War much as *The Wars* does to the First World War. The other *fictional* works I examine are *The Ash Garden, Burning Vision, The Wreckage*, and *The War Between Us*, two novels, one play, and one film that reconsider the war in the Pacific. Then in Chapter 8, I consider "Stones," *Fugitive Pieces, Hana's Suitcase, None Is Too Many*, and *Waiting for the Parade*, three fictional narratives and two plays about the war in Europe, and in Chapter 9 I turn to the auto/biographies and two films, each of which explores the war in Europe and, above all, highlights the complex blurring of home front and battle front domains during and after the war.[6] As I did with the First World War texts, here I focus critical attention on the construction of remembering and witnessing, and on debates about national identity in the context of the war.

## *OBASAN* AND THE CONFRONTATION WITH A FORGOTTEN PAST

When Naomi Nakane arrives in Granton, Alberta, to help her elderly aunt—Obasan—after her uncle has died, the old lady struggles up to the attic searching for something amid the layers of dust, dead flies, spiderwebs, and all those things, no longer wanted or used, that we relegate to such places. She finds her husband's ID card: Isamu Nakane #00556, with his picture showing him "young and unsmiling" beside the signature of an RCMP inspector. Obasan keeps the card, but this is not what she is looking for. Increasingly uncomfortable amid all the detritus from the past, Naomi reflects that "all our ordinary stories are changed in time, altered as much by the present as the present is shaped by the past....Our attics and living-rooms encroach on each other" (25). As indeed they do, and will, when the stories in *Obasan* gradually descend from the symbolic attic of things forgotten to reappear in the light of day with all their accumulation of dust, corpses, and memories.





When *Obasan* was published in 1981, it came as something of a shock to most Canadian readers because until then there had been very few attempts to portray the Second World War in Canadian fiction and there was nothing literary that exposed one of the most shameful aspects of the war on the home front. Earle Birney's *Turvey* (1949), Colin McDougall's *Execution* (1958), and Douglas LePan's *The Deserter* (1964) explored the soldier's experience, and Graham's *Earth and High Heaven* exposed Canadian anti-Semitism, but the story of Japanese Canadians was largely untold. Which is not the same thing as saying it was unknown. Nisei knew the story and so did their children, and information existed in mainstream newspaper archives and government documents, as well as in the memories of non-Japanese Canadians who had lived through the war on Canada's west coast or who had benefited, during and after the war, from the cheap farm labour, confiscated homes, businesses and fishing boats, of their Japanese-Canadian neighbours. But the story had been forgotten by the majority, erased from the official history of Canadians fighting against fascism. This process of forgetting began at war's end with the dispersal of Japanese families from the camps in the British Columbia Interior to points further east, the so-called "repatriation" of Japanese Canadians to a country few of them remembered or knew at all, if they were born here, and the refusal, until 1949, to allow those who stayed in the country of their birth to return to the coast.

There is a remarkable passage in *Obasan* that captures the power of erasure and forgetting, and it is so important to the novel and to my reading of it that I will quote at length. Naomi, who is well into the remembering of her past from her narrative present of September 1972, when her uncle dies, recalls a trip she took through British Columbia with Obasan, Uncle, and Aunt Emily in 1962. The trip was sort of a sentimental journey-cum-pilgrimage, though no one in the family spoke of it that way. It was Aunt Emily's idea, so perhaps she had more practical, documentary goals in mind. Whatever the motivation for the trip, what they find when they search "for the evidence of our having been" in or near Slocan, BC, is *nothing*. Not even ghosts:

> *I drove through what was left of some of the ghost towns, filled and emptied once by prospectors, filled and emptied a second time by the Japanese Canadians. The first ghosts were still there...their white bones deep beneath the pine-needle floor....Their buildings...still stood marking their stay. But what of the second wave? What remains of our time there?*
>
> *We looked for the evidence of our having been in Bayfarm, in Lemon Creek, in Popoff. Bayfarm and Popoff were farmlands in Slocan before the tar-paper huts sprang up. Lemon Creek was a camp seven miles away carved out of the wilderness. Tashme—formed from the names of Taylor, Shirras, and Mead, men on the BC Security Commission—also arose*

*overnight, fourteen miles from Hope, and as quickly disappeared. Where on the map or on the road was there any sign? Not a mark was left. All our huts had been removed long before and the forest had returned to take over the clearings. What remained the same was the smell of pine and cedar. The mountains too were unchanged except for the evidence of new roads and a larger logging industry. While we stood there in Slocan, we could hear the wavering hoot of a train whistle as we used to years before. But the Slocan that we knew in the forties was no longer there, except for the small white community which had existed before we arrived and which watched us come with a mixture of curiosity and fear. Now, down on the shore of Slocan lake, on the most beautiful part of the sandy beach, where we used to swim, there was a large new sawmill owned by someone who lived in New York. (117–18)*



What Kogawa creates in a passage like this—and throughout the novel—is a remapping of this obliterated landscape, a replacing of her community's story within a local and a much larger, reimagined landscape of Canadian cultural memory. Her Naomi finds the seemingly absent ghosts and tells their stories for herself and for us. Naomi cannot turn the clock back or change the past or bring those lost back to life, but she can and does interrupt, irrevocably, the process of forgetting and, by doing so, she insists that her readers and listeners—for Naomi is speaking to us—bear witness to things we did to others, in this case fellow citizens and neighbours.

*Obasan* opens on the evening of 9 August 1972, when Naomi and her uncle visit the coulee seven miles from the village of Granton, where she moved with Obasan and Uncle in 1951. She explains that they make this visit to the prairie, "which is like the sea," once a year at about this time. When she asks him why they come to this spot every year, he does not answer. Naomi has had few answers to her questions about the past from either him or Obasan and she has resigned herself to their silence, but this ritual visit and her uncle's repeated comment—"still too young" (3), even though she is now thirty-six and

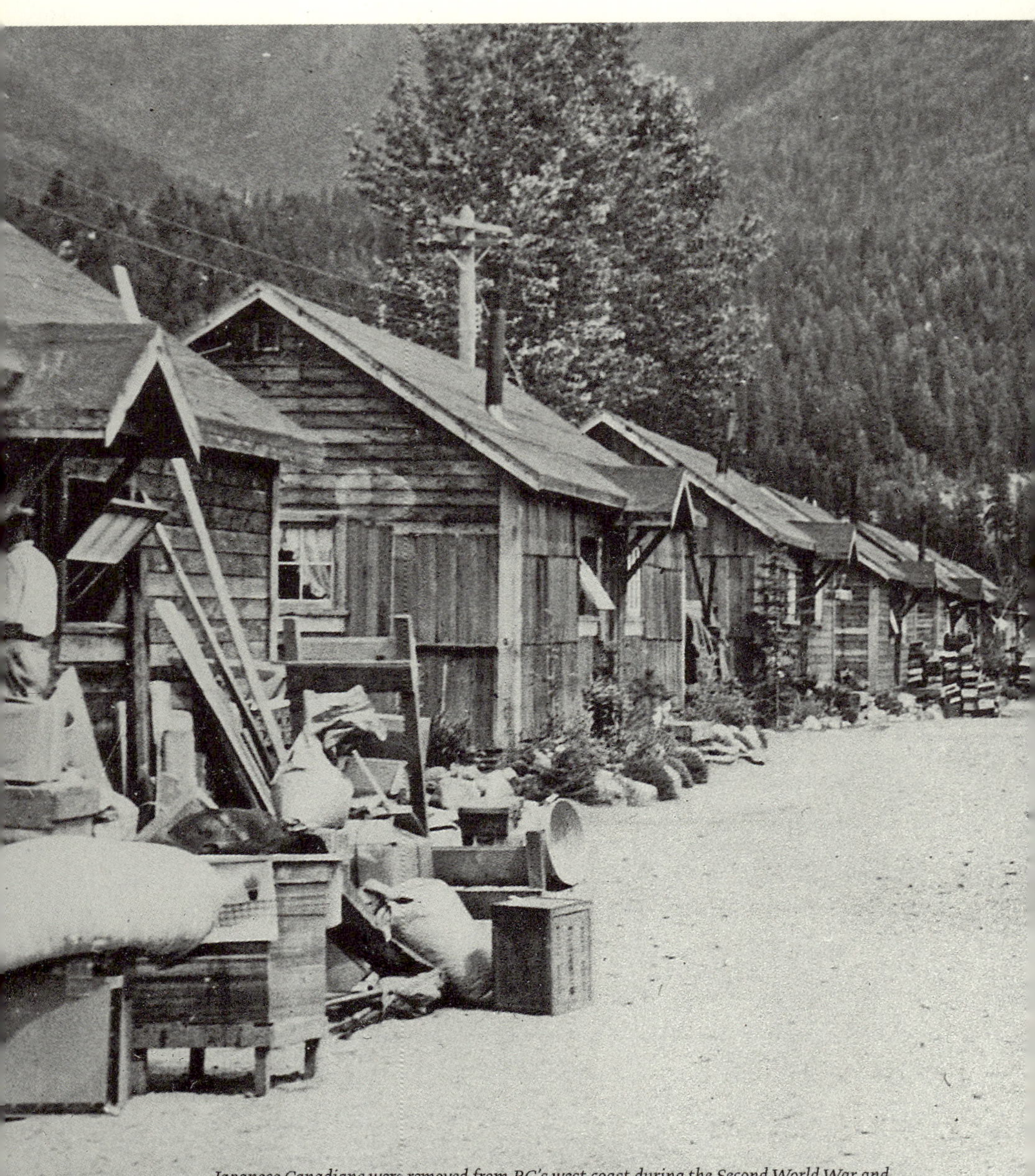

*Japanese Canadians were removed from BC's west coast during the Second World War and placed in internment camps. This archival photograph shows 28' x 14' shacks in the camp at Slocan, BC. Photographer unknown. Reproduced courtesy of the National Association of Japanese Canadians and Library and Archives Canada.*

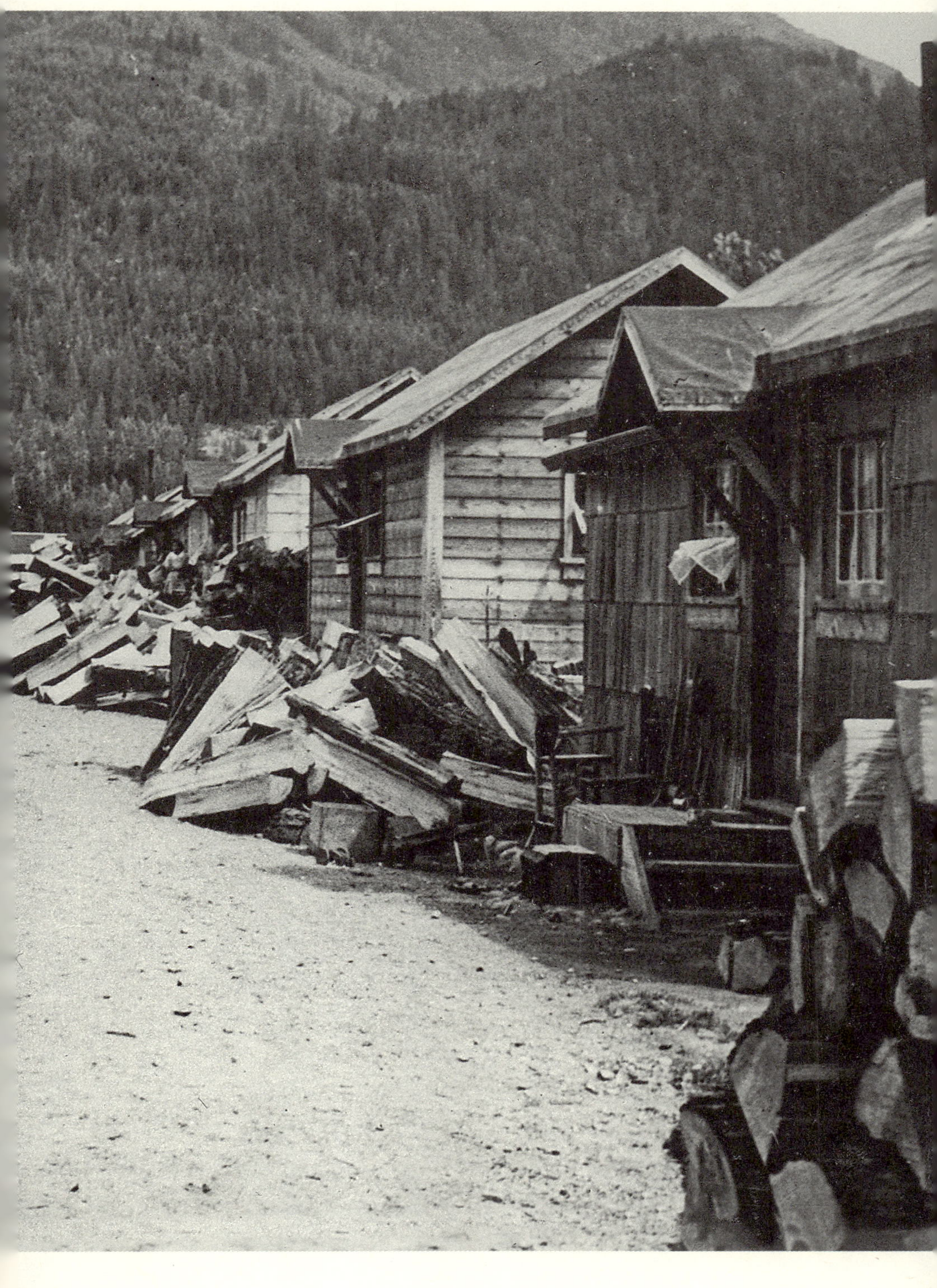

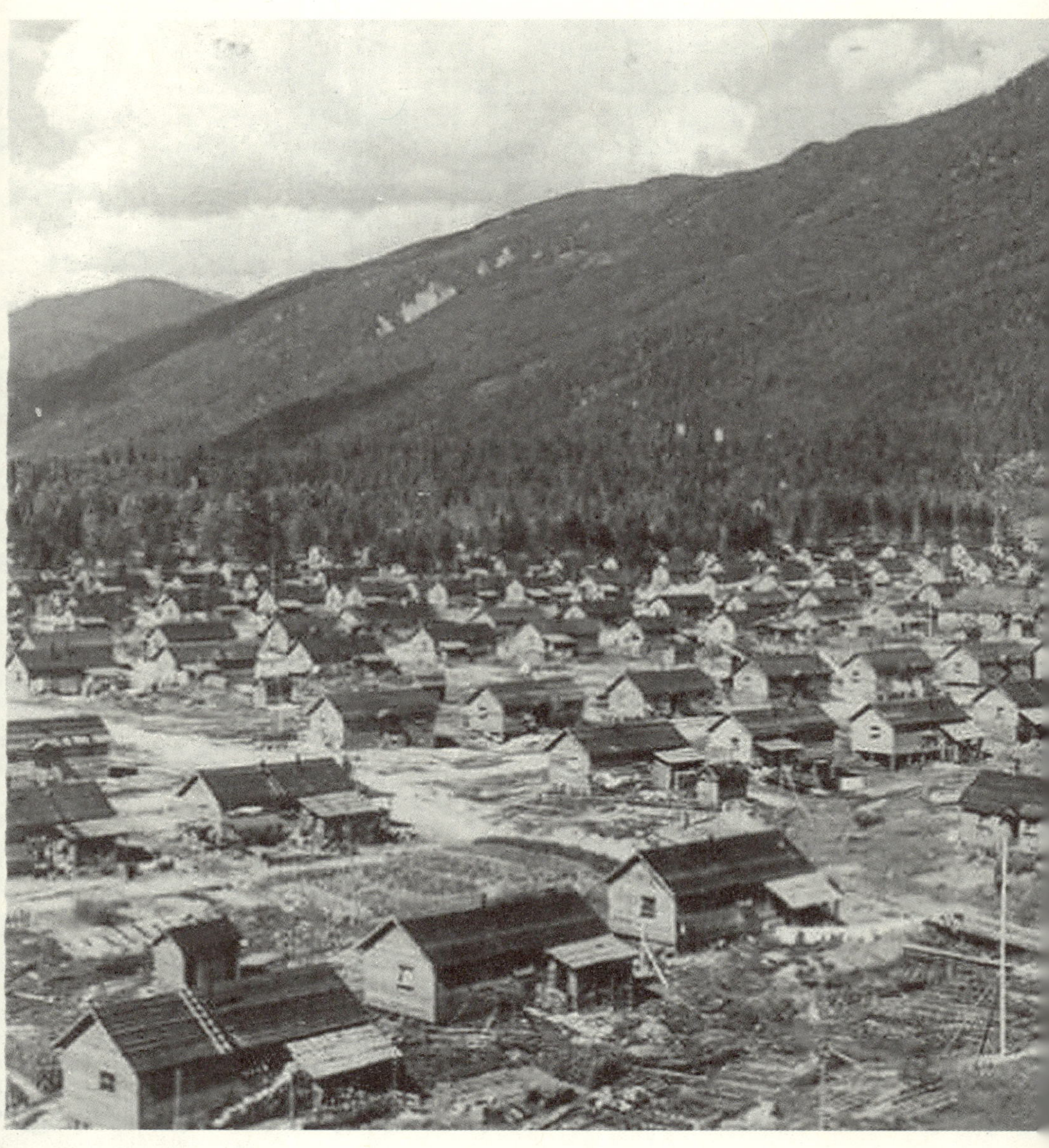

*Internment camp at Lemon Creek, BC, ca. 1942. Photograph: Rev. Yoshio Ono. Courtesy of the University of British Columbia Rare Books and Special Collections, Japanese Canadian Research Collection.*

not eighteen, her age when they first came to the coulee—represents our introduction to a landscape of memory in which we, like Naomi, have yet to find our way. The month is highly significant, however, because it was in August 1945 that the Americans dropped the atomic bombs on Japan: 6 August on Hiroshima and 9 August on Nagasaki. As a thirty-six-year-old teacher, Naomi must surely know this Second World War history, although at no point in her present narrative of 1972 does she examine that knowledge as a historical context for the disappearance of her mother. Uncle, Obasan, and Aunt Emily do know how these histories, public and private, are interconnected, but since August 1954, when Naomi was eighteen and Aunt Emily had visited Granton for the first time, bringing with her the weighty package with tragic news of Naomi's mother's fate, they have all kept silent "for the sake of the children" (219).





Although dates appear regularly in *Obasan*, they are never casual or merely personal; their meanings are important and multiple, always linking the past of the war to Naomi's present, always isolating strategic points of temporal connection between private and public history and between equally significant physical places: Marpole in South Vancouver, Hastings Park, Slocan, the Barkers' beet farm near Lethbridge, Granton, the coulee, with the Steveston fishery, BC's racism and wartime paranoia, Ottawa's War Measures Act and orders-in-council, Alberta and points further east like Toronto and Montreal, where Aunt Emily and Stephen will settle and build new lives. And looming like a threatening shadow in the distance, Japan, a foreign country that has pulled mother and grandmother away from their Canadian homes. In September 1941, Naomi's beloved mother left for Japan and what should have been a short visit; in December the Japanese bombed Pearl Harbor, bringing the Americans into the war and raising fears about a Japanese invasion along the west coast of Canada and the United States.[7]

As 1942 unfolds, it brings one injustice and outrage after another to Japanese Canadians living in Vancouver, and Kogawa charts these events through the intertextual device of dated quotations (selected by Naomi) from Aunt Emily's eyewitness accounts in letters to her absent sister, Naomi's mother, and entries in her diary: newspapers begin reporting that all Japanese Canadians are spies and saboteurs (82); Nisei are called "Japs" and "the enemy" (83); men born in Japan and without citizenship papers are being rounded up, including Naomi's Uncle Sam (84); "race persecution" (Aunt Emily's term) and agitation against people of Japanese origin mounts weekly (85); a curfew is imposed on Japanese Canadians, and signs appear saying "Japs Keep Out" (86); "young girls are...outraged by men in uniform," and Japanese Canadians are openly described as "a 'lower order of people'" (87), and finally a complete evacuation order comes into force as more and more men, women, and children are incarcerated in horse barns at Hastings Park (90–91). Nisei are labelled "enemy aliens" by the war office in Ottawa (92), and newspapers claim that "Japanese naval officers" are "living on the coast" (94). But Emily does not only criticize Caucasian Canadians; she names and singles out a traitor and collaborator within the Japanese-Canadian community—a Mr. Morii who lines his own pockets by working for the RCMP to identify and deliver Japanese Canadians into the hands of the authorities (90): "What a mess everything is," Emily writes. "Some Nisei are out to save their own skins, others won't fight for any rights at all. The RCMP are happy to let us argue among ourselves" (102). Perhaps the most disturbing aspect of this persecution and evacuation process, however, is the appalling conditions that the women are forced to put up with in the Hastings Park barns behind barbed wire, with "ten showers for 1,500 women" (99), sleeping in crowded quarters inches above a wooden floor over manure and maggots (99). What Emily describes, together with the dehumanizing labels and caricatured descriptions of "Japs" in the comic books young Stephen reads (101), amounts to what Giorgio Agamben calls a "state of exception" in which Canadian-born citizens of Japanese descent are reduced to the condition of animals, the *homo sacer* who can be eliminated with impunity by those in power.[8] Agamben is describing the Nazi dehumanization of Jews as vermin, which could and should be exterminated to preserve a healthy Aryan race in Germany, but Kogawa's Aunt Emily reminds us that Canada behaved in a similar, albeit less murderous, manner right here on home ground.

By May 1942, members of the Kato and Nakane families are separated and relocated to the BC Interior. Naomi, Stephen, and Obasan are put on a train destined for Slocan, "one of the best of the ghost towns" (105), and from this point on they will survive the war as internal exiles. It will be many months before Uncle joins them, more than a year before the children see their father, and twelve years before they see Aunt Emily again. The children will not resume their schooling for a year—in May 1943. The end of the war in the Pacific brings an enforced *choice* between "repatriation" to a foreign country, Japan, or further dispersal within Canada. Uncle and Obasan *choose* the latter and find themselves transported east to an Alberta sugar beet farm and a life of hard labour living in a small, uninsulated, one-room, chicken-coop hut (192). Before this removal, however, Naomi is awakened by a frightening dream in which "something has touched me....Something not human, not animal" (167). The war has finally ended and the day before her dream Stephen had run home shouting, "We won, we won, we won" (168), but Naomi's dream is an obscure warning (at least to a young child) of another event and the personal cost to her of winning this war. The nighttime visitation is her mother's spirit, for her mother is not yet dead, reaching out to this small Canadian daughter from amid the ruins of Nagasaki, and this dream marks the beginning of Naomi's haunting by her lost mother: "She is here. She is not here," the older Naomi recalls sensing, although the child only understands that "Something is happening but I do not know what it is" (107).

When Naomi returns to her present reflections in the coulee at the end of her story, she brings her reader/listener full circle back to where we were at the beginning of Chapter 2, on 13 September 1972. By this point, however, we have become informed secondary witnesses to her remembering. With her we have discovered what lies out there on the prairie beyond the coulee in the wide landscape of memory that contains Second World War history. We have listened as Nakayama-sensei reads and translates into English for Naomi, Stephen (and us) the letters hidden all these years in the grey cardboard folder Aunt Emily first brought to Granton in 1954. We hear Grandma Kato insist that "however much the effort to forget, there is no forgetfulness" (234), and we learn from her letter, dated simply 1949, exactly what happened to her and to her daughter, Naomi's mother. Instead of staying in Tokyo as originally planned, both women went to Nagasaki to help a niece with her new baby and they were in that city on 9 August 1945. Then Grandma describes the bombing, the wreckage, fire, destruction, the horrifying aftermath, and finding her daughter "naked [and] utterly disfigured": "Her nose and one cheek were almost gone. Great wounds and pustules covered her entire face and body. She was completely bald. She sat in a cloud of flies and maggots wriggled among her wounds" (239).

This woman is Naomi and Stephen's mother. She will survive her injuries, but she will keep her face covered by a cloth mask for the remaining years of her life, and she will ask that her children never be told (241). Some years later, Aunt Emily learns from a missionary that her sister has died because her name appears on a plaque, where a Canadian maple tree grows, but there is no date of death. Apparently Aunt Emily tried to bring her sister and mother home, but they wanted to bring the niece's orphaned child with them and the Canadian government refused (212–13). And so Naomi is left with her childhood memories, her dreams and nightmares, a few precious photographs, these tragic letters from her grandmother, Aunt Emily's documentation of injustice, and silence.

Clearly, this is not a war story in the way that Findley's *The Wars* is. There are no heroic or rebellious soldiers in *Obasan*, no actual battle scenes, no warfare as such. But *Obasan* is as much about war as *The Wars* (or *Execution*, *The Wreckage*, and *Fugitive Pieces*, for that matter) because it puts civilian collateral damage and the long shadow of aftermath and fallout centre stage. *Obasan* brings the Second World War home, as most of these post-1977 texts do, by demonstrating the lasting impact of the war on future generations of Canadians. It refuses to portray the war as a series of battles between men fighting in foreign countries with no consequences for those at home. In this way, as in so many others, *Obasan* stands for Canadian writing about the Second World War much as *The Wars* does for the Great War. Novels, plays, and films created after *Obasan*, whether they depict the war in Europe or in Asia, usually follow Kogawa's lead by foregrounding civilian suffering and the legacy for Canada of how we performed at home during the war, as much as how we performed abroad. *Obasan* also creates an extremely important landscape of memory in which it becomes not just possible but essential to see and pay attention to a history and a set of stories we tried to forget. As Grandma Kato discovered, "there is no forgetfulness." To say that Naomi is haunted by her absent mother and by the stories untold, even withheld from her, is to understate the case, and insofar as Naomi can be seen as representing a constitutive part of twentieth-century Canadian society (which surely she can), then her haunting is also ours, her ghosts speak to us as well and command our attention.

*Obasan* mobilizes most of those tropes I described in Chapter 1 as characteristic strategies for remembering war in these post-1977 texts. The wounds (emotional and physical), the fences and barbed wire, the suitcases, boxes, trunks that carry, yet hide, so many memories and secrets, the borders crossed and permeable are all there. Surprisingly, so are the trains, those sinister modes of transportation that now seem inseparable from the war in Europe and the Holocaust. Except that these are Canadian trains, the symbol of a national dream uniting a vast country, that are carrying "the despised rendered voiceless, stripped of car, radio, camera and every means of communication, a trainload of eyes covered with mud and spittle" (111). This train from Vancouver carries Naomi and what remains of her family "into the waiting wilderness" (111); the one they are forced to board in Slocan after the war carries them further still into a wilderness of hard labour

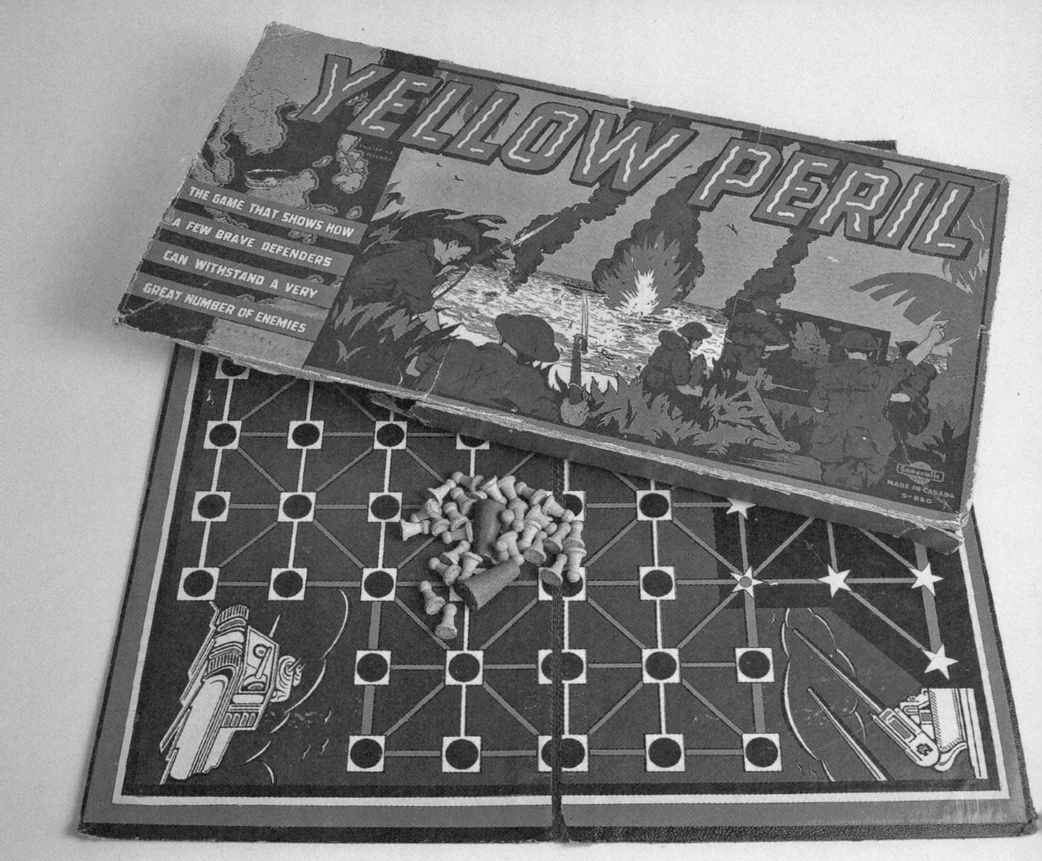


*This Somerville board game, "Yellow Peril," was popular during the Second World War. It appears on the Joy Kogawa website because of its relevance to* Obasan. *This image is reproduced, with permission, from the Galt Museum and Archives, P19970041915.*

and exile on the Alberta beet farm (179–81). The documents, photographs, letters (read and unreadable because in a foreign language), the fragments or, as Anne Michaels would call them, the fugitive pieces of memory, are all marshalled by Kogawa as she performs the difficult task of remembering and recreating the past. Many of the reproduced documents, whether ugly official letters or poignant, personal letters from Grandma Kato, become sites of secondary witnessing for the reader; they are testimonials to what happened then and pointed warnings about what could happen again.

I am puzzled by readers of *Obasan* who hear Naomi's voice as soothingly lyrical and her narrative as redemptive for her and for us.[9] To my mind, Naomi's voice is often angry and bitter (as it should be). When she does *sound* poetic or lyrical, the effect is due to the powerful imagery Kogawa uses to allow her character's pain and longing for a lost mother to break the heavy silence engulfing her. This is Naomi's private voice of memory: "Unless the stone bursts with telling, unless the seed flowers with speech..." (n.p.); "Mother, I see your face. Do not turn aside. Maypole Mother, I dance with a long paper streamer in my hand" (242); "But the earth still stirs with dormant blooms. Love flows through the roots of the trees by our graves" (243). Naomi's public voice, the one we must also attend to, is sharply different: "Time has solved few mysteries. Wars and rumours of wars, racial hatreds and fears are with us still" (78). She may not be as declamatory as Aunt Emily, who insists that "The Nazis are everywhere" (38), but she knows and makes sure we realize that a popular board game of the war years called "The Yellow Peril" is "a Somerville Game, made in Canada" (152).[10] This voice balances the personal one to guard against a reader's too easy appropriation of Naomi's grief. *Both* Naomi and Aunt Emily encourage us to remember our common past as Canadians, not only to sympathize *with* Naomi (she does not ask for our pity), but also to recognize, through this restored landscape of memory, how fragile our democratic freedoms are. Listening to *all* Naomi tells us elicits empathic unsettlement in a story that refuses redemptive closure.





How else can we receive the document that Naomi chooses to leave us with at the end of *Obasan*? This memorandum, dated April 1946, and signed by three members of the Co-operative Committee on Japanese Canadians—James M. Finlay, Andrew Brewin, and Hugh MacMillan—and sent to the Canadian House of Commons and the Senate, states the obvious in the clearest language: the orders-in-council calling for the deportation (euphemistically styled "repatriation") of "Canadians of Japanese racial origin" (248) "are based on racial discrimination" (249). They are "a crime against humanity" resembling the kinds of crimes for which German and Japanese war criminals were being tried in 1946 (249). They undermine the meaning of the democratic values for which

Canadians fought and died during the war, and they "constitute a threat to the security of every minority in Canada" (250). But the memorandum did not stop with that warning. In its final and most telling statement, and in words that reverberate back through *Obasan* (38), we are warned that these "Orders" "are an adoption of the methods of Nazism" (250). In other words, official Canada in 1946 continued to maintain Agamben's "state of exception" regarding Japanese-Canadian citizens. Naomi's Cassandra-like observation that "wars and racial hatreds and fears are still with us" (78) in 1972, when Naomi tells us her story and in 1980 when Kogawa writes her novel, continues to disturb, warn, and remind, to invite our empathy and unsettlement. As Aunt Emily knows, "the past is the future" (48).



Anne Wheeler's deeply moving film treatment of the Japanese-Canadian story, *The War Between Us*, ends with three members of the Kawashima family being loaded on to a truck and driven out of New Denver for *repatriation* to Japan.[11] Mr. Kawashima is a decorated veteran of the Great War, but this does not protect him from being labelled a Japanese national, along with his wife, and basically deported. Their daughter, Aya, is a Canadian citizen, born and raised in Vancouver, but she goes with her parents "to get them settled," as she tells her friend Peg Parnum, who has come to say goodbye. When Peg had protested this enforced repatriation to a devastated postwar Japan, an officious civil servant, Mr. McIntyre, reminded her that the war might be over, but the War Measures Act was still in force in Canada. And these two scenes—the departure and the confrontation with authority—each terrifying and heartbreaking, are powerful reminders that Canada denied democratic rights to many loyal residents and citizens during and after the war. The Kawashima family members, whom we come to recognize as good people *just like us* and as good neighbours by this late point in the film, exist in a state of exception regardless of how well they integrate with or come to love and be loved by the white families they live beside in New Denver. Only one member of this Japanese-Canadian family avoids *repatriation*. The son, Masaru, who like Aya is Canadian-born, is reminiscent of Stephen in *Obasan*. Mas rebels against the "Jap" label, refuses to speak Japanese, rejects his father's request that he accompany them to Japan, and elopes with the Parnums' daughter, Margaret. This young couple defies the taboo against interracial marriage and flees to Toronto where, one can only hope, they will be allowed to live happily.

*The War Between Us* is not, however, about young Mas and Marg. If it were, it would end up being a Canadian Romeo and Juliet story with a happy ending. The two main protagonists in the film are the little girl Mary-Jean Parnum and Aya, and they are based on two actual people who formed a lasting friendship during those years when Japanese-Canadians were relocated from Vancouver into the BC Interior. Wheeler dedicates the film to Frances Hicks (little Mary-Jean in 1940s New Denver) and Kana Enomoto, who could not return to Canada (her home and native land) until 1976. The deep bond that develops between the little girl and the young woman who arrived in her town, and then in her house as cook, babysitter, and housekeeper, begins almost as soon as the child sees Aya for the first time. Mary-Jean is too young for bigotry and racism. What she sees when she looks at Aya is a lovely, kind, elegant person who will listen to her stories and songs. What Aya recognizes is the innocence of the child, her honesty and generosity. They become friends.

The rest of the Parnum family will be won over by Aya and by the courage of her family, who carry on together despite their dislocation, impoverishment, and betrayal. Indeed, towards the end of the film Peg will ask herself and her husband, Ed: "How did this happen? How did we end up on the wrong side?" Over the course of the war, this couple has unlearned their prejudices against the "yellow peril" by living *with* Japanese Canadians. They have learned to love and respect them as fellow citizens and finally, through the marriage of Mas and Marg, as family; and they have gradually come to understand how dangerous government policies are, how much they have been manipulated by racist lies and propaganda, and how appallingly complicit they have been in this official brand of discrimination. None of this knowledge, however, changes history, and Wheeler sticks unflinchingly to the facts. Despite its obvious appeal to a viewer's emotions, the film does not provide a happy ending, a resolution, or even a gesture of reconciliation. Aya must go. Peg watches and weeps helplessly. Mary-Jean calls Aya's name and runs after the truck as it disappears around a bend in the road. The end.

The end except for a brief voice-over comment to remind us that among all those Japanese Canadians *repatriated*, relocated, and denied their rights, not one was a traitor or an enemy alien. This remark, given almost as an afterthought as the credits begin to roll, takes me back to the opening sequences of the film and reminds me of some crucial scenes and essential truths established along the way to this bitter ending. The film opens with crosscuts back and forth between the Kawashimas' home in Vancouver and the Parnums' home in their small town. While the filmic technique may not be striking, the contrasts are and these will be explored as the story unfolds. The Japanese family is sophisticated, well-educated, and well-dressed with their own business and a comfortable middle-class urban home; the white family, however, lives in a simple wood frame house without electricity. Ed Parnum is a blue-collar worker, decent but hardly well-educated, and soon out of work at the local mine. Peg is a simple woman, a country girl who plays the organ in church on Sundays and wears plain cotton dresses. Once Japan has attacked Pearl Harbor, however, everything changes, and Wheeler uses radio broadcasts and newspaper headlines to track the dates, the propaganda, and the orders-in-council calling for the removal of all people of Japanese racial origin from Vancouver and the coast.

When the townsfolk in the Interior learn that their town must accommodate hundreds of "Japs," they are horrified. As far as they know, these creatures carry diseases, cannot speak English, and are dangerous. Imagine the astonishment on all sides when the hapless Japanese Canadians arrive in town and get down from the open trucks transporting them. Dressed in their best suits, coats, and hats, they find themselves domiciled in sheds and chicken coops; they see their white neighbours as "hicks" or "savages." In one of the comic moments of the film, the Parnum family rushes out of their house and leaps about whooping with glee because they have just installed electricity, and Mas peers through the window of his family's shack to smile and observe—"the savages have discovered electricity."

As the months and years pass, the quiet war between these two groups of people forced to live side by side abates. The Japanese speak excellent English; Aya learns how to manage a wood stove (instead of the gas range she cooked on in the city); Marg learns from Mas that things called Cambridge and Oxford are universities he would like to attend. Better still, the young Japanese-Canadian men play hockey—well—and the New Denver team of mixed players wins the local game. And they can dance the jitterbug, something the local yokels have not even heard of. But if many of the young people meet on the common ground of teenage interests—and at least one pair falls in love—not all the town's residents accept the intruders and life for these dislocated people worsens. Ed Parnum's brother, a veteran who lost an eye at Dunkirk, hates the "Japs"; the government presence is always felt through the officious, cruel Mr. McIntyre, who is there to enforce all orders-in-council. When the Kawashimas learn that their Vancouver property has been auctioned off and that they must choose *repatriation* or relocation east of the Rockies, all touches of humour or fun evaporate. In what is, at least for me, the most telling scene in the film and the decisive nadir of the action, Mr. Kawashima, who has just agreed to be sent back to Japan, builds a bonfire outside the family's shack and, one by one, drops his army uniform, his officer's cap, and finally his medals into the fire. There is no dialogue in this scene, just an effective, low-key musical soundtrack underneath the sight of the fire consuming this man's Canadian identity. Then the camera moves in and holds a close-up of his handsome face lit only by the firelight to emphasize his grim pain and resolution. As perhaps only film can do for viewers, we are made secondary witnesses watching this man we have come to respect as he watches his life and his contribution to Canada go up in flames. We bear witness to the despair, pride, and anger embodied in this human being as he renounces the country that has betrayed and rejected him.

In *The War Between Us* Anne Wheeler has created a complex, nuanced, and very honest representation of the Second World War on the home front. The occasion is the removal of Japanese Canadians from the BC coast and their mistreatment by the Canadian government; however, the motivation of this film is ethical and exceeds this particular historical event. Through the plot, the cinematography, and the characters, who come to life for viewers through superb acting, Wheeler reminds us of our common humanity, of what connects us as individuals, families, citizens, and of our fragile democratic freedoms. She also explores the process of *un*learning stereotypes—about race, language, and culture, and about urban versus rural life—and *re*learning what we share and what we can achieve when we come to know each other. While the setting for this film is the Second World War and the landscape of New Denver, where the film was shot on location, the meaning of the film is that borders intended to separate us can be crossed, that we can learn mutual respect despite such borders, and that basic values of love, dignity, and shared experience can produce a national identity where orders and rules and restrictions cannot. To those who might say that *The War Between Us* is too emotional, even sentimental, that the curly red-haired kid is just too cute and the Japanese-Canadian woman just too good to be true, I would argue that this film achieves what no academic study or statistical report or legal maneuvering could ever achieve: it *shows* us what it means to be human. That this film is so difficult to see today is a shame. That we watch, instead, any number of combat movies about the war, signifies a dangerous failure of imagination and empathy. In this film, as in her other two films about the Second World War (*A War Story* and *Bye Bye Blues*), Wheeler imagines for us a landscape of memory in New Denver, in a POW camp, and on an Alberta farm, where ordinary Canadians struggled to understand, survive, and overcome what divides them and what diminishes them as human beings. She confronts, especially in *The War Between Us*, the creation under the War Measures Act of a state of exception within Canada and the willed forgetting of how we ended up—as Peg puts it—"on the wrong side."

## ETHICS AND WAR



### The Ash Garden



"With the bomb, ideas of right and wrong ceased to exist," an elderly Anton Böll tells the survivor of Hiroshima who has come to his Canadian home to interview him. "I know the world requires a certain payment from us all, pain and suffering, hunger, destitution, solitude, for the freedoms we enjoy. We have all paid," he insists, "or will. It is not right or wrong to have used the bomb. But it was necessary" (203). Anton Böll is a German physicist who escaped from Europe in 1940 thanks to the careful planning of Varian Fry, an American charged with getting intellectuals and artists out of Europe via Marseilles, the Pyrenees, and Spain.[12] When he makes this claim about the bomb, which he came to the United States to perfect with scientists working under Richard Oppenheimer for the Manhattan Project, it is August 1995 and he is sitting in the garden of his home near Pickering in the fictional town of Port Elizabeth. He is sitting with his back to the waters of Lake Ontario being interviewed by a fifty-six-year-old Japanese-American documentary filmmaker called Emiko Amai. Who Böll is and precisely how his life and that of Emiko's are connected will unfold slowly over the course of Dennis Bock's *The Ash Garden* and not be fully revealed until its closing pages. Although Bock does not pick up the story of the Second World War where Kogawa left it at the end of *Obasan*, nor has *Obasan* influenced *The Ash Garden* in any obvious way, there are, all the same, compelling parallels between the two works. One of the most important of these is the ethical debate captured in miniature by this fragment of Böll's comment. Another is the complex landscape of memory that Bock creates to connect the peaceful garden and the small-town Ontario retreat of Anton Böll and his wife Sophie, with haunting memories of a shattered Europe, of the surreal scenery of New Mexico, where Böll worked on the bomb, and the ash garden of Hiroshima to which he bears witness after the war. His memories of Hiroshima, as well as of numerous memorial gatherings at Columbia University and anti-nuclear demonstrations in New York, are preserved in dozens of reels of amateur film taken by Böll over four decades. It is these old films that he will screen for his visitor to illustrate what he witnessed and how he discovered her and was moved to intervene in her life.

Bock creates a third character in his novel, however, because the story is not only about an elderly scientist and a Japanese survivor. Sophie Heinemann, who married Anton Böll, was born in Linz, Austria, to a Jewish father and a Gentile mother. Realizing the danger facing them, her parents put sixteen-year-old Sophie on a train in 1938 to get her out of Europe and to safety, but they did not survive the Nazi genocide and she never saw or heard from them again. Sophie is the most enigmatic, troubling figure in the novel because we learn comparatively little about her and we see her primarily through her husband's and a third-person narrator's eyes. Evacuated from Germany via Hamburg on the ship SS *St. Louis*, she and 938 other refugees sailed to Cuba, where the ship was refused permission to unload its human cargo. The ship eventually returned to Europe, where England, France, Belgium, and Holland each accepted some refugees, but Bock does not explain exactly how his Sophie found herself in "Camp L," a Canadian internment camp in Cove Fields, close to the Plains of Abraham at Quebec City.[13] It is there, in 1943 at the age of nineteen, that she first sees the handsome young Professor Böll, who is visiting the camp. She decides that he may be her way out of her imprisonment as an "enemy alien." Apart from speaking German and being wartime exiles from Europe, the two have little else in common and their marriage, although close, is not a fulfilling one. Böll is consumed with his career and scientific ambition; as he will explain to Emiko, he did not flee Germany to protest Nazi atrocity but to advance his research (206). After the bombs have ended the war, he refuses to feel guilt—or so he insists—and yet he is obsessed with the past and with what he witnessed on his first visit to Japan weeks after the bombs were dropped. Whatever he needs now in his present life—forgiveness, reconciliation, atonement, understanding, praise—he will not let go of his career and the life-defining, history-making role he played in ending the war. His wife's trauma seems almost boring to him, her losses a matter of indifference. When Emiko challenges him after Sophie's funeral—"Did you ever know your wife, Professor?"—he finds her question "ridiculous" and presumptuous (253). But the answer to this question is: no. What he does know is Sophie's debilitating disease, systemic lupus erythematosus, a disease that will kill her by the novel's end.

*The Ash Garden* pivots between two significant dates—August 1945 and August 1995. The first date is still more precise: 6 August 1945, the day the *Enola Gay* dropped the atomic bomb on Hiroshima. Although the date of 6 August 1995 is signalled—it is the date on which Böll returns to New York City for the anniversary of Hiroshima and the lecture he gives in Fayerweather Hall at Columbia University—August 1995 is the longer present time of the narrative. It is the month of Böll's interviews with Emiko and of Sophie's fatal lupus attack, her death and funeral. This fiftieth anniversary is, therefore, the appropriate time for remembering and reflecting upon what happened on that day in 1945 and on how it changed the world as we knew it before the war. The Second World War, the Holocaust, and the bombing of Japan marked a far greater turning point in global affairs and a more absolute rupture with the past than the Great War but, for Canada, the impact of this war, its legacy and aftermath, would also be more ambivalent and troubled. In Bock's hands, the ethical dilemma posed by the measures taken to end the war finds its unlikely staging in a southern Ontario garden. August 1945 meets August 1995, not at a Holocaust memorial or in the Hiroshima National Peace Memorial Hall, but in the home of two elderly refugees from the war who have chosen this peaceful Canadian landscape as their final resting place and his site of confession. The house on Spruce Street in Port Elizabeth, looking out across Sophie's strangely sculpted garden and the garden paths leading down to the water, is at once a sanctuary and a carefully landscaped space in which Anton and Sophie can remember the past.





Central to their shared remembering is Camp L and their first secret encounter by the water in 1943, when she crept outside the barbed wire to meet him, but the couple also recalls revisiting the site after attending a postwar conference in 1957 at Pugwash, Nova Scotia.[14] Anton finds his way there easily; it is "exactly where he'd remembered it." But the place is abandoned:

> *They watched the hard-packed dirt compound for movement, empty but for a carpet of weeds that the fences and wire had been unable to withstand, waiting, possibly, for a ghost to swing open one of those wood-shack doors and rustle the tall weeds with his invisible feet....The door leading into one of the cabins on the right—had it been hers?—hung open and moved in the wind, as if the forms that haunted her memory lived on, persistent and invisible, still pacing from room to room. Shafts of light fell through the splitting wood of buildings uninhabited this last decade. The silent guard towers that had watched over the internees cast afternoon shadows along the dry earth.* (161–62)

Guard towers? Internees? Yes. The Camp L revisited by Bock's characters was one of several camps across Canada in which Germans, Austrians, and Italians were incarcerated during the war, and Sophie, as a German-speaking, Austrian-Jewish refugee, was classified as an "enemy alien."

Returning to this site prompts Sophie's memories of her time in the camp, her previous life in Europe until her parents put her on that train, and then her first rendezvous with Anton. Together they go down

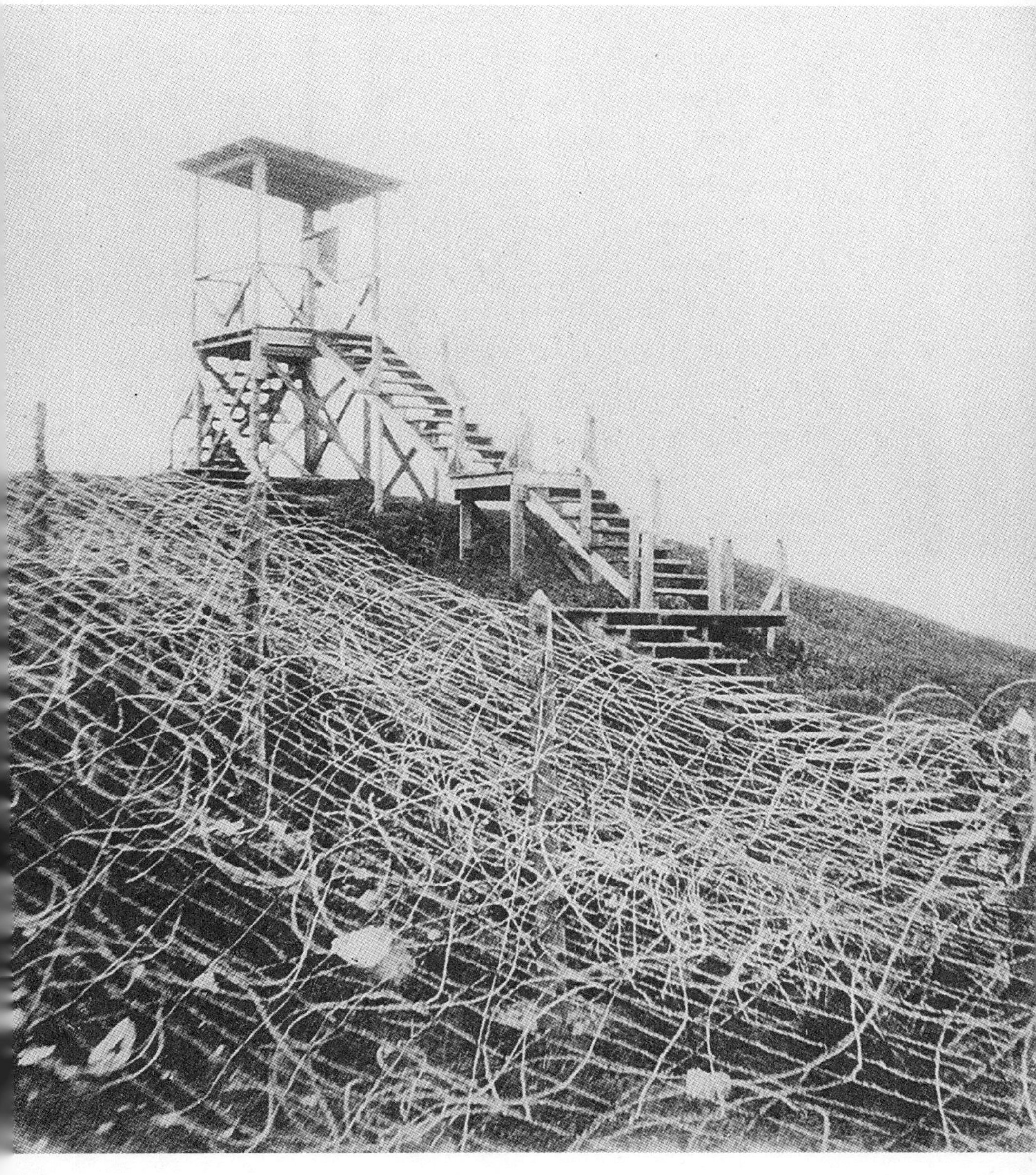

*Camp L, hastily set up in 1940–1941 near Quebec City, was used to hold so-called German-speaking "enemy aliens" deported from the UK as a potential security threat. Many of these people were in fact German Jews who fled Nazi oppression or were studying in England prior to the war. Sometimes these Jews were held in Camp L with Nazi* POWs *before being moved to other camps in Quebec or New Brunswick. Photographer unknown.* LAC/PA-143488.

to the river's edge beyond the barbed wire and make love, as if to superimpose a happier, more positive memory upon an otherwise traumatic landscape that no longer bears signs of a human past, unless it persists in the ghosts that haunt the place. Bock, however, reminds his readers that such places existed, not only for Japanese Canadians but also for other groups of people, some of whom were seeking refuge in Canada, like the Jews held in Camp L. This scene, in which multiple layers of memory are evoked in a Canadian landscape, is an example of Bock's narrative strategies for addressing the ethical questions raised in *The Ash Garden*. Camp L is what Pierre Nora would call a *lieu de mémoire* because it exists—it *was* real and there—but it is disappearing from lived history to become nothing more than a footnote (if that) in official Canadian history. By citing it through his characters and their memories, Bock puts it and what it meant back into the official story. He transforms the place into a *milieu de mémoire* that belongs, albeit with a comparatively minor claim on our attention, alongside the house and garden in Port Elizabeth, the rusty canisters holding Anton's amateur films, the desert landscape of Alamogordo, and ground zero at Hiroshima. He creates a Canadian landscape of memory that must be understood within the global remembering of the Second World War, and such a manoeuvre brings his characters, their life stories, and our attention back to the present of August 1995, the fiftieth anniversary of Hiroshima and Nagasaki, and the obsessions of Anton Böll and his attempt to explain his actions to Emiko.

Once he has agreed to be interviewed and has decided to show her the films he took when he visited Hiroshima from September to October 1945, an extraordinary realm of memory and confession opens up for Emiko. While the jerky, Charlie Chaplin-like images of people walking through "the ash garden of the city" (192) appear on the makeshift screen, Anton tells her that he has carried these film reels, these images, "around like family portraits" (192) and that they represent a "sort of diary" (193). But surely these are odd ways of thinking about the bomb and the destruction of the city. When Emiko presses him as to why he feels so personally connected to 6 August 1945, he replies easily that it is "my history too" and that he is one of the few left "who can admit to themselves that we did what needed to be done" (202). Emiko is, understandably, taken aback by this blunt, unapologetic honesty. She questions him more closely: did you film the devastation to show respect? To "document what had happened so others would know?" (204). He cannot answer. She persists: did you feel good about helping to end the war, do you feel you have a clean conscience? No, he replies: "You do not feel elation at the conclusion of a war. You do not feel pleasure" (205). It is after this exchange that the tension between the survivor and the perpetrator (if I can call Böll that) increases palpably. She wants to know why he left Germany, and his answer is disturbing: "I did not leave fascism as much as leave a place that could not accommodate my work" (206). She is incredulous and protests that he cannot have been ignorant about the Nazis, and she accuses him of absolving himself of responsibility (207). But Anton Böll is not a man to be accused or made to feel guilty. He turns the inquisition around: "Ask yourself why the Japanese fought as well as they did. Why there was virtually no domestic opposition" (207). She responds by saying that she was just a child of six at the time and that her parents were told lies, but he is relentless: "it is easy to say you were lied to. We were all lied to" (208). To bring Hirohito and Japan to its knees, the Americans *had to bomb* civilian targets because "it would be more effective. It would get the mission completed more quickly" (210). "Expediency won the war," he states flatly, "not justice" (211). And on this point, as on many others, this old man is speaking the truth.





After Sophie's funeral and before Emiko leaves Anton Böll, she realizes that this man has more to tell her. His final confession amounts to his *apologia*, his story of why she is here with him now and how he has atoned for his role in creating the bomb. During September and October 1945, Anton Böll visited hospitals in Hiroshima and came to know Emiko's grandfather, a medical doctor and her only surviving relative. He had actually tried to help the man relieve the suffering of his six-year-old granddaughter; now he expects her to thank him for remembering her and her grandfather and working to see that she was one of twenty-six young women chosen from among thousands to receive plastic surgery in the United States. Once she had arrived in the States, he followed her activities from a distance, watching her as the years passed and waiting for her to contact him. Emiko is not instantly full of gratitude, however; she is angry and appalled. She has been "spied on" for decades, "documented" by his camera, and now he screens these old films, his evidence, to prove that he deserves credit for finding her, convincing her grandfather to allow her to leave Japan for surgery, and for giving her a new life: "You were not simply chosen. I picked you. You were there [in the United States] because of me....I gave you this new life. Who you are is because of me" (261). Outraged by his hubris and claims, she gives him a rebuke instead of thanks: "*Who are you to do that?* What gave you the right?" (262). As far as she is concerned, he thought only of himself and *his* life and *his* "need to reconcile yourself with what you'd done" (262). She accuses him of kidnapping her life; he insists he gave her freedom and is now giving her the truth about herself: "That is my gift to you" (263).

When *The Ash Garden* ends, we are left with the knowledge that some meanings cannot be resolved, some acts cannot be explained, and that "absolution would never be extended" to Anton Böll by Emiko Asai. This novel is not, finally, about transcending or transforming history by restoring memory. There is no way for anyone to feel good about this past; there is no restitution possible. There is only the blunt truth that Japan capitulated, that Hitler was defeated, that the war was *won* by the Allies, but not before millions of innocent people had been murdered. As readers we listen to (we overhear) this frank discussion of who did what to whom and why, and we bear secondary witness to the suffering on both sides. *The Ash Garden* is not a novel lacking utterly in hope, however, and the hope we are left with arises in part from Böll's confession and Emiko's listening to, if not endorsing, it. A still more powerful site of hope lies in the recognition of connections between human beings over time and across space. Emiko has, in a sense, haunted Anton Böll, and the mysterious, wise Sophie has grasped the power of that haunting. It may be Böll who tells Emiko that "our lives are connected in ways you could never dream of" (258), but I believe Dennis Bock creates in Sophie Heinemann Böll that empathic witness to her husband's war, to his obsession and need, and before her death, to the need of this stranger, this filmmaker/survivor, Emiko, for recognition, acknowledgement, and connection. Sophie is the true ghost in this tragic narrative, the Austrian-Jewish refugee in Canada who is buried by a rabbi (a last rite recognizing who she is), but whose own story—whose life, in a sense—is never fully revealed.





### BEARING WITNESS IN *BURNING VISION* AND *THE WRECKAGE*

The next two texts, Marie Clements's play *Burning Vision* and Michael Crummey's novel *The Wreckage*, continue this process of connecting events and people across the familiar and hostile borders of war to demonstrate just how impossible it is to function as if what happened in one part of Canada, or in Asia, has no bearing on other parts of the country and the world, as if a loss experienced in one place has no repercussions elsewhere. Above all, this play and this novel confirm that contemporary Canadian responses to the events of the Second World War focus on ethical issues and on a revisiting of a past we thought we knew but about which we still have much to discover and understand. Each work achieves its chief impact by bearing witness to history, and central to my discussion of both works is a consideration of how they create fictional primary witnesses and construct, in performance and in narrative, the secondary witnessing function. *Burning Vision* tells the story of uranium mining and its journey from the Canadian Northwest Territories to the American Manhattan Project to the bombing of Nagasaki; it is also the story of official Canadian secrecy and complicity in the war and the refusal to acknowledge the impact of uranium mining on the Sahtú Dene of Great Bear Lake. *The Wreckage* is the story of several lives swept up in the maelstrom of the war, especially as that war developed in Japan, and Crummey takes his main male characters from Newfoundland and British Columbia to a Japanese POW camp, where one is a prisoner and the other is a soldier with Japan's Imperial Army serving as an interpreter in the camp: both are from *here*, both are Canadian (at least, the Newfoundlander is in the fictional present of 1994). Each work insists that we bear witness, and each urges us to respond with empathic unsettlement. Neither offers redemption, or makes things seem all right in the end, or holds out a promise of "never again."





In his study of uranium mining at Great Bear Lake, Peter van Wyck has a name for the route taken by the uranium-rich pitchblende ore minded at the Eldorado Mine on the eastern shore of Great Bear Lake in the Northwest Territories. The ore travelled south along the river and rail routes, through the Canadian landscape, to the processing plant in Port Hope on the shores of Lake Ontario, and from there it went further south to New Mexico and the Manhattan Project. Van Wyck calls this route "The Highway of the Atom" (6), and he means at least two things by this striking phrase. On the one hand, the highway is a literal metaphor—literal because the route that crossed Canada can still be traced, mapped, *found* on today's landscape, but metaphor because the atom would travel a much more abstract, scientific path from raw material to high-grade uranium to the atomic bombs dropped on Japan in August 1945 and a still more obscure toxic route into the environment, the food chain, and the bloodstream of the human population. I borrow this phrase to name the literary route that I am tracing from *Obasan* and Naomi's mother in Nagasaki to *The Ash Garden* and an elderly Anton Böll's ethical pride in his research, to the stories contained in *Burning Vision* and *The Wreckage*. Large stretches of this route—and certainly of this Canadian landscape—have been forgotten, willfully suppressed. As van Wyck points out, strategies for forgetting these stories and erasing the markers along the route have been pursued with energy.[15] But I want to show how our writers and artists are helping to connect the dots and how, in doing so, they put human beings and cultural memory back into the skeletal outline of this highway of the atom. One of the most frightening aspects of this reconnecting, retracing, and remembering is that we end up, relentlessly, back where we started: on home ground, in Canada, in the *lieu de mémoire* of Port Radium. Moreover, to quote van Wyck once more, this travelling is a warning: "The Highway of the Atom is a route along which the dead make a claim on the living. All of this [the ghosts, the forgetting, the remembering, the searching] makes a language of haunting seem perfectly reasonable" (153).





*Burning Vision* dramatizes the consequences of the Second World War and the bombing of Japan for the civilians in Canada and Japan who were caught up in that conflagration. Clements stages, so to speak, the highway of the atom. Despite its complex structure, stark symbolism, and expressionist techniques, however, the plot of the play stays close to historical facts, dates, and actual events, beginning with the discovery of uranium in the Canadian North. Gilbert and Charles Labine are credited with *discovering* pitchblende ore, which produced high-grade uranium, on the shores of Great Bear Lake in the Northwest Territories in 1930. A mine quickly developed at Port Radium, from where the ore was transported south. Most of the men mining and handling the sacks of ore were local Sahtú Dene, who moved their families to the site and lived in tents at Port Radium. The fine powder from the ore blew everywhere—into sandboxes, across the vegetation eaten by the migrating caribou herds, and into the food being prepared by Dene women. The sacks carried by the Dene stevedores leaked; tonnes of tailings accumulated on land and in the water. In short, radium contamination permeated everything in the environment. Moreover, it is believed that ore from that mine made its way into the American Manhattan Project.

After the Second World War, with the Soviet Union arming and the Cold War heating up—and long after it was clear what damage the atomic bombs had done in Japan—mining at Port Radium continued much as it had during the war. In 1952 the Crawley film company produced an "industrial documentary" called *The Highway of the Atom*, and the narrator of this film assured viewers that uranium from Port Radium "ended WWII."[16] It was not until the 1990s that the story of unusually high cancer rates and deaths among the Sahtú Dene in Deline began to emerge. As Peter Blow argues in his 1999 documentary film *Village of Widows*, too many Dene have died of cancer for there to be no connection with the mine, and the Deline Uranium Committee began seeking help from the federal government, as well as a kind of atonement or common ground with the Japanese survivors of Hiroshima and Nagasaki by visiting Nagasaki and participating in commemorative ceremonies.





Although Clements incorporates much of this information into her play, she transforms the story into a parable of life and death *for our times*. Underlying her complex, expressionist drama are many facts about the war in the Pacific, including the discovery of uranium, the mining operations that continued after the war, and the deaths from cancer of the miners, beginning in 1960. The cast is large, and some of the characters are named for historical figures of the period—Tokyo Rose (a Japanese-American "radio siren" whose real name was Iva Toguri), Lorne Greene, a well-known Canadian CBC radio announcer and actor nicknamed "the Voice of Doom" because the war news was so bleak, and the Labine brothers. Two other characters, who have symbolic roles, are simply called "Fat Man"—"an American bomb test dummy manning his house in the late 1940s and 50s" (13) and "Little Boy"—an "eight to ten years old" native boy who personifies "the... uranium found at the centre of the earth" (13). The through line of the plot is sustained in two key ways: through the onstage *presence* of a Dene Widow, who mourns the death of her husband from cancer as she tends her fire from which she evokes the visions that supply the scenes of the play; and by the *voice*, offstage, of the Dene See-er, a medicine man who speaks from the past of 1880 to the present of postwar devastation and threat and warns all who will listen that the black rock—the uranium-bearing pitchblende—should not be touched.

The play is set in a timeless realm of vision that merges past and present, here at Great Bear Lake with there in the United States or in Japan. As the map, which introduces the published text, suggests, the site of *Burning Vision* is a palimpsest of events in time and space that identifies important human connections. And the scenes are brief visions called up by the Widow as she stares into her fire to dream into reality the movements of memory, trauma, love, hatred, despair, and hope that define our humanity despite the pervasive rhetoric of racism and warmongering, the atrocities too often committed in the name of peace, and the ignorance and greed of individuals and colonial powers. The dramatic action occurs across four "movements," instead of in the conventional divisions of act and scene; they are titled, in turn, "The Frequency of Discovery," "Rare Earth Elements," "Waterways," and "Radar Echoes." Each of these titles carries multiple meanings, sometimes ironic and always both literal and metaphoric. Thus, to speak of the frequency of discovery is to identify the Geiger counter used to find uranium and radium but also to alert us to the arrogance of white men staking a claim to *discovery* of a place and a substance already known to the Dene (and known to be dangerous). "Waterways" is both the name of the place in Alberta, now called Fort McMurray (itself a site of resources, exploitation, and contamination), and the northern terminus of the railway connecting southern and northern Canada, the geographical point at which the river route north to Great Bear Lake—the waterway of the atom—began (van Wyck, 26–27). At the southern terminus sits Port Hope, Ontario, and the home landscape of Anton and Sophie Böll. Although one can identify enough of a linear through line, a plot, to follow the story of *Burning Vision* and to grasp the cause and effect tragedy of that story for the Dene and for Japanese civilians, the movements of the play work against a too simple development leading to a climax and a resolution. This play is not primarily about coming to terms with the past or finding closure (as we so often put it when we want to forget and move on), and so this structure in movements, which is held together by the repetition of images of circular movement, of sound effects, phrases and musical refrains, and the explosions of the bomb (which we hear four times), effectively resists dramatic resolution. Instead, the four movements overlap, repeat each other in key ways, and provide the reader or audience member with a multilayered, synaesthetic experience of time and space in which what was past is still present and what happened over *there* has "radar echoes" over *here*, today.





Clements captures this layering effect most succinctly in the stage instructions at the beginning of "Waterways—Movement Three." We read (or see and hear in a *tour de force* of stage design) "*The movement of scenes through, under, and over dangerous waters. Worlds swirling in brief currents that throw them together and then separate. SOUND: Dene and Japanese drums submerging in and out of the static propaganda, the sound score of western civilization building a country*" (75). And then we hear the voice-over of the Dene See-er, who speaks to us from 1880 to instruct us (through indirection) on how to listen to this strange play, and who will pronounce his warning in the fourth movement. But right here, at the start of Movement Three, he asks us to see and hear: "Can you read the air? The face of the water? Can you look through time and see the future? Can you hear through the walls of the world? Maybe we are all talking at the same time because we are answering each other over time and space. Like a wave that washes over everything and doesn't care how long it takes to get there because it always ends up on the same shore" (75).

And we can see; we can hear. Or at least we can learn to do so if we are attentive to the logic of Clements's vision. In the final moments of the play, the voices from around the world will answer each other to remind us of the Dene See-er's wisdom. What goes around comes around might be the trite formulation in English of the Dene See-er's words. But the message is clear: what you do today will come back to haunt you; you can never just send *it* away and be rid of *it*. Borders—*all* borders—are permeable.

*In this scene from the 2002 Firehall Arts Centre, Vancouver, premiere of Marie Clements's* Burning Vision, *the Miner (Marcus Hondro) dances with the Radium Painter (Erin Wells), who is now bald and dying. The production was directed by Peter Hinton, with set design by Andreas Kahre and lighting by John Webber. Photograph: Timothy Matheson. Reproduced with permission.*

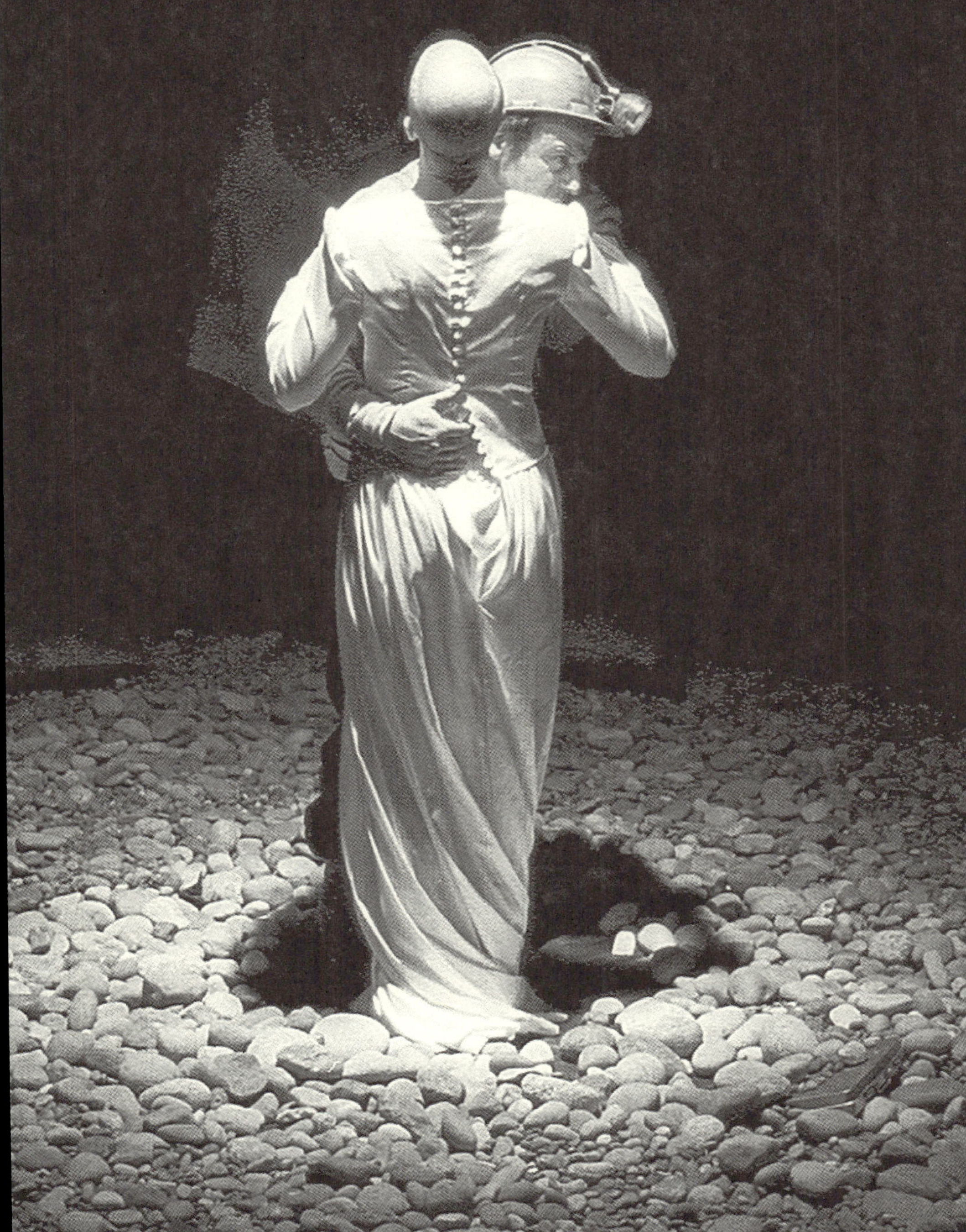

The voice of the Dene See-er reaches us from the distant past less as a ghostly presence, although by performing his words as voice-over he recalls a theatrical tradition of staging ghosts that goes back to Hamlet's father, than as an *embodied* voice of Dene history, wisdom, and cultural memory. But he is not the only ghostly presence called up by the Widow as she gazes into her fire. She will talk to her dead husband, missing and loving him and refusing to let go of his spirit until near the end of the play. The Labine brothers reappear from the past of 1930; the Japanese grandmother killed by the bomb returns to her grandson who sees himself as a child carried on her back; and perhaps the most disturbing of all these ghostly apparitions is that of one of the young women, who were called radium painters, when she comes back from the dead to circle around the mine's dark core; she glows more and more intensely as she moves and becomes bald from radiation poisoning.[17]

*Burning Vision* is the theatrical representation, a dramatization if you will, of a Canadian story about the mining of uranium, the contamination of Dene and southern Canadian lands, many deaths from cancer resulting from radiation poisoning, and the atomic devastation unleashed over Japan in August 1945—in short, the highway of the atom. This representation is not produced through a traditional plot (with beginning, middle, and end), but through the creation of a complex landscape of memory that draws on Dene storytelling, Canadian Second World War history, the international history of how the war in the Pacific ended, and the long postwar aftermath of the bombs. Some features in this landscape are well known, celebrated even. Others are not known or acknowledged. A central concern of the play, which makes it important for this study, is the forgotten story of how the Canadian government of the day took control of the mine in 1942 and, under cover of national security during wartime, secretly transported the precious ore from Great Bear Lake south along the highway of the atom. As Peter van Wyck explains, the archives of Eldorado Nuclear Limited are still closed to researchers (6–7, 117).

Restrictions on access to information about what happened between 1941–42, when the mine was reopened under government auspices (it became a Crown corporation in 1944), and 1960, when the mine closed operations and the cancer rates among the Dene began to become a worry, amount to a deliberate, and thus far effective, silencing of the story. As Canadian citizens we knew no more than the Dene stevedores carrying the leaking sacks of ore, but the full consequences of actions taken in our name to produce uranium, *made in Canada*, remain partially hidden, ghostly presences in the landscape of memory that Marie Clements recreates in her play, that Peter Blow documents in his film, and that Peter van Wyck struggles to map in his scholarly study.





Although *Burning Vision* is a serious issues-based play that does point fingers—as Rose says directly at the audience, "YOU'RE all so sorry [but] you can't really be sorry for something you don't want to remember, can you" (100)—the intensity of live production, the encompassing sound and lighting effects of the drama, the melding of voices in three languages (Slavey, English, and Japanese), and the composite characters from past and present, finally produce what I experienced *in performance* as an exhilarating testimony to human creativity and endurance.[18] Because the play opens with the atomic bomb exploding on Nagasaki, we are situated as secondary witnesses to a *shared* history of destruction and to the struggle to understand, survive, and maintain human values. Equally important, *Burning Vision* ends on a note of hope: the voice-over of the Slavey radio announcer is followed by the Japanese announcer, and then by an announcer whose English reveals what we have heard: "Hello Granddad, brother, sister, son, husband, father, cousin, nephew, friend, my teacher, my love...We love you and miss you" (122). And in the final words of the play, the Japanese survivor, Koji, answers this northern radio call: "They hear us, and they are talking back in hope over time" (122).

This promise of hope notwithstanding, *Burning Vision* is anything but a redemptive narrative. In the closing sequence of the play, set in some undetermined present, a bomb falls again, and the stage instructions inform us that "*a huge white light*" envelops the characters, leaving "*their world*" (and ours in the audience) in total "*blackness*" (119). When the stage lights come up again, we see that a "*black dust has settled over everything*" and the actor playing Fat Man has been replaced by "*a sack dummy*" looking the "*worse for wear*" (119). This explicit reminder of the past is followed by a hallucinatory montage of characters moving across a charred landscape, passing and merging with one another—Japanese Grandmother to Radium Painter to Dene Widow, who Koji, the Japanese boy *not* killed by the original blast over Nagasaki, addresses as *his* grandmother. The Dene Widow recognizes him as her "small man that survived. Tough like hope" (121), and she is finally able to release the haunting spirit of her dead ore-carrier husband. The hope Clements leaves us with, then, is shot through with warnings—that war is not over and done with, that grief and suffering continue, that healing is never complete, and that human beings who survive disaster and are alive today can, *must*, remember and learn from past experience. We must *listen* to the Dene See-er who tells us his terrifying vision of white men digging up the black rock, transforming it into a stick, and dropping "this burning" on people who "looked like us" (119): "I saw the future, and I was disturbed" (104).[19] In the final analysis, the responsibility to learn and act is ours. *We* are the ones who must uncover and acknowledge the facts about war, accept our share of responsibility for the fate of civilians on both sides, and bear witness to their stories. Clements leaves that ethical burden for us to carry, after the play is over, after the house lights come up, as we reflect upon the meaning, for today, of her burning vision.

What Clements does not consider, what she leaves out of her reckoning, is nonetheless immense. For example, there is no room on her large canvas for the fate of Japanese Canadians in Canada or for Canadian soldiers in Hong Kong and in POW camps, never mind the Chinese and other civilians massacred by the Japanese Imperial Army.[20] Kogawa told us something of the first story in *Obasan*, and other writers are beginning to open up other perspectives, but the most important of these new writers who address Canada's experience in the Pacific is Michael Crummey. Towards the end of his monumental novel *The Wreckage*, a grown daughter asks her seventy-year-old mother why she "would...choose that kind of trouble now?" (351). The mother is not sure herself, but she has, nevertheless, *chosen* to accept, indeed to embrace, "that kind of trouble." That "trouble" is a seventy-two-year-old man called Aloysious, or Wish for short, who is a Second World War veteran and a survivor of a Japanese POW camp near Nagasaki. The seventy-year-old mother and widow is Mercedes, who has returned to Newfoundland, where she was born, to scatter her husband's ashes on the occasion of the fiftieth anniversary of D-Day, 6 June 1944. Her husband was an American soldier stationed in St. John's during the war, but the man who drew her from her outport home to the city in 1940, the man she fell so deeply in love with when she was sixteen is Wish.





*The Wreckage* comprises a complex set of interwoven life stories, each of which has been shaped by the war in the Pacific, just as each was influenced, if not actually determined, by racism and bigotry at home. The third central character, with his own life story, is a Japanese Canadian who has joined the Imperial Army to fight for the glory of Japan and for an Asia liberated from white, Western influence. His name is Noburo Nishino and his made-in-Canada story is loosely based on that of a real person, Kanao Inouye (1916–1947), who was tried and executed for treason after the war.[21] To bring these complex narrative threads together across fifty-four years, not counting the equally complex, detailed backstories for each character's family, and two utterly separate worlds and cultures, Crummey creates a narrative divided into two sections: Part 1, beginning in 1940, sets the stage for the love, misunderstandings, and wartime separations that follow, and Part 2, set in 1994, explores the catastrophic consequences of the war in the Pacific for the lives of these otherwise ordinary Canadians. Uniting these two date-specific *present* times, is a host of repeated tropes, haunting phrases, and memories (often *re*-remembered and slightly distorted or reconstructed memories) to carry the weight of ethical purpose and narrative meaning in the text. But the point to keep in mind through my discussion of this novel is that it does not provide an easy resolution of the "trouble" Mercedes accepts by returning to Wish. We cannot put this work down with any reassuring sense of redemption for the characters, for Canada, or for ourselves.

To allay any misconception that *The Wreckage* will tell a story of star-crossed teenaged lovers from Newfoundland, Crummey opens the novel *in medias res* with Japanese soldiers in the jungle of Guadalcanal, just hours before their encounter with American troops.[22] But it will require several paragraphs before readers understand precisely where they are or on which side of the battle line: "He was never dry. Every day they abandoned field guns mired in mud. The tires and axles of ammunition carts disappeared in sludge and the shells for the guns still with them were carried by hand. Half a dozen men at the front of the column slashed a trail with machetes...Soldiers lost their footing on exposed roots...There was only river water to drink, and everyone in the company was miserable with dengue and with dysentery" (*The Wreckage* 1). The "He" that opens the book is Private Noburo Nishino and, despite his Japanese name, he understands English perfectly. When he hears a parrot crying "Yes sir!" (2), he realizes the Americans are close and warns his fellow soldiers. After their failed encounter with the enemy and three days of desperate retreat, a badly wounded Nishino is questioned by his commanding officer, Lieutenant Kurakake, about where he learned to speak English: "In Kitsilano," Nishino replies. "In Canada" (8).

After that startling announcement, the story shifts abruptly to Part 1 and the title "1940" and then to the subtitle "Wish." We are now in a makeshift cinema in the Cove on Little Fogo Island, Newfoundland; Wish is preparing to screen *The 39 Steps*, and the beautiful local girl he had hoped to see is watching him. If what these two feel cannot yet be called love, then it is certainly such a powerful sexual attraction that they will risk ostracization and violence to be together. Wish, who comes from a town on the southern shore of the Avalon Peninsula, is Roman Catholic; Mercedes, or Sadie, is Protestant. In 1940s Newfoundland everyone knows your religion based on where you were born, and no one will countenance a marriage between these two. While mention of the war now underway in Europe is made in passing by local men, it is not until Wish is driven from the community that he flees to St. John's and enlists. By the time Mercedes escapes to join him, turning her back on her family and her community's bigotry, he has already left for Halifax, and her long years of waiting for him begin.



From this point on, the narrative perspective shifts back and forth between Wish, who is captured in Singapore and interned in POW camps there and later near Nagasaki, and Mercedes, who waits in St. John's hoping for some word from him. She writes to him regularly, sending a photograph, with her promise that she will be there when he comes home. As so often happens in war stories, a photograph and a letter become potent talismans, symbols of hope, of a return to normalcy and home, and Wish cherishes her image and the few words that reach him through his years of starvation, forced labour, illness, and abuse as a prisoner of war. He survives this ordeal, but with no word from him, Mercedes comes to believe he is dead (she, in fact, receives a letter saying he is), and she marries the American soldier who has loved her loyally for years. The question that haunts the narrative almost to its end is why: why did Wish not write or call as soon as he was liberated? Why, when he reached Halifax in late 1945, did he not continue on to St. John's? The answer is inextricably bound up with his prisoner-of-war experience and his participation in the murder of Nishino. Indeed, Nishino, whose own story is inserted piece by piece between those of Wish and Mercedes, is *the* key figure in *The Wreckage*, the ghost who will haunt Wish, the third element so remote, so incalculable, so deadly, that will keep them apart. Until, that is, Wish is able to tell *all* his story, to testify as it were and bear witness, something he cannot manage until, at seventy-two in 1994, Mercedes asks him to tell her "What happened to you over there, Wish?" and she wants to know "everything" (302).

Before he releases his appalling story, Wish tells her that in Spanish her name "means compassion or mercy or some goddamn thing" (327), and in a way compassion or mercy is what she will give him by listening attentively "as if he was providing an affidavit, listing dates and events, victims and perpetrators and bystanders, answering questions to clarify, interpreting phrases, naming names" (327). His bearing of witness is, in turn, acknowledged and legitimated by her listening, by her willingness to be his secondary witness and, in this capacity, she serves as the reader's textual surrogate. What she cannot grant him is forgiveness or absolution. What he withholds from her is "the one detail" no one else knows (331). After Wish and his fellow prisoners were liberated, he and two close friends found Nishino hiding in the crypt of the French Temple not far from the camp, where Wish had previously delivered the ashes of dead POWs. They beat the interpreter to death with wooden clubs, removed objects from his pockets (including a First World War medal), and then they urinated on the corpse—at least two of them did. Wish was incapable of the act, not because he refused to carry out this final outrage on principle, but because he had developed a sudden erection, something he had not had in several years.

His incapacity, at once crude and incongruous—Crummey's description is "pedestrian and bizarre...freakish, inexplicable" (332)—should not, however, be dismissed as trivial. The resonance of this moment *for the reader* and the significance of Wish's erection for an interpretation of narrative meaning and ethical perspective in the novel is profound. This horrifying scene of urinating on the corpse echoes an earlier scene in Nishino's story *and* an early scene in Wish and Mercedes's relationship. While growing up in Vancouver, Nishino and his Japanese-Canadian friends experienced considerable racism, and on one occasion they struck back in the only way they could. The public swimming pool in English Bay was banned to boys like him; "No Japs" were allowed (189), but Nishino ingratiated himself with the white manager, who eventually allowed the boys into the pool early in the mornings provided they left well before it opened to the general public. Finally, on one morning, before they leave, "all four boys pissed into the clear water of the pool" (191). To grasp the significance of Wish's erection before Nishino's corpse, we must also recall one of his and Mercedes's clandestine meetings back in the Cove when she asked to see him naked. He stripped in front of her and although she had never seen a naked man before, let alone one sexually aroused, she understood and reached for him, but he moved away saying they would wait until they were married (177–78).





From this point in 1940 with Mercedes until the murder of Nishino five years later, Wish has linked his body, especially his sexual identity, with her and, in my reading of these parallel scenes, his overwhelming shame, even self-loathing, is so profound that he feels unable to return to her.[23] His contamination from the war is not only physical, the result of being forced to clean up the aftermath of the bombing of Nagaski; it is psychological and spiritual. Nishino, like Wish a victim of bigotry at home, has become his nemesis. To be sure, he has been told that his exposure to radiation at Nagaski will likely kill him, as it does his friend Harris, and he is haunted by his memories of the camp and of the devastation of Nagaski littered with charred bodies and dying women and children and later, while living temporarily in Chicago, by the sight of a young African American's battered face on the front page of the *Chicago Defender*, an image that evokes Nishino's dead face. But at the root of his refusal to return to Mercedes or to embrace any future happiness is this deeply personal crisis over the murder of Nishino.[24] This memory of wartime betrayal and atrocity has polluted and supplanted a memory of love and domestic fulfillment. This haunting by the past is among the most complex, intimate, and powerful ones I know of in recent remembered stories of war. The scars Wish carries are not on his body but *of* it and, thus, inescapable. No healing, no plastic surgery of the soul will remove or alter this past.

*Burning Vision* and *The Wreckage* have much in common besides their representation of the war in the Pacific. Both texts foreground the complex connections between here in Canada and there in Japan, between home front and battle front, between the violence and hatred of the war and the bigotry and persecution of peacetime Canadian (and Newfoundland) society. By insisting on these connections and using them strategically to advance and unify plot, this play and novel invite us to participate in remembering the war and discovering aspects of its factual history and traumatic aftermath, which we may not have known about or might prefer to ignore. These connections, together with the processes of remembrance and discovery, contribute to Canada's more general cultural memory of the war. But they do more than this because each narrative brings its characters, and us with them, *home* in the end. Each resists the temptation to leave war over there; each reminds us that our home and native land contributed to the war, not only by supplying uranium for bombs and soldiers for fighting, but also by sharing in the racism, bigotry, and violence that fuel all wars. Clements makes this point emphatically when she dramatizes the fatal effects of radium contamination and when her character, Round Rose, accuses *us* of being sorry for things we refuse to remember: "Selective memory isn't it? Let's be honest, hell, you can't even apologise for the shit you did yesterday never mind 50 years ago" (100). Crummey makes a similar point more obliquely when he has Wish keep the First World War medal found on Nishino's body. Ironically, tragically, this medal was won by Nishino's father, who fought for Canada in the Great War, as the inscription on the medal states. Whether intentional on Crummey's part or not, this medal recalls that scene in Anne Wheeler's *The War Between Us* in which the Japanese-Canadian veteran, about to be *repatriated* to Japan, burns his uniform and throws his medals into the flames.

Both works provide deeply moving examples of fictional, recreated primary witnessing (Clements through her Dene Widow; Crummey through Wish), and both serve as exemplary instances of secondary witnessing on the part of their creators who resist redemptive conclusions and insist that we—readers, audiences, contemporary Canadians generally—also perform the role of secondary witnessing and carry the ethical burden of remembering and understanding into the present. For the genre of drama, this passing of the burden is managed by a character (played in performance by a live actor) addressing the audience directly, as Round Rose does. In a novel, at least in *The Wreckage*, a character within the story—Mercedes—shows us what we must do: listen with empathic unsettlement, with compassion, and share the weight of memory. This sharing is made somewhat easier, or more accessible, because the *people* in both works are recognizable, average human beings who desire nothing more than to enjoy love, family, and peace. No one in either text is simply evil; Fat Man becomes almost sympathetic as the play develops and his terror over Cold War hostility is palpable, while Nishino's family past in Vancouver explains, if it does not excuse, his behaviour. By the same token, there are no heroes or heroics in either work; the sheer helplessness of all the characters, their grief, trauma, and loss, make them resonant figures of the human condition. And it is at this level of ordinary humanity that these works deliver their chief message, their excoriating damnation of war, because this is where we all live our daily lives. Quite simply, we can relate to them and their suffering.





Insofar as this play and novel hold out hope for a better, more peaceful future, they do so by bringing their fictional characters together across barriers of race, language, and religion, and by refusing the temptations of anger, recrimination, and retaliation. *Burning Vision* closes with a symbolic recognition of the Japanese survivor by the Dene Widow; *The Wreckage* ends with Mercedes and Wish united to face a belated and problematic future—together. In neither case is the past denied. To the contrary. The past of the Second World War is remembered, its ghosts acknowledged, and its history brought forward into our present of telling, performing, and reading. Like *A Nanking Winter*, in which a Chinese-Canadian playwright writes the horror of that massacre into contemporary Canadian life, or *Hana's Suitcase*, in which the Holocaust makes its way to Japan and finally to Canada in the form a Jewish child's suitcase or, most recently, in *The Promise of Rain,* in which another Canadian survivor of a Japanese POW camp must remember and bear witness to this past (including the brutality of a particular Japanese-Canadian interpreter) to save his sanity and his family, *Burning Vision* and *The Wreckage* ask us to bear witness. They implore us to face that terrible vision, to *see* the wreckage left behind by war for what it is, and to work through mourning to an informed cultural memory of war that embraces peace.



The central theme running through these works is that of erasure and forgetting. What happened to Camp L? Where was the "highway of the atom"? What happened to those towns with their shacks in the BC Interior, where the Japanese Canadians were interned? As Naomi tells us, no sign remains of her family's time near Slocan (*Obasan* 11–12): the huts have disappeared; no names appear on maps or roads; even their ghosts have been pushed aside by the ghosts of white miners. The Canadian landscape of memory seems to bear no trace of this made-in-Canada wartime past. And yet, as Grandma Kato knew, there can be no forgetting, and as Rose insists *we* cannot be sorry for things we refuse to remember. What these texts give their readers and viewers is a reawakening of collective, cultural memory because each in its own way, and through its generic conventions, recreates those erased landscapes and repopulates them. Each insists that war never stays over *there* and that it must be confronted *here*. Where official history and the general public have been blind to the scenes and deaf to the voices from the past, Canadian artists have picked up these "radar echoes" (as Clements calls them), done some extraordinary research into Canada's Second World War past, and then produced stories that capture aspects of what we have tried to forget—or did not know was even there to be remembered. Moreover, each text invites us to bear witness, to listen to the suffering of fictional characters who represent the experiences of actual individuals (in the cases of *Obasan* and *The War Between Us*) and of families and communities (in *The Ash Garden*; *Burning Vision;* and *The Wreckage*).

This is not to say that these works bring only bad news or accusations. To the contrary, each one strives for an ethical balance: not every Caucasian Canadian is seen as a racist; most ordinary Canadians were completely unaware of what was being mined at Eldorado under government auspices and then what was done with the material; all Canadians were subjected to intense propaganda that demonized the *Other*, whether that other person or group was in Germany, Italy, or Japan, or here on home ground; and all Canadians lost their democratic rights under the War Measures Act. Some Canadians resisted by protesting, signing petitions, or documents prepared by the signatories of the Co-operative Committee on Japanese Canadians' memorandum (*Obasan* 248–50). The ethical question raised by these post-1977 works boils down to this: what would *you* do? Under these circumstances and in light of what we can learn from the past, when we choose to remember it, what will you do should something like this happen again? None of these works allows a reader or audience member to indulge his or her emotional response, to identify with the victims and claim to be traumatized by their story (as LaCapra fears does occur with much retelling of trauma), and then to feel somehow absolved from responsibility. Instead, these works insist that we think as much as feel, that we experience an empathic unsettlement that prompts careful reflection. Each treads the very fine line between fact and fiction, history and story, emotion and reflection, in order to create a vision of a lived-in Canadian past that influences the present and the future. The Second World War shattered the lives of real people like Wish and Mercedes. It almost made the resumption of a lived-in present impossible for a man like Wish. And yet he does live, thanks to Crummey's imagination, to tell his story to the one person who will listen—and to us. Remembering and acknowledging the ghosts from his POW nightmare, especially that one Canadian ghost, illustrates both his dehumanization by war and, as it were, his *re*humanization through storytelling.

Like Mercedes, all we can do is listen and learn. This active engagement with our history and with remembrance is what John Murrell offers in *Waiting for the Parade*, the work I discuss in Chapter 8. While this play focuses on the home front to portray a group of women waiting for the war to end and their men to come home and to explore the many ways in which propaganda distorts the truth and twists perceptions during war, it also redirects attention to Europe and to Canada's wartime connections with a different set of borders and battles. In reality, of course, there were parades and celebrations and joyful reunions, but the aftermath of the war remained behind, unaddressed and unacknowledged. The aftermath persisted at home.

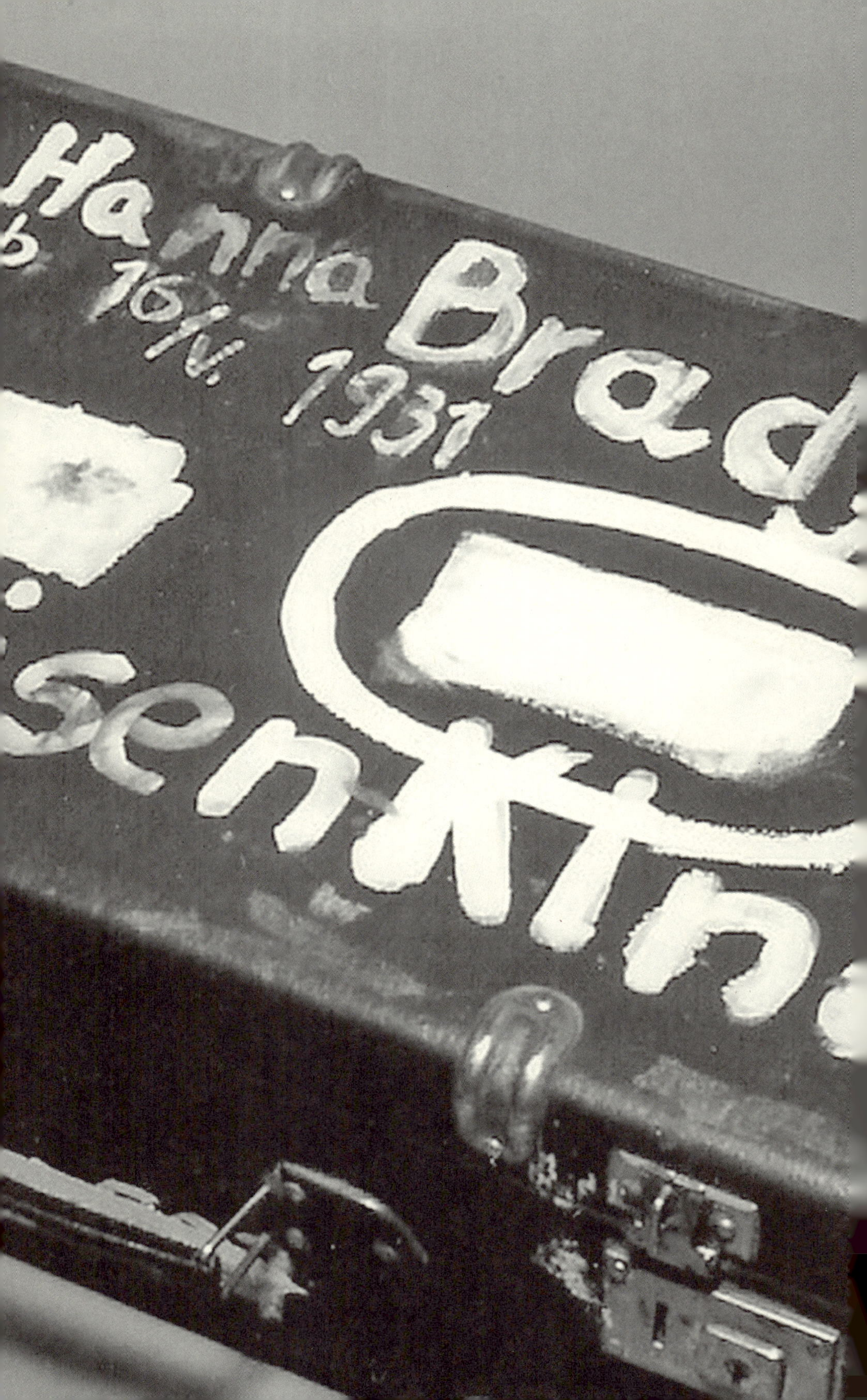
Hanna
1931

# 8
# The Promised Land

## Canada or Kanada?



HOW ARE CANADIANS remembering their Second World War history today? Who is doing the remembering? Newspapers run headlines over articles encouraging veterans to talk. "The Memory Project" strives to keep the war in Europe alive online, and in 2010 the country celebrated the Canadian Navy's centenary. On 5 May that year Canada made its last formal return to the Netherlands to remember those Canadians who liberated Holland in 1945, and a commemorative sculpture called "Wheel of Conscience" by Daniel Libeskind was installed at Pier 21 in Halifax as a reminder of a shameful aspect of home front history: the government's refusal to accept Jewish refugees. And yet we seem to have forgotten, or not quite grasped, the significance of staging an Olympic torch relay across the country for the 2010 Vancouver Winter Olympics, despite the historical fact that such a relay was not part of ancient Greek tradition. As John Allemang reminded readers in a *Globe and Mail* article, "This Is the Torch that Hitler Lit," the relay was invented by Hitler for the 1936 Berlin games.[1]

As these few examples of remembering—and forgetting—suggest, the process of creating a Canadian landscape of memory for the war in Europe has been somewhat hit and miss. People age and die, taking their stories with them. Younger generations choose to move on, to live in the present, to forget. Official military history tends to celebrate past glories or sufferings (like the tragic loss of Canadians at Dieppe) that led to later victories over enemies. As often as not today (more often than not, in fact), the popular press is quick to praise the military and slow to examine the complex contexts of past and current conflicts because criticism runs the risk of sounding unpatriotic, left-wing, or both. A case in point was Michael Valpy's 21 November 2009 article in the *Globe and Mail*, accompanied by a large, colour photograph of flag-waving Canadians applauding General Rick Hillier, chief of the defence staff, at a "Red Friday" rally in Toronto. Valpy called his piece "Invisible No More," and he tried to examine why "Canadians are reimagining their country as a military nation" (F1).





Although Valpy pointed out that the Canadian military is actively "engaged in information warfare" (F5) to enhance military culture, and despite his insistence that the decline of Canada's peacekeeping culture and self-image is worrisome, the visual impact of the article was pro-military; one had to read the small print to find the qualifications and cautionary details. Nevertheless, Valpy identified a critical shift in Canada's image, at least in its self-image at home. And his article raises another important question: if the military, the government, and the media are reimagining Canada as a warrior nation, instead of as a post-Second World War peacekeeping nation, where can one turn to find that larger picture of Canadian identity that reimagines, by remembering, our Second World War past as complex, contradictory, and more than a cause for self-congratulation and celebration? The literary works I turn to now remind their audiences and readers of much more than Canada's war in Europe against fascism.

Each of two plays—*Waiting for the Parade* and *None Is Too Many*—is set during the war but takes place at home, and in each the home front becomes a site of conflict and confrontation in its own right. The winners, however, are not soldiers, and the losers are not the enemy; one might say the losers are all of us.

## STAGING THE HOME FRONT

### Waiting for the Parade *and* None Is Too Many





To date, the Second World War has not attracted contemporary playwrights as much as the First. Among the reasons for this comparative lack of interest is the fact that it is still a bit too close in time for the degree of reflection that recreation often requires. It was also a more complex war, a more *total* war, and one in which Canadians were more deeply invested *as Canadians*, instead of as a British colony or as mere cannon fodder. With this investment came increased responsibility for our own decisions, actions, and inactions, and the playwrights have shown more concern for these responsibilities and the war's aftermath than with the terrible losses we incurred at Dunkirk, Dieppe, or even during the summer of 1944, following D-Day, in the battles to wrest Normandy from the Germans.[2] *Waiting for the Parade* premiered in 1977, the year that Findley published *The Wars*, but it was not the only play from the period to examine the Second World War. Margaret Hollingsworth's *Ever Loving* follows the lives of British and Italian war brides who, together with their Canadian husbands, hold a reunion in 1970 and remember their arrival years ago and their hopes for the future. For some, the years have been painfully disappointing; for all, they have meant a long struggle to adapt.[3] The husbands, however, fail to understand this struggle because, as one of them protests, "You should be grateful to be here. All of you...I fought for Canada. It's the greatest country in the world" (370).

In *Waiting for the Parade*, John Murrell digs deeply into the home front lives of his five female characters to expose a host of doubts, anxieties, and prejudices that permeate the tense atmosphere of one representative Canadian community in Alberta. The Calgary we see in Murrell's play is not part of the "greatest goddamn country in the world." At first glance, this play seems straightforward. The five women are all waiting when the play starts and four of them are still waiting at its end, when the war in Europe is over and the first soldiers are about to arrive in the city by train. Margaret, the oldest of the group, dies before her enlisted son arrives home and her younger son is released from prison for being anti-war and possibly a Communist sympathizer. Janet, whose husband did not enlist because of his radio work, takes on the role of domestic sergeant-major, drilling the women in air raid practice, leading them in rousing songs, and in making bandages and refreshments for the soldiers as they pass through town. The others dislike her bossiness, and she is both ashamed of her shirking husband and heartbroken by his infidelity. Eva is a schoolteacher and the potential saboteur of the group, despite her apparent shy nervousness. She is horrified when her grade ten students wear "Zap the Jap" buttons and she finally confronts her warmongering husband by ordering him out of the house with one of his own guns. She detests war, but she is generally despised for her pacifism; her students tell her she should be taken out and shot for her views. Catherine, whose husband is fighting, has a young child, but must work in a factory to make ends meet. When she receives a telegram informing her that her husband is missing in action, she begins an affair with a co-worker. And that leaves Marta. Marta Grauenholz is in many ways the fulcrum of the play because as a German Canadian she is viewed with open suspicion and hostility by Janet and Margaret and her home is attacked by neighbours who paint swastikas on the house and throw smoke bombs under the porch. Worse still, her father, and only relative, has been interned as an enemy alien suspected of being a Nazi sympathizer. By the time he is released from the camp he has lost his mind and he dies before the war ends. Marta's story illustrates the prejudice and hysteria whipped up by war propaganda, and her acceptance or rejection by the other women is the gauge of Canada's wartime domestic policies and behaviour.

Murrell did considerable research for this play by interviewing women who had lived through the war and shared their memories with him. So, although it is not a memory play (in the sense that *The Lost Boys*, *Vimy*, or *Burning Vision* are), it is a play that invites Canadian audiences and readers to remember events on the home front during the war. It contributes to Canadian cultural memory by filling in missing signposts in our landscape. Among the most significant of these is Murrell's collective portrait of women's experiences during the war. After many readings and discussions of the play, I have come to the conclusion that Murrell's five women are well presented, sympathetic spokespersons for their time and place.[4] When each woman addresses us directly in brief monologues, we are asked to see life from her perspective, to understand her emotion and trauma, to bear witness to her personal story and to learn from each and from their collective testimony. As a group these women stand for Canada, every bit as much as a group of soldiers might; as individuals they speak privately of their fear, loneliness, helplessness, and anger. And yet they are not—either singly or as a group—merely helpless. Janet cannot order them about indefinitely. They rebel against her authoritarian stance, as Eve does against her belligerent husband, and two of them—Catherine and Eve—embrace Marta, accepting her into their circle.

They must function, however, in the context and within the gendered, economic, and political constraints of their times, which Murrell evokes through their discussion of news reports, letters home, their war work and play (painting seams on their legs to suggest the silk stockings they cannot buy was a common practice), the movies they enjoy, especially with British heartthrob Leslie Howard (the son of a Hungarian Jew), the various forms of war propaganda they must deal with, as well as the constant "scuttlebutt" going the rounds. Murrell works references to key events into their conversations, from Dieppe to D-Day, from Pearl Harbor and the Alaska Highway to the atomic bomb, from King's assurances about no conscription to his reversal of that policy, the implementation of camps for "enemy aliens," and the anti-Communist attitudes of the day. But the drama of this play—its tensions and competing ideas and emotions—is performed most effectively through music.

Familiar war songs of the period are featured throughout the play, with particular attention given to "Wish Me Luck," "Now is the Hour," "The White Cliffs of Dover," and "Lily Marlene." "Lily Marlene," which Margaret, Catherine, and Eve rehearse early in the play, while Janet plays the piano, serves to remind them of what separates them from Marta. When she carries on singing *in German*, Janet remarks, "It never occurred to me, this song used to be one of theirs" (18). At which point Marta stops singing, turns to the audience for one of her brief monologues, and recounts how a Canadian officer reacted when she told him her full name. At first he thought she was Jewish and pulled his hand away from hers, "like he was burnt," but when she says no, he realizes that she is German. His response is shocking: "it's the Boche, right here on Centre Street" (19), he exclaims. Phrases like "one of theirs" and terms used in total ignorance as insults—"Jewish" and "Boche"—indicate that Marta and her father have been classified as Other, as not Canadian, as enemies. To drive this classification home, the women pick up "Lily Marlene" again with Marta singing in German and the others in English. At the piano, however, Janet tries to "*drown Marta out*" (19). The result is a battle of the lyrics, as the two languages "*tangle together*" to make "*discord*" out of the haunting melody and words of love.

But the lyrics of "Lily Marlene" are not the only ones that haunt this play and speak to us, in a present performance, about the past. Early in the play, and "*softly, very far away*" (14), a recording of Richard Tauber (1891–1948) singing an aria can just be heard. This music will fade, be replaced by other music, but keep returning. As it returns it establishes a crucial leitmotif and counterbalance to the simple-minded dualities of us/them, Canadian/German, pro- and anti-war being examined in this play. By Scene 9 we can hear Tauber more clearly and realize that he is singing the famous love song "Ach so fromm" from Friedrich von Flotow's romantic opera *Martha*:

> *Banger Gram, eh' sie kam*
> *Hat die Zukunft mir umhült,*
> *Doch mit ihr blühte mir*
> *Neues Dasein lusterfüllt.* (28)





In other words, Lyonel is singing of how, in his dreams, his sweetheart appears, fair like an angel and a lovely sight for his "lonely, longing, eyes."[5]

Unfortunately, however, Janet shows up in this scene to insist that Marta turn off such music because "a substantial number of people—are bothered by it" (29). Marta replies that this is not war music but a love song. But Janet persists: "The point is, nobody wants to hear it!" To which Marta can only say, "I want to hear it!" (30), which is tantamount to saying that she *is somebody*. However, the real point is that what Marta wants is irrelevant. The words are German and, therefore, offensive, regardless of what they mean. Murrell, who knows his opera, is making several further points here. Richard Tauber was an Austrian with Jewish ancestry and in 1933, after being assaulted by Nazi Brownshirts in Germany, he returned to Vienna, where he continued to sing with the Vienna State Opera until the *Anschluss* in March 1938. He then fled to England. Not only is Janet, and the other Calgarians she represents, attempting to silence a love song, she is also—albeit unwittingly—silencing the voice of a famous refugee artist, who sought and received asylum in England.

The irony of this Canadian ignorance about the broader context of racism and the intolerance it perpetuates on the home front surfaces repeatedly through the rest of the play. For example, when Eve protests the prime minister's introduction of conscription, Janet shuts her up with an order: "Tell them [the conscripts] they're fighting to preserve a way of life that's precious to you" (37). In the next scene, Marta re-enacts her visit to the local authorities (addressing *us* as if we are those authorities) to inquire about her father. When she is laughed at, she protests: "I have friends in this war—on our side! I read the casualty lists like everybody else! I am a Canadian citizen!" (40). Then, in the scene that follows this one, Margaret learns that her younger son has been arrested and jailed for distributing pamphlets described as "Communist anti-war propaganda" (44), and this persecution, like Marta's treatment and Eve's silencing, is taking place in a supposed democracy—the very kind of system the soldiers are "fighting to preserve."





These social and political ironies subside somewhat when Catherine receives a telegram announcing that her husband is missing in action. She believes he must be dead and laments not only his likely death but the fact that she has trouble seeing him clearly. With the passing months and years of the war, her Billy has vanished until she "can't remember what he looked like—at all. That's what hurts....Losing him—a little at a time" (62). This speech registers the deeply personal, emotional loss of war as it is experienced on the home front, and in doing so it provides a counterweight, almost a respite, to the more public, political tensions that continue to rise through the rest of the play. The long sixteenth scene contains the climax in what is, for the most part, an action-*less* play. The women are rehearsing what to do during a Japanese air raid. Janet is ordering them about, switching the lights on and off, timing their routines, and making Eve feel especially stupid. But when Catherine confronts her, Janet becomes furious: "The bloody Japanese," she shouts, are going to invade and that is why "the Americans are building their highway [the Alaska Highway] into the frozen North" (70). The rhetoric and accusations escalate until the two women attack each other physically. Their confrontation—ineffectual and silly—amounts to nothing, and yet Murrell uses this scene to demonstrate how the pent-up emotion, the tedium of waiting, and the impact of propaganda can operate on otherwise peace-loving, ordinary civilians, turning them into undignified bullies and pathetic victims. The fight, if one can call it that, may be a joke compared with Dieppe or D-Day, but it is a joke with a lesson all the same.

As the waiting draws to an end, we hear offstage battle noises that suggest radio reports on the Normandy invasion. The women huddle together centre stage "*terrified but still*" (76). When news arrives that a treaty has been signed, Eve rejoices by tossing neatly rolled Red Cross bandages into the air like streamers: "all quiet on the Western Front," she cheers. But Janet quickly squashes her enthusiasm: "The war is not over! What about the Japanese?" (88). Sadly, of course, she is right. Not only is the war in the Pacific not over, the atomic bombs are about to fall (92), the men are coming home from Europe with their own problems, and the repercussions of racism, grief, and trauma will set in. Marta is still not fully accepted by the others, although Eve will show her some kindness, and she is now alone (her father is dead), and Margaret died before seeing her sons again. Worse still, a cloud of apprehension hangs over the closing moments of the play. Tauber's voice is heard for the last time before it fades behind a snappy 1945-style dance tune, and the women—with the exception of Marta—dance once more. As the lights go down, even this dancing ends, and the women are left waiting while drums and a "*march grows louder and louder*" (90). The future is left hanging and ominous, but the memories from that era will cascade, as Lisa Appignanesi puts it, "through the generations in a series of misplaced fears, mysterious wounds, odd habits" (8).

When Jason Sherman accepted a commission from the Winnipeg Jewish Theatre in 1997 to create a play about Canada's response to Jewish refugees fleeing the Nazis, he faced a formidable challenge. His task was to create theatre based upon history, memory, and eyewitness accounts as these had been gathered together by Irving Abella and Harold Troper in their 1982 book *None Is Too Many: Canada and the Jews of Europe, 1933–1948*.

Sherman, born in 1962, is neither a soldier nor a survivor, neither an eyewitness to atrocity nor a victim. And he is not a historian. Nevertheless, in his play called *None Is Too Many* he has used his own craft, the resources and conventions of theatre performance, to dramatize one of the darkest aspects of Canada's Second World War history. The result is a powerful, political history play in which actual individuals from the 1930s and 1940s tell their stories, re-enact horrifying events, and confront, head-on, the anti-Semitism of Canadian policy and society. Saul Hayes, a Montreal laywer who would represent the Jewish case to the King government, is a key figure in Abella and Troper's book and the hero, or at least the main protagonist, in Sherman's play. The historical facts of what Canada did and did not do between 1937 and 1949 are set against the European context for these facts that stretches back to 1933, forward to Kristallnacht on 9 November 1938, the invasion of Poland in 1939, the fall of Vichy France in November 1942, the "final solution" at Auschwitz between 1943 and 1945, and to the displaced persons camps of 1946. Although these events cannot be explored in detail by Sherman, they provide the tragic backstory from which he selects striking moments to develop his Canadian story.

The crucial facts for the Canadian story are simple enough. In the 1930s and during the war years, Canada admitted only 4,381 Jewish refugees, even though the government knew by 1943 that a full genocide was underway. This number was significantly lower than for all the other countries who granted asylum to Jews fleeing Nazi Europe.[6] In the summer of 1939, Canada refused to allow the SS *St. Louis*, carrying 907 German Jews, to land; Canada was their last hope and they were returned to Europe, where most died. This is the failure remembered by Daniel Libeskind's sculpture "Wheel of Conscience" at Pier 21 in Halifax. It is also part of the story told by Bock in *The Ash Garden*.[7] In the fall of 1942, the Canadian government delayed any effort to rescue Jewish children orphaned in France until it was too late: the Nazis took over free France and 6,500 children were murdered (Abella and Troper 118). Why? Because anti-Semites held positions of authority in the Canadian government, from Prime Minister Mackenzie King, to his Quebec Lieutenant Ernest Lapointe, to Vincent Massey, Canadian High Commissioner to London, to the most fanatical of them all—the civil servant and gatekeeper in the wartime Ministry of Mines and Resources (also responsible for immigration), F.C. Blair, who was Director of the Immigration Branch of the Ministry. Blair is another central character in Sherman's play, the antagonist and embodiment of ordinary evil, opposite Saul Hayes.

To create a play out of this grim history, Sherman uses the theatrical conceit of witnessing. He sets his play in Ottawa in 1949, when Mr. Hayes is presenting his report to a special Senate Committee charged with finding ways to assist Jewish postwar immigration. Hayes, however, wants the committee to know as much of the background as possible. The audience members (and readers) are, therefore, positioned as the members of the committee who will receive the full report and hear Hayes's testimony. *We* become the secondary witnesses to the trauma experienced by people our country, by and large, refused to help. The play opens with a decisive scene between Saul Hayes and the committee chairman (call me Bob, he says to Saul). This man has read the report and wants Saul to cut certain unflattering details. Bob refuses to see why Saul would want to make accusations against Canadians (and the father of Canadians like himself) who fought and died in Europe for *his people*, especially when, he points out, "we're looking into how we can make things easier for your people, the survivors, to come over" (382). Clearly angry with Saul's insistence on presenting the full history, he questions Saul's motives for including such facts. Saul's response is that "it has to be on the record. It has to be known that, at a time when we needed your help most, it wasn't available" (382). Bob's next outburst is striking for both its insensitivity and its honesty: "Put yourself in my place," he argues. This country, "my friends, my neighbours, who, who sent their sons, who *lost* their sons, to defend...your people....I mean for God's sake, Saul, what do you think this war was about?" (383-84). It is, of course, insulting for Bob to ask

Saul to put himself in his place when he cannot do likewise, and yet it is also true that Canadians fought and died in this *good* war against fascist evil and racist murder. This confrontation between Bob and Saul captures the essence of the dilemma faced by both men. Each of them has a perspective on the past; each of them is trying to do the right thing now; each of them is, to different degrees, right. However, the final and shattering climax of this encounter comes at the end of the scene. Saul refuses to suppress the truth: "I'll give my brief. In full" (384), he states. To which Bob replies, "Well, it won't be believed" (384). This claim—you won't be believed—is precisely what survivors have been told, precisely what Kirmayer addressed when he insisted that a landscape of memory must be established before stories about limit experiences could be heard and acknowledged. The rest of Sherman's play produces such a landscape to test Bob's claim, and we will be asked to believe what we see, what we hear, what we *listen* to.

The play contains twelve scenarios, including the opening meeting between Hayes and the chairman, three of which are snapshots of Hayes's report to the Senate Committee in the play's present of 1949. I use the term scenario to describe the representation of actual past events because, unlike scenes in a realistic play, they do not function to explore character, develop interrelationships, or create a plot, so much as to present enacted, embodied evidence. They strike the reader, or audience member, as documents might do. For example, in one scenario we see a Jewish father arriving in Belgium in May 1938 to apply for immigration to Canada for his family; he is rudely rejected by an immigration officer because he is Jewish, but this officer suggests that if he and his family become Christians and bring their wealth to Canada, then he may be able to help them (388–89). In another, with the puzzling title "I Only Have Escaped," we learn, along with a Toronto family celebrating Hannukah in December 1939, the staggering truth captured by these words: a card has arrived from a relative in Warsaw with the single sentence—"Der Feter Yiuv ist *bei* uns" (400)—which makes no sense until the rabbi decodes the message, which refers to the Book of Job and means that only the writer of this message has survived a Nazi pogrom (402). This message is a cry for help and a warning, a voice reaching Canada almost from the grave, a plea to be understood and acted upon. Such a card was, in fact, sent from Warsaw and received by the Goldstein family in Toronto (see Abella and Troper, Chapter 3).

The scenario in which Hayes meets with Blair in his Ottawa office on 11 November 1942 is particularly disturbing. Not only is it Remembrance Day but also Hayes has come to finalize arrangements to rescue one thousand children in unoccupied France before the Nazis take over. Blair, however, is unsympathetic and skeptical. As far as he is concerned, these children are not really in any danger, the threat of "death camps" is mere "speculation" (406), and Mr. Hayes and the Jewish Congress are scheming to bring entire families to Canada. He argues and then bargains with Hayes, demanding that he "winnow away the list" until only five hundred names remain on it. Before such an unbelievable task begins, however, news arrives that the Germans have occupied free France and the Canadian government has severed diplomatic relations with the Vichy government. Now there is no need to choose which children will be saved and which will not; they will all perish. It is almost impossible to imagine a more horrifying scenario than this, but Sherman selects another episode from the Abella and Troper study to drive home his point about Canada's failure. This scenario, called "Welcome to Kanada," begins fairly innocently. The only sign that things are not what they might at first seem to be, rests with the spelling of Kanada. One by one, people arrive in front of an "officer," who welcomes them to Kanada and instructs them to leave their bags "there on the ground" (412). Within moments, his tone shifts from politeness to increasingly brutal commands that people strip naked and leave *all* their belongings behind before their heads are shaved. A man called "Mengele" shouts, "Links. Links. Recht. Links." (484) and we understand where we are: Auschwitz. But Sherman pushes the horror of the scenario further so that we, the committee members (audience and readers), can be in no doubt about what is happening and what we must believe. This "Mengele" addresses us directly to explain: "This part of the camp was called Kanada, because the prisoners whose task it was to oversee its operation believed Canada to be a land of great riches. You could say that many of those who died here made it to Kanada after all" (414). As Abella and Troper remind us, "To the condemned Jews of Auschwitz, Canada had a special meaning....It represented life, luxury and salvation; it was a Garden of Eden in Hell; it was also unreachable" (ix).

The title phrase "none is too many" comes not only from Abella and Troper but also from a statement actually made in 1945 by an unidentified Canadian immigration officer when he was asked how many Holocaust survivors would be allowed into the country.[8] That anyone could say such a thing, or think it, is unbelievable, but by the time Sherman brings us to the final scenario, where Hayes finishes his report to us, *we believe*. After the meeting is adjourned, the chairman thanks Saul and promises to increase the quota to "twenty thousand of your—of the displaced persons, effective immediately" (422), and he adds that a man could not have served his country better than Saul has, "not even on the battlefield" (422). Clearly, we are meant to see that Bob has listened, that he finally believes what he has been told. The two men then salute each other with the toast "L'chaim," and the play closes on a note of promise, hope, acceptance, and knowledge. However, there is one special comment that hangs over this happy ending like a dark cloud, and it is a warning to *always* remember and believe, a warning not to forget or suppress the past. Jason Sherman's Saul concludes his presentation to us with these words: "Beware the tyrant, I say. He does not live in a foreign land stained with blood; he lives amongst us, dripping with ink" (422).

If one thing stands out from all the attention paid to the wars by contemporary writers and artists, it is that the issues raised by reflection on the Second World War are still present, still begging for attention, still haunting the twenty-first century. A case in point is

Hannah Moscovitch's play *East of Berlin*, which premiered with Tarragon Theatre on 24 November 2007 but was not published until 2009. To go "east of Berlin" is to go to Auschwitz, and two young people in this play—a German Paraguyan man and a young Jewish woman from New York—make just such a trip in the 1960s. They have met in Berlin and fallen in love, but Sarah does not know the full truth about Rudi's past. Rudolf Klausener is the son of Dr. Rudolf Klausener, a former Nazi, a doctor in Auschwitz, and a war criminal. At first Rudi thinks that by loving Sarah he can make reparations for the sins of his father, that loving and marrying her will be "an act of...redemption" (56). He is, of course, wrong. When Sarah learns the truth, she leaves him and he returns to Paraguay, which is where he is as the play opens, standing outside his father's study door. *We* are constructed as primary witnesses to his anguish and guilt, and we are asked to approve his decision to go through the door and kill his father (75). Except that is not what he does. The plays ends with Rudi opening the door all right, but then he holds "*the gun up to his head*" (76). We do not hear a shot because the stage instructions call for an immediate blackout. When I saw the Vancouver production in February 2009, this sudden, surprise ending left me pondering Moscovitch's meaning: was this a symbol of an eye for an eye, a German child for all those murdered Jewish children? Was this simply a failure on Rudi's part to confront his father with the truth, to carry through on his responsibility as a secondary witness? Was it a futile appeal for sympathy, a self-indulgent posturing as a victim? Perhaps. But one point *is* clear from this final moment: either we face the past and its ugly facts or we will be forever haunted by what we refuse to believe, and the ghosts of that refusal will stalk future generations. *East of Berlin* is a memory play with an unequivocal, inescapable conclusion. One can never undo the past, make reparations, or achieve redemption. One can only—but it is a lot—pay attention, listen honestly and, with empathic unsettlement, bear witness, and remember.

## TRANSNATIONAL GHOSTS AND INTERGENERATIONAL HAUNTING

### *"Stones,"* Hana's Suitcase, *and* Fugitive Pieces

In some ways Michael Ondaatje's *The English Patient* seems like a good example of transnational ghosts and intergenerational haunting. I have decided not to focus on it, however, because the heart of its story involves issues tangential to Canadians on battle or home fronts during or after the war, and the most compelling *remembered* landscape is the Egyptian–Libyan desert. The main story is set toward the end of the war in Italy as the Allied armies march north behind the retreating Germans. Hana, the Canadian nurse who stays behind in the bomb-damaged Italian villa, San Girolamo, is caring for a burn patient too wounded to be moved and mourning Patrick, her father, whose story is told in *In the Skin of a Lion*, but who has been killed in France. Ondaatje brings another important figure from the earlier novel into the Italian villa; the thief Caravaggio appears out of the night and watches with and over Hana as she ministers to the dying man. Together, Hana and Caravaggio listen to the patient's confessional story; they perform, in a sense, as his secondary witnesses even though they do not address the reader and thereby model our witnessing.

But Kirpal Singh, known as Kip, a sapper with the British forces, Hana's brief affair with him, and the mysterious patient, whose story surfaces over the course of the narrative, are the chief protagonists in this transnational history of the war in North Africa and Europe, imperialism, and betrayal.[9] Memories of the war will continue to shape, even haunt, Hana and Kip, but the story of postwar aftermath is only touched upon in the closing moments of the novel. Kip, who learned from the war to reject the British Empire and European racial arrogance, will be living happily in India; Hana will be back in Canada, alone and it seems still grieving; the English patient, who is not English at all but Count Ladislaus de Almásy, will be dead. The extra-diegetic narrator who brings these characters and their stories together has no identity, except that of a chronicler and no national territory to defend. Like Almásy, the nationless patient, he exists beyond such categories. This is less a Canadian story than a story of postcolonial (notably East Indian) self-discovery and freedom: the former Empire, along with Europe, is on its knees; the future lies elsewhere.

By contrast, each of the texts I examine closely takes its readers to a Europe of the past but returns us firmly to Canadian home ground in the present. Each of the following narratives depicts children trapped by war, adults in the next generations who are haunted by the past and by their damaged childhoods, and first-person storytellers who are driven to speak, to bear witness, and to ask their readers to pay attention to their voices and their search for meaning. Each relies on memory and on commemorative gestures performed by adults for the past, for the lost children (and childhoods), to shape its narrative remembering. And each negotiates an uneasy coming to terms with post-memory. There are no happy endings, no absolutions, in these texts, just as there were none in *Obasan*, *The Ash Garden*, or *The Wreckage*. At most we are left with that disturbing quality of empathic unsettlement that urges us to reflect on the constant need for tolerance, acceptance, and remembrance as we struggle to build secure bridges to the future. In his story "Stones," Timothy Findley writes from the perspective of an adult son who witnessed the destruction of his father's psyche after the horror of Dieppe. In *Hana's Suitcase*, another adult narrator traces the history of a girl called Hana Brady who was murdered at Auschwitz, by retelling the story of a Japanese woman so determined to find out who Hana was that she locates Hana's surviving brother in Toronto. And in *Fugitive Pieces*, Anne Michaels creates a complex narrative weave of memory and voices across two generations of Jewish immigrants. She begins with a small boy rescued from the Nazis in Poland and wraps his story in the haunting of a grown son of survivors who is now living in Toronto but must uncover the past before he can live successfully in the present.

The first-person narrator in "Stones" is certainly not Timothy Findley in a precise autobiographical sense, but he closely resembles the man Findley was by the 1980s, and his childhood has much in common with Findley's.[10] The fictional auto/biographical speaker in this story is Ben Max, and by telling his own story he also tells his father's, his family's, and Canada's. Ben grew up "on the outskirts of Rosedale [in Toronto], over on the wrong side of Yonge Street" (195) and his parents owned a flower shop on Yonge. The present moment of his address to us is an unspecified month and year in the early 1980s, after his father's death. He has come to the beach at Dieppe carrying his father "in an envelope addressed to myself in Canada" (218) to release a small portion of his ashes onto the "red stones [that] look as if they have been washed in blood" (219). Once Ben has told us about this private ceremony, performed to fulfill his father's final request—but for other reasons as well—he confesses that he prefers to remember himself in the summer of 1939 at five years of age, walking with his family through the peaceful Sunday streets of Rosedale. He prefers to end "our story" with this early memory from a time when life was secure, when his parents were well and happy, and when the world held no threat. However, his and his family's story is mostly about the years between "the end of summer 1939" and the present, years that have brought grief and tragedy to Lily and David Max of Rosedale, Toronto, and their children.





The tragedy that struck this Canadian family is called Dieppe. David Max enlisted before the war started and without warning his family. As Ben remembers the moment when his father told them what he had done, he admits that he looks back on that scene "with some alarm" because he realizes that "my father was only twenty-seven years old—an age I have long survived and doubled" (200). By the time this father "was returned" (201) to his country and family on 14 February 1943, he was no longer the man he had been; he would never again be a loving husband and father. Ben describes his anticipation as the family waits in the Exhibition Grounds "to witness" the soldiers' arrival in the oval below the bleachers, and he recalls his disappointment at the absence of a parade and a band: "I wanted drums. I wanted bugles. Surely this ghostly, implacable sound of marching feet...was just a prelude...to cheering and the music blaring forth" (203). But it was not just a prelude, and that's Findley's point. The "ghostly, implacable sound" is the sound of history haunting the future. Of course, the reality of such a homecoming was beyond a child's comprehension because these men were "mostly casualties," scarred, bandaged, disfigured, and mutilated. He panicked, thinking his father was not there, which in a sense was true: "There was not a mark on his body, but—far inside—he had been destroyed. His mind had been severely damaged and his spirit had been broken" (203). When Ben asks his older brother what happened to their Dad, he receives a one-word answer: "Dieppe."





It will be many years before he realizes what that word signifies and how his father was broken at a place in France with that name. The intervening years are marked by one nightmare after another, which can be traced back to that place. Some of these horrors are public and social; others are private and domestic. No assistance is provided for soldiers like David Max who is suffering from post-traumatic stress, and their wives and children are left to manage on their own. To make matters worse, gangs of youths called "Zombies" roamed the Toronto streets beating up men in uniform, and a man like David would be arrested if he wore his military greatcoat in public.[11] Ben's adult reflection on this state of affairs is disturbing—"Our patriotism had come to that" (207). When David returns to the flower shop, he is stunned to see that the neighbouring butcher store, formerly owned by a friend called Oskar Schickel, has been taken over by someone called Arthur Reilly. He wants to know why, when "Oskar wasn't a German....He was a Canadian" (209). But, as Lily explains, it is enough that his name is German. Like Marta's father in *Waiting for the Parade*, this citizen has been stripped of his rights. At home, behind closed doors, David becomes a violent alcoholic who terrifies his youngest son and almost kills his wife. Because of this violence, he is assigned to the Asylum for the Insane on Queen Street, and after his release he refuses to return home; as Ben puts it, "my father never forgave himself" (215). He never forgave himself for attacking his wife and son, and he never forgave himself for his failure at Dieppe. When a brick is thrown through the window of Max's Flowers with the word "Murderer" printed on it, Lily finally decides to tell her children what happened on 19 August 1942 as Captain Max and his men approached the beach at Dieppe.

"My father never left his landing craft" (216), Ben tells us, but he also recalls what he learned later about the significance of Dieppe: "All but a handful of those who went into battle were Canadians. This was our Waterloo. Our Gettysburg" (215).[12] *Our*, that is Ben's, his listeners/readers, all of us, all Canadians. What one man remembers about his father's destruction at Dieppe is part of our cultural memory, but it is also a national story of loss and mourning—"a total and appalling disaster. Most have called it a slaughter" (216)—that few Canadians know much about. Findley brings Dieppe home in this story and shows how it permeated the private domain of the family and influenced future generations. The children who were traumatized, physically and emotionally, by the survivors of Dieppe, are forced to bear secondary witness to that "appalling disaster" by bearing primary witness to the disintegration of the soldier and his family. David Max failed to lead his men ashore on that August day. Watching the massacre of the first wave of troops, he froze and his men became sitting ducks. This is why another survivor threw a brick with the word "Murderer" through the shop window. When Ben confesses how his father swam away from the landing craft to be rescued by the HMS *Berkley*, he must also reveal the fact that most of the men left behind were "blown to pieces," and that once back in England those who survived confronted David Max with what he had done. Dieppe, his past, and his dishonorable discharge would haunt him for the rest of his life. The post-memories would then haunt his youngest son.

Ben insists that he has not come to Dieppe now "to relive the battle" or "to conjure ghosts" (219), although he tells us the ghosts of Dieppe are "palpable" (219). So why has he come? What does he achieve by taking his father's ashes to the beach? And what, more importantly, does he achieve by telling us this auto/biographical story? At the very least, he has reminded us about a terrible disaster in Canada's Second World War history, a tragedy (in the full sense of the term because it could have been avoided) forced upon us by British stupidity, inflexibility, and vanity. The Canadian commander Major-General Hamilton Roberts knew the plan was wrong; he protested, but was overruled by the British high command and obeyed his orders. Ben has also brought the consequences of that tragedy home to Canada and illustrated its profound impact on later generations—on the children. It is, however, Findley who has created this small, poignant narrative act of remembering with its peaceful gesture of acceptance and love. In "Stones," Findley imagines for us the red stones on the beach at Dieppe superimposed upon Rosedale's streets in a landscape that commemorates both places. Within the short span of a story, he evokes the elegiac mood through a form of prosopopoeia usually found in poetry.[13]



In her "Acknowledgements" to *Hana's Suitcase*, Karen Levine not only explains how she came upon Hana Brady's story but why she wanted to create the radio documentary and the book. Although narrated by an adult—Levine—and portraying a search across three continents and seventy years by another adult—Fumiko Ishioka—this story is about a small girl from Nove Mesto, Czechoslovakia, and about the importance of history. It is a story written for children of about nine or ten years of age, in the hope that, as Levine tells us, they "will learn from the story that history matters, and that despite the most unspeakable evil, good people and good deeds can make a difference" (111). Although the story ends on the positive note of discovery, it cannot be said to have a happy ending. Hana Brady was rounded up by the Nazis and transported to Theresienstadt concentration camp in 1942 when she was just ten; from there she was sent to Auschwitz and killed. Of the four members of her immediate family, only her brother George would survive the Holocaust. The suitcase, which gives the story its title, is both an actual, material artifact and a powerful metaphor. The physical object was sent from Auschwitz to Tokyo in response to the inquiries of Fumiko Ishioka, the co-ordinator of a small Holocaust Centre that opened in 1998. Fumiko believed she could best teach Japanese children about the Holocaust if she could loan some objects that had belonged to Jewish children. In 2000 the Auschwitz Museum sent her a package with a child's sock, a shoe, a sweater, a can of Zyklon B poison gas, and Hana's suitcase.[14] From there the questions multiplied and Fumkio began her quest. Who was Hana Brady? Why was she called a "Waisenkind"? The Japanese children wanted to know, and so did Fumiko. The past became an obsession for her and the suitcase became a metaphor for this desire to know, to find answers, to fill the emptiness in history with memories. When it arrived in Tokyo, it was empty and yet full of possibility, secrets, ghosts, and untold stories.

To tell the story of Fumiko's search is also to tell the story of the Brady family from Nove Mesto, and Levine does this by moving back and forth, chapter by chapter, between the early twenty-first-century present and the past of 1938–39 in Czechoslovakia as Hitler's troops arrive in the country and the restrictions on Jews increase. Without fanfare, Levine creates a narrative seesaw that pulls the past into the present of our reading, as well as the present of Fumiko's search. Slowly, inexorably, the Bradys' lives are squeezed: Jews must wear the yellow star; they cannot gather in public; the children cannot attend school and former non-Jewish friends avoid them. Meanwhile, back in Tokyo, Fumiko writes letters and gathers information: she learns that Hana was sent to Auschwitz from a place called Theresienstadt; she does research on this place and discovers that children held there were taught to paint and draw; "miraculously, 4,500 drawings created by these children had survived the war" (29); ever persistent, Fumiko asks for and receives photographs of five drawings by Hana from the archives of the Terezin Ghetto Museum.

As the noose tightens around the children held at Theresienstadt and the war draws to an end, so also does Fumiko's quest approach its climax. Her search takes her to Terezin in July 2000, where she plans to visit the museum to learn more about Hana. But it is a local holiday

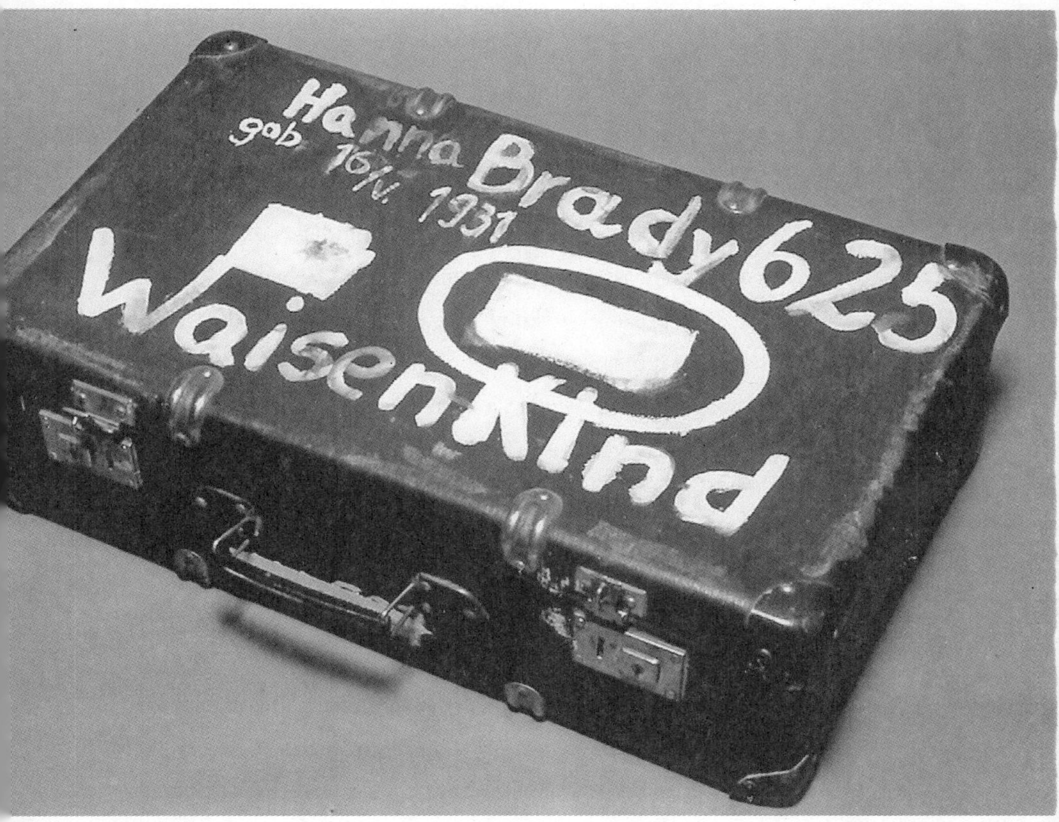


*Hana Brady's suitcase, labelled "Waisenkind" (orphan), inspired Karen Levine's award-winning novella* Hana's Suitcase. *This photograph is reproduced courtesy of Lara Hana Brady for the Hana Brady Family Legacy and the Tokyo Holocaust Education Resource Centre. Photograph © Tokyo Holocaust Education Resource Centre.*

and no one appears to be at work. Desperate, she enters the building and finds one woman in an office. She explains that she cannot come back another day because she must return to Prague to catch her flight to Tokyo tomorrow. The woman agrees to help her, and after examining lists of inmates at Theresienstadt they find Hana's name—Hana Brady, May 16, 1931. There is a neat check mark beside her name and beside all the other names on the page *except one*: "Brady, Georg, Schuler, 9.2.1928" (73). What might this mean? Levine delays her explanation and in the following chapter takes us back to 1943–44 and Hana and George's life in the camp. The children's ailing grandmother has arrived but old people are badly treated and the children can do little to help her. Within three months this beloved relative is dead and the two Brady children are alone again. They consult the "dreaded lists" that are regularly posted in every camp building: "Lists. Everywhere there were lists. The Nazis were systematic record keepers and they wanted all their prisoners to know it" (77). Of course, the children do not realize what it means when their names appear on these lists except that they will be leaving Theresienstadt by train for some place to the south. In September 1944, George's name is posted and Hana is devastated because she will be separated from him. When her name is posted, Levine imagines her feeling elated at the prospect of seeing George again. But as adult readers know, Hana and George have been transported to Auschwitz, and when Levine follows Hana through the infamous gate ("Arbeit macht frei") we fear the worst. The older girls are ordered to the right, the younger ones to the left (and directly to the gas chambers): "'Leave your suitcases on the platform,' the soldiers commanded. Through a wrought iron gate and under the watchful eyes of the surly dogs and uniformed men, Hana and her old roommates were marched off....They were ordered to enter a large building. The door closed behind them with a frightening bang" (81–82).

Then we return to the present of July 2000 as Fumiko repeats her question: "What does the check mark mean?" (83). It means that the person named is dead; Hana was killed at Auschwitz. But there is no check mark beside Brady, Georg, so this must mean that he survived. By searching further through the dusty records, the woman locates the name of George's bunkmate in the camp and realizes that this person is alive and may still be living in Prague. After a nerve-wracking series of last-minute phone calls and considerable help from Michaela Hjek, who works in Prague's Jewish Museum, they reach this man—Kurt Kotouc—who not only remembers George Brady, but has his address in Toronto. Hana's brother is alive and well. Fumiko will write to him from her Holocaust Centre in Tokyo. Once home she prepares a very carefully worded letter with photocopies of Hana's drawings and drawings made by her Japanese students. She knows that some Holocaust survivors cannot bear to talk about their experiences and that the shock of receiving her package could be terribly painful for George. However, after his initial surprise, George Brady responds by opening his heart and his memories to Fumiko. Levine then weaves George's story into Hana's and we realize that much of the information she can relate about the Bradys' lives has come from his memories. He was seventeen when Auschwitz was liberated and his story is one of extreme grief and eventual happiness because he left Europe, immigrated to Canada, and became a successful businessman with his own family. Although he has never dwelt on his past, he has kept a photograph album saved for him by an uncle, and now he sends photographs of Hana and the family—documents which are reproduced in Levine's book—to Fumiko with a long letter recalling his family's life in happier times.





The celebratory and commemorative conclusion to the story comes when George, accompanied by his daughter Lara, visits the Tokyo Holocaust Centre in March 2001. Now in his seventies, George Brady has in a sense reclaimed his past as a boy and a teenager, and he can now remember and share his stories with others. As he holds Hana's suitcase he weeps. But he also sees himself surrounded by a younger generation to whom Hana has "become so important, so alive," and he believes that these children are learning the values he cherishes—"tolerance, respect, and compassion" (105). It is as if Hana's empty suitcase has opened to reveal a treasure trove of historical knowledge in the form of personal memories and stories. As a metaphor for that past and those memories, it carries a message at once terrible and hopeful. Like a voice from the past—Hana's voice—it reminds us that the past cannot be undone but that we can learn from it by remembering and listening to the voice and its remarkable story. Of course, this is not just one person's story, not just an object signifying a *lieu de mémoire*. Through Levine's narration, it becomes a *milieu de mémoire*. The suitcase carries cultural memory as well as the personal stories of three generations, from Hana's parents to Hana and George to Fumiko and Karen Levine herself. By retelling it for children (and for the parents and grandparents who read it), Levine has constructed a powerful landscape of memory that connects Czechoslovakia in the 1930s and 1940s with Toronto and Tokyo in the twenty-first century.

In 2008 this landscape was transformed into a docudrama film called *Inside Hana's Suitcase* in which director Larry Weinstein juxtaposes archival footage with scenes of George and his daughter visiting Auschwitz in 2004 and gathering at the family cottage in Ontario, and through interviews with children in Toyko, Toronto, and Nove Mesto speaking in their own languages about what Hana's story means to them.[15] The afterlife of Hana's story, and Fumiko's search for her, continues to extend its reach across time and space, bearing witness to the past for a future badly in need of the values George Brady holds dear. If this afterlife represents a haunting of the present by the past, of Canada by the Second World War, then it is a haunting full of potential and even of hope.

*Fugitive Pieces* recapitulates all the issues and narrative strategies I have considered thus far. It is, moreover, the most ambitious and powerful fictional exploration of *Canadian* Holocaust survival that I have read to date.[16] To appreciate what Anne Michaels has accomplished with this novel, it is essential to identify the different storytellers and their interrelationships before considering the function of language and metaphor in the text.

The primary *author* is a young Toronto man called Ben, who we do not meet until the latter third of the story, but it is Ben who has found and organized the fugitive pieces of another man's life story: Jakob Beer. And Jakob's story opens out to include yet another man's story—the biography of Athanasios Roussos. To move from Ben back to Jakob and back to Athos is to move from Toronto in the 1990s back to Greece during the 1940s and back to a small town in Poland, where the Jewish Beer family lived in the 1930s. The life stories proper are introduced by an unidentified presence who writes in the middle voice of a historian-cum-biographer to give us a brief introduction (less than one page) to the bare facts of poet Jakob Beer's death. He was struck by a car in Athens in 1993, aged sixty, and his wife was also killed.[17] "They had no children" (n.p.). This presence (who I do not identify with Ben because of the style and voice) also provides another kind of information that we will need to remember as we move into the novel proper. It points out that "countless manuscripts—diaries, memoirs, eyewitness accounts—were lost or destroyed" during the Second World War, but that others were "deliberately hidden," while still others remain "concealed in memory, neither written nor spoken" (n.p.).[18] As we will discover, all three kinds of manuscript play a role in *Fugitive Pieces* because they constitute the pieces, or fragments, of elusive, fugitive memories held by the characters.



In the last sentence of this concise introductory note, we read that before his death Jakob Beer "had begun to write his memoirs"—*begun to write*. In other words, his auto/biography was surfacing from its hiding place in memory into written representation, but it was left incomplete by his death. When we turn the page, we find ourselves suddenly immersed in an early scene from someone's traumatic memory of war. This someone, who addresses us directly—"Bog-boy, I surfaced into the miry streets of the drowned city" (5)—plunges us back in time but, more importantly, back into scenes of almost unimaginable, unrepresentable horror. We will soon realize that this personal voice belongs to Jakob Beer, who is remembering himself as a seven-year-old child hiding from the Nazis and being rescued by a strange man from Greece called Athos. The following narrative reconstructs Jakob's memories of what happened in 1939, of how he was rescued, taken to Greece, and raised by the Greek scholar and geologist, and then how these two moved to Toronto after the war. Here, in Canada, they were finally safe: Athos taught at the University of Toronto and Jakob grew up, studied, lived, married his first wife, and established his career as a respected translator and poet. This life story exists in fragments, in bursts of memory and highly poetic imagery, that mirror Jakob's memory as he reworks, like a shuttle, his past and the tragedy that continues to haunt him and threatens to overtake his life in the present.

However, these fragments, found, assembled in a loosely chronological order, and published by Ben after Jakob's death, are much more than one man's life story. They constitute what Jakob calls "a biography of longing" (17) in which he struggles to recall and imagine a landscape of memory that will embrace (not simply include) the biography of his murdered family, especially his adored sister Bella, and the biography of Athos. This complex, relational auto/biography also covers many aspects of Second World War history and the terrifying haunting of the adult who cannot begin to outgrow the past until release, in the form of love, understanding, and peace of mind, come to him in his fifties, when he marries his second wife, Michaela. Jakob identifies the source of his crippling dilemma in the first fragment we read: "I did not witness the most important events of my life" (17).

The most important events of his life occurred in 1939, when he was seven, shortly after Germany invaded Poland. The Beer family was sitting at home quietly one evening, the mother sewing, the father resting, little Jakob listening to Bella discuss Beethoven, when shouting and loud noise were heard outside. Jakob was told to hide in the wall behind a cupboard, and then the door burst open. What he heard but could not see from his hiding place was the murder of his parents and the capture of his sister. This memory gradually becomes as clear as it can be through the repetition of the scene; new details are added (remembered) with each retelling. This primal scene is so powerful and incomprehensible that it will become part of Jakob, stuck in his flesh and spirit, part of his dreams, his imagination, his poetry, until the end of his life. When he crawled from his hiding place, he found his parents lying dead in pools of blood on the floor, but his sister was nowhere and he could not remember hearing her scream or speak. Eventually he ran from the house in terror and hid in the forests and fields by digging holes in the earth to lie in during the day. He was found by Athos—or, as Athos thinks of it, they found each other—at the edge of the excavations of Biskupin, the prehistoric Polish town abandoned roughly two thousand years ago but preserved by the bog into which it sank.[19] Athos was part of the scientific team unearthing the historic site after 1933, but when he saw the little bog-boy, he decided to save both their lives. Before the German soldiers destroy Biskupin and shoot or arrest the scientists (51), Athos gathers up Jakob and flees by car back to Greece. There, in his home on the island of Zakynthos he hides Jakob for the duration of the war. For Jakob to tell his own story, he must also tell Athos's story because "Athos was an expert in buried and abandoned places" (49). Little Jakob is just such a place, and once Athos has unearthed the child, he becomes his loving surrogate father, parent, companion, and teacher, the only person with whom Jakob can share his secrets.



Jakob's secrets, like his nightmares, are both terrifying and filled with terror. He is haunted by what he did not witness, by his confused memories of family, friends, and home, by the sudden shouting and banging on doors, by having to hide, even in Greece, when the Germans come to round up Greek Jews. Above all he is haunted by his beautiful, artistic older sister Bella, in part because he adored her and looked up to her and in part because he will never know what happened to her. Having been hidden and found, then hidden and found again, Jakob is haunted by this process, and in a sense becomes a lifelong fugitive. Consequently, his auto/biography does not take shape in a smooth, linear manner. It shuttles back and forth, like his memory, between the present of his memoir writing in the early 1990s and vivid, painful remembered scenes in the past, between the personal, secret life he lives with Athos and what he learns as an adult about the history of the Second World War, the Shoah, the long history of Jewish culture and persecution, and about geology, polar expeditions, and ancient civilizations (like the one at Biskupin).

For example, in the midst of remembering a private conversation with Athos about Polish synagogues, he will shift abruptly to the public knowledge, the history, he has acquired as an adult: "later, in Canada, looking at photographs of the mountains of personal possessions stored at Kanada in the camps, I imagined that if each owner of each pair of shoes could be named, then they would be brought back to life" (50). While there may be many responses evoked by such a comment, the idea that seizes my attention is the belief, still treasured by a man nearing sixty, in his younger self's stubborn faith in sympathetic magic, "the power of reversal" (50) by naming. By naming Bella he thought he could find her, or she him. And she does return to him, repeatedly, over the years, watching him, touching his back, whispering from her ghostly presence. Possibly the most poignant passage in Jakob's auto/biography is the last entry he makes before leaving the Roussos family house on Idhra with Michaela for the short trip to Athens, where the couple is killed. It is a heart-rending passage, conveyed in Jakob's passionate language, but also with economy, and Ben takes care that we get to read it, to hear Jakob's last words: "My son, my daughter: May you never be deaf to love. Bela, Bella: Once I was lost in a forest. I was so afraid. My blood pounded in my chest and I knew my heart's strength would soon be exhausted. I saved myself without thinking. I grasped the two syllables closest to me, and replaced my heartbeat with your name" (195). He saved himself by naming love.



At the time of producing this text, *Fugitive Pieces*, Ben is a professor at the University of Toronto, where he teaches courses in biography. He is also reasonably happy in his marriage to Naomi, who took his biography course and is well educated, but now seems occupied with domestic tasks and her devotion to Ben's parents. Ben's parents are Holocaust survivors who managed to immigrate to Canada after the war, buy a small house in Weston on the Humber River close to the city, and raise their only child, born in 1949, who they call Ben, "not from Benjamin, but merely 'ben'—the Hebrew word for son" (253). Ben's father teaches piano, a decided step down in life and career from "the once elegant student conductor in Warsaw" (248). And this father represents the source of Ben's deep unhappiness because, unlike Jakob's father-surrogate, Athos, this man is silent, angry, fearful, and full of despair. He is not an alcoholic, like Ben Max's father in "Stones," but he is a severely damaged, traumatized man, and he passes that trauma on to his son in the form of post-memories and first-hand memories.

One of the most disturbing memories that Ben's carries with him, as if he is unable to relinquish the complex pain it represents for father and son, involves the time when he threw a rotten apple in the garbage. His father retrieved it and insisted that the child eat it because it is food:





> *"Is an apple food?"*
> *"Yes."*
> *"And you throw away food? You—my son—you throw away food?"*
> *"It's rotten—"*
> *"Eat it....Eat it!"*
> *"Pa, it's rotten—I won't—"*
> *He pushed it into my teeth until I opened my jaw. Struggling, sobbing, I ate. (218)*

Not until years later, as Ben writes this auto/biography we are reading, is he able to comprehend what motivated his father to act like this, or to realize that his father's intense memory of starvation in the camps is now a part of his own post-memory of that starvation symbolized by a rotten apple—quite literally, the bitter fruit of persecution. It is small wonder then that Ben gravitates to his more responsive, loving mother, deeply resents his mother's affection for Naomi, and finds in Jakob Beer a father-like figure to respect and love. Ben's mounting resentment of Naomi's intimacy with his mother reaches its climax after her death and his father's suicide.

When Ben cleans out his parents' apartment, he finds a photograph he has never seen before: "I had left the clearing out of their bedroom for last. In the humidor, which he never used for cigars, in an envelope, a single photograph. We think of photographs as the captured past. But some photographs are like DNA. In them you can read your whole future" (251). There stands his father in front of a piano, a young man, holding an infant, and with a small girl clinging to his leg. His mother stands beside him: "On the back floats a spidery date, June 1941, and two names. Hannah. Paul. I stared at both sides of the photograph a long time before I understood that there had been a daughter; and a son born just before the action. When my mother was forced into the ghetto, twenty-four years old, her breasts were weeping with milk" (252).





The impact of this photograph catapults Ben, not only into the past he was not told about and the two young siblings who did not survive the ghetto, but also into the future. This photograph with its terrible revelation, its secrets withheld from Ben, its speaking silence, sets him on a quest that changes his life and enables him to produce his own compound auto/biography: his life story, Jakob's, Athos's, and many related stories of the war. When he returns home with this photograph and shows it to his wife, he realizes that his mother so trusted and cherished this daughter-in-law that she had shared her history and heartbreak with Naomi. Naomi has already seen the photograph and heard the story. Presumably Ben's mother hoped that Naomi would one day discuss this past with Ben, but he is so affronted by his exclusion from his family's life story that he withdraws from Naomi, his work, and even from life itself. Post-memory takes him over. To restore him, Naomi suggests he go to the house on Idhra, where Jakob had been visiting with Michaela, to search for Jakob's missing journals. If he can find them hidden among the hundreds of books and manuscripts left there, he will not only find Jakob, the man he reveres, he may also, just possibly, find himself.

Almost by accident, Ben finds the journals he was searching for, but he also finds something more, something foreshadowed by Jakob, something profoundly sad. As the biographer, who will prepare the larger auto/biographical story for us, his search for primary documents is amply rewarded. Before Athos and Jakob immigrated to Canada, Athos had moved his library and belongings from his house on Zakynthos to the Roussos family home on Idhra. However, he had never returned to sort, organize, or carefully shelve this wealth of material. After his death, Jakob has spent months on Idhra, dividing his time between the Toronto apartment and the Greek island; with each visit he adds to the accumulated material—the archive—but has no need to tidy it up. When he comes to Idhra with Michaela in 1992, a man finally happy enough to describe his past and how his lost sister haunts him, he simply stores the journals in which he begins his life story on a crowded shelf. For Ben, a stranger in the house, to locate them is akin to searching for a needle in a haystack or undertaking an archaeological dig. But one afternoon, Ben brings a woman—the American tourist Petra with whom he is having an affair—back to the house. She is the one responsible for going carelessly through the rooms, removing books, opening them, dropping them down helter-skelter, and it is when he tries to straighten up the mess she has created that Ben stumbles upon the journals.

Anne Michaels has imagined a rather bizarre sequence of moments of passion, betrayal, and rage on Ben's part as the steps that lead to this discovery. It seems almost as if Ben must fail to honour his wife's love and then recognize his guilt before he is capable of making amends to Naomi and becoming worthy of handling the story hidden in Jakob's journals. He has left Naomi alone in Toronto because he was jealous of his mother's trust in her daughter-in-law, full of pain and anger with his father's secrecy and remote coldness, and resentful of Naomi's affection for both of his parents. But Jakob's last words in the journal amount to prayerful advice about love: "May you never be deaf to love." (195). Caught up in self-pity and his affair, Ben has closed his eyes and ears to the love Naomi offers him. His violent outburst at Petra's thoughtless behaviour—her trespass—clears his heart and mind enough to, as it were, bring him to his senses.

Petra is, again by accident, responsible for the other discovery in the house on Idhra, one she makes with Ben. Together they enter Jakob and Michaela's bedroom and see their bed, which Petra thinks she and Ben will use. When she pulls back the cover, however, she and Ben find

> *Michaela's note where she'd left it. Planned as the surprise ending to a perfect day. Among the cushions, waiting for your discovery, the night you and Michaela never returned from Athens. Two lines of blue ink.*
>
> *If she's a girl: Bella*
>
> *If he's a boy: Bela (278–79)*





Ben does not comment on the meaning of this cryptic note. At this point he has still not found the journals; he is not worthy of finding them. Instead, he and Petra lie on the floor and in an act more akin to rape than love, he tells us that he pounds himself into her until he hurts them both and Petra cries in pain. But the message of love, left by Michaela for Jakob, is a sign, a warning, an exhortation that will connect Jakob's last words in the journal with Ben's life: Bel-la is the heartbeat of love and one must listen to one's heart—and to one's memory.

"On the map of history," Jakob writes in one of his journal entries, "perhaps the water stain is memory" (137). His journals, indeed, are like persistent, water stains of personal story slowly accumulating across the jagged map of Second World War history, and maps of history, as he knows from experience, "have always been less than honest" (137). Less honest even than geographical maps. From one of Athos's major books, written and published in Toronto and translated into Greek by Jakob, Jakob (and of course Ben too) has learned just how dishonest history can be and how dedicated to the truth one must be. *Bearing False Witness* is Athos's account of the fate of Biskupin. It "plagued" him, Jakob remembers; "It was his conscience; his record of how the Nazis abused archeology to fabricate the past" (104). The Nazis tried to erase the history of Biskupin because, by 1939, it had become famous as the site of a "Polish Pompeii," and as such it proved that a non-Aryan, ancient

European civilization existed in twentieth-century Poland (104). Himmler rejected such a history; it did not fit with the ideology of the Third Reich. His Bureau of Ancestral Inheritance (the SS-Ahnenerbe) was charged with replacing this history, just as German armies replaced the physical landscape of Poland, its place names and the landscape of Biskupin, with a pure Aryan, Neolithic Germanic history. To make matters worse, Athos learns that respected scientists, hired by Himmler, not only bore false witness about the evidence at Biskupin, but that they survived the war and continued to advance their careers. *Bearing False Witness* is Athos's water stain on the false map of Nazi history, his exposure of the lies, his own bearing witness to the truth he remembers seeing with his own eyes, unearthing with his own hands. And Jakob is the living testament to the memory of the bog, to the year 1939, and to the atrocity committed in his home and village.





Jakob remembers Athos telling him about these false witnesses and the attempt to erase Biskupin when the two were walking the streets of Baby Point, an area of Toronto that had once been "the site of an Iroquois fortressed camp" (104). Together they tried to imagine "an Iroquois attack" with "flaming arrows soaring above patio furniture" (105). And Athos tells Jakob about the Iroquois murder of Étienne Brûlé, a fur trader, while Jakob imagines "burning flesh" and "smoke rising in whorls into the dark sky" (105). He is stopped short by these thoughts, these images, however, because he knows now what happened in places like Auschwitz or Chelmno.[20] He is, as he notes in the journal, "ambushed, memory cracking open" (105). The strategy Michaels uses in this sequence of memories from the journals is similar to the way she has created the entire novel. She presents us with Jakob Beer, the writer, whose memories connect landscapes across time and space—there and then in Poland with here and then in Canada, there and more recently at Biskupin with here and now in 1950s Toronto. The true, faithful witness is the man or woman who can create such superimposed landscapes, who can see the past in the present and cherish it, who can hear absent voices and lost stories and respect them, pass them on, *believe* what they say. Such a witness (and auto/biographer) is like an archaeologist working through an archive, a site, reanimating the found objects of Biskupin, Baby Point, or even along the banks of the Humber River, which preserves the detritus of homes swept away when Hurricane Hazel struck Weston on 15 October 1954.[21]

*Bearing False Witness* is only one of the texts within the multitextual mapping of *Fugitive Pieces*, but it is the most important one, that is after Jakob's journals. Its title is an accusation and a warning; its methodology demonstrates how we should approach history; and its ethical stance provides an example—it models for the reader—of how to bear witness to the past while preserving as much as possible of individual and cultural memory without indulging in nostalgia or self-pity. Jakob's volumes of poetry are also worth noting, however, because they too perform the remembering and witnessing that produces a landscape of memory. Their titles—*Groundwork* (163), *Dilemma Poems* (210), *Hotel Rain* (213), and *What Have You Done to Time* (255)—are suggestive of the poet's grief, trauma, and struggle to cope with history and memory, even though we are not told much about the actual poems. *Groundwork* is the first volume, written before Jakob's first return to Idhra after the failure of his first marriage. *Groundwork* is the volume that Ben keeps on his desk after Jakob dies; it is the book that encourages him, after Naomi's suggestion, to visit Idhra and search for Jakob's story. *Groundwork* is about Jakob's past, about his lost sister, his murdered parents. It is also about the poisoned well of Nazi history, about policies that exceeded racism because non-Aryans, Jews in particular, were not spoken of as human beings but as "figuren" or "stücke," objects, debris to be burned, buried, disposed of (165). Here, as in *Obasan*, is another example of what Giorgio Agamben calls a state of exception under which a human being becomes a *homo sacer* who can be—indeed, will be—destroyed, without violating any law, to preserve the perceived health of the state.[22] Maurice Salman, Athos's friend, and Jakob's, has a much simpler term for the poems in *Groundwork*: "These aren't poems, they're ghost stories" (103). Like the landscapes that rise up through memory to connect past and present—Poland, Greece, Canada—these poems are revenants. We are not given them to read, and so we must imagine the terrifying ghosts about which Jakob writes.

Bella Beer is, perhaps, the ultimate ghost in the war fiction I have explored. Like Jakob we will never know for certain what happened to her, and being left to imagine her fate is both haunting and appalling. Her youth, her beauty, her musical talent and innocence, and her gender lead me, a female reader, to guess at a brutal gang rape by soldiers, followed by mutilation, murder, and finally complete erasure beyond my capacity to describe or even imagine. Such a death entails a degree of witnessing I want to refuse, and yet I am told, and I believe, that such things happened. The image of her murder and what it represents tests the limits of my empathic unsettlement. Nevertheless, I must pull back from an extreme emotional response or identification with her because *Fugitive Pieces* is not finally Bella's story and, in any case, such a response is ethically irresponsible. It is Ben's story and Ben is a character of my generation, a Canadian with whom I come to share the auto/biographies and histories he uncovers.

Like Ben, readers of *Fugitive Pieces* are secondary witnesses to Jakob's story, and like Ben we must also bear secondary witness (outside the text) to the trauma his parents experienced. Moreover, like Ben, we must come home and deal with what we have discovered about the past, over there, here and now, on home ground. Living here in Canada does not shield us from what happened or absolve us of the responsibility to listen. As the novel draws to its close, Ben's plane is preparing to land at Toronto's Pearson International Airport. Ben is an hour or so away from greeting his wife. As he looks down, he recalls a loving image of his mother and father—"As he eats, she strokes his hair" (294)—and he understands that he must not be deaf to the love awaiting him: "I see that I must give what I most need" (294). In other words, he must make reparation, not to the past, but in the present. The past cannot be changed, but the present and future can be made better.

*Fugitive Pieces* has been faulted for this *happy* ending and for the implication it carries of reconciliation, for putting the past away and moving on. Michaels has also been criticized for creating female characters who are mere symbols of long-suffering wives and mothers who tend their men, for creating male characters who objectify the women in their lives, and for employing an overly sensuous, lush language and imagery that are inappropriate for a story about the Holocaust.[23] While I understand these criticisms and reservations about the novel, they miss the central argument of the text by collapsing the author of the novel, the poet Anne Michaels, into the authors of the texts we read as *Fugitive Pieces*. Jakob Beer is a poet, a man who lives in and through language; the very syllables of Bel-la represent his heart's beat. He is, in a sense, a romantic as well as a survivor who experiences emotion so intensely, so powerfully that when he learns to speak and write, all that feeling must pour forth. Ben's voice is less emotional; his style is more abrupt, his paragraphs shorter, on the whole, than Jakob's. He is given, comparatively speaking, to fewer flights of imagery. He is rather more academic. Ben is, after all, Jakob's biographer, and it is Jakob's life that informs Ben's, and it is Jakob's hard-won wisdom that we must attend to.

Among the many profoundly wise observations that Jakob records in his journals, there is one that stands out for me as especially significant. I quoted part of the passage as an epigraph to this book—"History is amoral....But memory is moral" (Micheals 139)—but I want to return to it now to consider its wider import. "History and memory share events," Jakob tells us, but they are not the same...*events*:

> *History is amoral: events occurred. But memory is moral; what we consciously remember is what our conscience remembers. History is the Totenbuch, The Book of the Dead, kept by the administrators of the camps. Memory is the Memorbucher, the names of those to be mourned, read aloud in the synagogue.*
>
> *History and memory share events; that is they share time and space. Every moment is two moments.* (138)

If we agree with Jakob that history—perhaps that should be History—is the official records and facts found in a Book of the Dead, like those volumes in the Terezin Museum, an archive of inanimate data, then history is indeed a Totenbuch in which we will find objective details. But even these details must be received with caution. Athos's history of Biskupin, *Bearing False Witness*, reminds us that historians will, under certain circumstances, lie. Details like those in the lists at Terezin must be questioned, interpreted, reanimated. They must be *felt*. History must be infused with memory, with the names of those who will be mourned when we speak their names out loud and tell and listen to their stories. *Fugitive Pieces* is the *Memorbuch* that cradles the names and stories of those now dead who continue to haunt us, who insist that we make room for them here in this country, now.





Like "Stones," and *Hana's Suitcase*, albeit on a larger scale, *Fugitive Pieces* connects places in Europe with places in Canada. These connections are, I believe, central to the meaning of each text and provide keys to the ethical import of the stories they tell. The simplest formulation of this meaning is to say that people are connected both to the places they come from and the place in which they live now, that as individuals, as families, they carry those profound connections with them and that such connections produce the stories they tell about who they are. To gain access to such connected landscapes, to understand them, Findley, Levine, and Michaels work with childhood memories. Indeed, they work back and forth, over and through, such memories to create what Michaels so aptly calls "Memorbucher." The narrative process required to represent memory is never simply linear. To be sure, each text brings its storytellers into the present of recall, of writing, of reading, and on to Canadian home ground. However, the stories return, incessantly, to the remembered past—to the safe summer streets of Rosedale before the war, to those carefree days in Nove Mesto when Hana and George could just be kids, to those comforting Beer family moments when Bella played Beethoven and little Jakob listened, quietly, lovingly. By returning to the past, the narrative gathers up these moments (as well as the terrible ones) of memory for future generations and deposits them—like the broken bits of china found along the banks of the Humber River years after Hurricane Hazel—all around us. Like the children in these stories, we must remember to *find* them and pick them up.

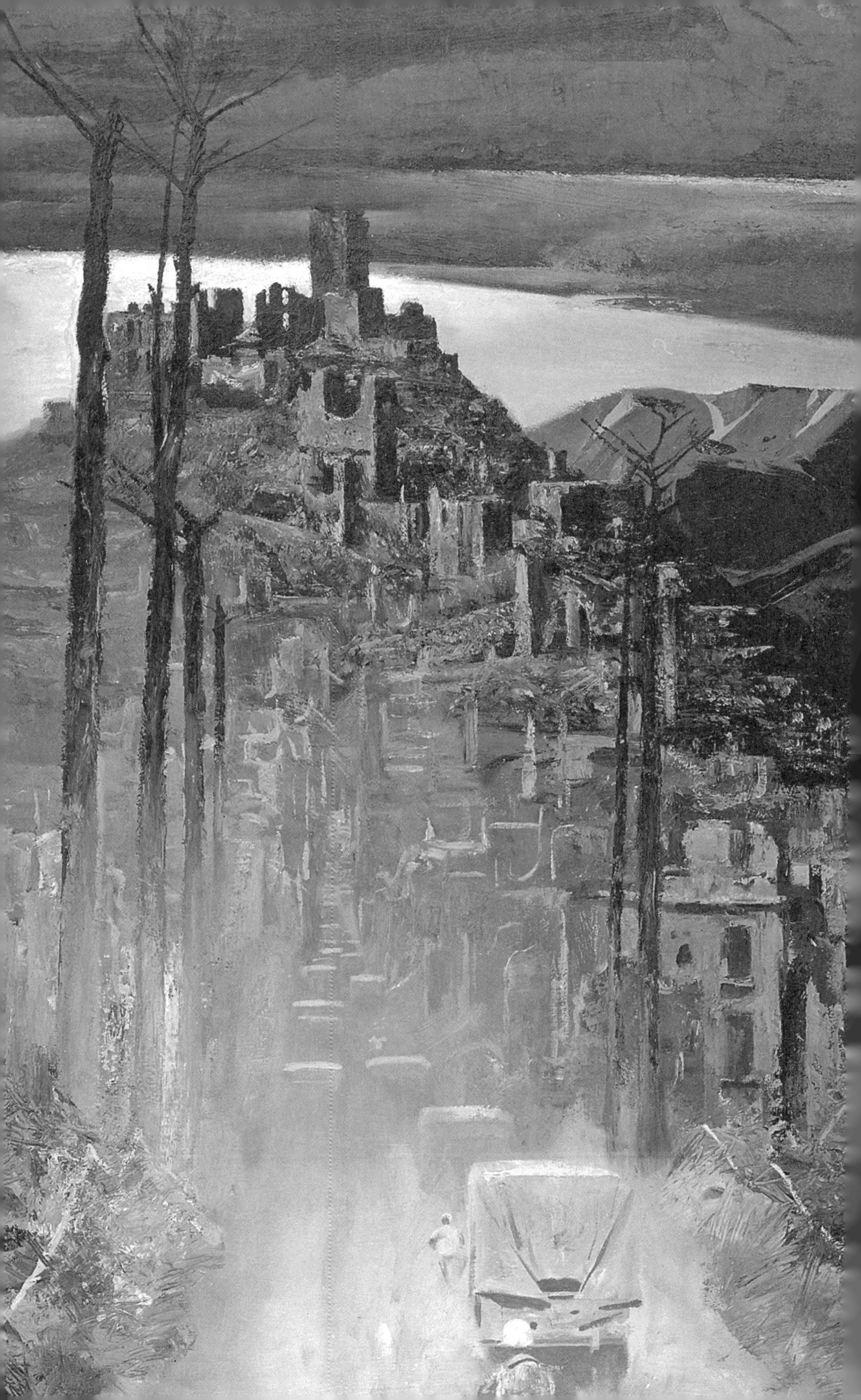

# 9
# Canada and the Aftermath of the "Good" War

## AUTOBIOGRAPHICAL TESTIMONY



*From Memoir to Documentary Film*

At the end of his memoir *A Wilderness of Days: An Artist's Experiences as a Prisoner of War in Germany* (1978), Maxwell Bates (1906–1980) reflects upon what he learned from his five years as a Canadian POW. Not surprisingly, he learned about freedom but in a rather different sense than one might at first imagine. "We had all learned much," he explains, and "what we had learned could not be learned in any other way": "Many of us had come to despise things we had valued before, and had learned to value things that we had despised or overlooked. It was up to us whether we lapsed back into the old grooves of hypocrisy, snobbishness and humbug. At least some of us had been freed" (133).

The art Bates created over the rest of his life attests to what he learned from his experiences of forced marches, near starvation, the constant presence of death, and hard labour in the camps. He did not return home to paint in the dominant Canadian tradition of landscapes empty of people. He painted people to portray their suffering or their hypocrisy and vanity, and when he painted people in a landscape he imbued both with a shared, uncanny quality of unsettlement and hauntedness.

Jonathan Browns characterizes Bates and his work as "melancholy": he "was haunted throughout his life by a persistent sense of loss" (n.p.). Although this melancholy cannot be attributed solely to the war, there is no doubt that like many returning soldiers, refugees, and Holocaust survivors, he was changed by his experience, saw peacetime, civilian life differently—and critically—and could never leave the war and its ghosts behind him. Browns claims that Bates "seemed unable to grieve" (n.p.), but I would rephrase that claim. It seems to me that he both bore unflinching witness to the war and to the home front aftermath and that he mourned the losses he experienced through his art, nowhere more so than in his figurative work, his self-portraits, and his illustrations for *A Wilderness of Days.*[1]

*A Wilderness of Days* is not a full-fledged autobiography. In it Bates does not tell his life story from his ancestors and family forward to the 1970s, when he decided to produce this volume. It is best described as a memoir of a short, intense, and devastating life-changing and future-defining experience. As a POW in Germany, he saw something of Marlow's heart of darkness and something of Geoffrey Firmin's hell, and he came back from that experience to tell us, to warn us, and to mourn. That much of what he shows us in his postwar art takes place *here*—on the Prairies, in Victoria living rooms, in a peacetime Canada—is essential because his paintings carry traces of the aftermath, of what can never be forgotten. This quality of aftermath in his memoir, as in many of his paintings, resembles the other non-fiction narratives considered in this chapter. Whether they are closer to full-scale auto/biography or more tightly focused on a few years of horror, all these texts insist on remembering and learning from the experience of war. And they all insist that those memories and lessons belong here and

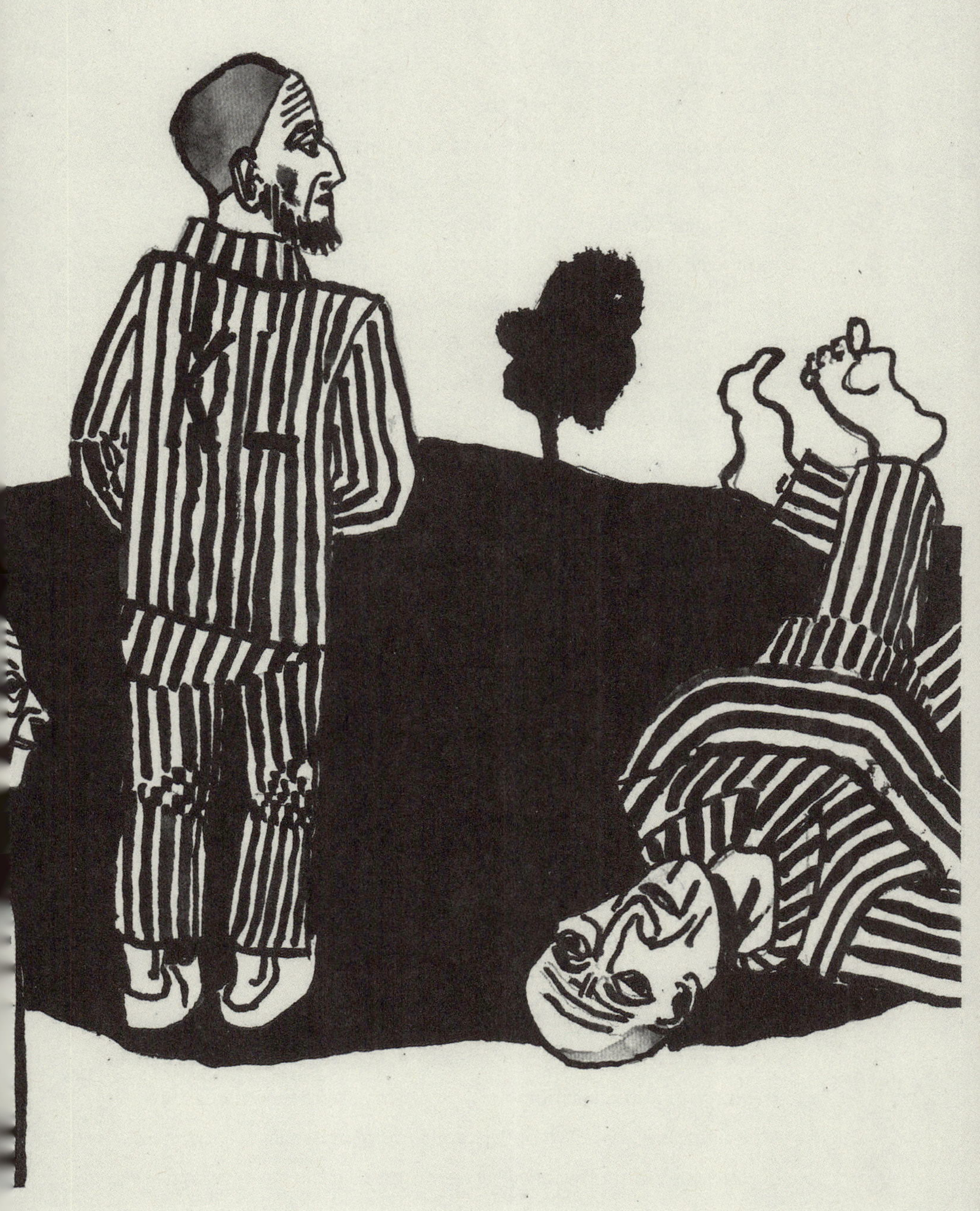

*This is one of several black-and-white drawings prepared by Maxwell Bates to illustrate his memoir* A Wilderness of Days. *In his account of his experiences as a prisoner of war during the Second World War, he includes a variety of scenes depicting daily camp life, German officers, and forced marches. About this drawing, he writes, "Prisoners who were too exhausted to keep up with the others, and who fell behind, were shot through the ears by a guard" (119). The drawing is reproduced courtesy of Mary Kintzle.*

deserve to be recognized as part of being Canadian. To describe these stories as haunted is to state the obvious. Less obvious is how they come to haunt and instruct us so many years after the war.

A large number of Second World War memoirs and autobiographies have appeared since 1977, but the two dozen or so I have read can be grouped into four, usually overlapping, categories: those written by men who served but wrote well after their return home; those written by Jewish men who survived the Holocaust and immigrated after the war or those who ended up here as "enemy aliens"; those by women who supported the war effort but were kept by social convention and regulation at arm's length (nurses, artists, correspondents); and those written by Canadians who are searching for their ancestors' stories, their family roots, their basic identity, in order to understand how the family past lingers in their personal Canadian present. This last group of texts reminds me of Ben's observation in *Fugitive Pieces* that "we think of photographs as the captured past. But some photographs are like DNA. In them you can read your whole future" (251).



Most of these texts reproduce documented historical facts about what happened when and where and to whom. They rely heavily on dates, place names, lists, and statistics. A few are carefully illustrated to assert authority and truth (I was there and saw that); and a few are what Susanna Egan calls "postmodern" because they foreground "the different disciplinary workings of memory, history, and autobiography" and rely on post-memory more than on first-hand experiences of war for their narratives (Egan and Helms 45). To demonstrate something of the generic scope of these non-fiction narratives, I focus on Charles Comfort's remarkable memoir *Artist at War*, Fred Bruemmer's auto/biography *Survival: A Refugee Life*, and Lisa Appignanesi's intergenerational auto/biography *Losing the Dead*.[2] Many of the narrative strategies and subgeneric categories developed in these non-fiction texts reappear in the documentary films discussed in the closing section of this chapter: *Return to Ortona* and *The Valour and the Horror*.

When Charles Comfort (1900–1994) went to Italy with the 1st Canadian Infantry Division in July 1943, he went as a war artist under the aegis of the Historical Section of the Canadian Military General Staff. His job was to record what he saw during the Italian campaign to take Ortona, break through the Adolf Hitler Line at Cassino, and participate in the liberation of Rome almost a year later. Neither he nor his fellow painters, Will Ogilvie and Lawren P. Harris, could have anticipated what they would experience. In addition to his sketches and paintings, Comfort kept a diary, and it is this record that lies behind his extraordinary memoir of the 1943–44 campaign called *Artist at War*. Among the many possible texts I might have chosen to examine, this one stands out. It is extremely well written, a classic of its genre—war memoir—that is both evocative and precisely detailed. It captures the scenes of battle and devastation at Ortona and later in the Liri Valley better than any other Canadian work of non-fiction or fiction I know, and it represents the process of remembering, notably through landscape scenes and images, as witnessed by the heightened perception of a professional painter. A visual artist who can achieve this degree of verbal power is rare because a painter's first language is pigment and brush or pencil strokes.





Another reason for choosing Comfort's memoir, however, pertains to the nature of the event and the fact that for decades Canada's Italian campaign has been neglected by scholars and artists. Of course, we can turn to Farley Mowat's very fine memoir *And No Birds Sang* and follow a brash young man north through Sicily into Italy listening to his shocked descriptions and sudden jolts into maturity.[3] We can also read Colin McDougall's *Execution*, which covers some of the same physical terrain and psychological horror as *Artist at War*, Michael Ondaatje's *The English Patient*, or Sandra Sabatini's *Dante's War*. But none of these novels captures the ordeal of bearing witness quite as effectively as *Artist at War* and none of them—not even *The English Patient* with its Canadian nurse, Hana—insists on comparative Canadian-Italian memories as pointedly as Comfort's narrative. I have chosen *Artist at War*, finally, because of its textual evolution from Comfort's 1943–44 field diary to the book's first publication in 1956 to its 1995 reprinting in a significantly modified new edition. With this new edition, the memoir reminds late twentieth-century and contemporary readers about Charles Comfort, his Second World War art (and by extension that of his fellow artists), and the importance of a campaign long overshadowed by events in France during 1943 and 1944.





Historian Mark Zuehlke specializes in the study of the Italian campaign and he argues that the battle of Ortona on Christmas Eve and Day in 1943 carries the same mythic significance for Canada in the Second World War as does Vimy Ridge for the First. In *Ortona: Canada's Epic World War II Battle*, Zuehlke traces the creation of this myth by reporters like Matthew Halton, who called Ortona "apocalyptic" (qtd. in Zuelhke 346), and he adds to the mythology by interviewing veterans, celebrating their bravery in the house-to-house street fighting that characterized the taking of Ortona from the Germans, and describing their successes as miraculous and legendary (Zuehlke 196–97). Although Ortona—the "Pearl of the Adriatic" (37)—at first seemed to have little military value, it became a viciously fought-over prize. It was destroyed as a result. In fact, Zuehlke describes Ortona as resembling a First World War No Man's Land, surrounded by a "landscape transformed by war into a charred, mud-choked hellhole" (148). For the military history of the Italian campaign, one cannot do better than to read Zuehlke's trilogy (*Ortona*, *The Gothic Line*, and *The Liri Valley*), where among a myriad of places, names, dates, and details one finds references to Charles Comfort sketching the devastation before him. For the artist's remembered response to events, however, one must spend time inside the world of *Artist at War*.

In his "Introduction: A Classic for Our Time," Eric Harrison, who was with Comfort in Italy, describes the memoir as "a redemptive classic for our time" (xv). Harrison also wrote the introduction to the first edition of *Artist at War*, but he revised his earlier commentary to address what he saw, in 1995, as challenges to Canadian identity, pride, and collective memory. Harrison protests that the Canadians in Italy have been forgotten, "deserted by the Press for the bigger stories" in France and on D-Day (xv), but he hopes that contemporary readers of the memoir will rediscover confidence in who they were and still are. I would not go so far as to call the memoir redemptive. Comfort does not find anything redeeming about the devastation wreaked on civilians, on the erasure of centuries of cultural treasure in art and architecture, and the slaughter of soldiers (German and Canadian). What his memoir does is *remind* us about a significant period in our Second World War past by allowing us to look through his astute eyes at the ugly violence of war and to register the impact of that violence through an emotional response to complex remembered landscapes immediately before him (and us) in Italy and back home in Canada where, by contrast, peace, serenity, and quiet still exist. Comfort's lesson is that we must remember, that we must look unflinchingly at reality and resist illusions of victory or grandeur, and that we consider, always, the price paid in war. The paintings Comfort created would not be anything like West's *Death of General Wolfe*, which Findley saw as glamorizing war and deceiving young men like Robert Ross.

The 1995 edition of *Artist at War* differs from the 1956 first edition and, before examining Comfort's narrative more closely, I want to reflect upon those differences. As Harrison claims, the book is "for our time," and the changes made for this edition are strategic. In addition to the updated introduction, the 1995 text contains an afterword by Comfort's grandson Charles Fraser C. Jackson (who prepared this edition), an insert of thirty-five colour plates not provided in 1956, Comfort's field notes for these pictures, a glossary of military terms and acronyms, two maps (one of southern Italy, one of the Liri Valley offensive, May 1944) showing the movement of various military divisions and corps from Messina and Calabria in the south northward to Ortona on the Adriatic and to Rome in the west. In his afterword, Jackson provides glimpses into a child's memories of a much-loved and respected grandfather, describes the "meticulous diary" Comfort kept and used in writing his memoir, and concludes with personal reflections on Comfort's death, his achievements, and his gifts of wisdom and art. In other words, Jackson remembers *the man* who created the paintings and the memoir and encourages us to do the same. Comfort's notes on the paintings included in this edition also bring the human being alive for readers, and one note in particular stands out. Comfort is reflecting on the "sheer horror and utter devastation of Cassino" (186) that he is struggling to present in what would become the painting *Route 6 at Cassino, Italy*: "Cassino is a lifeless, soundless ghostly ruin, with the deadly pallor of an eyeless skull, permeated with the stench of death" (187).

But if this painting and note foreground the man sitting amid rubble on his portable stool with sketching materials on a small makeshift easel, the covers to this edition *present* Charles Comfort directly. The front cover to the first edition carried a reproduction of *The Hitler Line* (see *Artist at War* plate 28), a tightly focused, intensely dramatic depiction of Canadian soldiers moving forward towards the viewer through a foreground wasteland of shattered tree trunks and smashed machinery and against a background of billowing black smoke, flashes from explosions, and an ominous dark sky. The men are emphatically identified as Canadian troops by the red badges on their left shoulders, but their faces and expressions are partially hidden by their helmets; they seem alert, watchful, even though we cannot see their eyes. This is a war painting. Not, to be sure, of the Benjamin West type, but still a war painting. These men are soldiers. The wasteland through which they walk is angry, broken, inhuman. *This* book is a war story.

By contrast, the front cover of the 1995 *Artist at War* carries a reproduction of Comfort's self-portrait. He is wearing a uniform, yes, but what confronts the reader is less a soldier than a man whose somber gaze engages us in thoughtful contemplation. This image reminds us forcibly of the artist and the individual man whose memoir we read. With this choice of cover, the narrative has been repositioned away from combat and towards reflection and memory. It is complemented,

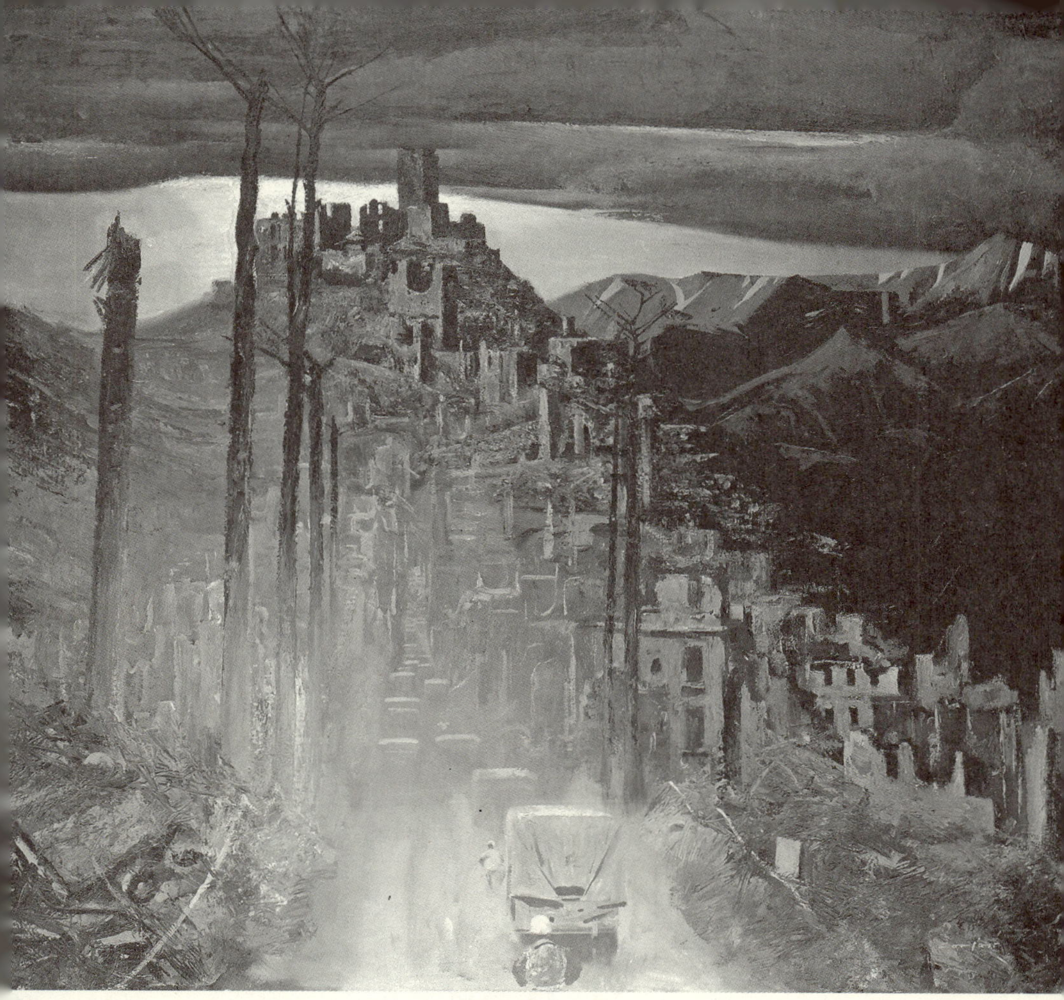

*Charles Comfort,* Route 6 at Cassino, Italy *(1944). o/c 101.6 x 121.9 cm. CWM #19710261-2275. Beaverbrook Collection of War Art. © Canadian War Museum. In his note on this painting, Comfort wrote, "For sheer horror and devastation Cassino surpasses anything I have seen in Italy"* (Artist at War *186).*

on the back cover, by a photograph of the artist, Captain C.F. Comfort, at work near Ortona on 8 March 1944.

Comfort's linear narrative of events is contained within a cyclic journey of departure, arrival, experience, and return. The man who returns to England at the end of the memoir, however, is different from the one who left full of anticipation in the summer of 1943. "Adventure had begun," he notes, "and with it that quality of lively excitation which surrounds the beginnings of every fresh wartime experience" (1). As his

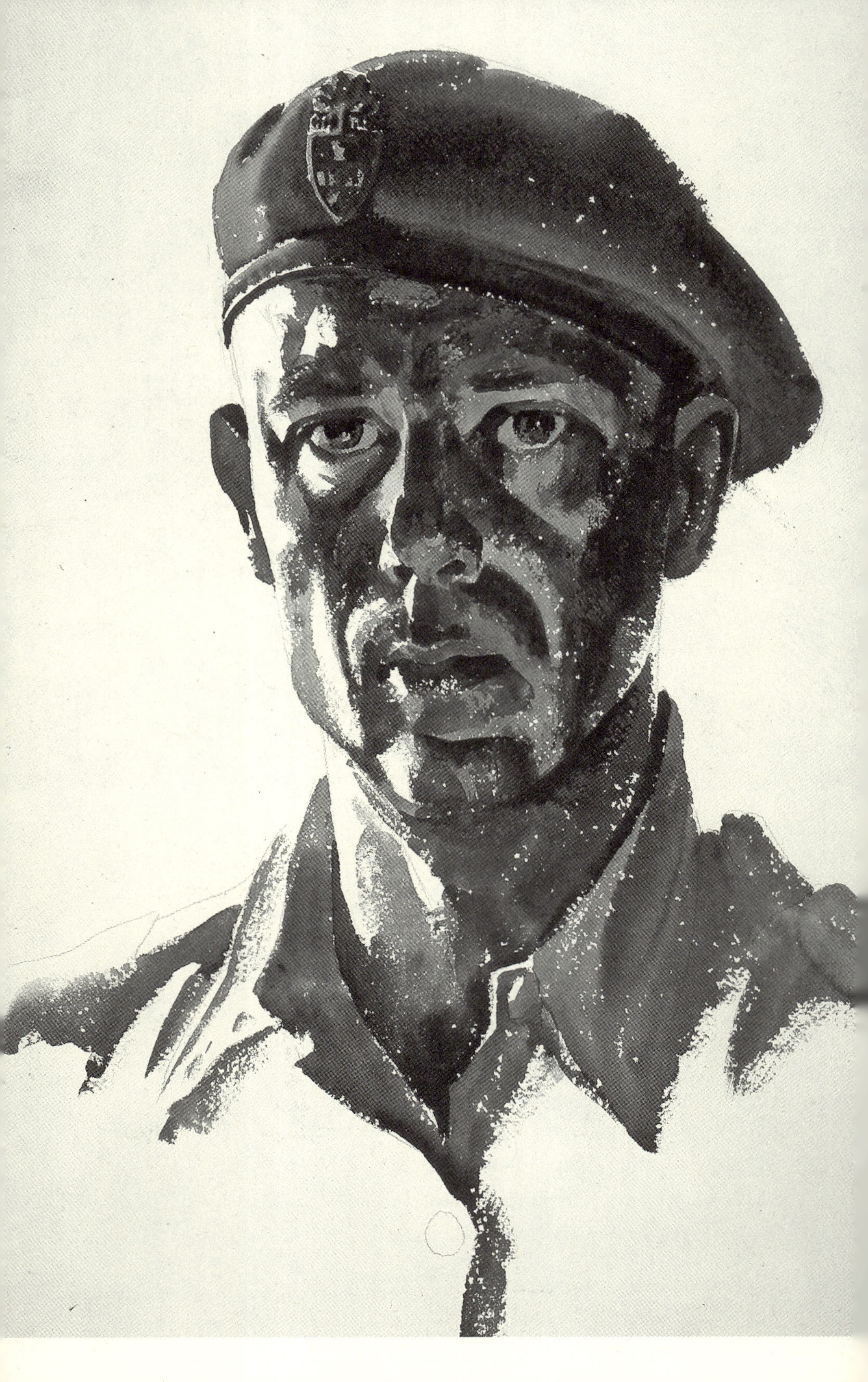

ship, the SS *Volendam*, leaves the Irish Sea headed for the Mediterranean, the men laugh, tell jokes, and sing. Comfort quotes these songs as the days tick by—"Roll out the barrel," "Bless them all, bless them all," "You are my sunshine," and eventually, inevitably it seems, "Vor der Kaserne, vor dem grossen Tor" (26). "Lili Marlene," that "extraordinary enemy love song" (47), will be the one he quotes most often until he stops mentioning songs because the soldiers no longer sing. The return trip is much more abrupt because he flies from Casablanca to an airfield in England. But even before landing, he registers the moment of sharp transition: "It was that massive air view of the Atlantic that had done it. A sudden dislocation of ideas and values had occurred as that great field of recollected associations rose out of the west. The Italian experience ended there. It was now a complete and unforgettable part of personal history" (166).





Although Comfort is not yet coming home but stopping in England for several months (he reached Halifax and his family on 25 December 1944), it is Canada he thinks of as he gazes at the Atlantic: Lunenberg, St. Margaret's Bay, Halifax, with the "mewing gulls" (168), ships, bell buoys, and sirens in the harbour, are waiting for him. This kind of connection will recur like a refrain in *Artist at War*. A scene in Italy will evoke the memory of a similar or sharply contrasting scene back home. And these connections between here and there, strange and familiar, too often decimated and quietly pristine, accumulate to produce a type of leitmotif of memory running through the narrative. In this way, Comfort attempts to make sense of what he sees in Italy by reminding himself (and us) of what we enjoy and of what Italy, Italian civilians, and our troops are suffering. He keeps home in mind as he brings his memories of war home.

< *Charles Comfort.* Major C.F. Comfort *(self-portrait, 1944). w/c 51.4 x 34.3 cm. CWM #19710261-2172. Beaverbrook Collection of War Art. © Canadian War Museum. This small, yet eloquent, watercolour self-portrait was reproduced on the front cover of the 1995 edition of Comfort's* Artist at War.

When his convoy finally leaves No.1 Canadian Base Reinforcement Depot in North Africa for Italy on 10 October 1943 at 08:15 hours, Comfort drops the excited present-tense voice he used to describe the start of this adventure. From here on he uses a first-person, past-tense voice of remembering to stress the fact that all sense of adventure is over and that a different kind of experience has begun. As he sails northward past Bari and up the Adriatic coast, he begins another type of narrative strategy that he will use for the remainder of the memoir to juxtapose his anchoring comparisons of Italian with Canadian scenes. He now comments extensively on the history of the Italian towns he passes, on the beauty of the landscapes with their orange and olive groves, the centuries of art and architecture held in the churches, towns, harbours, and castles. And he is horrified by the destruction he sees everywhere. For example, a side trip to Naples lays bare the shocking consequences of war: "We crossed on San Felice and passed the blackened remains of Santa Chiara. I was saddened that its glory had gone and that its calcined walls contained only the debris of that supreme example of baroque magnificence and the Gothic tomb of Robert the Wise. I remembered the almost carnival grandeur of Del Gaizo's décor, and those joyous anthems of moving colour in the ceiling by Francesco di Mura. Now it was gone, the accretion of seven centuries of artistic development consumed by fire bombs in one night" (40). Memories within remembering. What he saw before and what he sees now. And the contrast is both shocking and portentous.

Back at Campobasso, after the Naples experience, he places the city, liberated by Canadians and now nicknamed "Maple Leaf City" in recognition of its service as a rest centre for Canadian troops, by comparing it with home. It is similar in size to Lethbridge or Galt, he tells us, and one of its streets is "about the width of St. Catherine Street [in Montreal]" (30). However, he is fully aware that the serene beauty immediately around Campobasso "concealed the savagery of the battle proceeding from every inch of cover" (32). Although he cannot see the guns, the thunder of artillery is constant, and so is the loss of life. As he notes, tersely, he would establish contact with "spirited young men" (33) and then learn of their injuries or death. It was "a tragic pattern" to which he could not become inured (32).

But nothing prepares him for Ortona or Cassino. As he travels north with the troops, he describes the action in theatre metaphors of intense drama, bleak stages and "brutal properties" (57). Undamaged landscapes are like backdrops of wild "Laurentian beauty" (58) that contrast with terrain where fighting has occurred leaving shocking, wanton destruction. He recreates, in meticulous detail, scenes in the Moro Valley—precise colours, exact shapes, ruined vegetation, machinery, and bridges, and the incredible cacophony he endures while lying in a shallow trench through a "bowel-gripping nightmare" attack (62). Indeed, second only to the terrible things he witnesses, sound seems to have impressed Comfort more than anything else; mud, rain, cold, stench, hunger, all pale in comparison with "soul-shaking...spirals of dissonance" (65). At one point, he admits that he "had little desire to paint" (66), and he remembers a friend in Toronto who could not paint because of a barking dog (67). At another point, he remarks that he "felt suspended helplessly in some dense exhausting element where sound, and only sound, existed" (84).

Comfort's response to Ortona is both evocative and profoundly moving. He does not wax melodramatic or sentimental; his sentences are fairly short and unadorned, even though he is clearly reaching for the best image to convey the *feeling* of war. Because he was there as an artist, not a soldier, he did not take part in the merciless fighting in Ortona, but he saw what was left in the aftermath: the casualties lying in the shattered gardens of the Piazza Vittorio "grotesquely misshapen in death" (89), the once noble Via Monte Maielle reduced to "an abstraction of utter ruin" (103) from which a picture of Michelangelo, pierced by fragments of masonry, struggled to float free of the rubble, and the "intimate furnishings" of an apartment exposed to view with wash-stand, pictures, and a bed "dangling in upper space" (102). "I could not possibly paint, or even sketch, on that first dreadful visit" (103), is all he will say about his feelings. However, he notes at several points that he, like the troops, sustained himself by thinking of home. It was, ironically, Christmas, and even under these siege circumstances Christmas dinners were served of "Canadian turkey with dressing and vegetables" (99).[4]

After Ortona, in a chapter called "Hiatus," he has time for the reflection and contemplation he needs for his non-combatant work. Finally, he and Harris can find places to set up their sketching equipment and focus on recording (and interpreting) what they see. They must be constantly alert for concealed mines, traps, and enemy aircraft, but compared with what they witnessed in Ortona and would experience at Cassino, things were calm. In these circumstances, Comfort could wrestle with how to paint this war when the old formulas no longer made sense to him: "we were getting the raw material, the eye-witness experience, which should lend authority to anything we might eventually do" (113).





Cassino in the Liri Valley produced a still greater shock to Comfort. The significance of this part of the Italian campaign was twofold for him. First, the Canadians were mounting an attack on the Adolf Hitler Line defences and, second, the attack he witnessed was "the first major operation of the war wholly directed by a Canadian corps" (128). This would be, in Comfort's words, "the toughest battle Canadians had ever faced in any war" (129), and he is proud of his compatriots' success. *Briefly*. Because what he goes on to describe is worse than Ortona and he is filled with horror and something approaching guilt. The attack took place in May 1944, and the destruction of "trees in full foliage creates a far more sinister impression of devastation than those destroyed [at Ortona] in winter" (134). Everywhere he sees "lifeless rubble," from the great Benedictine Monastery of Monte Cassino to Cassino itself (see page 399): "For sheer horror and utter devastation I had not set eyes on its equal…it resembled…some imagined landscape on the moon" (135). As for the wasted monastery, he tells us that he cannot understand why it should have been destroyed "by our own generation" (135) after nearly 1,400 years of contribution to Western art and culture.

There are still more sites (and sights) of destruction and death that await him, but Cassino seems to have marked a personal nadir for Comfort. He notes that Pontecorvo has been reduced to a ghost town and he laments the dead still being pulled from under collapsed masonry, but he finds little solace in the military success of breaching the Hitler Line. His thoughts are with the missing and dead Canadians, the senseless destruction of cultural life, and, when he finally makes it to Rome, his relief because, since Montreal, "I had not seen a modern city which had escaped being crushed and burned" (141).





After Rome, Comfort will begin the last stage of this "adventure"—the circuitous route back to England and home—but he will carry with him these memories of Italy and the challenge of translating "the raw material, the eye-witness experience" into art. The art he ultimately produces does indeed bear witness to war, but his paintings, like this memoir, resonate in "our time" (as Eric Harrison put it) not for their celebration of military victories but for their testimony to the losses sustained in war—losses of life, to be sure, but also losses to art, history, and culture over centuries of creative human endeavour. In a matter of hours, or a few days, all this creativity can be erased, denied, desecrated, and destroyed by violence. The ruins of Ortona, Cassino, and Aquino, all depicted in the paintings reproduced in this edition of *Artist at War*, are Comfort's ghostly reminders, his warnings to future generations.[5] Like McCrae's dead, they appeal to us—"We are the dead"—but like Varley's famous First World War canvas, they ask us "For What?" (see page 36).

Even in the oils that depict human beings, Comfort issues a warning about the dehumanization of soldiers and their terrible vulnerability, which is an ironic remnant of their humanity. Thus, the troops camped below Campobasso in *Campobasso, Princess Louise Dragoon Guards in Foreground* (1945) are concentrated in a dark foreground and are faceless. The few soldiers crawling over a ruined road and past a burnt-out German tank in *Battle Scene—(Fantasy)—Villa Grande Road, Ortona Area* (n.d.) are barely distinguishable from the dust, mud, and smoke around them. The soldiers working their artillery in *Canadian Field Guns Near Ortona* (1945) or advancing towards the viewer in *The Hitler Line* (1944) lack individuality; they are serving a deadly function, caught up in a process of destruction that erases their humanity. As Laura Brandon notes, Canadian war artists were discouraged from depicting dead Canadian soldiers.[6] And as far as I know Comfort did not attempt such depictions. However, his *Dead German on the Hitler Line* (1944) is one of the most striking war pictures produced by Canadian Second World War artists. Here, in death, an enemy soldier gains a degree of tragic humanity denied in war. He does not have a name but his identity is easy to imagine. His tattered uniform, his sightless eyes, his grimace, his blonde hair, his lower body sinking into the charred earth, and his contorted, empty hands, all testify to the things Charles Comfort witnessed and wants future generations to remember and understand. Comfort does not portray a Nazi monster but someone's son, brother, possibly husband and father, although he seems very young.

Fred Bruemmer's *Survival: A Refugee Life* carries its author from memories of living with the Inuit of Bathurst Inlet back to his childhood in Latvia, where he was born in 1929 into a well-educated, very comfortable and loving Baltic German family as Friedrich von Bruemmer. He had three siblings and, miraculously, all four survived the horrors of war, imprisonment, labour camps, and the murder of their parents. The von Bruemmer parents were the last generation of a Baltic baron family with estates, power, and prestige, but after the First World War their way of life was vanishing, their ancestral home was taken over by the state and leased back to them, and then what was left of their former way of life was erased after the Second World War. Canadians know Bruemmer best through his many award-winning books and photography of the Canadian Arctic, its peoples, and its wildlife,[7] but his obvious passion for the North began with his arrival in Canada, and he tells that story in this 2005 memoir. As he comments early on in *Survival*, he was made homeless and stateless in

1939, when Hitler and Stalin "divided [his] world" (19), and he would remain a refugee until 1951, when he immigrated to Canada to work in a Kirkland Lake gold mine. In September of that year, he took his first real adult holiday. He was just twenty-two and while fellow miners fished, drank beer, or gardened at home, Bruemmer went north to Moosonee at the southern tip of James Bay.

This trip north, living with a trader and hunting with the local Indians, helped him decide what he should do with his future and how he could start a new life. "I loved those canoe trips on the great, lonely [Moose River]." He and his companions slept in the open and, as he listened to their stories, he realized that this was "their life...their land": "I loved those days and nights, roaming the northern forest with the Indians, camping in the wilderness. Perhaps in its freedom, its simplicity, its nearness to nature, it reminded me of the happiest time of my life, my childhood spent in Quellenhof" (267). By the time Bruemmer makes this connection explicit at the end of *Survival*, we can appreciate the significance of his joy "roaming the northern forest" because he has remembered and described his carefree roaming in Latvian and Polish forests as a boy, the almost indescribable shock of losing that life in that landscape, of fighting to survive in Russian labour camps, and then crossing a central European wasteland razed by advancing and retreating armies during and after the war. It is as if the landscape he recalls at James Bay and his landscapes of memory from childhood form a nurturing buffer around an ordeal he refused to reconstruct until, in this century at the age of seventy-six, he was ready to bear witness to the past.

Although I began by highlighting the framework of this memoir—from the Canadian present of remembering, to the European past and back again to Canada—the narrative itself is fairly straightforward and linear. And this is a *memoir*, not a full-fledged auto/biography. In it Bruemmer concentrates on the first two decades of his life set against the war-torn background of Baltic history. These are the years that shaped this man insofar as something that does not kill you may make you stronger. It is also not until late in the narrative, after the war ends, his release from the Russian labour camp, and his return to Soviet-controlled East Germany as a displaced person, that he mentions keeping diaries (229). Among the few possessions carried in two suitcases that he brings with him to Canada in 1951 are "dictionaries, books on animals, a paperback edition of Goethe's *Faust*, my diaries" (251). Presumably, these diaries provide the basis for his vivid memories of the years between 1939 and 1951, although it would have been almost impossible to keep any kind of record during his two years of forced labour. Although he does not say so, the diaries must date from the time of his release.[8]

One of the most moving of these memories involves the disappearance of his sister Hella. Once the von Bruemmer family had lost their ancestral lands, they moved into an apartment in Riga, but a love of countryside and forest was deeply ingrained, and in 1929 (the year Fred was born) his father bought a farm in northeast Latvia, which they called Quellenhof ("the place of the sacred spring") (32). In a pattern familiar to many Canadians, as soon as school closed for the year, an urban life was exchanged for a rural one. Summers were spent on the farm with the horses, cows, pigs, family dog, the local people who were like extended family, and the free run of fields, meadows, and woods. With the outbreak of the war, they left Quellenhof, never to return, and Bruemmer recalls crying when his mother explained that all Baltic Germans had to leave Latvia before the Soviet troops arrived. Beginning in 1939, and over the next short period, "84,000 Baltic Germans left Latvia and Estonia" (40). The von Bruemmers went to Poland, where the parents and their two youngest children, Fred and Hella, were assigned to an estate, formerly owned by Poles but now called Kleingraben. The Germans had renamed the Polish places they occupied when they invaded Poland. His elder sister had married and moved to Sumatra; his brother was fighting in the German army. For the next four years Fred went to school, did his best to avoid joining the Hitler Youth, and gradually came to understand something of the war when his brother came home wounded and he, with other schoolboys, was recruited to spend the summers digging anti-tank trenches.

When the Soviet troops invaded in January 1945, the worst period began. The von Bruemmer family attempted to flee once more, but they were trapped, arrested, and jailed by the Russians. His memories of what happened next are confused but vivid. He and his sister were separated from their parents; the family dog, having tracked them for miles and caught up, was shot, but not killed, by a callous young guard who laughed at the animal's agony. When an older guard put the dog out of its misery, Bruemmer recalls that "all that was left of my little dog was a small pile of bloody fur and shattered flesh in the snow" (67). Bruemmer then writes that the young guard called him and his sister crazy because they wept for a dog but not for their parents, who had just been shot, but if the children knew what had happened to their parents at that point, Bruemmer does not say so. Instead, when Hella tries to comfort him for the death of the dog, he states simply that "something broke": "Until that moment we had been rigid, frozen. Now it burst out, the grief, the fear, the despair of children who have lost all they loved, and we held each other and cried" (67). They are then marched to Poznan. It is dark in the city and Fred is pushed by a rifle butt, stumbles forward and, "when I turned around, Hella was gone" (67). Although he does not return to this scene later in the narrative, describe it as haunting him, or explain his fears for Hella, this moment of loss and separation stays with him until the two siblings are reunited after the war. The power of this scene and its impact, experienced and then remembered and told to us, is all the more forceful for its restrained telling. Unlike the tragic story of Bella and Jakob imagined by Anne Michaels in *Fugitive Pieces* or the factual story of Hana and George Brady in *Hana's Suitcase*, Hella and Fred's story has a happy ending. But the echoes across these fiction and non-fiction texts provide striking illustrations of the pain inflicted on children who survive such violent separations.

The next period in young Bruemmer's life starts abruptly that night when he finds himself, stunned and alone, imprisoned in a military camp. An older prisoner stands before him and asks, "What's the matter, boy?" (68), and thus began a strange, unemotional, but protective relationship between Bruemmer and the man known only as Karl. Without such a man it is unlikely that Bruemmer would have survived the next two years. First, Karl fed him from a private stash, then he warned him not to take off his boots when he slept because they would be stolen. When the guards arrived to register each prisoner, Karl advised him to lie: he is to say he was born in Berlin, not Riga, that he is twelve, not fifteen, and to drop the "von" from his name. These strategic shifts strip away signs of his true identity but the new identity will help him survive, and it will not be his last identity shift. The prisoners end up as slave labourers in the Soviet Union, and over the coming months Karl shows Bruemmer how to secure the best sleeping place on a train crammed with bodies, how to steal and fence the goods, how to procure extra rations of food, how not to confide in or trust anyone, and how to avoid the most brutal guards. Bruemmer becomes an adroit smuggler and is never caught. He survives an attack of dysentery, a disease that kills many men, because Karl filches extra bread and another prisoner, Manek, who is in a kind of partnership with Karl, knows how to heal "the shits" with "yarrow tea" and "oak-bark brew" (109). "It was my first victory," Bruemmer tells us. "So many others died. I lived. I was going to go on living. 'I will not die!' I kept repeating that" (109).

Most of his memories of the two camps he is in are, not surprisingly, horrible. Prisoners die and are immediately stripped by others who need clothes; the bodies are thrown outdoors in a heap and periodically carted away for burial in mass graves. These men and their graves are anonymous; they comprise thousands of those listed as *missing* after the war. Christmas was an especially difficult time in the camps. On the one hand, the prisoners were grateful to have survived and their meagre rations were slightly increased for that day. On the other,

Christmas songs, notably "Stille Nacht, Heilige Nacht" remind young Bruemmer of his lost family. These Christmas songs cracked what he describes as his "armour" because they evoked thoughts of loved ones when there was no love in a labour camp: "One thing I learned in prison: you don't think about the past and you don't dream about the future. You live for the day. All that matters is to survive this day" (142). He can only *place* these years in hell much later when he sees photographs of survivors from Auschwitz and Dachau and recognizes his younger self in their emaciation and in "the dull, passive stare of humans [who] have been destroyed by the absolute power of evil" (139).





Oddly enough, the prisoners rarely attempt to escape. If caught, their punishment is swift. For Bruemmer and Karl and Manek, life inside the second camp is tolerable because of their smuggling, thieving, and Bruemmer's ability to buy better food in local markets on those days when he is allowed out on his own. He recalls enjoying "the thrill of stealing," although he left the serious smuggling to Karl and Manek. After the war, and by his second spring behind barbed wire, he longs to be free, but Karl advises him to wait. Prisoners were slowly being released and as a boy of thirteen (and he is so thin and underdeveloped that he can still pass as three years younger than his real age) he was officially classified as a child. Children were released sooner than adult men. "Karl's advice, so long ago in Poznan, to make myself three years younger, had always helped me. Now it released me from prison" (163). Clearly, this hard, cold man is no Athos to Bruemmer's Jakob, and yet Bruemmer knows he "had been my guide, my friend, a sort of older brother. He had saved my life"(163). Writing and remembering so many years later, this is all Bruemmer will say, but the simple brevity is eloquent. Although deprived of family, love, home, identity, tenderness of any sort, and dignity, he knows how important to him this Karl has been. Later in the narrative he admits that he has become cold and remote himself, frozen into an unemotional instinct to survive.

After his release, and after the train passes through Poznan where so much personal loss occurred, he decides that he must once more modify his identity and move further from his Baltic roots. Because his spoken German would never pass as "Berlinisch," he decides to say he was born in Kalisz, Poland, but he keeps his new birth date. His younger age will yet again serve him well because the adults working with the refugees now flooding into the occupied zones of Germany will pity him. However, this change in place of birth represents another loss for him—the loss of his roots in a mother tongue that, after 1939, is a "dying dialect" spoken by about five hundred people all, like Bruemmer today, in their seventies. Along with those refugees who survived (and many did not) the crowded, disease-ridden, trains carrying them towards something called freedom, Bruemmer is unloaded in Frankfurt an der Oder and a refugee camp. This time, as he puts it, these pathetic souls are met with "blasts of Teutonic efficiency" (179). The food rations are better. It is possible to bathe, get medical care, and wear clean clothes (often ill-fitting but "you took what you got," 179). The clerk registering refugees takes down the particulars of his "invented—but hopefully safe—persona: Name: Friedrich Bruemmer; Born: January 27, 1933; Place of Birth: Kalisz, Poland; Profession: student; Parents' profession: both teachers, both dead; Relatives: no known relatives" (179–80).

Some of these details are true. His parents were dead and he did not know if any of his siblings were alive or, if they were, where to find them. Like millions of other ethnic German refugees, he had been *returned* to a Germany, indeed, to a Europe devastated by the war. Looking back on this state of things, Bruemmer describes it as "the greatest 'ethnic cleansing' program of modern times, perhaps of all time" (180). Twelve million ethnic Germans who had lived in central European countries now controlled by the Soviet Union were expelled and all their possessions confiscated.[9] Bruemmer says he had become one of the *Koffermenschen* or "suitcase people" (181) who carried all that remained of their former lives with them. But life will slowly improve for Bruemmer. Officials in charge of refugees single him out, take pity on his youth, and find him work repairing and cleaning a "plundered" estate near the city of

Cottbus, where he will soon be "adopted" by a teacher who lost her only son in the war. He begins to earn money by pawning smuggled books from the library of the estate and by teaching languages, and he starts the process of searching for the one sister who had married and moved to Sumatra before the war. This attempt sets in motion a process of reunion with his siblings, but the reunion he stresses is the discovery of his "dead sister" Hella. She heard from their elder sister that Bruemmer was alive and looking for them, so she obtained a pass from West Germany to visit him and found him living in Cottbus with his adoptive mother. His description of the two catching up on the lost years of their lives since 1939, and those of their two older siblings, is matter-of-fact and assembled from information gleaned over the months ahead. But clearly, finding Hella is a powerful moment, and realizing that all four are survivors is an immense relief.

Bruemmer's next challenge is to escape the Soviet zone and rejoin Hella and his brother Arist in West Germany. He succeeds, as he tells us, in "slipping through the iron curtain" and by the end of 1947 he settles into a tiny apartment in the village of Sehlde in Lower Saxony with his brother and his family. Bruemmer passes quickly over the next few years, his move to another West German town to live with former family friends, also Baltic German refugees, his return to school, and the restoration of his youth and ability to trust life: "School and family changed me; I belonged again. The death camp had damaged me. Something within me had atrophied and left me cold, cautious, callous, and old. Now, gradually, I became young again" (245). Once more he has been reborn, this time in preparation for the new life that awaits him in Canada. "My view of Canada was romantic, coloured by two books I had read as a child"; these are James Fenimore Cooper's *The Leatherstocking Tales* and Ernest Thompson Seton's *Wild Animals I Have Known*, which described a land of "Indians and wilderness, of wolves and coureurs de bois" (248). When he immigrated in December 1950 with his brother and Hella, he quickly realized that modern, southern Canada was not what Seton described, but his first holiday to the country around Moosonee revived memories of his childhood and revealed a northern Canada he would spend a lifetime exploring. From a young man without a home and a passport that labelled him "stateless," he begins again: "my persona changed. Friedrich von Bruemmer, Baltic German, became Fred Bruemmer, Latvian. I was a twenty-one-year-old high-school dropout" (250). Crossing Canada by train from Saint John, New Brunswick, to Kirkland Lake, Ontario, bears no comparison to the nightmare trains of Europe. He and Hella had window seats and beyond these windows lay endless forest and snow.





Bruemmer is clear about where he stands regarding this new country and home. He is "deeply grateful" (258). In the closing lines of *Survival* he writes,

*I had mined gold for fifteen months.*
*I had bought a motorcycle and a camera.*
*It was time to start another life. (270)*

Nevertheless, he will return to Europe, to Berlin, to Riga, to Dresden, and to Poznan. And he will write this memoir. Why? For whom does he tell this story of loss, terror, and survival? The reasons for writing are many, and some must be deeply personal. Bruemmer has not only survived, he has created a happy, successful life as a Canadian. He was luckier than many—in being protected by Karl, in being tough and intelligent, in speaking several useful languages despite an interrupted education, in receiving help from social workers in East Germany, and perhaps, above all, in being determined and resourceful by nature. So why revisit the past? Because all these lucky breaks and personal attributes have not freed him from the ghosts of a lost identity or the need to speak of his traumatic, dehumanizing experiences. He has come forward in the latter years of his life as Fred Bruemmer, Canadian author and photographer, to bear witness as only a survivor can. If the whole picture cannot be presented—and it is not in this memoir—then an extraordinarily vivid sense of what happened in Europe during and after the Second World War emerges from his testimony.

By telling contemporary Canadians (and his own children) about his life once Hitler and Stalin destroyed the world as he knew it, he reminds us of how blessed we are to be here and of how much immigrants like him carried with them in their psychological suitcases. There is very little overt anger in the pages of *Survival*, but this story is a profound indictment of war, ethnic and racial hatred, brutality, and what he calls "the absolute power of evil" (139). To survive such horror, to begin a new life and live it reverently, is to enact and embody the exact opposite of such evil. It is to re-establish a home in a new landscape while preserving a past landscape of memory; it is to live creatively in the face of destruction. It is to remember because to forget is impossible. It is, ultimately, to conjure hope from the fragments of despair by bearing witness.

Lisa Appignanesi provides several reasons for her decision to write *Losing the Dead*. Like Bruemmer, she wrote the book for her children so she could answer their questions about their grandparents. But she is more explicit than either Bruemmer or Comfort about her personal motivations and about the process of constructing a narrative based on conflicting memories, shifting identities, unacknowledged but necessary forgetting and silences, and a history lacking in archival evidence. Appignanesi claims that her generation was the last one to be born and grow up in the shadow of *the war*, which "will always be the Second World War" (5–6) for her and others like her. Therefore, she believes it is important to map that landscape of memory, post-memory, and forgetting, and to attempt a reconstruction of what influenced her Polish-Jewish parents who, in turn, influenced her. The most immediately pressing motivation for her writing, however, is her mother's Alzheimer's and her need, as a daughter, to bring a form of order—hence, of meaning or sense—to her mother's increasingly disoriented, fragmented memories. She will write, then, to help herself understand who she is and, as she says, to perform an act of "reparation" to her ailing mother, even though she recognizes that "the voyage into the past is always coloured by invention" and that memory is "a form of negotiation" (7). It is, she confesses, "for my own sanity that I decide to explore her past" (80).





After my first reading of *Losing the Dead*, I felt irritated with Appignanesi as an auto/biographer. I even wondered if she had not undertaken her "voyage into the past" to settle a score with a mother she resented.[10] The more I have thought about this text, however, the more I have come to appreciate this indomitable, survivor mother without whom none of Appignanesi's immediate family would have survived the war. Along with her father, brother, and maternal grandmother, she and they owe their lives to this woman I shall call (for simplicity's sake) Hena Borenstein.[11] Hena was apparently beautiful with blue eyes and blonde hair; when the time came she could pass as Aryan. She was also extraordinarily courageous and intrepid. The woman who emerges from Appignanesi's story was heroic. Her father, Aron Borenstein, seems to have been less able to cope with the horrifying events of the war or with the traumatic aftermath that remained with him through his life in Canada and later in England. He could not pass as Aryan and he could not protect his wife, young son, and parents from the Nazis, either in their small hometown or in Warsaw. Hena could lie easily and convincingly; Aron had difficulty doing so. Hena could hide her inner fear behind a cheerful bravado or a confident self-assertion when dealing with German, or later Russian, soldiers, the Gestapo, or German and Polish officials. Aron could not. In the postwar safety of Montreal, Hena relished telling stories of her exploits during the war, but her husband was usually silent about the past, always terrified when dealing with officials (even standard Canada–US border officials), and filled with rage. He hated Poles and Germans alike and never returned to Poland.

Although this father is a constant presence in *Losing the Dead* (and the parent Appignanesi seems to prefer and to resemble in colouring and features), his troubled ghost is not the main focus of her story. Lying behind the narrative of her parents' lives, and not confronted until near the end, is the suspicion that Aron Borenstein was not her biological father and that Lisa Appignanesi (née Elzbieta Borensztejn on 4 January 1946 in Łódź) was conceived in a liaison her mother had with a Russian KGB officer whose help during the occupation of Poland after the war was crucial for the family's survival. In 1981, on his deathbed, Aron called his wife a whore, but by then he was suffering from "diabetic delirium" (4) and had "transformed the ordinary London hospital ward where he lay into an SS camp" (3). In this state, he insisted that no one around him could be trusted except his daughter, and he begged her to help him escape. He reverted to speaking Yiddish, a language he had not used for decades, and he became obsessed with his war memories. These appalling scenes haunt the daughter, who can no more escape their influence and the long shadow they cast backwards over her "largely Canadian and largely happy childhood" (5). Her actual dilemma parallels that of Ben's and his parents' (especially his father's) in *Fugitive Pieces*. Caught by her father's tormented remembering and later her mother's forgetting, she finally decides to go back herself. By returning to Poland, to the war years, to her parents' past, to the archives that have survived, and to the few Poles who still remember her mother, she hopes to excavate the truth beneath the lies.

Appignanesi returned to Poland in 1997 with the express purpose of finding out what happened during the war so she could assess how those events shaped her family's life. She begins her story, however, with their arrival in Halifax on 27 April 1951. She has the official documents to confirm this fact, although even here the surname is unclear: Borensztejn? Borenstein? The writing is blurred. They have arrived after two years in France, where they fled in 1949, and little Lisa speaks a fluent five-year-old's French with a Parisian accent. They will settle in Montreal—her mother's decision. At first they are not well-off and move frequently, but Appignanesi recalls being fairly happy. However, her mother's frequent lies—changing names and personae, hiding their Jewish identity from their French-Canadian, Catholic neighbours, composing fictions for acquaintances—confuse and embarrass her. She does not understand why all this subterfuge and fabulation is necessary. The stories of war and survival recounted by her mother, and by family friends, contribute to her floating sense of vague guilt for "tainted origins" and a "bitter aura of shame" (35) that, in hindsight, she attributes to an oppressed group's internalization of an aggressor's contempt, which is then passed on, as if by osmosis, to the next generation. Her father's fears and unexplained anger further complicate the atmosphere at home, even though he is categorical about some things: "Poland is a cemetery" (72), a place loathed and never to be revisited; Canada is a haven for which he is grateful, a place for life, freedom, and the future.





On her first trip to Poland, a business trip, in 1988, she is not impressed with the country. Contemporary Polish constructions of their war history and their romantic depictions of Jews offend her. Her father was right; she leaves with no plan to return: "I hadn't counted on my mother's gradual and growing dotage to send me back" (77). But among her mother's fragmented memories is a lost brother, who the ailing woman sees again and again, on television, on the street, "everywhere"; for her, he is "a restless ghost, unburied" (78). This handsome brother, Adolf (or Adek) Lipszyc, was also blonde and blue-eyed, and he not only passed as Aryan during the war but also became a wealthy Warsaw businessman called Max Hiszcynski who hid Jews, forged passports, and saved many lives. He was a stunning success until his disguise collapsed, or someone reported on him, at about the time of the Warsaw Uprising, which began on 1 August 1944. Adek, alias Max, disappeared, or *was* disappeared.

For her trip to Poland in 1997, Appignanesi prepared carefully. She wrote ahead, set up meetings, asked for assistance in finding records and locating the streets and buildings where her parents had lived. Indeed, one of the most interesting aspects of this journey and its narrative reconstruction is the role played by archives. The process of consulting old yellowing file cards preserved in Warsaw's Jewish Historical Institute is by turns exciting, a bit like detective work, and disappointing, but she is able to confirm some names, their spellings, some dates, and a few addresses. She also discovers that her parents used several aliases with differing birth dates for each identity. She can find no record of her missing uncle, her mother's ghostly brother. She takes trains, usually old and dilapidated, to the towns outside Warsaw where her grandparents and parents had lived before and during the war, reflects on the ghosts and stories represented by these trains, which were such terrifying presences in her mother's stories (20, 102). In these towns—Grodzisk, Pruszków, and Łódź—she visits municipal registries and archives; she walks the streets searching for buildings only to find they have been torn down. At one point, in a run-down neighbourhood of Pruszków, she senses something carried by the odours of weeds and fruit, and in a fascinating conflation of times and places she remembers home but adjusts that memory: "I had always assumed these were smells of the Canadian countryside, but they are here, now, on this street" (108). They are, of course, both, but now she has a double sense of their significance. However, the house in which her parents had lived as refugees after the war is gone, "torn down and replaced by a public library" (109).

To provide context and missing information about the past, Appignanesi must rely on the history books. Where archives turn up little or nothing and where her mother's stories and failing memory complicate the stories and memories of friends, or her own and her brother's recollections of those stories, she must turn to the facts gathered, and interpreted, by historians. In this she resembles Robert Ross's biographer in *The Wars* who tells us "You begin at the archives" and "as the past moves under your fingertips, part of it crumbles. This is what you have" (5–6). So she must supplement these fragments, as does Findley, with research on the Warsaw Ghetto, the uprising there in May 1943, the trains to Treblinka, the mass murders and graves,

Auschwitz, Birkenau, and the history of specific buildings that survived the war, such as the Aleje Szuhca. This palatial edifice, formerly part of the Polish monarchy's estate in Warsaw, houses the Polish Ministry of the Interior in 1997, but during the war it was the headquarters of the Gestapo. This is where her father was taken after his arrest in 1944; it was from this hideous place that he was released when an SS doctor, whether in a stroke of miraculous good fortune or because the doctor was a Jew masquerading as a Nazi, corroborated his story that his missing foreskin was the result of an operation (177). Behind these walls and below the paved courtyard, history tells her, "hideous torture was enacted": "Here is the original site of my father's recurring nightmares, the location of his final delirium" (171). Here is where memory, story, primary and secondary witnessing, and history converge.

As we know from the opening chapters of *Losing the Dead*, the Borenstein family survived by escaping to Paris in early 1949 and then emigrating to Canada. By the end of this auto/biography, we have learned that Appignanesi's return to Poland in 1997 was part of her attempt to lose the dead (200). However, by writing this complex narrative of interconnected lives lived and lost, of multiple identities, trauma, and dislocation, she has not so much lost the dead as recovered them. By attending to what she calls the "ghost language" (217) of the war years that was internalized by her parents, she has uncovered and recuperated their life stories from Poland and Canada, along with her own. She now understands their "charade" of names and identities, why they sent her to convent schools, why they were so sensitive to anti-Semitism in Quebec, and why she grew up surrounded—confounded—by contradiction. All this she now understands as the "mirrorings of Polish-Jewish life...enacted on Canadian soil" (217).

Ghost language is an apt term for the haunting that Holocaust survivors passed on, simply by remembering but refusing to tell, or by remembering out loud obsessively, their experiences to their children. Hirsch calls this phenomenon post-memory, but to call it ghost language identifies the spoken/unspoken, heard/not heard (or denied) tension that defines such haunting. Appignanesi will never be able to prove that Aron Borenstein was, or was not, her father by revisiting the past and listening to the ghosts, so she opts to believe her mother, that master of survival fabrication, who insists that, of course, he is. And I, for one, am relieved by this. Somehow this *listening* to her mother confirms the older woman's role in her life and in the history of *the war*. It marks a listening-to-believe process that is fundamental to survival, and it adds voices, stories, human beings, to the landscape of memory that tells you who you are. It brings what happened there and then forward into the here and now for Appignanesi and, since she recounts this journey and listening publicly, also for us. One family's wartime Polish story assumes its rightful place in the larger history of postwar Canada.





At no point in *Losing the Dead* does she make the responsibility of listening more ethically charged than in her description of a story her father once told about eating animal instead of human feces in a Polish labour camp because near starvation meant that human excrement had no nutrients. When his Canadian relatives laughed at this story, Aron "ceased to speak and soon left the room" (128). His "disquisition on shit" (128) sounded preposterous in the safety and plenty of postwar Montreal. But recalling this story and its reception many years later, Appignanesi knows better: "There is something emblematic about this scene. It goes some way towards explaining my father's silence about his wartime experience. If you speak, not only are you forced to remember, but you meet with the incredulity of listeners. The incommensurability of wartime atrocities spoken of in the safety of an ordinary front room can seem like delirium or exaggeration....Largely, my father remained silent. His gestures, his displaced outbursts of rage, spoke for him."[12]

By listening and then telling as much as, as best, she can, Appignanesi performs the kind of auto/biographical remembering begun in fiction like *The Wars* and *Obasan*, developed further in *Fugitive Pieces* and *The Ash Garden*, and continued in non-fiction works like Fred

Bruemmer's *Survival*. She draws on many of the tropes and themes considered in previous chapters, and she does so with a contemporary acknowledgement of the theoretical terminology and postmodern narrative conventions usually employed by scholars—terms like trauma, haunting, memory-work, testimony, witnessing, and conventions like self-reflexivity, irony regarding the reliability of memory and the accuracy of history, and a deliberate foregrounding of the multiple layering of identities to capture something of the shifting aspects of truth. She reveals much about herself—her antipathies, jealousies, harsh judgements, and reconsiderations—and still more about a mother she enables her readers to know and admire. Although she comments (harshly I feel) that her mother's "ideal interlocutor is always and ever the Gestapo officer [hence the need to lie]" (34), she in fact constructs us, her own and her mother's listening readers, as her mother's ultimate interlocutors. Moreover, she gives us what Naomi struggles to find in *Obasan*, a mother's story that supercedes, precedes, and shapes a daughter's life story. And this is rare. With a few striking exceptions like *Obasan*, *Waiting for the Parade*, *The War Between Us*, or *Hana's Suitcase*, Canadian novels, plays, films, and memoirs of both wars grant pride of place to men—sons, fathers, husbands, lost uncles, brothers, veterans, prisoners of war, and soldiers' ghosts.[13] The female voice in war, and in our shared landscape of memory, is important but too often absent. It is also, and more often than not, a voice of courage and life-affirming hope. But one must dig deeply to find much hope in the documentary films with which I conclude this chapter on the Second World War. And one will look in vain for mothers, daughters, wives, or other women's voices.

## DOCUMENTING HISTORY, EDUCATING MEMORY

### The Valour and the Horror *and* Return to Ortona

If the popular press and the media are encouraging Canadians to reimagine "their country as a military nation" (Valpy), and if various writers of serious fiction, drama, and non-fiction provide us with what I see as a larger picture of Canadian identity that reimagines and remembers a highly complex, contradictory history of the Second World War and problematizes the basic notion that a nation's identity is forged in battle, then what contributions have recent documentary films made to this process? What do they contribute to the debate about memory, history, war, and identity? Many films about the war have been made since the early 1990s. At times it seems as if one cannot turn on the television (certainly not the History Channel), go online, or look through NFB brochures (or BBC ones for that matter) without finding war to be the popular subject.[14] And I am not speaking of news coverage of Afghanistan, the Middle East, or North Africa. The films being made are, like the online "Memory Project" and the *Globe and Mail*'s "Own a moment in history" gift photographs, about the two world wars.[15] They are documentary films that represent the *history* of Canadians in these wars and aim, as Graham Carr puts it, "to educate memory" by stimulating a viewer's empathy with the past through strategies of reconstruction and re-enactment (Carr 66–67).





All art is political; all art operates in the world to some degree. But these documentary war films, by virtue of their medium, their narratology and visual language, and their potentially wide dissemination, are more *overtly* political than, say, a novel like *Fugitive Pieces* or even *Obasan*, which contributed to a public, political debate. Moreover, by being so visible these films are open to attack from groups within society who disapprove of, or disagree with, their representation of historical events. Perhaps they are also held to a higher standard of accountability than a novel or a play because they are funded by the public purse and they make truth claims akin to those of autobiography and official History. Certainly, they deserve to be examined carefully and discussed critically *as what they are*—films, works of documentary art, texts that construct frames for the public remembering of the Second World War. If Graham Carr is correct (and I think he is) that such films play a significant role in educating memory, then we must take them seriously. We, that is all Canadian citizens, especially younger generations with increasingly tenuous links to the Second World War past, are the targeted consumers of these texts. They, like older generations, are meant to learn who we are today by remembering this history. We are *being educated* to understand certain things as more important than others and to recall them in specific ways.

The most important documentary to examine in the context of war, history, and memory is *The Valour and the Horror* directed by Brian McKenna and narrated by his brother Terence McKenna. *The Valour and the Horror* is a three-part documentary film, lasting approximately five hours, about Canadians in the Second World War. It premiered on prime time, Sunday evening, CBC Television in January 1992, when it provoked an uproar that had not happened previously (to my knowledge) and has not happened since. What's more, the CBC has never rebroadcast the original series. To view the films now, one must purchase them from the NFB. At the heart of the *Valour and the Horror* controversy lies the no man's land between fact and fiction, history and story, archives, documents, records, and artistic representation—some would say between truth and lies. Arguing for a *distinction* between these categories (for I do not believe one can be *defined*) involves issues of ethics and artistic convention—in this case, the conventions of historiography, documentary art, and performance. Where the furor over *The Valour and the Horror* ran aground was in its failure to address the ethics of *artistic* representation, and the filmmakers themselves invited such a failure by claiming at the start of each film that everything viewers were about to see was true: "There is no fiction."[16] They were attempting to seize the high ground of respect for facts, physical documents, eyewitness accounts, and archival images, but in doing so they devalued their own artistry. I will return to this crucial problem and to what has been called the "politics of war memory" (see Ashplant, Dawson, and Roper). First, however, I want to describe my response, as a secondary witness, to what I see when watching *The Valour and the Horror* and why I respond to the films with empathic unsettlement instead of uncritical, emotional identification or patriotism.

In the film series, the McKennas focus on three major aspects of the war. "Savage Christmas: Hong Kong 1941" is one of the earliest, detailed accounts we have of the fate of Canadians in the Pacific war; the film returns viewers to Hong Kong, remembers the massacre at St. Stephen's Hospital, revisits POW camps, and recounts many things we did not know, such as the story of Kanao Inouye (1916–47), the "Kamloops Kid," who played a major role as Nishino in Crummey's *The Wreckage*. In "Death by Moonlight: Bomber Command," the McKennas depict the RAF bombing of German cities, such as Hamburg, and reconstruct events from the perspective of two Canadian veteran bomber pilots who accompany the film crew; as with "Savage Christmas," this film presents a host of facts. It examines Bomber Command's decision to bomb civilian targets, and encourages viewers to feel horrified by such military decisions and disgusted with the British, especially Sir Arthur Harris, who developed the plan and ordered Canadian pilots (among others) to carry it out. "In Desperate Battle: Normandy 1944" tells the story of D-Day and the invasion of Normandy from the perspective of the Canadian forces on the ground. Among the most graphic and disturbing sequences in this film are the moments when two retired Canadian generals return to Verrières Ridge, near Caen, where troops from the Royal Highland Regiment of Montreal (the famous Black Watch) were slaughtered on 25 July 1944 (15 of 320 men survived) to retrace the decisions and errors that led to this calamity. There is also a deeply moving visit to the garden of L'Abbé Ardennes, which had been used by Kurt Meyer and the German 12th SS Hitler Youth as their headquarters; it was in this garden that Canadian POWs were abused and murdered in direct contravention of the laws of war set out in the Geneva Conventions. When one of the distinguished, articulate Canadian generals, Jacques Dextrasse's eyes fill with tears at this memory in this place, I find the appeal to my empathy (anger, outrage, grief) very strong. But even here, I believe, we are invited to respond ethically rather than emotionally. Certainly, I am unsettled by the sight of such a man remembering such an event, and I reflect on the reality of war, not on its reputed glory.

Each film is rigorously researched and carefully constructed; the strategies of representation used by the filmmaker and his team are many and complex. Some strategies are more effective than others—more convincing, more compelling, more informative—and some sequences in each film are more successful than others. That said (and allowing for the fact that I am not an expert in film studies), all three films are well done—not superb, not innovative, not prize-winning, but very good.[17] I am grateful to the McKennas for making them. They prompt me to question and reflect upon what I thought I knew about the war much more than other Canadian documentaries made before or since manage to do. Despite flaws, moments of sentimentality, a few awkward segues, and some clumsy re-enactments, at their best they produce in me some of the same reactions I have watching Andrzej Wajda's *Katyń* or Paul Verhoeven's *Zwartboek*. Through these films my memory is educated. I gain new information about the war, about the stupidity and challenges of actual battle, and about the capacity of those responsible for catastrophes or atrocities to blame others in order to save their reputations or advance their careers. And, yes, blame is laid: laid on the Japanese Imperial Army for its behaviour when it overran Hong Kong; laid on Bomber Harris for ordering the RAF (and RCAF) pilots to bomb German civilians so as "to destroy the will of the German people"; laid on General Guy Simonds for pigheadedly insisting that the Black Watch would advance on Verrières Ridge even when he knew the support plan and advance information were unreliable or simply wrong. We were told by journalists like Matthew Halton reporting on the Normandy invasion, that certain missions were glorious victories when they were not. They were, in fact, viciously fought, deadly, and hard-won at enormous cost (when they were won) to the Allies, the Germans, and French civilians in ancient cities like Caen, which was reduced to rubble but achieved no military objective.

Without undertaking a close analysis of film conventions, I want nonetheless to describe some of the strategies used in these films and consider their purpose. All three are documentaries, with elements of docudrama, and Terence McKenna explains at the beginning of each that what we are about to see is a "true story." Audience viewers are positioned as secondary witnesses to the truth depicted in narrative and images before them. They see and hear actors who represent actual soldiers, either by addressing them directly as the camera closes in on a face, or in scenes of preparation and battle re-enactment. One example of this re-enactment takes place when the men from the Black Watch of 1990 recreate what happened on 25 July 1944. Both categories of performance are presented, *in colour*, as occurring in the present; they are clearly contemporary reconstructions of past people and events. When an actor speaks, he performs the actual words of the soldier, taken from diaries or letters, in lines selected by the McKennas to serve the plot. Sometimes these performances are superb; sometimes they are contrived and awkward. Nicholas Campbell creates a fine portrait of a self-confident, superior and cold, Guy Simonds, and Graeme Campbell creates a thoroughly repugnant Arthur Harris. Archival photographs and jerky archival film footage, both of course in black and white, are interwoven with the contemporary scenes shot in colour. Music is heard throughout each film; it is an important element to which I will return. *Matériel* from the wars is featured—actual Lancaster planes, Sherman tanks, which are compared with the more powerful German Panzers, bombs, artillery, and other gear. The intention here is obvious: authenticity; we are looking at the *real things*. Juxtaposed with this pastness are the present aspects of the storytelling conveyed by veterans, not by actors. Within each film, two Canadian veterans return to the sites of their war experiences in order to remember, to describe their memories, and to discuss the past with each other while the cameras roll and we listen in.

In "Savage Christmas" the two men are Bob Clayton and Bob Manchester. Both were sergeants in Hong Kong, both were wounded, captured, interned for years in Japanese POW camps, and both survived. Mr. Clayton (just nineteen at the start of his tour of duty) is so deeply moved by his memories of the rape and murder of the nurses and the other atrocities committed in St. Stephen's Hospital that he becomes speechless and the camera turns away from him. Later he refuses to meet with Japanese veterans, at least one of whom was present during the St. Stephen's horror. The two veteran bomber pilots in "Death by Moonlight" are Doug Harvey and Ken Brown; Harvey joined the RCAF at nineteen, Brown at twenty. Harvey flew thirty missions over Germany in air battles that killed or injured one in every three air crews. Brown took part in the Allied attempt in 1943 to destroy dams essential to German war industries, a type of mission made famous in the 1955 film *The Dam Busters.*[18] Harvey and Brown reminisce about their missions and the suspicions they shared with fellow pilots and crews that the real statistics on fatalities were hidden from them and the public or the fact that the dam-busting raid Brown flew (to bomb the massive concrete and earthen work Sorpe dam) was a total failure, despite the hoopla in the British and Canadian press. Harvey and Brown are the two veterans who return to Hamburg in the early 1990s to meet with German survivors of "Operation Gomorrah," the code name for the destruction of Hamburg on 24 July 1943. But since the representation of this bombing mission became the veritable eye of the storm of protest against *The Valour and the Horror,* I want to examine it more closely in the context of the Senate inquiry into the film. Our veteran guides through "In Desperate Battle," which follows Canadian troops from Juno Beach to Verrières Ridge and Caen, are Radley Walters and Jacques Dextrasse, both of whom became decorated generals by war's end. Walters commanded a tank regiment; Dextrasse, just nineteen when he joined the Fusiliers Mont-Royal, would end an illustrious military career as chief of defence staff in Ottawa.

Of the six veterans who return, remember, and walk the viewer through the past, so to speak, Dextrasse is the most impressive. He is articulate, eloquent, wise, courageous and frank; he legitimates *The Valour and the Horror* through his participation. When he is moved to tears by an eyewitness account of the fate of Canadian POWs at L'Abbé Ardennes, when he speaks of his simple faith, when he admits that

Canadian troops also broke the Geneva Convention on the treatment of prisoners, when he describes his conviction that Hitler and the Nazis had to be stopped, and when he stands beside the grave of a sixteen-year-old soldier in the cemetery at Verrières and expresses his regret that such sacrifices are not known at home—I agree with, respect, and believe him. It is hard to imagine a more compelling spokesman for the values of democracy or a more sane judge of the terrible cost and horror of war than this man. I find it very difficult to understand how any viewer could think that Canadian soldiers were portrayed negatively, let alone as war criminals, in these films. But that is what some viewers alleged.





Reactions to music will differ immensely among listeners, and music used as background scores in films can be bland, sentimental, or very powerful. Music is always integral to a well-constructed film; it is part of the film vocabulary, embedded in and helping to shape the meaning of the narrative. Just as the voice-over narration by Terence McKenna carries the verbal through line of the historical sequence of events (identifying where we are, when, and who we see before us), so too does the music inform our ears with replays of popular tunes from the war, snippets of marching bands, and two key intertexts from classical music: Gabriel Fauré's *Requiem in D minor, Opus 48* and Ludwig von Beethoven's *Moonlight Sonata*. The popular songs take us back in time, even when they are performed by actors re-enacting life during the war; the marching bands and other music accompanying archival film footage and newsreel clips contrast with the recreated, enacted, past by signifying a past reality—and apparent factuality—of war. The classical music, however, performs a different and distinct function. Beethoven's *Moonlight Sonata*, with its slow, haunting opening chords in C sharp minor, is first played for us by the actor performing the role of a young French-Canadian officer. This man plays the piano for his hosts and fellow Canadians in the home of a wealthy, rather superior, British family. He suggests that these British are surprised by the talent and sophistication of a mere colonial. However, the gentle mood established by this music and the man's remembered performance, contrasts sharply—shockingly, in fact—with the repetition of this music as the RAF squadrons approach German cities at night, under moonlight, for their bombing raids. Peace abuts on war, beauty is threatened by appalling ugliness, life and creativity are pushed aside by the deathscapes of bombed buildings and charred bodies, the core values of civilization symbolized by Beethoven's music struggle for time and space in our minds with the barbarism of total war. And we are, surely, encouraged to think about such incommensurate experiences, to prefer one over the other.

The music that binds the entire three-part series and five hours of viewing together is the majestic *Requiem*.[19] We hear this at the start of each film. It returns and returns during each. And it swells over the final moments of "In Desperate Battle." Like the jovial, ironic war songs, or even like the playing of the sonata, introduced and performed for us by the young soldier/actor, the *Requiem* relies on the human voice singing the words from the mass for the dead. It voices a prayer for the dead and a lament for the living. It haunts the memory long after the films are over, and this haunting is a deliberate effect of the repetition, the return, over and over, to this music through the films. When I listen to this music now, I hear it as integral to *The Valour and the Horror*. When I review or remember the films now, this music saturates the story. By listening, remembering, being haunted, I pay attention and think. This music, like the films it inhabits, neither exalts war or warriors nor promises forgiveness or restitution. Instead, it serves to contextualize and humanize what was, with the Second World War, the most dehumanizing and evil of modern wars.

When the newly formed Senate Subcommittee on Veterans Affairs, chaired by Senator Jack Marshall, decided to investigate *The Valour and the Horror* in April 1992, it did so in response to loud complaints by veterans, some of whom had watched the January broadcast of the series. According to the committee report, their decision quickly "became almost as controversial as the film series itself" (3). Veterans argued that Canadian soldiers and pilots had been maligned and that the films were vitiated by errors of fact and a slanted, anti-military perspective. Critics of the subcommittee's decision saw the investigation as "an attack on freedom of expression" and a serious breach in the sacrosanct "arms-length relationship which exists between the Government and cultural agencies" (3). The Senate, however, went ahead with their investigation.

They set themselves three objectives: to allow veterans and their organizations a forum (something they already had in the media just like all citizens) in which to respond to "what they consider to have been a public, unfair and malicious slander of their conduct"; to listen to specialists in the military history of Canadians in the war and ascertain their views on the "historical methodology and merit" of the series; and, finally, "to inquire into the roles played by two public bodies, the National Film Board and the Canadian Broadcasting Corporation, in the conception, production, financing and decision to air as a documentary, a highly interpretive film series on a historical subject" (3). The key words in this third objective are "documentary," "interpretive," and "historical subject." And the claim behind these words is that history must not be touched by those who approach it interpretively while employing the tools of documentary. Only certain individuals (professional military historians?) have the right to write about a subject like the Second World War. No mention is made in the report of an effort to assess the artistic methodology and merit of the series. And the reason for this strategic oversight goes right back to the McKennas' claim in each film that they bring us true stories: "There is no fiction."

Given these objectives and the claims behind them, the findings of the subcommittee in its published report are predictable. The "authenticity" of the depictions was attacked, especially for "Death by Moonlight" and, to a lesser degree for "In Desperate Battle." The committee concluded that a "grave injustice" was perpetrated on veterans, that only professional historians were capable of assessing the value of such films—not "the arts and entertainment columnists" (44), and that the CBC failed in its responsibility to the Canadian taxpayer to properly vet and control the materials it commissions and broadcasts. The McKennas were accused of being anti-war, anti-British, and anti-establishment (26). On the one hand, concerns were expressed that "unsophisticated viewers" (presumably students too young to know better and adults too naïve to think critically) would believe Canada was "a nation of incompetents and murderers" (10). On the other hand, the inquiry itself would, some argued, "put a chill in the creative air" (35) and end up being, in historian Michael Bliss's word, an "inquisition."[20]





One of those who publicly protested the investigation of *The Valour and the Horror*, one of those lumped under the dismissive designation of "arts and entertainment columnists," was Timothy Findley, who called the films "brilliant" and reminded his readers that the series was painstakingly researched and "given the full support of the Chief of Defence Staff [Jacques Dextrasse]" (*Journeyman* 170).[21] And he went further: "It is an entirely responsible, fully documented and laudable piece of journalism—a landmark for which the majority of Canadians are grateful. If it were not controversial, it would be worthless; it would be mere propaganda. Propaganda, however, is what its opponents would have it be. Not to put too fine a point on it, they would prefer that it had lied. They object to its truths" (170). The problem, as Findley understood, was a battle over truth and lies and over whose version of the Truth must win the battle. Worse still, the battle itself was fought within the legitimating chambers of the Senate, instead of through the "normal" democratic process of "refutations and arguments carried out in public forums" (170). Rather than debate the pros and cons, opponents "have chosen" to censor the films and silence the McKennas (170), so that, as Findley puts it, Canadians can go on believing the lie that they "meant well" (171).

Among the recommendations submitted in the report are that "a disclaimer be boldly displayed" (60) on all those cassettes already distributed to the public to warn them that the treatment of the war in those films is only partly factual, represents the sole views of the filmmakers, and that military historians do not endorse these views and partial facts. Furthermore, the CBC is told that it must "fulfill its promise to the Canadian public not to rebroadcast *The Valour and the Horror*...in its original form" (60). The committee also recommends that a pamphlet be prepared, with assistance from a military historian, "which points out the inaccuracies and biases" (60) of the series, and that a "new group of film-makers [be asked] to produce another documentary on Canada's experience in the Second World War" (60).[22] An aspect of the films that seems to have especially rankled opponents, and that the subcommittee stressed, was the use of actors in dramatic sequences when films are representing important topics like war. Battle re-enactments were not singled out; presumably that form of performance was acceptable. But actors creating the characters of Bomber Harris or Guy Simonds was deemed unacceptable. Consequently, the committee recommended that in all future government-funded documentaries, experts be relied on to provide "accuracy and balance" and that dramatization never be used.





In their introductory chapter to *The Politics of War Memory and Commemoration* (Ashplant, Dawson, and Roper, 3–85), the co-editors of the volume describe the current proliferation of interest in the two world wars and locate the roots of this interest in a so-called "anniversary boom" (4) and in the "unresolved legacy of the Nazi war of national expansion and ethnic 'purification'" (5), which fuels contemporary wars. They also call for the enhancement of ways in which the wars are remembered so as to integrate oral history and life story methods, and to move beyond national narratives that idealize soldiers and marginalize non-combatants, especially women (21–22). However, they sound a warning about the uncritical reliance on personal experience or on victims' stories because such stories carry an immense emotional power that is difficult to manage and can distort complex issues. This risk is, in part, what LaCapra addresses when he calls for narratives—historical and artistic—to resist the indulgence in empathy and the temptation to offer uplifting resolutions to experiences that exceed such resolution. LaCapra describes empathic unsettlement as the best response such narratives can aim for, and I have returned to this concept frequently in my discussion because I agree and see most of my texts inviting just such a response.

Unfortunately, Ashplant, Dawson, and Roper do not analyze the arts per se or attempt to draw distinctions and connections between non-artistic and artistic modes of commemoration. The title of their volume, however, is a forceful reminder that remembering war is political, and the furor over *The Valour and the Horror*, the Senate report, and the consequences of their recommendations exposes the dangerous reality of this politics. One side sought to control the story by claiming access to objective Truth and silencing all dissenting voices; the other side sought to problematize such claims and absolutes by giving voice to a range of life stories, personal experiences, and relative truths. The end result was certainly moving, but did the mobilization of empathy spill over into emotional excess and subjective distortion?

That *The Valour and the Horror* has weaknesses and flaws is clear. It pays scant attention to the causes of the war, ignores the home front, marginalizes and trivializes women, and forgets the contributions made by many groups except for white anglophone and francophone men. But it also contributes enormously to a broad understanding of war in general and of Canadians in the Second World War in particular. Instead of seeing veterans portrayed as incompetent murderers, I see them portrayed as honest, fair-minded, intelligent people who bear considerable trauma, and as models of what Jacques Dextrasse calls moral courage. The men I refer to are primarily the six veterans who walk me through their remembered landscapes, now peaceful and almost beyond recognition, of the war.

Since "Death by Moonlight" and its depiction of Sir Arthur Harris and the bombing of Hamburg drew the most intense criticism, let me consider one scene from that film to argue my response to the entire series. Towards the end of the film, Brown and Harvey revisit Hamburg and they meet with two women, elderly like themselves, who survived the incendiaries that burned what bombs did not destroy. These four people stand quietly, facing each other. The camera moves in on their faces in turn. One woman, sixteen at the time, recalls seeing a child and mother melted into the asphalt of the road and she asks the men what they think. They reply by saying that as pilots they could not see what took place on the ground and were not informed by those in command who should have known. And they reflect on their own ages, barely out of their teens, at the time. They insist, gently, that the Nazis had to be stopped. There are no accusations made, no apologies asked for or given. No one assumes guilt or asks for forgiveness. Instead, the second woman takes Brown's hand, he holds her hand with both of his, they look at each other and agree in a few words that this is enough—to be able to stand together, listen to one another, and remember. No one weeps. To do more would be wrong. Reparation is beside the point.





This brief scene captures for me the ideal of empathic unsettlement. The result of this scene is an enhanced understanding. The response to it can only be an ethical one because it captures our acknowledgement of what, as Atwood says, we do to others and not just what others have done to us (see page 3). How does one evaluate such a moment? By falling back on statistics, on obeying orders, on German atrocities? And who is best equipped to interpret this moment? McKenna, thankfully, is quiet and I can interpret it for myself. I see two truly exceptional men remembering and two brave women refusing to claim victimization. The scene embodies, for me, the central meaning and purpose of the series. We are informed about the war, its aftermath, and aspects of Canadian participation, and we come to appreciate what words like valour and horror convey. Our memories are educated, not only about facts and dates, but also about human nature. Educating memory is never neutral, never not political, but in these films artists dare to supplement what is—and is not—revealed in the history books by the experts by integrating personal perspectives, voice, and stories into their narrative.

Compared with *The Valour and the Horror, Return to Ortona* is a short, simple, non-interpretive documentary. It runs for twenty-six minutes and was prepared by the CBC and distributed in 2001 as a special addition to the series *Canada: A People's History*.[23] The storyline is also simple: a small group of Canadian veterans of the battle to wrest Ortona from the Germans in December 1943—the same battle Charles Comfort witnessed and painted—returns to the Italian city to visit the cemetery and meet with a group of German paratroopers who fought against them in the street-to-street, house-to-house nightmare that was Ortona. They are all elderly men now, in the present filming of their return, but they have all agreed to make this return in the interests of friendship and reconciliation. The word *reconciliation* is frequently repeated in this film.

But *Return to Ortona: A Battlefield Redemption*, as the subtitle describes it, differs from *The Valour and the Horror* in many more important ways than length. There is a narrator, present through a voice-over, who leads us through events, from the opening sequence on a bus as the "Canadian boys" arrive in Ortona to the closing moments when the veterans visit the cemetery and this narrator walks on a street in the contemporary, rebuilt city and identifies himself. The voice we have been listening to belongs to David Halton, son of Matthew Halton, the Canadian reporter who covered the war and reported on major battles in which Canadians fought—Dieppe, Ortona, the invasion of Normandy, the liberation of Holland. Matthew Halton is the reporter identified by the McKennas in *The Valour and the Horror* as not reporting the truth about defeats, casualties, and catastrophes. In *Return to Ortona*, his son describes his father's reports from Ortona and *re-presents* him as heroic, like the soldiers he accompanied. This film does not use actors or re-enactments. Present sequences are in colour and archival footage—used sparingly—is black and white. There is very little music, and the most significant song, introduced late in the film, is "Lili Marlene," sung by Marlene Dietrich. "Silent Night" makes a brief appearance because it was sung at the Christmas 1943 dinner. The primary focus of the film is the old men of 2001 who return, share their memories and a meal, shake hands, and are—so we are led to believe—reconciled. A secondary, less obvious, focus is on the process of reporting. Because David Halton returns to report on this reunion, the act of reporting becomes inseparable from the history of the war and we are encouraged to trust in and accept both the authenticity of this return and the father's original war work. This Halton stands in for and vouches for that one.





Other aspects of this journey back to the past are at least as important as the Halton father and son and the hoped-for reconciliation of old warriors. As David tells us, some of the elderly Canadians are "ready to salute their old enemies," but others are not: some can forgive but not forget. One German veteran, Hugo Bauer, is devastated by this return. Halton describes him as "the most traumatized" of the German vets, and Herr Bauer weeps at the memory of the horror of those days. For him, he explains, Christmas is a hopeless season; he feels dead at that time of year. Once the ice is broken, however, and a celebratory meal is served to commemorate the makeshift Christmas dinner served in 1943, an interesting set of observations surfaces into the main plot of the film. One man who was responsible for shelling a medieval church into rubble to rout the Germans using it explains that at the time the church did not matter: the Germans had to be removed. Now, all these years later, he admits that he has been haunted by the ghosts of that church and of Ortona. By returning he hopes to lay these ghosts. Another Canadian shows off a ring he has kept as a souvenir from the battle only to be told by a German vet that the ring belonged to a German paratrooper. This moment is tense and awkward, and is hastily passed over. What remains unsaid is that the ring became a trophy when it was cut from a dead man's hand. Then one German points out that they were not enemies but opponents, as if that distinction could possibly account for what took place in Ortona. And Halton acknowledges that scores of Italian civilians were killed or left homeless by a battle for a city of "minor strategic value" to both sides.

This film is profoundly moving. As a viewer and secondary witness, I sympathize with these "gentlemen" (another word used frequently). Clearly, they have suffered; they are haunted by Ortona, by what they witnessed, by those they lost, and by things they did. They are brave to make this return journey together, to meet in peace, shake hands, share memories, and break bread. I wish them well and hope this reunion brings them, as individuals, some modicum of peace. But what else can I respond to here and what has been forgotten, passed over, in this attempt to heal old wounds? What, in fact, has happened to history and how does the myth of return, controlled by a carefully staged process of remembering, educate memory? What do we learn from this film or, to put it bluntly, would these men do once more what they did then? I might try to address these questions by pointing to what is left out in the film—the home front, women and children, the reasons for Canadians being in Italy in the first place, the war against fascism and Hitler, the appalling destruction of the city and its historic buildings, and the enormous cost to Italian civilians.[24] Or I might criticize the investment of Halton, the son, in celebrating (restoring?) the reputation of his father, but the bare mention of doubts about this emphasis on father-son loyalty and pride seems disloyal and mean-spirited. Catch-22. What I fall back on then, indeed what most perplexes me, is the notion of return itself.

*Return to Ortona* is not about the past as such, let alone the Second World War; it is about "old warriors" returning to the site of their former battle, to their remembered landscape. Returning physically invites further remembering but shapes, focuses, and restricts the memories it elicits, blocking some and allowing others. Returning is invested with commemorative associations of pilgrimage, religious ritual, and thus of worship and forgiveness—the film's subtitle is not an afterthought: *Return to Ortona: A Battlefield Redemption*. Return, enclosed tightly within a frame of anxious arrival and relieved, even jovial, departure, offers closure, a goodbye to all that. Viewers, along with the veterans, can now move on, having buried the past and greeted each other as friends. The horrors of Ortona, of war more generally, can be and have been redeemed, the narrative circle, completed. There is nothing left to say; no untidy doubts or questions remain to haunt this particular, poignant landscape of memory.

And yet, and yet...my nagging questions persist: what or who has been redeemed? Why is redemption needed or wanted? How has redemption been achieved by this return and by the filming of the return? When I want to remember Ortona, I return to Charles Comfort's *Artist at War* and Mark Zuehlke's *Ortona*, to eyewitnessing and historiography. I am skeptical about redemption and pilgrimage—or redemption by means of pilgrimage—because the former seems irrelevant to the circumstances of Ortona and the latter seems self-indulgent *for me as a secondary witness*. For the viewer, *Return to Ortona* replaces thought, reflection, analysis, and empathic unsettlement with un-self-critical emotion. And yet...I am not able to simply dismiss the reconciliation performed in this film, and I keep in mind the words of one Canadian veteran (a pastor with the "Van Doos") who forgives but does not forget. Despite my grave misgivings about this film and my skepticism about the unexamined claims it makes for reconciliation, redemption, and peace, it is gratifying to watch these men reach out to each other and remember. Perhaps younger Canadian viewers will be encouraged to reflect upon how war has damaged and haunted these men. Perhaps they will take pride in the fact that the initiative to invite the surviving German paratroopers to meet them in a now peaceful, rebuilt Ortona, was Canadian. Perhaps they will understand that this distant place in a foreign country holds significant value in our landscape of memory, that it is, in a sense, part of Canada's story. Perhaps they will endorse this demonstration of reaching out across an abyss of memory, history, language and background, as a Canadian value. Perhaps.

If all I had to work with was this film, however, or the CBC series *Canada: A People's History*, to which this film serves as a kind of coda, I would lack an essential critical context within which to remember Ortona or the war. Compared with the treatment of the war in *The Valour and the Horror* or the Italian campaign in *Artist at War*, *Return to Ortona* provides a sanitized, narrow focus on history and it privileges one particular set of memories and one way of remembering over others. To think back over the texts I have examined in these chapters is to realize that in most of them the people (the characters) return—for example, Jakob and Ben in *Fugitive Pieces*, the Dene in *Burning Vision*, Uncle and Naomi in *Obasan*, Lisa Appignanesi in *Losing the Dead*, each set of veterans in *The Valour and the Horror*, but especially Doug Harvey and Ken Brown in "Death by Moonlight." Indeed, I would say that the process of returning—to the past, to memories, to the streets, houses, cemeteries, to the archives and fragments and testimonies that Robert Ross's biographer works with—structures these narratives and gives them meaning. Not redemption, not peace, not necessarily or always reconciliation, but meaning.

To educate memory, in the best sense of the word educate, we need as many perspectives and as many artistic representations of returning to momentous events, which determine our lives, as possible. Simply to document, as if the documentary act were not itself a fiction, man-made, created from experiences, crumbling archival fragments, and personal memories, is not enough. We must interpret the past, weigh what happened, reconsider, listen, bear secondary witness. Expanding cultural memory to establish a flourishing landscape of memory constitutes an ethical process, not a fact-gathering one. If we believe that the Second World War was a *good* war, then we cannot shy away from embracing and discussing what we did and why.

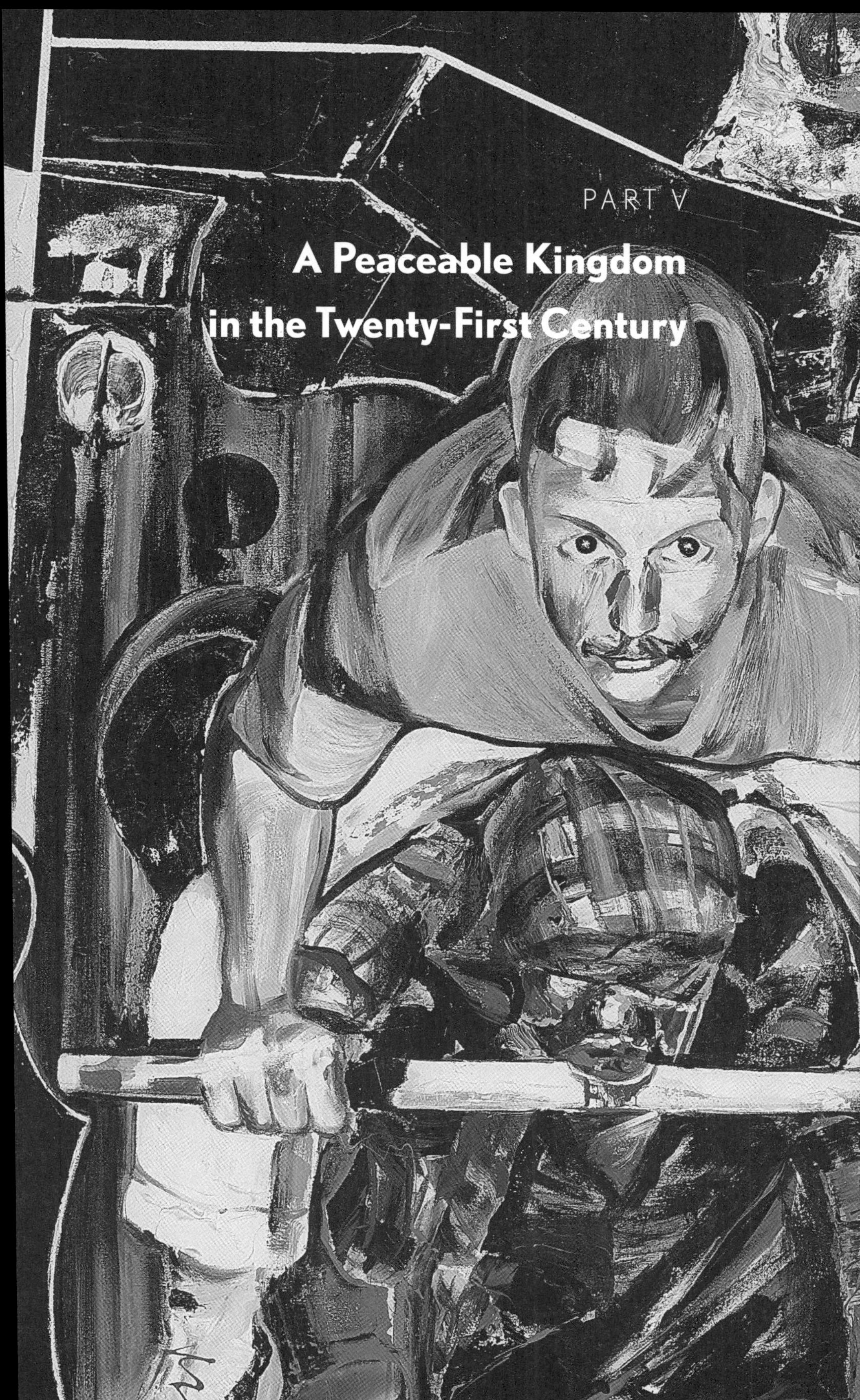

PART V

# A Peaceable Kingdom in the Twenty-First Century

So why have I written this?
To sound a warning?
To suggest that if such things
happen in one civilized country,
they may happen in others?
But thousands have sounded
the same warning before me.



**Hugh MacLennan**

*Voices in Time*, 294

My FIRST act of revolution:
to remember.



**Judith Thompson**

*Such Creatures*, 16

The past can only be managed.
With remembrance.
With accountability.
With justice—however frail,
however inadequate,
however imperfect.



**Erna Paris**

*Long Shadows: Truth, Lies, and History*, 464

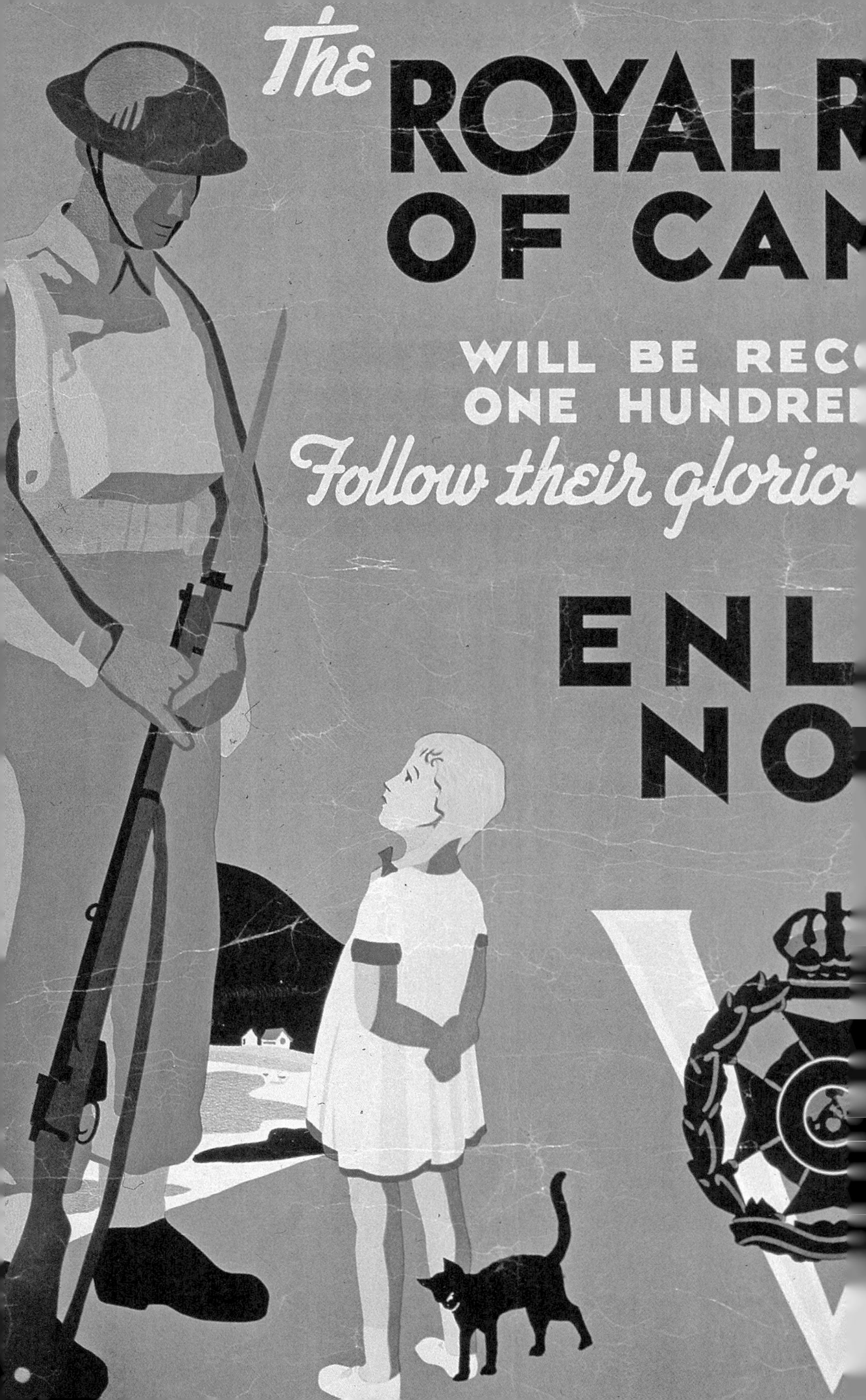
The
ROYAL R
OF CAN
WILL BE REC
ONE HUNDRE
Follow their glorio
ENL
NO

# 10
# Remembering War; Finding Peace?

## Some Conclusions



ALTHOUGH MOST of my attention in previous chapters was devoted to work produced in the last century, I have, from time to time, come forward beyond my 2007 end date as I follow writers and artists into the present. I have done this for several reasons. As of 2011 and the withdrawal of Canadian troops from Afghanistan, that war continues and new wars erupt in the Middle East. The facts and realities of past and current wars are still with Canada and the international community. It should not be surprising, then, that scholars, artists, and journalists continue to explore the subject of war, to ask what has been learned, and to reflect upon the past. As Ian McKay and Jamie Swift point out in *Warrior Nation* (11–15), official Canadian history today celebrates war *heroes* for their valour and sacrifice; new immigrants taking their citizenship oaths are schooled, as never before, in our military past; appeals are made to veterans of the Second World

War to share their memories while they can, and veterans' obituaries or interviews with elderly veterans appear with haunting regularity.

Not long ago, my attention was caught by a full-page obituary for William Allister, artist and veteran, who died at eighty-nine in 2008. Allister survived forty-four months in a Japanese POW camp, and after the war he became an artist dedicated to painting, as he put it, "towards peace."[1] More recently, on 9 August 2010, the CBC's *The National* rebroadcast a 1998 interview with another POW, John Ford, who returned to the camp near Nagasaki to remember the "poor souls" held in the camp with him *and* the civilian victims of Nagasaki who were killed by the bomb. The war is "never over" for him, he explains, and he hopes nothing like the camps or the bombs will happen again. Such responses represent one kind of reaction to war and they are a welcome antidote to spectacles like Steven Spielberg and Tom Hanks's television mini-series (also screened in Canada) *The Pacific*, which portrays the American war in the Pacific with a level of violence, barbarism, and savagery unrivalled by earlier combat films. Responses by men like Allister and Ford also constitute a more honest, flexible reaction to Canada's military history than the angry reaction, by military mothers, to a recent anti-war video; these mothers forced the filmmakers to erase the script's reference to cannon fodder and then called for the video to be banned from the Internet.[2] Other recent artistic productions are more complex—and more ambivalent, if not directly critical—in their representations of war. New British works like the play *War Horse* and P.J. Harvey's album *Let England Shake* return to the Great War to remind viewers and listeners about that terrible past in the context of twenty-first-century war and terror. And the 2008 Dutch film *Winter in Wartime* (*Oorlogswinter*) portrays life in a Dutch town under the Nazis from the rare perspective of a thirteen-year-old boy and as anything but heroic.[3] Between October 2010 and February 2011, Berlin's Deutsches Historisches Museum mounted the controversial and challenging exhibition *Hitler und die Deutschen: Volksgemeinschaft und Verbrechen* (*Hitler and the Germans: Nation and Crime*) in an effort to contextualize the rise of Nazism through a retrospective look at the arts, media, photography, and memorabilia of the period and to expose the lure of this past for neo-Nazis.

Contemporary Canadians also return to the First World War in their efforts to remember, understand, and honour—if not precisely to celebrate—those who fought or lived through a war we have learned to see as central to a history of the nation. Kenneth Brown's play trilogy "Spiral Dive," which premiered in Edmonton in January 2011, is just one example of the ongoing obsession with the two world wars. Inspired by the playwright's childhood memories of elderly (and traumatized) men around him and by the stories his grandfather told about Vimy and its aftermath, the trilogy is an epic dramatization of Canadians at war.[4] Sally Stubbs's play, *Herr Beckmann's People*, presents the Second World War from a fairly unique perspective—at least, as regards a Canadian representation of the war. The chief protagonist, Anna Epp, a German-Canadian artist living in British Columbia, returns to postwar Germany in 1969 to see her aging mother, a former concert pianist, and her dying brother. Her return not only brings her face to face with the hardships endured by German civilians during and after the war but it also forces her and her mother to confront their dead husband and father's collaboration with the Nazis and her mother's refusal to leave Germany because it might jeopardize her career. Anna realizes that no one can claim the high road of innocence during such times and that she cannot escape or easily reject the family's past by immigrating to Canada. Like so many other characters in the plays, novels, and films I have considered, Anna's ghosts live on in war's aftermath and want their stories told.

Canadian scholars also keep exploring the military past to reassess what happened, analyze new information, and debate received truths. Jean-Louis Cohen's *Architecture in Uniform: Designing and Building for the Second World War* (2011), the comprehensive catalogue accompanying the Canadian Centre for Architecture's April to September 2011 exhibition, is an exhaustive and fascinating exploration of the many ways the war produced contemporary gadgetry, housing, and social engineering. Recent works by authors like Mark Bourrie, Suzanne Evans, Nathan Greenfield, Randall Hansen, Bohdan Kordan, Margaret MacMillan, Jonathan Vance, and Mark Zuehlke further demonstrate the value of remembering and studying the impact of the two wars.

The most interesting (and troubling) study, however, is Susan Fisher's *Boys and Girls in No Man's Land: English-Canadian Children and the First World War* (2011). A moment's reflection on how the home front must have been managed during the two wars is a reminder that children were influenced by the distant conflict. Fathers and older brothers did not come home or, when they did, they were often physically and psychologically damaged. Timothy Findley presents this reality as a child experiences it with stunning clarity in "Stones," the story I discussed in Chapter 8. Iconic posters from both wars are sharp visual reminders of how children were used to boost recruitment: "Daddy, what did YOU do in the Great War?" that little girl asks so innocently, while her brother plays with his toy soldiers at their father's feet, and in "Remember Hong Kong!" a sweet, blonde girl with her cat symbolizes what all good Canadian men must protect from the savage Japanese. Neighbours and friends were plunged into mourning by news arriving in letters; blackout curtains, parades, food stamps, and the collecting of scrap metal were all activities that disrupted a normal childhood routine. What Susan Fisher examines is much more profound and far-reaching. Through her close examination of school curricula and popular children's literature before, during, and after the war, Fisher demonstrates just how pervasive the militaristic message was. Canadian boys were being trained to be soldiers, to think of Empire first and be proud of their Anglo-Saxon ethnicity as superior to all others. They were told that valour and sacrifice for a greater, British ideal was manly and proper. This was the world in which a young man like Findley's Robert Ross grew up. Adults who protested the war and its propaganda were threatened, persecuted, and silenced.[5] In short, boys and girls were brainwashed and exploited at home and at school.

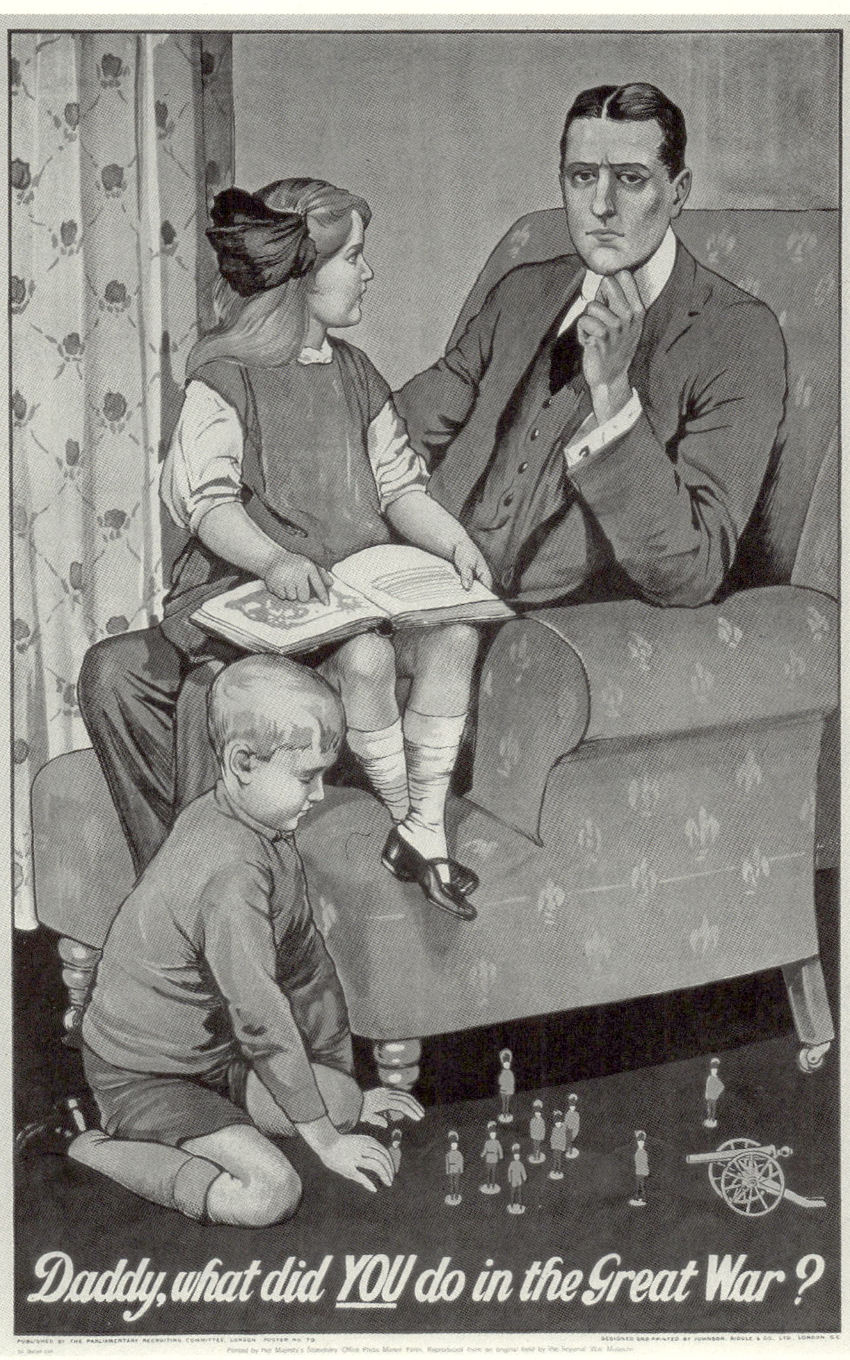


*Pages 453–454: Colourful posters were effective propaganda tools. These two aimed at recruiting men by depicting children's pressure on them. Above: "Daddy, what did* <u>YOU</u> *do in the Great War?"* CWM *#19720028-007. © Canadian War Museum. This famous image aims to shame a father into joining up for the First World War.*

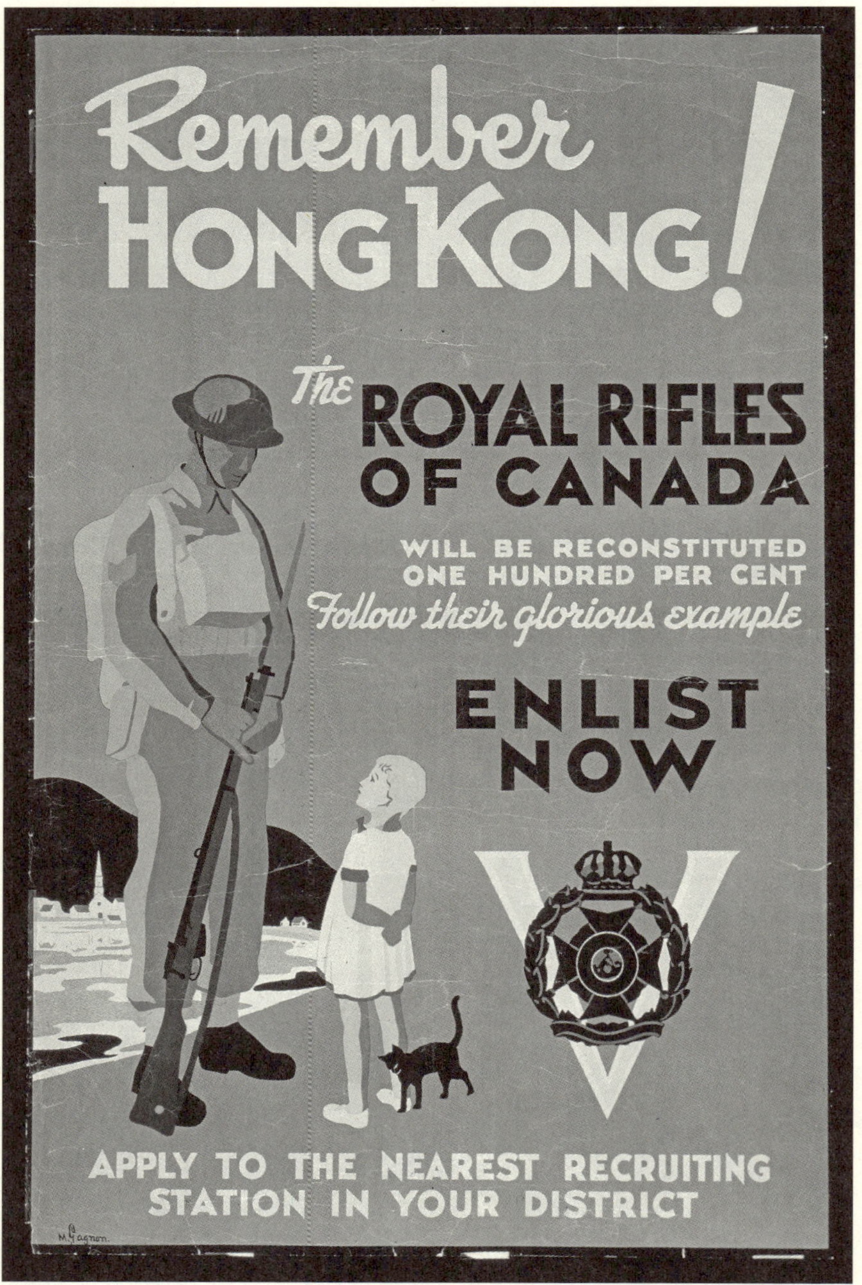


*"Remember Hong Kong!" CWM #19750317-153. © Canadian War Museum. The horror of what happened to Canadian soldiers (and Chinese civilians) when Japan invaded Hong Kong became a rallying cry for recruiting more troops. At stake, or so this image implies, are the pretty blonde children at home.*

However, Fisher does not look exclusively at the past. In her final chapter, she comments on the surge in contemporary Canadian writing about war for children. I have also noted this proliferation of works aimed at young readers, but the long list Fisher provides in her appendix (259–61) is surprising. Although she is careful to stress the differences between this literature and that of the Great War period—today's has less militaristic rhetoric, more realistic portrayal of death and suffering, and greater focus on the individual on both battle and home fronts—the fact remains: we are experiencing a "powerful resurgence of the First World War in the Canadian imagination" (251). To the questions why and why now, Fisher offers some familiar answers: we need to remember those involved or directly connected with the war before they die, and a critical reassessment is increasingly possible with the distance gained as time passes. But she adds to these a possible explanation that I find especially interesting—the place granted the Great War in Canada's "national mythology" as a coming-of-age story. She observes that "to claim descent from the men and women who were part of that struggle is to announce a particular sort of Canadian identity" (253). I would push this observation, with which I agree, further. The Great War has often been remembered and imagined by Canadians, including those writing since 1977, as a unifying myth of the nation and one about which we can and should feel proud. At times of national stress, it is strategically and psychologically useful to turn to such myths of proud national identity, even though, as Fisher makes clear, this can only work for "a particular sort" of Anglo-Canadian identity.

If we are haunted by First World War ghosts, then that haunting is both a blessing and a curse, or so our literature from *The Wars* and *Vimy* to *Mary's Wedding* and *Broken Ground* claims. Findley, Thiessen, Massicotte, and Hodgins all provide us with a vision of the war that locates some hope for the future in the process of cultural remembering of the past, in bearing witness to past actions—at home and abroad—and to listening to the stories (imagined but also based on facts) of individuals who died or who survived the trauma of war to help build a stronger country. The landscape of memory produced by these creative reimaginings of the Great War, while never simply positive or mindlessly celebratory, reveals and underscores qualities of survival, strength in the face of great odds, a capacity to find understanding (if not quite *meaning*) through remembering, and the power to believe, as Mary does in *Mary's Wedding*, in the promise of future peace. There are qualifications aplenty in my last sentence, but I cannot speak as positively about the vision captured by those works that struggle to represent Canada in the Second World War.

Among the many conclusions I draw from the wealth of material contemporary Canadians have produced on both wars since 1977, this distinction between the representation of the two wars is key. Despite criticisms of the rhetoric and lies that seduced young men like Robert Ross into the Great War and the horrors experienced during and after that war, Canadians continue to find much to celebrate in their contribution to that war effort. Deaths on the battlefield were rarely noble—as Vanderhaeghe shows us in *Dancock's Dance*—but Canada did emerge from the war a stronger and more united nation than it had been before the war. Even allowing for the angry resistance of Quebec, a man like Talbot Papineau could be seen as a national hero and a national loss, as Sandra Gwyn reminds us. The aftermath on the home front was clearly difficult and too often poorly managed, but recent works do not avoid, or tidy up, those realities. Hodgins explores the postwar failures of Canadian society as much as the endurance and hope that enabled veterans and their families not just to carry on, but to help build the new nation. Representations of the Second World War, whether because of its greater complexity and mechanization or because it is still too close to the present, are less celebratory and more critical—even accusatory in a play like *Burning Vision*—of Canadian society, the government of the day, and the actions of Canadian troops in specific theatres of war. *We* (Canada as a nation) made some serious mistakes during that war by interning certain groups of citizens, by adopting a tacit (if not overt) policy of anti-Semitism, by hiding the truth about the role Canada played in supplying uranium to the Manhattan Project and refusing responsibility afterwards for the human costs at home, and by attempting to silence filmmakers who dared to consider the possibility that Canadians were involved in bombing civilian targets in Germany. Works like *Obasan*, *None Is Too Many*, *The Ash Garden*, and *The Wreckage*, and the documentary film *The Valour and the Horror* expose attitudes, events, and actions during the war that are less than admirable.





However, if Canadians hope to understand who and where they are in this century, then an honest debate about the past is essential. If the works of art about either war tell us anything, it is this: we must work at remembering so we can create—and continue to create—a landscape of memory that sustains us, that is as alive, as complete, as powerfully informing, and as ongoing as possible. And so, this is one more crucial conclusion I have reached through the course of this study: as Judith Thompson and Erna Paris tell us (see epigraphs to Part V, this volume), *we must remember*. "Can you see me, yet?" Findley's Cassandra asks. Why do I write, if not to warn, MacLennan's narrator in *Voices in Time* asks (see the first epigraph to Part V). Of course, one cannot warn without remembering, and a warning is useless if it is not heard. Therefore, seeing and listening to the voices—so often the ghostly voices of witnesses—is an essential act of participation in the present landscape. And we must try to pay attention with empathic unsettlement, which leads me to another large conclusion I would draw from what the artists give us. As they assume ethical responsibility to the historical past by bearing witness, by imagining characters who bear witness or who are secondary, second-generation witnesses, so we are asked to bear witness to history with empathy, accountability, and remembrance.

Beyond these few large conclusions lie many smaller, specific ones about recurrent symbols and images, about representations of the home front and of children, and the themes, not only of bravery and sacrifice, but also of prejudice, betrayal, and violence. But I do not wish to repeat here the points made in earlier chapters. That Canada remains a society haunted by its war history seems clear. What Canadians do with this haunting, once they acknowledge it, is the basic challenge before all of us. Instead, I prefer to conclude by reconsidering some of the aesthetic and ethical parameters of the artistic representation of war by looking briefly at three post-2007 texts that reimagine the Second World War: *Far to Go*, *Such Creatures*, and *Beatrice & Virgil*. These three works illustrate some of the new and yet familiar directions Canadian writers are exploring as they continue to develop our landscape of memory. To one degree or another, each of these texts, two novels and one play, start where Findley left off with *The Wars*, a work that I see as an absolutely fundamental influence on the later novels and plays. They begin by stressing the importance of individual and cultural memory, and by searching through the remnants of the past—the archive—for answers to questions and more generally for understanding; they all respect the facts of history while creating new, at times surprising or even shocking artistic solutions to Adorno's old question: how does anyone write poetry—make art—after Auschwitz? I might have chosen other examples to conclude with. There is no shortage of material, and it keeps appearing.[6] But these three share much, while being interestingly different and very accomplished, so they provide precisely the textual evidence I watch for and learn from.

The publication in 2010 of Alison Pick's novel *Far to Go* seemed like a gift—a gift to me as I reflected on all the fiction and non-fiction about Canada and the Second World War I had read for this study, and a gift to the future for all readers who want to remember this history and honour those who were lost, murdered, or survived to come to this country. *Far to Go* tells a terrifying and heartbreaking story. It does not have a happy ending. It does not offer absolution, transcendence, or even what I might call hope unless one finds hope, as I do, in the processes of remembering and storytelling. Perhaps this is why the novel received scant attention when it appeared and was ignored when awards were handed out. It is a painful and challenging novel, but it is so beautifully crafted and so honest that I predict it will survive to influence future Canadians' representation of war, of civilians caught up in war and of the Holocaust and its aftermath in Canada.

The title alerts a first-time reader to expect a story about children; as the nursery rhyme tells us, "Thursday's child has far to go." And this story is about children, one little boy in particular, who with other Jewish youngsters was evacuated from Czechoslovakia to the United Kingdom on the Winton *Kindertransport*. Sir Nicholas Winton, a British stockbroker, set up this escape system in 1938 to take children from Prague by train to the coast and then by ship across the Channel to foster homes in Great Britain.[7] Winton saved 669 Jewish Czech children in this way before the last train, which left Prague on 3 September 1939, was turned back because Germany had invaded Poland. All this is fact. The fictional hero of the novel is Joseph (Pepik) Bauer (1933–2008), put on a train at the age of six by his desperate parents, who would never see or hear from their son again. He ended up orphaned in Great Britain. They were murdered in Auschwitz. The fictional woman who finds Joseph decades later in Montreal and tells his story is a retired history professor at Concordia University whose research specialty has been the *Kindertransport*, the history of the Czech and Sudetenland Jews and, more generally, the testimony of Holocaust survivors.[8] Her name is Anneliese (Mueller) Bauer, born in Prague in 1940, and she is Joseph's half-sister, his only surviving relative.

The third essential protagonist in this story/research/history is the reader. Professor Bauer uses that flexible English pronoun *you* in much the same way as Robert Ross's biographer does, except that the "you" in *Far to Go* exists inside and outside the text and is addressed more intimately than is the case with *The Wars*. The elderly Joseph, who is dying of cancer, is her immediate audience and, as we—her larger audience of listening readers—learn at the end, she has created the fictional threads of the story for Joseph in the final months of his life. But, at the beginning of the story's journey, before we appreciate just how far we must all go on the train of memory with this professor, or who the child she loved was, she warns us not to expect redemption or renewed faith in the goodness of humanity: "There are few things in life...that turn out for the best, with real happy endings" (6). And she reminds her readers of something else: "if I've learned one thing over my very long career," she says, "it is this: we research what we recognize. We are looking into our own darkness" (6).





The darkness that Pick and her professor illuminate involves betrayal, anguish, love, terror, unfathomable cruelty, and survival. To throw light on this abyss, she (they) relies on memory, an archive of letters, facts, names, dates, lists, a haunting photograph, and a diamond watch. But the archive can only provide the framework, the bare bones, of the story. To enter the darkness located by research requires imagination and empathic unsettlement. Much of Anneliese Bauer's professional research has involved listening to *and believing* the stories (the testimony—a term she resists) of survivors. She has embraced the role of secondary witness to their witnessing, and from this experience she is able to imagine how to fill in the blanks in Joseph Bauer's story. By imagining his story—not merely his history—she discovers, throws light on, her own life story. She conjures up the thirsty ghosts who haunt her dreams and appear in the margins of her archival research. She brings them alive: Pavel Bauer, Anneliese Bauer, little Pepik, his lost baby sister, and their loving nanny Marta Mueller. In other words, and like many of the novels, stories, and plays I have examined, this one is a fictional auto/biography that produces truths because its creators (Pick, of course, but also Professor Bauer) so powerfully weave together the archive of history with personal memory and imagination. Anneliese (Mueller) Bauer, narrator, Canadian professor, half-Jewish survivor of the Holocaust, can *make up* this story for her newly found half-brother and herself because she respects historical facts but accepts their limitation; she does not allow facts to silence memory and imagination.

As she moves back and forth between the present of 2007–08 in Montreal and the past of 1938–39 in a small town in Sudetenland, and then in Prague, she shifts her attention. In the present she speaks directly to us, never more so than in the closing chapter, which Joseph does not live to hear her read to him. In the past, she disappears as the auto/biographical narrator behind her story, a story, however, that is tied to history by the letters interspersed through it. Each of these *real* documents is dated, addressed, and signed by a Bauer family member or relative, but at the end of each a reader learns of the writer's fate—"Died Birkenau, 1943" (5). One letter, addressed by Mrs. Bauer to her son Pavel (Joseph and Anneliese's father) is heavily redacted; the elderly woman who wrote it also vanished: "Died Birkenau, 1943" (51). The most devastating of these letters, however, is the one Pavel Bauer wrote in June 1939 to his little son, weeks after the child was carried out of his life on the *Kindertransport* and not long before he and his wife were rounded up and sent to the death camps. In it he writes of how they all, including Nanny Marta (the non-Jewish governess), miss him, how they all send kisses and long to hear from him, and of how quiet the house is without him. Pavel writes that he is thinking of setting up Pepik's beloved toy train set once more because "A train will always remind me of you" (271). At the bottom of this letter, which little Pepik never received and Joseph only holds when Anneliese gives him these documents, we read: "(FILE UNDER: Bauer, Pavel. Died Auschwitz, 1944)" (271)—a statement at once factually correct and a lie (Pavel did not simply die; he was murdered) that hides more than it reveals.

*Far to Go* deserves a more thorough analysis than I can give it here. Among its many rich themes—betrayal, search for family and identity, Holocaust aftermath (especially for children), hauntedness, ghosts, and memory, the limits of history, and the power of imagination—witnessing is the one I shall end by stressing. To be sure, this beautiful novel speaks back to *The Wars, Obasan, Fugitive Pieces, Hana's Suitcase,* and even Kreisel's *The Betrayal* in its themes, its images (although no one has imagined the fascination and terror of trains better than Pick), its auto/biographical narration and its respect for historical facts. But the single most telling aspect of this novel, the juncture it produces between aesthetics and ethics, is Professor Bauer's bearing of secondary witness.

In 2008 she is sixty-eight, and after Joseph's death she is once more alone, but it is never too late to gather her own earliest memories of her mother Marta Mueller and speak out about what she knows as a scholar and has witnessed at second hand. In the final, brief, confessional coda to the novel, she tells us how and where she made up parts of the story and she explains why she has offered it to us, her listening readers: "What I'm telling you—haltingly, I realize—is that this is just one way it might have happened. Nothing is certain, save what meets us at the end....It might seem morose to end with the dead, but I am thinking of posterity. I don't have to tell you the reason for this. Soon there'll be nobody left to remember" (308). Nobody, that is, except us. As we run our eyes down the final list of names with their relentless death dates—1943, 1942, 1941, 1943...43...43...(309)—we must bear witness to the expanding landscape of memory *gifted* to us by this Canadian writer and her professorial witness.

Judith Thompson has never hesitated to confront the most difficult of subjects in her plays. From *The Crackwalker* (1980) and *Lion in the Streets* (1991) to *Palace of the End* (2008), she has put courageous, troubled women facing violence on the streets at home or war and terrorism abroad on the stage to remind her audiences of harsh realities we might prefer to ignore.[9] For example, that our capacity for sadistic cruelty, like our need to give and receive love, is not confined to one class of people or to foreigners beyond our borders, and that Canada is in no way immune to prejudice and violence, whether these aspects of life reach us through the media, through the haunted lives of refugees from war seeking peace and safety here, or through the aftermath of our home-grown history. Thompson is by no means the only contemporary Canadian playwright to address issues raised by recent wars. Plays like *The Monument*, *Incendies* (*Scorched*), and *A Line in the Sand* come immediately to mind. In *Such Creatures* (2010), however, she has attempted something quite daring (especially for a non-Jew and a non-survivor)—not simply to juxtapose but to *relate* the Holocaust to school gang wars that erupt on Canadian city streets. I am not certain that she succeeds in this ambitious attempt, but I am certain that *Such Creatures* is an important play, worthy of serious attention. I also believe that it represents one of the ways in which twenty-first-century Canadians—those whom Pick's Professor Bauer realizes may easily forget the Holocaust when all the survivors and their children have died—will reimagine the Second World War and their responsibility to the past.

*Such Creatures*, which premiered at Theatre Passe Muraille in January 2010 and was published later that year, is a short two-hander. Only two characters appear on a basic, flexible set that suggests a Toronto "*inner-city park* [with] *high-rises*" that can be "*transformed into elements...found in a concentration camp*" (3). Blandy, whose full name is Bernadette, is a mixed-race teenager from a broken and abusive home in the Vaughn and St. Clair area of Toronto. She finds her only comfort (an illusion as it turns out) in hoping she belongs to a gang of tough girls who would never betray her. Sorele is a Canadian Jew of Polish ancestry (a woman who reminds me of the Polish-Canadian survivor Anna Heilman),[10] who returns to Auschwitz to mark the fortieth anniversary of her liberation by the Russians in January 1945. She was thirteen when transported to the extermination camp, and she survived until her rescue two years later, at which point she weighed sixty-three pounds, had lost her hair and teeth, and no longer looked alive. She was, then, the age that Blandy is now in the present of the play. But what else, beside gender and age, could these two possibly have in common? What could they conceivably say, or give, to one another? In 1985 Sorele is a middle-aged woman with cancer and a memory full of ghosts. By comparison, Blandy has barely lived.

Thompson slowly establishes several connections between the two as each delivers her separate opening monologue. Chief among these connections is their performances in school productions of Shakespeare. After much swearing and sarcastic resistance, Blandy agrees to play the role of Hamlet (she sneers that no boy would act in such a thing because it is “so friggin’ gay” [5]) only to find that she “gets” Hamlet, his isolation, his problems with parents, his misery and self-doubt, his rage; her “backstory” resembles his—or so she believes (9). Sorele had played the role of Miranda in *The Tempest* just before being rounded up and sent to the death camp.[11] Sorele remembers this happier time in her Warsaw school and she still recalls the lines from the play that were so appropriate during her incarceration. Auschwitz was a terrifying island ruled by a monstrous Prospero and she, like the other Jewish girls in her cell, were reduced to the condition of Caliban. However, remembering the play, both its subject and the happy normalcy of a school production, helped her to survive then and restores her desire to live now: “I had to conjure my world in my mind, my island, the real true world, and I would do that by Remembering.... My FIRST act of revolution: to remember” (16).

Thompson gradually introduces phrases and images that further link her two women. Both use positive memories to sustain them and to fight back against oppression and violence. Blandy clings to the memory of her loving grandmother and, in the slang of her time and place, insists that she is “not gonna be some frickin’ rabbit sittin’ in a cage waiting to be cooked” (17). Sorele recalls vividly her rejection of the Nazi reduction of her and the other girls to bare life: “Wait here, cockroaches,” the SS guards shouted, “by night you will be ash” (26), but the girls refused to obey the order to beat one of their group. They refused and retained their humanity and loyalty. She also remembers and recounts her role in the historic 1944 Auschwitz uprising that climaxed with the blowing up of a crematorium: “While the SS were running around like chickens, we threw the grenades and bombs we had made at the crematoria. Crematorium FOUR was blown up. DESTROYED. Thousands and thousands of lives spared because of us. FIVE not-so-silly teenaged girls” (33).[12] Both women are haunted—Blandy by the ghosts of her abusive father and drug-addicted mother, and Sorele by the ghosts of those who did not survive Auschwitz, most importantly her sister. Each describes her hope that a miracle will take place to inspire, sustain, and rescue her.

Although the play begins with separate monologues, the two voices and stories gradually interrupt and complement each other until a verbal counterpoint emerges and they finally interact physically and speak the closing line of the play together. Sorele has found the strength to continue her fight with cancer by remembering the horror she survived as a girl and the inspiring courage of her sister who slashed the throat of an SS man with a hidden blade as he prepared to hang her. While Blandy waits for the approaching gang to attack her, she *"assumes the voice of Sorele's sister"* (48) to shout that the SS will die like cockroaches but she will die with dignity: "You can never touch our souls!" she cries (48). Blandy is then savagely beaten by the gang and left in a heap when the girls run away, but Sorele goes to her aid as the fifteen-year-old she once was by stepping through the barriers of time and space that separate them to comfort Blandy. The stage instructions make this moment of performance dramatic and clear: "*They help each other up,* SORELE *becoming her fifty-five-year-old self. They look at each other,*" and say together: "We defy augury" (49). Sorele has not only remembered her survival of Auschwitz but has summoned the strength she discovered there in human loyalty, the refusal to betray others, and the defiant courage of her murdered sister, to help Blandy in the present.

Whether or not Thompson's interweaving of a story of Holocaust survival with the need to survive the war on contemporary inner-city Toronto streets is entirely convincing or even, some might say appropriate—can one equate Auschwitz with urban gang violence in Canada?—her ethical point rings true. Remembering empowers one to resist oppression, violence, and degradation; it helps a person overcome the dehumanization inflicted on those classified as *other* and persecuted. One can, and must, Thompson tells her audiences, learn from the past, especially a past as haunting and terrible as the

Holocaust. We must never forget or participate in such crimes. Like Sorele and Blandy, we can celebrate a shared humanity. Perhaps the great distance in time and experience that separates these two women is part of Thompson's strategy, after all, because the greater the difference the easier it is to see another as other. To overcome such distinctions is part of their triumph.

If it is true that "we research what we recognize" as "our own darkness" (*Far to Go* 6), then in *Such Creatures* Thompson has probed that darkness and insisted that it is neither over and done with nor safely *over there* in someone else's country. Canada, she tells us, cannot be a peaceable kingdom unless its citizens *know* that darkness, see it for what it is and make room for it in a collective landscape of memory. We must learn to recognize hatred, prejudice, and ignorance and deal with them through memory, empathic unsettlement and, like Sorele with Blandy, direct action. Sorele is a fictional witness to atrocity; so is Blandy. Are they so different after all? And is Canada really a Never-Never Land without thirsty ghosts, where darkness never existed, and such evils as anti-Semitism never surface? Judith Thompson's answer is no. Her characters in *Such Creatures* are like Cassandra in *Can You See Me Yet?* warning us, imploring us to listen. By bringing the memories of a Holocaust survivor on to contemporary Toronto streets and stages (and to other cities and theatres as the play travels), Thompson introduces new voices into a human and specifically twenty-first-century Canadian history.

In his novel *Beatrice & Virgil* Yann Martel pursues a somewhat different path into the nightmare of the Second World War that nonetheless serves to keep memory and the lessons of Holocaust survival alive. The novel opens with an almost essay-like reflection upon the question that drives the entire narrative: how does a twenty-first-century writer—specifically, Canadian writer Henry L'Hôte—tell a story about the Holocaust? As the narrator tells us, Henry is working on his third novel after the great success of his second, but his publisher and agent have doubts. This third novel is rather unusual. It is about the Holocaust and it is in two distinct parts—a fiction and an essay. Henry wants it published as a flip book, "a book with two sets of distinct pages that are attached to a common spine upside down and back-to-back to each other" (6). The cover would be the same on the front and the back, with one side upside down—or so he imagines. And Henry has clear, rational reasons for wanting his flip book: his fiction and non-fiction are intimately related; one is not more important or truthful than the other. Henry rejects the notion that fiction lies and non-fiction tells the truth.

When I picked up *Beatrice & Virgil* for the first time I was surprised because the front and back covers on the dust jacket are almost identical except that one is upside down and is marred by an ugly black-and-white box with the bar code and the word "FICTION." Am I holding in my hands the very book that this fictional Henry has written? Is Henry the real name (or the pen name) for Yann Martel? Well, yes and no. Henry is not, as far as I know, the real-life Yann, but the book I am holding and reading is, indeed, the book Henry will write *after* he has had the terrifying experiences I am going to read about. *This* book is his remembered account of what happened. Just how much this *Beatrice & Virgil* overlaps with the book Henry's publisher rejected is never made clear. We are told categorically, however, that Henry's "flip book concerned the murder of millions of civilian Jews...by the Nazis" (9). He is obsessed with the Holocaust and desperately trying to approach that history in a new way: "Henry's double book was about the ways in which that event was represented in stories" (9). He had read extensively and knew full well that "historical realism" was the dominant approach and that the few exceptions to this were Art Spiegelman's *Maus*, David Grossman's *See Under: Love*, and Martin Amis's *Time's Arrow* (10). But Henry wanted to create an "artful witness" (11) to atrocity, even though he is neither Jewish nor related to a survivor; he wanted, with his novel, to take poetic licence with, of all subjects, the Holocaust. Why?

During the lunch meeting in an upscale London restaurant, poor Henry goes from excitement to despair as the assembled group—publisher, editor, agent, historian—grills him and it becomes clear that they do not like his book. They ask repeatedly—what is the book about? Although they do not listen to his thoughtful answer and find it easy to dismiss, we should pay close attention to what Henry says: "My book is about a new choice of stories. With a historical event, we not only have to bear witness, that is, tell what happened and address the needs of ghosts. We also have to interpret and conclude, so that the needs of people *today*, the children of ghosts, can be addressed. In addition to the knowledge of history, we need the understanding of art" (15). In response, the group at lunch complains that the "novel lacks drive and the essay lacks unity" (17), but what I suspect they really object to is Henry's way of telling this particular story. If we, the readers of *Beatrice & Virgil* (the novel Henry does give us), keep this crucial explanation of purpose in mind as we read, then I believe we will understand and appreciate the story that Henry (and Yann) create. We will revisit the history of terrible events from the war that must not be forgotten and we will open ourselves to the "understanding of art." We will listen, today, to the ghosts and we will bear witness—secondary witness to be sure and witness mediated through the power of memory and art—but witness all the same.





The story that unfolds after this introduction is one that will shake many readers to their emotional and ethical foundations and offend others.[13] It is by any account a bizarre story. Audacious. Horrifying. It is an autobiographical fiction relayed by an unnamed narrator about how Henry met a mysterious and threatening taxidermist in some unnamed European city and inherited (after a fashion) an animal allegory in the form of a play about the Holocaust. The play has two main characters: Beatrice is a donkey and Virgil is a howler monkey, and these two creatures exist in a Beckettian-style play reminiscent of *Waiting for Godot* or *Endgame*. This play intertext occupies a key position in Henry's own life story (as he recalls it), and theatre performance and theatrical metaphors are of central importance to the novel as a whole.

After that lunch in London, Henry leaves the restaurant devastated. Five years of work on his novel have just been rejected. He walks in

Hyde Park, calls his wife back in Canada, and concludes that he must stop writing. When he returns home, he and Sarah decide to spend a year abroad. Although the narrator is coy about their city of choice—New York? Paris? Berlin? (and perhaps it does not matter much)—I see them in Berlin. Canadians do not go abroad to the United States. Wherever it is, they settle in: she gets a work visa as a nurse; he is a "resident alien, a rightless ghost" (21) who must now fill his life with other activities than writing. He returns to studying the clarinet; he takes up acting and helps out with a local theatre company; he waits table in a bistro. They get a puppy and a kitten from a local pound. Sarah becomes pregnant and they begin to anticipate the joy of a baby. Meanwhile, he answers the mail from readers of his second, successful novel about animals (echoes of *Life of Pi*) that reaches him from his Canadian agent and London publisher. Then, one day, a package arrives containing a marked-up copy of Gustave Flaubert's story ("The Legend of Saint Julian Hospitator" 30–43) and a fragment of a play with two characters called Beatrice and Virgil discussing the virtues of pears (44–51).





Henry has been tracked down by the taxidermist, whose name is also Henry, and from this point on our Henry's life turns into a kind of terrifying ghost story. He is puzzled by this strange package, disturbed by the Flaubert story about Julian who enjoys murdering all types of animals but is saved at the end because he is generous to a leper (Christ in disguise); Julian is then made a saint without expressing a word of remorse for his lifetime of brutality to animals. And he is intrigued by the characters in a play who chat away about pears. The brief note attached to these documents contains a request for unspecified help, a name, and an address, which happens to be in a nearby area of the city. When Henry walks to the address (the street number is 1933), he finds himself at a store called Okapi Taxidermy run by the solitary man who sent the package. This Henry, a taxidermist in his early eighties, lacks interest in people or events beyond his own work and his play, which he calls *A 20th-Century Shirt* (134). In his workroom he has a stuffed donkey he calls Beatrice and a stuffed howler monkey he calls Virgil: they are, he says cryptically, "my guides through hell" (75).[14] He also explains to our Henry that his taxidermy work resembles the task of the historian: "I am extracting and refining memory from death. In that I am no different from a historian" (96). His play, however, is less history than allegory or fable; it is an attempt at art, but he has come to an impasse and needs Henry's professional help.





The more Henry learns about the play, which the old man insists on reading aloud to him, the more certain he becomes that this strange play is about the Holocaust. Clues abound, from the terror felt by the animals to the striped shirt image of the landscape they live in; these creatures are starving, hence their obsession with food, and they are hiding from people who persecute and want to exterminate them. They recall being subjected to appalling torture and having witnessed what one would certainly describe as a pogrom, and after debating what to call the events they are living through, they decide on "The Horrors" (136). What's more, they ponder an essential question about the Holocaust: "How are we going to talk about what happened to us one day when it's over?" asks Beatrice, repeating Virgil's earlier question (112). To which Virgil replies, "that's assuming we survive" (133). As Henry gradually recognizes the true subject of this play text, he also begins to suspect the true identity and intentions of its author. The man is so sullen and uncommunicative, except in his demands for assistance with his play, that Henry comes to the conclusion that he is not a Jewish survivor struggling to tell his story, but a former Nazi torturer and murderer—one of the young men who, in the play, attacks and mutilates the two animals—who wants redemption after the fact without admitting his guilt or expressing remorse. One clue to this possible identity comes in the form of an address on a list in the old man's play: "68 Nowolipki Street" (149). As Henry recalls from his previous research on the Holocaust, this street exists in Warsaw and is the address at which the historical documents bearing witness to life in the Warsaw Ghetto were hidden by Emmanuel Ringelblum

(1900–1944), the Jewish historian who bore witness to the fate and treatment of his people and whose work was published in 2006 as *Notes from the Warsaw Ghetto.*[15] Henry returns to the store and demands information about this address, which the old man claims is an imaginary place thought up by Beatrice, where "every trace of the Horrrors would be filed away and saved" (172). Of course, Henry knows better. Although he does not say so exactly, Henry appears to suspect that this cold, selfish old man has either stolen some of these precious Jewish documents to pass off as his own invention or now sees himself as a Saint Julian figure worthy of redemption because of his Holocaust allegory or, as Henry also realizes, he "is using the Holocaust to speak of the extermination of animal life" (173). It is this last possibility that seems to be the final straw for Henry.





But if the old man has been hiding his true identity, so has our Henry. When he returns to the taxidermy store to confront the old man, to refuse to help him further, and to throw the play manuscript down in disgust, he is shocked to find the taxidermist quick to accuse him of hiding his real name: "What else are you hiding?" he demands (171). Henry L'Hôte—our author—used a pseudonym when writing his successful novel, so he too has protected his real identity from fans, readers, and inquisitors like this man. When Henry finally admits that he does not want to help the man, will not take his play, and turns to leave, the man stabs him twice in the abdomen. Seriously injured and bleeding profusely, Henry staggers out to the street. As the ambulance arrives to carry him to hospital, he looks back at the store to see it engulfed in flames and the old man grinning at him from the window. The store burns rapidly, with the man and his play manuscript inside it—"A howling inferno" (183), a true holocaust and a fitting death.

But this is not the end of Henry's story. He survives, recovers, and is profoundly changed by his experience. He returns to writing. He writes the text we have just read, a text that bears witness, that tells his autobiography, and that recreates the past in and for the present of 2010. He writes a novel containing what Henry can remember and then recreate of the old man's animal allegory play. However, Henry inflects *his* version of things rather differently from the original. He calls the entire novel-memoir-history-play *Beatrice & Virgil* (not *A 20th-Century Shirt*), and his text is unquestionably about the Holocaust. Henry's animals are his way of remembering and reimagining that terrible past for the present, of telling the story in a new way.

There is one more element in this moving tale. Henry has also written a text called "Games for Gustav" and this text consists of thirteen boxes that are appended to the novel. The title comes from Beatrice; it is the name she gives to the corpse of a boy the two find (196). She and Virgil want to play games for the boy's sake, to remember, and in an odd-sounding way, celebrate him. The games Henry imagines, however, are not playful or peaceful. They are appalling. The first twelve boxes contain brief descriptions of frightful dilemmas, all recalling actual situations from the Holocaust, followed by a question. The essence of all these questions is this—in such a circumstance what would YOU do? The most shocking (to my mind) is the one in which a parent can reach better air if he or she steps on the head of his or her dead daughter: "Do you step on your daughter's head?" (n.p.). But the twelfth game-box question is the most haunting: a doctor offers you a pill that will erase memory so that you forget your suffering, losses, and "entire past. Do you swallow the pill?" (n.p.). The box for game thirteen is empty.

As I stare in disbelief at this thirteenth box, I long to fill it with something. To imagine another such tormenting question, however, is too awful. But then I realize that Yann Martel has already enabled me to understand that the box need not be filled with life-and-death questions of this sort. It can and is, preferably by far, a blank space for remembering. We can refuse the pill of forgetting, just as Henry has. We can share in the memory-work of history and art by bearing our own secondary witness to the ghosts that follow this, and other, Canadian authors as they embrace their own and this country's hauntedness. I have halted my memory-work of analysis and listening with *Beatrice & Virgil* because I believe that it succeeds in its high task of writing poetry and fiction and drama after Auschwitz. Moreover, it opens up the future with that empty box as an invitation to readers to continue the work of creating a landscape of memory. Martel refuses to provide the last word on a subject that cannot be concluded but that still demands our empathic unsettlement.

This novel is not set in Canada. Unlike the other works I have considered, even a memoir like Comfort's where reassuring memories of home surface into the war artist's story or *The English Patient*, where Hana and Caravaggio share memories of their Canadian past, Canada is hardly mentioned. Henry L'Hôte, his surname surely a sign of his own "hospitator" activities, not only carries his home country with him in his travels, but also chooses to *host* the other Henry's story within his own and to expand his personal horizon of memory to include the wider world.[16] The crossing of Canadian borders to embrace a wider reality is a pervasive feature of these post-1977 war representations, especially when writers and artists reconsider the Second World War. This seems to me central to the meaning of these works, a meaning forcefully presented by Martel in *Beatrice & Virgil*. Canada is not, never was, immune from the rest of the world. Canadians are responsible for their decisions and actions at home and abroad, and what happens over there has repercussions here. Thirsty ghosts and memories do not stay put in the past or in foreign places; there is no magic pill for forgetting. What this extraordinary novel, like *Such Creatures* and *Far to Go*, shows us, is that the business of remembering and trying to understand is part of the here and now, of Canada in the twenty-first century, and that Canadians will continue to discover new ways of telling the stories about the two world wars. If we can still believe in Canada as a peaceable kingdom—and that is a large IF—then it can only be peaceable by recognizing history as fully as possible and by establishing a landscape of memory full, rich, and sustaining for all Canadians. When Henry does return home, he will bring this story with him. We will listen to him and believe, and the landscape will make room for him and for all those who have yet to write, read, bear witness, and remember.

Geoffrey Hartman has said that the Holocaust does not belong exclusively to Jewish history because it is integral to European history and that this history, and its stories, is of "the utmost consequence to every thoughtful person" (*The Longest Shadow: In the Aftermath of the Holocaust* 67). I would expand upon this compelling assertion to say that the history and stories of the *entire* Second World War (with atrocities and massacres of civilians in Europe and Asia) continue to hold enormous importance for "every thoughtful person." I also agree with Susan Gubar who writes, in *Poetry After Auschwitz: Remembering What One Never Knew*, that permission "to speak or write" about the war and the Holocaust "consists precisely in our inhabiting of the post-1945 period" (57). Alison Pick, Judith Thompson, and Yann Martel write about what they never knew and tell stories about a war that contemporary Canadians cannot possibly *know*. Nevertheless, such stories are part of being Canadian, just as Canada exists within an international global community. Where the First World War stories and history still remind readers, despite caveats and complications, that Canada attained a sense of national pride and identity through that war, the picture of the Second World War emerging from 1977 or 1981 (with *Obasan*) to the present, places Canada firmly in that wider world and questions Canadian policies and actions at home and abroad. This is the wider world, and our responsibility to it, captured so powerfully and honestly by a painter like Gertrude Kearns in her Somalia series or in her Kandahar pictures (see pages 46–47).[17] In the twenty-first





> *Gertrude Kearns,* Somalia 2, Without Conscience *(1996). o/c 287.2 x 114.3 cm. CWM #19990022-001. Beaverbrook Collection of War Art. © Canadian War Museum. Here Kearns depicts Master Corporal Clayton Matchee torturing Somali teenager Shidane Arone, who died from his injuries. Private Kyle Brown photographed the torture and Kearns's painting is based on this frequently reproduced photograph. This crime marked a nadir for a Canadian peacekeeping mission.*

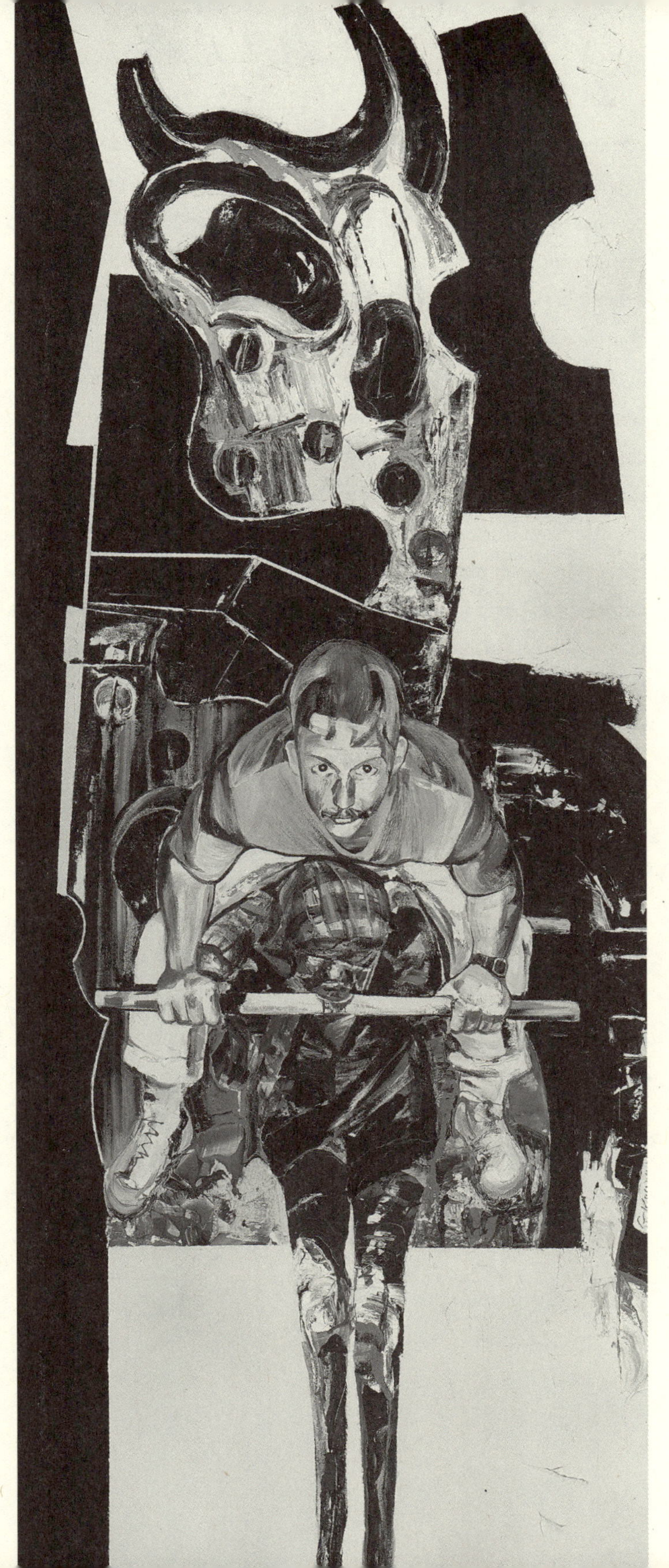

century, our landscape of memory must make room for more than a narrowly nationalistic story or a benign, peaceful one, precisely because of Canada's shift from a postwar peacekeeping role to an active involvement in new wars. Henry Kreisel understood that Canadians existed in that world as early as 1969 in *The Betrayal*, a story and a title charged with new significance today—as Kearns shows.

In ways almost impossible to quantify or label, those who returned from fighting, nursing, and reporting in both wars helped to define the country Canada is today—its industry, its cultural and social institutions, its policies and its communities—and we have inherited this country from those who lived and worked here before us.[18] But the borders between here and there, past and present are never fixed; the landscape is never finished. Novelists from Pick to Bock and Martel, playwrights from Chan and Stubbs to Thompson, along with filmmakers, painters, and artists working in other media, continue to explore those borders, to reimagine what borders include or exclude, and to remember the stories that are never finished. By representing the history and the stories of the wars, the artists also shape—and produce—the Canada of today. Moreover, they do this important cultural work not through combat but through memory. They help build a home for the imagination. Ted Chamberlin describes this kind of Canadian home perfectly when he tells us that "Whatever and wherever it is, home is always border country, a place that separates and connects us, a place of possibility for both peace and perilous conflict" (3). Home is where we recognize, and take responsibility for, a shared landscape of memory.

# Notes

## 1 Landscapes of War



1. In *In Search of* Alias Grace, Atwood discusses contemporary Canadian historical fiction and her own novel. She draws a distinction between the nineteenth century, which she describes as invested in memory, and the twentieth century, which she sees as "memory-denying" (13), and she considers the recent turn to historical fiction as a response to this wish to deny or forget the past.
2. When it was first shown, this film elicited violent criticism from veterans, even though it relied on two distinguished veterans to present its disturbing reassessment of Allied aggression in the bombing of Hamburg and in other attacks on German civilians. Attempts were made to curtail release of the film and to vilify the filmmakers. I discuss the film, and reactions to it, in detail in Chapter 9.
3. For an interesting discussion of the idea that Canada sees itself as a peaceable kingdom, see William New's "Beneath the Peaceable Kingdom."
4. This American film, released in 1961 and starring some of the major actors of the day (Spencer Tracey, Burt Lancaster, Marlene Dietrich, and Richard Widmark, for example) about the trial of Nazi judges was a feature film intended for a mass audience. However, it included documentary footage, taken by American soldiers, of corpses piled high in concentration camps and bulldozers pushing them into mass graves. This material was shocking under any circumstances and was certainly a terrifying visual element in a mainstream film from the 1960s.
5. Some of the pre-1977 works are Earle Birney's *Turvey*, Tom Hendry's *Fifteen Miles of Broken Glass*, Colin McDougall's *Execution*, Henry Kreisel's *The Betrayal*, and of course Hugh MacLennan's *Barometer Rising*. Some of Raymond Souster's

war poems were published in his *Selected Poems* (1972), but he had published war poetry in the 1960s. Souster fought with the RCAF from 1941 to 1944 and wrote extensively about the war; his work has been neglected and deserves careful reassessment. I will return briefly to McDougall, MacLennan, Kreisel, and Souster in later chapters. Memoirs by Second World War veterans warrant closer attention; for my discussion of Comfort and others, see Chapter 9.

6. In 1917 the day was very cold and wet, snow was falling, the battleground was an appalling mess of mud, dead and dying men and horses, rats, and no birds sang. I return to this reality when discussing Joseph Boyden's *Three Day Road* in Chapter 3. In 1936 thousands of mourning Canadian veterans and families travelled to France for the unveiling, but the day was rainy and cold and apart from newspaper and radio reports, Canadians at home had little first-hand sense of the occasion. The country and world had moved on, new wars were erupting and looming; the attention of most Canadians was focused elsewhere.



7. French Canadians were not the only Canadians to resist conscription for either war, so it is problematic to construct Quebecers as alone in this regard. By the same token, and given the period I discuss, it would be inappropriate to pretend that either war was a foundational myth, or could be recruited to serve such a purpose, for contemporary Quebec. While the First and Second World Wars function well as narratives—myths even—of the nation for English-speaking Canada, they do not have the same traction in Quebec. The only successful unifying myth for Canada (insofar as any myth can succeed in this context) is the discourse of the North; see my analysis in *Canada and the Idea of North*. The wars represented by francophone writers are either earlier ones—the so-called Battle of the Plains of Abraham or the War of 1812—or very recent ones. An especially striking example of the latter is Wajdi Mouawad's play *Incendies* (*Scorched*), which was also an award-winning film.

8. I am thinking here of films like *Joyeux Noël*, *The Lives of Others*, *Paradise Road*, and *The Thin Red Line*, of novels by such different writers as Pat Barker, Sebastian Faulk, Shirley Hazzard, Marc Levy, Ian MacEwen, Irène Némirovsky, and Kurt Vonnegut, and a number of important memoirs by men and women like Primo Levi, or of cultural histories like Iris Chang's *The Rape of Nanking*. I return to a few of these works in passing, but my focus in this book is on Canada. For critical studies of other literatures and the arts, see Buitenhuis, Cobley, Crosthwaite, Eksteins, Fussell, McCormick and Perry, Malvern (2001), Michalski, Middleton and Woods, Santner, Schama, Stanzel and Löschnigg, Winter, and Young.

9. Hirsch distinguishes post-memory from memory "by generational distance" and from history because of its "deep personal connection," and she insists that post-memory is "mediated" through "imagination and creation" (22).
10. This famous question is often cited by scholars and, as LaCapra notes in *History and Memory after Auschwitz*, it is often misunderstood (181). See Theodor Adorno's *Negative Dialectics* (362) for the full passage and context.
11. Few Canadian war artists painted the dead and as official war artists they were instructed not to depict Canadian war dead. Varley is something of an exception here in that he deliberately chose not only to depict dead soldiers but also to portray them as mixed in with, barely distinguishable from, the muddy, devastated landscape. See studies by Brandon, especially "Shattered Landscape: The Great War and the Art of the Group of Seven," Osborne, and Tippett.
12. A recent English-language video program quotes Dix's belief in this important witnessing role of the artist; see Reiner Moritz's *Otto Dix: The Painter Is the Eyes of the World*. Among the many German writers and painters who fought and survived the Great War, most came back as profoundly traumatized and disillusioned as Dix, but in works like his series of etchings called *Der Kreig* (1924) Dix put a human face on the tragedy of war for the average young man swept up in its mindless horror. Although not Jewish, Dix was persecuted by the Nazis and spent the war years living in Switzerland. Many of his paintings were confiscated as examples of degenerate art; his critical views of German militarism and industrial modernization were deemed unacceptable.
13. This video archive contains a collection of filmed testimonies and autobiographical accounts of the Holocaust by survivors interviewed by professional psychologists and psychotherapists. Dori Laub, a co-founder of the Fortunoff Video Archive, one of the best-known psychoanalyst-interviewers and a survivor himself, discusses the Archive in "An Event Without a Witness."
14. In his interview for *Canvas of War*, Bayefsky (1923–2001) comments on his drawings from Bergen-Belsen and tells us that such sights convinced him to be an artist. This testimony is also quoted in Laura Brandon's "Reflections on the Holocaust" (67).
15. At the University of British Columbia, seminars or classes devoted to the study of the Holocaust have been rare but programs in Jewish Studies were well established across Canada (and at UBC) by the 1990s, and the oldest centres, departments, or programs for Jewish Studies are at the University of Manitoba, McGill, Concordia, the University of Toronto, and York University; see Richard Menkis, "A Threefold Transformation." To my knowledge, Canadian war literature has rarely been deemed a viable doctoral thesis topic in Canadian English departments. One early exception to this neglect is Crawford Kilian's 1972

thesis. The experience of my colleague, Laurie Ricou, is more representative: when he wanted to study Canadian war literature at the University of Toronto in the early 1970s he was told there was none and persuaded to drop the idea. Between 2005 and 2010, I directed three theses on Canadian literature and the First World War.

16. A number of articles have appeared in which the Canadian novels and poetry written by veterans (and nurses) of the First World War are being re-examined with a new awareness of the early twentieth-century canon, and literary trends of the period between the wars are gradually emerging; see, for example, studies by Hill, Holmes, and Thompson.



17. McDougall's *Execution* was reprinted in 1972 and again in 2005, and *Barometer Rising* has never gone out of print or been entirely forgotten because MacLennan's other works keep him before the public eye; however, novels like Earle Birney's *Turvey* and Douglas Le Pan's *The Deserter* are rarely mentioned or studied, and few Canadians have read or seen a production of Tom Hendry's anti-war play *Fifteen Miles of Broken Glass*.

18. On the military history of Newfoundland, which was not part of Canada until 1949, see Nicholson and Gilbert, but for more personal stories of the impact of the war on Newfoundland, see David French's play *Soldier's Heart* and David Macfarlane's memoir *The Danger Tree*. The first collection of Canadian war poetry was edited by John Garvin in 1918; later collections were compiled by Colombo and Richardson in 1985, and by Callaghan and Meyer in 2001.

19. These are some of the scholars whose work has been especially useful to me, but the research on these subjects is vast, interdisciplinary, and international.

20. For discussion of *The Valour and the Horror*, see Bercuson and Wise, and also Findley's response to the "reactionary opposition" to the television broadcast in his essay "The Valour and the Horror." As Findley notes, the "resentment" aroused by the McKennas' "brilliant," "landmark" film was based on the fact that it explored the truth about Allied bombing of Hamburg, Dresden, Berlin, and finally Hiroshima and Nagasaki (169–70). The film told us things we had decided to forget and reflected on the suffering we inflicted as well as the suffering we endured. I discuss the film in Chapter 9, together with films made later, like *Canada Remembers* and *Return to Ortona*, which toe a more politically correct line by eliding or ignoring Allied aggression or, as in the latter film, by framing the story of violence, death, and destruction, in a narrative of memories shared by elderly German and Canadian veterans who agree to mourn together, shake hands, and leave the past behind them.

21. This reference to 130,000 killed in the bombing of Dresden, a figure given by David Irving in *The Destruction of Dresden* (1963) has recently been disputed;

see Randall Hansen, who puts the figure at 35,000 (245–46). The higher figure is used by Kurt Vonnegut in *Slaughterhouse-Five*.

22. The term discursive formation is Foucault's in *The Archaeology of Knowledge*, and I develop this concept in *Canada and the Idea of North* as the discursive formation of North. The discourse of the two wars has become as important to the production of a Canadian identity as the idea of North—and as constantly changing and as urgent in the twenty-first century.

23. Although I cannot swear that I did not see this painting prior to 1979, I am certain I saw it that year both in Robertson's book and in the travelling exhibition, "A Terrible Beauty," when it came to the Burnaby Art Gallery in January 1979.

24. In *A Painter's Country*, Jackson writes that "the little thirty-inch canvas by Paul Nash, entitled 'Void,' expressed more about war than all the big twenty-foot canvases put together" (50). Derwent Wood's *Canada's Golgotha* (1918), bronze, 83 x 63.5 cm, depicts a Canadian soldier crucified and surrounded by mocking Germans. The story of Germans having crucified a Canadian made for spectacular propaganda, but it has always been denied by Germany and soon became so contentious (and disputed by Canadian soldiers) that the sculpture was withdrawn from exhibitions. Laura Brandon includes a full-page illustration of the piece in *Art or Memorial?* (128).

25. The Commonwealth War Graves Commission lists 956 cemeteries and memorials from the two world wars in Belgium and northern France alone. Driving through this landscape of memory in the summer of 2009, stopping frequently to visit these *lieux de mémoire*, was an experience I shall never forget and believe every generation should have. Although I paid most attention to Canadian sites like Vimy, Beaumont-Hamel, and tiny Bourlon Wood Cemetery, nestled peacefully among fields and sheltered by woods and hedges, I also paid my respects at major British sites and at two severe, unvisited German cemeteries for the dead of the Great War. However, the sites I found most memorable and disturbing were the landscapes around Vimy and Beaumont-Hamel, where the lush grass covers, but cannot hide, the mounds and ridges of a countryside torn and gouged by war.

26. Cardiff's mention of feet washing up on British Columbia beaches refers to the bizarre sequence of such events between 2007 and 2009. Beginning in August 2007, single running shoes with the remains of feet began washing up along BC's coast. By October 2009, there were seven such findings. News coverage was extensive, but to date forensic analysis has only matched some of the pairs and no identifications have been announced.

27. The spring 2010 issue of *Canadian Art* carries a Thauberger image on its cover showing four Canadian women in fatigues and carrying weapons running towards the camera with an airbase in the background. Thauberger spent several weeks in the spring of 2009 as a war artist with the Canadian Forces in Kandahar, and these images of female troops are part of the work she has completed; see the article by Deborah Campbell for the illustrations and some commentary by the artist.
28. This painting is reproduced by Laura Brandon in *A Brush with War* (45); see also the article for the *Globe and Mail* by Val Ross, who touches on the chilly reception given some of Kearns's work by the military.
29. This comment and others are quoted in Deborah Campbell's article (64–65), and I read many more in the book kept for the occasion. The majority were protests by people who resented having such an image put in their way. The title of the piece is a military term for reconnaissance, and the soldiers Thauberger photographed were doing reconnaissance training, albeit they had to stage this shot for her because she was not allowed to photograph them during training.

## 2 Landscapes of Memory

1. There are two different versions of *J'accuse*; the silent film appeared in 1919 and the sound film in 1938. I am describing the 1938 film for which Gance made important changes to the story to address the approach of the Second World War. The 1938 film employs some dramatic expressionist effects—double exposures, chiaroscuro, tight close-ups—to portray Jean's fury and despair, and these scenes exist in sharp contrast with almost documentary-style footage of battle scenes, news headlines, and re-enactments. For further discussion of the film, see Jay Winter, *Sites of Memory, Sites of Mourning* (133–38). According to Winter, by 1923 almost two million people had seen the 1919 silent film.
2. Kirmayer is James McGill Professor and director of Social and Transcultural Psychiatry at McGill University, a position that necessitates working across traditional disciplinary and departmental boundaries, and his thinking on questions of trauma and memory in this important essay has provided very useful context for me in both teaching and theorizing representations of war. Although his analysis of categories of memory and practical treatment of post-traumatic disturbances extends well beyond my applications, his attention to language, metaphor, and cultural manifestations of traumatic memories demonstrates the relevance of his concept for artistic and cultural memory-work.
3. Kirmayer's discussion of types of memory and modes of managing trauma (notably through suppression, repression, and dissociation) is more technical

than I have intimated here. His emphasis is on how we recall extreme traumatic events and, more importantly, how we cope with them, work through such experiences, and move forward towards healing.

4. The massacre of roughly twenty thousand Polish officers and intellectuals by the Russians in the forest of Katyń in 1940 was blamed on the Germans until some Soviet records were opened and what many Poles knew to be true could finally be verified and acknowledged. It was not until April 2010, however, that Wajda's film was broadcast on Russian television and the historical truth, thereby, brought to the attention of Russians. The occasion for this screening was the 10 April 2010 crash near Katyń of the airplane that was carrying Poland's president and many other leaders to the first joint commemoration of the massacre.



5. In both *History and Memory after Auschwitz* and *Writing History, Writing Trauma*, LaCapra examines the problems inherent in witnessing and listening to trauma victims. On the one hand, he recognizes the importance of the victim's being *heard* or listened to, if he or she is to work through the mourning produced by a traumatic experience instead of becoming trapped in the repetition of traumatic memories, which Freud identifies with endless melancholia; on the other hand, he warns against the danger of listeners (secondary witnesses) appropriating the victim's trauma and seeing themselves as equally traumatized. See his comments in *History and Memory* (11–15, 184–96) and in *Writing History* (64–78).

6. Discussions of a so-called ethical turn in literature and literary and cultural studies often begin by criticizing modernist, and even more emphatically postmodernist, texts for sidestepping ethics. Paul de Man was seen as representing this refusal of ethics, and then the discovery of his Nazi connections from his war years in the Netherlands was considered a likely personal reason for his theoretical avoidance of ethics. Suffice to say that this setting up of oppositions and straw men is simplistic. While there has been a discernible re-emphasis on the ethical dimensions, potential, and even responsibility of literature and the arts since the 1980s, especially in works representing war, ethical problems were never absent from postmodernism. This is a large and still debated subject. For discussions of ethics in contemporary writing (notably works that can be seen as postmodern) see Hutcheon, LaCapra, Nünning, and Wyile's "Making a Mess of Things"; on de Man, see Felman; on Findley, see Krause.

7. I have not listed expressionism here because, despite its techniques of distortion and stylization, some expressionist strategies are very effective in depicting the horrors of war; see Löschnigg on German First World War poets. Moreover, there are links between realist and esxpressionist aesthetics that do not exist, for example, between realism and surrealism. I have analyzed

expressionism at length in *Regression and Apocalypse*. In his essay "Between the Extreme and the Everyday," Rothberg develops a theory of "traumatic realism" that I find productive. He insists that traumatic realism distrusts modernist experimentation and postmodernist pastiche because it will not or "cannot free itself from the claims of mimesis and it remains committed to a project of historical cognition through the mediation of culture" (67).

8. An especially heated debate still swirling around postmodernist fiction involves the perception that a postmodern novelist is ducking ethical issues by hiding behind self-conscious textual acrobatics instead of confronting artistic responsibilities to referentiality and the trauma of real events. This debate surfaced energetically around Findley's Second World War novel *Famous Last Words*.



9. For a discussion of the Historian's Debate, see Huyssen (30–38), LaCapra, *Writing History* (44), and Santner, who provides a detailed summary (46–52).

10. Beginning in the 1970s with Umberto Eco, Stanley Fish, and Wolfgang Iser, theories of reader response and the analysis of textual, notably novelistic, strategies for addressing and involving the reader in an active "configuration of meaning" (Iser's term; see *The Implied Reader* 287–88), became widely accepted principles of critical analysis. More recent theoretical work on trauma, haunting, and witnessing, draws on aspects of reader response theory (whether semiotic—Eco—psychoanalytical—Fish—or phenomenological—Iser) even when it does not acknowledge or discuss these theories. Certainly, I take as a given that readers and viewers of the works I discuss are meant to participate in the work of producing meaning, not only because these works are highly self-conscious (often self-reflexive and postmodern), but because the reader/viewer response opens the way to ethical dimensions of the reading/viewing experience that may carry over from the fictional world to the *real* one.

11. I insert Bakhtin's term "dialogics" into this process because I always find it both more accurate and more productive when I want to identify literary, social, cultural exchanges that exist in and by virtue of their discursive interlocutions. Bakhtin was one of the first among twentieth-century thinkers to stress the necessity of addressability in social practices, of the relationship between speaker and listener, who responds in dialogue, and the representation of this dialogism in the novel. See Bakhtin's *The Dialogic Imagination* and my use of his theories in *Canada and the Idea of North* (24–26).

12. In Primo Levi's words, "we, the survivors, are not the true witnesses....Those who did so [but who did not survive]...have not returned to tell about it...they are...the submerged, the complete witnesses" (83–84).

13. Oliver offers a feminist philosopher's analysis of masculinist constructions of subjectivity and of subject/object hierarchies. She draws on the work of

Emmanuel Lévinas to support her non-adversarial, multisensory articulation of a more hopeful, non-violent ethics or "new vision," as she calls it (204–07). While I find it difficult to share her vision, I think that post-Second World War Western society has too easily accepted the arguments of ethnologists like Konrad Lorenz and sociologists like Robert Ardrey. Lorenz, a survivor of a Russian POW camp in the Second World War, published *On Aggression* in 1966 and Ardrey published *The Territorial Imperative* the same year. Both books portray human aggression as normative and inescapable; both were enormously popular and influential during the latter period of the Cold War, and it may well be time to challenge their assumptions and conclusions.



14. I discuss Detaille's painting and its use in Thomson's play in the next chapter. Longstaff, an Australian painter, created his piece in 1931 to mark the creation of Walter Allward's monumental Vimy Memorial, and his depiction of the dead soldiers rising from the Douai Plain to gather at the monument recalls Allward's dream in which he claimed to see dead soldiers filing by to assist the living. This painting now hangs in a prominent position in the Hall of Remembrance, which houses the Vimy Memorial maquettes, in the Canadian War Museum. My thanks to Jan Lermitte for bringing this work to my attention.
15. My quarrel with Fussell concerns his narrow focus on a subset of British war poets as representative of all the best and new in literary responses to the Great War. He is contemptuous of McCrae's "In Flanders Fields," when a careful reading of the poem demonstrates its poetic qualities and its connections with a traditional and dominant response to the war. For thoughtful and detailed analyses of the poem, see Nancy Holmes's excellent study "'In Flanders Fields': Canada's Official Poem," and the 1998 NFB film *John McCrae's War: In Flanders Fields*, which contains commentaries on the poem by British and Canadian scholars.
16. For a fresh—and chilling—look at the attractions, dangers, and politics of contemporary re-enactment culture in virtual and real time, see Alan Filewod's "Warplay: Spectacle, Performance, and the (Dis)Simulation of Combat."
17. Winter's claim to the term "memory boom" (*Remembering War* 1), ignores the fact that Huyssen coined the term in 1995. That said, Winter's stress, in this book, on interpreting the role of remembrance from the local, small-scale, and personal perspective is important (150). It is a perspective that enters the landscape of memory in many important ways and can often be lost in the dominant discourse of official, national history. Many very recent commemorative events have turned to private letters, journal entries, individual, and ordinary stories of loss and suffering to supplement and modify the public

record. Winter discusses the very popular collection of German soldiers' tales edited and published by Philipp Witkop (104–10), and an example of this local and small-scale perspective in Canada is the "The Memory Project," which is examined by David Williams; see my following summary of Williams.

18. The dispute over changing the flag from the Canadian Red Ensign, which Canada had used since the 1890s and under which Canadian troops fought during both wars, was fierce. It took Lester B. Pearson, himself a Second World War veteran and the prime minister of Canada in 1964–65, to persuade angry veterans that the change was necessary and good for Canada. Repatriation of the constitution, which had resided in Whitehall, occurred under Pierre Elliott Trudeau's watch in 1982, and the adoption of "Canada Day" for our national holiday on 1 July took place in 1982. Ironically, the first of July is also the date commemorated in Newfoundland, which joined Canada in 1949, to mark the day, in 1916, when the Newfoundland Regiment was decimated at Beaumont-Hamel. The date plays an important role in David French's *Soldier's Heart*.



19. Worrying about identity is something of a Canadian obsession, and not without reason. Because of our geography, sharing what has been (though less so in this century) the longest, undefended border in the world with a superpower, our protracted colonial history, and the powerful, distinct status of Quebec, means that a strong, unified, national identity has not taken root in this country. Too many Canadian thinkers have commented at length on this situation for me to summarize their arguments here, and many Canadian writers and artists have explored or even satirized our so-called colonial cringe; this situation will surface in some of the war texts examined in the following chapters, for example, in *Billy Bishop Goes to War* by John Gray and Eric Peterson. For discussion of national identity in the context of literature and the arts, see Margaret Atwood's *Survival*, Northrop Frye's *The Bush Garden*, William New's *Land Sliding*, Grace's *Canada and the Idea of North*, and works by Laura Moss, Herb Wyile, and Joyce Zemans. In *On the Art of Being Canadian*, I have selected three foci for exploring national identity, one of which is the representation of war; see Chapter 2, "Theatres of War."

20. In "Concepts and Methods for the Study of Literature and/as Cultural Memory," Erll and Nünning provide an invaluable overview of the theoretical continuities and developments in cultural memory studies, particularly in the context of literature and always with a view to the interdisciplinary parameters of cultural memory. They outline three current approaches to the study of literature and memory as "the memory *of* literature," "the concept of memory *in* literature" (13), and "the concept of literature as a medium of cultural memory," that is "the mediality of literary texts and their functions in the formation

and transformation of cultural memories" (14). While I will certainly discuss examples of the incorporation and representation of memory in my texts, I am most interested in examining "the mediality" of these texts for the production of Canadian cultural memory of the two wars.

21. The contributors to *La Grande Guerre* examine works by well-known writers like Claude Simon, Blaise Cendrars, and Henri Barbusse, but they also draw attention to other contemporary writers and artists with whom I am not familiar. The volume addresses important gaps in my knowledge, not only by expanding the repertoire of writers and texts dealing with war, but also by inserting the Belgian and French perspectives into the broader discussion of the subject.

22. As the editors explain, the European Commission supports transnational research in the form of European Thematic Network Projects. The ACUME (Approaching Cultural Memory) network on cultural memory brought over eighty European partners together in an interdisciplinary and comparative study of cultural memory. The Bologna conference on remembering war was one event in the network's research program; see Lamberti (2–3).

23. Stanzel and Löschnigg, Buitenhuis, and Cobley were among the first literary scholars to provide the kind of comparative, international perspective on war (notably on the Great War) that is becoming more familiar today. The Second World War is slowly attracting similar attention; see, for example, *European Memories of the Second World War* edited by Helmut Peitsch, Charles Burdett, and Claire Gorrara.



## 3 Novels

1. After the battle on the Plains of Abraham in 1759 when the British General Wolfe defeated the French General Montcalm, small skirmishes and defensive actions occurred in 1812 and 1837, but the only event that can qualify as approaching a civil war or a serious military conflict on Canadian soil was the so-called Riel Rebellion and military suppression of the Métis in 1885.

2. I do not make this comparison, however, because Caron's novel has not influenced a line of war novels in Quebec or anglophone Canada, and because its ethical and psychological import is restricted to the narrator. While *The Draft Dodger* is certainly a memory-work in which the First World War story of Uncle Nazaire is overheard and remembered by his twenty-five-year-old nephew Jean-François, who is dodging the Vietnam draft, the narrative structure of the novel is less complex than *The Wars* and the story itself is less applicable to a community or national situation (Canadian or Québécois).

3. After her dismissal, Leah realizes that she has shed "any lingering illusions she might have entertained about the justice of the war or the possibility of

playing some mitigating role as a nurse" (143). In his acknowledgements, Poole lists the only book he knows of about the role of Canadian women overseas: *The War Diary of Clare Gass, 1915–1918*, edited by Susan Mann (317). Thiessen's nurse is called Clare and his character is inspired by the same diary. However, the figure of the First World War Canadian nurse as a fictional character can be traced back to *The Wars*, and she reappears with exceptional power as Augusta Moffat in Urquhart's *The Underpainter* (1997); see also my comments on Paul Gross's film *Passchendaele*.

4. Cumyn is writing a trilogy (or tetralogy) about the two wars with his hero Ramsay Crome as the central figure.



5. I find these novels troubling for their sexism and for the weakness of the female characters. Although one might argue that the sexist attitude of the men in these novels is part of the era in which they lived, it is not contextualized as specific to time and place or placed in a qualifying perspective. The women characters in these novels are awkwardly drawn and unconvincing; they are presented as selfish, predatory, lacking in understanding, or simply as sex objects.
6. In one particularly long and informative passage (257–61), Jim recalls and reflects on his experiences, the terrible deaths he has witnessed, and the losses of friends he works with as a stretcher-bearer. How this voice reaches us is not made clear in the narrative, but it is fairly certain that Jim will not be able to tell Grania these things when he returns. Certainly, he would not have been allowed to send such reflections home in a letter and no one serving overseas was supposed to keep personal diaries.
7. There is an extensive theoretical literature on autobiography and I have drawn on this work in my study *Inventing Tom Thomson*, my Pollock biography, *Making Theatre*, and in my essay "Performing the Autobiographical"; see also work by Eakin, Egan, and Gilmore.
8. The representation of actual, historical people alongside fictional characters is a common feature of war writing. Findley was the first to do this extensively in *The Wars*, and all subsequent Canadian war novels and plays follow his example to some degree. To be sure, this strategy is also a hallmark of historical fiction more generally.
9. I see this novel as about the Canadian north—as far north as Lake Superior that is—even more than a story about the Great War. However, Austin is not worthy of that landscape, as Rockwell Kent makes clear when he describes Austin's landscapes as hellish. For my discussion of the images of North and the concept of a northern narrative, see *Canada and the Idea of North* (184–225).

10. Like so many works in which the war features as an aspect of background or historical context, the First World War is not the only factor leading to James Piper's violent behaviour and his rape of his daughter, but it does hover there and infect his and his children's story. He tries to escape into the war but, despite his wife's prayers that he will die there, he returns even more damaged than when he left.

11. That said, it is worth recalling that the so-called fantasy story of "The Blind Assassin," which functions as an intertext in this novel, has striking parallels with wars in ancient Mesopotamia; see Dyer, *War* 240. I suggest that Atwood is in fact tracing a long human obsession with warfare, at least as far as males are concerned. 

12. Entire book-length studies have been devoted to *The Wars*, which, together with *Famous Last Words*, has attracted considerable critical attention. See, in particular, work by Brydon, Krause, Pennee, Vauthier, and York. It is a pleasure to acknowledge all these studies, which have been helpful to me in developing my approach to this iconic text. 

13. Fussell was the first to mount this argument with respect to British literature and insofar as he remains an influence his ideas go unchallenged. However, recent scholars have demonstrated the continuities and complexities of pre-war and Great War impact on the arts and Western culture more generally. See Eksteins, *Rites of Spring*, and Winter, *Sites of Memory, Sites of Mourning*.

14. Lorraine York is mistaken when she insists that we are deliberately not told the narrator's gender; however, her larger point about Findley's desire to keep the question of gender open and therefore inclusive is still valid (see *Introducing Timothy Findley's* The Wars 81–84). In later work, like *The Telling of Lies*, he creates a very effective female narrator. Pennee has also called this narrator a biographer, as well as a researcher and a "fictionist" (39), but she does not explain why the term is helpful for understanding the narrator's role.

15. I am thinking especially of his novel *The Telling of Lies* but also of his comment in *Journeyman* that his job as a writer is "to seek and to confront the truth" (170). Findley often creates fictional autobiographical narrators for his novels; see in particular, *Famous Last Words* and *The Telling of Lies*.

16. Gérard Genette's analysis of narrative levels in fiction is still the best and most precise one I know of; see *Narrative Discourse* (227–43). The intradiegetic narrator functions within the first, or main, level of diegesis, which is, according to Genette, narrated by an extradiegetic narrator (228). In *The Wars* this narrator resembles an omniscient chronicler, or historian, who shares the storytelling with Robert's biographer (the intradiegetic narrator). For a useful analysis of

Genette's narrative levels in war novels, see Cobley, in particular her discussion of *The Wars* (104–09).

17. Longboat (1887–1949) was from the Six Nations Reserve at Ohsweken, Ontario. He was a legend in his day, the winner of many competitions, and in 1907 the winner of the Boston Marathon. In 1911 he set a professional record in the fifteen-mile race, and he served during the war as a dispatch runner. A young man like Robert would have followed his career in the newspapers and also been aware of the racist criticisms levelled at this very independent-minded athlete.



18. The original suggestion that soldiers urinate on their handkerchiefs and hold them over their faces has been attributed to Canadian Captain Francis Scrimger of 14th Battalion Royal Regiment. Scrimger, a doctor who had studied at McGill with John McCrae, realized that the first gas used by the Germans at Ypres on 22 April 1915 was largely chlorine and that, therefore, the ammonia in urine would cause the chlorine to crystallize, thereby providing some protection to men who did not have gas masks. See the discussion of this matter by Graves in *A Crown of Life*, 187–88.

19. In this theme of betrayal, *The Wars* resembles the film *Joyeux Noël* in which three sons from both sides of the conflict will be betrayed by fathers: the German officer is punished by his kaiser; the Scots officer is rejected by his church; and the French officer, in what I found the most distressing of the betrayals, is abandoned by his own father, a French general. Their crime has been to sanction the fraternizing in No Man's Land of their soldiers during that first Christmas on the Western Front. Findley has been categorical about the rape scene; he sees it as symbolizing what civilization and the fathers' generation did to young men. For his comments on this scene, see the interview with Aitken, "Long Live the Dead," 91.

20. *The Wars* is replete with carefully distributed facts about the war, including key battles up to June 1916, weapons (the infamous Ross rifle) and *matériel*, and actual people from the period. Virginia Woolf and her pacifist friends will make an appearance; the Toronto streets and the church where Mrs. Ross stages her protest are accurate, as are many other references—for example, to Benjamin West's *The Death of General Wolfe*, the burning of the Canadian Parliament buildings, and Robert's hero Tom Longboat. Findley scholars have often commented on his ability to mix fact and fiction, right down to the smallest detail; it is a hallmark of his art, and I discuss it further in this chapter and in *On the Art of Being Canadian* (71–75). One must proceed with caution, however, and not necessarily take him at his word: Mauberley in *Famous Last Words* is a consummate liar and an elaborate fiction; see Shields's essay "Mauberley's Lies."

21. Several scholars have debated the issue of Findley's position as a postmodernist writer of metafiction (see especially Brydon, Krause, and Pennee), and this is not the place to rehearse the debate. As I have been insisting, however, post-1977 Canadian novels and plays about war must, and do, respect the facts of history. They also rely heavily on realist narrative strategies, even when they are challenging and rewriting official military history. For an important discussion of contemporary Canadian historical fiction and its narrative strategies and relationship to historiography, see Wyile's *Speculative Fictions*, especially Chapter 1; for his discussion of *The Wars* as a historical novel and as historiographic metafiction, see pages 140–44. When I say that Lady Juliet's fiction helps make Robert real to readers, I am paraphrasing Robert Kroetsch's famous comment that "the fiction makes us real" (63).



22. The original Parliament buildings were completed in 1877 in the nineteenth-century Gothic revival style. Fire destroyed these buildings in 1916 and the grand central tower was rebuilt in 1917; in 1933 it was renamed the Peace Tower.
23. Evans does a fine job of tracing the co-opting rhetoric and iconography of maternal sacrifice of the son for the state (or a cause) from biblical times to the present with the invention of the "Silver Cross Mother" in 1919 (7–8). As she points out, this latter figure of the mother is never hysterical or protesting (never a woman like Mrs. Ross), because she is being used by the state and the military to honour her child's sacrifice in war and to sanctify the struggle "by ensuring that we remember—but not too much" (157). Despite all our talk of peace and, in Canada, our celebration of peace—for example, in the 1992 unveiling of the Canadian Monument to Honour Peacekeepers, or in the Peace Tower—Evans's reminder that pacifist women were "reviled in their day" (159) is important. She writes that "the stories of Canadian mothers from the war were grounded in a patriotic and patriarchal social context reflected in images of mothers and women supporting the war effort that appeared on posters, in advertisements, and in initiatives such as the White Feather Campaign" (159).
24. The Canadian Soldier Settlement Board was established in 1917 to assist returned soldiers who had served abroad with the Canadian Expeditionary Force and other servicemen who could qualify. Men had to apply under the Settlement Act and be screened for fitness, moral character, assets, and farming capabilities. If passed, they were granted loans up to a maximum of $7,500 for the purchase of Dominion lands set aside for veterans. By 1921, the board had accepted 43,000 applications, most of which were for settlements in Alberta and Saskatchewan. There were two such settlements in British Columbia: one in the Interior and the other on Vancouver Island; see also note 28.

25. Matthew's refusal to return to teaching after the war is connected in his mind with the misleading rhetoric of poets like Tennyson and Kipling. "Sometimes," he explains, he listens to Maude trying to convince him that "there was still some sense in teaching youngsters the poems of Kipling, say, for the pleasure of imagining a life where I might still believe she was right" (44). Kipling would lose his own son in the war and modify his views on war as a result. It is Kipling's words that appear on the memorials in Imperial War Graves cemeteries: "Their Name Liveth for Evermore." For further discussion of propaganda by what Pierre Berton calls "literary liars," see *Marching as to War* (166–68); see also Buitenhuis.
26. The notion that a Canadian hero is different from the swashbuckling, aggressive, win-against-all-odds American hero has been around for some time; see, for example, Margaret Atwood's discussion in *Survival* (34–35 and 165–74). Matthew Pearson conforms to this concept of the Canadian protagonist with particular emphasis placed on his ethics and rather extreme sense of personal responsibility and guilt for tragedies he could never have stopped. In this way he further typifies the figure of a Canadian solider-as-hero and resembles Robert Ross and Xavier Bird in *Three Day Road* or Esau in *Soldier's Heart*.
27. Wyatt Taylor's story is one of several subplots in the novel. He has travelled across Canada to find Nora Macken, who had promised to marry him after the war, and he stays in the settlement to help the returned soldiers clear the massive stumps from their fields. As an explosives expert, he knows how to blast the stumps with greater accuracy than men like Mac, who is killed trying to do this on the day Taylor arrives. Like the others, Taylor represents the breadth of Canada found in the community because most of the men and their families have moved west from the east coast, Ontario and Quebec, and the Prairies to take up the government's offer of free land.
28. These excerpts from Hodgins's article "Finding Merville" demonstrate the impact on him of his first visit to the French village. He returned at a later date for a longer visit, spoke with an old-time resident who told him stories told by his father and recalled that the farmers' fields were fertilized by human bodies; this man also told him that the skeleton of a Canadian soldier, still wearing its dog tag, had recently surfaced nearby. Signs of the trenches and of No Man's Land were still visible. Hodgins was impressed by the place and by how much it reminded him of home. He would return home to write *Broken Ground* out of this experience.
29. Useful information is available about the northern Canadian concept of the Windigo, but some serious, racist misconceptions also continue to crop up. The Windigo is a figure of warning against greed and the purpose of Windigo

stories is to warn children against giving in to selfish greed, especially in times of scarcity during winter. This is not the place for a discussion of the meaning of the Windigo, but in brief I can note that once a person has given in to the Windigo spirit and tasted human flesh, he or she goes mad and becomes a Windigo that will attack and eat other human beings. Such dangerous creatures must be killed to save a community, and the killing of a Windigo must be carried out in strict, sacred ways by a shaman with the power and purity to cleanse a community from such contamination. For further information see Colombo's *Windigo*, Marano, Ray and Stevens, and Schwarz. Another major work in which the Windigo looms large is Tomson Highway's *Kiss of the Fur Queen* in which the Windigo is represented by the priests of the Roman Catholic Church who prey on native children and by the insatiable consumerism of white southern Canadian society.



30. Niska asks her friend Joseph Netmaker to write a letter to Xavier that she dictates in English, but his punctuation is faulty. Her message is that he "must return home" because he is "the last in our family line," and he must do what he needs to do to survive, even if he has to kill others; she tells Xavier that Elijah also knows this (301). However, when the letter reaches Xavier and is read to him, he is told that the letter says: "you are the last of your family" and that "God understands if you must kill Elijah" (318). This is why he believes Niska is dead and that, when the time comes, he will kill Elijah.
31. Before the final scene with Elijah, when the Canadians are ordered to advance across an open field, Xavier rebels. He tears off his ID and shouts that he is "not a part of this stupid army" (364–65). This is how he comes to be found later carrying Elijah's ID and medals but without his own dog tag. The gestures may seem slight, even gratuitous, but their significance is immense. While Xavier is mistaken for Elijah, he is in a sense not living as himself; he is estranged from himself and the identity Niska must restore to him.
32. There are many points at which a scene in France or Flanders will cause Xavier to think of home or where what he sees from the canoe will bring images of the battlefields back to him. For example, the burned forest beside the river with its stunted trees and "blackened tree stumps" looks to Xavier "just like the dead trees of Ypres" (110). This associative technique is used often by Boyden to connect home front and battle front landscapes.
33. The scene is among the more tragic in the novel and marks a significant turning point for Xavier who will never forget the unnecessary violence of killing two helpless people; see pages 304–06. This terrible moment connects, through imagery and Xavier's response, with the earlier scene when innocent birds are destroyed; see pages 257–58.

34. Francis Pegahmagabow was an Ojibway from Parry Sound and enlisted with the original 1st Battalion. With the Military Medal and two bars, he is the most decorated First Nations solider in Canadian history. He worked primarily as a sniper and had a record of 378 kills. However, when he returned to Canada he was denied land under the same Settlement Act that Hodgins describes in his novel, and he was treated in a racist and insulting manner by white authorities. He was an Indian and thus seen as a ward of the state, denied his rights and a full pension, and he suffered from both physical wounds and post-traumatic stress disorder (PTSD). He became an activist for native rights and died in 1952 at just sixty-four years of age. For a full discussion of his life during and after the war, see Hayes's *Pegahmagabow: Legendary Warrior, Forgotten Hero.* Boyden does not make Corporal Pegahmagabow a character in his novel, but his name comes up frequently (e.g., 24, 246, 286–88), and Elijah is jealous of this other Indian who is such a famous sniper.

## 4 Theatres of War

1. Gray has explained that he and Peterson chose the narrative form of memory and storytelling because Canadian audiences were comfortable with the form: "Canadians don't much like listening in on other people's conversations. They think it's impolite. This plays havoc with the basic convention of theatre itself, so what do you do? Well, you drop the fourth wall and you simply talk to the audience" ("Preface" to *Billy Bishop*, 6).
2. My allusion here is to the speech Hamlet makes to Horatio after he has spoken with his father's ghost: "There are more things in heaven and earth, Horatio, / Than are dreamt of in your philosophy" (*Hamlet* II, scene 1, lines 166–67). There are, as well, few more compelling ghosts than King Hamlet, who has come back from the grave in full armour to insist that his son remember him; but see below my discussion of the ghost in *Dancock's Dance.*
3. *Oh! What a Lovely War* was created by Littlewood, Charles Clinton, and London's Theatre Workshop. It is one of the best and most popular satiric treatments of the Great War; it premiered in London on 19 March 1963. Designed as a Pierrot and circus show with songs, dance routines, and projections, the play provides a savage critique of the war, the vanity and stupidity of the generals, of capitalist greed, and government lies and propaganda.
4. In his preface to the published text, Gray describes what happened to the play when it was produced in the United States, where a *real* First World War plane sat on the stage. With the heads of the Joint Chiefs of Staff, the CIA, the FBI. and the American Air Force sitting in the audience, this Canadian play became a pro-war spectacle devoid of irony or comic satire; it was transformed into a

play about the American Dream, and Gray and Peterson quickly grew "weary of the American Dream" (13). The play died on Broadway because it was of no interest to Americans who, as Gray notes, did not win this war (15). It was much more successful in the UK.

5. The Canadian Military Service Act making service compulsory for males between twenty and thirty-five came into force on 29 August 1917. Although exemption for conscientious objection on religious grounds was permitted, the pressure to sign up only increased. This conscription policy split the House of Commons and divided Canada, particularly francophone and anglophone Canadians, in a dangerous way.



6. Despite seeing this production and reading and teaching this play, I remain troubled by what strikes me as structural incoherence and a vague, inconclusive ending. The play actually closes with a chorus of the characters singing "A Song" that seems intended to be a version of "O Canada" and the words of this song seem meant to celebrate the overcoming of everybody's misery: "A hundred years of progress / A century for us / Oh, Canada!" (127–28).

7. David French has written five plays about generations of the Mercer family: *Leaving Home* (1972), *Of the Fields Lately* (1973), *Salt-Water Moon* (1984), *1949* (1988), and *Soldier's Heart* (2002). We meet Jacob in the first play, when he is an older, angry man living in Toronto and pining for Newfoundland, but it appears to have taken French three decades to get back to the roots of his story and what caused the son to leave home and his family.

8. As recently as 2008 when McKenna released *The Great War*, one of the young descendants of Talbot Papineau who appears in the film and grew up in Newfoundland, weeps at Beaumont-Hamel as she sings the "Ode to Newfoundland" and tells her companions that because of what happened there on 1 July 1916 her "smiling land" had no choice but to become part of Canada.

9. Flowerdew (1885–1918) was born in England but immigrated to Canada. He was living in British Columbia when war broke out and, like many Canadians of British origin, was quick to enlist.

10. Massicotte did extensive research to create his play, and as a reviewer for the *New York Theatre Wire* noted, if one didn't know that bayonets and aeroplanes co-existed in the same war, this play shows that they did. It also dramatizes the deadly futility of that co-existence for those using horses and bayonets. *Mary's Wedding* has proven very popular in Canada and abroad and is frequently remounted; it has won many awards and been widely taught. It has been adapted as an opera, which premiered with the Pacific Opera Company in November 2011. Among many other plays and scripts, Massicotte has written

an anti-war play based on T.E. Lawrence and Robert Graves called *The Oxford Roof Climber's Rebellion* (2006), and he is working on a stage play based on the Holocaust opera, *The Emperor of Atlantis (or Death's Refusal)*, composed by Viktor Ullmann with libretto by Peter Kien during their incarceration in Theresienstadt in 1943. Both men were murdered at Auschwitz.

11. Munnings (1878–1959) was a British painter famous for his drawings and paintings of horses. He worked for Lord Beaverbrook's War Art Program, which is how he came to paint this romantic canvas of the charge at Moreuil Wood. The painting is now in the Canadian War Museum.

12. This representation of the fraternization that occurred along the Western Front during that first Christmas is often referred to in fiction and it is the heart of the film *Joyeux Noël*, in which the officers on each side of the battle lines will pay dearly for allowing their men to sing and celebrate together in No Man's Land.

13. The text of *The Lost Boys* is extremely interesting and useful for anyone reading, studying, or wanting to produce the play. In it, Thomson reproduces pictures of his uncles, their mother, German soldiers, gravesites, and other images relevant to the play. Thomson himself appears in a photograph accompanying the note on the author at the end of the text and this makes it easy for those not familiar with his face to see exactly how much he resembles his great-uncle George.

14. Chamberlin attributes this quotation to a Tsimshian elder speaking Gitksan (*If This Is Your Land* 1).

15. *Vimy* premiered on 25 October 2007 on the Maclab Stage at the Citadel Theatre in Edmonton. The production was a stunning success, with Clare played by Daniela Vlaskalic, Will by Matt Busby, Sid by Phil Fulton, J.-P. and Bert by Vincent Hoss-Demarais, Mike and Claude by Sheldon Elter, and Laurie by Billy MacLellan. James MacDonald directed, with co-designers Bretta Gerecke and Narda McCarroll. Brian Dooley served as dramaturge, and in his "Afterword" to the published text he speaks of the battle as crucial for Canadian identity and sums up the play as Thiessen's "dramatic elegy to a defining moment in Canadian history" (81).

16. In her excellent edition of the war diary of Clare Gass (1887–1968), Susan Mann provides a wealth of information about Canadian nurses in the First World War and many details about the life and work of Gass. Among those details is the fact that, while training in Montreal, the Nova Scotia-born Clare became particularly fond of her second cousin, Laurence Gass, an engineering student at McGill, and that he is the "Laurie" mentioned in Clare's diary (xix). Lieutenant Laurence Gass was killed at Vimy Ridge. Clare learned of his death

on 18 April, and the only entry in her diary for that day was: "Laurie!" (166). She made no entry on the 19th, and on the 20th noted the death of one of her brothers. Susan Mann describes Laurence Gass as "an exceptional young man" (287) and, judging from his picture, he was handsome (288). Clare never married, but she did keep Laurie's picture with her through her long life. Clearly there was a romantic connection between the cousins, but Thiessen has invented a much more serious relationship for his Clare and Laurie.

17. The Vimy Glide is the term used to describe the way the infantry had to move forward, one hundred yards every three minutes, keeping carefully behind artillery barrages sent over their heads to weaken the German lines. If the men ran too quickly, they would be caught by artillery firing from behind them; if they were too slow they would be in the way and lose the advancing line they started with. The scene in which the men re-enact practising this glide is one of the few moments of humour in the play (see 43–44).





## 5 "Away to the War and Back Again"

1. I will refer to the autobiographical writing I explore as auto/biography to emphasize the fact that these works are never simply the life stories of one individual but of a family, a group, a community or, in some texts, of the country. Memoirs are narrower and more personal stories than auto/biographies. As a rule they cover only a small portion of an individual's life—in politics or during the Holocaust, and so forth. Auto/biography always includes the narrator's story within, or alongside, the larger story of those around him or her. It goes without saying, I hope, that auto/biography is not truth but a fictional creation with close ties to the facts and events and lives of actual people.

2. I choose these two because of their wide dissemination on national television and then as DVDs, but also because they provide interesting examples of documentary appeals to younger audiences by involving individuals from that generation in the process of remembering. Other documentaries include *The Battle of Vimy Ridge*, the six-part series *For King and Country, Forgotten Warriors, And We Knew How to Dance: Women in World War I, John McCrae's War: In Flanders Fields, Front Lines: The Private Faces of War*, and the First World War segments of *Canada Remembers*.

3. The 1982 excellent film of Findley's *The Wars*, directed by Robin Phillips with Brent Carver as Robert Ross and a score created by Glenn Gould, featured several major actors, among them Martha Henry, William Hutt, and Jackie Burroughs. The film has been withdrawn from circulation, however, and is no longer available for viewing. The 1986 film *Going Home*, directed by Terence

Ryan and starring Nicholas Campbell, is a powerful treatment of the 1919 Canadian mutiny in a Welsh demobilization camp. The mutiny was brutally repressed and information about what happened was kept secret for decades; see my discussion of the film in *On the Art of Being Canadian* (75–77 and 78–79).

4. I have taken all quotations from the DVD and checked accuracy against the actual film.
5. See my discussion of "The Memory Project" and of David Williams's analysis in Chapter 2.
6. Berton describes General Arthur Currie's anger at being ordered to use the Canadians to capture Passchendaele Ridge and his disgust at the stupidity and waste of the campaign. Currie inspected the battlefield ahead of time and was shocked at the mess he found. He predicted major losses and Berton describes him as "bitter and heartsick" after the battle (*Marching as to War* 187). Passchendaele was not worth the cost.
7. This story, never proved, inspired a sculpture by Derwent Wood called *Canada's Golgotha* (1918). The piece, which is now in the Canadian War Museum, was exhibited in 1919 and then, as a result of German protests and lack of hard evidence that any such atrocity took place, it went into storage, where it stayed until 1992. For a discussion of this controversy and an image of the sculpture, see Laura Brandon's *Art or Memorial?* (30).
8. In 1995 the CBC, in conjunction with the NFB, made a fifty-minute film based on *The Danger Tree*. Macfarlane narrates the story, which, in this version, focuses closely on the war and its meaning for Newfoundland. This film is now difficult to see, but I was fortunate to locate a copy and I am quoting here from the film. In his 1 July 2006 article for the *Globe and Mail*, "July 1, 1916: The Somme of All Loss," Macfarlane marks the ninety-year anniversary of the tragedy and reminds readers that, for Newfoundland, Beaumont-Hamel has mythic importance.
9. The Canadian Movement developed after the war and led to the formation of many pan-Canadian clubs and organizations such as the Canadian Institute for International Affairs, the Canadian League, and the League of Nations Society; see Gwyn, 488–89. The Canadian League had a right-wing element that was rabidly anti-Communist, but Claxton was successful in lobbying the Ontario government to repeal the law that forbade French-language instruction in the province—the very law that so infuriated Henri Bourassa.
10. This poem is not bitter, finally, but celebratory, and it should be better known than it is. Published in 1969, it is another example of the secondary witnessing by a non-combatant that I have been discussing in this chapter.

## 6 Living in a Haunted World

1. I have discussed the question of war in Lowry's works, especially in *Under the Volcano*, in my essay "Remembering Tomorrow."
2. Lowry lived on the west coast of Canada from 1939 to 1954; he tried to enlist in Vancouver but was rejected. He always insisted that he was not a pacifist and that he had seen Hitler as an evil threat since the early 1930s, but his vision of life was deeply non-aggressive, and I find it hard to imagine how he would have coped in an army.
3. Among the many other works I might consider in this chapter are Wendy Lill's *The Fighting Days* about women's struggle to get the vote against a background of anti-Communist hysteria; Timothy Findley's *The Butterfly Plague*, which follows the rise of Nazism in Germany and demonstrates how such thinking infiltrates North America; Sharon Pollock's *The Komagata Maru Incident*, a play that focuses on the infamous treatment of Sikh immigrants to Canada, who were refused entry in the summer of 1914 and forced to return to India, but stages that event in the context of German espionage in the lead-up to the First World War; Wayson Choy's *The Jade Peony*, which tells the story of growing up in Vancouver's Chinatown in the context of the 1930s, when Chinese Canadians watched helplessly as Japan invaded their former home and hatred between Chinese and Japanese Canadians erupted in Vancouver's streets; Judy Fong Bates's auto/biography *The Year of Finding Memory* about her own return to China to find the story of her parents' escape from a war-torn China and their attempt to find peace in Canada; and Eric Siblin's *The Cello Suites*, in which the great Pablo Cassals and the conflict in Spain meet against the backdrop of Bach's music.
4. Bruemmer is best known to Canadians for his books about the Canadian Arctic; he spent many years travelling and photographing the circumpolar world, and his work and photography bring its beauty and fragility to our attention.
5. Eksteins's study of the Great War, *Rites of Spring*, is a major interdisciplinary exploration of the forces building up in Europe prior to the war and the long-range cultural results of the war. It deserves to be better known.
6. The Communist Party of Canada was founded in Guelph, Ontario, in 1921. It became a legal party in 1924 but was banned in 1939 and harassed by police during the 1920s and 1930s: meetings were broken up, offices raided, and activists suspected of being Communists were arrested and, if foreign-born, deported. Canadian Communists played a role in the Winnipeg Strike and the On to Ottawa Trek, as well as supporting the Republican cause in Spain. Canadians have recently learned that during the Cold War, the government

instituted a secret anti-Communist policy known as PROFUNC, under which anyone deemed suspicious as a possible security threat could be arrested, interned, and shot if they tried to escape. I first heard about this policy on the CBC program *The Fifth Estate*, which aired on 14 October 2010. PROFUNC, which stands for "PROminent FUNCtionairies of the communist party," was not abolished until 1980.

7. The cast for the premiere of *Can You See Me Yet?* included Frances Hyland as Cassandra, Helen Burns as Alma, Maggie Griffin as Rosemary, Judy Marshak as Annie, Doris Petrie as Doretta, Amelia Hall as Maudie, Lawrence Aubrey as Franklin, Larry Reynolds as Clare, William Webster as Edward, Clare Coulter as Enid, and Edward Atienza as Doberman. Marigold Charlesworth directed, with sets by Pat Flood. The play opened on 1 March 1976 at the National Arts Centre in Ottawa.



8. This woman existed, as did most of the characters and bit players in Bock's version of Bethune's life; however, her precise identity (was she a spy or not?) and the extent of her connection with Bethune are debated. According to Michael Petrou, Kasja Rothman fled Spain for Mexico after Franco took power; she died there thirty years later and was neither a spy nor a fascist (164–67). Petrou makes no mention of a child she might have had with Bethune, but they did have an affair. Bock chooses to make her the great love in Bethune's life and the mother of this daughter to whom he addresses the auto/biography. Bock also imagines her as killed by the Republican forces, who believe she is a fascist spy, soon after giving birth to the child.

9. The Second Sino-Japanese War, beginning in 1937, merged with the Second World War, and General Chiang Kai-shek was Allied commander-in-chief in China through the war. He faced mounting opposition within China and the Chinese Communist Party's Red Army conducted successful resistance operations against the Japanese and mounted a major offensive in northern China. After the war, the Nationalists under Chiang Kai-shek were weak and the Communists under Mao Zedong were poised to take over the country. The result was a civil war that ended with the Nationalists banished to Taiwan and the Communists in control of China; the Cultural Revolution would follow.

10. I discuss the artistic process of making icons of these real people in Chapter 3 of *On the Art of Being Canadian*. Emily Carr and Mina Benson Hubbard have also been reinvented until today they are iconic figures.

11. For recent studies by experts on China see *Scars of War*. As Diana Lary and Stephen MacKinnon note in their introduction to the book, "There are no war cemeteries in China" (8) and silence about memories too painful to recall

prevails. This book appeared in 2001 and since then signs of change in China's willingness to remember are beginning to appear in films, memorials, and acknowledged cemeteries.

12. Iris Chang's life and death are troubling. Although well-educated and a successful writer, she suffered from depression and had a nervous breakdown in 2004. The reasons for this lie in her constant work to promote her third book and the nature of her ongoing research into the treatment of Chinese Americans. She became an activist pressing for Japan to acknowledge its atrocities in China, and after her suicide a bronze statue of Chang was erected in Nanjing.

13. John Rabe established the Nanking Safety Zone, which included several embassies and Ginling College and sheltered around 200,000 Chinese. He had lived and worked in China from 1910, spoke Chinese, and loved the country. He took photographs of the atrocities, made a film while there, and kept a diary. When he returned to Germany in 1938 he gave public lectures on the state of affairs in China and wrote to Hitler asking him to help by persuading Japan to stop its massacre. The Gestapo were not impressed, however, and Rabe was detained and his film confiscated; he was allowed to keep his photographs and diaries. Denounced by the Allies, and arrested by the British and the Russians, he was declared "de-Nazified" in June 1946, but his health was broken and he died in 1950. His tombstone in Berlin was moved to Nanjing as part of a memorial to the massacre, and his former residence in the city was restored as a memorial hall and opened in 2006. His diaries have been translated and published under the title (in the UK) of *The Good German of Nanjing* (1998) and the film *John Rabe*, directed by Florian Gallenberger, was released in 2009. Rabe's story and his reputation are slowly being recuperated. Minnie (Winnifred) Vautrin went to China as a missionary in 1912 and helped to found Ginling College. During the worst of the raping and massacre the college, built to house 200 to 300 girls, sheltered around 10,000 women. Vautrin returned to the United States and, unable to forget her experiences there, she committed suicide in 1941. A documentary film called *Nanking* was released in 2007 and is based on Iris Chang's book. The most impressive film about the massacre to date is Lu Chuan's *City of Life and Death* (2009). In it Chuan depicts much of the atrocity that took place while using a kindly young Japanese soldier as his witness to the horror and as a form of ethical barometer for events. At the end, this man kills himself after freeing two Chinese hostages (one a child). The film was shot in black and white in a chronological present.

## 7 "Made in Canada"

1. Although the Communist Party of Canada (CPC) was legal as of 1921, party leader Tim Buck and other party members were persecuted and jailed during the war. Joe Wallace (1890–1975), a CPC member, writer, journalist, and poet was incarcerated at Petawawa during the war and, according to James Doyle, was reported to have protested when he heard himself and fellow political prisoners described by prison officials as "enemy aliens" by replying that they were not "enemy aliens" but "Canadian anti-fascists" (Doyle 164). Wallace was put in solitary confinement for this telling of truth. As early as 1933, the agitprop play *Eight Men Speak* was closed by Toronto police after one night's performance (on 4 December 1933) because it was deemed by the authorities to be dangerous. The play uses abstract characters and stylized scenes to portray the 1932 arrest of Canadian Communists and the attempted assassination of Tim Buck during a riot in Kingston Penitentiary; Buck had no part in the riot (see Doyle 130–31; see also Toby Ryan 43–47).
2. From today's perspective, this 1949 novel strikes me as uncomfortably pro-Zionist, and in it Klein does not explore how or under what circumstances the state of Israel was created after the war. At the same time, this novel is remarkably contemporary in its narrative strategies. By using a first-person narrator on a personal search to find his uncle and the past, he produces the kind of haunted, witnessing auto/biographer figure so familiar today in works about the Second World War, and in this sense *The Second Scroll* is a more sophisticated narrative than *Earth and High Heaven*.
3. Among other historians, academic and popular, to write about Canada's participation in the war, see works by Bercuson, Broadfoot (1974), Keshen, McCormick and Perry, and Pierson. I discuss Bercuson and Wise on *The Valour and the Horror* later, and Zuehlke's *Ortona* is, to date, our best major study of that battle.
4. Earle Birney (1904–1995) served with the Canadian army in personnel selection during the war and spent three years in England, Belgium, and Holland. Among his writings about the war are the novel *Turvey* and the poems in his 1945 volume *Now Is Time*, one of the most powerful being "The Road to Nijmegen" (42–43). Birney returned after the war to build an important career as a poet and an academic and he seemed less traumatized by his experiences in Europe than many.
5. Colin McDougall (1917–84), who enlisted with the Princess Patricia's Canadian Light Infantry and won a Distinguished Service Order, fought in the Italian campaign. He became registrar at McGill University after the war. *Execution* won a Governor General's Award for fiction in 1958 and it is his only novel, but it is a moving account of Canadian Major John Adam's experience (loosely

based on McDougall's) during the campaign and his inability to save a young soldier from execution by firing squad. McDougall's account is based on the actual execution for murder of Private Harold Pringle on 5 July 1945 (see Clark's *A Keen Soldier*). Canada's policy of executing its own soldiers is also criticized by Jack Hodgins in *Broken Ground* and by Vern Thiessen in *Vimy*.

6. Although there are, to date, fewer post-1977 novels, plays, auto/biographies, biographies, and films exploring the Canadian experiences in the Second World War than in the First, there are still too many for me to examine each in detail. Inevitably, I have had to make difficult choices, but I have been guided in my selection by my decision to focus on texts that create strong home front landscapes while remembering the war in the Pacific or in Europe. For my brief consideration of Michael Ondaatje's *The English Patient*, see Chapter 8; for my analysis of Robert Lepage and Ex Machina's *Seven Streams of the River Ota*, see Grace, "Playing Butterfly"; Timothy Findley's *Famous Last Words* and *The Telling of Lies* both explore the Second World War, but neither directly addresses Canadians in the war nor the Canadian home front. Other works of interest include Bacque's *Our Father's War*, Finucan's *The Fallen*, Humphrey's *Coventry*, Huston's *Fault Lines*, Itani's *Requiem*, Marlatt's *Taken*, and Sabbatini's *Dante's War*; and plays by Chislett, Moscowitcz, Rossi, Stubbs, and Thompson (*Such Creatures*) also address home front or Holocaust issues. I consider *Such Creatures* in Chapter 10.

7. These fears were real, if also exaggerated by the media. The Imperial Japanese Navy and Airforce were active along the Canadian and American coasts between Alaska and California during the war. On 20 June 1942, a Japanese submarine, I-26, fired twenty-one shots at the Estevan Point lighthouse on Vancouver Island in an effort to knock out wireless communication; they occupied and held two of the most westerly of the Aleutian Islands (Attu and Niska); they bombed Dutch Harbor, an Alaskan fishing village; and by July 1943, 5,300 Canadian troops had sailed north from Vancouver Island to help the Americans drive the Japanese out of the Aleutians. The reputation of the Japanese as vicious killers preceded them after their assault on Hong Kong in December 1941 (right after Pearl Harbor), so anxieties and hostility had roots in experience for Canadians. For a discussion of activities along the Pacific coast, see Brendan Coyle's *War On Our Doorstep*. The legacy of this Japanese activity was not only a move to militarize the Canadian Northwest and to allow increased American military presence on Canadian soil, but also an apparent justification for persecution of Japanese Canadians living in coastal areas. As Coyle is quick to point out, accusations of spying and treachery were "groundless" and "outright racist" (71), and as Ken Adachi confirms in *The Enemy That*

*Never Was*, anti-Asian prejudice had longstanding roots in "white" Canada and the Second World War added fuel to this simmering racism. I find it curious that Kogawa does not allow either Naomi or Aunt Emily to reflect on the actual presence of Japan in our coastal waters or to acknowledge the atrocities committed by the Japanese military in Hong Kong or, for that matter, in China during the Imperial Army's 1937 invasion. There were good reasons for dreading the Japanese military.

8. In *Homo Sacer* and *State of Exception*, Agamben argues that Nazi ideology first stripped German Jews of their rights as citizens and their property, then used propaganda to dehumanize them as less than human—as vermin or insects—then moved to incarcerate them *within* the German state, before more aggressively moving to genocide. According to Agamben, Jews were reduced to the condition of "bare life" (*Homo Sacer* 8) within a state of exception (a condition, but also a place like the concentration camp, where groups in society are isolated beyond the safeguards of laws and constitutions in a kind of stateless no man's land), and could, therefore, be "*killed and yet not sacrificed*" with impunity (*Homo Sacer* 8, 82). He goes on to warn that "in our age, the state of exception comes more and more to the foreground as the fundamental political structure" (*Homo Sacer* 20); see also *State of Exception* (2, 39, and 52). The Canadian government instituted several orders under the War Measures Act that resemble the preparatory steps taken by the Nazis, and they subjected German and Italian Canadians to treatment similar to that experienced by Japanese Canadians.

9. For varying responses to *Obasan*, see studies by Banerjee, Brydon, Davidson, Deer, Goldman (128–40), Howells, Kamboureli, Karpinski, McFarlane, and Merivale. To my mind, Karpinski makes the most productive contribution to recent discussions of the novel by stressing its representation of trauma, testimony, and cultural memory; she sees Naomi as a gendered survivor whose personal trauma exposes official history. Kamboureli argues, as do I, that the novel does not *conclude* with a resolution of injustice and trauma, but ends with both the historical and personal issues left open-ended.

10. The Canadian Somerville Games Company did indeed produce a popular board game called "Yellow Peril", but the term "Yellow Peril" dates back to the late nineteenth century and was commonly used in twentieth-century popular culture to refer to Chinese villains like Fu Manchu. The idea of Asians as the "Yellow Peril" could be found everywhere by the 1930s, from novels, films, and comics to pulp fiction. It is a pleasure to thank my colleague, Glenn Deer, for his assistance with this reference.

11. Wheeler has made, to date, three films about the Second World War. The best-known of these is *Bye Bye Blues* (1989), a feature film based on her mother's experience as a pianist at home during the war years. *A War Story* (1981) is a docudrama that explores her father's experience as a doctor in a Japanese POW camp; it is narrated by Donald Sutherland and takes the actors and film crew back to Japan to revisit the site. Like *The War Between Us*, this film is almost impossible to see today. *The War Between Us* was filmed on location in New Denver, BC, with a script prepared by Sharon Gibbon. Wheeler worked closely with the local community and with the Nikkei Internment Memorial Centre in New Denver, and as the filming progressed people became actively interested and involved in the process. In the end, the film is as much a biography/history of a town as it is a story of the war. Mieko Ouchi plays the role of Aya with Robert Ito as her father Mr. Kawashima. For Wheeler's comments on the war and her sources of inspiration for these films, see "Perspectives on War" in *Bearing Witness*.

12. In *Villa Air-Bel*, Rosemary Sullivan describes Varian Fry's work to get artists and intellectuals out of Europe through Vichy France via the safe house of the villa outside Marseilles. From Marseilles Fry arranged for his refugees to take escape routes out of France through Spain and Portugal to freedom—if they were successful—in North America. Among some of his most famous clients were Max Ernst, Marc Chagall, and André Breton. Walter Benjamin would commit suicide before completing his escape.

13. Today the site of Camp L appears to be a golf course. However, it existed and was one of twenty-six such prison camps for persons of German or Italian "racial origins." For an especially disturbing and important account of the camp and of how the German-Jewish refugees were treated there and in Camp N in Sherbrooke, Quebec, see Walter Igersheimer's memoir *Blatant Injustice: The Story of a Jewish Refugee from Nazi Germany Imprisoned in Britain and Canada during World War II*. *Blatant Injustice* is one of the few published memoirs to document Canadian imprisonment of European refugees, and it did not appear until 2005, but see also Koch and Kreisel ("Diary of an Internment"). As the 2012 catalogue and exhibition, *Enemy Aliens*, at Vancouver's Holocaust Education Centre confirms, no female refugees were held at Camp L. For an account of Italian Canadians who were interned as "enemy aliens," see Mario Dulani's moving story of his arrest and incarceration in *The City Without Women: A Chronicle of Internment Life in Canada during the Second World War* and John Murrell's play *Waiting for the Parade*. The SS *St. Louis*, a ship in the Hamburg-America Line, sailed from Hamburg on 13 May 1939 carrying almost one thousand Jewish refugees to Cuba; however, the ship was not allowed to land or the passengers

to disembark in Havana, so it was forced to return to Europe, where countries there accepted groups of refugees. For a description of the fate of the ship and its refugees, see Abella and Troper, 63–66; Canada was one of the countries that refused to allow the passengers to disembark, so Bock's Sophie would have arrived in Canada via Europe.

14. Pugwash, Nova Scotia, is the small town where a group of scientists met for the first time in 1957 to discuss the threat of nuclear arms and possible war. Now known as the Pugwash Conferences on Science and World Affairs, the conferences continue to address major issues facing the world. In 1995 the organization won the Nobel Peace Prize. Boch's Anton Böll attends the founding conference.





15. Van Wyck notes, with frustration, the restrictions and practical hurdles put in the way of any researcher who wants to study the thirty-four metres of records belonging to Eldorado Nuclear Limited held in Library and Archives Canada (6–10), and he thinks of his book, written against these restrictions, as exposing "a very Canadian exercise in forgetting" (12).

16. *Highway of the Atom* was one of many "industrial documentaries" made by Crawley Films. Labelled production #491, it was shot in November 1951 and finished in July 1952; the sponsor was the Northern Transportation Company, which explains the boosterish tone of the piece. My thanks to James Forrester and Paul Harris for the emails that provided this information on a now largely forgotten film. I would also like to thank my colleague Peter van Wyck for bringing the film to my attention in the first place. This colour film invokes an illustrious history of white explorers opening up the North to trade routes, industrial development, and progress. Contemporary mining and engineering feats are likened to the heroic endeavours of Alexander Mackenzie, and southern technology and science are touted as "carrying life to the North." The heroine of the film is the tug boat called the *Radium Franklin*, a new member of the Radium fleet, on her maiden voyage from the shipyards in Vancouver, up to Waterways, Alberta, to the Mackenzie River, and across on the Bear River to Fort Franklin (Deline) on Great Bear Lake. The North, while filmed as always beautiful, under sunny skies, is described by the narrator as "trackless" and empty; the Indians are stevedores who cannot read or write, and no mention is given of their families or communities; and we are told that the mine at Port Radium is "the very source of the power of the atom" that ended the war and is now changing the world. I make these quotations of the film's narrator from my viewing of an old copy of the film; more detailed information is not available.

17. Van Wyck describes the actual practice of radium painting by the American Radium Dial Company, which established a factory in 1922 to paint numbers on clock faces that would glow in the dark. The company hired young women to do this work and they had no protection from the materials they used. Cancer rates escalated among the women and a famous lawsuit focused on the "emaciated, cancer-ridden body of a dial painter, Catherine Donahue" (92). In the play, this figure is especially striking and disturbing because she is so vulnerable and innocent—and yet is dying.

18. The play premiered at Vancouver's Firehall Theatre on 26 April 2002 with Margo Kane playing the roles of the Dene Widow and the Japanese Grandmother, Allan Morgan as Fat Man, Hiro Kanagawa as Koji, and Dene Elder George Blondin performing as the Dene See-er. The production was directed by Peter Hinton, with set design by Andreas Kahre and lighting (a crucial component in the action of this play) by John Webber. The opening explosion was an effective way of plunging an unsuspecting audience into the darkness, noise, and shuddering impact of a bombing experience, and when this is repeated towards the end of the play, the audience is forcibly reminded of the events leading up to the first dropping of the bomb. For me these two shocks served to emphasize my role as a secondary witness above and beyond my already clear witnessing position as an audience member.

19. In *When the World Was New* (78–79), George Blondin retells the Dene medicine man's story of his vision and warning about white men coming to their land and taking the black rock to use it elsewhere to create the atomic bombs from the mysterious and dangerous substance. Blondin, who played the role of the Dene See-er in the premiere of *Burning Vision*, delivers this story in the third and fourth movements of the play.

20. Perhaps it is unfair to ask a playwright to do more than Clements achieves in her play, but I do find that the absence of any attention to the causes of the war or to Japanese atrocities creates a problem for the ethical dimensions of her otherwise very powerful drama.

21. Inouye, who was known as the "Kamloops Kid," was a Canadian citizen born in Kamloops, British Columbia; he was studying in Japan when war broke out and was conscripted into the Imperial Army, where he served as an interpreter and prison camp guard in Hong Kong's notorious Sham Shui Po POW camp. He became known for his unusual brutality, notably to Canadian prisoners of war, and several Canadian POWs testified at his trial that he was responsible for the torture and death of at least eight Canadians. At his trial, Inouye claimed that he had been a victim of racist abuse in Canada. For further historical information on Inouye, see Greenfield's study of Canadian POWs in *The Damned*

(376–79). Crummey departs considerably from these facts in creating his character Nishino, but the basic outline is there: Nishino enlists in the Japanese army, is subject to racism in Vancouver, is brutal to the prisoners, and hates all Canadians with fierce intensity. His death, however, is not the result of a formal trial for war crimes, and Crummey's invention of his murder by liberated POWS is a crucial element in Wish's story. Herb Wyile comments on the racist treatment of Nishino in Vancouver in his discussion of the "ethical turn" in recent literature; see "Making a Mess of Things" (826–27).

22. The Guadalcanal Campaign, code-named "Operation Watchtower," took place between August 1942 and February 1943. It was won by the American Marines and the Allied forces, and ended by pushing the Japanese army into a long and costly retreat. Crummey has observed the historical facts as the basis for this opening section of his novel, but there is no indication I am aware of that a Japanese Canadian serving with the Imperial Army was present. Crummey has invented his character Nishino; see note 21.

23. In a more thorough analysis of the images and echoes in the text, one might well develop a different interpretation of Wish's behaviour. One might ask, for example, why he cannot see in his inability to urinate on the dead interpreter an unconscious rescue from further complicity in degrading another human being. In such a reading, Wish's refusal to seduce the sixteen-year-old girl because he loves and respects her, despite his sexual drive, serves as the sign of his body's remembrance of her presence, which saves him from an equally sinful act. In the final analysis, Crummey leaves this sexual echo, along with many other echoes and memories in the novel, unresolved and ambiguous.

24. What Wish sees in the newspaper is the report and photograph of fourteen-year-old Emmett Till (1941–1955) who was savagely beaten and murdered in Mississippi for whistling at a white woman. Photographs of the corpse confirm that his face was reduced to a pulp, much as we are told Nishino's was.

## 8 The Promised Land

1. See Allemang's discussion of this history in his 24 October 2009 piece. He not only reminded Canadians of the Nazi creation of the relay, but he also noted that the Berlin games were memorable for their obvious anti-Semitism and other racial prejudices. For Canadian fictional representation of these games see Findley's *The Butterfly Plague* and Dennis Bock's *Olympia*. To the best of my knowledge, Allemang's facts were ignored and effectively dismissed by supporters of the games and the torch relay. However, the Vancouver Holocaust Education Centre mounted a special exhibition—"More Than Just Games:

Canada & the 1936 Olympics"—in an effort to inform people and contextualize the games.

2. Dunkirk, Dieppe, and D-Day, from the Canadian landing at Juno Beach to Verrières Ridge and Caen, are examined by military historians from Berton to Granatstein and Morton; for a moving film account of Dieppe, see the 1993 CBC film *Dieppe*, directed by John Smith, and for descriptions of Canadians in Normandy, see Ted Barris and Antony Beevor. Beevor calls Dieppe a "murderous fiasco" (77), and of Juno Beach he says that Canadians were "determined to take revenge for the Dieppe raid" (130–31).

3. For a striking depiction of the war bride subject, see the film *The War Bride* directed by Lyndon Chubbuck and starring Anna Friel as the young Englishwoman who marries a Canadian soldier, Charlie, only to find that his ranch on the Prairies is a remote, weatherbeaten house where his impoverished mother and sister live. These two women greet the ebullient Lily, newly arrived from London and carrying her small daughter, with hostility and resentment. Life is hard for these women and they make it hard for their daughter-in-law. Things do not improve when a traumatized Charlie returns home. That Lily finally prevails over her unloving relatives and harsh surroundings provides a rather sunny conclusion to a reality that was often bitter.

4. Murrell interviewed hundreds of women from Calgary and environs who had lived through the war years, and from these interviews he developed the five characters in his play. Theirs, he felt, was the "great, untold story" of Canadians in the Second World War (see Picard). Since its premiere in 1977, *Waiting for the Parade* has become a classic, much loved by general audiences. My students, however, criticize Murrell's portrayal of women, finding them nostalgic stereotypes with little relevance for the twenty-first century. This response to the play misses a key point: Murrell's historical reconstruction of the 1940s, in addition to informing us about our past, exposes racist and sexist attitudes of the period that could surface again.

5. Friedrich von Flotow's *Martha* is a romantic opera with libretto by Wilhelm Friedrich. Some of the arias, such as the title solo "Martha" and "The Last Rose of Summer," remain favourites in the repertoire. The lines we hear Tauber singing in the play—"Ach so fromm, ach so traut"—are from "The Last Rose of Summer" in which the hero, Lyonnel, describes a dream in which he lives with the beautiful Martha as his love.

6. According to Abella and Troper, Canada accepted fewer than 5,000 Jewish refugees between 1933 and 1945 and had "the worst record for providing sanctuary" (x). Other countries accepted many more: for example, the United States accepted more than 200,000; Palestine, 125,000; Great Britain, 70,000;

Argentina, 50,000; China, 25,000; Chile, 14,000 (x). See also Joe King's *From the Ghetto to the Main*, in which he provides the following statistics on Canada's acceptance of refugees: "1935—880 Jews allowed in; 1936—619; 1937—584; and 1938-39, on the eve of World War II, 890" (208).

7. See my discussion of *The Ash Garden* (319-27, this volume) and Bock's description of the ship (134-38). Abella and Troper also describe the fate of the ship and its passengers (63-65).

8. Although the person who made this racist remark has not, to my knowledge, been positively identified, Joe King states that it was Blair (*From the Ghetto to the Main* 208). Blair has been quoted as saying that "Jews and other undesireables would never be admitted" into Canada (Abella and Troper 147).



9. An analysis of ghosts and bearing witness is possible with *The English Patient*, but the novel belongs to a different discussion—one about post-national fiction and politics—than mine in this book. The same is true of other works I have chosen not to consider: Findley's *Famous Last Words*, Huston's *Fault Lines*, and Sabatini's *Dante's War* are not set in Canada and do not feature Canadian war stories or landscapes of memory. A novel that should be remembered here, however, is Henry Kreisel's *The Betrayal* (1964). Set in Edmonton after the war, it explores the aftermath of the Holocaust, the impact of that horror on survivors in Canada, and the impossibility of leaving war and atrocity behind when one lives in the seemingly innocent landscapes of Canada. As one character, Professor Lerner, realizes: "Here it was, the whole horror of the recent European past, in this apartment [Lerner's apartment in Edmonton], where on the whole I live a peaceful, contented, relatively happy life. Here now were the old ghosts, and I was, whether I wanted it or not, involved" (*The Betrayal* 43-44). In another context, I might trace the fictional representation of the impact of the Holocaust in Canada back to Kreisel's novel. Hugh MacLennan revisits this impact in his historical novel *Voices in Time*.

10. Although "Stones" is not an auto/biographical story per se, the two world wars were major events in Findley's life and his family's history. The family had lived in Rosedale and Findley's father did enlist in the Second World War. The novel *You Went Away* comes much closer to depicting the impact of the war on Findley and his parents.

11. The term "Zombies" was used for men conscripted to serve Canadian home defence under the National Resources Mobilization Act (NRMA) of 1940. The term was pejorative and carried the stigma of cowardice because such men did not volunteer for active service overseas. They wore drab uniforms and, as Findley notes, sometimes engaged in violence against soldiers home on leave. By the war's end, many thousands of NRMA men had been sent overseas.

12. Granatstein and Morton provide a devastating description of "the charnel-house of Dieppe," where of the "4,943 Canadians [who] set off from England, 2,211 returned, almost half of whom had never gone ashore" (208). Between 300 and 400 men were evacuated from the beaches—a fraction of those who landed and died there (*Canada and the Two World Wars* 209). To read their description of the beaches or to visit them today is to be stunned by the madness of the Allied plan: "every Dieppe beach was commanded by almost unassailable cliffs, and...tanks could not operate effectively on pebbled beaches" (209). Dieppe was a slaughter and, with the exception of the 1979 CBC documentary *Dieppe* (see Terence Macartney-Filgate), it did not receive general public discussion and analysis in Canada by Canadians until the 1990s. John Smith's CBC film *Dieppe* was shown in 1993, five years after Findley published the volume *Stones* and four years after Granatstein and Morton examined the subject in *A Nation Forged in Fire* (1989), which forms part of their 2003 volume *Canada and the Two World Wars.*



13. As I noted in Chapter 2, prosopopoeia is often a strategic trope in the literature I consider. Paul de Man calls it "the trope of autobiography" because it produces "the fiction of an apostrophe to an absent, deceased, or voiceless entity, which posits the possibility of the latter's reply and confers upon it the power of speech" (75-76). In "Stones," Ben addresses us but he also speaks to his first addressee—his dead father—who speaks back to him through memory and ashes. Findley's most striking image of this spectral addressivity occurs with the envelope holding his father's ashes that Ben addresses to himself; it is *as if* (for this simile is carried by a metaphor—the envelope with its message/ashes—for speech) his father could speak to him from these ashes, reminding him to scatter the ashes on the beach at Dieppe...or else. "*I* am the dead," David Max reminds his son, as if to echo McCrae's dead. Levine also relies on prosopopoeia to bring Hana Brady back to life, but Anne Michaels deploys the trope throughout *Fugitive Pieces* in an almost dizzying representation of narrators' voices speaking to each other and to readers in apostrophe to the dead and in reply by the dead.

14. In her "Afterword" Levine tells us that the original suitcase was "destroyed, along with many other objects from the Holocaust, in a suspicious fire in Birmingham, England in 1984" (108). The one sent to Fumiko was, therefore, a replica of this original. However, this fact was not revealed until 2004, when George Brady visited Auschwitz, and it makes very little difference to the impact and purpose of Hana's story. Indeed, one might even argue that the fate of the original was overcome, as Hana's fate could not be, by its complex afterlife.

15. In addition to the original radio program created by Levine, this award-winning children's book, and the docudrama film by Weinstein, Hana's story has also been made into a play. Through these various genres and media it continues to travel the world and inform younger generations of Canadians and others.
16. I have selected Michaels's novel for close analysis because of its quality but also because it deals so explicitly with a *Canadian* landscape haunted by its characters' memories of the war. See note 9. Another novel that depicts the aftermath, in Canada, of the Holocaust is Alison Pick's *Far to Go* (2010), and I briefly address this text in Chapter 10.



17. The term "middle voice" helps to locate an appropriate voice for Holocaust historiography; it is neither the passive, impersonal voice of the historian nor the more intimate, self-referential voice of the auto/biographer. English does not have a grammatical middle voice between the active and passive voices; therefore, in English a writer must find a discursive way (as Hayden White and Roland Barthes have argued—see LaCapra, *Writing History, Writing Trauma* 18–20) to represent events that is neither simply referential to physical reality nor merely intransitive and self-referential. The result is an in-between position of personalized, yet factual, narration that conveys a degree of undecidedability. Vincent Pecora gives a thoughtfully critical assessment of ethical claims for the middle voice, and LaCapra cautions against a too easy stress on its value. I agree, especially when the subject is war, atrocity, and the Holocaust, or when the art is historical (fiction, drama, painting, film). In such instances, an artist must respect objective facts *as facts*.
18. This description of hidden manuscripts refers to, among other similar documents, the famous "Notes from the Warsaw Ghetto"; see *Notes from the Warsaw Ghetto: From the Journal of Emmanuel Ringelblum*. Later in the novel we learn that Ben's parents were incarcerated in the ghetto.
19. Biskupin is one of the oldest archaeological sites in central Europe. Scientists believe the site, a fortified wooden village, located on an island in Lake Biskupin, near Poznan in Poland, was built by a highly developed Slavic civilization called Lusatian that existed across central Europe over 2,700 years ago. It was first discovered in 1933 when people spotted wooden poles sticking up from the water. Excavations began soon after and continued up to the German invasion of Poland. The Germans attempted to claim the site as an early Germanic one and destroyed evidence to the contrary. After the war, the site was carefully reconstructed and is now open to tourists. In addition to the historical significance of Biskupin and its strategic role in the story of Athos and Jakob, Michaels builds some of her most important extended metaphors

of history and memory as sites for archaeological excavation on the story of Biskupin, which symbolizes the need for individuals to search for and uncover truths buried in the earth, in stories, or in archives.

20. I discussed Claude Lanzmann's film *Shoah* in Chapter 2, but recall it here, with its remembrance of events at Chelmno and description of Jewish prisoners forced by the Nazis to dig up mass graves or burn the still living bodies of fellow Jews to destroy the evidence of their atrocities and the witnesses to this evidence because Michaels's Jakob describes just such an outrage (52). The entire novel is built, in a sense, on the extended metaphor of a landscape that hides and reveals such histories; its multiple narrators not only bear witness to such scenes but insist on the ethics and archaeology of memory-work. For another fictional representation of mass grave atrocity that evokes the Holocaust, see Dodd's novel *Jew*.



21. Michaels describes the devastating impact of Hurricane Hazel, which struck the suburb of Weston, where Ben and his parents were living in 1954, causing the river to flood and sweep homes and people away (*Fugitive Pieces* 243–46). Detritus from the disaster continued to surface over the years, and Michaels uses this actual event as a metaphor for a landscape of memory in the novel.
22. Agamben presents his concept of the *homo sacer*, the person who is first stripped of defining human characteristics so he can be killed with impunity and whose death carries no legal consequences or socio-religious value for the state that eradicates him, in both *Homo Sacer* and *State of Exception*.
23. Among the best analyses of *Fugitive Pieces* are essays by D.M.R. Bentley, Méira Cook, and Susan Gubar. Each of these critics addresses the issues that have troubled readers of the novel, from its highly metaphoric, lush style to its representation of gender, and its portrayal of the Holocaust. In "Regarding the Pain of Women," James Young examines some of the particular challenges that artists face when attempting to represent the suffering, objectification, sexual abuse, and trauma of women during the Holocaust.

## 9 Canada and the Aftermath of the "Good" War

1. Bates was deeply influenced by German expressionist art and had studied with the great German painter Max Beckmann in New York in 1949–50, when Beckmann was in exile from Germany. Bates's use of symbolism and figuration bear close resemblance to Beckmann's.
2. Among the other memoirs and auto/biographies that I cannot discuss are works by Arnold, Judy Bates, Bluman, Colville, Den Hertog and Kasaboski, Dulani, Eksteins, Igersheimer, Kipp, Kwan, Mowat, and Naves. For an analysis

of Canadian Holocaust auto/biographical narratives, see Egan and Helms, and Chapter 6 of Egan's *Burdens of Proof.*

3. There is no doubt that this battle experience had a lifelong impact on Mowat. He was nineteen years old when he enlisted with the 2nd Battalion of the Hastings and Prince Edward Regiment (the "Hasty Pees"), and the violence, carnage, and constant danger were both shattering and maturing. The war changed him; he could not slip back into civilian life and chose instead to go north, where he began his discovery of Canada's arctic landscapes and peoples that would inspire so much of his subsequent work. He concludes *And No Birds Sang* by confessing that he wept at the sight of a friend whose face was "empty...under its crown of crimson bandages" and he wonders if he wept for this man or for himself and for "those who would remain" (242–43). In this sentiment he is like those who Maxwell Bates describes as freed by their war experiences from the hypocrisy of home.
4. Zuehlke reproduces some striking photographs of Christmas during the war in Italy and he provides a detailed account of the dinner in Ortona (300–27).
5. All these paintings are reproduced in a colour plate insert to *Artist at War*, and some have been reproduced in *Canvas of War*; see, in particular, pages 118–19.
6. Laura Brandon discusses the representation of dead soldiers by Canadian war artists in "Above or Below Ground?" and she calls Comfort's dead German the "most shocking" of the fourteen depictions of corpses.
7. See, for example, *Seasons of the Eskimo*, *Arctic Animals*, and *Arctic Memories: Living with the Inuit*.
8. Nowhere does Bruemmer explain how he can remember events, names, and dates so precisely, and he does not claim to have drawn on his diaries for the memoir. When the diaries are mentioned, he does not describe them or comment upon why he started keeping them.
9. Although it is understandable that Bruemmer would feel deeply about this expulsion, he does not mention the fate of the Jews, including German Jews, nor does he examine the role Germany played in arousing such hatred among non-Germanic peoples in several central European countries. He cites MacMillan in *Paris, 1919* in support of his figure of twelve million and his chief target is Stalin and the brutality of the Soviet Union. See his discussion in Chapter 17 (178–81).
10. Appignanesi allows that she is not the best of daughters, that she is impatient with her mother's demands and repetitions, and that she looks a lot like her dark-haired, dark-eyed, large-nosed father and, therefore, can never be a beauty like her mother. It is noteworthy, I think, that she does not include a single photograph in the book, although she describes photographs and surely knows

that most memoirs and auto/biographies feature photographs. She returns to the story of a mother with dementia and the horrors of the Holocaust in her novel *The Memory Man*, but the auto/biography is a better-written narrative than the rather contrived detective-style story in the novel. For a discussion of *Losing the Dead*, see Egan and Helms, 39–45.

11. Changes in names, dates of birth, and addresses are a constant feature in this story because such changes enabled the Borensteins to hide their Jewish identity and blend in with the local Polish population. Hena also changed the name from Borenstein to Borens when they lived in a small town in Quebec so as not to alert the local Catholic French Canadians, who were not keen to have Jews among them. These aliases would cause Appignanesi considerable trouble when she went to Poland to search through archives for facts about the family; see pages 28 and 38–40. But they also spelled survival and inevitably led to an ongoing sequence of camouflaging lies.
12. Appignanesi goes on to connect this scene with Primo Levi's description of survivors not being believed when reporting what they saw and experienced in *The Drowned and the Saved* (see *Losing the Dead* 129), and this experiencing of disbelief is a common theme in war memoirs and testimonials.
13. For the Second World War memoirs and auto/biographies in which women play central roles, see works by Arnold, Blumen, Den Hertog, Raab, and Ravel, and the nurses' accounts in *Women Overseas*, edited by Day, Spence, and Ladouceur.
14. Among the many recent Canadian films about the war is the three-part *Canada Remembers* series produced by the Canada Remembers Committee of Veterans Affairs and the NFB. Released in 1995, it comes with a resource guide with references to books by military historians and other experts. *Canada's War in Colour*, another three-part series, was broadcast on CBC Television in 2005. Like *Canada Remembers*, the series is upbeat and non-controversial. As recently as 2008, the NFB released *On All Fronts* and mounted a special campaign to advertise its commitment to documenting the war. Other films are listed in the bibliography.
15. On 18 December 2010, the *Globe and Mail* ran a full-page advertisement about these photographs (A18). For prices starting at $199.00, one could go online to "select prints from any of the four available collections" from the newspaper's archives. To my eye, the images featured in the ad are simply propaganda and they offer a crass attempt to cash in on—and promote—the contemporary military bandwagon. One picture shows a Canadian soldier "battered and bloodied by war yet still heroic"; another shows two fresh, unscarred sailors kissing a girl as they celebrate V-J Day in Toronto; and in the most manipulative photograph, a happy soldier and father—no signs of trauma or injury—stands with

his pretty wife and two young children under the headline "Peace at Last." All four are well-dressed and facing into the full light of a promising future. There are no signs of strain, grief, loss (of his comrades or her good wartime job) here.

16. All quotations from the voice-over narration or individual comments and dialogue of the film are my own and are based on close study of the films. There are no page references.

17. Although close comparisons are beyond my expertise or scope here, I would suggest that strategies, such as contemporary interviews, return to sites of memory and catastrophe, and re-enactments, used by Ophuls and Lanzmann (who eschews the use of archival materials and re-enactments), or by Ken Burns in his epic treatment of the American Civil War, are borrowed by the McKennas.





18. *The Dam Busters*, a famous 1955 British film, portrays "Operation Chastise" in which the RAF tried to blow up the Möhne, Eder, and Sorpe dams using bouncing bombs. The Sorpe withstood the attack because of its construction.

19. Fauré (1845–1924) composed his *Requiem* between 1887 and 1890, and it exists in three versions, each one more heavily scored for orchestra than the one before. Given these dates, it is obvious that he did not have either world war in mind while writing. Nevertheless, it is an appropriate choice (from among many great requiems, for example, by Mozart and Verdi) for these films because one of the most anguished remembered scenes of death in the third film took place in a French abbey garden. The McKennas may well have had more reasons than this for choosing Fauré—for example, the famous soprano aria *Pie Jesu* is a unique element in the piece, and the composer wanted to convey something greater about humanity with his treatment of the mass than to dwell on death and religious ritual—but whatever their reasons, it is we the viewing listeners who will respond in personal ways.

20. In a footnote on page 5 we can read: "Professor [Michael] Bliss, one of the most vocal critics of the Senate Sub-Committee [he is one of our most distinguished historians, but not a military historian], labelled the investigation...an 'inquisition,' and argued that it was a 'menace to the liberal, unfettered flow of controversial opinion that is, and ought to be, the glory of a free society." Amen. At least Bliss received a footnote for standing up to this pernicious committee in the name of the same freedoms the soldiers fought to protect.

21. Findley's discussion of the film and the Senate inquiry first appeared in the *Journal of Canadian Studies* 25.4 (Winter 1992–93) as a special editorial, but my quotations are from its reprinting in *Journeyman.*

22. See note 14 for the titles of some of these films. Judging from what David Bercuson and S.F. Wise say in *The Valour and the Horror Revisited*, only academic

historians believe in scholarship and "rational analysis" (9), and they state, unequivocally, that the film "is bad history" (10). They impugn the motives of the filmmakers, dismiss the "requiem-like choral music" (presumably this is what they know about Fauré), and describe the use of Beethoven's *Moonlight Sonata* as resembling "a Hollywood recreation of the Charge of the Light Brigade" (49). They admit that Canadians do not know their own history, but they cannot see that academic historians may be part of the problem.

23. *Canada: A People's History* is a thirteen-part docudrama series prepared by the CBC. It provides a broad overview of centuries of Canadian history with segments on the two world wars. This highly dramatized celebratory series does attempt to be inclusive of women, First Nations, settlers, and immigrant populations.





24. Halton and Ted Griffiths (an organizer of the reunion), who operated one of the tanks that shelled a medieval church, reducing it to rubble, stand in the Piazza San Francesco before the rebuilt church to reflect upon the terrible necessity of levelling this medieval treasure to force the German snipers out.

## 10 Remembering War; Finding Peace?

1. In addition to painting, Allister published a memoir of his years in a POW camp called *Where Life and Death Hold Hands* (1989), but it is his philosophy that strikes me as extraordinary and wise. He is quoted in his obituary as follows: "Forget—no. But forgive—yes, if forgiving could encompass disapproval. To really understand war was to forgive, to grasp the nature of the illness, the historic path of the virus in the bloodstream of a nation....Open the gates of war anywhere, and hellish monsters roam the earth" (Hawthorne S15). For further descriptions of Allister, see Nathan Greenfield's *The Damned*; Greenfield draws extensively on Allister's memoirs.
2. This video, "The Afghan Mission," was attacked by military mothers who were outraged by the lines of one actress, playing a mother mourning her dead son, who comments that if she had known she was providing cannon fodder by having children she might never have had any. The Quebec women who made the video to protest government policies were then assailed by angry politicians, as well as military mothers, who called for a ban on the video. This recent episode recalls the reaction of veterans and politicians to *The Valour and the Horror* and illustrates the censorship that is practised in Canadian democracy. See the article by Alexandre Robillard for more details.
3. *Winter in Wartime* is based on the 1972 semi-autobiographical novel *Oorlogswinter* by Jan Teslouw. The film tells the story of a teenager in a small Dutch town during the hunger winter of 1944–45. When a British pilot is shot

down near the town, the boy and his companions want to hide and assist him. But the Germans are searching for the man and begin to round up the town's officials to force someone to step forward and reveal where the pilot is. Eventually the boy's father, the mayor of the town, is executed because no one will speak up. Then the boy discovers that a beloved uncle is actually a Nazi collaborator and he shoots this uncle. The film, like the novel, focuses more on the hard lessons of human behaviour during the extreme situations of war and on the terrible aftermath of the war for a family than on actual combat. In this sense it is an especially interesting perspective on the war because it is not a combat movie but a thoughtful remembering of the ethical choices made, or not made, during a time of crisis.



4. I have not had a chance to see the trilogy, which has yet to be published, but in her review Marsha Lederman praises the scope and provides some context for Brown's creation of these three plays. Judging from advertisements about the trilogy, it would seem that Brown has provided a Second World War response to *Billy Bishop Goes to War.*
5. It comes as something of a shock to be reminded that veterans' groups, as early as 1928, tried to control the story of the Great War by calling for a ban on Harrison's *Generals Die in Bed,* but even more disturbing is that fact that teachers who attempted to provide a wider context on the war than the official militaristic version were threatened with dismissal (Fisher 60). A Winnipeg pacifist, Alice Chown, was threatened with imprisonment in a jail or an insane asylum if she refused to shut up (Fisher 225).
6. I continue to be impressed with the quality and quantity of works being published and performed about both wars. However, while the Great War is still an important subject for Canadian writers—Stephen Massicotte's play *The Oxford Roof Climber's Rebellion* is an example—more and more attention is being given to the Second World War. Hannah Moscovitch's *East of Berlin* and Sally Stubbs's *Herr Beckmann's People* are two fine examples of plays that dramatize the aftermath of the war and the second generation of survivors' sense of hauntedness and guilt. Andrew Borkowski's story collection, *Copernicus Avenue,* brings the war home to Canada through the traumatic memories of Canadian immigrants, and memoirs and scholarly studies appear with regularity.
7. The *Kindertransport,* or Refugee Children's Movement, began on 15 November 1938—shortly after Kristallnacht—when a group of British Jewish leaders convinced the UK to admit Jewish children under seventeen into the country as refugees. Over the nine months prior to the outbreak of war, the UK accepted thousands of such children from Nazi Germany, Austria, Poland, Danzig, and Czechoslovakia. These youngsters were taken into foster homes, orphanages, or

settled on farms. Very few ever saw their parents again. The trains leaving from Prague were organized by the British stockbroker Nicholas Winton, who set up his headquarters in a hotel in Wenceslas Square. Winton was born in England to German-Jewish parents and later in life, when his work to save Jewish children was revealed, he received many accolades. He was knighted in 2002 and is named a "British Hero of the Holocaust" (as a Jew he could not be honoured as a "Righteous Gentile").

8. The university in Montreal is not named in the novel, but I am assuming it is Concordia University because Concordia is the home of MIGS (Montreal Institute for Genocide and Human Rights Studies). The archives house an extensive collection of Holocaust diaries, manuscripts, memoirs, and interviews with survivors. These can be consulted online at the Concordia University Archives.



9. Thompson's first play, *The Crackwalker*, presents the lives of young people struggling to find some degree of normalcy and happiness in the face of mental disability, abuse, poverty, and social degradation. *Lion in the Streets* depicts an average Canadian neighbourhood as a kind of purgatory in which the ghost of a murdered girl haunts the streets. Scenes of violence, revenge, misogyny, and terror erupt through the safe-seeming surfaces of ordinary life. *Palace of the End*, however, is most notable for reaching beyond a Canadian setting into the larger world of violence and terrorism in Iraq. This play consists of three distinct but related stories in the form of monologues. Each monologue is based on actual news stories about people involved in the conflict—American soldier Lynndie England, British weapons inspector Dr. David Kelly, and the Iraqi Communist Nehrjas Al Saffarh. The most excoriating of these personal stories is the third one because Nehrjas describes her rape and torture by Saddam Hussein's secret police and the brutal torture, before her eyes, of her young son. The real woman was killed when the Americans bombed her home during the first Gulf War. Arsinée Khanjian's performance of this role in the 2008 Canadian premiere by Canadian Stage Company at the Berkeley Street Theatre in Toronto was simply breathtaking. *Palace of the End* won the Amnesty International Freedom of Expression Award in 2009 and was called a "theatrical Guernica" (Coates and Grace, *Canada and the Theatre of War*, vol. 2, 149).

10. In her 2002 autobiography, Anna Heilman tells the story of her ordeal in Auschwitz and her role, with other teenaged girls, in the uprising. Before her death from cancer in 2011, Heilman was a social worker in Ottawa and might well have helped girls like Thompson's Blandy; see note 12.

11. The play's title is from *The Tempest*, a play that stresses the word *creature* to explore the boundaries between the human and non-human. Sorele gives

Miranda's famous speech towards the end of the play: "O brave new world, / that has such people in't!" (*The Tempest* V, i, lines 183–84 and *Such Creatures* 49). Of the two Shakespeare plays used as intertexts in *Such Creatures*, *The Tempest* strikes me as the more significant, in part because of Caliban, who is robbed of his lands, degraded to subhuman status and attempts to revolt, and in part because of the ambivalent status of the concept of a "new world" for today's ears. Canada is not a new world, of course, and it is not free of evil and violence.

12. Thompson has drawn on historical facts for Sorele's story of revolt in Auschwitz-Birkenau. Although she does not mention Heilman as a source for these events, Heilman may well have been an inspiration for the character of Sorele. On 7 October 1944, the 12th Sonderkommando Unit planned to stage their revolt. A group of young women who worked in a munitions factory had smuggled gunpowder to the men who made crude hand grenades for the attack; there were also knives and small axes hidden in the crematoria. By the time the revolt was suppressed, crematorium 4 was damaged beyond repair. The young women were captured, raped, and tortured, but they refused to give up the names of living accomplices; four of these girls were hanged by the SS in front of the assembled women's camp.

13. While I do not conflate Henry L'Hôte with Yann Martel, it is a fact that *Beatrice & Virgil* received a very negative review in the *New York Times* by Michiko Kakutani, who found Martel's treatment of the Holocaust "misconceived and offensive" because, in her view, it trivialized the Holocaust (C1). Other reviews are more favourable and *Goodreads* blog comments range from raves to condemnations.

14. *Beatrice & Virgil* is a highly intertextual work. The Flaubert story is just one example of this method; the references to Dante's *Divine Comedy* constitute another. Allusions to contemporary works like Spiegelman's *Maus* and, more significantly, Emmanuel Ringelblum's archive, also provide useful context for the novel as well as for the role of documents in the text. I discuss Ringelblum in note 15.

15. Emmanuel Ringelblum (1900–44) was a Polish-Jewish historian incarcerated in the Warsaw Ghetto. He and his family escaped the ghetto after the uprising but were later found and executed, together with the family that hid them, by the Gestapo. While held in the ghetto, he organized the preservation of diaries and other documents about what was happening to the Jews, and this archive was hidden in three milk cans and ten tin boxes. In December 1960, in a cellar of a ruined house at 68 Nowolipki Street, Warsaw, two of the milk cans were found with precious documents; the third can has not been found to date. For a discussion of the history surrounding Ringelblum and for the English

translation of documents first published in 1952, see *Notes from the Warsaw Ghetto*, translated and edited by Jacob Sloan.

16. The word "hospitator" is interesting. Derived from *hostis* and related to hospice, it indicates a person who receives or entertains a stranger, or a guest, hospitably. Flaubert's title is sometimes given as "Saint Julian the Hospitaller," a more familiar term, but the point is the same: by welcoming the leper (Christ in disguise) Julian became a hospitator, a host, and thus a saint. Martel has several reasons for using the story as an intertext (the significance of the non-human animal world, the horror of war and slaughter, the need to find redemption), but it is as a host and hospitator that Henry L'Hôte most recalls Julian. By making room within his own imagination for the ruthless taxidermist and his grisly play, Henry has embraced some of the most leprous events of the twentieth century.

17. Laura Brandon reproduces several of Kearnes's pieces in *A Brush with War*, together with the work of other contemporary Canadian war artists. To my eye, her large, unflinching images of atrocity and appalling injuries are the most challenging of these works. In the Somalia painting she exposes what Canadian soldiers inflicted on others; in her Afghanistan paintings she depicts the injuries they received. See her *What They Gave* (2006) in *A Brush with War* (66–67); "Scenes from the Front" by Val Ross; and pages 46–47 (this volume).

18. As far as the two world wars are concerned, the list of those who returned, or who immigrated (through Camp L or after the Second World War) to participate in Canada's history, is impressive. Just a few of the names on any such list would include: Pierre Berton, Earle Birney, Fred Bruemmer, Brooke Claxton, Alex Colville, Charles Comfort, Arthur Currie, Modris Eksteins, Leslie and Cecil Frost, Clare Gass, Matthew Halton, Anna Heilman, Harold Innis, Henry Kreisel, A.Y. Jackson, Farley Mowat, Harry Somers, Raymond Souster, and Fred Varley. The list in Eric Koch's memoir about Camp L, *Deemed Suspect* (258–60), is equally impressive.

# Bibliography

## Primary Sources



### Fiction


Appignanesi, Lisa. *The Memory Man*. Toronto: McArthur & Co., 2004.

Atwood, Margaret. *The Blind Assassin*. Toronto: Random House, 2000.

Bacque, James. *Our Fathers' War: A Novel*. Toronto: Exile Editions, 2006.

Bird, William R. *Ghosts Have Warm Hands*. Ottawa: Clark, Irwin, 1968. Orig. *And We Go On*. 1930.

———. "Sunrise for Peter." 1946. Whitaker 20–34.

Birney, Earle. *Turvey*. 1949. Toronto: McClelland & Stewart, 1989.

Bock, Dennis. *The Ash Garden*. Toronto: HarperCollins, 2001.

———. *The Communist's Daughter*. Toronto: Harper Perennial, 2006.

———. *Olympia*. Toronto: HarperCollins, 1998.

Borkowski, Andrew J. *Copernicus Avenue*. Toronto: Cormorant, 2011.

Boyden, Joseph. *Three Day Road*. Toronto: Viking, 2005.

Caron, Louis. *The Draft Dodger* [*L'Emmitouflé* 1977]. Trans. David Toby Homel. Toronto: Anansi, 1980.

Carrier, Roch. *La Guerre, Yes Sir!* 1968. Trans. Sheila Fischman. Toronto: Anansi, 1970.

———. "Son of a Smaller Hero." Trans. Sheila Fischman. Whitaker 232–35.

Crummy, Michael. *The Wreckage*. Toronto: Anchor, 2005.

Cumyn, Alan. *The Famished Lover*. Fredericton, NB: Goose Lane, 2006.

———. *The Sojourn*. Toronto: McClelland & Stewart, 2003.

Dodd, D.O. *Jew*. Toronto: Exile Editions, 2010.

Donaldson, Allan. *Maclean*. Halifax, NS: Vagrant, 2005.

Edugyan, Esi. *Half-Blood Blues*. Toronto: Thomas Allen, 2011.

Findley, Timothy. *The Butterfly Plague*. 1969. Toronto: Penguin, 1986.

———. *Famous Last Words*. Toronto: Clarke Irwin, 1981.

———. *The Piano Man's Daughter*. Toronto: HarperCollins, 1995.

———. "Stones." *Stones*. Toronto: Viking, 1988. 193–221.

———. *The Telling of Lies*. Markham, ON: Viking, 1986.

———. *The Wars*. Toronto: Clarke, Irwin, 1977.

———. *You Went Away*. Toronto: HarperCollins, 1996.

Finucan, Stephen. *The Fallen*. Toronto: Viking, 2009.

Galloway, Steven. *The Cellist of Sarajevo*. Toronto: Alfred A. Knopf, 2008.

Gélinas, Gratien. *Tit-Coq*. Montreal: Les Éditions Beauchemin, 1950.

Graham, Gwethalyn. *Earth and High Heaven*. 1944. Toronto: Cormorant Books, 2003.

Gross, Paul. *Passchendaele*. Toronto: HarperCollins, 2008.

Harrison, Charles Yale. *Generals Die in Bed*. 1930. Hamilton, ON: Potlatch, 1975.

Hodgins, Jack. *Broken Ground*. Toronto: McClelland & Stewart, 1998.

Humphreys, Helen. *Coventry*. Toronto: HarperCollins, 2008.

———. *The Lost Garden*. Toronto: Harper Flamingo, 2002.

Huston, Nancy. *Fault Lines*. Toronto: McArthur & Co., 2007.

Hutton, June. *Underground*. Toronto: Cormorant, 2009.

Innes, Stephanie, and Harry Endrulat. Illus. Brian Deines. *A Bear in War*. Toronto: Key Porter Kids, 2008.

Itani, Frances. *Deafening*. Toronto: Harper Perennial, 2003.

———. *Requiem*. Toronto: HarperCollins, 2011.

Klein, A.M. *The Second Scroll*. 1951. Toronto: McClelland & Stewart, 1969.

Kogawa, Joy. *Obasan*. Toronto: Penguin, 1983.

Kreisel, Henry. *The Betrayal*. Toronto: McClelland & Stewart, 1964.

———. *The Rich Man*. 1948. Calgary: Red Deer Press, 2006.

Lawson, Mary. *The Other Side of the Bridge*. Toronto: Knopf, 2006.

LePan, Douglas. *The Deserter*. Toronto: McClelland & Stewart, 1964.

Levine, Karen. *Hana's Suitcase*. Toronto: Second Story, 2002.

Lotz, Jim. *Killing in Kluane*. Markham, ON: Paper Jacks, 1980.

Lowry, Malcolm. *Under the Volcano*. 1947. New York: Harper Perennial, 2007.

MacDonald, Ann-Marie. *Fall On Your Knees*. Toronto: Knopf, 1996.

———. *The Way the Crow Flies*. Toronto: Knopf, 2003.

MacLennan, Hugh. *Barometer Rising*. 1941. Toronto: McClelland & Stewart, 1958, 1989.

———. *Voices in Time*. Toronto: Macmillan, 1980.

Major, Kevin. *No Man's Land*. Toronto: Doubleday, 1995.

Marlatt, Daphne. *Taken*. Toronto: Anansi, 1996.

Martel, Yann. *Beatrice & Virgil*. Toronto: Knopf, 2010.

McCauley, G.F. *Soldier Boys*. Burnstown, ON: General Store Publishing, 2003.

McDougall, Colin. *Execution.* 1958. Toronto: McClelland & Stewart, 1972. 2004.

Michaels, Anne. *Fugitive Pieces.* Toronto: McClelland & Stewart, 1996.

———. *The Winter Vault.* Toronto: McClelland & Stewart, 2009.

Milner, Donna. *The Promise of Rain.* Toronto: McArthur & Co., 2010.

Ondaatje, Michael. *The English Patient.* Toronto: McClelland & Stewart, 1992.

Palka, Kurt. *Patient Number 7.* Toronto: McClelland & Stewart, 2012.

Pick, Alison. *Far to Go.* Toronto: Anansi, 2010.

Poole, Michael. *Rain Before Morning.* Madeira Park, BC: Harbour Publishing, 2006.

Ravel, Edeet. *Your Sad Eyes and Unforgettable Mouth.* 2008. Toronto: Penguin, 2009.

Sabatini, Sandra. *Dante's War.* Toronto: Key Porter, 2009.

Stenson, Fred. *The Great Karoo.* Toronto: Doubleday, 2008.

Urquhart, Jane. *The Stone Carvers.* Toronto: McClelland & Stewart, 2001.

———. *The Underpainter.* Toronto: McClelland & Stewart, 1997.

Whitaker, Muriel, ed. *Great Canadian War Stories.* Edmonton: University of Alberta Press, 2001.

Willson, Beckles. *The Redemption.* New York: G.P. Putnam, 1924.



## Non-Fiction (Autobiography, Memoir, Biography)

Appignanesi, Lisa. *Losing the Dead.* Toronto: McArthur & Co., 1999.

Arnold, Gladys. *One Woman's War: A Canadian Reporter with the Free French.* Toronto: James Lorimer, 1987.

Bates, Judy Fong. *The Year of Finding Memory.* Toronto: Random House, 2010.

Bates, Maxwell. *A Wilderness of Days: An Artist's Experience as a Prisoner of War in Germany.* Victoria, BC: Sono Nis, 1978.

Bishop, William A. *Winged Peace.* Toronto: Macmillan, 1944.

———. *Winged Warfare.* New York: George Doran, 1918.

Bluman, Barbara Ruth. *I Have My Mother's Eyes: A Holocaust Memoir Across Generations.* Vancouver: Ronsdale Press, 2009.

Bruemmer, Fred. *Survival: A Refugee Life.* Toronto: Key Porter, 2005.

Calder, Robert. *A Richer Dust: Family, Memory and the Second World War.* Toronto: Viking, 2004.

Chong, Denise. *The Girl in the Picture: The Story of Kim Phuc, the Photograph and the Vietnam War.* Toronto: Penguin, 1999.

Clark, Andrew. *A Keen Soldier: The Execution of Second World War Private Harold Pringle.* Toronto: Knopf, 2002.

Colville, Alex. *Alex Colville: Diary of a War Artist.* Comp. Graham Metson and Cheryl Lean. Halifax, NS: Nimbus Publishing, 1981.

Comfort, Charles. *Artist at War.* 1956. Pender Island, BC: Remembrance Books, 1995.

Dallaire, Roméo. *Shake Hands with the Devil.* Toronto: Random House, 2003.

Day, Frances Martin, Phyllis Spence, and Barbara Ladouceur, eds. *Women Overseas: Memoirs of the Canadian Red Cross Corps.* Vancouver: Ronsdale Press, 1998.

Den Hartog, Kristen, and Tracy Kasaboski. *The Occupied Garden: Recovering the Story of a Family in the War-Torn Netherlands.* Toronto: McClelland & Stewart, 2008.

Dickson, Paul Douglas. *A Thoroughly Canadian General: A Biography of H.D.G. Crerar.* Montreal: McGill-Queen's University Press, 2007.

Douglas, Tom. "Behind Enemy Lines." *The Beaver* 89.5 (October–November 2009): 28–33.

Dulani, Mario. *The City Without Women: A Chronicle of Internment Life in Canada during the Second World War*. Trans. Antonio Mazza. Oakville, ON: Mosaic Press, 1994.

Eksteins, Modris. *Walking Since Daybreak: A Story of Eastern Europe, World War II, and the Heart of Our Century.* Boston: Houghton Mifflin, 1999.

Fabijančić, Tony. *Bosnia: In the Footsteps of Gavrilo Princip.* Edmonton: University of Alberta Press, 2010.

Findley, Timothy. *Inside Memory: Pages from a Writer's Notebook.* Toronto: HarperCollins, 1990.

———. *Journeyman: Travels of a Writer.* Ed. William Whitehead. Toronto: Harper Flamingo, 2003.

———. "The Valour and the Horror." *Journeyman* 168–71.

Fleming, R.B., ed. *The Wartime Letters of Leslie & Cecil Frost, 1915–1919.* Waterloo, ON: Wilfrid Laurier University Press, 2007.

Gass, Clare. *The War Diary of Clare Gass, 1915–1918.* Ed. Susan Mann. Montreal: McGill-Queen's University Press, 2000.

Graves, Dianne. *A Crown of Life: The World of John McCrae.* St. Catharines, ON: Vanwell Publishing, 1997.

Gwyn, Sandra. *Tapestry of War: A Private View of Canadians in the Great War.* Toronto: HarperCollins, 1992.

Hancock, Glen. *Charley Goes to War: A Memoir.* Kentville, NS: Gaspereau Press, 2004.

Hayes, Adrian. *Pegahmagabow: Legendary Warrior, Forgotten Hero.* Huntsville, ON: Fox Meadow, 2003.

Heilman, Anna. *Never Far Away: The Auschwitz Chronicles of Anna Heilman.* Calgary: University of Calgary Press, 2002.

Hodgins, Jack. "Finding Merville." First published in *Comox Valley Record* vol. 11, no. 44 (1996). www.jackhodgins.ca/findingmerville.htm.

Hughes, John McKendrick. *The Unwanted: Great War Letters from the Field.* Ed. John Richard Hughes. Edmonton: University of Alberta Press, 2005.

Igersheimer, Walter J. *Blatant Injustice: The Story of a Jewish Refugee from Nazi Germany Imprisoned in Britain and Canada during World War II.* Montreal: McGill-Queen's University Press, 2005.

Ignatieff, Michael. *True Patriot Love: Four Generations in Search of Canada.* Toronto: Viking, 2009.

Jackson, A.Y. *A Painter's Country.* Toronto: Clarke, Irwin, and Co., 1958.

Kipp, Charles D. *Because WE are Canadians: A Battlefield Memoir.* Ed. Lynda Sykes. Vancouver: Douglas & McIntyre, 2003.

Kitigawa, Muriel. *This Is My Own: Letters to Wes and Other Writings on Japanese Canadians, 1941–1948.* Ed. Roy Miki. Vancouver: Talonbooks, 1985.

Koch, Eric. *Deemed Suspect: A Wartime Blunder.* Toronto: Methuen, 1980.

Kreisel, Henry. "Diary of an Internment." *Another Country: Writings by and about Henry Kreisel.* Ed. Shirley Neuman. Edmonton: NeWest Press, 1985. 18–44.

Kwan, Michael David. *Things That Must Not Be Forgotten: A Childhood in Wartime China.* Toronto: Macfarlane, Walter & Ross, 2000.

MacDonald, Laura M. *Curse of the Narrows: The Halifax Explosion, 1917.* Toronto: HarperCollins, 2005.

Macfarlane, David. *The Danger Tree: Memory, War, and the Search for a Family's Past.* 1991. Toronto: Vintage, 2000.

——. "July 1, 1916: The Somme of All Loss." *Globe and Mail* 1 July 2006: F1, 4.

McClung, Nellie. *In Times Like These.* 1919. Toronto: University of Toronto Press, 1972.

Mowat, Farley. *And No Birds Sang.* Toronto: McClelland & Stewart, 1979.

——. "I Remember Italy." *Globe and Mail* 6 November 2004: F1, 4.

——. *Otherwise.* Toronto: McClelland & Stewart, 2008.

Nemni, Max, and Monique Nemni. *Young Trudeau, 1919–1944: Son of Quebec, Father of Canada.* Trans. William Johnson. Toronto: McClelland & Stewart, 2006.

O'Shea, Stephen. *Back to the Front: An Accidental Historian Walks the Trenches of World War I.* Vancouver: Douglas & McIntyre, 1996.

Querengesser, Tim. "The Day the Nazis Came North." *UpHere* (October/November 2009): 72, 74.

Siblin, Eric. *The Cello Suites: J.S. Bach, Pablo Casals, and the Search for a Baroque Masterpiece.* Toronto: Anansi, 2009.

Souster, Raymond. *Jubilee of Death: The Raid on Dieppe.* Ottawa: Oberon, 1984.



## Poetry

Atwood, Margaret. "The Loneliness of the Military Historian." *Morning in the Burned House.* Toronto: McClelland & Stewart, 1995. 49–53.

Birney, Earle. "The Road to Nijmegen." *Now is Time.* Toronto: Ryerson Press, 1945. 42–43.

Brault, Jacques. *Suite Fraternelle.* Ottawa: Éditions de l'Université d'Ottawa, 1969.

Callaghan, Barry, and Bruce Meyer, eds. *We Wasn't Pals: Canadian Poetry and Prose of the First World War.* Toronto: Exile Editions, 2001.

Colombo, John Robert, and Michael Richardson, eds. *We Stand On Guard: Poems and Songs of Canadians in Battle.* Toronto: Doubleday, 1985.

Comfort, Charles. *The Moro River and Other Observations.* Hull, QC: Privately published, 1970.

Davey, Frank. *Back to the War.* Vancouver: Talonbooks, 2005.

Garvin, John W., ed. *Canadian Poems of the Great War.* Toronto: McClelland & Stewart, 1918.

Keefer, Janice Kulyk. *Midnight Stroll.* Holstein, ON: Exile Editions, 2006.

Lighthall, W.D. "Canadian Poets of the Great War." *Transactions of the Royal Society of Canada.* 3rd series. Ottawa: RSC, 1918.

McCrae, John. *In Flanders Fields and Other Poems.* Toronto: William Briggs, 1919.

——. "In Flanders Fields." *In Flanders Fields and Other Poems* 29.

——. *In Flanders Fields.* Collected by Sir Andrew McPhail. Guelph, ON: John McCrae Birthplace Society, n.d.

Morgan, Jane, and Walter Morgan, eds. *Soldier Poetry of the Second World War.* Oakville, ON: Mosaic Press, 1990.

New, William H. "My Vancouver Starts." *Touching Ecuador.* Lantzville, BC: Oolichan Books, 2006. 52.

Nowlan, Alden. "Ypres: 1915." *Notes for a Native Land: A New Encounter with Canada.* Ed. Andy Wainwright: Ottawa: Oberon Press, 1969. 100–02.

Souster, Raymond. "The Dresden Special." *Selected Poems of Raymond Souster.* Ottawa: Oberon Press, 1972. 108.

Struthers, Betsy. *Censored Letters.* Oakville, ON: Mosaic Press, 1984.

## Drama, Music, and Installation

Brown, Kenneth. "Spiral Dive." Unpublished trilogy script. 2011.

Brown, Kenneth, and Stephen Scriver. *Letters in Wartime. The West of All Possible Worlds: Six Contemporary Canadian Plays.* Ed. Moira Day. Toronto: Playwrights Canada Press, 2004. 339–81.

Cardiff, Janet, and George Bures Miller. *The Murder of Crows.* Sound installation. Nationalgalerie im Hamburger Banhof, Berlin, 2008.

Chan, Marjorie. *A Nanking Winter.* Toronto: Playwrights Canada Press, 2008.

Chislett, Anne. *Quiet in the Land.* Toronto: Playwrights Canada Press, 1981.

Clements, Marie. *Burning Vision.* Vancouver: Talonbooks, 2003.

Coates, Donna, and Sherrill Grace, eds. *Canada and the Theatre of War.* 2 vols. Toronto: Playwrights Canada Press, 2008, 2010.

Faroud, Abla. *Game of Patience.* Trans. Jill MacDougall. Coates and Grace 2:7–36.

Findley, Timothy. *Can You See Me Yet?* Vancouver: Talonbooks, 1977.

——. *The Trials of Ezra Pound.* Winnipeg: Blizzard Publishing, 1995.

"Flowers for Nellie." Writer/director John Chipman. *The Current*. CBC Radio. 26 November 2007.

French, David. *1949*. Vancouver: Talonbooks, 1989.

——. *Leaving Home*. Toronto: Anansi, 2002.

——. *Soldier's Heart*. Vancouver: Talonbooks, 2002.

Garneau, Michel. *Warriors*. Trans. Linda Gaboriou. Vancouver: Talonbooks, 1989.

Glick, Srul Irving. "I Never Saw Another Butterfly." Performed by Maureen Forrester. *Srul Irving Glick: Canadian Composers' Portraits*. CMC Centrediscs, 2006.

Gray, John, and Eric Peterson. *Billy Bishop Goes to War*. Vancouver: Talonbooks, 1981.

Hendry, Tom. *Fifteen Miles of Broken Glass*. Vancouver: Talonbooks, 1975.

Hollingsworth, Margaret. *Ever Loving*. Coates and Grace 1:298–371.

Hunter, Maureen. *Wild Mouth*. Winnipeg: Sirocco Drama, 2008.

Kerr, Kevin. *Unity (1918)*. Vancouver: Talonbooks, 2002.

Lepage, Robert, with Ex Machina. *Seven Streams of the River Ota*. London: Methuen, 1996.

Lill, Wendy. *The Fighting Days*. Vancouver: Talonbooks, 1985.

Luengen, Ramona (composer), and Anne Hodges (libretto). "Naomi's Road." Vancouver Opera Company Commission, 2005.

Massicotte, Stephen. *Mary's Wedding*. Toronto: Playwrights Canada Press, 2002.

——. *The Oxford Roof Climber's Rebellion*. Toronto: Playwrights Canada Press, 2006.

Moscovitch, Hannah. *East of Berlin*. Toronto: Playwrights Canada Press, 2009.

Mouawad, Wajdi. *Scorched*. Trans. Linda Gaboriau. Toronto: Playwrights Canada Press, 2005. Coates and Grace 2:188–250.

——. *Wedding Day at the Cro-Magnons*. Toronto: Playwrights Canada Press, 1994.

Murrell, John. *Waiting for the Parade*. Vancouver: Talonbooks, 1980.

Pollock, Sharon. *Fair Liberty's Call*. Toronto: Coach House, 1995.

——. *Getting It Straight*. *Sharon Pollock: Collected Works, Volume 2*. Ed. Cynthia Zimmerman. Toronto: Playwrights Canada Press, 2006.

——. *Man Out of Joint*. *Sharon Pollock: Collected Works, Volume 3*. Ed. Cynthia Zimmerman. Toronto: Playwrights Canada Press, 2008.

——. *Sweet Land of Liberty*. *Sharon Pollock: Collected Works, Volume 1*. Ed. Cynthia Zimmerman. Toronto: Playwrights Canada Press, 2005.

Rossi, Vittorio. *Paradise by the River: The Story of Petawawa: An Historical Drama in Three Acts*. Vancouver: Talonbooks, 1998.

Sanger, Richard. *Not Spain*. Toronto: Playwrights Canada Press, 1994.

Sher, Emil. *Hana's Suitcase: Hana's Suitcase on Stage/Original Story by Karen Levine; Play by Emil Sher*. Toronto: Second Story Press, 2006.

Sherman, Jason. *None Is Too Many*. *A Terrible Truth II*. Toronto: Playwrights Canada Press, 2003. 82–155; Coates and Grace 1:377–422.

———. *Reading Hebron.* Toronto: Playwrights Canada Press, 1997.

———. *Three in the Back, Two in the Head: A Play.* Toronto: Playwrights Canada Press, 1995.

Somers, Harry. *North Country: Four Movements for String Orchestra.* 1948. *The Spring of Somers,* CBC, 1996.

Stubbs, Sally. *Herr Beckmann's People.* Winnipeg: Sirocco, 2011.

Thiessen, Vern. *Einstein's Gift.* Toronto: Playwrights Canada Press, 2003.

———. *Vimy.* Toronto: Playwrights Canada Press, 2008. Coates and Grace 1:221–94.

Thompson, Judith. *The Crackwalker. The Other Side of the Dark: Four Plays by Judith Thompson.* Toronto: Coach House, 1989. 15–71.

———. *Lion in the Streets.* Toronto: Playwrights Canada Press, 1990.

———. *Palace of the End.* Coates and Grace 2:352–82.

———. *Such Creatures.* Toronto: Playwrights Canada Press, 2010.

Thomson, R.H. *The Lost Boys.* Toronto: Playwrights Canada Press, 2002; Coates and Grace 1:5–53.

Thomson, R.H., with Martin Conboy. "Vigile 1914–1918 Vigil." Canada's National History Society. Government of Canada. 16 December 2008. Web.

Vanderhaeghe, Guy. *Dancock's Dance.* Vancouver: Talonbooks, 1996; Coates and Grace 1:162–220.

Verdecchia, Guillermo, and Marcus Youssef. *A Line in the Sand.* Vancouver: Talonbooks, 1997; Coates and Grace 2:41–86.

Wagner, Colleen. *The Monument.* Toronto: Playwrights Canada Press, 1993; Coates and Grace 2:91–145.

Watts, Irene N., ed. *A Terrible Truth: Anthology of Holocaust Drama.* 2 vols. Toronto: Playwrights Canada Press, 2003, 2004.

Wright, Richard, and Robina Endres, eds. *Eight Men Speak.* Co-created by Oscar Ryan, E. Cecil-Smith, Frank Love, and Mildred Goldberg. *Eight Men Speak and Other Plays from the Canadian Workers' Theatre.* Toronto: New Hogtown Press, 1976. 21–89.

## Film

*The 49th Parallel.* Dir. Michael Powell. General Films, 1941.

*Aces: A Story of the First Air War.* Dir. Raoul Fox. NFB, 1993.

*And We Knew How to Dance.* Dir. Maureen Judge. NFB, 1993.

*Ararat.* Dir. Atom Egoyan. Miramax and Alliance Atlantis, 2002.

*Bye Bye Blues.* Dir. Anne Wheeler. Alberta Motion Picture Development Corporation, NFB, and Téléfilm Canada, 1989.

*Canada: A People's History.* 13-part series. Prod. Mark Starowicz. CBC, 2001.

*Canada Remembers.* 3-part series. Dir. Terence Macartney-Filgate. NFB, 1995.

*Canada's War in Colour.* 3-part series. Dir. Karen Shopsowitz. CBC, 2005.

*Canvas of War: The Art of World War II*. Dir. Michael Ostroff. Sound Venture Productions. NFB, 2000.

*The Danger Tree*. Dir. John McGreavy. NFB/CBC, 1997.

*Dieppe*. Dir. John N. Smith. CBC, 1993.

*Dieppe*. Dir. Terence Macartney-Filgate. Script by Timothy Findley and William Whitehead. Narrator Douglas Rain. CBC, 1979.

*Emotional Arithmetic*. Dir. Paolo Barzman. Seville Pictures, 2008.

*Entre les lignes/Front Lines: The Private Face of War*. Dir. Claude Guilmain. NFB, 2008.

*Far From Home: Canada and the Great War*. Dir. Richard Nielsen. NFB, 1997.

*The Final Mission: The Story of the U-190*. Dir. Alain Vèzina. NFB, 2006.

*For King and Country: Canada's Soldiers in the Second World War*. Dir. Gilbert Reid. Narrator R.H. Thomson. History Channel, November 2004.

*Forgotten Warriors*. Dir. Loretta Todd. NFB, 1996.

*Fugitive Pieces*. Dir. Jeremy Podeswa. Maximum Film Distribution, 2007.

*Going Home*. Dir. Terry Ryan. Canada/UK. CBC/BBC Wales/NFB, 1986.

*The Great War*. Dir. Brian McKenna. CBC, 2007.

*Highway of the Atom*. Crawley Films, 1952.

*Inside Hana's Suitcase*. Dir. Larry Weinstein. Christal Films, 2008.

*John McCrae's War: In Flanders Fields*. Dir. Robert Duncan. NFB, 1998.

*The Last 100 Days*. Documentary. Dir./Prod. Richard Nielsen. NFB, 1999.

*The Liberation of Holland*. Dir. Alan Mendelsohn. CBC, 2005.

*Map of the Human Heart*. Dirs. Vincent Ward and Louis Nowra. Miramax Films, 1993.

*Passchendaele*. Dir. Paul Gross. Alliance Films, 2008.

*Return to Ortona: A Battlefield Redemption. Canada: A People's History*. Special Documentary Edition. Prod. Mark Starowicz. CBC, 2001.

*Sam's Army*. Documentary. Prod. Richard Nielsen. NFB, 1999.

*Savage Christmas: Hong Kong 1941. The Valour and the Horror*, Part 1.

*Shake Hands with the Devil*. Dir. Roger Spottiswoode. Seville Pictures, 2007.

*The Snow Walker*. Dir. Charles Martin Smith. Lions Gate Films, 2004.

*The Valour and the Horror*. 3-part series. Dir. Brian McKenna. NFB/CBC, 1992.

*Village of Widows*. Dir. Peter Blow. Lindum Films, 1999.

*Vimy Remembered: Vimy Ridge 90*. Dir. Fred Parker. Toronto: CBC Home Video, Morningstar Entertainment, 2007.

*Voices of War Series*. Dir. T.J. Healy II. NFB, 2005.

*The War Between Us*. Dir. Anne Wheeler. Troika Productions, 1994.

*The Wars*. Dir. Robin Phillips. Score by Glenn Gould. Nielsen-Ferns International, Polyphon Film und Fernsehgesellschaft, 1983.

*A War Story*. Dir. Anne Wheeler. NFB, 1993.

*Wedding in White*. Dir. William Fruet. Cinépix Films, 1972.

## Secondary Sources


Abella, Irving, and Harold Troper. *None Is Too Many: Canada and the Jews of Europe, 1933–1948.* Toronto: Lester & Orpen Dennys, 1982. Rpt., Toronto: University of Toronto Press, 2013.

Abley, Mark. "Of War and Regeneration." *Canadian Geographic* 125.6 (2005): 58–64.

Adachi, Ken. *The Enemy That Never Was: A History of the Japanese Canadians.* Toronto: McClelland & Stewart, 1991.

Adorno, Theodor. "Commitment." 1962. *The Essential Frankfurt School Reader.* Eds. Andrew Arato and Eike Gebhardt. New York: Continuum International, 2005. 300–18.

———. *Negative Dialectics.* Trans. E.B. Ashton. New York: Continuum, 1973.

Agamben, Giorgio. *Homo Sacer: Sovereign Power and Bare Life.* 1995. Trans. Daniel Heller-Roazen. Stanford: Stanford University Press, 1998.

———. *Remnants of Auschwitz: The Witness and the Archive.* Trans. Daniel Heller-Roazen. New York: Zone Books, 1999.

———. *State of Exception.* 2003. Trans. Kevin Attell. Chicago: Chicago University Press, 2005.

Aitken, Johan. "'Long Live the Dead': An Interview with Timothy Findley." *Journal of Canadian Fiction* 33 (1981–82): 79–83.

Allemang, John. "This Is the Torch that Hitler Lit." *Globe and Mail* 24 October 2009: F1.

Amigoni, David. *Victorian Biography: Intellectuals and the Ordering of Discourse.* London: Harvester Wheatsheaf, 1993.

Amis, Martin. *Time's Arrow.* New York: Viking, 1991.

Anderson, Benedict. *Imagined Communities: Reflections on the Origin and Spread of Nationalism.* London: Verso, 1983.

Antze, Paul, and Michael Lambek, eds. *Tense Past: Cultural Essays in Trauma and Memory.* New York: Routledge, 1996.

Ashplant, T.G., Graham Dawson, and Michael Roper, eds. *The Politics of War Memory and Commemoration.* London: Routledge, 2000.

Assmann, Jan. "Collective Memory and Cultural Identity." Trans. John Czaplicka. *New German Critique* 65 (Spring/Summer 1995): 125–33.

*Atonement.* Film. Dir. Joe Wright. Universal Pictures, 2007.

Atwood, Margaret. Afterword. *The Journals of Susanna Moodie.* Toronto: Anansi, 1970. 62–64.

———. *In Search of* Alias Grace: *On Writing Canadian Historical Fiction.* Charles R. Bronfman Lecture in Canadian Studies. Ottawa: University of Ottawa Press, 1996.

———. *Moving Targets: Writing with Intent, 1982–2004.* Toronto: Anansi, 2004.

———. *Survival: A Thematic Guide to Canadian Literature.* Toronto: Anansi, 1972.

Auden, W.H. "In Time of War." *Collected Shorter Poems, 1930–1940.* London: Faber & Faber, 1950. 279–80.

Auger, Martin F. *Prisoners of the Home Front: German POWs and "Enemy Aliens" in Southern Quebec, 1940–46.* Vancouver: UBC Press, 2005.

Avery, Donald. "Ethnic and Class Relations in Western Canada during the First World War: A Case Study of European Immigrants and Anglo-Canadian Nativism." Mackenzie 272–99.

Backhouse, Constance. *Colour-Coded: A Legal History of Racism in Canada, 1900–1950.* Toronto: University of Toronto Press, 1999.

Bacque, James. *Crimes and Mercies: The Fate of German Civilians Under Allied Occupation, 1944–1950.* 1977. Vancouver: Talonbooks, 2007.

Bailey, Anne Geddes. *Timothy Findley and the Aesthetics of Fascism.* Vancouver: Talonbooks, 1998.

Bailey, Anne Geddes, and Karen Grandy, eds. *Paying Attention: Critical Essays on Timothy Findley.* Toronto: ECW Press, 1998.

Bakhtin, M.M. *The Dialogic Imagination: Four Essays.* Ed. Michael Holquist. Trans. Caryl Emerson and Michael Holquist. Austin: University of Texas Press, 1992.

——. *Speech Genres and Other Late Essays.* Trans. Vern W. McGee. Eds. Caryl Emerson and Michael Holquist. Austin: University of Texas Press, 1986.

Bal, Mieke, "Light Writing: Portraiture in a Post-Traumatic Age." *Mosaic* 37.4 (2004): 1–19.

Bal, Mieke, Jonathan Crewe, and Leo Spitzer. *Acts of Memory: Cultural Recall in the Present.* Hanover, NH: University Press of New England, 1999.

Bance, Alan. "Sexuality, Gender and the First World War: The Impact of War on Sexual *Mores* and Sexual Consciousness in Britain and Germany." Stanzel and Löschnigg 405–24.

Banerjee, Chinmoy. "Polyphonic Form and Effective Aesthetic in *Obasan.*" *Canadian Literature* 160 (Spring 1999): 101–19.

Barbusse, Henri. *Under Fire.* Trans. W. Fitzwater Wray. London: Dent, 1965.

Barenboim, Daniel. *Knowledge Is the Beginning: The Ramallah Concert.* Dir. Paul Smaczny. EuroArts DVD, 2006.

Barker, Pat. *The Eye in the Door.* 1993. New York: Plume Penguin, 1995.

——. *The Ghost Road.* 1995. New York: Plume Penguin, 1996.

——. *Regeneration.* 1991. New York: Plume Penguin, 1993.

Barnholden, Michael. *Circumstances Alter Photographs: Captain James Peters Reports from the War of 1885.* Vancouver: Talonbooks, 2009.

Barris, Ted. *Victory at Vimy: Canada Comes of Age, April 9–12, 1917.* Toronto: Thomas Allen, 2007.

Beevor, Antony. *D-Day: The Battle for Normandy.* New York: Viking, 2009.

Behrend, Hanna. "'Seedcorn Must Not Be Ground Down': Vera Brittain's and Käthe Kollwitz's Responses to the First World War." Stanzel and Löschnigg 425–45.

Bell, John. *Guardians of the North*. Exhibition catalogue. Ottawa: National Archives of Canada, 1992.

Bemong, Nele. "A State Just Out of the Cradle, but with Age-Old Recollections: The Memory-Shaping Function of the Belgian Historical Novel." Nünning, Gymnich, and Sommer 113–27.

Benedict, Ruth. *The Chrysanthemum and the Sword: Patterns of Japanese Culture*. Boston: Houghton Mifflin, 1946.

Benjamin, Walter. *Illuminations: Essays and Reflections*. Ed. Hannah Arendt. Trans. Harry Zohn. New York: Schocken Books, 1968.

Benson, Eugene. "Interview with Timothy Findley." *World Literature Written in English* 26.1 (1986): 107–15.

Bentley, D.M.R. "Anne Michaels' *Fugitive Pieces*." *Canadian Poetry* 41 (Fall/Winter 1997): 5–20.

Bercuson, David L., and S.F. Wise. *The Valour and the Horror Revisited*. Montreal: McGill-Queen's University Press, 1994.

Berton, Pierre. *Marching as to War: Canada's Turbulent Years, 1899–1953*. Toronto: Anchor, 2002.

———. *Vimy*. Toronto: McClelland & Stewart, 1986.

Bhabha, Homi K., ed. *Nation and Narration*. London: Routledge, 1990.

Bliss, Michael. "After 1918: From Chaos to Mackenzie King." *We Remember*. Spec. issue of *The Beaver* 88.5 (October–November 2008): 22–23.

Blocker, Jane. *Seeing Witness: Visuality and the Ethics of Testimony*. Minneapolis: University of Minnesota Press, 2009.

Blondin, George. *When the World Was New: Stories of the Sahtú Dene*. Yellowknife, YK: Outcrop, 1990.

Blunden, Edmund. *Undertones of War*. 1928. Chicago: University of Chicago Press, 2007.

Bölling, Gordon. "Acts of (Re-)Construction: Traces of Germany in Jane Urquhart's Novel *The Stone Carvers*." *Refractions of Germany in Canadian Literature and Culture*. Eds. Heinz Antor, Sylvia Brown, John Considine, and Klaus Stierstorfer. Berlin: Walter de Gruyter, 2003. 295–317.

Borstad, Lane. "Walter Allward: Sculptor and Architect of the Vimy Ridge Memorial." *JSSAC* 33.1 (2008): 23–38.

Bourrie, Mark. *The Fog of War: Censorship of Canada's Media in World War Two*. Vancouver: Douglas & McIntyre, 2011.

Boychuk, Rick. "Sovereignty and War." *Canadian Geographic* (November–December 2005): 15.

Boyden, Joseph. "Pushing Out the Poison." Wyile, *Speaking* 219–40.

Boyne, John. *The Boy in the Striped Pajamas: A Fable.* New York: Random House, 2006.

Brandon, Laura. "Above or Below Ground? Depicting Corpses in First and Second World War Official Canadian War Art." Grace, Imbert, and Johnstone 93–106.

———. *Art and War.* London: I.B. Taurus, 2007.

———. *Art or Memorial? The Forgotten History of Canada's War Art.* Calgary: University of Calgary Press, 2006.

———. "Artist at War: Jack Shadbolt (1908–1998)." *Canadian Military History* 8.3 (1999): 59–61.

———. *A Brush with War: Military Art from Korea to Afghanistan.* Ottawa: Canadian Museum of Civilization Corp., 2009.

———. "The Canadian War Memorial That Never Was." *Canadian Military History* 7.4 (1998): 45–54.

———. "Carl Schaefer, War Artist 1903–1995." *Canadian Military History* 4.2 (1995): 88–91.

———. "Emotion as Document: Death and Dying in the Second World War Art of Jack Nichols." *Material History Review* 48 (Fall 1998): 123–30.

———. "Genesis of a Painting: Alex Colville's War Drawings." *Canadian Military History* 4.1 (1995): 100–04.

———. "The Group of Seven and the Great War." *Peindre la Grande Guerre.* Paris: Cahiers d'études et de recherches du musée de l'Armée, 2000. 113–25.

———. "In Memoriam: Aba Bayefsky, Official War Artist, 1923–2001." *Canadian Military History* 10.2 (2001): 69–70.

———. "Making Memory: *Canvas of War* and the Vimy Sculptures." *Canada and the Great War.* Ed. Briton C. Busch. Montreal: McGill-Queen's University Press, 2003. 203–15.

———. "Maurice Cullen: A Newfoundland Artist of the Great War." *ArtsAtlantic* 17.2 (200): 44–47.

———. "Naming Names: The War Art of Atlantic Canada." *ArtsAtlantic* 13.1/13.2 (1995): 31–33, 35–37.

———. "Normandy Summer, 1944: D-Day and after in Canadian Art." *Canadian Military History* 3.1 (1994): 26–36.

———. "Obituary—George Campbell Tinning, War Artist, 1910–1996." *Canadian Military History* 5.2 (1996): 57–61.

———. "Obituary—Orville Fisher: Official War Artist (1911–1999)." *Canadian Military History* 9.1 (2000): 56–59.

———. *Pegi by Herself: The Life of Pegi Nicol MacLeod.* Montreal: McGill-Queen's University Press, 2005.

———. "Ready for the Unexpected? The War Art of Edwin Holgate." Pepall and Foss 92–100.

———. "Reflections on the Holocaust: The Holocaust Art of Aba Bayefsky." *Canadian Military History* 6.2 (1997): 67–71.

———. "Resurrection: Images of Belief in Canada's War Memorials." *Revelations: Bi-Millenial Papers from the Canadian Museum of Civilization.* Eds. Robert B. Klymasz and John Willis. Hull: Canadian Museum of Civilization, 2001. 42–52.

———. "The Second World War Paintings of Lawren P. Harris (1910–)." *Canadian Military History* 2.2 (1993): 28–32.

———. "Shattered Landscape: The Great War and the Art of the Group of Seven." *Canadian Military History* 10.1 (2001): 58–66.

———. "Tom Wood: Naval Artist (1913–1997)." *Canadian Military History* 7.2 (1998): 65–70.

Brecht, Bertolt. *Mother Courage and Her Children: A Chronicle of the Thirty Years War.* London: Methuen Drama, 2009.

Brewster, Hugh. *At Vimy Ridge: Canada's Greatest World War I Victory.* Toronto: Scholastic, 2006.

Brewster, Murray. "Ottawa Too Cheap on Arctic, Critics Charge." *Globe and Mail* 12 September 2007: A8.

*A Bridge Too Far.* Film. Dir. Richard Attenborough. United Artists, 1977.

Bridgewater, Patrick. "The German Painters of the First World War." Stanzel and Löschnigg 517–39.

Broad, Graham. "Shopping for Victory." *The Beaver* 85.2 (April–May 2005): 40–45.

Broadfoot, Barry. *Six War Years, 1939–1945: Memories of Canadians at Home and Abroad.* Toronto: Doubleday, 1974.

———. *The Veterans' Years: Coming Home from the War.* Vancouver: Douglas & McIntyre, 1985.

———. *Years of Sorrow, Years of Shame: The Story of Japanese Canadians in World War II.* Toronto: Doubleday, 1977.

Broich, Ulrich. "World War I in Semi-Autobiographical Fiction and in Semi-Fictional Autobiography: Robert Graves and Ludwig Renn." Stanzel and Löschnigg 313–25.

Brown, Laura S. "Not Outside the Range: One Feminist Perspective on Psychic Trauma." Caruth, *Trauma* 100–12.

Browns, Jonathan. "Melancholy/Mélancolie: Maxwell Bates." Ottawa: Ottawa Art Gallery, 2001.

Bruce, Jean. *Back the Attack! Canadian Women During the Second World War—At Home and Abroad.* Toronto: Macmillan, 1985.

Bruhns, Wibke. *My Father's Country: The Story of a German Family.* 2004. Trans. Shaun Whiteside. Toronto: Anchor, 2009.

Brydon, Diana. "A Devotion to Fragility: Timothy Findley's *The Wars.*" *World Literature Written in English* 26.1 (1986): 75–84.

———. "'It Could Not Be Told': Making Meaning in Timothy Findley's *The Wars*." *The Journal of Commonwealth Literature* 21.1 (1986): 62–79.

———. "*Obasan*: Joy Kogawa's 'Lament for a Nation.'" *Kunpipi* 16.1 (1994): 465–70.

———. *Timothy Findley*. New York and London: Twayne and Prentice Hall, 1998.

———. *Writing on Trial: Timothy Findley's* Famous Last Words. Toronto: ECW Press, 1995.

Buitenhuis, Peter. *The Great War of Words: British, American, and Canadian Propaganda and Fiction, 1914–1933*. Vancouver: UBC Press, 1987.

Burns, Robert J. "Bombs in the Bush." *The Beaver* 84.6 (December-January 2004–05): 41–44.

Busch, Briton C., ed. *Canada and the Great War: Western Front Association Papers*. Montreal: McGill-Queen's University Press, 2003.

Butler, Judith. *Precarious Life: The Powers of Mourning and Violence*. London and New York: Verso, 2004.

Butlin, Susan. "Landscape as Memorial: A.Y. Jackson and the Landscape of the Western Front, 1917–1918." *Canadian Military History* 5.2 (1996): 62–70.

———. "Women Making Shells: Marking Women's Presence in Munitions Work 1914–1918—The Art of Frances Loring, Florence Wyle, Mabel May, and Dorothy Stevens." *Canadian Military History* 5.1 (1996): 41–48.

Byers, Michael. "Sovereignty Will Solve the Northwest Passage Dispute." *Globe and Mail* 11 August 2007: A17.

Caballero, Carlo. *Fauré and French Musical Aesthetics*. Cambridge: Cambridge University Press, 2001.

Cahén, Fritz Max. *Men Against Hitler*. Adapted with introduction by Wythe Williams. Indianapolis: Bobbs-Merrill, 1939.

Calder, Angus. *Disasters and Heroes: On War, Memory and Representation*. Cardiff: University of Wales Press, 2004.

Campbell, David. *Writing Security: United States Foreign Policy and the Politics of Identity*. Minneapolis: University of Minnesota Press, 1992.

Campbell, Deborah. "War Artist: Althea Thauberger on the Cultural Front Lines." *Canadian Art* 27.1 (Spring 2010): 62–67.

Campbell, Rebecca. "'We Gave Our Glorious Laddies': Canadian Women's War Poetry, 1915–1920." MA thesis University of British Columbia, 2007.

*Canadian Military History*. Founded in 1992 and published by the Laurier Centre for Military Strategic and Disarmament Studies. Waterloo, ON: Wilfrid Laurier University Press.

Canton, Jeffrey. "The Whole Lake Beneath: Timothy Findley." Daurio 59–68.

Carr, Graham. "War, History, and the Education of (Canadian) Memory." Hodgkin and Radstone 57–78.

Caruth, Cathy. "An Interview with Robert Jay Lifton." Caruth, *Trauma* 128–47.

———. *Unclaimed Experience: Trauma, Narrative and History*. Baltimore: Johns Hopkins University Press, 1996.

———, ed. *Trauma: Explorations in Memory*. Baltimore: Johns Hopkins University Press, 1995.

Chamberlin, J. Edward. *If This Is Your Land, Where Are Your Stories? Finding Common Ground*. Toronto: A.A. Knopf Canada, 2003.

Chambers, Ross. "Orphaned Memories, Foster-Writing, Phantom Pain: The *Fragments* Affair." Miller and Tougaw 92–111.

———. *Untimely Interventions: AIDS Writing, Testimonial, and the Rhetoric of Haunting*. Ann Arbor: University of Michigan Press, 2004.

Chang, Iris. *The Rape of Nanking: The Forgotten Holocaust of World War II*. 1997. New York: Penguin, 1998.

Chang, Jui-te. "The Politics of Commemoration: A Comparative Analysis of the Fiftieth-Anniversary Commemoration in Mainland China and Taiwan of the Victory in the anti-Japanese War." Lary and MacKinnon 136–60.

Charon, Milly. *Worlds Apart: New Immigrant Voices*. Dunvegan, ON: Cormorant Books, 1989.

Christov-Bakargiev, Carolyn. "The Murder of Crows." 2008. *The Murder of Crows*. Berlin: Nationalgalerie im Hamburger Banhof, 2009. 16–23.

Christy, Norm. *For King and Country: The Canadians at Arras, August–September 1918*. Ottawa: CEF Books, 2005.

———. *For King and Empire: The Canadians at Passchendaele, October to November 1917*. Ottawa: CEF Books, 2007.

Churchill, Caryl. *Seven Jewish Children, a Play for Gaza*. London: Hern Books, 2009.

*City of Life and Death*. Film. Dir. Lu Chuan. China Film Group, 2009.

*The Civil War*. Film. Dir. Ken Burns. PBS. 23–27 September 1990.

Clarkson, Adrienne. "Eulogy for Canada's Unknown Soldier." *Canadian Literature* 179 (2003): 15–21.

Coates, Ken. "The Great Canadian Sovereignty Charade." *Up Here* (May–June 2007): 54–57, 61–62.

Coates, Ken, P. Whitney Lackenbauer, William Morrison, and Greg Poelzer. *Arctic Front: Defending Canada in the Far North*. Toronto: Thomas Allen, 2008.

Cobley, Evelyn. *Representing War: Form and Ideology in the First World War*. Toronto: University of Toronto Press, 1993.

Cohen, Jean-Louis. *Architecture in Uniform: Designing and Building for the Second World War*. Montreal: Canadian Centre for Architecture, 2011.

Collins, L.J. *Theatre at War, 1914–18*. London: Macmillan, 1998.

Colombo, John Robert, ed. *Windigo: An Anthology of Fact and Fiction*. Saskatoon, SK: Western Producer Prairie Books, 1982.

Compton, Anne. "Romancing the Landscape." Ferri, *Jane* 115–43.

Connerton, Paul. *How Societies Remember.* Cambridge: Cambridge University Press, 1989.

Cook, Méira. "At the Membrane of Language and Silence: Metaphor and Memory in *Fugitive Pieces.*" *Canadian Literature* 164 (Spring 2000): 12–33.

Cook, Tim. *Warlords: Borden, Mackenzie King, and Canada's World Wars.* Toronto: Allen Lane, 2012.

———. "The Great War of the Mind." *Canada's History* [formerly *The Beaver*] 90.3 (June-July 2010): 18–26.

———. "Hope in Hell." *We Remember.* Spec. issue of *The Beaver* 88.5 (October-November 2008): 16–18.

———. *Shock Troops: Canadians Fighting the Great War, 1917–1918.* Toronto: Viking, 2008.

Copp, Terry. "U-boats in the St. Lawrence." *Globe and Mail* 6 November 2004: D14–15.

Coyle, Brendan. *War on Our Doorstop: The Unknown Campaign on North America's West Coast.* Surrey, BC: Heritage House, 2002.

Criglington, Meredith. "Urban Undressing: Walter Benjamin's 'Thinking-in-Images' and Anne Michaels' Erotic Archeology of Memory." *Canadian Literature* 188 (2006): 86–102.

Crosthwaite, Paul. *Trauma, Postmodernism, and the Aftermath of World War II.* New York: Palgrave Macmillan, 2009.

*The Dam Busters.* Film. Dir. Michael Anderson. Pathé, 1955.

*Days of Glory (Indigènes).* Film. Dir. Rachid Bouchareb. The Weinstein Company and IFC Films, 2006.

Daurio, Beverley, ed. *The Power to Bend Spoons: Interviews with Canadian Novelists.* Toronto: Mercury Press, 1998.

Deer, Glenn. "The New Yellow Peril: The Rhetorical Construction of Asian Canadian Identity and Cultural Anxiety in Richmond." *Claiming Space.* Ed. Cheryl Teelucksingh. Waterloo, ON: Wilfrid Laurier University Press, 2006. 19–40.

Delisle, Esther. *The Traitor and the Jew.* Trans. Madeleine Hébert. Montreal: Robert Davies Publishing, 1993.

Delisle, Jennifer. "'For King and Country': Nostalgia, War, and Canada's Tomb of the Unknown Soldier." *The Dalhousie Review* 85.1 (2005): 16–32.

De Man, Paul. "Autobiography as De-Facement." *The Rhetoric of Romanticism.* New York: Columbia University Press, 1984. 67–81.

D'haen, Theo. "European Pasts, American Presents: Literary Memory, Period Memory, and Didactic Paradigms." Nünning, Gymnich, and Sommer 29–39.

Dickson, Paul. "The Forgotten General." *The Beaver* 89.4 (2009): 25–26.

*Disaster at Dieppe.* Spec. issue of *The Beaver* 89.4 (2009).

Dix, Otto. *Der Krieg.* 1929–32. Zwinger Neues Galerie, Dresden.

Dooley, Brian. Afterword. *Vimy*. Toronto: Playwrights Canada Press, 2007. 80–88.

Doyle, James. *Progressive Heritage: The Evolution of a Politically Radical Literary Tradition in Canada*. Waterloo, ON: Wilfrid Laurier University Press, 2002.

Dubinsky, Karen. "*Polytechnique*: What We Remember, What We Invent, What We Forget." *Academic Matters* (May 2009): 25–27.

Duffy, Dennis. "Let Us Compare Histories: Meaning and Mythologies in Findley's *Famous Last Words*." *Essays on Canadian Writing* 30 (1984–85): 187–205.

Du Prey, Pierre de la Ruffinière. "Allward's Figures, Lutyens's Flags and Wreaths." *JSSAC* 33.1 (2008): 57–64.

———. "Vimy Reveille." *JSSAC* 33.1 (2008): 3–4.

Dyer, Gwynne. *Climate Wars*. Toronto: Random House, 2008.

———. *War*. 1985. Toronto: Random House, 2004.

Eakin, Paul John. *How Our Lives Become Stories: Making Selves*. Ithaca: Cornell University Press, 1999.

Eco, Umberto. *The Prague Cemetery*. Trans. Richard Dixon. Boston: Houghton Mifflin Harcourt, 2011.

———. *The Role of the Reader: Explorations in the Semiotics of Texts*. London: Hutchinson & Co., 1981.

Egan, Susanna. *Burdens of Proof: Faith, Doubt, and Identity in Autobiography*. Waterloo, ON: Wilfrid Laurier University Press, 2011.

———. "History Revisited: Holocaust Autobiography in Canada." Unpublished paper, 2004.

Egan, Susanna, and Gabriele Helms. "Generations of the Holocaust in Canadian Auto/Biography." *Auto/biography in Canada: Critical Directions*. Ed. Julie Rak. Waterloo, ON: Wilfrid Laurier University Press, 2005. 31–51.

Eksteins, Modris. *Rites of Spring: The Great War and the Birth of the Modern Age*. Boston: Houghton Mifflin, 1989.

*Empire of the Sun*. Film. Dir. Steven Spielberg. Warner Brothers, 1987.

*"Enemy Aliens": The Internment of Jewish Refugees in Canada, 1940–1943*. Exhibition catalogue. Vancouver: Vancouver Holocaust Education Centre, 2012.

English, John. *Citizen of the World: The Life of Pierre Elliott Trudeau*. Vol. 1. Toronto: Knopf Canada, 2006.

Erll, Astrid, and Ansgar Nünning. "Concepts and Methods for the Study of Literature and/as Cultural Memory." Nünning, Gymnich, and Sommer 11–28.

Eubanks, Charlotte. "The Mirror of Memory: Constructions of Hell in the Marukis' Nuclear Murals." *PMLA* 124.5 (2009): 1614–31.

Evans, Suzanne. *Mothers of Heroes, Mothers of Martyrs: World War I and the Politics of Grief*. Montreal: McGill-Queen's University Press, 2007.

Fallada, Hans. *Every Man Dies Alone*. Trans. Michael Hoffmann. Brooklyn, NY: Melville House Publishing, 2009.

Faludi, Susan. *The Terror Dream: Fear and Fantasy in Post–9/11 America*. New York: Henry Holt, 2007.

Faulks, Sebastian. *Birdsong*. London: Random House, 1993.

———. *Charlotte Gray*. London: Vintage, 1999.

Farney, James, and Bohdan S. Kordan. "The Predicament of Belonging: The Status of Enemy Aliens in Canada, 1914." *Journal of Canadian Studies* 39.1 (Winter 2005): 74–89.

Fauré, Gabriel. *Requiem, Op. 48, D Minor*. New York: Philips, 1995.

Felman, Shoshana. "Education and Crisis, or the Vicissitudes of Teaching." Caruth, *Trauma* 13–60.

Felman, Shoshana, and Dori Laub. *Testimony: Crises of Witnessing in Literature, Psychoanalysis, and History*. New York: Routledge, 1992.

Ferri, Laura. "A Conversation with Jane Urquhart." Ferri, *Jane* 15–41.

———, ed. *Jane Urquhart: Essays on her Works*. Toronto: Guernica, 2005.

*F.H. Varley: A Centennial Exhibition*. Edmonton: Edmonton Art Gallery, 1981.

Fick, Steven, and Alyssa Julie. "À la carte: Slicing the Polar Pie." *Canadian Geographic* (January–February 2008): 40–41.

Figley, Charles K. *Mapping Trauma and Its Wake: Autobiographic Essays by Pioneer Trauma Scholars*. New York: Routledge, 2006.

Filewod, Alan. "The Face of Re-enactment: A Photo Essay." *Canadian Theatre Review* 121 (Winter 2005): 9–16.

———. *Performing Canada: The Nation Enacted in the Imagined Theatre*. Kamloops, BC: Textual Studies in Canada, 2002.

———. "Warplay: Spectacle, Performance, and the (Dis)Simulation of Combat." Grace, Imbert, and Johnstone 17–27.

Findley, Timothy. "Alice Drops her Cigarette on the Floor...(William Whitehead Looking over Timothy Findley's Shoulder)." *Canadian Literature* 91 (Winter 1981): 10–21.

———. "The Banks of the Wabash." *Story of a Nation: Defining Moments in Our History*. Toronto: Doubleday Canada, 2001. 144–75.

Fisher, Susan R. *Boys and Girls in No Man's Land: English-Canadian Children and the First World War*. Toronto: University of Toronto Press, 2011.

———. "The Study of War." *Canadian Literature* 179 (2003): 10–14.

Fletcher, Martin. *The List*. New York: St. Martin's Press, 2011.

Flynn, Michael. "Searching for Alternatives: Autobiography and Masculinity at the Bimillenium." Strozier and Flynn 239–49.

Foster, Lois, and Anne Seitz. "Official Attitudes to Germans during World War II: Some Australian and Canadian Comparisons." *Ethnic and Racial Studies* 14.4 (1991): 474–92.

Foucault, Michel. *The Archaeology of Knowledge and the Discourse on Language.* Trans. A.M. Sheridan Smith. New York: Pantheon Books, 1972.

Francis, Daniel. *National Dreams: Myth, Memory, and Canadian History.* Vancouver: Arsenal Pulp Press, 1997.

Freud, Sigmund. *Beyond the Pleasure Principle.* Trans. and ed. James Strachey. New York: Liveright, 1961.

———. "Mourning and Melancholia." *The Standard Edition of the Complete Psychological Works of Sigmund Freud*, vol. 14. Trans. James Strachey, Anna Freud, Alix Strachey, and Alan Tyson. London: Hogarth Press; Toronto: Clarke Irwin, 1957. 238–58.

———. "Remembering, Repeating and Working-Through." *The Standard Edition*, vol. 12 (1911–1913):147–56.

Friesen, Joe. "The Race to Claim the Arctic: 'The Outcome Will be Determined by Simple Power.'" *Globe and Mail* 20 October 2007: A8–9.

Frye, Northrop. *The Bush Garden: Essays on the Canadian Imagination.* Toronto: Anansi, 1971.

Fussell, Paul. *The Great War and Modern Memory.* New York: Oxford University Press, 1975.

Gabriel, Barbara. "'The Repose of an Icon' in Timothy Findley's Theatre of Fascism: From 'Alligator Shoes' to *Famous Last Words.*" Bailey and Grandy 149–80.

Garay, Kathy. *Peace and War in the 20th Century.* 2008. McMaster University Library Archival Collection. http://pw20c.mcmaster.ca.

Geiger, Jeffrey. "Taking Aim: New Documentary and War." *Zeitschrift für Anglistik und Amerikanistik: A Quarterly of Language, Literature and Culture* 2.2 (2008): 153–73.

Genette, Gérard. *Narrative Discourse: An Essay in Method.* Trans. Jane E. Lewin. Ithaca: Cornell University Press, 1980.

Giacobazzi, Cesare. "'Contaminated Memory in Günter Grass' *My Century*: Literary and Journalistic Accounts of War." Lamberti and Fortunati 103–14.

Gibelli, Antonio. "Memory and Repression: Psychiatric Sources and the History of Modern War." Lamberti and Fortunati 59–73.

Gibson, Graeme. "Timothy Findley." *Eleven Canadian Novelists Interviewed by Graeme Gibson.* Toronto: Anansi, 1973. 115–49.

Gilbert, Martin. *The Battle of the Somme: The Heroism and Horror of War.* Toronto: McClelland & Stewart, 2006.

Gilbert, Sandra M. "Soldier's Heart: Literary Men, Literary Women, and the Great War." Higonnet, Jenson, Michel, and Weitz 197–226.

Gill, Douglas, and Ulrich Schneider. "Mutiny as a Theme in English and German Literature on World War I." Stanzel and Löschnigg 365–82.

Gilmore, Leigh. *The Limits of Autobiography: Trauma and Testimony.* Ithaca: Cornell University Press, 2001.

Goldman, Marlene. *Rewriting Apocalypse in Canadian Fiction.* Montreal: McGill-Queen's University Press, 2005.

Gordon, Neta. "The Artist and the Witness: Jane Urquhart's *The Underpainter* and *The Stone Carvers.*" *Studies in Canadian Literature* 28.2 (2003): 59–73.

———. "Time Structure and the Healing Aesthetic of Joseph Boyden's *Three Day Road.*" *Studies in Canadian Literature* 33.1 (2008): 118–35.

Grace, Sherrill. "Bearing Witness and Cultural Memory: Canadian Representations of War in the Pacific." Grace, Imbert, and Johnstone 107–20.

———. "Border Crossings in Contemporary Canadian Responses to the Two World Wars: *Famous Last Words* and *Burning Vision.*" *Riding/Writing Across Borders in North American Travelogues and Fiction.* Ed. Waldemar Zacharasiewicz. Vienna: Verlag der Österreichischen Akademie der Wissenschaften, 2011. 369–89.

———. *Canada and the Idea of North.* Montreal: McGill-Queen's University Press, 2001, 2007.

———. *On the Art of Being Canadian.* Vancouver: UBC Press, 2009.

———. "Playing Butterfly: Henry David Hwang and Robert Lepage." *A Vision of the Orient: Texts, Intertexts, and Contexts of Madame Butterfly.* Eds. Jonathan Wisenthal, Sherrill Grace, Melinda Boyd, Brian McIlroy, and Vera Micznik. Toronto: University of Toronto Press, 2006. 136–51.

———. "Performing the Autobiographical Pact: Towards a Theory of Identity in Performance." *Tracing the Autobiographical.* Eds. M. Kadar, Linda Warley, Jeanne Perreault, and Susanna Egan. Waterloo, ON: Wilfrid Laurier University Press, 2005. 65–79.

———. *Regression and Apocalypse: Studies in North American Literary Expressionism.* Toronto: University of Toronto Press, 1989.

———. "Remembering Tomorrow: Lowry, War and *Under the Volcano.*" *Strange Comfort: Essays on the Work of Malcolm Lowry.* Vancouver: Talonbooks, 2010. 189–213.

Grace, Sherrill, Patrick Imbert, and Tiffany Johnstone, eds. *Bearing Witness: Perspectives on War and Peace from the Arts and Humanities.* Montreal: McGill-Queen's University Press, 2012.

Granatstein, J.L. "Dieppe: A Colossal Blunder." *The Beaver* 89.4 (2009): 16–24.

———. *The Last Good War: An Illustrated History of Canada in the Second World War, 1939–1945.* Vancouver: Douglas & McIntyre, 2005.

———. *Who Killed Canadian History?* Toronto: Harper Perennial, 2007.

Granatstein, J.L., and Desmond Morton. *Canada and the Two World Wars.* Toronto: Key Porter, 2003.

Granfield, Linda. *In Flanders Fields: The Story of the Poem by John McCrae.* Illus. Janet Wilson. Markham, ON: Fitzhenry & Whiteside, 2002.

———. *Remembering John McCrae: Soldier-Doctor-Poet.* Toronto: Scholastic, 2009.

———. *Where Poppies Grow: A World War I Companion.* Markham, ON: Fitzhenry & Whiteside, 2002.

Grant, Shelagh D. *Polar Imperative: A History of Arctic Sovereignty in North America.* Vancouver: Douglas & McIntyre, 2010.

Graves, Robert. *Goodbye to All That.* Rev. ed. Harmondsworth, Middlesex: Penguin, 1960.

Gray, Charlotte. "Feminists on the Home Front." *We Remember.* Spec. issue of *The Beaver* 88.5 (October–November 2008): 24–26.

Greenfield, Nathan M. *Baptism of Fire: The Second Battle of Ypres and the Forging of Canada, April 1915.* Toronto: HarperCollins, 2007.

———. *The Damned: The Canadians at the Battle of Hong Kong and the POW Experience, 1941–45.* Toronto: HarperCollins, 2010.

Greenstein, Michael. "Perspectives on the Holocaust in Henry Kreisel's *The Betrayal.*" Neuman 284–92.

Grossman, David. *See Under: Love.* Trans. Betsy Rosenberg. New York: Picador, 1989.

Gubar, Susan. "Dis/Identifications: Empathic Identification in Anne Michaels' *Fugitive Pieces*: Masculinity and Poetry after Auschwitz." *Signs: Journal of Women in Culture and Society* 28.1 (2002): 249–76.

———. *Poetry After Auschwitz: Remembering What One Never Knew.* Bloomington: Indiana University Press, 2003.

———. "Prosopopoeia and Holocaust Poetry in English: The Case of Sylvia Plath." Miller and Tougaw 112–28.

Hall, Lynda. "Remembrance of Things Past and Present." Interview with John Murrell. *Canadian Theatre Review* 79/80 (Summer/Fall 1994): 120–23.

Hansen, Randall. *Fire and Fury: The Allied Bombing of Germany, 1942–45.* Toronto: Doubleday, 2008.

Hartman, Geoffrey H. *The Longest Shadow: In the Aftermath of the Holocaust.* Bloomington: Indiana University Press, 1996.

Hawthorne, Tom. "William Allister, 89. Soldier and Actor." *Globe and Mail* 29 November 2008: S15.

Hayes, Geoffrey, Andrew Iarocci, and Mike Bechthold, eds. *Vimy Ridge: A Canadian Reassessment.* Waterloo, ON: Wilfrid Laurier University Press, 2007.

Hazzard, Shirley. *The Great Fire.* New York: Farrar, Straus and Giroux, 2003.

Herman, Judith. *Trauma and Recovery.* 1992. New York: Basic Books, 1997.

Hibberd, Dominic. "Attitudes to Germany in the Work of Wilfred Owen and Other British Poets of the First World War." Stanzel and Löschnigg 223–34.

Highway, Tomson. *Kiss of the Fur Queen.* Toronto: Doubleday, 1998.

Higonnet, Margaret Randolph, Jane Jenson, Sonya Michel, and Margaret Collins Weitz, eds. *Behind the Lines: Gender and the Two World Wars.* New Haven: Yale University Press, 1987.

Hill, Colin. "Generic Experiment and Confusion in Early Canadian Novels of the Great War." *Studies in Canadian Literature* 34.2 (2009): 58–75.

Hillger, Annick. "'Afterbirth of Earth': Messianic Materialism in Anne Michaels' *Fugitive Pieces.*" *Canadian Literature* 160 (Spring 1999): 28–45.

*Hiroshima: Why the Bomb Was Dropped.* Film. Narrated/Dir. Peter Jennings. ABC News, 1996.

Hirsch, Marianne. *Family Frames: Photography, Narrative, and Postmemory.* Cambridge, MA: Harvard University Press, 1997.

———. "Marked by Memory: Feminist Reflections on Trauma and Transmission." Miller and Tougaw 71–91.

Hodgkin, Katharine, and Susannah Radstone, eds. *Contested Pasts: The Politics of Memory.* New York: Routledge, 2003.

Holmes, Nancy. "'In Flanders Fields': Canada's Official Poem: Breaking Faith." *Studies in Canadian Literature* 30.1 (2005): 13–33.

"Hotel Modern." *KAMP.* 2009. Theatre Group Hotel Rotterdam. www.hotelmodern.nl.

Howells, Coral Ann. "'History as She Is Never Writ': *The Wars* and *Famous Last Words.*" *Kunapipi* 6.1 (1984): 49–56.

Hucker, Jacqueline. "'After the Agony in Stony Places': The Meaning and Significance of the Vimy Monument." Hayes, Iarocci, and Bechthold 279–90.

———. "Lest We Forget: National Memorials to Canada's First World War Dead." *Journal of the Society for the Study of Architecture in Canada* 23.3 (1998): 88–95.

———. "Vimy: A Monument for the Modern World." *JSSAC* 33.1 (2008): 39–48.

Hulcoop, John F. "'Look! Listen! Mark My Words!': Paying Attention to Timothy Findley's Fictions." *Canadian Literature* 91 (Winter 1981): 22–47.

Humbert, Agnès. *Résistance: A Woman's Journal of Struggle and Defiance in Occupied France.* 1946. Trans. Barbara Mellor. London: Bloomsbury, 2008.

Hutcheon, Linda. *A Poetics of Postmodernism: History, Theory, Fiction.* New York: Routledge, 1988.

Huyssen, Andreas. *Present Pasts: Urban Palimpsests and the Politics of Memory.* Stanford: Stanford University Press, 2003.

———. *Twilight Memories: Marking Time in a Culture of Amnesia.* London: Routledge, 1995.

Imbert, Patrick. "Le paradigm intérieur/extérieur et la violence nationaliste en Amérique latine." *La Langue de Bois* 47 (2001): 75–88.

———. "Peace and War: Public Language, Specialized Language, and the Media." *Semiotica* 99 1.2 (1994): 29–51.

Imposti, Gabriella Elina. "'God's Playground': Poland and the Second World War in Wajda's Cinema." Lamberti and Fortunati 235–54.

Ingham, David. "Bashing the Fascists: The Moral Dimensions of Findley's Fiction." *Studies in Canadian Literature* 15.2 (1990): 33–54.

Iser, Wolfgang. *The Implied Reader: Patterns of Communication in Prose Fiction from Bunyan to Beckett*. Baltimore: Johns Hopkins University Press, 1978.

Ivekovic, Sanja. Installation. "Mohnfeld/Poppy Field." *Documenta 12*, 2007.

*J'accuse*. Film. Dir. Abel Gance. Pathé, 1919. Sound release version, 1938.

Jakovljevic, Branislav. "Theatre of Atrocities: Towards a Disreality Principle." *PMLA* 124.5 (2009): 1813–19.

Jenkins, Karl. *The Armed Man: A Mass for Peace. The Platinum Collection*. London: EMI, 2007.

*John Rabe*. Film. Dir. Florian Gallenberger. Twentieth Century Fox, 2009.

*Journal of the Society for the Study of Architecture in Canada (JSSAC)*. Spec. issue on Vimy 33.1 (2008).

*Joyeux Noël*. Film. Dir. Christian Carioun. Sony Picture Classics, 2005.

*Judgment at Nuremberg*. Film. Dir. Stanley Kramer. United Artists. Roxlom Films, 1961.

Kakutani, Michiko. "From 'Life of Pi' Author, Stuffed-Animal Allegory about Holocaust." *New York Times* 12 April 2010: C1.

Kaldor, Mary. *New and Old Wars*. Cambridge: Polity Press, 1999.

Kamboureli, Smaro. "The Body in Joy Kogawa's *Obasan*: Race, Gender, Sexuality." *Scandalous Bodies: Diasporic Literature in English Canada*. Don Mills, ON: Oxford University Press, 2000. 175–221.

Karpinski, Eva C. "The Book as (Anti-)National Heroine: Trauma and Witnessing in Joy Kogawa's *Obasan*." *Studies in Canadian Literature* 31.2 (2006): 46–65.

*Katyń*. Film. Dir. Andrzej Wajda. ITI Cinema, 2007.

Kear, Jonathan. "Spectres of the Past, Inhabitations of the Present: Jochen Gerz and the Problem of Commemoration." Lamberti and Fortunati 193–214.

Kershaw, Alex. *The Envoy: The Epic Rescue of the Last Jews of Europe in the Desperate Closing Months of World War II*. Cambridge, MA: Da Capo Press, 2010.

Keshen, Jeffrey. *Saints, Sinners, and Soldiers: Canada's Second World War*. Vancouver: UBC Press, 2004.

Kilian, Crawford. "The Great War and the Canadian Novel, 1915–1926." PHD diss. Simon Fraser University, 1972.

King, Joe. *From the Ghetto to the Main: The Story of the Jews of Montreal*. Montreal: Montreal Jewish Publication Society, 2000.

King, Nicola. *Memory, Narrative, Identity: Remembering the Self.* Edinburgh: Edinburgh University Press, 2000.

King, Norman. *Abel Gance: A Politics of Spectacle.* London: British Film Institute Publishing, 1984.

King, Ross. "White Feathers and Tangled Gardens." *Canadian Art* (Winter 2009): 75–81.

Kipling, Rudyard. "Recessional." 1897. *Rudyard Kipling: Complete Verse.* New York: Anchor, 1989. 327.

Kirmayer, Laurence J. "Landscapes of Memory: Trauma, Narrative, and Dissociation." Antze and Lambek 173–98.

Kitagawa, Muriel, and Roy Miki, eds. *This Is My Own: Letters to Wes and Other Writings on Japanese Canadians, 1941–1948.* Vancouver: Talonbooks, 1985.

Klein, Ruth, ed. *Nazi Germany, Canadian Responses: Confronting Antisemitism in the Shadow of War.* Montreal: McGill-Queen's University Press, 2012.

Klovan, Peter. "'Bright and Good': Findley's *The Wars.*" *Canadian Literature* 91 (Winter 1981): 58–69.

Koch, Phil. "Wait for Me, Daddy." *The Beaver* 88.4 (August–September 2008): 18–19.

Kollwitz, Käthe. Sculpture. *Die Eltern* (1932). Roggevelde Cemetery, Belgium.

Konody, P.G. "On War Memorials." *Art & War: Canadian War Memorials.* London: Canadian War Records Office, 1919. 5–16.

Kordan, Bohdan S. *Enemy Aliens, Prisoners of War: Internment in Canada during the Great War.* Montreal: McGill-Queen's University Press, 2002.

Kosok, Heinz. "Aspects of Presentation, Attitude and Reception in English and Irish Plays About the First World War." Stanzel and Löschnigg 343–64.

Krause, Dagmar. *Timothy Findley's Novels: Between Ethics and Postmodernism.* Wurzburg: Königshausen & Neumann, 2005.

Kroetsch, Robert. "A Conversation with Margaret Laurence." *Creation.* Toronto: New Press, 1970. 53–63.

Kröller, Eva-Marie. "The Exploding Frame: Uses of Photography in Timothy Findley's *The Wars.*" *Journal of Canadian Studies* 16.3–4 (Fall/Winter 1981): 68–74.

Krystal, Henry. "Trauma and Aging: A Thirty-Year Follow-Up." Caruth, *Trauma* 76–99.

Labayle, Eric. *Les Canadiens à Vimy: 9 avril 1917.* Louviers: Ysec Éditions, 2001.

LaCapra, Dominick. *History and Memory after Auschwitz.* Ithaca: Cornell University Press, 1998.

———. *Writing History, Writing Trauma.* Baltimore: Johns Hopkins University Press, 2001.

Laghi, Brian. "Arctic Sovereignty: Passage's Thaw a Recipe for Chilly Foreign Relations." *Globe and Mail* 10 July 2007: A4.

Lamberti, Elena. "The Experience of War and the Search for Identity in the US Narratives of World War I and World War II." Lamberti and Fortunati 115–28.

Lamberti, Elena, and Vita Fortunati, eds. *Memories and Representations of War: The Case of World War I and World War II.* Amsterdam: Rodopi, 2009.

Langer, Lawrence. *The Holocaust and the Literary Imagination.* New Haven: Yale University Press, 1975.

Lanzmann, Claude. "The Obscenity of Understanding." Caruth, *Trauma* 200–20.

Lary, Diana. "A Ravaged Place: The Devastation of the Xuzhou Region, 1938." Lary and MacKinnon 98–116.

———. "War and Remembering: Memories of China at War." *Beyond Suffering: Recounting War in Modern China.* Eds. James Flath and Norman Smith. Vancouver: UBC Press, 2010. 262–87.

Lary, Diana, and Stephen MacKinnon. Introduction. *Scars of War.* Lary and MacKinnon. 2–15.

Lary, Diana, and Stephen MacKinnon, eds. *Scars of War: The Impact of Warfare on Modern China.* Vancouver: UBC Press, 2001.

Laub, Dori. "Bearing Witness, or the Vicissitudes of Listening." Felman and Laub 57–74.

———. "An Event Without a Witness: Truth, Testimony and Survival." Felman and Laub 75–92.

Lawson, Robert. "German Representations of Canada and Canadian Soldiers: Karl Bröger's *Bunker 17,* Wolfgang Borchert's 'Billbrook,' and Rainer Kunad's *Bill Brook.*" *British Journal of Canadian Studies* 20.2 (2007): 275–88.

*Le chagrin et la pitié: Chronique d'une ville française sous l'Occupation.* Film. Dir. Marcel Ophuls. Milestone Film and Video, 1969.

Lederman, Marsha. "The Master of 'Blatant Artifice' Speaks." *Globe and Mail* 24 May 2008: R7.

Levi, Primo. *The Drowned and the Saved.* Trans. Raymond Rosenthal. New York: Vintage International, 1989.

Levine, Allan. *King: William Lyon Mackenzie King—A Life Guided by the Hand of Destiny.* Vancouver: Douglas & McIntyre, 2011.

Levy, Marc. *The Children of Freedom.* Trans. Sue Dyson. Toronto: HarperCollins, 2008.

*Literature and War.* Spec. issue of *Canadian Literature* 179 (Winter 2003).

Littlewood, Joan, Theatre Workshop, and Charles Clinton. *Oh! What a Lovely War.* London: Methuen, 1965.

*The Lives of Others* (*Das Leben der Anderen*). Film. Dir. Florian Henckel von Donnersmarck. Sony, 2006.

Löschnigg, Martin. "Expressionist-Artillerist: 'Poet' and 'Soldier' as Conflicting Role Models in German Avant-Garde Poetry from the First World War." Grace, Imbert, and Johnstone 79–92.

———. "Intertextuality, Textuality and the Experience of War: David Jones's *In Parenthesis* and Otto Nebel's *Zuginsfeld*." Stanzel and Löschnigg 99–119.

MacKay, Marisa. *Modernism and World War II*. Cambridge: Cambridge University Press, 2007.

Mackenzie, David, ed. *Canada and the First World War: Essays in Honour of Robert Craig Brown*. Toronto: University of Toronto Press, 2005.

MacKinnon, Stephen. "Refugee Flight at the Outset of the Anti-Japanese War." Lary and MacKinnon 118–34.

MacLeod, Peter. "Women of War." *The Beaver* 89.4 (2009): 28–34.

MacMillan, Margaret. *Paris, 1919: Six Months that Changed the World*. New York: Random House, 2003.

Malkin, Jeanette R. *Memory-Theatre and Postmodern Drama*. Ann Arbor: University of Michigan Press, 1999.

Malpede, Karen. "Theatre at 2000: A Witnessing Project." Strozier and Flynn 299–308.

Malvern, Sue. "Art and War: Truth or Fiction?" *Art History* 19.2 (1996): 307–12.

———. *Modern Art, Britain and the Great War: Witnessing, Testimony and Remembrance*. New Haven: Yale University Press, 2004.

———. "War, Memory and Museums: Art and Artefact in the Imperial War Museum." *History Workshop Journal* 49 (Spring 2000): 177–203.

Manguel, Alberto. "On the Art of Detection: An Interview with Timothy Findley." *Descant* 33.4 (Winter 2002): 22–32.

Marano, Lou. "Windigo Psychosis: The Anatomy of an Emic-Etic Confusion." *Current Anthropology* 23.4 (August 1982): 385–412.

Marshall, Brenda. "Meta (Hi)Story: Timothy Findley's *Famous Last Words*." *The International Fiction Review* 16.1 (1989): 17–22.

*Max Manus*. Film. Dirs. Joachim Rønning and Espen Sandberg. D Films, 2008.

McAndrew, Bill, Bill Reading, and Michael Whitby. *Liberation: The Canadians in Europe*. Montreal: Éditions Art Global, 1995.

McConnon, Aili, and Andres McConnon. *Road to Valour: A True Story of World War II Italy, the Nazis, and the Cyclist Who Inspired a Nation*. Toronto: Doubleday Canada, 2012.

McCormick, Ken, and Hamilton Darby Perry. *Images of War: The Artists' Visions of World War II*. New York: Orion Books, 1990.

McEwan, Ian. *Atonement: A Novel*. Toronto: Seal Books, 2007.

McFarlane, Scott. "Covering *Obasan* and the Narrative of Internment." *Privileging Positions: The Sites of Asian American Studies*. Eds. Gary Y. Okihiro, Marilyn Alquizola, Dorothy Fujita Rony, and Wong K. Scott. Pullman: Washington State University Press, 1995. 401–11.

McGoogan, Ken. "Arctic Ambitions." *The Beaver* 88.2 (April–May 2008): 22–23.

———. "What Would Franklin Think?" *Globe and Mail* 29 September 2007: T1.

McKay, Ian, and Jamie Swift. "Fighting Words: Museum Name Change a Sign of Our Times." *Canada's History* (February–March 2013): 50.

———. *Warrior Nation: Rebranding Canada in an Age of Anxiety.* Toronto: Between the Lines, 2012.

McLuhan, Marshall, and Quentin Fiore. *War and Peace in the Global Village.* Toronto: Bantam, 1968.

Menkis, Richard. "A Threefold Transformation: Jewish Studies, Canadian Universities, and the Canadian Jewish Community." *A Guide to the Study of Jewish Civilization in Canadian Universities.* Ed. Michael Brown. Toronto: York University, 1998. 43–69.

Merivale, Patricia. "Framed Voices: The Polyphonic Elegies of Hébert and Kogawa." *Canadian Literature* 116 (Spring 1988): 68–82.

Messiaen, Olivier. *Quatuor pour la fin du temps.* 1941. Deutsche Grammophon, 2000.

Michalski, Sergiusz. *Public Monuments: Art in Political Bondage, 1870–1997.* London: Reaktion, 1998.

Middleton, Peter, and Tim Woods. *Literatures of Memory: History, Time, and Space in Postwar Writing.* Manchester: Manchester University Press, 2000.

Miller, Nancy K., and Jason Tougaw, eds. *Extremities: Trauma, Testimony and Community.* Chicago: University of Illinois Press, 2002.

Mills, Catherine. *The Philosophy of Agamben.* Montreal: McGill-Queen's University Press, 2008.

Milroy, Sarah. "Painter with a Wounded Soul." *Globe and Mail* 2 January 2008: R1–3.

Moritz, Reiner E., Dir. *Otto Dix: The Painter Is the Eyes of the World.* Poorhouse Productions, 1989.

Morton, Desmond. *Fight or Pay: Soldiers' Families in the Great War.* Vancouver: UBC Press, 2004.

———. *A Military History of Canada.* Edmonton: Hurtig Publishers, 1985.

Morton, Desmond, and J.L. Granatstein. *Marching to Armageddon: Canadians and the Great War, 1914–1919.* Toronto: Lester & Orpen Dennys, 1989.

Moss, Laura, ed. *Is Canada Postcolonial? Unsettling Canadian Literature.* Waterloo, ON: Wilfrid Laurier University Press, 2003.

Mosse, George. *Fallen Soldiers: Reshaping the Memory of the World Wars.* New York and Oxford: Oxford University Press, 1990.

Mulhallen, Karen. "A Conversation with Timothy Findley." *Descant* 44.3 (Winter 2002): 33–48.

*The Murder of Crows.* Exhibition catalogue for Janet Cardiff and George Bures Miller. Berlin: Freunde Gutter Musik Berlin, 2009.

Myers, D.G. "Responsible for Every Single Pain: Holocaust Literature and the Ethics of Interpretation." *Comparative Literature* 51.4 (Fall 1999): 266–88.

Nadj, Julijana. "Fictional Metabiographies as Genre Memory and Genre Critique: Biographers Between Abandonment and Affirmation." Nünning, Gymnich, and Sommer 187–99.

Neary, Peter. "'Without the Stigma of Pauperism': Canadian Veterans in the 1930s." *British Journal of Canadian Studies* 22.1 (2009): 31–62.

Nelles, H.V. *The Art of Nation-Building: Pageantry and Spectacle at Quebec's Tercentenary.* Toronto: University of Toronto Press, 1999.

Némirovsky, Irène. *Suite Française.* Trans. Sandra Smith. New York: Knopf, 2006.

Neufeld, James. *Lois Marshall: A Biography.* Toronto: Dundurn Press, 2010.

Neuman, Shirley, ed. *Another Country: Writings by and about Henry Kreisel.* Edmonton: NeWest Press, 1985.

New, William H. "Beneath the Peaceable Kingdom." *Canadian Literature* 91 (Winter 1981): 2–8.

——. *Land Sliding: Imagining Space, Presence, and Power in Canadian Writing.* Toronto: University of Toronto Press, 1997.

——. "Notes Towards a Reading of *The Terracotta Army.*" *Gary Geddes: Essays on His Works.* Ed. Robert G. May. Toronto: Guernica, 2010. 104–39.

Nicholson, G.W.L. *The Fighting Newfoundlander: A History of the Newfoundland Regiment.* 1964. Montreal: McGill-Queen's University Press, 2006.

Nora, Pierre. "Between Memory and History: *Les Lieux de Mémoire.*" Trans. Marc Roudebush. *Representations* 26 (Spring 1989): 7–25.

——. *Realms of Memory: Rethinking the French Past.* Vol. 1. Trans. Lawrence D. Kritzman. New York: Columbia University Press, 1996.

Novak, Amy. "Textual Hauntings: Narrating History, Memory, and Silence in *The English Patient.*" *Studies in the Novel* 36.2 (Summer 2004): 206–31.

Novak, Dagmar. *Dubious Glory: The Two World Wars and the Canadian Novel.* New York: Peter Lang, 2000.

Nünning, Ansgar, Marion Gymnich, and Roy Sommer, eds. *Literature and Memory: Theoretical Paradigms, Genres, Functions.* Tübingen: Francke Verlag, 2006.

Oliver, Dean F., and Laura Brandon. *Canvas of War: Painting the Canadian Experience, 1914 to 1945.* Vancouver: Douglas & McIntyre; Ottawa: Canadian War Museum, 2000.

Oliver, Kelly. *Witnessing Beyond Recognition.* Minneapolis: University of Minnesota Press, 2001.

Osborne, Brian S. "The Iconography of Nationhood in Canadian Art." In *The Iconography of Landscape: Essays on the Symbolic Representation, Design and Use of Past Environments*. Eds. Denis Cosgrove and Stephen Daniels. Cambridge: Cambridge University Press, 1988. 162–78.

——. "Warscapes, Landscapes, Inscapes: France, War, and Canadian National Identity." *Place, Culture and Identity: Essays in Historical Geography in Honour of Alan R.H. Baker*. Eds. Iain S. Black and Robin A. Butlin. Québec: Les Presses de l'Université Laval, 2001. 311–33.

"Own a Moment in History." Advertisement. *Globe and Mail* 18 December 2010: A18.

*Paradise Road*. Film. Dir. Bruce Beresford. Village Road, 2000.

Paris, Erna. *Long Shadows: Truth, Lies, and History*. London: Bloomsbury, 2001.

——. *The Sun Climbs Slow: The International Criminal Court and the Struggle for Justice*. Toronto: Vintage, 2008.



*Paris 1919: Inside the Peace Talks that Changed the World*. Film. Dir. Paul Cowan. Canada/France co-prod. NFB, 2008.

Patterson, Ian. *Guernica and Total War*. Cambridge, MA: Harvard University Press, 2007.

Pecora, Vincent P. "Ethics, Politics, and the Middle Voice." *Literature and the Ethical Question*. Ed. Claire Nouvet. Spec. issue of *Yale French Studies* 79 (1991): 203–30.

Peitsch, Helmut, Charles Burdett, and Claire Gorrara, eds. *European Memories of the Second World War*. Oxford: Berghahn Books, 1998.

Pennee, Donna Palmateer. "Imagined Innocence, Endlessly Mourned: Postcolonial Nationalism and Cultural Expression in Timothy Findley's *The Wars*." *English Studies in Canada* 32.2 (2006): 89–113.

Pepall, Rosalind, and Brian Foss, eds. *Edwin Holgate*. Montreal: Montreal Museum of Fine Arts, 2005.

Pesce, Sara. "Film and War Imaginary: The Hollywood *Combat* and Cultural Memory of World War II." Lamberti and Fortunati 223–34.

Petrou, Michael. *Renegades: Canadians in the Spanish Civil War*. Vancouver: UBC Press, 2008.

Picard, Carol. "Murrell Play Stands Test of Time." *Rocky Mountain Outlook* 27 October 2005: 40.

Pierce, John. "Constructing Memory: The Vimy Memorial." *Canadian Military History* 1.1–2 (1992): 5–8.

Pierson, Ruth Roach. *Canadian Women and the Second World War*. Ottawa: Canadian Historical Association, 1983.

——. *"They're Still Women After All": The Second World War and Canadian Womanhood*. Toronto: McClelland & Stewart, 1986.

Pirie, Bruce. "The Dragon in the Fog: 'Displaced Mythology' in *The Wars*." *Canadian Literature* 91 (Winter 1981): 70–79.

PMLA. *Special Topic: War* 124.5 (October 2009).

Portelli, Alessandro. "The Massacre at the Fosse Ardeatine: History, Myth, Ritual, and Symbol." Hodgkin and Radstone 29–41.

Porter, Anna. *The Ghosts of Europe: Journeys Through Central Europe's Troubled Past and Uncertain Future.* Vancouver: Douglas & McIntyre, 2010.

———. *Kasztner's Train.* Vancouver: Douglas & McIntyre, 2007.

Pratt, Mary Louise. "Harm's Way: Language and the Contemporary Arts of War." *PMLA* 124.5 (October 2009): 1515–31.

Prokofiev, Sergei. *Voyna I mir. War and Peace.* Chandos Records, 2000.

Pynchon, Thomas. *Gravity's Rainbow.* New York: Viking Press, 1973.

Raab, Elisabeth M. *And Peace Never Came.* Waterloo, ON: Wilfrid Laurier University Press, 1997.



Rabe, John. *The Good German of Nanking: The Diaries of John Rabe.* Ed. Erwin Wickert. Trans. John E. Woods. New York: Knopf, 1998.

Rae, Patricia, ed. *Modernism and Mourning.* Lewisburg, VA: Bucknell University Press, 2007.

Ralph, Joel. "Vimy Revisited." *The Beaver* 87.2 (2007): 36–41.

*The Rape of Europa.* Film. Dirs. Richard Berge, Bonni Cohen, and Nicole Newnham. Diglbeta, 2006.

Ravel, Maurice. *Le Tombeau de Couperin.* London: EMI, 1975.

Ray, Carl, and James R. Stevens. *Sacred Legends of the Sandy Lake Cree.* Illus. Carl Ray. Toronto: McClelland & Stewart, 1971.

*The Reader/Der Vorleser.* Film. Dir. Stephen Daldry. Weinstein Co., 2008.

Remarque, Erich Maria. *All Quiet on the Western Front.* 1928. New York: Fawcett, 1958.

Renov, Michael, ed. *Theorizing Documentary.* New York: Routledge, 1993.

Rhiel, Mary, and David Suchoff. "Introduction: The Seductions of Biography." *The Seductions of Biography.* Eds. Mary Rhiel and David Suchoff. New York: Routledge, 1996. 1–11.

Rhodes, Shane. "Buggering with History: Sexual Warfare and Historical Reconstruction in Timothy Findley's *The Wars.*" *Canadian Literature* 159 (Winter 1998): 38–55.

Ricou, Laurence. "Obscured by Violence: Timothy Findley's *The Wars.*" *Violence in the Canadian Novel since 1960.* Eds. Terry Goldie and Virginia Harger-Grinling. St. John's, NL: Memorial University Press, 1981. 125–37.

Ringelblum, Emmanuel. *Notes from the Warsaw Ghetto.* Trans. and ed. Jacob Sloan. New York: ibooks, 2006.

Roberts, Carol. *Timothy Findley: Stories from a Life.* Toronto: ECW Press, 1994.

Robertson, Heather. "Beauty Buried Alive." *We Remember.* Spec. issue of *The Beaver* 88.5 (October–November 2008): 20–21.

———. *A Terrible Beauty: The Art of Canada at War.* Oshawa, ON: James Lorimer & Co. in association with the Robert McLaughlin Gallery; Ottawa: National Museum of Man, 1977.

Robertson, Megan. "Environments of Memory: Bio-Geography in Contemporary Literary Representations of Canada and the Great War." MA thesis University of British Columbia, 2008.

Robillard, Alexandre. "Women's Group Edits Anti-War Video after Outcry." *Globe and Mail* 9 October 2010: A9.

Ross, Val. "Scenes from the Front." *Globe and Mail* 28 August 2006: R1–2.

Rothberg, Michael. "Between the Extreme and the Everyday." Miller and Tougaw 55–70.

Roze, Anne, and John Foley. *Artois: Paysages de la Grande Guerre/Landscapes of the Great War.* Anvers, Belgium: Les Champs de la Mémoire, 2007.

Ryan, Andrew. "A War of Racism and Terror." *Globe and Mail* 13 March 2010: R5.

Ryan, Toby Gordon. *Stage Left: Canadian Theatre in the Thirties, A Memoir.* Toronto: CTR Publications, 1981.

Said, Edward. *Culture and Imperialism.* New York: Vintage, 1994.

Sangster, Joan. "Mobilizing Women." Mackenzie 157–93.

Santner, Eric L. *Stranded Objects: Mourning, Memory, and Film in Postwar Germany.* Ithaca: Cornell University Press, 1990.

Saunders, Max. "War Literature, Bearing Witness, and the Problem of Sacralization: Trauma and Desire in the Writing of Mary Borden and Others. Lamberti and Fortunati 177–91.

Saunders, Tim. *Juno Beach.* Montreal: McGill-Queen's University Press, 2004.

Schama, Simon. *Dead Certainties (Unwarranted Speculations).* New York: Knopf, 1991.

Schoentjes, Pierre, ed. *La Grande Guerre: Un siècle de fictions romanesque.* Genève: Librairie Droz, 2008.

Schultze, Bruno. "Fiction and Truth: Politics and the War Novel." Stanzel and Löschnigg 297–311.

Schwarz, Herbert T. *Windigo and Other Tales of the Ojibways.* Illus. Norval Morrisseau. Toronto: McClelland & Stewart, 1969.

Schwarz-Bart, André. *The Last of the Just.* 1959. Trans. Stephen Becker. New York: Overlook Press, 2000.

Scobie, Stephen. "Eye-Deep in Hell: Ezra Pound, Timothy Findley, and Hugh Selwyn Mauberley." *Essays on Canadian Writing* 30 (1984–85): 206–27.

Sebald, W.G. *On the Natural History of Destruction.* 1999. Trans. Anthea Bell. Toronto: Vintage Canada, 2004.

Sedgwick, Eve Kosofsky. *Between Men: English Literature and Male Homosocial Desire.* New York: Columbia University Press, 1985.

Servais, Raoul. "L'empreinte 14–18." Schoentjes 393–96.

Shaw, Martin. *War and Genocide: Organized Killing in Modern Society.* Cambridge: Polity Press, 2003.

Sheffield, R. Scott. "Aboriginal Contributions to Canadian Culture and Identity in Wartime: English Canada's Image of the 'Indian' and the Fall of France, 1940." *Hidden in Plain Sight: Contributions of Aboriginal Peoples to Canadian Identity and Culture.* Eds. David R. Newhouse, Cora J. Voyageur, and Dan Beavon. Toronto: University of Toronto Press, 2005. 405–18.

Sherriff, R.C. *Journey's End.* Harmondsworth: Penguin, 1983.

Shields, E.F. "Mauberley's Lies: Fact and Fiction in Timothy Findley's *Famous Last Words.*" *Journal of Canadian Studies* 22.4 (1987–88): 44–59.

———. "'The Perfect Voice': Mauberley as Narrator in Timothy Findley's *Famous Last Words.*" *Canadian Literature* 119 (Winter 1988): 84–98.

Shipley, Robert. *To Mark Our Place: A History of Canadian War Memorials.* Toronto: NC Press, 1987.

Shirinian, Lorne, ed. *Under Fire: The Canadian Imagination and War.* Kingston, ON: Blue Heron Press, 2004.

*Shoah.* Film. Dir. Claude Lanzmann. New Yorker Films, 1985.

Silcox, David P. *David Milne: An Introduction to His Life and Art.* Richmond Hill, ON: Firefly Books, 2005.

Smit, Ester, and Dinand Webbink. *De Propaganda Oorlog: Oorlogs-affiches en Verzetsdrukwerk, 1940–1945.* The Netherlands: Deventer Stadsarchief, 2009.

Smith, Julian. "Restoring Vimy: The Challenges of Confronting Emerging Modernism." *JSSAC* 33.1 (2008): 49–56.

Spargo, Clifton R. *The Ethics of Mourning: Grief and Responsibility in Elegiac Literature.* Baltimore: Johns Hopkins University Press, 2004.

Spiegelman, Art. *Maus: A Survivor's Tale.* 2 vols. New York: Pantheon Books, 1973, 1986.

Stamp, Gavin. "The Imperial War Graves Commission." *JSSAC* 33.1 (2008): 5–22.

Stanley, Jo. "Involuntary Commemoratives: Post-traumatic stress disorder and its relationship to war commemoration." Ashplant, Dawson, and Roper 240–59.

Stanzel, Franz K. "'The Beauty of the Bayonet': Hand-to-Hand Combat in English and German Poetry." Stanzel and Löschnigg 83–95.

———. "'In Flanders Fields the Poppies Blow': Canada and the Great War." *Difference and Community: Canadian and European Cultural Perspectives.* Eds. Peter Easingwood, Konrad Gross, and Lynette Hunter. Amsterdam: Rodopi, 1996. 213–26.

Stanzel, Franz K., and Martin Löschnigg, eds. *Intimate Enemies: English and German Literary Reactions to the Great War, 1914–1918.* Heidelberg: Universitätsverlag C. Winter, 1993.

Stein, Janice Gross, and Eugene Lang. *The Unexpected War: Canada in Kandahar*. Toronto: Viking, 2007.

Stravinsky, Igor, and Charles Ferdinand Ramuz. *The Soldier's Tale*. 1918. Nimbus Records, 1986.

Strozier, Charles B., and Michael Flynn, eds. *The Year 2000: Essays on the End*. New York: New York University Press, 1997.

Sturken, Marita. "Personal Stories and National Meanings: Memory, Reenactment, and the Image." Rhiel and Suchoff 31–41.

——. *Tangled Memories: The Vietnam War, the AIDS Epidemic, and the Politics of Remembering*. Berkeley: University of California Press, 1997.

Sullivan, Rosemary. *Villa Air-Bel: World War II, Escape, and a House in Marseille*. Toronto: HarperCollins, 2006.

Summers, Alison. "Interview with Timothy Findley." *Canadian Literature* 91 (Winter 1981): 49–55.

Sunahara, Ann Gomer. *The Politics of Racism: The Uprooting of Japanese Canadians During the Second World War*. Toronto: James Lorimer, 1981.

Taylor, Tom. *Glimpses: World War II, West Vancouver through the Paper and the Eyes of the Paper Boy*. Vancouver: Private publication, 2004.

Thamer, Hans-Ulrich, and Simone Erpel, eds. *Hitler und die Deutschen: Volksgemeinschaft und Verbrechen*. Dresden: Sandstein Verlag, 2010.

*The Thin Red Line*. Film. Dir. Terrence Malick. 20th Century Fox, 1998.

*The Third Man*. Film. Dir. Carol Reed. British Lion Film Corporation, 1949.

Thompson, Eric. "Canadian Fiction of the Great War." *Canadian Literature* 91 (Winter 1981): 81–96.

Thomson, Denise. "National Sorrow, National Pride: Commemoration of War in Canada, 1914–1945." *Journal of Canadian Studies* 30.4 (1995–96): 5–27.

*Timothy Findley & the War Novel*. Spec. issue of *Canadian Literature* 91 (Winter 1981).

Tippett, Maria. *Art at the Service of War: Canada, Art, and the Great War*. Toronto: University of Toronto Press, 1984.

——. "British and Canadian Art and the Great War." Stanzel and Löschnigg 540–53.

Todorov, Tzvetan. *The Conquest of America: The Question of the Other*. New York: Harper and Row, 1984.

Tompkins, Joanne. "Canadian Theatre and Monuments: Memorializing and Countermemorializing in *The Death of General Wolfe*, *Angélique*, and *Sled*." *Canadian Theatre Review* 115 (Summer 2003): 5–11.

Trout, Stephen. *On the Battlefield of Memory: The First World War and American Remembrance, 1919–1941*. Tuscaloosa: University of Alabama Press, 2010.

*The True Glory: From D-Day to the Fall of Berlin*. Film. Dirs. Carol Reed and Garson Kanin. 1945. Re-release, Imperial War Museum, London, 2009.

Trumpener, Katie. "Memories Carved in Granite: Great War Memorials and Everyday Life." *PMLA* 115.5 (2000): 1096–1103.

Tuchman, Barbara W. *The Guns of August*. 1962. New York: Presidio Press, 2004.

*Unspeakable: The Artist as Witness to the Holocaust*. Exhibition catalogue. London: Imperial War Museum, 2008.

Urquhart, Jane. "Confessions of a Historical Geographer." Wyile, *Speaking* 79–103.

Valpy, Michael. "Invisible No More." *Globe and Mail* 21 November 2009: F1, 5.

Vance, Jonathan F. *Death So Noble: Memory, Meaning, and the First World War*. Vancouver: UBC Press, 1997.

——. "Remembering Armageddon." Mackenzie 409–33.

——. "The Soldier as Novelist: Literature, History, and the Great War." *Canadian Literature* 179 (2003): 22–37.

Van der Kolk, Bessel, and Onno van der Hart. "The Intrusive Past: The Flexibility of Memory and the Engraving of Trauma." Caruth, *Trauma* 158–82.

Van Schoonneveldt, Léon. "The Moral Witness in the Field of Cultural Remembrance." Nünning, Gymnich, and Sommer 236–47.

Van Wyck, Peter C. *The Highway of the Atom*. Montreal: McGill-Queen's University Press, 2010.

Varon, Jeremy. "Probing the Limits of the Politics of Representation." *Absence/Presence: Critical Essays on the Artistic Memory of the Holocaust*. Ed. Stephen C. Feinstein. Syracuse: Syracuse University Press, 2005. 12–38.

Vauthier, Simone. "The Dubious Battle of Story-Telling: Narrative Strategies in Timothy Findley's *The Wars*." *Gaining Ground: European Critics on Canadian Literature*. Eds. Robert Kroetsch and Reingard Nischik. Edmonton: NeWest Press, 1985. 1–39.

Vigna, John. "The Conductor of the Cellist of Sarajevo." *Trek* (Summer 2009): 18–20.

Vincent, Thomas B. "Canadian Poetry of the Great War and the Effect of the Search for Nationhood." Stanzel and Löschnigg 165–75.

Viol, Claus-Ulrich. "Constructions of Fascism in British Cultural History: From Fancy-Dressers to Missing Links." *ZAA* 57.2 (2009): 177–93.

Von Flotow, Friedrich (composer), and Friedrich Wilhelm Riese (librettist). *Martha, oder Der Markt zu Richmond*. EMI Classics 2009.

Von Habsburg, Francesca. "Collecting: The Last Temptation." Interview with Janet Cardiff. *The Murder of Crows* exhibition catalogue 39–41.

Vonnegut, Kurt, Jr. *Slaughterhouse-Five, or the Children's Crusade*. New York: Dell, 1969.

Wajda, Andrzej. "Director's Statement." 2007. http://katyn.netino.pl/en.

Walker, James W. St. G. "Race and Recruitment in World War I: Enlistment of Visible Minorities in the Canadian Expeditionary Force." *Canadian Historical Review* 70.1 (1989): 1–26.

Walters, Guy. *Berlin Games: How Hitler Stole the Olympic Dream.* London: John Murray, 2006.

*The War.* Film. Dir. Ken Burns. PBS, 23 September 2007.

*The War Bride.* Dir. Lydon Chubbuck. Great Britain: Prism Leisure Corp., 2004.

Wasserman, Jerry. "Remembering Agraba: Canadian Political Theatre and the Construction of Cultural Memory." *Signatures of the Past: Cultural Memory in Contemporary Anglophone North American Drama.* Eds. Marc Maufort and Caroline De Wagter. Brussels: Peter Lang, 2008. 101–14.

Waterston, Elizabeth Hillman. *Blitzkrieg and Jitterbugs: College Life in Wartime, 1939–1942.* Montreal: McGill-Queen's University Press, 2012.

Watson, Alexander John. *Marginal Man: The Dark Vision of Harold Innis.* Toronto: University of Toronto Press, 2006.

Weintraub, Stanley. "The Peace of 1914. Christmas Truce." Stanzel and Löschnigg 381–400.

West, Rebecca. *The Return of the Soldier.* 1918. New York: Random House, 2004.

Wheeler, Anne. "Perspectives on War." Grace, Imbert, and Johnstone 189–203.

Whittaker, Robin C. "Fusing the Nuclear Community: Intercultural Memory, Hiroshima 1945 and the Chronotopic Dramaturgy of Marie Clements's *Burning Vision.*" *Theatre Research in Canada* 30.1–2 (2009): 129–51.

Wild, Paula, with Rick James. *The Comox Valley: Courtenay, Comox, Cumberland and Area.* Photography by Boomer Jerritt. Madeira Park, BC: Harbour Publishing, 2006.

Williams, David. *Confessional Fictions: A Portrait of the Artist in Canadian Novels.* Toronto: University of Toronto Press, 1991.

———. "A Force of Interruption: The Photography of History in Timothy Findley's *The Wars.*" *Canadian Literature* 194 (2007): 54–73.

———. *Media, Memory, and the First World War.* Montreal: McGill-Queen's University Press, 2009.

*Winter in Wartime.* Film. Dir. Martin Koolhoven. Isabella Films, 2008.

Winter, Jay. *Remembering War: The Great War Between Memory and History in the Twentieth Century.* New Haven: Yale University Press, 2006.

———. *Sites of Memory, Sites of Mourning: The Great War in European Cultural History.* Cambridge: Cambridge University Press, 1995.

Wright, Robert. *Virtual Sovereignty: Nationalism, Culture and the Canadian Question.* Toronto: Canadian Scholars Press, 2004.

Wyile, Herb. "Making a Mess of Things: Postcolonialism, Canadian Literature, and the Ethical Turn." *University of Toronto Quarterly* 76.3 (Summer 2007): 821–37.

———. *Speaking in the Past Tense: Canadian Novelists on Writing Historical Fiction.* Waterloo, ON: Wilfrid Laurier University Press, 2007.

———. *Speculative Fictions: Contemporary Canadian Novelists and the Writing of History.* Montreal: McGill-Queen's University Press, 2002.

———. "Windigo Killing: Joseph Boyden's *Three Day Road.*" *National Plots: Historical Fiction and Changing Ideas of Canada.* Eds. Andrea Cabajsky and Brett Josef Grubisic. Waterloo, ON: Wilfrid Laurier University Press, 2010. 83–97.

Yaeger, Patricia. "Consuming Trauma; or, the Pleasures of Merely Circulating." Miller and Tougaw 25–51.

Yang, Daqing. "Atrocities in Nanjing: Searching for Explanations." Lary and MacKinnon 76–96.

York, Lorraine. *Front Lines: The Fiction of Timothy Findley.* Toronto: ECW Press, 1991.

———. *Introducing Timothy Findley's* The Wars. Toronto: ECW Press, 1990.

Young, Alan. "'We Throw the Torch': Canadian Memorials of the Great War and the Mythology of Heroic Sacrifice." *Journal of Canadian Studies* 24.1 (1990): 5–28.

Young, James E. *At Memory's Edge: After-Images of the Holocaust in Contemporary Art and Architecture.* New Haven: Yale University Press, 2000.

———. "Regarding the Pain of Women: Questions of Gender and the Arts of Holocaust Memory." *PMLA* 124.5 (2009): 1778–86.

Zemans, Joyce. "Envisioning Nation: Nationhood, Identity and the Sampson-Matthews Silkscreen Project: The Wartime Prints." *Journal of Canadian Art History* 19.1 (1998): 7–47.

———. "Establishing the Canon: Nationhood, Identity and the National Gallery's First Reproduction Program of Canadian Art." *Journal of Canadian Art History* 16.2 (1995): 6–35.

Zuehlke, Mark. *Ortona: Canada's Epic World War II Battle.* Vancouver: Douglas & McIntyre, 1999.

*Zwartboek [The Black Book].* Film. Dir. Paul Verhoeven. A-Film, 2006.



## Websites

*Images of a Forgotten War.* nfb. www3.nfb.ca/ww1.

*Canadian Virtual War Memorial.* Veterans Affairs Canada. www.veterans.gc.ca/eng/remembrance/memorials/canadian-virtual-war-memorial.

*Welcome to the Memory Project.* www.thememoryproject.com.

# Permissions



**Appignanesi, Lisa,** *Losing the Dead*

Copyright © Lisa Appignanesi. Excerpt used by permission.

**Atwood, Margaret,** *The Blind Assassin*

Excerpt from *The Blind Assassin* by Margaret Atwood, copyright © 2000 by O.W. Toad, Ltd. Used by permission of Doubleday, an imprint of the Knopf Doubleday Publishing Group, a division of Random House LLC. All rights reserved.

© Margaret Atwood (2000), *The Blind Assassin.* Bloomsbury Publishing PLC. Excerpt used by permission.

**Bock, Dennis,** *The Ash Garden*

© Dennis Bock (2001) *The Ash Garden.* Bloomsbury Publishing PLC. Excerpt used by permission.

Excerpt from *The Ash Garden* © 2001 by Dennis Bock. Published by HarperCollins Publishers Ltd. All rights reserved. Used by permission.

Excerpt from *The Ash Garden* © 2001 by Dennis Bock. Used by permission of Alfred A. Knopf, an imprint of the Knopf Doubleday Publishing Group, a division of Random House LLC. All rights reserved.

**Bock, Dennis,** *The Communist's Daughter*

Excerpt from *The Communist's Daughter* © 2006 by Dennis Bock. Published by HarperCollins Publishers Ltd. All rights reserved. Used by permission.

Excerpt from *The Communist's Daughter* © 2006 by Dennis Bock. Used by permission of Alfred A. Knopf, an imprint of the Knopf Doubleday Publishing Group, a division of Random House LLC. All Rights reserved.

**Boyden, Joseph,** *Three Day Road*

Excerpt from *Three Day Road* by Joseph Boyden. Copyright © Joseph Boyden, 2001. Reprinted by permission of Penguin Canada Books Inc.

Excerpt from *Three Day Road* by Joseph Boyden, copyright © 2005 by Joseph Boyden. Used by permission of Viking Penguin, a division of Penguin Group (USA) LLC.

Excerpt from *Three Day Road*, by Joseph Boyden. The Orion Publishing Group, London. Used by permission.

**Chan, Marjorie,** *A Nanking Winter*

Excerpt from *A Nanking Winter* © Marjorie Chan, Playwrights Canada Press, Toronto ON. Reprinted by permission of the publisher.

**Clements, Marie,** *Burning Vision*

Excerpt from *Burning Vision* by Marie Clements © 2003 Marie Clements, Talon Books Ltd., Vancouver, BC. Reprinted by permission of the publisher.

**Gray, John and Eric Peterson,** *Billy Bishop Goes to War*

Excerpt from *Billy Bishop Goes to War* by John MacLachlan Gray with Eric Peterson © 1981 John MacLachlan Gray and Eric Peterson, Talon Books Ltd., Vancouver, BC. Reprinted by permission of the publisher.

**Hodgins, Jack,** *Broken Ground*

Excerpt from *Broken Ground* by Jack Hodgins. Copyright © 1998 Jack Hodgins. Reprinted by permission of McClelland & Stewart. Canada.

Excerpt from *Broken Ground* by Jack Hodgins (McClelland & Stewart Limited, 1998). Copyright © 1998 Jack Hodgins. With permission of the author.

**Hodgins, Jack,** "Finding Merville"

"Finding Merville" by Jack Hodgins first published in the *Comox Valley Record*, vol. 11, no. 44. Copyright © 1996 Jack Hodgins. Excerpt used with permission of the author.

**Macfarlane, David,** *The Danger Tree: Memory, War, and the Search for a Family's Past*

Excerpt from *The Danger Tree* © 2000, 2014 by David Macfarlane. Published by HarperCollins Publishers Ltd. All rights reserved. Used by permission.

© David Macfarlane, 2001, *The Danger Tree*, Walker Books. Excerpt used by permission of Bloomsbury Publishing Inc.

Excerpt from *The Danger Tree: Memory, War, and the Search for a Family's Past* by David Macfarlane (Macfarlane Walter & Ross, 1991). Copyright © 1991 David Macfarlane. With permission of the author.

**Martel, Yann,** *Beatrice & Virgil*

Excerpt from *Beatrice & Virgil* by Yann Martel. Copyright © 2010 Yann Martel. Reprinted by permission of Knopf Canada.

Excerpt from *Beatrice & Virgil: A Novel* by Yann Martel, © 2010 by Yann Martel. Used by permission of Speigel & Grau, an imprint of Random House, a division of Random House LLC. All rights reserved.

Excerpt from *Beatrice & Virgil* by Yann Martel (Knopf, 2010). Copyright © 2010 Yann Martel. With permission of the author.



**Massicotte, Stephen,** *Mary's Wedding*

Excerpt from *Mary's Wedding* © Stephen Massicotte, Playwrights Canada Press, Toronto, ON. Reprinted by permission of the publisher.

**Michaels, Anne,** *Fugitive Pieces*

Excerpt from *Fugitive Pieces* by Anne Michaels. Copyright © 1996 Anne Michaels. Reprinted by permission of McClelland & Stewart.

© Anne Michaels, (1997) *Fugitive Pieces.* Bloomsbury Publishing PLC. Excerpt used by permission.

Excerpt from *Fugitive Pieces* by Anne Michaels © Copyright 1996 by Anne Michaels. Used by permission of Alfred A. Knopf, an imprint of the Knopf Doubleday Publishing Group, a division of Random House LLC. All rights reserved.

**Murrell, John,** *Waiting for the Parade*

Excerpt from *Waiting for the Parade* by John Murrell © 1980 John Murrell, Talon Books Ltd., Vancouver, BC. Reprinted by permission of the publisher.

**Sherman, Jason,** *None Is Too Many*

Excerpt from *None Is Too Many* © Jason Sherman, Playwrights Canada Press, Toronto, ON. Reprinted by permission of the publisher.

**Souster, Raymond,** "The Dresden Special"

Excerpt from "The Dresden Special" is reprinted from *Collected Poems of Raymond Souster* by permission of Oberon Press.

**Thiessen, Vern,** *Vimy*

Excerpt from *Vimy* © Vern Thiessen, Playwrights Canada Press, Toronto, ON. Reprinted by permission of the publisher.

**Thomson, R.H.,** *The Lost Boys*

Excerpt from *The Lost Boys* © R.H. Thomson, Playwrights Canada Press, Toronto, ON. Reprinted by permission of the publisher.

# Index

Page numbers in *italics* refer to illustrations.

Other Titles from The University of Alberta Press

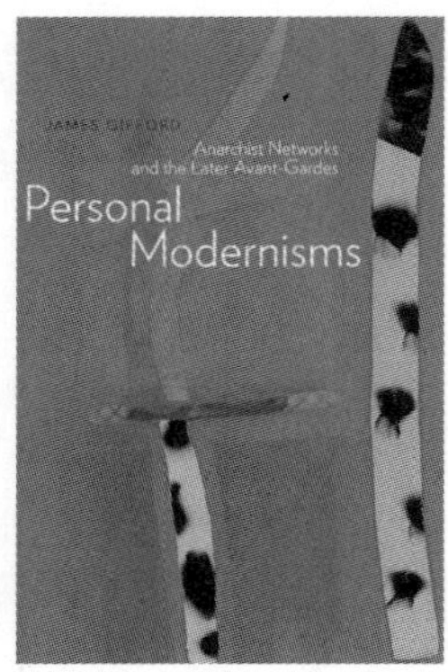


**Personal Modernisms**

*Anarchist Networks and the Later Avant-Gardes*

JAMES GIFFORD

978-1-77212-001-1 | $34.95 (T) paper

978-1-77212-009-7 | $27.99 (T) EPUB

978-1-77212-010-3 | $27.99 (T) Kindle

978-1-77212-011-0 | $27.99 (T) PDF

320 pages | Notes, bibliography, index

Modernist Literature/Literary Criticism/Anarchist Studies

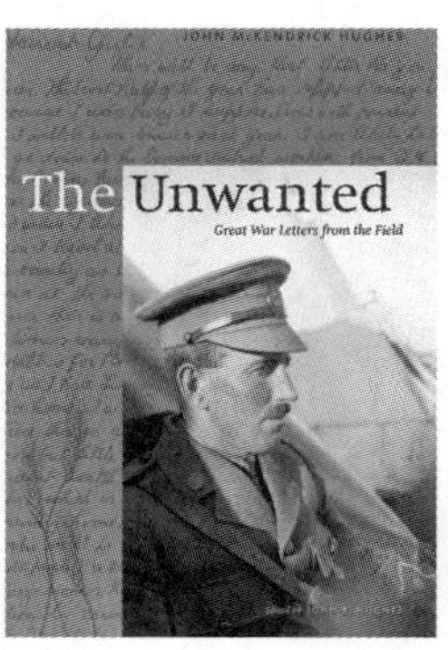


**The Unwanted**

*Great War Letters from the Field*

JOHN MCKENDRICK HUGHES

JOHN R. HUGHES, Editor

416 pages | B&W photographs, maps, notes, bibliography, index

978-0-88864-436-7 | $32.95 (T) paper

History/War/Agriculture

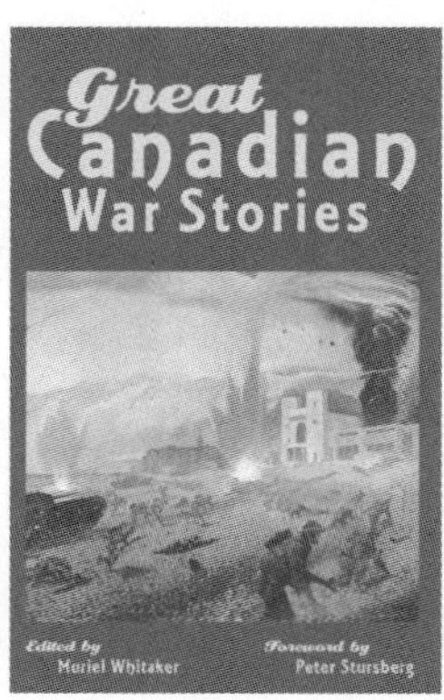


**Great Canadian War Stories**

MURIEL WHITAKER, Editor

PETER STURSBERG, Foreword

978-0-88864-383-4 | $19.95 (T) paper

296 pages

Literature/Short Stories